THE ROUTLEDGE HANDBOOK OF
COMMUNICATION AND BULLYING

The Routledge Handbook of Communication and Bullying provides an essential and unique analysis of bullying and anti-bullying efforts from a communication perspective. Drawing upon communication theory and compelling empirical research, this volume offers valuable international perspectives of this pervasive concern, examined within varied contexts. In addition to providing exemplary data-based scholarship, the *Handbook* is comprised of first-hand accounts of those who have been bullied, adding an important pragmatic and complementary dimension to the topic. This anthology serves as a useful resource for educators, administrators, managers, and other stakeholders who are challenged with this difficult social issue. Responding to the various charges emanating from the National Communication Association's (NCA) Anti-Bullying Project, this collection constitutes a valuable foundation from which to draw as conversations about bullying continue around the globe.

RICHARD WEST is Professor in the Department of Communication Studies at Emerson College in Boston. At the national level, Rich is Past President of the National Communication Association (NCA) and past President of the Eastern Communication Association (ECA), the oldest professional communication organization in the country. Rich's scholarship intersects family, communication, and identity; he is the co-author of several books in multiple editions (*IPC: Interpersonal Communication*; *Gender and Communication/3rd edition*; *Understanding Interpersonal Communication: Making Choices in Changing Times*; *Perspectives on Family Communication*; and *Introducing Communication Theory: Analysis and Applications*). He is also co-author of *An Introduction to Communication* (Cambridge University Press) and *Interpersonal Communication* (Sage Publications). Rich is the recipient of various distinctions, including Emerson's Norman and Irma Mann Stearns Distinguished Professor, Illinois State University's Outstanding Alum in Communication Studies, and NCA's Bernard J. Brommel Award in Family Communication.

CHRISTINA S. BECK is Professor in the School of Communication Studies at Ohio University. Dr. Beck is Past President of the National Communication Association (NCA). As part of her *Enhancing Opportunities* NCA Presidential Initiative, she established the NCA Anti-Bullying Project. Beck has also served as President of the Central States Communication Association, Editor of *Communication Yearbook* (volumes 30–33), and Book Review Editor for *Journal of Health Communication: International Perspectives*. Beck has published four award-winning books in the areas of health communication and gender: *The Lynching of Language: Gender, Politics, and Power in the Hill-Thomas Hearings*; *Partnership for Health: Building Relationships between Women and Health Caregivers*; *Communicating for Better Health: A Guide through the Medical Mazes*, and *Narrative, Health, and Healing: Communication Theory, Research, and Practice*, in addition to numerous journal articles and book chapters.

THE ROUTLEDGE HANDBOOK OF COMMUNICATION AND BULLYING

Edited by Richard West and Christina S. Beck

NEW YORK AND LONDON

First published 2019
by Routledge
711 Third Avenue, New York, NY 10017

and by Routledge
2 Park Square, Milton Park, Abingdon, Oxon OX14 4RN

Routledge is an imprint of the Taylor & Francis Group, an informa business

© 2019 Taylor & Francis

The right of Richard West and Christina S. Beck to be identified as the authors of the editorial material, and of the authors for their individual chapters, has been asserted in accordance with sections 77 and 78 of the Copyright, Designs and Patents Act 1988.

All rights reserved. No part of this book may be reprinted or reproduced or utilized in any form or by any electronic, mechanical, or other means, now known or hereafter invented, including photocopying and recording, or in any information storage or retrieval system, without permission in writing from the publishers.

Trademark notice: Product or corporate names may be trademarks or registered trademarks, and are used only for identification and explanation without intent to infringe.

Library of Congress Cataloging-in-Publication Data
A catalog record for this book has been requested

ISBN: 978-1-138-55235-7 (hbk)
ISBN: 978-1-315-14811-3 (ebk)

Typeset in Bembo
by Apex CoVantage, LLC

Printed and bound in Great Britain by
TJ International Ltd, Padstow, Cornwall

CONTENTS

Foreword by Christina S. Beck	*viii*
Preface	*x*

PART I
Foundations of Bullying and Communication Research   **1**

1 Coming to Terms with Bullying: A Communication Perspective   3
Richard West and Lynn H. Turner

2 Building Better Models to Understand Bullying   13
Brian H. Spitzberg

3 Communication Ethics and Bullying   22
Janie Harden Fritz

   Voices for Visibility: The Resilient You   30
Keith Berry

PART II
Contexts of Bullying
★★**Bullying, Culture, and Identity**★★   **35**

4 Bullying and the Influence of Race, Ethnicity, and Culture on
Personal Violations   37
Tina M. Harris and Anastacia Janovec

5 How Dominant Group Members Can Transform Workplace Bullying   46
Robert J. Razzante, Sarah J. Tracy, and Mark P. Orbe

Contents

6 Cyberbullies, Bullying, and the Young in India 57
Rajesh Kumar

Voices for Visibility: Disciplining the Immigrant Body Through Collective Bullying 64
Wilfredo Alvarez

★★Workplace Bullying★★ 71

7 Disciplining the Office: The Past, Present, and Future of Communication Research on Bullying 73
Stacy Tye-Williams

8 The Theory of Bullying Conflict Cultures: Developing a New Explanation for Workplace Bullying 81
Nathalie Desrayaud, Fran C. Dickson, and Lynne M. Webb

9 Understanding Workplace Bullying from Two Perspectives: The Case of the Persian Gulf and the United States 93
Renee L. Cowan and Jaime E. Bochantin

10 Great Leadership in Business Does Not Compensate Idle Management in Workplace: Leadership, Organizational Culture, and Workplace Bullying in Startups in Japan 104
Masaki Matsunaga

11 Coping with Workplace Incivility: A Qualitative Study of the Strategies Targets Utilize 116
Jennifer S. Linvill and Stacey L. Connaughton

Voices for Visibility: It's More Than Personality Clash: The Escalation of Bullying 127
Anonymous

★★Bullying in the Academy★★ 133

12 U.S. K–12 Bullying Prevention Policy: A CHAT Analysis 135
Geoffrey Luurs

13 To Tell or Not to Tell: Bullied Students' Coping and Supportive Communication Processes 145
Carly M. Danielson and Lucas J. Youngvorst

14 Bullying in Academia Among College Professors 155
Alan K. Goodboy, Matthew M. Martin, Carol Bishop Mills, and Cathlin V. Clark-Gordon

Contents

15 Tensions Within Bullying and Career Resilience in Higher Education 164
Sean Eddington and Patrice M. Buzzanell

Voices for Visibility: Middle School Bullies Using Lies to Incite a Fight 173
Garry Bailey

★★Bullying Within/Across the Lifespan★★ 177

16 Exploring Bullying Experiences Among Immigrant Youth in Canada 179
Rukhsana Ahmed

17 A Look at Bullying Communication in Early Childhood: Towards a
Lifespan Developmental Model 188
Thomas J. Socha and Rachel Sadler

18 Verbal Aggressiveness as Bullying in the Emerging Adult Sibling Relationship 198
*Scott A. Myers, Carrie D. Kennedy-Lightsey, Christine K. Anzur, James P. Baker,
and Sara Pitts*

19 Bullying in Seniors' Communities: What's Identity Got to Do With It? 210
Loraleigh Keashly

★★Cyberbullying★★ 219

20 Defining Cyberbullying: Analyzing Audience Reaction to Anti-Bullying
Public Service Announcements 221
Kelly P. Dillon and Nancy Rhodes

21 Examining Cyberbullying Bystander Behavior 230
Sarah E. Jones and Matthew W. Savage

22 Textual Harassment as a Form of Bullying, Drama, and Obsessive
Relational Intrusion 241
Erin M. Sumner, Nicholas Brody, and Artemio Ramirez Jr.

Epilogue: Looking Forward 253
Christina S. Beck and Richard West
References 255
Contributors 299
Index 309

FOREWORD

A few months ago, the Parent Teacher Organization (PTO) paid for all of the students at my daughter's elementary school to attend a movie. When Ellie-Kate, a fourth grader, got home from school, she described the movie as "sad at the start but good at the end." The film, *Wonder*, does present an affirming message with a happy ending, stressing the importance of kindness, inclusivity, and acceptance as children came to admire and appreciate a new student, Auggie, with a craniofacial difference (National Public Radio, 2013, September 12).

Unfortunately, other individuals do not fare as well as the fictional Auggie and his fellow students who opted to "choose kind." According to the 2015 Youth Behavior Risk Survey conducted by the Centers for Disease Control (CDC), "20% of high school students reported being bullied on school property in the 12 months before the survey. Additionally, 16% of high school students reported they have been bullied electronically in the past 12 months" (Centers for Disease Control, n.d.). Moreover, the Workplace Bullying Institute released the startling findings of the 2017 U.S. Workplace Bullying Survey. The survey revealed that "19% of Americans are bullied [in the workplace], another 19% witness it, [and] 61% of Americans are aware of abusive conduct in the workplace" (Namie, 2017, para. 3).

According to the CDC (2016), bullying involves "aggression that is physical (hitting, tripping), verbal (name calling, teasing), or relational/ social (spreading rumors, leaving out of group)" (para. 2), potentially resulting "in physical injury, social and emotional distress, and even death" (para.5). Indeed, as we read the evening paper or scroll through Facebook, we all too commonly find yet another tragic account of a young person who purportedly had been bullied to the point of taking his or her own life (No Bullying.com, 2014, February 25).

Communication Discipline Response

In September, 2014, I was skimming Facebook at the end of a long day, and I stumbled on to a thread about a teen in my area who had passed away. I didn't recognize the name, but, as the mom of four daughters (including two who were still in school at the time), I felt drawn to click through the comments. Stunned, I read posts suggesting that she had been bullied.

We live in a small, tight-knit, rural community, nestled in the heart of Appalachia. I don't know why I used to have such a sense of (what turned out to be false) security in that description. As I've come to realize, people can opt to be cruel anywhere—small towns or large cities, elementary schools or corporations, during interactions with other children or senior citizens or family members

Foreword

or strangers. Bullies can target individuals that they know well or terrorize people that they have only encountered online.

As I stared at that Facebook thread back in the fall of 2014, my heart broke for that young girl, her family, her friends, and her school, and I grew angry. How could we allow such abusive interactions to ensue? What could we do? How could we make a difference?

As the then-Second Vice President of the National Communication Association (NCA), I recognized that even vile, negative comments constitute "communication." Physical actions and posts on message boards clearly comprise communicative acts. Although other organizations had certainly initiated anti-bullying efforts prior to that moment (ranging from celebrities in the STOMP Out Bullying campaign to the United States government through stopbullying.gov), the public dialogue regarding bullying lacked an integral voice—the Communication discipline.

Notably, several individual scholars in the Communication discipline (including a number of the contributors to this anthology) had already been researching and writing about bullying and communication, but we needed a platform for synthesizing and sharing that scholarship in a systematic manner. Getting our research and resources into the hands of educators, counselors, administrators, etc. necessitated strategic planning for action and advocacy.

I shared my concerns with colleagues on the NCA Executive Committee, and, with their approval, I founded the NCA Anti-Bullying Project and appointed the NCA Anti-Bullying Task Force, under the leadership of Keith Berry and Renee Cowan. Through this project, individuals from various scholarly traditions in our discipline join together with the goal of employing Communication-based insights to better understand and address the multifaceted, complex social problem of bullying. This team continues to seek ways of utilizing what we know about communication to make a difference in the lives of those who have been affected by bullying and to partner with stakeholders to prevent future incidents. As part of this initiative, we have established the NCA Anti-Bullying Resource Bank, conducted multiple community outreach and engagement programs, and connected scholars from across our discipline with shared commitments to educating, empowering, and equipping individuals with resources for addressing varied dimensions of this problem in diverse contexts.

The *Routledge Handbook of Communication and Bullying* spotlights scholarly contributions from the Communication discipline on this serious societal issue. Chapters in this anthology draw from Communication-based theories and concepts to offer insights about communicative practices that affected individuals orient to as bullying in five broad contexts—Bullying, Culture, and Identity; Workplace Bullying; Bullying in the Academy; and Bullying Across the Lifespan, and Cyberbullying. Notably, contributions to this volume stress not only the theoretical and scholarly implications of this research but also the pragmatic opportunities, affirming what we could and should do with these insights. Additionally, this anthology constitutes a state-of-the-discipline review for Communication-based research on bullying. As such, it also sets an agenda for what remains to be learned from a Communication perspective about these disturbing and dark communicative practices known as "bullying."

Christina S. Beck, Ohio University

PREFACE

The stories are haunting and all-too-real:

> *A group of boys bully Leena, a teenager with a significant acne problem, on social media. Within two weeks, Leena hangs herself in the basement of her Tennessee home.*

> *A fellow employee harasses Henry, a transgender employee at a big-box store in Minnesota, so much that he feels forced to quit his job, causing him to lose his apartment, and start prostituting on the streets.*

> *Wanda, a 74-year-old early dementia resident in a Tokyo nursing home, faces her roommate's wrath whenever she refuses to do as the roommate demands, such as fetching or cleaning her shoes.*

> *A group of girls bullied Jessica, a middle-school student in Florida, so badly that she jumped to her death from atop a cement silo.*

Not a week goes by without a tragic story related to bullying. Indeed, the subject of bullying appears in local, state, national, and international headlines. To be sure, bullying episodes trend on social media, grab the attention of news desks, provoke comments from politicians, and continue to resonate across the globe. Whether face-to-face or online, bullies and their targets/victims have sparked important discussions related to civility and other-centeredness. These difficult dialogues have captured the attention of an array of various stakeholders, including academic leaders, social workers, human resource professionals, social media experts, celebrities, and psychiatrists, among others.

Regrettably, as the literature reveals, anti-bullying initiatives report mixed levels of success. Although many programs utilize the ever-popular Olweus approach (named after a pioneer who is generally credited with introducing bullying to research), the model adheres to a Nordic orientation, limiting its application to other parts of the world (Kalman, 2011; Yamada, 2010). The results of other programs to reduce online bullying have also been somewhat ineffectual. For instance, cyberbullying across the globe is responsible for nearly a 90% rise in young people seeking support in the UK alone (Khomami, 2016).

Over the years in which conversations about bullying have appeared, popular culture has taken a front seat at the theatre of the absurd, raising awareness while also often sensationalizing this serious societal problem. Television, social media, and publications have interrogated the topic with memorable headlines. Yet, not all of the information on bullying is anecdotal or sensationalistic. Psychological, sociological, economic, biological, and philosophical perspectives have been offered, too, resulting in work that has been important for both reflection and intervention.

Despite the important conclusions gleaned from some of this scholarship across the disciplines, ironically, Communication has remained relatively quiet during academic and public dialogues about bullying. Unequivocally, bullying constitutes a communicative act, with verbal, nonverbal, and computer-mediated communication behaviors characterizing its existence (see West & Turner, this volume). Although some scholars in the Communication discipline have contributed to our understanding of communicative processes and practices pertaining to bullying, we have lacked an examination of what we know thus far and an agenda for concepts and issues requiring additional research. Until now.

We conceived and planned *The Routledge Handbook of Communication and Bullying* to fill this gap in the literature. This book strives to include representative theoretical and practical scholarship, and it comprises the first comprehensive collection dedicated to investigating the intersection of bullies, bullying, and the communication processes. The research contained in this compendium speaks to the theoretical and pragmatic notions embedded in bullying. In particular, the contributing authors unpack this insidious behavior as they provide both conceptual understanding and relevant life experiences.

Sectionalizing a concept as complex as bullying may seem futile, but it is necessary if we are to articulate the vastness of the research. Further, the scholarship contained within this book necessitates clear lines of demarcation as we introduce the various contexts, methods, and rationales. In addition, presenting a delineated approach to bullying enables us to explore its prevalence, depth, breadth, causes, types, and implications. Therefore, in this anthology, we aim to familiarize readers with the underlying influence of the communication process on bullying and its various manifestations, as well as consider various prevention and intervention strategies.

Communication scholarship pertaining to bullying spans theoretical, meta-theoretical, and heuristic traditions. The contributors in this volume present a template of scholarly considerations, including where, why, and how bullies function in a number of different communities. Each essay also addresses the nuances associated with bullying behavior, ensuring a thorough treatment of this vital and ubiquitous topic.

We organized chapters into two different parts and subdivided even further into subsections. First, operating under the assumption that a topic as complex as bullying requires us to understand its foundations, we begin with Part I (Foundations of Bullying and Communication Research), which contains three chapters that explore three fundamental issues related to bullying, as well as a personal reflection essay. Chapter 1, authored by Richard West and Lynn Turner, commences the discussion of bullying by situating the term in the Communication discipline. This chapter provides a framework for examining it and discussing representative contexts in which bullying occurs, and it offers one model (Holistic Model) for consideration. In Chapter 2, Brian Spitzberg investigates bullying by invoking the interdisciplinary nature of the concept. Similar to other foundational chapters, he presents several challenges to discussing the concept from a Communication vantage point. Janie Harden Fritz (Chapter 3) delineates the ethical issues surrounding bullying, an important theme that merits additional attention in the literature. Fritz posits that bullying should be understood from a virtue ethics perspective, a position suggesting that, when a person is bullied, a person's well-being is jeopardized. Keith Berry (*Voices for Visibility*) closes this section by discussing the notion of resiliency and how it functioned for him, as a target/victim of bullying. His autoethnographic account intersects compelling issues of identity, well-being, pain, and suffering.

The chapters in Part II of the *Handbook* unpack particular contexts in which bullying appears. In this portion of the book, we sought not only representation, but also efficiency in presentation. To

Preface

this end, the 19 chapters and three *Voices for Visibility* include a cross-section of numerous areas and experiences and provide a powerful synthesis of the state of the discipline regarding Communication-based research on this issue. Moreover, this part of the volume charts an agenda for next steps as our discipline takes a seat at the scholarly table, affirming the consequentiality of communication for understanding, addressing, and preventing bullying incidents.

Four chapters comprise efforts to understand "Bullying, Culture, and Identity," a subsection highlighting the importance of the individual and various fields of experience. Chapter 4, authored by Tina Harris and Anastacia Mae Janovec, embraces a cultural framework as the authors review the literature associated with bullying, race, and ethnicity. The authors argue that reflecting upon the research will empower others to develop anti-bullying policies and initiatives. In Chapter 5, as they investigate bullying acts, Robert Razzante, Sarah Tracy, and Mark Orbe examine the movement from Co-Cultural Theory to Dominant Group Theory. In particular, Razzante et al. conduct an analysis to understand how Dominant Group Theory can disrupt or impede workplace bullying. Chapter 6, authored by Rajesh Kumar, examines cyberbullying in India. In the chapter, Kumar suggests that with the rising use of the internet in the country, opportunities for bullying are flourishing. He posits that cyberbullying reduction can occur if parents begin to engage themselves more fully with their children as they interact online. Finally, Wilfredo Alvarez (*Voices for Visibility*) articulates a personal narrative as an Afro-Indigenous-European Caribbean native. In this provocative examination, Alvarez elucidates how verbal microaggressions, among other behaviors, become part of the everyday experiences of immigrants living in the U.S.

In a section spotlighting "Workplace Bullying," we feature five research-centered chapters and one personal reflection essay. Stacy Tye-Williams (Chapter 7) surveys the literature on workplace bullying. Discussing a range of topics, she proposes that the conversation about bullying embraces not only a traditional research approach, but also a more imaginative one. In Chapter 8, Nathalie Desrayaud, Fran Dickson, and Lynne Webb propose Bullying Conflict Cultures Theory. Focusing on the academic workplace, the team examines cultures that are more prone to bullying and suggest that if a culture is more open to disagreements, bullying is more opportunistic. Considering bullying from two cultural perspectives (the Persian Gulf and U.S.) (Chapter 9), Renee Cowan and Jaime Bochantin discuss bullying from a human resource professional perspective. The authors take a critical/power-based view and detail both stark similarities and differences between the two societies. In Chapter 10, Masaki Matsunaga presents an analysis of responses from hundreds of employees at dozens of Japanese start-ups. In this research, he argues that various leadership styles influence the workplace environment, which, in turn, can impact bullying behavior in that environment. Chapter 11, authored by Jennifer Linvill and Stacey Connaughton, offers a constructionist meta-theoretical framework to understand coping mechanisms of workplace incivility. They also consider matters related to social support and potential bullying behaviors. In our third *Voices for Visibility* account, an anonymous academic author elucidates a troubling journey toward tenure. The author articulates several questionable and untoward behaviors experienced along the way, each underscoring the fact that the college environment, as a workplace, is not immune from bullying.

The third area of this volume focuses on research related to Bullying in the Academy. This section include four studies and one personal reflection essay. Geoffrey Luurs (Chapter 12) compiles an assessment of bullying prevention programs in North Carolina. In his analysis, he employs Cultural-Historical Activity Theory (CHAT) to identify the strengths and weaknesses of the various programmatic policies. In Chapter 13, Carly Danielson and Lucas Youngvorst examine the coping processes and mechanisms that bullied students use. In addition to offline practices, the authors also identify various CMC venues that both alleviate and exacerbate the challenges facing bullied students.

Specifically looking at college professors, Alan Goodboy, Matthew Martin, Carol Bishop Mills, and Cathlin Clark-Gordon (Chapter 14) found that workplace bullying occurs in environments with higher job demands, lower control over work, and lower social support from supervisors.

xii

Goodboy et al. note that job dissatisfaction, job stress, and a desire to leave result when individuals are exposed to such hostile environments. In Chapter 15, Sean Eddington and Patrice Buzzanell delineate research related to bullying at the college level. In addition, Eddington and Buzzanell present an imagined conversation in which the two discuss the parameters and implications of bullying in higher education. This subsection closes with a fourth personal essay (*Voices for Visibility*) written by Garry Bailey. In this reflection, he introduces us to the notion of middle school intimidating bullying behavior by girls. The narrative includes the interplay among children, their parents, classmates, and the school system.

We devote the fourth subsection to "Bullying Within/Across the Lifespan." Four chapters span a number of different communities, including young immigrants, preschoolers, siblings, and senior citizens. Chapter 16, authored by Rukhsana Ahmed, utilizes focus group analysis to understand how Canadian immigrant youth view bullying. The group members concede that bullying is inextricably linked to discrimination based on religion, sexual identity, race, and gender. Thomas Socha and Rachel Sadler, in Chapter 17, contend that bullying is a developmental, dark side, lifespan communication phenomenon, depicting a strategic effort to be aggressive to others. Socha and Sandler argue that Communication scholars are well-positioned to investigate the various life trajectory points where/when bullying occurs, beginning with early childhood. In Chapter 18, Scott Myers, Carrie Kennedy-Lightsey, Christine Anzur, James Baker, and Sara Pitts examine an often-overlooked and under-explored population: the adult sibling relationship. The team researched verbal aggression, in particular, to investigate the extent to which siblings bullied other siblings during their childhood. In Chapter 19, Loraleigh Keashly articulates the need to study bullying in senior communities. Embracing a Communication perspective, the research highlights peer-to-peer bullying as a response to a senior's identity threat, a threat underscored by rigid cultural ageism and stereotypes.

The final area of the *Handbook* focuses on the online bullying that characterizes so much of contemporary bullying efforts. The three chapters revolving around cyberbullying present an array of topics, each central to any discourse related to this intimidating and ruinous behavior. In Chapter 20, Kelly Dillon and Nancy Rhodes analyze the mediated-CMC-bullying intersection by addressing the efficacy of public service announcements related to the responsiveness and prevention of bullying. They utilize a Symbolic Interactionist and a mental models approach to understand the differences between lay and academic interpretations of bullying. In Chapter 21, Sarah Jones and Matthew Savage analyze focus groups of college students who had witnessed cyberbullying behavior. The team examined the responses to these bystanders and conceptualized a typology of bystander actions and bystander types. Our final chapter by Erin M. Sumner, Nicholas Brody, and Artemio Ramerez (Chapter 22) elucidates the various consequences of text messaging constructed to bully another. The chapter emphasizes important harasser motives involved in the online bullying.

When we began *The Routledge Handbook of Communication and Bullying*, we envisioned one fundamental goal: to showcase exemplary communication scholarship related to bullying. Contributions to this book herald the integral nature of Communication theories, concepts, and behaviors for grappling with the serious social issue of bullying. We hope that this anthology provides a theoretical, empirical, and pragmatic springboard for further scholarly investigations and activism efforts. We believe that this anthology constitutes an important contribution for the Communication discipline and for broader public dialogues about best practices for a) responding to bullies, b) encouraging involvement in prevention efforts, and c) supporting individuals who experience such abusive situations.

Finally, this state-of-the-discipline book celebrates the diversity of scholarship available in the field. To this end, we encouraged variation in methodological genres, conceptual approaches, and current and emerging themes pertaining to the menacing behavior of bullies. Moreover, we proudly include a wide array of scholars from varied geographical, cultural, and institutional backgrounds. In doing so, we present a collection of distinguished Communication scholars who have employed a

Communication lens for understanding bullying culture and practices. As such, this book serves as a foundation for those seeking the most salient research conclusions regarding one of the most critical topics resonating across the globe.

A Special Note of Appreciation

We recognize that a book of this nature required the involvement of scores of people. First, we are indebted to the scholars whose work appears in this *Handbook*. Throughout the editing process, we became more impressed and even more enthusiastic about what we were reading. We are convinced that the empirical, theoretical, and practical scholarship will be academic touchstones for future research. These writers have honestly and responsibly addressed themes related to bullying that remain aligned with the myriad of cultural conversations taking place.

We also thank Routledge and their production teams. We appreciated the levels of support we received from the very beginning and deeply appreciate the encouragement from an international publisher of this caliber.

We also extend our gratitude to our respective personal and professional communities. Rich, as always, is inspired by his mother, Beverly, a woman with tenacity, grit, and kindness. She was relentless in protecting and supporting him during his frequent bouts of childhood bullying. He also thanks his life partner, Chris—the human equivalent of love, friendship, and support. Christie offers special thanks to her husband, Roger C. Aden, and daughters, Brittany, Chelsea Meagan, Emmy, and Ellie-Kate. Their patience and understanding made her involvement in this project possible.

In closing, we hope that this book inspires additional research about and engagement with this serious problem. Communication scholars hold the potential to make a difference in our world, and bullying in particular, constitutes an issue for which our research can truly impact lives.

PART I

Foundations of Bullying and Communication Research

1

COMING TO TERMS WITH BULLYING

A Communication Perspective

Richard West and Lynn H. Turner

We live in a culture that tends to thrive on the humiliation of others (Martocci, 2015). As a result, bullying is prevalent in all aspects of life and at all ages (Monks & Coyne, 2011). We hear about bullies and bullying behaviors in myriad contexts and through multiple venues. Comedians like Chris Rock and Stephen Colbert humorously muse about the value of bullying for toughening kids up and getting important social changes through Congress. It's virtually impossible to attend to any popular media for more than an hour without reading or hearing the word "bully." Further, scholars from a variety of disciplines, including education, sociology, psychology, and communication, have trained research attention on the concept.

Despite this ubiquity, the definition of bullying is often unclear or contested. And, although most scholars aim to incorporate a foundational understanding of the term in their research, both consistencies and inconsistencies in the literature exist. To begin, typically, Western scholars have defined bullying as resting on three specific criteria: A bully seeks to inflict *intentional harm* through *repeated unwanted actions* (verbal or physical) directed toward an individual who is of *lesser power* (e.g., physical, emotional, financial, etc.) than the bully (e.g., Olweus, 1997; Monks & Coyne, 2011; Stopbullying. gov, n.d.). Still, research, interviews, and experience affirm that bullying can involve repeated behavior and, occasionally, a one-time offense (Monks & Coyne, 2011). Bullying may not need repetition if fear of repeated attacks is apparent (Stopbullying.gov, n.d.). In addition, bullying behavior is not always directed toward one individual. Rather, it can be deployed upon a group, including women and members of co-cultures (Orbe, 1998; Priest, King, Bécares, & Kavanagh, 2016; Rivers & Duncan, 2013). This targeted action is sometimes referred to as *bias bullying* (Smith, 2011), or what some scholars identify as the "thorny issues around what causes and constitutes bullying, [including] how to think differently about overlapping phenomena such as racism, sexism, homophobia, or sexual harassment" (Mishna, 2012, p. 53). Finally, some have argued that bullying may not need an uneven power dynamic (Smith, 2011), a conclusion that undercuts earlier and contemporary conceptions of the behavior. Bullying can occur between peers of the same age or social class, co-workers of the same standing, or individuals of the same sex. Therefore, a traditional definition, though widely used, has a variety of challenges associated with it.

And the inconsistencies seem to continue. For instance, the term *bullying* was originally used solely to describe children's hurtful play among peers (Monks & Coyne, 2011), and the majority of the literature using the term still discusses children from kindergarten through high school (e.g., Waasdorp, Pas, Zablotsky, & Bradshaw, 2017; Coulter, Herrick, Friedman, & Stall, 2016; Jara, Casas, & Ortega-Ruiz, 2017; Mishna, 2012; Monks & Coyne, 2011; Ofe, Plumb, Plexico, & Haaka,

2016; Olweus, 1997; Smith, 2014). However, bullying occurs not only during K–12 but also prior and subsequent to the school years (Garlough, 2016; Quinn, 2015; Reigle, 2016). Children may begin bullying in the first few years of their life, although these actions may not actually constitute bullying, because researchers question whether children so young can have malicious intent or if they are just mimicking behaviors they see others exhibiting (Monks & Coyne, 2011; Tattum & Herbert, 1997).

Research on bullying has expanded beyond schools to include cyberbullying, cultural mores, workplace bullying, legal issues, and bullying within senior (elderly) communities (Bonifas, 2016; Quinn, 2015). Further, after individuals exit high school, the terminology for bullying changes to a focus on harassment and abuse. Perhaps this is due to legal reasons, since many U.S. states have created laws to punish bullying behaviors, even if the perpetrator is below 18 years old (Levi, n.d.; Stopbul lying.gov, n.d.). The necessity of holding perpetrators accountable in a court of law (Garlough, 2016) establishes clear definitions for terms like harassment and abuse.

Given ever-changing environments where bullying is found, technological advances enabling bullying to occur in cyberspace, and policy-legal evolutions in interventions around bullying, some writers contend that developing a universal definition and interpretation of bullying is difficult and, at times, inappropriate and unnecessary (Bazelon, 2014). Moreover, if a definition does not clearly suit the needs of students, employees, or individuals, organizations must modify it in order for policies to be created (Reigle, 2016). Research has found that when children, teachers, and parents are asked for their definitions of bullying, they often provide different definitions from one another and from the researchers (Monks & Coyne, 2011). For instance, children are more likely to conflate bullying with any type of aggression than are adults. In addition, some writers caution that the social construction of bullying using a Western lens is not always applicable to non-Western cultures (Moon, 2000).

It is incumbent on scholars to provide clear lines of demarcation and appropriate parameters within their own research projects. Valid theories and measurement tools begin with clear conceptual definitions. While it may not be possible or desirable to create a universal definition for bullying, it is critical to posit a specific definition for each individual study and clarify how the definition is congruent with the theory and method utilized in the study.

Bullying is immensely crucial in the lives of not only the target/victim but also the bully and their respective communities (Randall, 1997; Quinn, 2015). Vulnerable groups are the most at risk (Mishna, 2012). In addition, the nature of bullying and its numerous impacts require scholars and practitioners to grapple with its definition, even if we conclude that it's impossible to create a single definition for all situations. As communication researchers, we are uniquely well-suited for this task, and yet, the task is quite challenging.

Bullying as Communication

Bullying behavior, bystander behaviors, and the ways to reduce or eliminate the harmful effects of bullying are communicative in nature (Berry, 2016). Whether through verbal or nonverbal/physical codes, bullies employ communication tactics to achieve their intent (Lutgen-Sandvik & Tracy, 2012). In addition, bullying necessarily requires a sender, a channel, and a receiver or audience. The sheer act of bullying is tantamount to significant noise in a communication channel. Senders, channels, receivers, and noise are all key components in any communication model (West & Turner, 2017), and yet, scholars fail to assert this fundamental template in their research. Moreover, cyberbullying and cyber-aggressions are tantamount to communication episodes (e.g., computer-mediated communication, CMC). Finally, anti-bullying programs and initiatives, too, require expertise in communication skills such as forgiveness, understanding, and empathy (www.stopbullying.gov, n.d.). It is clear, then, that bullying is profitably viewed through a communication lens that employs an understanding of foundational elements.

Models representing the communication process are rarely explicit in communication scholarship. Interestingly, however, the field of communication traces its roots to the various features of these models, and they remain particularly apt to consider in dialogues about bullying. Discussions related to relevant aspects of communication such as communication contexts and effects help scholars to frame their understanding of bullying and assist practitioners as they conceptualize and construct effective interventions around bullying.

Despite these assertions, the communication field has entered this difficult dialogue quite late, and as this anthology attests, our research is just beginning to influence how scholars understand bullying. In the research that does exist, communication scholars have studied bullying by employing a variety of frameworks, including: relational/family (Berry & Adams, 2016; Matsunaga, 2009), workplace (Cowan, 2009), and educational (Goodboy, Martin, & Rittenour, 2016). And while this research has been important in many ways, no clear or consistent thread exists demonstrating scholarly efforts to interpret the bullying concept. In fact, researchers have examined bullying from myriad vantage points, including those of parents (Smorti, Menesini, & Smith, 2003), HR professionals (Cowan, 2012), customer service workers (Bishop & Hoel, 2008), and bystanders (Brody & Vangelisti, 2016), among others. If we accept the assumption that bullying is complex and appears in different forms, it seems necessary to establish some sort of "clarification model" so that discussions and analyses might be more aligned with communication research.

In the remainder of this chapter, we present research on bullying in three contexts (school, workplace, and senior communities) and provide a concrete exemplar illustrating each. We conclude with an illustration of how a holistic model of communication can usefully frame this research. Our approach, therefore, grounds the reported research in praxis. As Hollis (2016a) notes, "theories provide solid backdrops," and yet, for those who experience bullying, "there is nothing theoretical about the experience" (p. 22). We believe that an approach respecting both the theory and experience of bullying responds to Craven, Marsh, and Parada's (2013) assertion that theory, research, and practice cannot be separated from one another; if one area is weak, all are impaired. In addition, this chapter serves as an overview of the various environments in which bullying occurs and a precursor to the research that will be offered throughout the remainder of the book. Of necessity, this review includes many sources outside the communication field.

A Contextual Approach

To provide an efficient snapshot of the bullying concept and induce its definition, we articulate three primary environments in which the behavior is typically explored and explained: schools, workplaces, and senior centers. We provide representative conclusions and make no claim that we are exhaustive in our review. We limit the majority of our review to those studies that are theoretical, and we are not exploring the popular culture conversation on bullying (which is quite expansive and didactic in nature). Further, as Randall (1997) observes, "the roots of much bullying are nurtured in the homes of perpetrators where aggression is learned and honed by deviousness into bullying" (p. 5). Therefore, one definitional insight that comes along with Randall's comment is that bullying is not a fully formed schemata, but rather often follows along developmental stages, allowing for both expansion and extinction of the behavior. In that spirit, we begin our discussion with the context where the largest portion of research exists: the schools.

Schools

Most of the research on bullying in the U.S. didn't begin until the 1990s, which was the time when scholars realized that boys who shot their classmates, such as the two shooters at Columbine High School in Colorado, had previously been bullied in school. Schools are enclosed spaces where large groups of individuals spend significant amounts of time together, making them opportunistic sites for multiple forms of bullying. Researchers have posited a number of different conclusions related to bullying in the schools. We begin our discussion with what scholars have concluded about bullying during the earliest school years.

Preschool

Although scant research focused on bullying in preschool in the past, recently it has become an area of growing research interest. Pepler and Cummings (2016), for example, posit that 2–5-year-olds are immature, and consequently, children may not recognize when power is being exerted upon them or when they're exerting power over others. Some research indicates that bullying in preschool is different than what is observed with older children. Specifically, preschoolers tend to be more likely to use direct forms of bullying such as hitting, name calling, and comments such as "you can't play with us" compared to the more indirect methods, such as spreading rumors, adopted by older children in school (Monks, 2011).

Preschool Bullying: Manuel

While playing at the water table, Manuel continues to splash water at Lydia, making her cry. He sees his friends, Luke and Albert, laugh, and in turn, Manuel continues to throw handfuls of water at the girl. Maggie, one of the preschool teachers, immediately escorts Manuel out of the room, telling him his behavior was unacceptable and mean. She stresses to Manuel that he needs to go back to apologize to Lydia and shake hands.

Much of the research related to preschoolers adopts a developmental-relational perspective (Lerner, 2012; Lerner & Callina, 2014). Applying this model to bullying, Pepler and Cummings state that scholars and practitioners need to understand:

> the complex, dynamic, and continuous interactions between an individual child's characteristics (genetic, neuro-physiological, and developing social-emotional capacity) and experiences in key social relationships (with parents, other caregivers, and peers) as well as in broader contexts (family, school, community) and broader systems (culture, media, and political climate).
>
> *(p. 37)*

In other words, because young children are introduced to so many potentially influential agents in their early years, the heterogeneity of their bullying experiences needs to be considered before drawing definitive conclusions. Further, researchers have concluded that 4-year-old children are likely to conform to the values and social opinions of other children around them (Haun & Tomasello, 2011), even when they know that the opinion is wrong. Additionally, researchers (Nassem & Harris, 2015) note that children in early childhood experiment with their power potential by bullying their peers and will often cease bullying when they learn from adults (parents, teachers, etc.) and their peers that it is unacceptable. Thus, preschoolers tend to experiment with bullying, and at this age, bullying is a pliable and changeable behavior.

Middle School

Sometimes called "the drama years" (Kilpatrick & Joiner, 2012), middle school remains a prime location for bullies to flourish. At this educational level, bullying is considered to be a group phenomenon, involving the bully, the target/victim, and the bystanders (Datta, Cornell, & Huang, 2016). Themes related to popularity and status (Wright & Li, 2013) are embedded in discussions of bullying for young children in grades 6–8. Adolescents at this stage draw upon their self-appraisals and other situational factors to determine how to cope with the bullying.

At this point in their educational trajectory, students begin to use social media to bully others for attention, among other reasons (Hicks, Jennings, Jennings, Berry, & Green, 2018). Cyberbullying is a topic that resonates across people's lives, but it seems to have its genesis during the middle school years. During the middle school years, cyberbullying is undertaken via apps such as Instagram, Snapchat, and YouTube and serves as an opportunity to digitally harass someone, post hurtful information and/or images, embarrass peers, or spread rumors (Martin, Wang, Petty, Wang, & Wilkins, 2018). Cyberbullying seems to increase as middle schoolers age and, in one study, as grade level increased (from seventh grade to eighth grade), so did instances of cyberbullying (Şentürk & Bayat, 2016).

Smith (2014) reports on studies showing that family factors influence children of middle school age in myriad ways related to bullying in the school. The researcher distills three themes: (1) a difficult home environment, featuring significant parental conflict, providing a bullying role model; (2) excessive parental control, resulting in children being unprepared to stand up to bullies; and (3) domestic abuse, prompting children to accept or to mete out violence.

The aforementioned discussion suggests that bullying in middle school is multifactorial and functions as a result of a confluence of factors, namely a desire for popularity, a predilection for social media, and family factors such as parental conflict.

Middle School Bullying: Paige

Deciding that she was among the best dressed at school, Paige tells her friends during lunch about the shoes that Samantha is wearing. As the girls go past Samantha's lunch table, they laugh in unison, with Paige yelling: "Shoes for Sale! Samantha's Shoes for Sale!" Sam feels scared and looks down at her cell phone, hoping the episode will end quickly. Later, however, Sam finds that Paige took a picture of her shoes and posted them on Instagram with the caption: "See Sad Samantha's Stinking Shoes!"

High School

Research examining bullying in high school (grades 9–12) is quite sparse, with only 31 studies looking at bullying in the U.S. focused on this cohort (Azeredo, Rinaldi, de Moraes, Levy, & Menezes, 2015). Bullying investigations have studied both face-to-face and cyberbullying, although the research is more anecdotal than empirical. At the secondary level, similar to the middle school level, scholars continue to view bullying as a group experience (Edwards & Batlemento, 2016). Much of the research centers on the characteristics of the bully and the effects of bullying upon target/victims. From a theoretical standpoint, scholars have adopted a social-ecological approach, suggesting that there is a relationship among the individual and their family, community, and school (Bronfenbrenner, 1979). Thus, attitudes and behaviors related to bullying are influenced by a dynamic interplay of both academic and non-academic stakeholders (Merrin, Espelage, & Hong, 2018).

With respect to the high school bully, a number of characteristics have been identified. A bully is more likely to engage in alcohol consumption and smoking (Nansel, Craig, Overpeck, Saluja, & Ruan, 2004), consider suicidal ideation (Hinduja & Patchin, 2010), carry a weapon (Nansel et al., 2004), feel social isolation (Juvonen, Graham, & Schuster, 2003), and, while identifying as extroverts, score low on agreeability assessments (Maunder & Crafter, 2018). High school bullies tend to be healthier and stronger than those not involved in bullying (Wolke, Woods, Bloomfield, & Karstadt, 2001) and enjoy elevated peer group status (Vaillancourt, Hymel, & McDougall, 2003).

The target/victim of a bully has also been investigated. First, high school is a time of identity development (Smith, 2014). As a result, when teens manifest identities that are outside the mainstream of their high school classmates, they often become the targets of bias bullying. Racial harassment, faith-based bullying, homophobic/LGBT bullying, bullying the differently abled, and so forth, all constitute bias bullying, also known as *identity-based bullying* or *prejudice-driven bullying*.

The literature related to high school bullying also examines the effects of bullying. This research notes that the effects are both short and long term. Most profoundly, exposure to high school bullies results in significant health-related problems. Gini and Pozzoli (2009) found that target/victims are more likely to develop colds, sleeping problems, headaches, and stomach aches. In addition, bullied high school youth are prone to anxiety disorders and consider self-harm and suicide (Lereya et al., 2013) to a greater degree than those who are not bullied.

While there has not been a significant amount of empirical work related to high school bullying behavior, it seems clear that bullying taking place in high schools generally moves beyond one person bullying another and into pack or group bullying. Individuals begin to manifest various identities at this stage, resulting in GLBT youth, teens with disabilities, and teens of color disproportionately targeted for bullying.

High School Bullying: Jake and Jason Foster

As twins, the Foster boys were known throughout their school for their identical looks. Yet, they were also known as the biggest bullies in the high school. Both football players, the boys were popular and loved walking the hallways, which featured posters of them as members of the football team. One day, however, the two were with a group of other players and saw Toby, a small-framed transgender junior. The players circled Toby around his locker, calling him names and telling him not to leave the school alone at the end of the day. Toby, petrified and too nervous to tell school administration, called a ride-sharing program once the next class started and headed home three hours before the end of the day.

College

When students attend college, bullying behavior does not cease. Further, some research indicates that if students had been bullied in high school, there is a residual impact that they carry into college with them, negatively influencing their first-semester transition experiences (Goodboy, Martin, & Goldman, 2016). Bullying in college has been called a "pervasive social problem" (Brock, Oikonomidoy, Wulfing, Pennington, & Obenchain, 2014, p. 516), although there is little empirical work on bullying at the college level. What research there is points to a variety of issues. First, bullies continue their behavior from middle and high school into the college environment (Adams & Lawrence, 2011), and bullying is often viewed as a "rite of passage" (p. 4). In addition to this privileged characteristic, other themes emerge in the literature. For instance, target/victims of bullying experience fear and feelings of exclusion, isolation, or perceptions related to abuse, ridicule, alienation, and loneliness (Adams & Lawrence, 2011).

Because college is replete with group opportunities and activities (classroom projects, residence halls, Greek life, etc.), a group mentality takes on an even more pronounced role than in earlier academic levels. To this end, the bystander effect has been studied as it relates to college students. Palmer and Abbott (2018), for instance, found that bias bullying occurs quite frequently in college, and they note that bystanders were more likely to help when the target/victims were members of the same group to which they belonged. The researchers conclude that in-group/out-group identities could help inform anti-bullying initiatives.

With respect to cyberbullying, texting and interactions on social media are the primary ways in which college students bully others (Lund & Ross, 2017). In one study, 90% of respondents noted that they were likely to report cyberbullying to institutional officials and much less likely to confront the cyberbully or the target/victim (Luker & Churchak, 2017). Further, only 10% felt prepared to handle bullying episodes at their college/university. Contrary to popular anecdotes, researchers (Obermaier, Fawzi, & Koch, 2016) concluded that in some cyberbullying episodes, the number of bystanders makes no significant difference in terms of the desire to intervene unless the episode is viewed as an "emergency." In that situation, bystanders were more likely to intervene.

As we noted earlier, little bullying research has been conducted with college students. However, it seems apparent that college-aged populations are influenced by their peers in ways both seen and unseen. Given the proclivity of college students to use social media, bullying via technology remains critical. At times, college students will intervene to confront the bully, but they must be motivated by the episode's severity and their own similarity to the target/victim.

College Bullying: Nola

The five friends sitting in their teacher education class all knew that they would, one day, be teachers. As the self-appointed group leader, Nola took it upon herself to tell the others what their tasks would be for their final group assignment. She told three of the group members that they should try to meet outside of class and Nola worked out times they could do this. When the fourth member, Emma, asked about the times, Nola told her that she couldn't meet with the others because Emma "smelled like an Italian restaurant! You're all garlic-smelling!" Nola later posted an Instagram picture of Emma with a garlic clove and a chef's hat with the caption: "Mangia, Emma!" Emma was so embarrassed. She felt helpless and awkward.

Workplaces

The workplace is an environment where adults live out much of their daily lives. Like schools, and despite telecommuting, most workplaces are enclosed spaces where individuals from various backgrounds come together to accomplish various tasks. This dynamic can—and often does—result in a working environment that is ripe for bullying. However, workplaces are subject to federal and state laws governing workers' civil rights. A worker has the right to be free from harassment, hostility, and/ or discriminating events that constitute workplace bullying (Feeley, 2013). In some cases, though, the legal protections simply result in workplace bullying that is very subtle and indirect as the bully doesn't want to risk getting caught and facing disciplinary action or job loss (Kuykendall, 2012).

Few populations at work garner as many bullying attempts as the GLBT population, of which more than 36% report being bullied at work (Kirton, n.d.); over 56% of those bullied report that it is done repeatedly (Schef, n.d.). As one author notes, there is a "workplace epidemic" of bullying GLBT employees (Picchi, 2017). To receive legal support, a target/victim usually has to be a member of a federally protected class (race, color, sex, gender, religion, age, disability status, genetic information, country of origin). One personal characteristic not on the list is sexual orientation/identity.

In 1998, President Bill Clinton outlawed discrimination of federal civilian employees who are GLBT. Nearly every year since then bills have been introduced to add sexual orientation to the Employment Non-Discrimination Act, but they have failed to pass, leaving GLBT people without legal protection. The good news is that in 22 states, Guam, Puerto Rico, and the District of Columbia, employment discrimination is prohibited on the basis of sexual/gender identity. The bad news is that in 28 states, someone can be fired for being GLBT (Kaplan, 2014).

Some research indicates that employees feel rather powerless when confronted with bullying at work, even when they do have legal protections (Tye-Williams & Krone, 2017). In this study, the researchers found that employees felt that advice often given for dealing with workplace bullying (such as "stay calm" and "be rational") made no difference in their own situations or actually made things worse. Workplace bullying, similar to other bullying, frequently pertains to a power differential between the bully (e.g., supervisor, co-worker, etc.) and the target/victim. Bullying in the workplace typically includes an aggressor's attacks on another's personal and professional performance and/or on the personal features or characteristics of an employee (Duffy & Yamada, 2018).

Like schools, the workplace is not inoculated from bullying. In fact, research shows that bullying continues to be a major problem. Research shows that workplace bullying results in loss of productivity, diminished health, and psychological stress. Overall, we can conclude that bullying is likely to occur in workplaces that are lacking in transparency, accountability, guidance, and an appropriate reward structure (O'Farrell & Nordstrom, 2013).

Workplace Bullying: Henry and Quentin

Working as a night stocker at Walmart with only a high school diploma, Henry sometimes worried about the future. Yet, he was more than happy in his personal life. Henry had recently gotten married, and he and his husband, Eric, were enjoying married life. His happiness ends each night, however, when he gets to work and listens to his boss, Quentin, spew anti-gay language at him ("Hey, sexy, did you and Eric do your 'man-bob' last night?!"), all the while claiming he was just joking ("We have to stay awake around here at 3 a.m.! We need a little comic relief"). But Henry always felt helpless, knowing that his co-workers were laughing at him, not with him. He was pretty sure that the hatred many felt toward him for being gay could erupt into violence at any time. He also knew that with his credentials, his work options were quite limited.

Senior Living Communities

Images of bullying generally connote kids at school and employees at work. Yet, few recognize that bullying in the elderly (e.g., over 65 years of age) community has emerged as equally problematic (see Keashly, this volume). When discussing seniors residing in support communities (e.g., retirement homes, senior centers, assisted living facilities), the research on bullying (e.g., elder abuse) is scarce, however. Perhaps one reason accounting for this scholarly absence is the fact that staff in retirement centers may be anxious about providing information regarding resident behavior for ethical and legal reasons.

We've already noted that bullying knows no boundaries. And, in addition to young people in schools and people in their workplaces, perhaps no other context is more vulnerable to bullying than senior living communities. Still, as gerontologists, sociologists, and social workers try to grapple with the bullying of and by elders, the humiliating behaviors continue. It is important to point out that resident-on-resident bullying needs to be considered in tandem with the fact that 50% of residents in nursing homes and assisted care facilities suffer from some form of dementia or cognitive impairment (Alzheimer's Association, 2017).

Bullying, in the world of aging seniors, is quite similar to bullying in the world of the students and workers. Like the school and the workplace, bullying in senior residential contexts includes yelling, hitting, pushing, rough handling, and pulling hair, among others. But for seniors who actually live with each other, the bully has other options as well. Physical bullying can also mean preventing a target/victim from riding in an elevator or hitting another on the knees with a cane. Psychological bullying includes isolating seniors from others, bossiness, insulting physical abilities such as sight and hearing, and engaging in rumors or gossip, among others. Further acts of bullying include shunning those who are new residents, telling residents that they are not welcome to sit at their table, rummaging through personal belongings, threatening revenge if the resident tells the staff, and repeated episodes where older residents are often uninvited to events or tables with younger residents ("You can't hear like we can, so sit somewhere else") (Podnieks, 2008).

Research related to seniors living in residential communities is replete with examples that characterize elder bullying between a stressed caregiver and a dependent patient (Bergeron & Gray, 2003). Yet, other researchers note that we should diminish the value of this kind of discussion because stress alone doesn't account for many bullying episodes. Further, excusing bullying by attributing it to stress fails to hold bullies accountable and serves to direct funds to improving the caregiver's situation, rather than to the target/victim's needs/resources (Brandl & Raymond, 2012).

Some research characterizes bullying as an act that undercuts the dignity of the senior. In particular, the bullying process results in self-isolation of the target/victim. Targets/victims of bullying in senior centers report higher levels of loneliness, depression, and suicide ideation (Benson, n.d., Teo, 2012). Further, seniors who have been bullied experience Post-Traumatic Stress Disorder (PTSD) and other disorders, including social phobias, panic disorder, and obsessive-compulsive disorder (Dobry, Braquehasis, & Sher, 2013). Ogle, Rubin, and Siegler (2013) looked at exposure to trauma such as bullying in senior communities and found that bullying targets are more vulnerable to other maladies, including sleep disturbances, higher anxiety levels, and other health problems.

Despite sparse research so far, examining bullying in senior communities is of paramount importance. It is clear, however, that seniors who are bullied will likely remain silent, both fearing repercussions and believing that they will be a burden to family members and/or friends. Bullying in senior communities is as serious as, if not more than, bullying in schools and in workplaces. Seniors have unique needs and, because of their limited physical and intellectual abilities, are frequently targeted for bullying.

Senior Residential Bullying: Myra and Liz

The 80+-year-old roommates at the city's nursing home facility have been living together for two weeks. But Liz—a resident for nine years—continued to tell Myra—a new resident—that she needed more space in the room. Liz demanded that Myra put all her belongings in one drawer while Liz took three. "And, sometimes, you need to get me dessert when we watch TV. We call that the new kid on the block," Liz laughed. Myra definitely didn't want to cause problems, especially because she knew of Liz's hotheaded reputation. Myra acquiesced, trying to not to cry as she remembered happier times with her late husband and feeling ashamed that she was now viewed as her roommate's servant.

A Holistic Approach to Bullying

Although communication scholars have just begun investigating bullying, it is, as we noted earlier, a behavior anchored in communication. In addition to acknowledging the value of context, we advanced the belief that the communication process informs bullying behavior, identifying a sender (bully), receiver (target/victim), channel (online, face-to-face), and noise (the bullying act) as key ingredients. In other work (West & Turner, 2017, 2019), we have argued that the complexity of communication can be understood using a holistic lens. In doing so, we conclude that several additional components are critical to understanding communication: culture, history, and effect. Each has, to some degree, relevancy to our discussion of bullying and provides additional understanding of bullying as a communication process.

With respect to *culture*, we believe that the rules, norms, and patterns of communication are instrumental as we try to understand bullying. Whether school/classroom rules, workplace norms, or types of communication patterns, bullying depends on the cultural climate surrounding the process. Bullying exists when the culture allows or encourages the behavior. In rare circumstances, bullying can occur organically, with no previous recognition of conditions or situations that may explain the bullying.

The notion of *history* refers the historical period in which the bullying behavior is undertaken and viewed. For instance, although scholarly discussions of bullying date back over 50 years ago (Ciavarella, 1968), scholars and participants have viewed it (and defined it) differently over time. Early conceptions of bullying saw it primarily as a behavior undertaken by children without too many lasting consequences (Mishna, 2012). Currently, bullying is conceptualized much differently. An historical marking allows us to see that we are investigating a behavior that remains pivotal today—perhaps even more so, given technological advances. Clearly, bullying has intrigued researchers for decades, and this historical understanding provides us with a snapshot of the concept's (unfortunate) durability.

A third and crucial factor from a holistic vantage point is the consequence, or *effect*, of bullying. Throughout this review, we see scholars shining a light on various consequences of bullying. Whether psychological, emotional, physical, or physiological, bullying behavior has a significant effect upon the system (environment) and subsystems (people/relationships) where it occurs. This effect cannot be understood as anything but adverse. Not one short- or long-term benefit arises from any bullying episode, and understanding the effect(s) of bullying is of paramount importance if there are to be opportunities for intervention.

A holistic approach to understanding bullying is rooted in the transactional nature of communication, a communication model whereby individuals simultaneously send and receive messages. Taking a holistic approach allows us to acknowledge the additional elements that provide insight into the bullying process. Understanding all of the components related to the bully, the bullying, and the environmental conditions helps us as we build a definition of the concept. Fully mapping the concept is the first step as researchers disentangle the complexity related to bullying.

Conclusion

The primary aim of this chapter has been to focus on how a communication perspective provides a unique entree to the conceptual framework of bullying. By presenting a representative overview of three contexts in which bullying occurs, we have offered a way to define bullying. Exploring the research in these three contexts illustrates how bullying communication manifests across key moments in the lifespan. Our school lives (preschool, middle school, high school, and college), workplace experiences, and elderly years while residents in senior communities are all important markers in the trajectory of bullying behaviors.

As noted throughout this chapter, communication research related to bullying is sparse and embryonic. The scholarship contained within this anthology allows us to view bullying as a communicative practice. The insidiousness of the behavior and the professional and personal challenges related to investigating its various embodiments are clear. We remain confident that communication scholars will be key to helping not only those who work to eradicate bullying but, most importantly, the targets/victims as well.

2

BUILDING BETTER MODELS TO UNDERSTAND BULLYING

Brian H. Spitzberg

Still proximal to the inflection point between the past millennium and the next, we continue to struggle to find a position from which to grasp the full implications of our pace of change. Our technologies seem to be evolving at a much faster rate than our personal, societal, and cultural abilities to grasp their multifaceted roles in our lives. We are so enamored of the affordances allowed by new media that the primary functions of the message become the ground to the figure of the medium, despite the decades intervening since the "hypodermic" analogy and the McLuhan conjecture of the medium as the message. Yet, we are still a tribal species, evolved with adaptive tendencies to seek status and group identity despite the occasional maladaptive effects of such motives. Bullying represents one of these tendencies that continues to challenge the better angels of our nature, in both our experiences and our ability to understand our experiences.

This chapter seeks to place a few highly selective signposts in charting a course through this rapidly changing territory. The intent is to suggest some general recommendations for using theory and measurement more productively in the pursuit of comprehending the phenomenon of bullying and cyberbullying. The guiding assumption is that theory building is beneficial to this process of understanding, and understanding is important to the process of intervention and prevention (Raskauskas & Huynh, 2015). The chapter is organized around four colloquial maxims: (1) you don't know what needs to be studied until you know what has been studied; (2) you won't find what you're not looking for; (3) measure what you theorize and theorize what you're measuring; and (4) verification should yield theoretically to falsification.

Bullying is a form of aggression (Randall, 2001). Yet, surprisingly little of the rich history of research into aggression in general is referenced in the bullying literature specifically. Only the occasional reference is made to Berkowitz (1962) or Bandura (1973), and even less to more contemporary theoretical work (e.g., Tedeschi & Felson, 1994). Even most of the intimate partner violence, psychological abuse, and communicative aggression literature is relatively untapped in the study of bullying. This would be understandable to some degree if bullying were an entirely distinct theoretical, legal, or empirical construct. It is not clear that bullying currently qualifies as such.

There are excellent analyses of the definitional issues involved in studying bullying and cyberbullying (e.g., Bauman, 2013; Bauman, Underwood, & Card, 2013; Craven et al., 2013; Crawshaw, 2009; Grigg, 2010, 2012; P. K. Smith, del Barrio, & Tokunaga, 2013; Turner & West, this volume; Volk, Dane, & Marini, 2014). P. K. Smith et al. (2013; see also Swearer, Siebecker, Johnsen-Frerichs, & Wang, 2010) identify three core criteria of bullying: (1) an intent to harm, (2) a specific target, and (3) imbalance of power. They note a common fourth criterion: (4) repetition. Of these four distinct criteria, the intent criterion is common to all forms of aggression; the specific target and repetition are generally common to related crimes such as stalking and sexual harassment; and the criterion of power imbalance is relatively common to most sexual harassment. The conclusion, which seems conceptually reasonable if not entirely empirically reasonable, is that bullying is a *subtype* of aggression.

Despite the general agreement that "it is essential that consensus be reached on a precise definition" (Bauman, Underwood & Card, 2013, p. 41), and despite the degree of "emerging consensus in the Western research tradition" regarding these criteria (P. K. Smith et al., 2013, p. 27), the terminological morass continues to expand. As an illustration of the nomenclature trees that may be obscuring the theoretical forest of bullying research, consider the concept generator illustrated in Table 2.1. All these terms exist in the literature. The table is intended to function somewhat similarly to the Tansey wheel (Freeman, 1993). The artist Mark Tansey created a wheel with three concentric revolving circles, with nouns on the inner circle, verbs and participles on the middle, and the outer ring populated by phrases or subjects, many of which derived from critical theory. By spinning the wheels, up to 5,832,000 possible sentence combinations arise. This table facilitates drawing a conceptual weft thread through the concepts to illustrate both conceptual possibilities and redundancies.

The table reflects several modifiers relevant to bullying: (1) the modality of bullying refers to features such as face-to-face or technological harassment; (2) the code or signal system involved represents such features as communicative/verbal or physical/nonverbal codes; (3) the contextual factors involved reflect various situational or functional features such as the culture, relationship, gender, motive or function, or demography of the bullying; (4) the intensity level represents the interest in occasionally differentiating the severity of bullying (e.g., minor or severe); (5) the aggression type is the most differentiated column and reflects a diverse landscape, including behaviors such as exclusion/isolation, outing, sexting, or privacy intrusion; (6) the coping strategies employed by the target are derived from a conceptual coding system developed for stalking management (Spitzberg & Cupach, 2014), representing six possible responses to bullying, such as: freezing (unmoving), rumination (moving inward), seeking social support (moving outward), moving against (counterbullying), avoidance (moving away), or negotiation or pleading (moving with); (7) the outcome level of bullying represents the locations of bullying effects, such as a meaner world (cultural/societal), costlier justice or litigation (institutional/organizational), entangling third-party relationships (social network), relationship turbulence (relational), or personal trauma (individual/ personalogical); and, finally, (8) the type of outcome represents the specific form of the effects of bullying, such as general disturbance (posttraumatic stress disorder), physical (injury, sleep or eating disorder), affective (anxiety, fear), cognitive (lowered self-esteem, distrust), behavioral (disrupted daily routines), social (disrupted social and familial relationships), resource (expenses or finances), spiritual (loss of faith), ambivalent (both enabling and disabling experiences), and resilience (traumatic growth).

Any given study or program of study may take any given total or partial path through this conceptual loom. Most, however, skip a number of the warp threads. More importantly, many studies fail to take into account the research populating the rest of the loom as if it is irrelevant. Some of the loom may be irrelevant, but unless the entire conceptual tapestry and fabric is understood, it is difficult to know the contribution of any given thread.

You Won't Find What You're Not Looking For

The topography of the "dark side" perspective to the social sciences is defined by the two dimensions of normative and functional ambivalence (Figure 2.1). The normative dimension refers to the degree to which individuals or collectives subjectively view a phenomenon as good or evil, desirable or undesirable. The functional dimension refers to the degree to which a phenomenon empirically and objectively facilitates or debilitates an organism's or group's functional vitality or ability to survive and thrive. When crossed, these dimensions map a four-quadrant territory.

Table 2.1 Concept-Generator for Cyber-Aggression

Technology/Modality Modifier	Code/Target Modifiers	Contextual/ Criterion Qualifiers	Intensity/ Severity Qualifiers	Aggression Types	Coping Strategies	Outcome Level Modifier	Outcomes
		• Culture/ Nationality		• Abuse • Aggression			• General Disturbance
• Cyber(space)-	• Communicative	• Relationship (dating, peer, celebrity, etc.)		• Bullying • Coercion • Control/ Power/ Dominance	• Unmoving	• Cultural/ Societal	• Physical Health
• Digital	• Direct/Indirect	• Demographic (child, teen, adolescent, etc.)	• Minor	• Denigration • Exclusion/ Isolation (social) • Flaming	• Moving Inward	• Institutional/ Organizational	• Affective Health
• E-(lectronic) • Internet	• Psychological • Relational	• Fear-inducing • Functional (instrumental, expressive, impulsive, controlled, etc.)	• Moderate	• Grooming • Harassment • Humiliation • Incivility • Impersonation • Intimidation	• Moving Outward	• Social Network • Personal/	• Cognitive Health
• Masspersonal	• Social	• Gender(ed)-based/ Sexual	• Severe	• Intrusive/ Invasive • Microaggressions	• Moving Against	• Relational	• Behavioral Disturbance
• Mobile/Device/ Smartphone • Online	• Verbal vs. • Physical/FtF	• Individual vs. Group • Power Asymmetric • Repeated/ Pattern		• Mobbing • Ostracizing • Outing • Pestering	• Moving Away		• Social Health
• Technological/ Techno-		• Revenge (porn) • Threatening • Unwanted		• Pursuit • Rumors • Sexting • Solicitation • Stalking	• Moving With	• Individual/ Personalogical	• Resource Health
				• Snooping/ Stealth • Surveillance/ Monitoring • Terrorism • Trolling			• Spiritual Health
				• Vicarious bullying • Victimization			• Ambivalence
				• Violence			• Resilience

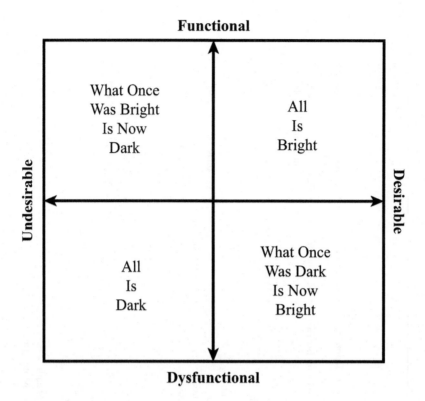

Figure 2.1 The Topography of the Dark Side

Most bullying research and theory occupies the normatively undesirable and functionally debilitating domain where everything is considered dark and damaging. Almost certainly, on the scales of almost any cost-benefit analysis, most bullying deserves to veer in this direction. Bullying is too often damaging in ways that align with the general cultural conceptions of its harms. Bullying victimization is related to diminished academic achievement (Kessel Schneider, O'Donnell, Stueve, & Coulter, 2012), obesity (DeSmet et al., 2014), depression and suicidality (Bauman, Toomey, & Walker, 2013; Holt et al., 2015; Messias, Kindrick, & Castro, 2014; Reed, Nugent, & Cooper, 2015; Sampasa-Kanyinga, Roumeliotis, & Xu, 2014; Schenk & Fremouw, 2012), school violence (Leary, Kowalski, Smith, & Phillips, 2003; Sommer, Leuschner, & Scheithauer, 2014), and bullying perpetration (Chapin & Coleman, 2017).

The theoretical problem is that studies that do not look for functional ambivalence or phenomenological experiences of the desirable aspects of bullying will not find them. Out of hundreds of studies on stalking, for example, only a small handful even ask whether or not any positive or beneficial outcomes arose from the experience (Spitzberg & Cupach, 2014). In the bullying research, for example, several isolated studies indicate that bullying may be curvilinear to social competence, peer popularity, and status (Andreou, 2006; Kisamore, Jawahar, Liguori, Mharapara, & Stone, 2010; Puckett, Aikins, & Cillessen, 2008). Bullying is a means to achieve one of the most prized possessions in social life, and under various circumstances and in the eyes of certain groups, it appears to be an appropriate and effective path to chart for such purpose. Furthermore, bullying victims may experience adversity, but research indicates that adversity itself tends to be curvilinear to well-being and psychological adjustment over the long term (Keinan, Shrira, & Shmotkin, 2012; Mancini, Littleton, & Grills, 2016; Seery, Leo, Lupien, Kondrak, & Almonte, 2013). A moderate amount of adversity is likely to build resilience and capability for managing further adversity. Yet, most studies do not test for curvilinearity because they do not know to look for it, and they do not know to look for it because most theories of bullying do not hypothesize such a relationship, mired as they are in linear thinking.

We only find what we are looking for, and we tend to only measure what our ideologies permit. It may seem difficult to ask what the benefits of bullying are, but only by asking such dark side questions can theory accommodate the kinds of findings that arise. If, for example, it is found that bullying is a path to popularity, then theoretically it enables the subsequent question: Are there ways to better facilitate popularity that do not involve bullying?

Measure What You Theorize; Theorize What You're Measuring

Although bullying research has generally not rooted itself extensively in the broader field of aggression research, its operational legacy is clearly a close hybrid of more traditional forms of aggression research. Bullying is typically conceptualized as a set of aggressive behaviors, but its conceptualization is often not translated into its operationalization. There are several issues that need continuous attention in researching bullying.

First, the conceptual definition of bullying must correspond rigorously to the operational definition of bullying. If the scholarly consensus is that bullying requires four criteria (intent to harm, specified target, power asymmetry, repetition), then these four criteria need to be measured independently in any study before any behavioral content of bullying is measured. In our research on stalking, for example, we generally asked several questions to construct the Venn diagram of stalking as it was differentiated from its close relative of obsessive relational intrusion (Spitzberg & Cupach, 2014). These questions inevitably ended up excluding many people who experienced behaviors identical to stalking victims, but who did not meet legal criteria of stalking (i.e., fear and repetition), leading to a problem long recognized in both the stalking and the rape literature representing unacknowledged forms of victimization (Spitzberg, 2017). That is, many people may have engaged in or been victimized by bullying-type behaviors, but do not recognize such behavior as "bullying." Others will believe themselves as having been bullied or having been a bully, yet not engaged in such qualifying behaviors.

A second problem is the reliance on behavior item lists and factor analytic methods when attempting to define the topographical territory of bullying. A common legacy of the intimate partner violence, harassment, stalking, and similar cognate areas of research is that measures of bullying are often comprised by a list of behaviors rated on a scale of their reported frequency of occurrence. At least two problems with these approaches require consideration.

The first problem with behavior lists is that, assuming a comprehensive inductive process was undertaken to sample the entire domain of bullying, when such a list is scaled by frequency, it must be sensitive to the definitional criterion of repetition (Rivers, 2013). This means that there must be a true zero-point (never experienced or perpetrated the behavior), a single-experience (experienced or perpetrated once), and some variability in the remaining options (e.g., more than once; or, 2 to 5 times, 6 to 10 times, more than 10 times). The single-experience response option becomes important for studying diversity across tactics as well as repetition within tactics. Only such response scales allow application of criteria of repetition across both time/context and type of behavior. This tends to involve ordinal rather than interval scaling, but the impact on most statistics will likely be minor. Once the scaling is properly set up to assess repetition, then introductory material can operationalize the other criteria of bullying, such as power asymmetry, attributed intent and target specificity. This scaling approach allows the measure to accommodate certain conceptual features of the phenomenon (i.e., repetition).

A second problem with behavior lists is the assumption that factor analysis represents a theoretically sound approach to conceptualizing bullying types and, thereby, developing the contents of bullying theory. Behavior items represent observed indicators, and factors or principal components represent latent variables. But seldom do researchers ask what those latent variables represent from a theoretical perspective. As one example among many, Doane, Kelley, Chiang, and Padilla (2013) use factor analysis to identify four victimization and four perpetration factors (public humiliation, malice, unwanted contact, deception). These items are scaled on a frequency scale (never, less than a few times a year, a few times a year, once or twice a month, once or twice a week, or every day/almost every day). The resulting subscales can be summed within or across factors, depending on whether the research interest is in types of bullying or overall bullying. Reliability analyses assess the internal consistency of these factors under the assumption that reliability is necessary for validity. However, this assumption applies to scales but not indexes (Streiner, 2003). In a scale, the ratings of items are thought to be the manifestations of an underlying trait or latent construct. That is, ratings are caused by that underlying but not directly observed variable. In the Doane et al. scales, factor analysis assumes that there is a "deception" or a "public humiliation" motive or function that causes the responses to those items. Yet, this does not make much intuitive sense. Instead, those behavioral items would seem more logically representative of an index, in which the more of these items experienced, the more that a given outcome is caused (e.g., deception victimization, public humiliation). The items cause the latent construct, rather than the latent construct causes the item responses.

This is somewhat similar to many of the approaches to mental and behavioral disorders in the *Diagnostic and Statistical Manual (DSM)* of the American Psychiatric Association. For example, there are eight criteria for PTSD in the *DSM* 5.1, and several of these criteria require only one or two of several indicators to be observed to qualify that criterion as relevant to a diagnosis of PTSD. But, it need not be assumed that these criteria and indicators collectively represent a reliable scale—it is simply assumed that the more of these indicators, the more likely they *constitute* PTSD. Negative affect, hypervigilance, intrusive thoughts, and difficulty sleeping are both symptomatic and constitutive of the syndrome. These indicators may or may not be numerically correlated at the individual level in time and space, but collectively they still index the syndrome's intensity or severity.

To the extent that bullying is operationalized by a behavioral index, it may not be appropriate for factor analytic models that presuppose intercorrelation and reliability within factors. Domain representation frameworks may also suffer from such dimensional problems, although they appear more theoretically grounded than typical factor analytic approaches (Card, 2013). We discussed the distinction between scales and indexes at length in our work on measuring obsessive relational intrusion and stalking (Spitzberg & Cupach, 2014) and proposed that more conceptual or theoretical grounds be employed when formulating measures of harassment. This may open up alternative ways of thinking about what bullying behavior is accomplishing for its perpetrators and in what ways it may be influencing its victims.

A third set of issues regarding current measures of bullying is that it becomes easy to overlook what we have yet to assess. By way of a heuristic device, Cone's (1978) behavioral assessment grid can be adapted (Spitzberg, 2015) to reveal a variety of approaches to operationalizing bullying that have yet to be explored fully (Figure 2.2). Bullying motivation and affect, knowledge and cognition, and behaviors or skills are all relevant to a full comprehension of bullying perpetration or victimization. Yet, many bullying measures reflect only one of these domains. These domains may be operationalized through very direct means or very indirect means. Indirect means range from projective or interview techniques requiring substantial inference from the individual's interpretations. Most research employs self-reference or other-reference surveys. Some studies examine case records of school counselors or behavioral disruption records. More direct methods include direct observation in natural contexts, role-play or simulation methods, recording of artifacts (e.g., scraped emails, YikYak posts, or tweets), physiological indicators such as stress response to negative message exposure, or criterion-based (e.g., PTSD symptoms). Both these domains and directness options can vary by various universes of generalization, whether a given measure generalizes across external features

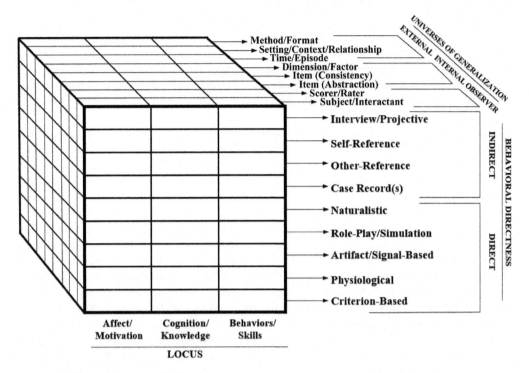

Figure 2.2 Behavioral Assessment Grid

(i.e., different methods, contexts, or times), internal features (i.e., dimensions, items), or observers (i.e., participants or observers/raters).

In summary, it is advisable to look at what scholars are measuring before considering what they *say* they are studying or theorizing. If it is not in the measure, it cannot be evidence for the theory. If the measure is not consistent with the theory, the theory cannot be tested. This raises the process of theory testing more generally.

Verification Should Yield Theoretically to Falsification

Sir Karl Popper has been much maligned by many contemporary scholars in the social sciences, but his most distinct contribution was perhaps never needed more than in the current context of public (dis)trust of science. Popper (Pigliucci, 2013; Popper, 1974; 1980) essentially intended to proffer a distinction between pseudo-science and science. The key difference is that science takes risks of being wrong by approaching theory from a falsificationist approach, whereas pseudo-science approaches theory from a verificationist approach, seeking evidence in favor of its precepts. In the former camp are most "hard sciences," in which theories make precise predictions, such that test situations can be devised in which the prediction is found to survive or fail strict tests of observation. In the latter camp are theories ranging from astrology to psychoanalytic or interpretive theories, in which evidence can always be fit to the theory. The essential ethos of science is that if it is wrong, its authors must accept that it is wrong, discard the previous conjectures, and move onto more fruitful and risky theoretical ventures.

A mark of pseudo-scientific approaches are discussion sections that focus the lion's share of their content on the results that were supported or partially supported and giving short shrift to those results that produced null findings. For Popper, null findings are the only results of direct scientific

Brian H. Spitzberg

merit, in the sense that they permit the discarding of invalid theory, or at least the formulation of auxiliary hypotheses that advance the theoretical program of research. In contrast, he argues,

> it is easy to obtain confirmations, or verifications, for nearly every theory—if we look for confirmations ... Every "good" scientific theory is a prohibition: it forbids certain things to happen. The more a theory forbids, the better it is.

Thus, "every genuine *test* of a theory is an attempt to falsify it, or refute it" (Popper, 1980, p. 22; italics in original). The question in reading theory in bullying research is whether it is making predictions that are at genuine risk of being wrong if in fact they are wrong.

There are several theories that are sprouting in the bullying field, most of them hybridized from a variety of theories that originated in other domains of social science (Marini & Volk, 2017; Postigo, González, Montoya, & Ordoñez, 2013; Zych, Ortega-Ruiz, & Del Rey, 2015b). A fuller review of such theories is beyond the scope of the present chapter, but a number deserve note, including comprehensive theory-social-ecological theory, social information processing theory, general strain theory, social learning theory (Espelage, Rao, & Craven, 2013), attachment theory, socio-cultural theory, evolutionary theory (Monks et al., 2009; Volk et al., 2014), general theory of crime (Marcum, Higgins, & Nicholson, 2017; Marcum, Higgins, & Ricketts, 2014), social capital theory, dominance theory, humiliation theory, organizational culture theory (Evans & Smokowski, 2016), and self-determination theory (Lam, Law, Chan, Wong, & Zhang, 2015). There are also conjectures that appear more as hypotheses or nascent models rather than theoretical systems. These would include studies of speculations such as online disinhibition or anonymity effects (e.g., Barlett, Gentile, & Chew, 2016), routine activities theory, structural role theory (Craven et al., 2013), cyclic process (den Hamer, Konijn, & Keijer, 2014), theory of mind (Espelage, Hong, Kim, & Nan, 2017), catastrophe theory (Escartín, Ceja, Navarro, & Zapf, 2013), theory of reasoned action (Doane, Pearson, & Kelley, 2014), Heider's balance theory (Standen, Paull, & Omari, 2014), group process theories (Hymel, McClure, Miller, Shumka, & Trach, 2015), and trait configurations such as the dark triad (Smoker & March, 2017). Most of these theoretical endeavors represent either relatively narrow slices of the bullying phenomenon or more conceptual organizational heuristics rather than precise formal statements of conditional interrelationships among constructs. It is suprising the extent to which the communication field has failed to investigate the bullying concept. We have been overly reliant upon other fields to inform us.

As new media infiltrate our lives, they are transforming much of the face of bullying theory and measurement. Scholars continue to come to grips with the extent to which such media are fundamentally distinct from previous forms of interaction (e.g., Hall, 2016; O'Sullivan & Carr, 2017) and attempt to formulate theories that grasp the extraordinary reach of media effects (e.g., Spitzberg, 2014). Likewise, scholars of bullying are attempting similar projects to differentiate bullying from cyberbullying, just as prior research attempted to differentiate stalking from cyberstalking (e.g., Cavezza & McEwan, 2014; Dempsey, Sulkowski, Nichols, & Storch, 2009; Dooley, Pyżalski, & Cross, 2009; Erdur-Baker, 2010; Forssell, 2016; Gradinger, Stohmeier, & Spiel, 2009; Kraft & Wang, 2010; Nobles, Reyns, Fox, & Fisher, 2014; Pereira, Spitzberg, & Matos, 2016; Pyżalski, 2012; Sheridan & Grant, 2007; Sontag, Clemans, Graber, & Lyndon, 2011; Spitzberg & Hoobler, 2002).

Again, drawing from research and theory outside the realm of bullying and aggression may assist such endeavors. For example, O'Sullivan & Carr (2017) propose that masspersonal communication represents an empirically identifiable space between perceived accessibility and personalization dimensions interaction. This conceptual space suggests the potential intersections of individual-versus-group and technological effects of access and psychological targeting that may distinguish bullying from cyberbullying. Other work on affordances (Brandtzæg, 2010; Evans, Pearce, Vitak, & Treem, 2017; Feaster, 2010, 2013; Schrock, 2015; Sutcliffe, Gonzalez, Binder, & Nevarez, 2011), cyber motives (Wang & Chang, 2010), or communicative functions identifiable in mediated texts (Ludwig & de Ruyter, 2016) offer ripe theoretical materials for theorizing the potential distinctions between realspace and cyberbullying, if any there are to find. What make cyberbullying distinct from face-to-face bullying are the same dimensions that allow their intersection and amplification of personal and proximal realspace interaction. This research also has the potential to identify particularly well-adapted coping strategies based on the modality of bullying (Eterovic-Soric, Ashman, Mubarak, & Choo, 2017; Nyborg et al., 2016; Tokunaga & Aune, 2017).

In summary, theories need to do more than be a repository for the accumulation of data that "partially" support the theories. Instead, theories need to propose bold, risky predictions. When these predictions are not supported by the research, then scholars need to hold the theories accountable to the data, and articulate new falsifiable auxiliary hypotheses rather than ad hoc excuses.

Conclusion

Bullying and cyberbullying are relatively ubiquitous experiences (Näsi, Keipi, Räsänen, & Oksanen, 2015). Yet, it seems a little strange to claim with certainty that we can estimate with precision the prevalence of something that still presents so many conceptual and empirical quandaries. Ongoing theoretical development of the construct would benefit from careful scholarly and empirical attention to issues surrounding the relevance of various conditions and criteria of bullying as a conceptual category of behavior, and in relation to its many cognate cousins in the aggression family tree. Bullying perpetration theory will also be advanced by extending models to include components that tap (1) motivation and affect components, (2) knowledge and cognition components, (3) skill and behavioral components, (4) contextual components, including cultural, chronological, relational, situational, and functional constructs, and (5) outcome components. Many of these components will also serve bullying victimization models.

Theories are the lingua franca of social science. Sophisticated methods, estimates of prevalence of problems, and the success of interventions are important, but the relative status and progressiveness of a field of study are the power, precision, and heurism of its theories. The theoretical tools of the past and present will need to be married to the appropriate methods to forge the strongest conceptual models to chart the course of future scholarship.

3

COMMUNICATION ETHICS AND BULLYING

Janie Harden Fritz

Relationships are central to human well-being, providing comfort, connection, support, and meaning throughout the lifespan. Relationships can also be sources of intense distress and pain. One particularly distressing relationship occurring across the lifespan is bullying. The communicative phenomenon of bullying is an ever-present reminder of the dark side of interpersonal interaction (e.g., Spitzberg & Cupach, 1998, 2007). Bullying demonstrates the power of communication to bring harm to human beings. Continuing research on the causes and consequences of bullying highlights the multifaceted nature of this phenomenon. Multiple contextual, social, structural, and personal factors contribute to bullying and its outcomes, inviting careful analysis of the varied dimensions of this problematic and complex interpersonal process. An examination of bullying from a communication ethics perspective reveals why bullying is not only pragmatically harmful but also problematic from a broader perspective rooted in philosophical understandings of the good for human beings.

Communication Ethics

Bullying results in short- and long-term harm. This harm emerges from communicative practices of bullying across contexts ranging from childhood (e.g., Hymel & Swearer, 2015, De Lara, 2016) to adult professional life (e.g., Lutgen-Sandvik, Namie, & Namie, 2009; Lutgen-Sandvik, Tracy, & Alberts, 2007). Research on bullying highlights the importance of considering bullying from the perspective of communication ethics. The subfield of communication ethics emerged formally in the 1980s and has grown in importance over the last few decades. Although communication ethics is typically associated with "clearly communicative phenomena as deception, openness, [and] free expression," communication ethics encompasses an increasingly broad domain of phenomena (Cheney, Munshi, May, & Ortiz, 2011, p. 1). Indeed, communication itself can be understood to have "inherently moral or ethical dimensions," a position that can be traced back to Plato, who considered how messages can seduce and corrupt (Cheney et al., 2011, p. 1).

Postmodernism's deconstruction of foundations for morality and ethics, such as universal moral principles and individual moral autonomy, has generated challenges for scholarly work in communication ethics (B. C. Taylor & Hawes, 2011). However, we experience life as a moral enterprise, involving judgments about right and wrong (C. Taylor, 1989). Despite disagreements about issues of right and wrong human communicative behavior, we must make ethical judgments with whatever resources we have at our disposal. We are called to be thoughtful ethical communicators, acknowledging the messiness of human life and the reality of multiplicity of goods; one singular communication ethics stance is not within reach (Arnett, 2011). To begin, communication ethics perspectives, theories, and frameworks provide us with argumentative parameters to engage questions arising from different understandings of the good guiding human communities and individual lives.

Ethical practices are habituated and typically operate implicitly, with understandings of right and wrong guiding communicative choices with minimal awareness (e.g., C. Taylor, 1989). We work from taken-for-granted assumptions about justice and care, rights and obligations, and autonomy and choice. We become mindful of these assumptions when they are violated or when we are faced with a situation in which (1) competing alternatives for communicative action present themselves, (2) a decision must be made, and (3) one or more of those decisions violate ethical principles but may be attractive for securing desired outcomes. Hence, communication ethics becomes salient, according to Johannesen (2001), when persons face a conscious behavioral choice regarding means and ends, when that choice can be judged according to standards of right or wrong behavior, and the outcome holds significant consequences for others. From this perspective, bullying can be assessed within a traditional purview of communication ethics. The next section addresses several ways to think about communication ethics in the context of bullying, beginning with elements of Johannesen's (2001) coordinates of consequences, right and wrong behavior, and communicative choice.

Bullying: Implications for Communication Ethics

As other chapters in this volume assert, bullying brings about deleterious consequences for persons bullied, the extended groups of which bullied persons are a part, and bullies themselves. Work-place bullying generates destructive consequences for persons and organizations (Hoel, Sheehan, Cooper, & Einarsen, 2011; Tye-Williams, this volume), and childhood bullying experiences have enduring negative consequences in many domains for both targets of bullying and bully perpetrators (Eisenberg, Gower, McMorris, & Bucchianeri, 2015; Spitzberg, this volume). Some of these consequences emerge from the process of interaction, in which repeated practices of destructive communication work reflexively to make such practices more likely through labeling by others or self-labeling, reinforcing the bully identity and associated behaviors (deLara & Garabino, 2003; Duck, Foley, & Kirkpatrick, 2006; Fast, Fanelli, & Salen, 2003). Furthermore, bullying may perpetuate itself in that those who are bullied may become bullies themselves (Haynie et al., 2001; Turner & West, this volume).

Current understandings of bullying recognize it as a violation of the dignity and implicit value of human beings, a foundational principle of most ethical, moral, and religious systems serving as a minimalist universal standard for human conduct across cultures (e.g., Christians & Traber, 1997). Its communicative manifestations are broad, including ostracism, demeaning comments, threats, and aggressive utterances (e.g., Einarsen, Hoel, Zapf, & Cooper, 2011b; Olweus, 1993a). We understand bullying to be wrong, violating ethical expectations by denying another person respect and acknowledgement (e.g., Hyde, 2005). We could consider such violations breaches of interpersonal justice, a refusal to grant others what is owed to them as human beings. Planalp and Fitness (2011) discussed such ethical implications connected to the human need for interaction and the experience of mutual care (p. 137). Although cultural practices often lead to violation of these norms, lack of adherence does not relativize or invalidate them. Cultural variations may occur in specific embodiments of these minimal standards while conforming to their underlying principles (e.g., Appiah, 2006).

The question of communicator choice between means and ends raises a question important to how scholars and practitioners conceptualize bullying and the assumptions that undergird ethical frameworks. For example, intentionality is a contested term, included in some, but not all, definitions of bullying (Einarsen et al., 2011b; Keashly & Jagatic, 2011; Turner & West, this volume). Some scholars interrogate the issue of agency in the act of bullying; for example, Horton (2016), in his brief history of the study of bullying, urged a wide view focused on the broader social and institutional context of power relations within which bullying emerges, rather than on the individual person alone. Behavior associated with bullying, when envisioned as unintentional, may shape the nature and extent of consequent harm experienced by those bullied (Keashly & Rogers, 2001, cited in Keashly & Jagatic, 2011). For example, if I attribute a repeated pattern of aggressive behavior toward me as stemming from cultural differences in communication styles rather than as a desire to bully me, I may reinterpret the behavior and be less distressed. The question of extent of accountability and responsibility for choice may vary with age of the bully perpetrator, as well as with other demographic factors. Recent research, for example, suggests that vulnerable populations, such as gay, lesbian, bisexual, and transgender youths, are more likely than their straight counterparts to be both perpetrators and targets of bullying (Eisenberg et al., 2015; Peguero, 2012).

In some ethical systems, such as virtue ethics, individuals enact decisions not through a calculation of means and ends or rational choice but through habituation—one's character inclines toward virtue or vice through repeated practice. For example, my colleague may not have to think twice if I come to her to apologize for a wrong that I have done. Her inclination to be magnanimous and forgive me may be her first impulse if it is habituated as part of her character. Stewart (2011) noted that many of our treatments of communication ethics are insufficient because they do not take into account the temporally situated nature of ethical choice. In the end, we must attend not only to a given decision at one point in time, but to what comes next, so our responsibility for choosing is ongoing and inflected in complicated ways. With these caveats in mind, regardless of intention to harm and the nature of our choosing, the target experiences bullying as problematic, and bullying does result in negative personal and organizational consequences. Finally, we do make choices about actions to take, even as those choices bring about differently configured contexts to which we must then respond anew.

From a communication ethics perspective, scholars and practitioners must agree on how and why bullying violates ethical standards of communication with others so that coordinated efforts can be directed toward combating these practices. Just as such efforts are directed toward other communicative violations of human dignity such as sexual and racial harassment, so must efforts be directed toward mitigating the practice of bullying (Kinney, 2012). The National Communication Association (NCA), for example, generated a code of ethics that ostensibly guides its members, highlighting principles for ethical communication to provide a common, public center of professional agreement about acceptable and unacceptable communicative behavior, an explicit good protected and promoted for this academic group. This code of ethics, the NCA Credo for Ethical Communication, has been applied to organizational contexts as a touchpoint for ethical communicative behavior in the workplace (e.g., Fritz, 2013a). Likewise, school bullying has become a rallying point for development of programs for prevention and anti-bullying policies (e.g., National Center for Mental Health Promotion and Youth Violence Prevention, 2011; P. Smith, Ananiadou, & Cowie, 2003; Luurs, this volume; U.S. Department of Health & Human Services, 2014b).

Because scholars and practitioners conceptualize bullying in the context of dyadic relationships (e.g., Einarsen et al., 2011b), it falls within the scope of interpersonal communication ethics. Interpersonal communication ethics focuses on communicative practices that hold implications for the flourishing of a relationship and the relational partners (Fritz, 2016). For instance, honesty is an important ethical practice in personal relationships connected to intimacy (LaFollette & Graham, 1986). Much interpersonal communication research, and hence issues of interpersonal communication ethics, focuses on close relationships (e.g., Planalp and Fitness, 2011). However, professional and role-related relationships are also sites within which persons seek and secure both constitutive, or internal (e.g., self-worth, friendship, love), and external (e.g., assistance with tasks, information) life goods. The bullying that occurs in personal and professional relationships compromises those goods by generating hurt and emotional pain, taking energy away from tasks, and reducing the quality of life of persons bullied.

Workplace bullying is relevant to organizational communication ethics as well because of its implications for organizational culture and climate as well as for individual outcomes (Arnett, Fritz, & Bell, 2009; Fritz, 2013b; Seeger, 1997). In the corporate context, bullying becomes a matter relevant to leadership ethics, given the responsibility of organizational leaders to protect and promote the good of institutional settings (Arnett et al., 2009; Fritz, 2014). Organizational leaders who take action to stop bullying demonstrate commitment to a bully-free workplace and offer hope for those who experience bullying.

Communication Ethics Frameworks

A focus on contextual areas, as locations for bullying, highlights elements relevant to conceptualizations of bullying as unethical communicative behavior specific to particular sites of human interaction. Concentrating on specific locations for bullying helps identify harms specific to those contexts and highlight issues of ethics relevant to those harms. Bullying in the context of school, the workplace, or in private relational contexts may emphasize different issues relevant to the good of persons, relationships, and/or institutions and point to ethical considerations tied to those issues. For example, as Kahle and Peguero (2017) noted, "understanding and addressing bullying victimization that occurs in schools is essential for establishing a safe and healthy learning environment for all youth" (p. 324).

Ethical frameworks for decision making derive from specific assumptions about the nature of the good, with each representing a particular bias or standpoint on the good (Arnett et al., 2009). These frameworks define general principles guiding decision making and are not necessarily tied to particular contexts. However, some ethical frameworks fit particularly well with particular contexts. For instance, virtue ethics has been highlighted as a fitting approach to professional ethics because of similarities in the concerns each system brings to its understanding of the human community, its purpose, or *telos*, and the accountability and obligation of persons to the greater social good (e.g., Oakley & Cocking, 2001). Bullying may be approached fruitfully from multiple ethical frameworks. Therefore, in order to explicate bullying as unethical communicative behavior, I review several approaches to communication ethics, limiting my treatment to deontological, utilitarian, codes, procedures, and standards, and virtue-based ethics, noting how each perspective provides resources for understanding bullying as a violation of communication ethics. The following is limited to the workplace context, recognizing, however, that the general principles may also be applied, with some modification, to other contexts that are seeking to remedy bullying behavior.

Communication Ethics Frameworks Applied to Bullying

Deontological Ethics

Each ethical framework rests on particular assumptions relevant to the human good. Kantian deontological, or duty-based, ethics focuses on duties understood as universal principles (Arnett et al., 2009). Kantian duty-based ethics is based on considering how the human community would function if everyone performed a particular action subject to ethical prohibition, such as lying. If everyone were to lie, language itself would lose its meaning for the human community. One of the most recognized ethical injunctions associated with deontological ethics is to treat people as ends, never as means.

The unethical nature of bullying in any context rests in the bully's treatment of another human being as a means to an end. In the context of the workplace, Kinney, drawing on the work of Dillard (e.g., Dillard, 1990; Dillard, Segrin, & Harden, 1989), suggested that persons with goals for advancement may place those goals as primary, particularly if they see no other way for advancement. Use of negative influence strategies, aggression, manipulation, and other bullying behaviors directed against others become means to a desired end. For instance, bullies may threaten or coerce colleagues to do extra work on a particular project in order to advance bullies' interests. This aggressive action against others makes those others a means to a desired end, thereby violating deontological ethics.

The context of childhood bullying can also be understood from a deontological perspective. To the extent that bullies in the school context direct their destructive efforts at others in order to gain power, recognition, or material goods, as in the case of instrumental targeting (e.g., Faris & Felmlee, 2014), other children become means to ends. In the case of those provocative victims who may elicit bullying (Olweus, 1993a), the end sought by the bully may be to stop the annoying behavior, but in a way that fails to honor the humanity of the provoking victim. For example, Sandra has victimized Eliza again and again by snatching away her lunch and devouring the chocolate-chip cookies. One day, Eliza decides to get revenge by baking stones into the cookies. This time, when Sandra bites into what she thinks is a tasty chocolate-chip cookie that she has confiscated from Eliza, she breaks a tooth.

To the extent that structural and cultural factors in the workplace environment foster bullying behavior, and to the extent that organizational leaders fail to take action against it, the organization itself could become hostile to the persons who work there. The result is an uncivil culture (Pearson & Porath, 2009) marked by fear (Rayner, 1999, cited in Hoel et al., 2011). In this case, the organization could be understood as treating people as a means to an end. Despite the contracted nature of work for pay, an implicit understanding of organizational life honored at least in theory is that employees are valued participants in the process of accomplishing organizational goals, not mere means to ends. The popularity of approaches to management such as servant leadership (Greenleaf, 1977) and the status of corporate social responsibility as a recognized benchmark for corporate ethics in the West (Christensen, Morsing, & Thyssen, 2011) indicate at least an espoused commitment on the part of organizations to the value of human beings as ends rather than means. These approaches to leadership and management suggest that workplaces do value persons as ends rather than means. To be consistent with professed ethical values, such workplaces would also seek to prevent bullying in order to promote the value of persons as ends rather than means.

Utilitarian Ethics

Often held up as a contrast to duty-based ethics, utilitarian ethics measures ethical action by the extent to which a given decision secures the greatest good for the greatest number of persons. Utilitarian ethics rests on an assumed shared good, similar to deontological ethics. In the workplace context, to the extent that bullying compromises the productivity and other contributions of the person being bullied, the organization suffers to some degree, not just the one bullied. In addition, those witnessing the bullying may suffer specific harm, as suggested by Porath and Erez's (2009) study of the effects of observations of rudeness on bystanders in a workplace context. Their results showed that employees who witnessed rude behavior in the workplace exhibited decreased performance, creativity, and organizational citizenship behaviors and were more likely to think in aggressive terms. The cost of both workplace incivility (Pearson & Porath, 2009) and workplace bullying (Hoel et al., 2011) appear to be significant.

It could be argued that a utilitarian ethic in the workplace could promote the behavior of mobbing, in which multiple persons direct coercive, abusive, or controlling action toward another person for a perceived violation of cultural norms or workplace expectations (e.g., Leymann, 1996). The phenomenon of rate-busting documented in early industrial settings, for instance, comprises one example. In rate-busting, one person works far beyond the expected productivity of others. Such a high level of performance might be seen to jeopardize the wages paid to everyone and thereby prompt the wrath of co-workers, who attempt to slow down this highly productive rule violator. In this case, the bullying or mobbing would be directed toward protecting the good of the many, defined as the workers. The question then focuses on the means by which the greater good is protected. A deontological approach results in a different outcome than a utilitarian ethic, given the duty-based injunction against treating people as ends rather than means.

A utilitarian ethic raises questions about the standard upon which understandings of "the greater good" is based: the greater good for whom? The workers? The organization? The leaders? The community? In the case of school bullying, because of the disruption to learning that happens as a result of bullying practices, bullying is pragmatically useless for the greater good. In this context, stakeholders elevate the good of learning over the good sought by the bully, whether that good is self-esteem, power, or some other outcome. Given the nature of the educational system, the publicly announced purposes of the enterprise provide a standard to define the good, which is governed by public oversight, such as school boards and state and federal regulations. In the case of the corporation, although organizational goals and purposes protect productivity, those performing the work hold expectations about what a reasonable rate of work might be, which might be at variance with those of management. Perceived injustice may shape understandings of the greater good in ways at variance with representatives of the organization. The issue of publicly stated standards moves the discussion to another framework for ethics: codes, procedures, and standards.

Codes, Procedures, and Standards Approaches to Ethics

A codes, procedures, and standards (CPS) approach to ethics looks to agreed-upon guidelines generated by a group, such as an organization or professional community, to define ethical principles applicable to members of that organization or group (Arnett, 1987; Arnett et al., 2009; Chesebro, 1969). Policies against bullying provide a standard against which behavior can be measured and perpetrators called into account (Kinney, 2012). From this perspective, bullying is unethical because it violates the public standard of expectations for ethical communicative behavior. When anti-bullying policies become a vital element of an organization's mission, organizational leaders can model support for the mission by enforcing the policy, thereby connecting word and deed and inspiring employees' intent to comply with organizational ethical standards (Fritz, O'Neil, Popp, Williams, & Arnett, 2013). In school settings, adoption of policies against bullying provide a public display of expectations for student behavior, an explicitly stated commitment on the school's part to provide a safe learning environment for all students.

Virtue Ethics

The fourth and final framework for application to the phenomenon of bullying is virtue ethics. Virtue ethics has experienced a resurgence of attention over the last two decades in many fields of study, including the broad field of communication (Fritz, 2018). Virtue ethics looks to the idea of a human *telos* anchored in excellences of various types, focusing on the notion of human flourishing or well-being. From this perspective, we can potentially identify human capabilities and capacities that, when developed, permit human beings to express and exhibit these excellences to varying degrees. The goods of human life become criteria for evaluating practices leading to excellence. Through development of moral character, in which right actions become habituated, the virtuous person is inclined toward right action, embodying the good through prudential judgment and practical wisdom. The question representing virtue ethics is "What would a good person do?"

From a virtue ethics perspective, bullying behavior is not virtuous, but demonstrative of vice. In classical Aristotelian virtue ethics, bullying could be considered a violation of temperance, showing appropriate restraint, or magnanimity, a form of generosity. Some might consider bullying a form of cowardice, the vicious counterpart of courage. Bullying behavior does not contribute to human excellence through any of the goods proper to human beings. The focus in virtue ethics is on practices of excellence that both define the good and lead to human flourishing.

Childhood bullying enacts practices that define the worst a human being can be and develops corrupt character in the perpetrator, while creating conditions under which human well-being is thwarted. Some recipients of bullying behavior in both work-related and school-related contexts may respond with—or further develop—resilience and resourcefulness (e.g., Hinduja & Patchin, 2017; MacIntosh, Wuest, Gray, & Aldous, 2010). Such attributes and practices are valuable for human life, leading to strength and self-efficacy. In this case, the bullying behavior becomes an element of the environment requiring practical wisdom, or phronesis. Phronesis guides the one bullied through unwanted circumstances, making the unpleasant experience into an opportunity to gain strength or to learn (Hinduja & Patchin, 2017, point in this direction). Bullying behavior, however, remains in the category of vice, regardless of responses to it.

One approach to organizational life from a virtue ethics perspective is professional civility (Fritz, 2013a, 2013b). Professional civility protects and promotes productivity, or the work accomplished in and on behalf of the organization; place, or the organization and its mission and purpose; and persons, the employees who carry out the work of the organization. The professional civility framework was generated in response to the crisis of incivility in the workplace (Fritz, 2013b) but holds implications for more intense forms of problematic behavior. From a professional civility perspective, bullying compromises goods of the workplace in several ways.

When persons are bullied, their productivity likely suffers (Cowan & Bochantin, this volume; Hoel et al., 2011). Not only is the instrumental end of productivity compromised, but the *telos* of the practice defining the good of the product or service is lessened in value because the person working on the task is not performing as well as might be possible if the bullying were not taking place. Bullying thereby damages productivity as the purpose of the organization and the inherent goods connected with the product, service, or other outcome defining productivity as an element of professional practice or craft excellence (Fritz, 2013a). Bullying practices, as suggested earlier, can compromise organizational culture and climate. Intentions to leave the organization and absenteeism and effects on those witnessing bullying will also be detrimental to the organization (Hoel et al., 2011, pp. 136–137). Threats to the good of persons are perhaps the most documented results of bullying (Hogh, Mikkelsen, & Hansen, 2011; Lutgen-Sandvik et al., 2007). Damage to physical and psychological health indicates compromised human well-being. These effects are particularly pernicious from a virtue ethics perspective, since the well-being of the human person is tied to meaningful engagements in the world, including the experience of work.

Ethical Responses to Bullying

Thus far, this chapter's focus has centered on bullying behavior as a violation of communication ethics. Yet, an equally important avenue to consider relates to ethical responses to bullying. If perpetration of bullying behavior is unethical, then it rests with the leaders in various environments where bullying takes place (schools, workplace, etc.) to identify both macro- and micro-level practices in order to address this problem. Failure to ameliorate or eliminate unethical contact perpetuates problematic practices and encourages further bullying. As noted earlier and elsewhere (Luurs, this volume), educational institutions are developing policies to address prevention of and responses to bullying, including programs that focus on the whole person. These programs, although working within the framework of a CPS rubric, possess content closer to a virtue ethics approach. That is, schools provide children with opportunities to develop responses and practices of resilience that become part of their character, resources for living that tap their capabilities (e.g., Hinduja & Patchin, 2017).

In the workplace context, officials and scholars are beginning to address bullying. Scholars are calling for anti-bullying policies (see Cowan, 2011; Cowan & Bochantin, this volume), and some highlight the necessity of recognizing bullying as interpersonal violence, with accompanying sanctions (Kinney, 2012). Cowan's research reveals that many organizations do not have policies targeted explicitly to bullying behavior. If they understand bullying as a violation of ethics, then they should employ the strategy of adopting policies that explicitly define and target bullying behavior. From a CPS approach, adoption and enforcement of these standards constitutes a formal approach to ethics operating through identification and sanction. From a deontological perspective, these policies contain within them the recognition of the value of human beings as ends rather than means, with inherent dignity demanding respect. From a utilitarian perspective, anti-bullying legislation works to the ethical end of the greatest good for the greatest number: Everyone benefits from a defined good articulated and enforced by the organization. From a virtue ethics perspective, such policies encourage and support the well-being of organizational participants.

As bullying behavior decreases, opportunities for positive experiences in the workplace can increase. Lutgen-Sandvik, Riforgiate, and Fletcher (2007) provided vivid evidence of the deeply meaningful and even joyful experiences that working with others can bring. Workplaces that protect and promote the good of productivity, persons, and the place of work itself contribute to human flourishing by working against workplace bullying. The long history of public education's quest to protect and promote the good of learning for some of the most vulnerable members of society—children—highlights the role of dedicated professionals in service to the greater good of society and its members through development of human potential (Brubacher & Rudy, 1997). Educational institutions continue their noble purposes as they enact and enforce policies against bullying and find ways to develop resourcefulness and resilience in their charges. Through these approaches to the unethical behavior of bullying, our institutions can meet multiple goods despite the messiness and complexity of human existence. Communication ethics scholarship contributes resources—both ancient and contemporary—to the ongoing quest for the human good, highlighting communicative practices that are problematic and those that hold the potential for healing, moving us in the direction of a more caring culture that promotes personal and communal well-being.

VOICES FOR VISIBILITY
The Resilient You

Keith Berry

You are living in a time when school bullying is an omnipresent societal problem that shapes the lives of youth, especially youth of difference. Cultural discourse on bullying is commonplace. News anchors routinely convey dramatic stories about the latest youth who were bullied at school. Also, you hear others who are around you, those whom you know and are strangers to you, interacting about/through bullying issues. These conversations are often deeply emotional ones. Indeed, the corrosive impact bullying has on youth's well-being has rendered this issue a topic *du jour* in communication (Berry, 2016). As a result, it is rare for many days in your lived experience to pass you by you when don't hear stories about harsh violence committed against yet another vulnerable body and being.

Your engagement over time with this discourse and these interactions has exposed you to the ways in which bullying is, at least in part, a problem concerning youth identity. A cast of characters comprises the bullying storyline and includes "bullies," "victims," "bystanders," "parents," and "teachers," just to name a few. In addition, attributes assigned to these characters and their actions, especially concerning those who are victimized through bullying, matter to the stories you're hearing and helping to co-construct. "Jocks bullied him because he is gay." "Choir kids bullied her because she stutters." "Cheerleaders bullied her because of the way she looks." These and other appraisals are uttered regularly and often without equivocation, as if they represent unquestionable certainties. In these ways, bullying discourse, much like bullying itself, is infused with loaded labels pertaining to youth's social location or subjectivity.

Your research and teaching at the intersections of relational communication and cultural identity, inquiry that you primarily conduct by using autoethnography, ethnography, and phenomenology, lead you to be keenly interested in the ways this communication serves to frame the youth who are bullied, primarily how it renders them "victims." You notice mediated and interpersonal accounts about bullying most often stressing the pain and suffering they endure. They demonstrate how bullying changes youth, and these changes are usually unwelcomed and harmful. Much of your own research and writing on bullying in which you explain this subset of peer aggression as a problem that is decidedly communicative, and rooted in formative processes of identity negotiation (Berry, 2016), has focused on the damaging role bullying plays in constituting and re-constituting (i.e., making and remaking) youth into victimized beings. You have learned that this emphasis is commonplace in much of the research literature you've read on bullying. But this reliance on prioritizing the negative doesn't surprise you. After all, you believe bullying is a concrete instantiation of unethical and socially unjust communication, which, in turn, mindlessly harms youth who are less able to defend themselves. You want your work to help prevent bullying and shine a light on how destructive this problem really is to youth's ability to live well—openly, freely, and mindfully in the moment. You convey this negative because it is real and ubiquitous, and you hope your work will help to make a difference in people's lives.

At the same time your research and teaching has also led you to identify bullying as cultural issue that, much like cultural issues generally, is performed through canonical storylines (see Berry, 2016; Berry & Adams, 2016). With your current story here in mind, you believe the emphasis on the negative dimensions to bullying represents a *normative* storyline that most often directs people's attention to certain factors when orienting to bullying and bullying prevention, and away from other possible factors. Consequently, you wonder what alternate social locations are being taken for granted through this singular emphasis on harm and the negative, more generally.

While this normative orientation, indeed, serves to reveal the darkness that feels, to you, to be inseparable from bullying, your life and work have taught you that it also concomitantly *conceals alternate stories* about what it looks like and means to perform as bullying victims, including stories that speak to more positive and affirming factors of bullying, factors that exist *in tandem* with youth pain and suffering. With this in heart, you decide to write a handbook chapter that will explore moments of resilience and even happiness and joy that were part of your experiences with being bullied in your youth. You convey this story because you hope to expand the storyline concerning bullying, communication, and identity by advocating a re-imagination of the multiple selves possible, and often necessary, in experiencing and enduring bullying. You convey this story because you have come to believe the bullying story is far more complex and layered than many people, including you, sometimes suggest.

★ ★ ★

You were bullied in middle school and high school (see Berry, 2016) in ways that taught you at an early age that identity labels, and identity generally, matter a great deal to yourself and others. Other kids (boys, mainly) bullied you based on your physical appearance. You were a chubby boy off and on during your youth. Boys honed in on your weight and didn't often miss a chance to use words against you like "blubbo-lard," "fat ass," and other variations of fattist-based humor and aggression. In addition, you moved through the world with a graceful gait; you were more gentle and not as physical than most of the other boys you knew. Also, you spoke with an equally graceful and gentle voice, softer than most of the other boys. These ways of being provided boys with fodder to use when bullying you. To them you were a "fairy," or at the very least you were not "tough." Physical attacks sometimes accompanied the boys' verbal attacks. Although these boys never beat you up in ways that left you black and blue or at the hospital, as they did to other kids like you, they did occasionally find enjoyment in pushing you against lockers and shoving you in the hallways. Even more, many boys loved to intimidate you with the *threat* of violence. Their promise of hurting you felt real and scary, leading you to be vigilant of your surroundings and to avoid them at all costs.

To add dis-ease and an ongoing sense of confusion to your experiences with this bullying, you often felt "different" as a kid. These feelings exacerbated your experiences with being bullied and made you an attractive target to boys who bullied you. You were different, but you didn't know why you had those thoughts and feelings, and you had a hard time talking through those feelings with parents and friends. Your parents tried valiantly to help you reconcile these feelings. Yet, it wouldn't be until you were in your early 20s when you would realize feeling and being "different" primarily related to your being a gay boy, and then a gay teenager, in a heteronormative world that successfully thwarted, to put it gently, your being able to acknowledge and be open and proud of who you are and love. In these ways, your youth in bullying was further confounded by your being in the contested and complicated space of the "closet" (Adams, 2011), a most problematic, even though hidden, dimension to your story.

Yet, while your youth was filled with bullying that at times harmed you, and that produced unwanted and impactful feelings of dis-ease, you also lived with a backstory, so to speak, that was filled with various ways of performing that tended to keep you well, or at least well enough. These were ways of relating, largely with yourself, and being as a boy that you performed outside of the spotlight of the kids at school, and in some cases, even your family. In this sense, you lived within a "secret apprenticeship" (Garfinkel, 1967), exploring the possibilities for performing the graceful, gentler, and softer you; that is, the you who was abject to others, but instinctive and more fluid to you. It was through this backstage apprenticeship that you learned to be *the resilient you.*

The resilient you came to life when you performed as teacher for some of your friends, boys and girls, in your neighborhood. Your mother, aunt, and one of your grandmothers were teachers, so they were partially responsible for inspiring these performances. However, there was more to these enactments, particularly in terms of the sort of relating with others they entailed. For instance, you often would try to teach Spanish to your friends, even though you were only in your first year of Spanish class in middle school. You put these kids in a circle and had them recite certain Spanish words and phrases: "Hola." "Adios." "Me llamo es. . . (fill in the blank with their name)." "Me gusta limonada." You adored how they would mimic how you acted and the authority and power demonstrated therein; how you had to correct them from time to time, and their openness to your feedback; how you were helping them to practice a language different than English, one that would help you and them enter into a different and special world; and how their respect for your teaching, even if they didn't really mean it, made you feel respected and like a teacher, someone who had something to give to others, something for which they felt appreciative and happy. As teacher, you were embraced, even if your students didn't like the homework you gave them.

The resilient you also came to life at home and in the washroom. There, under the premise of your needing to urinate, you would sometimes experiment with your mother's makeup. Once you securely locked both of the washroom doors behind you, double checking to make sure they were truly locked, so as to be confident you would not be detected by others, you would play with your favorites—her foundation, powder, and sometimes lipstick. You would start by applying the base and then adding some powder. You didn't hold back either. You figured if you were going to use it, you wanted to really see what it would feel and look like. When you did try lipstick, you usually only applied it to one lip. That way you could see what it looked like on your face without taking things too far. Overall, when playing with her makeup, you felt pretty and fancy. Your skin looked soft and your lips shiny. You felt sophisticated. You loved the way it felt on your skin, too. Restrictive gender roles and rules outside of this room kept you from ever telling someone about how makeup was prevalent within your apprenticeship process. Still, performing in this way allowed you to free yourself, even if just for a few secretive minutes, from paralyzing and exclusionary ways of performing "boy" that dominated your life outside of the apprenticeship and in everyday public life. You never felt like you were a girl, and you don't look back at yourself today and wonder if you were transgender. Nonetheless, you felt more comfortable doing these things to/with your body than you did attempting to do the things boys and men needed to do, such as playing sports and hitting on girls.

Yet also, the resilient you came to life when you took a shower each night after dinner. There, you would pretend you were the announcer voice for television commercials. As you stood in the shower, you read the flowery language on the bottle of your mom's soap. Hidden by the loud sounds of the shower water hitting the plastic shower walls, you announced boldly, "This soap offers daily silkiness. It's for noticeably soft skin and contains white peach and orange blossoms. Revel in the feeling of irresistibly soft skin that invites the touch. Silkiness. Elegance. Delicateness. This soap is for you!" There, in the shower, you felt more open to utter the consonant "s" in prolonged and exaggerated ways (i.e., effeminate and non-real-boy-like), and to use fabulous words like "silky," "elegance," and "delicateness." There, in the shower with your exposed and unguarded chubby body, you performed these words repeatedly, each time trying to accentuate a different letter or word, and with tones that

Voices for Visibility

you *wanted to use* rather than those you had to keep from using out of fear of being policed for gender violations. Your parents would at times ask why you were taking such long showers, sometimes expressing their concern about wasting water. However, you showered un-phased. To you that performance allowed for a glorious and wet safe space in which, even if just for that part of the day, you felt like you could be playful and not have to be vigilant of how you sounded or looked. In that space, you felt cleansed from the dirt that you'd accumulated while being at school that day. You felt free.

The resilient you came to life most frequently when you were in bed each night trying to fall sleep. Then you listened to your favorite songs on cassette tapes, which you played on the double cassette boom-box you received for Christmas one year, a gift that was formative in multiple ways in your gender training (see Berry, 2013, 2016). This musical bedtime resilience entailed your visualization— vivid and detailed imagination work—of you performing on stage. One of your favorite settings had you performing as one of the backup dancers during a concert of The Pointer Sisters, a hit R&B singing group of the 1980s. On stage you knew every word to their songs—"Jump for My Love" and "I'm So Excited" being two of your favorites. You would imagine yourself on stage with the sisters. Although you didn't wear a dress like they would wear in their music videos, you sang every note with them and moved seductively underneath the covers, mimicking how they moved on stage. You sang through the songs with them, blasting out with excitement the words to the songs' choruses, sometimes to the point your parents would call into your room and ask you to keep your volume down. While the Pointer Sisters were your most common inspirations, you also performed with other singers and groups, including Culture Club, Michael Jackson, and Huey Lewis and the News. Whichever song you sang, you felt happy, and sometimes joyously so, to be able to escape into the imaginative world of these musical performances. During those visualizations you were someone who others in your life would barely be able to recognize, but someone you who you loved to be.

While these practices helped to sustain you, creative visualization also had a partner technique that you developed and came to rely on: visualizing hardship while in bed. You would often visualize yourself in conflict situations in which you lost, ruminating about what you said that would lead to others' harsh attacks. Later in college, you would also visualize yourself "coming out" as gay to the people who were closest to you, only to be scorned for doing so and, at times, jettisoned from their lives. To be sure, imaginations have limits and, while positive in some ways, can take a deep toll in others.

★ ★ ★

The above four ways of performing the resilient you may not have allowed you to forget about being bullied or your dis-ease from feelings of difference generally. But they were definitive moments of your bullying story that demonstrated you being well, thriving, and in some cases feeling at peace and joyful. They were important to your story, too. Granted, you did not feel comfortable enough to share these performances with others, save for your times as a teacher. Also, moments of dis-ease often overshadowed these resilient moments. After all, you were quite good at visualizing the pain and suffering you felt was inevitable to your being rejected for being yourself. Regardless, the resilient you showed creative and resourceful performances of selves that conditioned your existence in real ways that mattered. As such, they demonstrate that multiple modes of being can appear within bullying and its aftermath, not only the ones that entail harm and damage, and, thus, further underscore the complexities of bullying and its impact on youth identity and well-being. As Schrag (1997) writes on the issue of subjectivity,

> [W]e are dealing not with a single unitary, sharply defined portrait, but rather with a portrait that is itself curiously diversified. What thus appears to be at issue is a multiplicity of profiles and perspectives through which the human self moves and is able to come into view.
>
> *(p. 1)*

Thus, telling your story here makes you think about the possibilities for learning about and responding to bullying, and for "doing" bullying research and teaching, that can come into being if others are willing to locate and reflect on similar moments that might comprise many people's stories.

You also think about how performances of the resilient you most often occurred in more isolating ways. Save for moments of teaching Spanish to friends, these ways of performing and staying well enough occurred outside of face-to-face interaction. Now it is important to mark that moments of being by yourself are not divorced from the influence and presence of others. Gergen (2009) writes,

> [V]irtually all intelligible action is born, sustained, and/or extinguished within the ongoing process of relationship. From this standpoint, there is no isolated self or fully private experience. Rather, we exist in a world of co-constitution. We are always already emerging from relationship; we cannot step out of relationship; even in our most private moments we are never alone.
>
> *(p. xv)*

However, the deep and inevitable intertwinement of human lives doesn't change the fact that you performed these resilient identity practices outside of the presence of others. In the here-and-now this leads you to ask: What would have happened if you made your performative choices more public? For instance, how would the makeup play have been received by others? If negatively, how would that response further shape the dis-ease you felt? Were the shower and makeup practices better left as performances for one, enactments whose main audience was your self-as-other? While you don't regret a single thing about those performances this many years later, you do take pause concerning the ways you felt it necessary to keep these things secret. You cringe when remembering the need for you as a young boy to have to be so vigilant in your apprenticeship. You wonder how life might have been different throughout your youth, how life might be different now, had you felt allowed and free to be open.

You end this story with a mindful awareness and caution about the complexities involved with advocating a more multilayered orientation to the identi*ties* inherent to, and performed within, bullying. Moving forward with this position—that multiple possible selves are present, influential, and need to be talked about concerning bullying, not just the ones speaking to the pain and suffering of being victimized—matters a great deal. The extent to which you emphasize resilience risks your de-emphasizing and disregarding the pain and suffering intrinsically connected to, and accentuated by, bullying. In turn, your doing so risks disconfirming the vulnerable youth of difference being bullied. And yet, by more circumspectly exploring the identities of bullying, and, thus, by resisting singular and static portrayals of the victims of bullying, and for that matter, all characters who are involved in this corrosive problem (e.g., those who bully, educators), you stay honest to the communicative and constitutive nature of bullying practices, one that assumes bullying, much like communication, to be contextual, contingent, and subject to change and variation.

Whichever ways you use to move forward with understanding bullying's hold on vulnerable youth, and the consequential ways you talk about this problem, you still understand that bullying typically not only involves hardship, but also the admirable task (and achievement!) of having found your way resiliently through harmful interactions and relationships, as well the role of secret performances in helping youth to survive.

PART II

Contexts of Bullying
★★Bullying, Culture, and Identity★★

4

BULLYING AND THE INFLUENCE OF RACE, ETHNICITY, AND CULTURE ON PERSONAL VIOLATIONS

Tina M. Harris and Anastacia Janovec

Literature on bullying reveals a trend that is quite similar to most social science research: Race/ethnicity and culture are individual and collective characteristics rarely explored by scholars (Peguero & Williams, 2013; Stone & Carlisle, 2017). As a discipline, social science research typically involves the use of convenience sampling of homogeneous (i.e., majority of White American) college students. While the findings might illuminate greater understanding of a given phenomenon, they blatantly fail to address the important role that qualities such as race/ethnicity play in human interaction and interpersonal relationships. This deficiency could be achieved by including racially/ethnically diverse populations in these studies. The findings may reveal that their experiences with a phenomenon are qualitatively different from those of people from the majority group (i.e., Whites). Nevertheless, social science research usually occurs within homogenous environments (i.e., a predominantly White institution), thus decreasing the likelihood that the experiences of racial/ethnic communities will be both included and reflected in the conclusions drawn from the findings, a detail of particular importance to bullying research. Specific attention must be given to a more inclusive approach to research on this increasingly important social issue.

Scholars affirm a basic acknowledgement and recognition that race/ethnicity and, indeed, culture inform not only our identities and understandings of ourselves but also how we choose to interact with people who differ from us. This issue is critical in light of the recent findings from a Southern Poverty Law Center (2016) national survey of public school teachers on their perceptions of students after the 2016 presidential election. According to the SPLC website, teachers reported "that the [political] primary season was producing anxiety among vulnerable students and emboldening others to new expressions of politicized bullying." Politicizing bullying means that individuals have used bullying as a context for addressing the larger issue of politics rather than it being a very serious issue. These findings demonstrate that, even in one political context, students reported heightened anxiety and are targeted as bullying victims because of their race, ethnicity, culture, and religion.

Our review of the existing research on race and bullying has revealed what we believe are two distinct trajectories that scholars have followed in an effort to understand how racial group membership influences experiences with bullying. The first trajectory involves studies using race as the primary variable (Connell, El Sayed, Gonzalez, & Schell-Busey, 2015; Felix & You, 2011; Fleschler Peskin, Tortolero, & Markham, 2006; Larochette, Murphy, & Craig, 2010; Lewis & Gunn, 2007; Mendez, Bauman, Sulkowski, Davis, & Nixon, 2016; Peguero & Williams, 2013; Schumann, Craig, & Rosu, 2013; Shin, D'Antonio, Son, Kim, & Park, 2011; Spriggs, Iannotti, Nansel, & Haynie, 2007; Wu,

Lyons, & Leong, 2015). In some instances, race has been utilized either interchangeably or coupled with ethnicity (i.e., race/ethnicity). Employing race as a variable in this way is common in social science research. As we illustrate in the next section, race and ethnicity refer to human characteristics related to biology and ancestry, respectively. Race refers to biological traits, such as, skin, nose, and hair texture and is used in relation to a larger people group. In contrast, ethnicity refers to ancestral lineage (i.e., Korean, Indian) and establishes within-group differences. Current research findings show that bullies are responding to race/ethnicity as cultural markers in very similar ways.

The second trajectory is more expansive and uses a broader conceptualization of race, per se, by including ethnicity as well as culture, religion, and socioeconomic status as qualities that make a person susceptible to bullying (Edwards, Kontostathis, & Fisher, 2016; Fisher et al., 2015; Garnett, Masyn, Austin, Williams, & Viswanath, 2015; Goldweber, Waasdorp, & Bradshaw, 2013; Kahle & Peguero, 2017; Mueller, James, Abrutyn, & Levin, 2015; Pan & Spittal, 2013; Rodriguez-Hidalgo, Ortega-Ruiz, & Monks, 2015; Scherr, 2012; Stone & Carlisle, 2017; Wang, Leary, Taylor, & Derosier, 2016). This research is complex and nuanced and often includes use of the umbrella term "diversity." As such, race becomes a less salient aspect of bullying while still being applicable to larger racial populations. Our review of literature includes an overview of inter- and cross-disciplinary research that falls into these categories.

This specific area of racial bullying research provides further evidence that bullying constitutes a widespread social issue affecting an array of people from diverse cultural backgrounds. In this chapter, we attend to the interplay of race/ethnicity and culture as they manifest in these troubling interpersonal altercations, thus highlighting the paucity of attention that is typically given to bullying and race. Thus, it fills a void in the literature by acknowledging the human diversity that exists in our world. Research on this topic is important in light of findings that people who identify as members of historically marginalized groups often experience higher rates of bullying than do majority group members (Larochette et al., 2010; Mendez et al., 2016; Peguero & Williams, 2013; Wang et al., 2016). Moreover, this area of research will likely grow, given the current socio-political climate of the U.S. (Southern Poverty Law Center, n. d.). Although currently scant and sporadic social science research on race and bullying has been produced, the findings that do exist comprise statistics and personal narratives that offer a compelling rationale for more inclusive bullying research. Such an approach to bullying scholarship will aid in both unpacking the cultural complexities of bullying and serving as a catalyst for the eradication of bullying as a serious social issue plaguing many segments of society.

Race as a Social Construct

Before discussing the relationship between bullying and race, it is important to understand the broader societal context within which race as a social construct was born.

Many people conceptualize race as a physical descriptor of humans without acknowledging or recognizing its relationship to power, privilege, and systemic oppression. While race in the context of bullying is not racism in its truest form, it results from biased and prejudiced thinking that a person is socialized to espouse. Racism is the intersection of racial prejudice and societal power; thus, in order for a person to be racist, they must have societal power, which is directly related to their membership in the majority group. According to Orbe and Harris (2015), racism is "the systematic subordination of certain racial groups by those groups in power" (p. 10), meaning that the numerical majority (i.e., macroculture) has societal power, and if members have racial prejudice, then that group is the only one that can be racist. In the U.S., the majority group is Whites, and as this definition indicates, they are the only group that is capable of being racist. This does not mean that all Whites in the U.S. are racists. Rather, as a collective, they are the only racial group that can be racist or perpetuate racism. In terms of people of color (i.e., microcultures), they can have racial prejudice, or "inaccurate and/or negative beliefs that espouse or support the superiority of one racial group" over others (Orbe &

Harris, 2015, p. 10). As such, when people act on their racial prejudice, they engage in racial discrimination, and unlike racism, all people can have racial prejudice and practice racial discrimination.

Defining these terms helps us to provide an essential general understanding of systemic oppression. Notably, for the purposes of our chapter, we primarily operationalize "race" as physical markers or characteristics (i.e., skin color, eye color, hair texture) used to distinguish one people group from another. This distilled definition captures the very basic grasp of race that children have in relation to bullying. While bullying behaviors might technically be considered racist according to the definition outlined above, it is best to describe them as being *racial*, or of having to do with race. Indeed, it is equally important to underscore the societal and institutional implications that this pattern of negative behavior has for all parties involved and beyond.

Despite their reference to different qualities, scholars often use "race," "ethnicity," and "culture" synonymously or interchangeably. Race comprises a social construction used to place people into value-based categories, while ethnicity refers to "a cultural marker that indicates shared traditions, heritage, and ancestral origins" of a people group (Orbe & Harris, 2015, p. 9). Orbe and Harris defined culture as the "learned and shared values, beliefs, and behaviors common to a particular group of people" (p. 9). Each concept refers to a unique aspect of people groups and distills them down into very simple terms, which, to some extent, is how children cognitively interpret and perceive others (Orbe & Harris, 2015). People subconsciously attend to physical human qualities that suggest one's race or ethnicity and look for behaviors and artifacts to determine what constitutes a culture. Many children and adults view the world in the same way, giving little or no thought to the power dynamics that are at play (Orbe & Harris, 2015). Systemic oppression is largely responsible for societies placing value on groups and people. However, the research on bullying and race shows that bullying in this context is primarily based on the distilled definition that is accepted by the lay public (Connell et al., 2015; Felix & You, 2011; Fleschler Peskin et al., 2006; Larochette et al., 2010; Lewis & Gunn, 2007). (Further discussion on race as a social construction is provided in the following section of this chapter.) The factors that contribute to bullying are primarily interpersonal (i.e., peer-to-peer) and not institutional. As such, the literature presented will be from this vantage point.

Bullying and Race

According to Wu et al. (2015), children who choose to bully often times use physical cues stereotypically associated with a person's perceived or actual race, ethnicity, or culture as criteria for committing interpersonal violence against their peers. These findings are consistent with other studies. The scholars conclude that, although children do not yet have the cognitive skills essential for fully understanding the systemic nature of racism, they are making race-based decisions when they choose to engage in bullying behaviors. Moreover, their bullying is symptomatic and reflective of familial, societal, and institutional ideologies (Felix & You, 2011). Scholars doing this type of research acknowledge the systemic nature of bullying despite not focusing on it in their scholarship. Instead, they direct their attention to the fact that students employ a value-laden racial hierarchy when they choose to bully, acknowledging that bullying can occur at any point throughout one's lifetime and in various social and professional contexts.

As Schumann et al. (2013) noted, racial bullying differs from other types of bullying in that a person is targeted specifically because of their out-group membership. The victims are usually not a part of the dominant racial/ethnic group. Schumann et al. based their findings on Geographical Information Systems data gathered from 20,021 students in grades 6–10. They primarily concluded that "community diversity was associated with prevalence of racial victimization" (p. 959). In other words, when students lived in a community where they were in the numeric minority, they faced a greater likelihood of being a victim of race-based bullying. This type of bullying is different from others in that one's phenotype or physical features such as skin color, facial features, hair, and eye color are cultural markers a perpetrator(s) uses as criteria to enact bullying behavior. This pattern of behavior should not be surprising, given the history of institutionalized slavery and internment camps in the U.S. In these specific instances (among many others), fear of the proverbial other served as the driving force behind the mistreatment of Africans and Japanese Americans who were believed to be genetically inferior. More broadly, this racist ideology related to minority groups has trickled down into how people groups interact with each other, which is why racial discrimination and other forms of systemic oppression have been able to survive. Bullying remains a troubling behavior, and, as Schumann et al. argued, addressing race is of paramount importance when discussing the bully and their behavior.

Race as an Influencing Factor

Currently, limited research exists on racial bullying (Pan & Spittal, 2013), yet those studies offer compelling evidence that race constitutes an influential factor on the in-school violence that a student may face (Larochette et al., 2010; Mendez et al., 2016; Peguero & Williams, 2013). Bullies pick on victims because they do not perceive them as part of the "in crowd," placing them under harsh scrutiny because of their "otherness" or social status (i.e., peer preference/group) (Wang et al., 2016). The perpetrator frequently targets a victim for not possessing qualities or attributes deemed "desirable." Bullying itself is a form of violence, and, when confounded by race, the interpersonal violence creates a double layer of isolation, which speaks to the overwhelming effect that bullying can have at a very critical time in a person's life. Granted, bullying can occur well into adulthood (for related arguments, see Socha, this volume), but in this discussion, attention is placed primarily on the relationship between the educational environment and culture.

The fact that one's race/ethnicity sometimes triggers a verbal or physical assault in elementary and/or high school is not a startling finding, particularly given the history of racial/ethnic injustices throughout the world. Nevertheless, this relationship is striking, given that the perpetrators are so young. Race increases a child's risk level for being bullied (Larochette et al., 2010). Larochette et al.'s Canadian-based study of 3,684 students and 116 principals yielded confirmatory findings of the relationship between race and bullying, concluding that the individual factors of race and sex placed an individual at greater risk for being bullied. One uplifting takeaway from this study was that these bullying risks and occurrences decreased when students were in supportive schools that had significant racial/ethnic diversity.

Mendez et al. (2016) found similar results in their study of racial bullying. In their qualitative study, Mendez et al. determined that intraracial, or within-group, bullying is another form of race-based bullying that adversely effects school-aged children. In this instance, Mexican American students were targeting Mexican immigrant students, which was largely attributed to their linguistic differences and ethnocentrism. The Mexican American students either reported—or were perceived—as espousing an air of superiority over their same-race/ethnicity peers. An example of within-group bullying might be English-only speaking Mexican American students who have assimilated to the dominant culture with negative perceptions of Spanish-only speaking or bilingual Mexican students. The English-only students may look down on the other Mexican students because they hold stereotypical beliefs about Mexican immigrants and wish to distance themselves from these peers specifically because of the shared ethnicity between the different groups.

Mendez et al. (2016) identified bullying cycle, isolation, alienation, and school factors that contributed to the behaviors of Mexican American students who engaged in bullying. All four are important and disconcerting, but the perceived or desire to perpetuate the bullying cycle is particularly striking. This finding suggests that a cultural norm condones and allows the perpetuation of abusive behavior targeted at a vulnerable population. Attacking the victim's racial/ethnic identity has far-reaching consequences for the mental, physical, and emotional well-being, a topic we revisit later in this chapter.

As noted previously, racially based bullying is not a historically unique phenomena, but is severely influenced by the context surrounding the behavior. Felix and You (2011) explained that racial bullying differs from bullying in general in that bullies target victims for an unchangeable attribute. Bullying provides an extreme means for gaining social control over others in an attempt to "shape a person's behavior into what is considered a social norm" (p. 870). Felix and You found that, for Native American and African American students in California, racial/ethnic bullying occurred with higher frequency and in the form of physical victimization, respectively. It also transpired at a higher rate than all other ethnic groups, which Felix and You attributed to being in the numerical minority and a product of a country that is associated with "systematic, widespread societal oppression and racism" (p. 871). Felix and You explained that racial bullying can be mitigated in part by a racially/ethnically diverse student population, as that would allow for increased intergroup contact, "which increases the chance of cross-ethnic friendships" and "may lead to changes in stereotypes and behaviors, which can reduce cross-ethnic peer victimization or ethnic discrimination" (p. 872). This solution may appear idyllic, but there is still a lack of clear understanding of the factors that contribute to a perpetrator's decision to actively engage in bullying behaviors.

Marginalized Status Triggers Victim Status

When students of color are in the numerical minority, they automatically have a marginalized status (Goldweber et al., 2013; Stone & Carlisle, 2017; Wang et al., 2016; Peguero & Williams, 2013). They are at risk for racial bullying regardless of "urbanicity," which, according to Goldweber et al. (2013), refers to whether or not a school is urban (i.e., non-urban). Peguero and Williams (2013) used data from the Education Longitudinal Study of 2002 to understand the role that stereotypes play in bullying victimization. Their findings revealed a clear relationship between bullying victimization and race/ethnicity. The stereotypes of interest were related to "family socioeconomic status (SES), test scores, and interscholastic sports participation" (p. 545). These factors "predict students' educational success" and are "factors linked to bullying in schools" (p. 559). In the study, when students of color (SOC) did not conform to racial and ethnic stereotypes, they experienced an increased likelihood of being bullied.

Peguero and Williams' (2013) findings also showed that, when they were involved in interscholastic sports, Asian American and Latino American students were more likely to be bullied. The reverse was true for Caucasian American and Black/African American students, thus leading Perguero and Williams to determine that interscholastic sports functions as a form of insulation or protection for them. Through this important study, the authors offered compelling and comprehensive bullying data validating the assumption that, in many instances, beliefs about and attitudes towards racial/ethnic minorities is directly related to victimization.

Research on bullying in relation to the racial/ethnic makeup of the local community has revealed three distinct patterns that scholars have identified as being directly related to their study of the intersection of bullying and race. The scholars offer evidence that these homogenous communities directly impact the interpersonal interactions and subsequent bullying experiences of the students in the numerical minority (Felix & You, 2011; Fisher et al., 2015; Goldweber et al., 2013; Pan & Spittal, 2013; Rodriguez-Hidalgo et al., 2015. The studies that have been conducted on bullying have fallen into one of the following patterns: (1) focus on predominately White institutions (PWI) or non-diverse schools (e.g., monoracial, homogenous) (Larochette et al., 2010; Schumann et al., 2013), (2) focus on multiracial schools where the minority groups are in the majority (Connell et al., 2015; Gage, Prykanowski, & Larson, 2014), or (3) problem-focused bullying in racially diverse communities (Pan & Spittal, 2013). Each pattern reveals varying degrees of marginalization in the research itself, in that the racial/ethnic diversity of the students themselves is either (purposely) excluded or recognized as a contributing factor to the experience with bullying itself.

The few studies specifically focusing on racial bullying yield important yet conflicting results. For example, in response to the acknowledgement of the lack of research on the impact of school diversity in types of bullying behaviors that occur, Fisher et al. (2015) conducted a study on this very topic. The study involved 4,581 middle school students, the majority of which were Caucasian Americans (86.4%), with African Americans accounting for 10.6% of the students surveyed. Fisher et al. concluded that Caucasian American students experienced bullying at a higher rate than did African American students, which is not surprising given that an overwhelming number of the student population was Caucasian. Thus, it stands to reason that they would experience disparity in terms of bullying. It is the case with most studies on bullying that a vast majority of participants identify as Caucasian Americans and very likely attend homogenous schools (Connell et al., 2015).

In their study of bullying in the United Kingdom, Lewis and Gunn (2007) offered evidence that conflicts with that of Fisher et al. (2015). Lewis and Gunn used the workplace as the context for understanding bullying and found that, when comparing the bullying experiences of Caucasian Britons and racial/ethnic minority respondents, racial/ethnic minorities were "more likely to label themselves as suffering from bullying behaviours than their White counterparts," and that their Caucasian British colleagues engaged in "subtly different patterns of bullying behavior towards White and ethnic victims" (p. 641). These findings support the fact that race/ethnicity is indeed a factor in bullying. Bullies frequently act on their prejudices and biases when choosing to verbally or physically assault someone, even as adults.

Notably, Mendez et al. (2016) acknowledged that same-race bullying is also a troubling pattern; however, people of color more likely encounter bullying when they are enrolled in schools or contexts where the numerical majority are primarily Caucasian American. Moreover, people of color interpret their experiences through multiple lenses or standpoints. As King (1988) explained, marginalized individuals have a "both/or" orientation to the world, and in the case of students of color, their experiences center around their race, gender, or raced-gender. As such, they have the advantage and disadvantage of relating to both worlds because of their multiple consciousness, yet standing apart because of differences. By extension, they live as a raced individual and find ways to balance living simultaneously in two different worlds.

Intersectionality and Race in Bullying

As previously discussed, very little research on bullying exists that solely looks at race. Instead, researchers explore race in addition to other human characteristics, including ethnicity, culture, socioeconomic status, and community. Such studies are important because they acknowledge that people are implied beings and are a product of their various communities (i.e., family, neighborhood, school, city, etc.). Connell et al. (2015) provided one study that explores intersectionality. According to Garnett et al. (2014), intersectionality comprises a theoretical framework that "advocates studying the mutual and simultaneous construction of various social categories" (i.e., race, class) in order to "identify the unique patterns of oppression that might stem from the various intersections of claimed and perceived identities" (p. 1226). They were specifically interested in intersectionality and perceptions of and experiences with bullying. Garnett et al.'s findings offer confirmation that the both/or orientation is critical to understanding racial bullying. This research supports the notion that confounding factors make race-related bullying experiences sometimes more complex than one might first believe.

Connell et al.'s study (2015) revealed slight differences across racial/ethnic groups. Caucasian American and Asian American youth commonly reported perceived victimization, while African Americans were more likely to report actual bullying and less likely to report perceived bullying. According to Connell et al., "an individual's ethnicity represents status and can contribute to the power deficit for bullying victims," which means they are "exhibiting characteristics that make them vulnerable" (p. 808). Thus, as a result of being in the minority, people of color are forced to have a heightened awareness of their out-group membership status. This experience is compounded by racial stressors that they experience in their local community. Connell et al. also found school climate and school diversity to be factors that impact bullying. Connell et al. concluded their study by encouraging teachers and administrators at homogeneous schools to not only have an awareness of the role a marginalized status (i.e., race/ethnicity) plays in bullying practices, but to identify ways to make their students of color feel safe and connected to their schools.

In addition to race, socioeconomic status is a confounding factor in bullying for some students, but not for all students of color. According to Fleschler et al. (2006), when socioeconomic status is coupled with race/ethnicity, an even greater likelihood of experiencing bullying emerges. Fleschler et al. sampled African American and Hispanic American students at urban schools and found that, while 15.3% of them were bullying victims as compared to Caucasian American students (10.1%), they also reported being bully-victims (8.6% vs. 3.7%) and bullies (8% vs. 6.5%). Fleschler et al. noted in their conclusion that life stressors, as well as normal adolescent tensions, adversely affect segments of the student population. Thus, race/ethnicity, along with other factors, contribute to bullying experiences.

Peguero and Williams (2013) also studied SES and race in the context of bullying and found that students were often bullied because of their family's SES, among other characteristics. They found that, when African American and Latino American students were of a high SES, they were subjected to bullying, while their high SES Caucasian American and Asian American peers were not. Overall, Peguero and Williams determined that SES was a "potential risk factor for bullying victimization among youth from stereotypical economically disadvantaged backgrounds" (p. 568). These findings appear contradictory, yet they demonstrate the extent to which Caucasian American students are (sub)consciously allowing their racial biases to function as motivating factors in their bullying behaviors.

Other studies have found that the quality of peer and family relationships impact instances of bullying. In their research, Spriggs et al. (2007) found that African American victims of bullying had stronger relationships with their classmates as compared to their Caucasian American and Hispanic American peers. They suggested that bullying, as well as other experiences with being an out-group member, forced students in their study to seek additional coping mechanisms (i.e., support systems and social networks). Family and school contexts were robust predictors of involvement with bullying, such that the stronger the relational ties and association with the school, the less likely an African American student was bullied. While Spriggs et al. identified some differences across groups in this study, they found that relational and institutional connections are equally important for students of all racial/ethnic groups.

Stone and Carlisle (2017) also explored the relationship between race and bullying but included the variable of youth substance use, with the goal of better understanding the origins of, or catalysts for, bullying from the vantage point of the perpetrator. They found that "racial bully perpetrators were most likely to have used cigarettes, alcohol, and marijuana, followed by youth in the mixed victim/perpetrator group" (p. 23). When analyses were stratified by race, it was revealed that, when non-Hispanic Caucasian American and Hispanic American youth were the perpetrators or perpetrator-victims of racial bullying, they were also greater consumers of cigarette, alcohol, and marijuana. This finding suggests that the students might be bullying because they view their classmates who are of a different race as some type of threat.

Recognizing the importance of intersectionality, other scholars have conducted research exploring racial bullying along with such factors as weight and sexual identity. According to Kahle and Peguero (2017), the likelihood of being bullied or victimized was lower for African American females and males and greater for Asian American females and males of all other non-Caucasian racial/ethnic groups in contrast to their Caucasian American counterparts. In terms of weight, Kahle and Peguero found that underweight females were less likely to be bullied and that racial bullying likelihood was higher for underweight Asian American and other race/ethnicity males. These findings underscore the relationship between weight and bullying, noting that students who are overweight are victimized more than "average weight" peers (Kahle & Peguero, 2017). Further, when other factors are considered, the potential increases for individuals to become a victim of bullying.

Mueller et al. (2015) also considered intersectionality and bullying. Their query gave specific attention to race, gender, sexual identity, and mental health. Their study of experiences with bullying found that "White and Hispanic gay and bisexual males, White lesbian and bisexual females, and Hispanic bisexual females were more likely to be bullied than were White heterosexual adolescents" (p. 980). Additionally, according to Mueller et al., "Black lesbian, gay, and bisexual youths' vulnerability to being bullied was not significantly different from that of White heterosexual youths. Black and Hispanic heterosexual youths were less likely to be bullied than were White heterosexual youths" (p. 980). As their analysis suggested, race and sexual identity played a role to the extent of which person was bullied. Thus, the more different they were from the Caucasian American heterosexual students, the greater the likelihood of becoming a bullying victim.

Sexual identity comprises a type of out-group, and in the Mueller et al. (2015) study, Caucasian American students who were not heterosexual appear to be associated more with their marginalized status and out-group membership, which is similar to the experiences of students of color. Thus, it may be inferred that the privileges associated with their race (i.e., not being bullied) were lost when bullies were aware of their sexual identity. Sexual identity is not an easily identifiable human characteristic as is race. Thus, when a person's group membership in a marginalized and stigmatized group becomes known, they are at a greater risk for being ostracized and bullied, which was evidenced in this study. The Mueller et al. (2015) findings support other studies on race and bullying, while offering insight into how intersectionality increases risks for bullying.

Effects of Bullying on Students of Color

Victims of bullying can experience adverse side effects that can impact their overall well-being. The effects become even more pronounced and are often times psychological when the bullying is race-based. According to Wu et al. (2015), racial bullying in the workplace may be responsible for racial/ethnic minorities' sensitivity to future discrimination. Other consequences include, but are not limited to, increased sensitivity of race/ethnic-based rejection (Wu et al., 2015), suicide ideation, depression, and completed suicide (Edwards et al., 2016), clinically diagnosed depression (Garnett et al., 2014), and relational isolation (Spriggs et al., 2007; Stone & Carlisle, 2017). While other factors might contribute to these negative outcomes or consequences for victims, evidence from the aforementioned studies affirm the assumption that people of color experience adverse mental health consequences because of their marginalized societal and academic status. Their both/or orientation potentially causes them to contend with oppressive forces impeding and derailing their academic and personal success at a very critical point in their young lives.

Other studies on the effects of race-based bullying have found that bullying victims who are a part of a marginalized racial/ethnic group have very likely been affected emotionally and mentally in ways that their Caucasian American peers are not. As Garnett et al. (2014) noted, students of color risk encountering not only racial discrimination but discrimination based on sexual identity, weight, or possibly both. Garnett et al. revealed that students' level of potential discrimination intensified in proportion with the number of classes that they take, also increasing the likelihood of deliberate self-harm and suicidal ideation. Students who experienced multiple forms of discrimination "had significantly higher depressive symptoms compared to the low discrimination class" (p. 1225). These findings were also consistent with a study by Rodríguez-Hidalgo, Ortega-Ruiz, and Monks (2015), who discovered "that those adolescents from cultural minority groups are at heightened risk [for bullying]" and experience "cultural victimisation, multi-victimisation, [increased] frequency, and level of negative feelings" as well as lower self-esteem (p. 8).

T.S. Pan and Spittal's (2013) study yielded similar findings, but included religion, which is also a type of culture where members have shared beliefs, values, and traditions. Religious identities are often times associated with a person's ethnicity (i.e., Jewish identity); the researchers accounted for this by studying ethnocultural and religious bullying in urban China. Pan and Spittal found that taken together, these layered forms of bullying cause psychological distress and can take the form of any of eight health-related outcomes: "suicidal ideation, suicide planning, depressive symptomology, anxiety symptomatology, fighting, injury intentionally inflicted by another, smoking and moderate/ heavy alcohol consumption" (p. 685). The results are consistent with those of other studies, in that victims were at risk for a compromised mental health status. Shin et al. (2011) offer additional support for this observation and explain that "bullying among Korean/Asian American adolescents and their related mental health issues need to be addressed in a comprehensive context of their discrimination experiences, acculturation, family and school environments" (p. 873).

Mueller et al. (2015) and many other researchers have found that students of color and LGBTQI+ youth are at risk for many other mental health issues such as low self-esteem/stress (Rodríguez-Hidalgo et al., 2015; Wu et al., 2015), substance abuse (Stone & Carlisle, 2017), and alienation/ isolation (Spriggs et al., 2007; Peguero & Williams, 2013; Yoon, Sulkowski, & Bauman, 2016); however, the consequences are significantly more pronounced for racial/ethnic minorities. These studies provide insight into the effects of bullying in ways that the vast majority of the bullying studies do not. Moreover, scholars are making important efforts to unpack a very complex and important social issue occurring in the U.S. and around the world.

Bullying and Race: Interventions for a Critical Social Issue

As our review has shown, the topic of *bullying and race* is a critical social issue that is being studied by scholars from various disciplines. Overall findings indicate that not only are students of color dealing with the stress of being a potential bullied individual, but these targets are forced to identify ways to cope with the abuse (Garnett et al., 2015; Mendez et al., 2016). Currently, there is a dearth of research on this aspect of bullying. Yet, the literature offers some evidence indicating that race-based bullying is a reality for many students in schools around the globe.

The findings articulated in this chapter offer greater insight into this national and international issue and the ways in which bullying adversely affects historically marginalized groups. The research also provides evidence of a strong relationship between race and bullying despite there being limited research on this important topic (Pan & Spittal, 2013). The literature does succeed in illuminating the various types of bullying many people experience, and when a victim is targeted because of their race, ethnicity, or culture, it has serious impact on them (Larochette et al., 2010; Mendez et al., 2016; Peguero & Williams, 2013). The studies offer support for the fact that victim status is due to a person not being of the majority group (i.e., Caucasian American); thus, their "otherness" places them at greater risk for being bullied by their peers (Wang et al., 2016).

According to the Southern Poverty Law Center (2016), racial bullying and hate crimes are on the rise in the U.S. Therefore, it is quite possible that there will be an increase in schools in particular. The scholars studying this issue recognize the importance of this area of research, particularly since it has a direct impact on individuals (Larochette et al., 2010), communities (Schumann et al. (2013), and institutions (Schumann et al., 2013; Yoon et al., 2016). Hopefully, our review of these studies has instigated attention to a social issue that, as Scherr (2012) explained, will be eliminated with help from students, parents, administrators, and scholars whose work translates into societal interventions for a very vulnerable population.

5

HOW DOMINANT GROUP MEMBERS CAN TRANSFORM WORKPLACE BULLYING

Robert J. Razzante, Sarah J. Tracy, and Mark P. Orbe

Over the last two decades, the Communication discipline has become a leader in research that explains, defines, operationalizes, and theorizes bullying (Lutgen-Sandvik & Tracy, 2012). Similar to studies of harassment, discrimination, and abuse, the bullying literature has been largely motivated by a desire to analyze this interactional "bad behavior" so that it ostensibly may be eradicated. Less clear, however, is the specification of (1) behaviors that should fill the void when bullying behavior declines and (2) the processes by which "good behavior" might most effectively be inspired and created. This chapter works to contribute to this gap in research by identifying communication actions of dominant group members that may disrupt bullying practices. In doing so, the study extends Co-Cultural Theory (Orbe, 1998) toward the applied conceptualization of Dominant Group Theory (Razzante & Orbe, 2017).

The chapter begins by providing a brief review of relevant workplace bullying research (for additional information on workplace bullying, see Cowan & Bochantin, this volume; Tye-Williams, this volume). The chapter then connects this workplace bullying research to Dominant Group Theory, showing how dominant group members may communicate with targets of workplace bullying (a type of co-cultural group) in ways that result in: (1) reinforcement of oppressive structures, (2) impediment of oppressive structures, and/or (3) dismantling of oppressive structures. We affirm that, through their micro-level interactions, dominant group members have the opportunity to create, maintain, or transform (anti-)bullying practices in the workplace. We demonstrate this key point at the heart of the chapter when we provide a constructed vignette and an analysis that illustrates how dominant members' specific communicative practices could reinforce an environment of workplace bullying or, instead, inspire environments (both micro-level and macro-level) that are characterized by perspective-taking, compassion, microaffirmations, and effective conversations for action. Focusing on both these micro and macro discursive moves underscores the value of examining anti-bullying practices within the framework of communication as constitutive, wherein dominant group members have particular agency to both reinforce, impede, and/or dismantle oppressive structures and discourses. Finally, as discussed in our conclusion, we designed our analysis to leave readers feeling inspired and informed to practice preferred ways of being so as to disrupt abuse and create humane organizing practices.

Moving From Critiquing the Problem to Inspiring Transformation

Similar to much of the organizational literature that has concentrated on problems and deficits (Sekerka, Comer, & Goodwin, 2014), most workplace bullying research has focused on analyzing and critiquing problematic features and effects of abusive interactional behavior at work. Primary questions that workplace bullying scholars have studied include (1) how abuse manifests, (2) how employees respond, (3) why it is so harmful, (4) why resolution is so difficult, and (5) how it might be resolved (Lutgen-Sandvik & Tracy, 2012). All but the last question focus on its related problems—which, of course, exist many at multiple layers of organizational interaction. Bullying manifests in micro-level interactions when people gossip and spread rumors. Meso-level workplace policies, most of which concentrate on demographic-based harassment (e.g., age, sex, race), have not sufficiently disciplined "equal opportunity" workplace jerks. Macro-level discourses, such as television shows that glorify tough bosses who yell "you're fired," normalize harsh behavior. Moreover, corporate climates, built through specific rituals, norms, and communication, institutionalize competitive harassing behavior due to unquestioned (and mythical) assumptions that bullying might increase productivity (Keashly & Jagatic, 2003).

Although scant, some research focuses on solutions for intervention and change. At the macro-level, this work has come in the form of scholars aligning with activists and making the name "workplace bullying" public via news stories, Wikipedia entries, and white papers. The phrase "workplace bullying" entered the English lexicon in the early 1990s and began to gain traction in the United States in the mid-2000s (Lutgen-Sandvik & Tracy, 2012). Public scholarship has increased general awareness of bullying and built momentum for anti-bullying laws (Namie, Namie, & Lutgen-Sandvik, 2010). What's more, the concept has moved from a state of denotative hesitancy to one that exists in material representations like documentary movies, specialized institutes, and 702,000 Google hits in .36 seconds (as of spring 2018). At this point, it's safe to say that the term *workplace bullying* has gained popular traction. At the meso-level, and with mixed results, human resource professionals have moved toward incorporating specific anti-bullying language into organizational policies (Cowan, 2011; Cowan & Bochantin, this volume). However, policy changes do not equate with parallel culture modifications. Despite policies that forbid certain behaviors, employees are often confused about the ways they *should* be interacting to create a humane workplace. Indeed, even when employees know that they have witnessed bad behavior and try to help, they oftentimes tell the target of abuse to just quit, fight back, or simply blow it off—advice that many targets of bullying do not view as helpful (Tye-Williams & Krone, 2017).

That said, some types of communication are ameliorative. Co-workers corroborating and reporting workplace bullying lends credibility to targets' stories. Just talking with and providing social support to co-workers is also valuable, whether or not such talk leads to active resistance. After sharing their stories in focus groups with other bullying targets, nearly every participant said they felt much better and realized the problem was experienced by others (Tracy, Lutgen-Sandvik, & Alberts, 2006). Further, conversations with supportive co-workers including collective fantasies about revenge (Tye-Williams & Krone, 2015)—even more than talking with family, researchers, or friends—seem to make a positive difference (Lutgen-Sandvik, 2006). Although this talk may not do anything to change the abuse or bully's behavior, it allows employees to reframe the situation and maintain a preferred identity (Lutgen-Sandvik, 2008).

However, is there something beyond *feeling better* that can be accomplished through communication? Can certain communicative behaviors disrupt bullying and create positive change? One promising direction has been the move toward bystander training, in which workgroups learn how to provide immediate feedback in poignant workplace interactions, increase positive communication, and re-source problematic behavior (Foss & Foss, 2003; Scully & Rowe, 2009; Wajngurt & Keashly, in press). Another area lies in sexual harassment research. Researchers have provided specific recommendations in terms of what bystanders can do when they observe harassment, depending on whether they want to correct problematic behavior or affirm positive behavior, and ranging in the immediacy and involvement of the response (Bowes-Sperry & O'Leary-Kelly, 2005). In the face of harassing behavior, a high immediate, high involvement response would be to immediately name the offense and ask the actor to stop. A high immediate, low involvement response would be to inter-rupt the incident and redirect the parties. Meanwhile, a low immediate, high involvement response would be to report the offender formally, and a low immediate, low involvement reaction would be to privately counsel the target about the experience (Bowes-Sperry & O'Leary-Kelly, 2005).

This past research shows what to do to stop negative behavior. Yet, what type of behavior should unfold in its place? Some scholars have focused on affirmation. For example, as a correlate to bystander response to offensive behavior, Bowes-Sperry and O'Leary-Kelly (2005) provided a variety of exam-ples of affirming positive behavior, such as public praise, private praise, formal commendation, or simply using body language to show approval. In her work on building a respectful workplace, Tehrani (2001) argued that the importance of recognition and reward in achieving organizational cultural change cannot be overestimated. She suggested that such reward need not be financial and might come in the forms of certificates, medals, and recognition "in the appraisal process where appropriate objectives are set to assess the levels of respect shown to colleagues and teams" (p. 151). Positive organizational scholar Dutton (2003) introduced the framework of high quality connections, which are characterized by respectful engagement, task enabling, trusting, and play. Indeed, work can be a source of positive emotional experiences, allowing workers to feel safe, respected, valued, trusted, and inspired (Lutgen-Sandvik, Riforgiate, & Fletcher, 2011).

In contrast to workplace bullying that can suck the life out of employees, brief interactional encounters have the potential to energize, support, and buffer. That said, little communication research has incorporated studying positive behavior alongside the negative bullying behavior, and that which has done so suggests that the relationship of positive and negative behavior is complex. When negative interactional behavior is low, positive organizational factors have beneficial effects. However, when bullying levels are high, positive relational patterns have decreased effects on mental health, intent to leave, and stress (Lutgen-Sandvik, Hood, & Jacobson, 2016).

In short, workplace bullying research in the field of communication has focused primarily on describing and explaining the sustenance of the problem. Knowing about the negative is certainly important. However, simply recognizing the problem does not guarantee that an organization can survive, much less thrive. An unrealized promise exists in exploring how people may most effectively treat others with kindness and respect and how organizations might promote this type of behavior. As such, we must move our research from exploring the problematic consequences of bullying to how it might be ameliorated. One potential avenue for doing so is when typically powerful and dominant group members step in to transform abusive workplace situations—something we turn to next.

Dominant Group Theory

An extension of Co-Cultural Theory (Orbe, 1998), Dominant Group Theory (DGT) considers the diverse ways in which majority group members—those individuals who are White, male, hetero-sexual, Christian, able-bodied, middle- or upper-class, and/or cisgender—communicate within a society where their social location is steeped in privilege. The theory emerged from a synergistic review of key literature (e.g., DeTurk, 2011; Sue et al., 2007) and qualitative data from two recent studies (Orbe & Batten, 2017; Razzante, 2017). Within this section, we outline the key concepts of DGT in order to demonstrate its applicability to anti-bullying.

Five Premises of DGT

Five epistemological assumptions inform the fundamental ideas of DGT. First, a hierarchy exists in each society that privileges certain groups of people based on their majority group standing (e.g., White, heterosexual, and/or male). Second, in contrast, others (e.g., people of color, LGBTQ persons, and/or women) are marginalized as co-cultural group members. Third, dominant group members may represent a diverse set of experiences; however, they all share a similarly privileged societal position (for related arguments, see also Harris & Janovec, this volume). Fourth, the diversity of dominant group members cannot be ignored with essentialist thinking. Fifth, and finally, dominant group members negotiate their privilege when communicating with others. These five premises inform the other theoretical concepts—factors, communication orientations, and dominant strategies—that comprise DGT.

Six Factors Influencing Dominant Group Communication

As reflected in the five premises, the communication of dominant group members—despite the privilege that they have in common—is not always the same. Instead, it can take multiple forms. Mirroring the concepts of Co-Cultural Theory (Orbe, 1998), DGT describes six factors that influence the communication of majority group members: communication approach, interactional outcome, field of experience, abilities, perceived costs and rewards, and situational context (Razzante & Orbe, 2017).

Like Co-Cultural Theory, DGT identifies two primary factors in majority group communication: communication approach and interactional outcome (Razzante & Orbe, 2018). *Communication approach* focuses on the tone of messages as demonstrated on different points along a continuum. A nonassertive communication approach, which prioritizes others' needs and expectations over one's own, sits on one end. An aggressive communication approach lies on the other end; it signifies instances when individuals put their own needs and expectations above those of others. In the center of the continuum is assertiveness. An assertive communication embraces a balance between attending to the needs and expectations of self and others. *Interactional outcome* involves the effect that dominant group communication has for self and others living in a hierarchical society. According to DGT, three outcomes exist: (1) reinforcing existing oppressive structures (i.e., supporting the status quo in terms of institutional racism, sexism, etc.), (2) impeding existing oppressive structures (i.e., communicating in ways that counter everyday prejudice and discrimination of co-cultural group members), and (3) dismantling existing oppressive structures (i.e., using one's privilege to fight against institutional policy and practice that provides unearned entitlements) (Razzante & Orbe, 2018).

DGT combines the three components of communication approach and interactional outcome to produce nine different communication orientations that dominant group members assume in their communications with others (see Razzante & Orbe, 2017). Adoption of one communication orientation over another is informed synergistically by the other four factors. For instance, *field of experience* (the sum of an individual's life events) includes messages from family and friend and, socialization through various organizations, as well as past and current experiences with co-cultural and dominant group members. *Abilities*, or a person's capability to communicate in different ways, comprises another influential factor in dominant group communication. This particular factor draws attention to the reality that not all majority group members have the same skill levels or opportunities to enact each of the different strategies (discussed in next section). In short, the competency levels of dominant group members—like their co-cultural group counterparts—vary significantly.

The fifth factor influencing dominant group communication is *perceived costs and rewards* (Razzante & Orbe, 2018). Every form of communication, when enacted by a particular person in a specific situation, will have some effect on them as individuals. Not all "costs" (e.g., social isolation, guilt, public condemnation) and "rewards" (e.g., continued social privilege, self-fulfillment) will be perceived the same by all majority group members. Instead, particular perceptions of different costs and rewards depend largely on the field of experience and interactional outcome of particular individuals. The final factor is *situational context*, an important consideration in dominant group communication (Razzante & Orbe, 2018). Broadly conceptualized, situational context involves a number of issues, including physical environment, geographical location, interpersonal and small group dynamics and time and seasonal circumstances. People do not typically select one specific way to communicate in all situational contexts (Orbe, 1998). Instead, depending on a combination of different factors, different forms of communication may be used in different situations. When responding to bullying in the workplace, a dominant group member's communicative response draws from these six influential factors. Next, we explore how anti-bullying practices manifest in relation to these six factors.

Dominant Group Communication Orientations and Strategies

The final core concept of DGT involves communication orientations that are comprised of different dominant group communicative strategies (Razzante & Orbe, 2018). As described earlier, two factors—communication approach and interactional outcome—intersect to formulate nine different dominant group communication orientations. A communication orientation is a specific stance that dominant group members assume during their everyday interactions. Each communication orientation is primarily defined through the sub-factors of specific interactional outcomes (*reinforce, impede,* or *dismantle oppressive structures*) and communication approaches (*nonassertive, assertive,* or *aggressive*). Scholars associate particular dominant group messages with each orientation, as we describe next. Through our exploration of communicative strategies, we agree with and complicate Tye-Williams and Krone's (2017) point that privileged individuals and potential anti-bullies have access to a variety of responses to bullying. DGT helps to understand how power and privilege can be used as a means to disrupt bullying while also recognizing that the reproduction of workplace bullying can occur, too.[1]

According to Razzante and Orbe (2018), nine dominant group communication orientations exist. *Nonassertive reinforcement* represents an approach that is covertly complicit in its support of dominant oppressive structures. Remaining neutrally silent is one dominant group strategy associated with this orientation (see Table 5.1). Other majority group members whose communication behaviors reinforce oppressive societal structures might be more assertive in their messages (Razzante & Orbe, 2018). An *assertive reinforcement* orientation works to balance the needs and expectations of both dominant group and co-cultural group members. However, given the inherent advantages of their majority group status, individual communication ultimately reinforces oppressive societal structures. Two strategies, resisting majority group essentialism and redirection, are reflective of this stance. For example, a dominant group member might deflect the fact that marginalized co-workers are being bullied by making known the ways he/she is bullied instead. A final communication orientation associated with reinforcing oppressive societal structures is *aggressive reinforcement*. This stance prioritizes a dominant group member's desire to maintain or strengthen existing power dynamics with little or no consideration given co-cultural rights, needs, and desires. Endorsing the status quo, dismissing co-cultural concerns, and blaming the victim are strategies consistent with this stance. These strategies especially manifest when a dominant group member ignores bullying in order to maintain hierarchical power within the workplace.

Impeding oppressive structures stresses the importance of interpersonal messages that disrupt manifestations of oppression in everyday interactions. *Nonassertive impediment* features dominant group messages that counter existing prejudice and discrimination against co-cultural group members—albeit in covert, indirect ways (Razzante & Orbe, 2018). The primary dominant strategies that are a part of this orientation are engaging in self-reflexivity and recognizing one's own privilege. That is, a dominant group member might impede bullying practices by becoming aware of the ways he/she contributes to bullying him/herself. Alternatively, an *assertive impediment* orientation strives for a balance between self and others' concerns during attempts to counter co-cultural prejudice and discrimination. Several different dominant group strategies, defined in Table 5.1, promote impeding oppressive structures through an assertive communication approach: affirming co-cultural concerns, educating others, and setting an example for others. For more aggressive majority group members, another alternative exists. Individuals who adopt an *aggressive impediment* orientation are not overly concerned with dominant group perceptions; instead, their priority is their effort to promote change in the everyday lives of co-cultural group members. Scholars associate two particular dominant strategies with this orientation: confronting oppressive rhetoric and microaffirmations (Razzante & Orbe, 2018). As such, assertive impediments can be conceptually aligned with emerging research on active bystander training (Foss & Foss, 2001; Scully & Rowe, 2009; Wajngurt & Keashly, in press).

Nonassertive dismantling seems like an oxymoron: How can a dominant group member dismantle dominant oppressive structures passively? Yet, one strategy has been identified: sacrificing self (see Table 5.1 for definition). This particular strategy prioritizes the needs of co-cultural group members over one's own needs (Razzante & Orbe, 2011). An *assertive dismantling* orientation to dominant group communication maintains a balance of self- and other needs while invoking societal change. Challenging oppressive ideologies, identifying as a co-cultural ally, and assuming responsibility for action are dominant strategies central to this orientation. Furthermore, an ideal dismantling

Table 5.1 Sample Dominant Group Strategies by Communication Orientation

	Sample Strategy Description
Nonassertive Reinforcement	
Ignoring one's privilege	A lack of awareness of, or outright refusal to acknowledge, the societal privilege that comes with dominant group status
Remaining neutrally silent	Recognition of oppression but not speaking out to avoid conflict
Assertive Reinforcement	
Redirection	Highlighting aspects of one's identity that reflect disadvantage as a means to deemphasize one's own privilege
Resisting group essentialism	Objections to criticisms by others that generalize majority group members into one large homogenous group
Aggressive Reinforcement	
Endorsing the status quo	Communicative messages that rationalize, support, and/or endorse existing ideologies, values, and oppressive institutions
Dismissing co-cultural concerns	Communicative messages that regard co-cultural concerns as trivial, illegitimate, or outright false
Victim blaming	Assigning responsibility to co-cultural groups to remove themselves from oppressed positions
Microaggressions	Everyday exchanges that feature denigrating messages to others because of their co-cultural identities
Nonassertive Impediment	
Recognizing one's privilege	Verbal acknowledgements of one's own societal privilege that increase awareness for others
Engaging in self-reflexivity	Ability and willingness to reflect on the consequences of individual thoughts and actions as dominant group members
Assertive Impediment	
Affirming co-cultural concerns	Acknowledging the legitimacy and magnitude of co-cultural issues and the realities of societal oppression
Educating others	Drawing from one's own growth—cognitively, emotionally, spiritually, etc.—to facilitate growth in others
Setting an example for others	Communicating in ways that can serve as a model for other dominant group members

(*Continued*)

Table 5.1 (Continued)

	Sample Strategy Description
Microaffirmations	Everyday exchanges that feature affirming messages to others because of their co-cultural identities *when considering* others' desires or wishes on how to be affirmed
Aggressive Impediment	
Confronting oppressive rhetoric	Explicitly naming, without regard to others, dominant group messages as ignorant, hurtful, and/or discriminatory to co-cultural group members
Microaffirmations	Everyday exchanges that feature affirming messages to others because of their co-cultural identities *regardless of* others' desires or wishes on how to be affirmed
Nonassertive Dismantling	
Sacrificing self	Efforts to challenge institutionalized oppression that come with significant personal cost
Assertive Dismantling	
Challenging oppressive ideologies	Questioning the legitimacy of policies that unfairly discriminate against co-cultural group members
Identifying as co-cultural ally	Communicating in ways that challenge policies that negatively affect co-cultural group members
Assuming responsibility for action	Assuming an action-oriented approach that utilizes one's own privilege to work against systems that foster that very privilege
Aggressive Dismantling	
Forcing	Pushing your agenda to advocate for societal change with little to no regard for dominant group members' concerns

of oppressive structures may emerge through what Dutton (2003) referred to as "high qualitative connections," where workplace anti-bullying efforts emerge through assertive strategies that cultivate respectful engagement, task enabling, and trust. The final communication orientation is *aggressive dismantling* (Razzante & Orbe, 2011). Majority group members who are determined to fight institutional oppressive structures with little to no concern for others (including both dominant group and co-cultural group members) enact dominant group strategies, such as using one's privilege and forcing. An aggressive dismantling of oppressive structures may manifest when a dominant group anti-bully uses their position of privilege to advocate and implement anti-bullying norms while not consulting with co-cultural members. Such an approach may ultimately do more harm than good.

Dominant Group Theory (Razzante & Orbe, 2017) provides a useful theoretical framework to illuminate the communicative choices that dominant group members can take in response to workplace bullying. As noted previously, organizational literature has focused on problems and deficits (Sekerka et al., 2014), while workplace bullying research has primarily focused on identifying and critiquing bullying practices. DGT offers a theoretical framework that continues to locate and demystify workplace bullying *while also* identifying ways dominant group members can use their positions of privilege to eliminate workplace bullying. As such, our approach to this chapter addresses the call for looking for ways that workplace bullying can be resolved (Lutgen-Sandvik & Tracy, 2012). The following sections provide a constructed vignette that, with its analysis, examines how different dominant group member behaviors could impact, normalize, or transform workplace bullying.

Transforming Workplace Bullying

Constructed Vignette: Paws for Love

The following constructed vignette is fictionalized but draws from data contained in existing workplace bully research (e.g., Lutgen-Sandvik, 2006, 2008; Tracy et al., 2006; Workplace Bullying Institute, 2010). Among other things, this research demonstrates how bullying comprises a ritualized escalatory behavior and often intersects with other identity characteristics (e.g., subordinates, women, and racial minorities are more likely to report bullying, whereas supervisors and dominant group members more likely engage in bullying behaviors). Given our interest in how dominant group members might influence workplace bullying, we include clear reference to demographic and identity characteristics in the narrative. Furthermore, and perhaps most importantly, many workplace bullying targets describe that part of the challenge in telling their story is that their experience is just too horrific and fantastic for others to find credible. We suspect that some readers will find this case unbelievable. However, targets of bullying report even more extreme tales. We offer the narrative to set up our analysis of how dominant group members perpetuate, but might also intervene in and potentially transform, workplace bullying.

★ ★ ★

As Sofia got ready for work that morning, she felt that all too familiar pit growing in her stomach. She had been working as a technician in her small town's veterinarian office—Paws For Love—ever since she had graduated from the local technical college several years earlier. She loved dogs and cats—especially Chihuahuas, since they reminded her of her native Mexico. Sofia had never been that talkative or outgoing and sometimes felt as though she connected better with animals than with people. That said, she had always gotten along with her co-workers despite some self-acknowledged social awkwardness. Up until three months ago, being a vet tech had been her dream job.

So why the change? The highly regarded founder of Paws for Love, Dr. Karen Lewis, had recently retired and hired a new manager to take her place, Dr. Williams. Dr. Sam Williams was a White, burly, middle-aged man who had been the fraternity brother of Dr. Lewis' nephew. He was gregarious, loud, sociable, and he told everyone to call him "Dr. Fun."

Whereas the office had been a place of peaceful pleasantness before, "Dr. Fun" played not-so-funny practical jokes and laughed so maniacally that he immediately made Sofia feel uncomfortable. In his first week on the job, he guffawed so loudly that an injured puppy shrank into the corner of the room. Assuming that he just did not realize his effect on the puppy, Sofia had suggested, "Dr. Williams, I think you may be scaring the animals a little bit." He ignored her comment during the appointment, but, as soon as the client and puppy left the room, his smile turned to a sneer. He said, "Listen, little miss mousy Mexi, I'm the boss around here now. I'm fun. I'm loud. You're quiet, and a bit boring. NEVER tell me what to do." Sofia, shocked and dumbfounded, could not believe her ears.

Several hours later, the now-retired founder Dr. Lewis happened to stop in the office as she occasionally did. Dr. Williams turned on his charm, telling her how well that things were going since she had retired. Sofia tried to pull Dr. Lewis aside, hoping she could talk to her about Dr. William's behavior. However, there was no such opportunity. On the way out, Dr. Lewis said, "Sofia, you look concerned. I hope you'll share any upset you have with your new boss." Over the next few weeks, the surprise insults from Dr. Williams continued to rain down when she least expected it—oftentimes wrapped in the guise of humor. Sofia began to hate work, and she felt powerless. Yet, it was the only vet office in their small town, and, with Dr. Lewis retired, there was no one with authority who might talk to or discipline Dr. Williams.

The only other person regularly in the office was James, who had been working the front desk for six months—a job he took to make ends meet during a "gap year" between college and law school. Sofia had come to appreciate James' friendly demeanor, great attitude, and positive outlook on life.

Plus, with his all-American good looks and easy smile, he was fantastic at calming anxious animals and clients.

One particular morning when Sofia arrived at work, she lingered at James' front desk. Here, she was safe from Dr. William's abusive behavior because his offensive insults were reserved for private interactions in the back examination room. However, eventually she knew she had to face Dr. Williams.

As Sofia wandered toward the examination room to set it up for the day, James began to wonder why she seemed to be increasingly on edge. Sofia had always been a woman of few words, but, lately, she had seemed almost scared to go back and start her work for the day. James decided to wheel his receptionist chair so he could see and hear what was going on in the examination room down the hallway. James knew that Dr. Williams was working in the back operating room—an area that had a separate door to the examination room. Suddenly, he heard Dr. Williams enter the room where Sofia was setting up.

Even with her back to the door, Sofia heard it click. Dr. Williams had arrived, and Sofia had no way of knowing his mood for the day. Would he leave her alone, or was she going to be the object of his abuse? She busied herself with sanitizing the thermometer and setting up the scale, refusing to look up. She mumbled, "Good morning," but Dr. Williams managed to get close enough to her to reach over and lift up her chin. Forcing her to look at him in the eye, he half smiled, cocked his head, and said, "Don't you know that it's bad manners to not look your boss in the eye?" She shook herself free and said, "Yes sir." He said, "Please, do not call me sir. I want you to call me Dr. Fun, and I want you to treat me as if I am fun. Not all this moping around. Is that part of your upbringing or something? You're in America now, time to start acting that way!" Sofia could feel tears well in her eyes and sweat break out under her arms. She thought to herself, "Sofia, just endure this, and soon the animals and clients will be here and you will be safe again."

Overhearing this exchange, James knew he had to make a decision. He knew that, technically, he was a low power employee with no formal authority. However, Dr. Williams always treated James with respect, saying how much they had in common, inviting him to happy hour, and asking about James' experience playing college football. Meanwhile, he showed no such interest in Sofia, and James saw Sofia becoming a shell of herself in the face of the racial slurs and sarcastic, bullying behavior. James knew that Dr. Williams would probably listen to him if he said something, but was that really his responsibility? What was he going to do?

★ ★ ★

The preceding constructed vignette offers an example of workplace bullying at Paws for Love. James and Dr. Williams are both native-born White men, whereas Sofia is a woman of color who immigrated to the U.S. as a young child. While keeping in mind that identity is complex and multifaceted, in the following analysis, we primarily focus our attention on race/ethnicity, gender, nationality, age, and socioeconomic status. Our protagonist, James, is the key figure through which we apply Dominant Group Theory. We ask, as a dominant group member in terms of race and gender, how might James use his positionality to disrupt Dr. Williams' bullying antics? Drawing from DGT, we explore the variety of ways in which James might reinforce, impede, or dismantle the oppressive structure of workplace bullying at Paws for Love.

As a native-born White man, James can reinforce workplace bullying in several ways. First, he could engage in nonassertive reinforcement by *remaining neutrally silent*. In essence, James could recognize that he could, and should, do something, but he might fail to mobilize himself to act. In other words, he could acknowledge that Dr. Williams oppresses Sofia through continuous bullying. However, recognizing that he could be ostracized by Dr. Williams (a significant perceived cost for a young employee) could influence James to keep quiet. James might also engage in aggressive reinforcement through *dismissing co-cultural concerns*. In this case, James might insist that Sofia is being too sensitive and should get over Dr. Williams' "playful nature." His field of experiences, steeped in White male privilege, might fail to spark empathy and understanding of Sofia's anxiety as co-cultural target of Dr. Williams' bullying. Even though James may enact two different dominant group behaviors, both communicative choices lead to the same interactional outcome: a reinforcement of workplace bullying.

In addition to his ability to reinforce workplace bullying, James also has the potential to impede a workplace environment that marginalizes Sofia. First, James might assertively impede through *educating others*. That is, James might draw from his experiences being one of the few White players on a majority Black football team to help Dr. Williams realize that not everyone finds the same behaviors as fun. Such communication might be able to teach Dr. Williams about his comments' implications when coming from a position of power and privilege. Depending on his communication abilities and the specific situational context of Paws of Love, James' field of experience might also aggressively impede through *confronting oppressive rhetoric*. That is, James might engage in assertive impediment through enacting several *microaffirmations* on behalf of Sofia. For example, James might know that Sofia feels more empowered to confront Dr. Williams' oppressive rhetoric herself when she is physically in the presence of others, especially with someone like him whose cultural location is similar to the bully. Yet, he also knows that, in the past, Sofia's assertions alone have not had any impact on Dr. Williams' behaviors. As such, James might walk over and stand beside Sofia in solidarity when she challenges Dr. Williams herself—making sure that all parties know that he supports her and identifies the doctor's behaviors as abusive.[2]

Finally, James might engage in communicative behaviors that work toward the dismantling of workplace bullying. He might specifically engage in nonassertive dismantling through *sacrificing self*. For example, James could sacrifice self by whistleblowing—by finding a way to be in touch with Dr. Lewis, even though she is retired. In whistleblowing, James risks losing his job or being stigmatized as the office snitch. Yet, James might be willing to make this choice, given his commitment to social justice. If James does not feel comfortable whistleblowing, given his understanding of the perceived costs and rewards associated with that choice, he might engage in assertive dismantling through *identifying as a co-cultural ally*. Rather than merely affirming Sofia's concerns through interpersonal interactions, James might put his empathy into action by approaching Dr. Lewis and advocating for organizational policy changes that condemn workplace bullying and make such behaviors punishable up to termination. While Sofia may understand James' efforts, she may also see his actions as unnecessary (e.g., she didn't want Dr. Williams to be fired, just to stop bullying her). Accordingly, she may critique his well-intentioned attempts as enacting change that he thinks is best—with little regard to her own desires. As such, James might valuably instead initiate an anti-bullying campaign around work that raises awareness and mobilizes his colleagues in the eradication of workplace bullying by Dr. Williams and others. Consulting first with targets of workplace bullying is crucial for intervening ethically.

As a dominant group member,[3] James could draw from various levels of societal privilege as he negotiates his awareness of workplace bullying. Depending on his abilities, field of experience, and perceived costs and rewards, James could employ a number of different dominant group strategies to reinforce, impede, and/or dismantle workplace bullying. The key element here is the insight that DGT provides in terms of understanding the variety of interactional outcomes possible as a result of a dominant group member's communication. Of course, each communicative strategy will have its own set of interactional outcomes rooted in the particular set of dynamics present in a specific situational context. No rule of thumb guides every situation.

Conclusion: Advocating for an OPPT-in Approach to Power and Privilege

This chapter employed Dominant Group Theory as a theoretical framework to build upon the research in bullying bystander training (Scully & Rowe, 2009; Sajngurt & Keashly, in press), organizational strengths (Cooperrider & Godwin, 2012), and positive emotion at work (Avery, Wernsing, & Luthans, 2008). Dominant Group Theory can valuably illuminate structures of workplace oppression and how dominant group members can strategically use their positionality for transformative change. We hope that DGT may provide a theoretical launching pad to both explain and inspire individual actions toward more equitable, affirming, and bullying-free workplace environments.

While we assert the utility of DGT for understanding the potential communicative responses to workplace bullying, we also believe that simply "knowing more" about intervention strategies is not sufficient for inspiring new and habitual ways of acting and being. As delineated in Tracy and colleagues' ontological-phenomenological- phronetic-transformative (OPPT-in) approach, to transform life as lived, our theories and scholarship must provide access to seeing the world anew (Tracy, Franks, Brooks, & Hoffman, 2015). Thus, more so than scientifically proving the efficacy of certain practices, our scholarship holds unrealized promise to inspire people to ask new questions and try out specific ways of being and acting (Tracy & Donovan, 2018). A good test of OPPT-in scholarship and pedagogy is whether, as a result of it, people themselves practice transformed ways of talking or being. This perspective differs from most scholarship that leaves people *knowing* about certain frameworks and equipped to *argue, analyze,* or *theorize.* It also steps beyond leaving people able to *apply* or *teach* the framework. We hope that this chapter's constructed vignette and description of potential responses inspires readers to practice new ways of interacting and strive to create just workplaces that promote human flourishing.

In particular, we encourage research that privileges the nuanced voices of individuals whose lived experiences resist easy conceptualizations of "bully" or "bullied." Accordingly, we call for critical pragmatist research that reveals the complex messiness of context-based individual-personal-cultural identities and their impact on communicative behaviors. Utilizing autoethnography (Boylorn & Orbe, 2014) to learn about people's stories regarding workplace bullying, for example, can inspire the type of transformation for which we advocate. Various potential methodological approaches exist; however, the common denominator is to create scholarship that informs and inspires simultaneously. We desire for this chapter to be a small contribution toward that ultimate goal.

Notes

1 As Dr. Brenda J. Allen (2017) advises, everyone is response-able, but all responses are responsible.
2 James' communicative behaviors here offer an important point of nuanced analysis. In the context of DGT, all dominant group behaviors are understood in terms of their interactional outcome. As such, the perceptions of James' use of microaffirmations are receiver-oriented. That is, others in the situational context—both co-cultural group and dominant group members—determine what an affirming message might be. In this example, James' communicative behavior is affirming to Sofia, due to prior understanding of how Sofia wishes to be affirmed in times of distress. For microaffirmations to be most effective, dominant group members and co-cultural group members should inform each other on how they can affirm one another in times of distress. Without prior communication, James risks reinforcing Sofia's marginalization through potentially patronizing behavior (see Razzante & Orbe, 2018).
3 Within this brief narrative, we have focused on salient identity markers associated with nationality, ethnicity, and gender. It is important, however, to recognize the multidimensional nature of identities, including how individuals negotiate positions of privilege and disadvantage simultaneously (J. N. Martin & Nakayama, 1999). For instance, while James has some privilege in terms of race and gender, he may also be at a social disadvantage based on age, socioeconomic status, and other aspects of his identity. In this regard, his privileged identities must be understood in a particular context; for example, he may be situated as a co-cultural group member (based on age, class) when interacting with Dr. Williams.

6

CYBERBULLIES, BULLYING, AND THE YOUNG IN INDIA

Rajesh Kumar

Introduction

Development of communication and information infrastructure over the years in India has led to a rise in access to and use of these technologies and services. With the government's priority agenda to connect every village in India with internet facilities in coming years, communication network expansion and its uses are likely to rise further. According to a report titled "Internet in India 2017," published by the Internet and Mobile Association of India (IAMAI, a non-profit industry body) and IMRB International (a multi-country market research company), the number of internet users in India is expected to reach to 500 million by June 2018. Internet penetration in urban India was 64.84% in December 2017 as compared to 60.6% in December 2016. Moreover, Rural Internet penetration has grown from 18% in December 2016 to 20.26% in December 2017. Significantly, this report noted that young men and college-going students were the primary users of the internet.

Internet use among youth have also proliferated because of the success of social media platforms that have become an indispensable part of young people's lives. With more and more households getting access to internet and digital information resources, corresponding concerns emanating out of digital consumption also need to be addressed without any delay and with added caution. One of the major concerns arising out of this digital boom in India is an increasing incidence of cyberbullying. Eighty-one percent of Indian children between the age of 8 and 16 years are active on social media networks, and, of these, 21% have reported being bullied online; this was higher than Australia, the U.S., and Singapore (Intel Security India, 2015). *First Post* (17 June 2016) reported that Indian teens faced the biggest risk of cyberbullying among Asian countries, and close to one in two parents believed that their children were safer from bullies on a playground than online. This scenario is giving rise to parental concern about their children as they grow up. It is natural for parents to grow concerned, because childhood and adolescence are the prime development phases of children's lives; lessons learned and experiences gathered in childhood are retained throughout their lives. Parents worry about what their children are experiencing and what are they exposed to during their developmental phases. Therefore, some sort of intervention on the part of parents, teachers, educational institutions, and governments in relation to internet use by the young is the urgent need of the hour (Snakenborg, Acker, & Gable, 2011). This chapter presents and analyzes the incidence of cyberbullying in India and how it can be tackled, especially through parental mediation of digital media use by the younger members in families.

Cyberbullying in India

Bullying in India manifests itself in different forms, such as school bullying, workplace bullying, sibling bullying, office bullying, online bullying, etc. Among all these, cyberbullying is one of the most frequently employed. Dr Debarati Halder, Managing Director of the Center for Cyber Victims, defines cyberbullying as "online harassment that involves hurling harsh, rude, insulting, teasing remarks through the message box or in open forums targeting one's body shape and structure, educational qualifications, professional qualifications, family, gender orientation, personal habits and outlook" (as cited in Sen, 2016).

The risk for Indian kids of being cyberbullied has increased over the years. Instances of cyberbullying have been much higher in India in comparison to that in other Asian countries. India ranks highest among many other Asian countries in cyberbullying, with 53% of internet-using children between the ages of 8 and 17 having faced some form of online bullying more than once (Norton Cyber Security Insights Report, 2016). India ranked third highest in incidents of cyberbullying in the world, after China and Singapore, according to a survey report by Microsoft Corporation. About 7,600 children in the age group of 8–17 years, drawn from 25 countries, participated in this survey. Survey participants were asked only about "negative online experiences" because cyberbullying may have different connotations in different socio-cultural context; Indians may find something (video, text, pictures) offensive that may not be seen as such by the British or by people of other nationalities. From India, 22% of children surveyed indicated that they had experienced bullying online in some form or other. Indian parents feel that online bullying is more disturbing and long-lasting as compared to other forms of bullying. Since online posts are permanent, parents worry that online content with the intent of bullying may revisit the kids and harm them in the future as well (Microsoft Corporation Survey, 2012).

Several social activists, doctors, police officers, and psychologists have observed that the increase in cyberbullying seems to have kept pace with the growth of internet penetration in India. Cases of minors being convicted of posting slanderous comments or pornographic pictures on Facebook or other social media sites are increasing; many are being sent to reformatory homes as well. The fact that cyberbullying can occur anonymously makes it an even more dangerous act, as victims may never know who instigated an act with the intent of bullying (*Deccan Herald*, 2015). Thus, cyberbullying has turned into a major concern in India that needs to be tackled without further delay. The best way to prevent online bullying is to sensitize young people in terms of internet etiquette, morals, and cyber laws. It has also become imperative that parents mediate internet use by the young members in their families (Hunter, 2011). Therefore, different measures to tackle cyberbullying need to be explicated.

Tackling Cyberbullying

Youth have to be educated about online safety in a fashion similar to how they are taught to protect themselves offline. Online safety also includes teaching children how to avoid risks that can place them in vulnerable situations related to cyber offenses (Hunter, 2011). A web education platform for sensitizing stakeholders to reducing bullying, www.NoBullying.com, suggests different endeavors to contain cyberbullying in India. In 2013, an Indian teen from Chicago, Trisha Prabhu, read about a cyberbullying incident in Florida that caused the suicide of an 11-year-old student. Prompted by this report, Prabhu launched software named ReThink in order to combat the problem of online bullying. ReThink is an innovative project that approaches bullying issues from a bully's point of view. It is based on the assumption that the younger population often say and do things impulsively because of peer pressure or without understanding the ramifications of what they do online. Using context-sensitive word-screening, the ReThink software filters through a teen's message, prompting him or her when they are likely to post potentially hurtful messages. This filter provides the youth time to consider the consequences of their actions and change their mind about posting something negative about others. In addition to reducing the number of cyberbullying victims, the ReThink program has the potential to modify a bully's behavior, curtailing future cyberbullying.

Testing of the program took place at a Google Science Fair in 2014. Prabhu conducted 1,500 trial runs in her school and evaluated the results. Approximately 93.4% of trial participants chose not to post negative comments after having had time to reconsider. "ReThink enables teens to become better digital citizens," says the 15-year-old inventor, who is passionately promoting her program in national and international forums.

The Times of India (2015) reported that the Central Board of Secondary Education (CBSE), which governs a significant number of schools in India, has directed school administration to form anti-bullying and anti-ragging committees. With over 17,000 CBSE-affiliated schools in the country, this decision could make a positive impact in combating bullying in school. This committee will comprise the vice-principal of the school, school doctor, counselor, senior teacher, legal representative, and representatives from the school's parents' and teachers' association. CBSE schools are required to warn students through a public display board that strict action will be taken against acts of bullying. These anti-bullying committees can be especially helpful for new entrants to the school as they are often targeted for bullying by existing students. Under this new initiative, bullies may be subjected to warnings, fines, suspension, or expulsion as appropriate and relevant.

By noticing some common signs, parents and teachers may contain cyber abuse faced by the young members in their families or schools and help them through any ordeal they may be encountering. These signs include a lack of interest in using computers or connected devices; sudden closure or removal of their social networking accounts; mood swings after reading texts, pictures, video, etc., online; loss of interest in going to school; sudden drop in grades and reports of poor school performance; secretive behavior about activities online; sudden outbursts of emotions; deteriorating health without any reason; sleep disorder, etc. (Hunter, 2011). Parents can also seek professional counseling for their children, if required, to help the child overcome the psychological effects of abusive acts online. Moreover, parents should also mediate the use of digital media and services by the younger members in their families (Snakenborg et al., 2011).

Parental Mediation: Experiences and Experiments

In recent years, there has been increasing interest in the processes through which parents facilitate the development of their children. Jacobson and Crockett (2000) identified how parental monitoring ensures children's development and welfare. Through their research, they found a significant correlation between parental monitoring and a variety of children's developmental indicators such as grade point average, lower levels of adolescent depression, and so on. Today, the internet is not merely an information resource but also a virtual platform or assembly forum of people. People form online groups to discuss issues, chat, and socialize among themselves, at times anonymously. While in some cases such virtual forums are enriching and convenient for business, virtual classrooms, and social networking, certain age groups, particularly children and adolescents, are vulnerable to such platform assemblies. This makes parents concerned about their children's activity online (Snakenborg et al., 2011).

The concern parents have is justified, as research into children's internet information skills show that children lack the evaluative and strategic skills to evaluate the utility or reliability of information derived from internet (Kuiper, Volman, & Terwel, 2008; Walraven Brand-Gruwel & Boshuzen, 2009). The EU Kids Online survey (targeting 11–16-year-olds) suggests that children know more than their parents about the internet (Livingstone, 2002). The scenario in India is more difficult to handle as young children here are quite a bit smarter than their parents when it comes to the use of digital tools and services. In fact, two generations exist together—"digital natives" and "digital immigrants." The former refers to the Gen "Y" or Millennial, and the latter refer to parents born considerably before the onset of the internet and its popular uses (Bittman, Rutherford, Brown, & Unsworth, 2012). Today, children have innate ability and curiosity for using information and communication tools and services available through internet. Children may use internet for different purposes including gathering new knowledge and information. But there have been instances when parents interpret their children's use of ICT tools and internet as the loss of academic focus and determination. Here arises a conflict situation between children's desires and aspirations and parental interpretation of the whole scenario (Kumar, 2016).

Since parents have a significant role to play in containing cyberbullying, they must devise some means to regulate internet use by their children. Here comes the role of parental mediation. Parental mediation refers to the solicitation, counseling, monitoring, and intervention in the use of these technological tools and devices to ensure the young one's online safety and to facilitate optimum utilization of these tools and services. However, there has been scant evidence of parental control and supervision over the use of digital media by the younger generation. Earlier studies and empirical results on concept and practices of parental mediation in the context of television and videogame use by children provide us with elements of a concise mediation theory (Mendoza, 2009). While discussing "parental mediation," three types emerge: restrictive mediation, active mediation, and co-use of media. Each was validated empirically and found to be applicable to both television and videogames (Austin, 1993; Bybee, Robinson, & Turow, 1982; Koolstra & Lucassen, 2004; Nikken & Jansz, 2006; Van der Voort, Van Lil, & Peeters, 1998). Restrictive mediation implies exercising control over the amount of time children spend on media and also over their media consumption. Active mediation is instructive or normative and amounts to sharing critical comments, including the explanation of complex content (Austin, Bolls, Fujioka, & Engelbertson, 1999; Valkenburg, Krcmar, Peeters, & Marseille, 1999). Co-use amounts to watching or playing together as a deliberate strategy to share children's media use (Van der Voort, Nikken, & Van Lil, 1992). Thus, the conceptualization of parental mediation in earlier studies established that parents could use at least these three different types of mediation to guide their children spending time on television and videogames.

However, it is yet to be concluded whether parental mediation is as applicable in the case of new media use by the young people as it is to watching television and playing videogames. Using digital media has increasingly turned into a solitary activity for all members of the networked household, whether in separate spaces, including children's bedrooms, or on mobile platforms (Kennedy & Wellman, 2007). Among adolescents, this pattern is evident in respect of surfing the web as well as using other media like mobiles, etc. (Holloway & Valentine, 2003; Livingstone & Bovill, 2001; Rideout, Foehr, & Roberts, 2010). This individualization, however, problematizes mediation, as it is difficult, if not impossible, for parents to apply active mediation or to engage in co-use under these circumstances.

Applying restrictive mediation also is less straightforward in the case of private online access. Various studies and analyses by Kirwil (2009), Lee and Chae (2007), Lwin, Stanaland, and Miyazak (2008) and Warren and Bluma (2002) investigating parental mediation of new media use by youth indicate that traditional parental mediation styles are applicable to internet use. In general, these researchers followed a deductive approach in which they drew items or scales from television research and used these in an adjusted form to measure defined styles of internet mediation. Nikken (2011), in his study on parental mediation of young children in Europe, found that mothers are more prominent mediators and, basically, that all types of parental mediation are more often applied by mothers. Furthermore, less educated parents set more content restrictions on their children's internet use and more often apply active mediation. The parents' own experience with the internet has a parallel in the amount of general restrictions they put on their children's web surfing, i.e., parents who went online less often tried to restrict the child's online behavior to a greater degree. Furthermore, parents with more computer or internet skills more often installed technical applications on the computer for online safety. Single parents did not differ from parents in nuclear families with regard to their mediation practices. The findings in this study, however, indicate that because of the low levels of know-how of mothers regarding information and communication technologies (ICTs), they express their inability to significantly intervene in the usage and access of ICTs by youth. Parents express their due concern for all the events associated with cyberbullying, morphing, caricature, and harassment that might occur in the online activities of their children. L. S. Clark (2011) suggested that, in addition to active, restrictive, and co-viewing as parental mediation strategies, future research needs to consider the emergent strategy of participatory learning that involves parents and children interacting together with and through digital media.

There have been very few studies in relation to parental mediation practices in India. Kumar (2016), in a study titled "ICT uses by 14–20-year-olds in India: Imperatives of parental intervention," determined that "discussion with the young ones" comprised the best of all mediation strategies to be applied by the parents. In her study of Indian teens, Sridhar (2001) discovered that, when chatting online, teens were interacting with strangers most of the time. Many were also ignorant of the dangers of revealing their identities to strangers online. Hence, with the aid of personally owned and individually used digital media tools and services, Asian youths today have considerable autonomy in broadening and managing their social lives, free from parental oversight. On several occasions, an inability to draw the line between online and offline existence has been an event of inconvenience to youth and their families. Several popular shows are aired in India that take due consideration of issues such as cyberbullying, cyber molestation, and harassment, such as *Webbed* (MTV), among others. Some studies have been done in various Asian countries that have concluded that Asian parents lack the ability to effectively mediate their children's digital media use. A study by Komolsevin (2002) of Thai children's use of the internet concluded that half of the parents interviewed did not supervise their children's internet usage, while one-quarter of them did not even know what their children used the computer for. Another study by Guntarto (2001) revealed that in some parts of Indonesia parental control is almost impossible as youth media consumption did not occur in the presence of family, e.g., in rural areas where children access the internet via community kiosks. In a study in rural Malaysia, Razzali (2002) also found that parents were ignorant of the internet and thus failed to prohibit their children from visiting cybercafes where they might be using the internet inappropriately. Rananand (2002) concluded that most Thai parents were computer-illiterate and felt embarrassed about discussing computer-related issues with their children. Similarly, T.M.P. Nguyen and T.Q.C. Nguyen (2002) determined that the majority of the Vietnamese children they interviewed had learned about the internet from their friends; those who had been briefed by their parents were in the minority. These children exploited their parents' ignorance of the internet and used stolen accounts to access the internet, thereby escaping parental knowledge of their online activities. Thus, it is obvious that the disparity between parental and child knowledge of digital tools and services impacts negatively on the parents' traditional roles as gatekeepers, guides, and teachers.

Instances of cyberbullying have proliferated because of social media phenomena. Youth have been frequent users of social networks and micro-blogging sites, but often they fail to understand and analyze the impact of their activities on these platforms. boyd (2014) has captured the views, emotions, and experiences of the teens in an interesting and intriguing fashion:

> Teens are passionate about finding their place in society. What is different as a result of social media is that teens' perennial desire for social connection and autonomy is now being expressed in *networked publics*. Networked publics are publics that are restructured by networked technologies. As such, they are simultaneously (1) the space constructed through networked technologies and (2) the imagined community that emerges as a result of the intersection of people, technology, and practice . . . Just because teens can and do manipulate

social media to attract attention and increase visibility does not mean that they are equally experienced at doing so or that they automatically have the skills to navigate what unfolds. It simply means that teens are generally more comfortable with—and tend to be less skeptical of—social media than adults. They don't try to analyze how things are different because of technology; they simply try to relate to a public world in which technology is a given.

(pp. 8, 13)

Therefore, with increasing use of digital media by the young, parental mediation in some form becomes imperative. It is evident from the aforementioned research that many youth require parental intervention and/or mediation in their digital media use. The form and process of mediation may differ depending upon socio-cultural and demographic variation, but undoubtedly, it is needed at this time. This is especially the case because young children are vulnerable to content across this largely "ungoverned" digital space, and they often fail to understand how this content may impact them psychologically, socially, and culturally.

Summary and Suggestions

In recent times, concerns arising out of digital media use by the young have increased. These concerns encompass use of the internet particularly and the risks posed to youth by its use. The safety of young children gives rise to considerable public anxiety, even moral panic, over childhood freedom and innocence, all compounded by uncertainty and fear of the power of new and complex technologies. Unlike in the West, the governments and civil society in India have not shown much concern about the social ramifications of digital media uses by the young. In fact, it has never been a priority on the agenda for our governments, as far as formulating some policy or legislation pertaining to this issue is concerned.

For broadcast and print sectors, much concern has been expressed, and multiple regulatory bills have been introduced to keep pace with changing communication technologies and media expansion. But no such approach has been observed in terms of the expansion of the internet and the use of digital media tools and services. The IT Act enacted by the Indian government covers the broad areas and deals with anyone misusing ICT-enabled devices and the internet to malign someone's image, create tensions between communities, practice hate speech, or jeopardize national security and welfare. However, acts and legislations for securing our young population in terms of their access and usage of digital tools and services are not in place, and we desperately need it in some form or other. Ignoring such concerns can place our generation next at risk in both predictable and unpredictable ways.

Therefore, it is time for the government and we as citizens to start working on evolving methods to protect our young children from digital malaise, while also facilitating its optimum utilization, as Christian Sandvig (2006) has advanced in his ideas on internet architecture: "The unsettled character of today's advanced communications systems is not our burden; it is our chance to act" (p. 115). Importantly, we must recognize the fast-changing, malleable character of the media form; it is so malleable that it will be difficult to figure out through which route it enters our children's sphere. The changing technological media landscape makes this challenging, but we cannot afford to ignore it. One challenge lies in the fact that the internet is largely ungoverned. Schmidt and Cohen (2013) observed that the

internet is the largest experiment involving anarchy in history. Hundreds of millions of people are, each minute, creating and consuming an untold amount of digital content in an online world that is not truly bound by terrestrial laws. This new capacity for free expression and free movement of information has generated the rich virtual landscape we know today.

The authors proceeded to describe the internet as the "world's largest ungoverned space" (p. 3). The power of this space has been best captured by Solis (2007). Solis argued that

> there has been a fundamental shift in our culture and it has created a new landscape of influencers and an entirely new ecosystem for supporting the socialization of information—thus facilitating new conversations that can start locally, but have a global impact.
>
> *(para. 3)*

"Digital India," a campaign initiated by the present government of India, aims to connect every citizen through broadband services and more so through the smartphone, which is a gadget used in privacy and isolation. Though it's a highly commendable initiative, it also makes parental monitoring and intervention in digital media use by the young more challenging. This aspect of the newly emerging scenario must also be taken into consideration while empowering citizens with easy access to digital technology and services as envisaged in this project.

The parental mediation model recommends a few strategies to be practiced for effective monitoring of our children when they use digital tools and services. Discussion and intellectual enlightenment should be the purpose of the guardians' monitoring and mediation. Every mediation practice has certain advantages and limitations as well; there is one specific mediation strategy that can ensure marvelous results. We must look at different strategies and amalgamate them in an effective manner. For example, placement of digital media gadgets at someplace common in the house will help to reduce undesirable use. If we apply time-specific restriction as well, it further limits misuse such as music and movie downloads, visiting inappropriate sites and content, posting inappropriate content and bullying, etc. Participating in the usage of digital tools by the young and supervising their usage can prove beneficial in helping children grow familiar with computer-mediated communication, drawing optimum benefits and ensuring their safety from cyberbullying. Finally, as parents, one ultimate objective should be to develop a sense of rationality among our children, not fear. Therefore, parents must discuss digital media use with their children, particularly the internet and the benefits or harm it may entail. Last but hardly least, for protecting young children against online harassment, parents must enhance their own knowledge of digital tools and services, since several studies have found that a lack of digital literacy in parents has been a major impediment in parental interventions in digital media use by young people.

Acknowledgement: Some portions of this chapter were derived from the report of a major research project of this author sponsored by Indian Council of Social Science Research (ICSSR), N.Delhi, India.

VOICES FOR VISIBILITY
Disciplining the Immigrant Body Through Collective Bullying

Wilfredo Alvarez

"Stop talking that shit!!!"
A high school peer's response when he overheard me speaking Spanish to another peer.

"What the hell is wrong with this guy's accent? (laughter)"
A person's response when he heard something that I said in a group conversation.

"You have done well enough to be here; that is very good for a Hispanic."
A professor's response when discussing my performance as an instructor.

Some synonyms for the word "bullying" include "mistreatment," "intimidation," "harassment," "oppression," and "victimization," to name a few. In my experiences as an immigrant, I have felt "bullied" by host society members since the time I arrived in the United States as an adolescent. I believe my status as an immigrant is a central catalyst for my unsettling interpersonal encounters with host society members. My experiences with what I call "collective bullying" began the moment that I became institutionalized upon my arrival to the United States. In my case, it was high school in inner city New York.

Soon after my arrival, I realized that my colored immigrant body and foreign accent had a particular significance to many people in this country. This significance was displayed in the verbal violence that many felt the need and freedom to perpetrate against it. A type of violence that I continue to experience to this day, over 20 years after a high school peer told me to "stop talking that shit!!!" in response to me speaking my native language in public (i.e., Spanish). This particular instance, however, was different from the ensuing subtle, but no less hurtful, type of verbal microaggressions (Nadal, 2011; Rivera, Forquer, & Rangel, 2010) that I experienced thereafter and that I argue can function as mechanism to discipline immigrant bodies in everyday interactions (Foucault, 1990).

In this chapter, I discuss how host society members (i.e., people born and raised in the United States regardless of ethnic background, but particularly members of the dominant group—in this case, White European Americans) enact power, intimidation, and aggression communicatively in their mundane interactions with immigrants. I highlight my personal experiences with what I call "collective bullying" to underscore some of the ways that host society members engaged in bullying behaviors against me. Overall, I illuminate how, in an ethnically diverse society such as the United States, immigrant bodies can become the target of collective bullying. I conclude by underscoring some of the main consequences and significance of bullying for individuals and communities.

Bullying as a Collective Endeavor

Bullying behaviors, for the purposes of this chapter, are communicatively enacted, occur in public, and display the hallmarks of power, intimidation, and aggression (Lutgen-Sandvik, 2006). The harmful effects of bullying have been well documented (Bowes, Wolke, Joinson, Tanya Lareya, & Lewis, 2014; Takizawa, Maughan, & Arseneault, 2014; Thornberg, 2015). Bullying also occurs in diverse social contexts and affects people in different social roles (Monks & Coyne, 2011). Definitions of bullying almost always encompass some type of aggressive behavior from a "bully" towards a "target" over a prolonged period of time, which sometimes results in long-lasting harmful effects such as anxiety, depression, and even suicidal ideation (Berry & Adams, 2016). Bullying also includes a power differential and one party's intention to abuse the power imbalance (Lutgen-Sandvik & Tracy, 2012).

Collective bullying occurs when aggressive and intimidating behaviors stem from groups of people and not individuals (Thornberg, 2015). For instance, in the workplace, a person could be bullied by various colleagues, including their bosses, over prolonged periods of time (Lutgen-Sandvik & Tracy, 2012). The bullying experiences that I describe below do not show bullying behaviors happening from one particular individual over a time period but, instead, occurring as a collective endeavor from the group to which I refer as "host society members." This type of bullying, however, displays similar dynamics as individual bullying—perceived power differentials, microaggressive behaviors, and public intimidation from a "dominant" toward a "nondominant" group member (Nadal, Griffin, Wong, Hamit, & Rasmus, 2014).

Immigrant-Host Encounters: Collective Bullying as Disciplinary

Foucault (1990) described "discipline" as mechanisms of power that regulate social actors' thoughts and behaviors through subtle means. This type of disciplinary power keeps people subjugated within a system of power relations (Foucault, 1977). In the context of my immigrant experience in the United States, several events illustrate what I refer to as the "collective bullying" perpetrated against me ("target") by host society members ("perpetrators"). In the following narratives, I describe how bullying is communicatively and subtly enacted and contextually situated across various stages of my life as an immigrant. Throughout these narratives, I illuminate the nuances and seriousness of bullying as a social problem, and subsequently, I discuss implications of this social phenomenon for individuals and communities.

"Stop Talking that Shit!!!"

I often say that coming to the United States through a place like New York City was both a blessing and a curse. A blessing because there was much cultural diversity and I felt that I could go incognito for most of the day; a curse because I had to negotiate the vast cultural differences on a daily basis. Suffice it to say, navigating everyday interactions comprised a great communication challenge. That situation required me to be mindful of social and cultural cues to which I was not privy. In addition, I was primarily communicating in my native language. This state of affairs came with unforeseen consequences.

High school in the Bronx, New York, served as a fitting preface of things to come for life as an immigrant. Though I could pass (Spradlin, 1998) given the large number of Latin American immigrants in the area, I could only do so insofar as my linguistic abilities allowed me. When some people perceived that English was not my native language, their responses were sometimes belligerent (see related work by Nadal et al., 2014). My experience with a peer who one day overheard me speaking Spanish to another peer is emblematic of my experiences during this phase of my life as a newly arrived immigrant.

On this particular day, I was having a conversation with a peer about a school assignment, in Spanish. Suddenly, I hear someone say in a very loud tone, stop talking that shit!!! Not only was his tone of voice screechingly loud, but he also approached me and screamed those words right in my ear. He also postured his body as if physical contact would follow the aggressive verbal tone. I froze, momentarily. It took me several seconds to process what had just happened. The peer with whom I was talking seemed stunned as well. So what is significant about this interaction? First, the aggressive and threatening tone and body posture were shocking and intimidating. Also, the psychological effects of this exchange lasted for a very long time (Takizawa et al., 2014).

As a newly arrived immigrant, during that time, I was still experiencing the vulnerable state of cultural transition and adaptation or culture shock (Kim, 2005). I felt that every one of my actions was under constant scrutiny, and I still feel that way today. I continue to live with the feeling that everything I do is under someone's careful watch, waiting to call me out whenever something I do or say stands outside of the cultural norm. Whenever someone calls me out in public, I feel doubly distressed. Getting called out in public because of my language use is painful and embarrassing for me.

Similar experiences have happened many times since then. Those experiences have stirred feelings of anxiety, aggression, self-hate, low self-esteem, and deep insecurities, among others. Related to my insecurities, in the moments when people highlighted my linguistic deficiencies or my cultural differences, being a foreigner became richly magnified. So much so that in a visit to my psychotherapist, she suggested that I might be suffering from PTSD stemming from a collection of past experiences with verbal and nonverbal microaggressions over a particular time period in my life. I share some of those episodes in the following narratives.

"What Is Wrong With This Guy's Accent?"

Nonverbal messages often communicate more powerfully than verbal messages. Nonverbal channels have mediated many of my interactions with host society members. These channels include paralinguistic behaviors such as voice tone, volume, and pitch, eye behavior, and facial expressions, as well as body language such as postures, gestures, touch, etc. The following episode further highlights my experiences with what I characterize as collective bullying. This time, someone highlighted my linguistic differences by making fun of my foreign accent. This type of behavior is also emblematic of experiences that I have had with many host society members since my arrival in the United States.

I was at a party, having a conversation with a group of people when a man paused to ask the group, "What is wrong with this guy's accent?" and proceeded to laugh out loud. Both his facial expression and tone of voice when he asked the question communicated disgust. His frowning sent a message of rejection. I considered what this person might have meant based on the manner in which he asked the question. Was there a subtext here of any kind? As thoughts raced through my head, I pondered how to respond in a competent manner considering the context. I reminded him of my country of origin (Dominican Republic) and native language (Spanish). He seemed disinterested in any information that I shared with him. After the embarrassment and anger I felt in that moment, I realized that I needed to stay away from that person the rest of the evening. I was afraid my anger would have gotten the best of me following that hurtful exchange.

Like a slow water drip, I noticed those subtle instances of microaggression kept happening in routine interactions with host society members. That man at the party placed a strong emphasis on the word "accent," as if wanting to emphasize my distinctiveness in that context. In each of my experiences with verbal aggression, the verbal and nonverbal messages operated in concert to express unease with my linguistic performance, particularly how I pronounced words in English. Those individuals' reactions are symbolic of various issues operating at the signification level.

My accent, a paralinguistic device, is a seed of meaning through which individuals make sense of and assign significance to my complex being. The party episode shows that how I talk has implications for how people respond to me. More specifically, my accent functions as a trigger for host society members to be verbally aggressive, as dialect is one of the most common ways in which in-group and out-groupness is constituted and negotiated in U.S. society (Lippi-Green, 2003). Over time, my interactions with host society members, and primarily Whites, created a context of discursive closure (Deetz, 1992). My ability to express myself in complicated ways was constantly restricted by my perception of the insular idea people had of me. This context of discursive closure was mediated in part by my phonetic language use, which seemed to give some people a license to engage in bullying behaviors, primarily verbal aggression.

Because of the consistency and vitality with which I endured verbal and nonverbal attacks, I felt that the onus was on me to adapt to my surroundings; I experienced "coping fatigue" (Cose, 1993). Host society members' (non)verbally aggressive behaviors disciplined and regulated my social performances in powerful ways (Foucault, 1990). I wanted to be my genuine self but could not due to having a constant fear of repudiation. In social occasions, I noticed that I engaged in "passing" behaviors to reinforce others' expectations of me at the expense of my individual integrity (Spradlin, 1998).

In the aforementioned narratives, host society members' comments represent distancing at the group level, enactments of ethnolinguistic vitality (Giles & Sassoon, 1983). Their remarks embody the presumed and automatically expected normativity, purity, and ideal within communication systems imbued with the ideology of White supremacy. In these particular instances, bullying is projected as xenophobic discourse that signifies that speaking in particular "standard" forms is a norm that is always "natural" and "neutral" in relation to others (B. J. Allen, 2011). Subtle mundane communicative behaviors, in tandem with macro-level systems of signification, perpetuate a disciplinary structure that determines where, when, and how immigrant bodies become unintelligible (Butler, 1994), uncivilized (Cisneros, 2008), and a threat (Chavez, 2008) to the host society establishment. My lived experiences illuminate some of the ways that those disciplinary processes are constituted through routine communication with host society members.

"That Is Very Good for a Hispanic."

In their taxonomy of racial microaggressions, Sue and colleagues (2007) presented *Ascription of Intelligence* as one of the main themes. This "ascription" occurs when dominant group members believe people of color to be less intelligent. The following narrative is symbolic of experiences that I have had with host society members where they display assumptions of inferiority and lesser intelligence. One day, I was sitting in an auditorium at a teaching workshop. A veteran and venerated professor, a master teacher and scholar, was facilitating the workshop, a dynamic and engaging presentation. I approached the professor after the presentation to introduce myself and to ask some questions about pedagogy. I also wanted to get some advice as I was experiencing much confusion and uncertainty about my new role as a college instructor—the so-called impostor syndrome. A few minutes into our conversation, the professor says to me, "You will be fine; you have done well enough to be here. That is very good for a Hispanic."

I stood there, bewildered and unresponsive, wondering what to say and in what manner. Part of me felt that there was nothing that I could say or do to remedy the situation—for some strange reason, I felt this state of inertia in responding to host society members' insulting statements throughout my time in this country. Maybe part of me just felt the impotence that many immigrants feel when dealing with verbal aggression. How does a person fight a systematic barrage of xenophobic statements? This feeling can be all consuming after dealing with injuring experiences over a prolonged period of time. I experienced a sense of overwhelmedness that rendered me emotionally incapacitated. Cose (1993) referred to this state as "coping fatigue" in *The Rage of a Privileged Class*. In response to the professor's comment, I remember trying to end the conversation so that I could leave and go wallow in my grief. What I found most disturbing about the professor's remarks, and what has been consistent in encounters with many host society members, was that this person seemed utterly unaware of the problematic nature of his remarks.

This professor's troubling words represent another example of the type of bullying behavior that I have experienced throughout my years living in the United States. Interestingly, however, I have also noticed that many people's verbally aggressive behaviors have come across as unabashedly unremorseful. As I consider my experiences over the years, the consistency and variety of verbally aggressive behaviors suggest that the problem lies beyond ignorance; this treatment seems to be part of a culture. In sum, my experiences with many host society members show that their verbal and nonverbal behaviors have been intentional in their aims to hurt me due to my immigrant status, ethnicity, and language use. The professor's subtle yet perturbing assumptions and communicative choice about my ethnicity and ability to perform academically offer an instance of how "collective bullying" has been a constitutive feature of my interactions with host society members over the years.

Coping With the Consequences of Collective Bullying

The effects of bullying can last for a long period of time after the person has endured the torment (Takizawa et al., 2014). For instance, visits to the psychologist suggest that I have experienced the following feelings due to my negative experiences with host society members over prolonged periods of time: anxiety, anger, low self-esteem, insecurity, self-doubt, and hate towards others, just to name a few. These behaviors are not atypical of people who have experienced bullying (Samnani & Singh, 2012). This list of negative emotions is also not surprising considering that many immigrants already find themselves in vulnerable places due to their perception of being "the other." In this concluding section, I discuss the disciplinary power of subtle communicative acts, social roles, psychological effects, and changing cultures of bullying as central themes to underscore the significance and consequences of systemic and systematic bullying.

My experiences with bullying display some similarities; those behaviors can be subtle, and they can come from people in positions of authority, peers, and people in subordinate institutional roles. My experiences also show that bullying behaviors can be mediated by beliefs and assumptions people have about others, which highlights the symbolic nature of verbally aggressive behaviors. For example, my experiences illustrate that perceived cultural hierarchies exist based on language use and ethnicity and the ways those hierarchies are normalized through disciplinary communicative behaviors. In this sense, symbolic meaning and value negotiation take the place of physical power and coercion that we often see in schoolyards' bully-target dynamics (Thornberg, 2015). Regardless of deployment type, bullying behaviors can have detrimental psychological effects on bullies' targets.

Negative affect and low self-esteem are some of the main effects of bullying behaviors (Coyne, Chong, Seigne, & Randall, 2003; Samnani & Singh, 2012). According to Samnani and Singh (2012), "Negative affect can be described as a tendency to experience emotions that include anxiety, fear, sadness, and anger" (p. 583). Furthermore, some correlation exists between low self-esteem and feelings of vulnerability and bullying behaviors (Matthiesen & Einarsen, 2001). Research also shows that Hispanics/Latinos/as are the targets of bullying more repeatedly than Whites (Fox & Stallworth, 2005). My experiences with microaggressive bullying behaviors and their psychological consequences reinforce these findings. Taken together, research findings support how my experiences with verbally aggressive behaviors have caused much emotional turmoil, including feelings of mental distress, anxiety, anger, depression, and low self-confidence. What researchers have also learned about the effects of bullying is that they not only affect bullies and their targets, but also people in their interpersonal networks (i.e., family, friends, and co-workers) (Berry & Adams, 2016; Lutgen-Sandvik & Tracy, 2012).

Bullying research has determined that the effects of bullying can influence targets' interpersonal relationships (Vega & Comer, 2005). In my case, bullying deeply affected my romantic relationship as well as friendships and work relationships. I found myself incessantly irritable about living in this country and asking myself the question "Why did they [my parents] bring me here?" Still today, I have recurring thoughts about what life could be like had I not left my native country. The mental distress and emotional fatigue that I have experienced due to repeated verbally microaggressive behaviors took a toll on my spouse, which reached its apex when she asked me one day to "please go see the therapist; I am just tired of this situation." I could sense a similar degree of fatigue and overwhelmedness from my close friends. One of them politely advised me to go back to my native country at least once a year because he thought "it would be beneficial to my psyche." Overall, my repeated harmful interactions with host society members have taken an emotional toll on me over the years. Inevitably, those behaviors had ripple effects that not only affected me psychologically, but also people in my interpersonal networks.

Bullying is one of the most pervasive and insidious social problems of our time (Berry & Adams, 2016; Lutgen-Sandvik & Tracy, 2012; Samnani & Singh, 2012). Bullying behaviors comprise communicative deployments that hurt individuals and groups of people. My experiences as an immigrant interacting with host society members over the years show that some bullying behaviors can be subtle and stem from diverse groups of people, which makes it a complex issue to intercept and address before it escalates into violence. For this reason, it is important to continue advancing lines of research that explore antecedents, processes, outcomes, and contexts of bullying. Second, it is important to challenge detrimental discourses about (Latino/a) immigrants in popular culture texts (Chavez, 2008; Cisneros, 2008). Those messages are powerful mechanisms that shape how people conceptualize and perceive immigrants and specifically Latino/a immigrants. Research on stigmatized groups and microaggression is also a significant line of research to consider. Although much of this research has focused on racial minorities (Blacks, Latinos/as, and Asians), less research focuses on microaggressions against recent immigrants from different parts of the world (Nadal, 2011).

In closing, bullying can be a collective practice when it is created and maintained through a communication system that sanctions its execution in routine interactions. Given this dynamic, cultures that challenge bullying behaviors can be created. People must be mindful of how we are complicit in contributing to this system. As a system of meanings that produces disciplinary institutions and structures of power (Foucault, 1990), each person is responsible for understanding such systems and engaging in mindful strategic actions that disrupt or at the very least undermine it. In sum, bullying constitutes a collective endeavor that requires individuals, particularly those in positions of power, to consider the extent to which they are complicit in contributing to systems of disciplinary power through our communication with those who are less powerful.

Becoming more aware and assuming responsibility for the violence we perpetrate on others either consciously or subconsciously will ensure that instead of perpetuating cultures of violence, we can create communities of appreciation and cultures of compassion, empathy, and respect for both self and others. People can reach this goal by becoming more aware of the processes and products of each comment, judgment, and action as we negotiate power in the episodic spheres, moments, and encounters that make up everyday life.

★★Workplace Bullying★★

7

DISCIPLINING THE OFFICE

The Past, Present, and Future of Communication Research on Bullying

Stacy Tye-Williams

According to Heinz Leymann (1996), one of the early scholars of workplace bullying, "in the societies of the highly industrialized western world, the workplace is the only remaining battlefield where you can 'kill' each other without running the risk of being taken to court" (pp. 172–173). Given its harmful nature, not surprisingly, over the course of several decades, researchers in a variety of disciplines have drawn attention to the human and organizational costs of bullying and other forms of aggressive communication in the workplace (Lutgen-Sandvik, Tracy, & Alberts, 2007). Much of this research draws on psychological perspectives, although education and management scholars have also been key producers of scholarship on this topic. All of these perspectives have been useful in advancing awareness and knowledge. However, it is important to highlight the contributions that have been made specifically by Communication researchers, particularly given that workplace bullying is by its very nature a communication phenomenon. Put another way, bullying behaviors are inherently communicative (e.g., gossip, threats, insults, silent treatment, physical intimidation), and communication also comprises the predominant tool with which bullying can be resisted and corrected.

The centrality of communication guided the development of this chapter. As such, I primarily selected research conducted by Communication scholars. Additionally, in keeping with the focus of this *Handbook*, I selected research specifically examining workplace bullying. I recognize that a myriad of terms are related (e.g., ostracism, incivility) but, given the limited space of the chapter and continued construct profusion and confusion (Keashly & Jagatic, 2011), this chapter concentrates on scholarship that explores communication and workplace bullying. I centered the discussion on communicative strategies for addressing it, hence the title "Disciplining the Office." This chapter begins with a discussion of the historical roots of workplace bullying research, next explores individual, interpersonal, organizational, and macrosocietal strategies for addressing it, and concludes with imagining the possibilities for future research.

A Brief History of Workplace Bullying Research

Andrea Adams, a BBC journalist and author, is credited with first garnering widespread attention to workplace bullying in the UK and uncovering the devastating nature of workplace bullying (Namie & Namie, 2009). Adams coined the term *workplace bullying* in 1988. Before the term's conceptualization, most targets considered any unfair treatment as, for instance, "office politics" or "just the way things are" in corporate life (Lee, 2000). Naming the phenomenon brought awareness to what was previously a silent epidemic and became a major turning point in generating discussion and research focused on workplace bullying.

In terms of academic work, Heinz Leymann (1990), a psychologist, was instrumental in situating workplace bullying as a topic of research. His initial research explored nurses who attempted suicide as the result of difficult workplace experiences. This study led him to realize the devastating nature of bullying, or what he called mobbing, in the workplace. Consequently and subsequently, throughout his career, Leymann devoted his attention to the psychological effects of bullying on employee well-being. Since that time, the contributions from the field of psychology have been vast (e.g., Baillien, Escartin, Gross, & Zapf, 2017; Crawford, 1997; Einarsen et al., 2011b; Leymann, 1996). Smith (1997) argued that useful lessons can be learned about adult bullying by analyzing school bullying. As a response, early research was often linked to and/or drew upon research on schoolyard bullying (Pörhölä, Karhunen, & Rainivaara, 2006; Smith, Singer, Hoel, & Cooper, 2003). Business and management scholars have also been instrumental in shaping our understanding and awareness (D'Cruz & Noronha, 2010; Fox & Spector, & Miles, 2001). Despite early criticism that workplace bullying was little more than a trendy research line, it has found prominence among academic and working professionals alike (Einarsen et al., 2003). Much of the early research was conducted in Scandinavian countries (Einarsen, 2000) and the United Kingdom (Lee, 2000). However, a few researchers in the United States contributed to these early conversations as well. Communication scholars entered into the conversation in the late 1990s and early 2000s (Keashly, 1997; Keashly, 2001; Lutgen-Sandvik, 2003). Much of the early research focused on defining it (Keashly, 1998), determining its prevalence (Lutgen-Sandvik et al., 2007), examining risk factors (Harvey & Keashly, 2003), and mapping out the contours of the involvement of various actors in bullying situations (Namie, Namie, & Lutgen-Sandvik, 2010). Communication scholars have also been instrumental in developing remedial strategies rooted in the experiences of mistreated workers.

Levels of Construction

Some targets I have worked with over the years have likened the experience of being bullied as similar to enduring a natural disaster such as a tornado or hurricane. In one telling example, a participant referred to the bully as "the vortex of evil" (Tye-Williams, 2005). The severity of natural disasters is measured by levels of destruction (e.g., F5 tornado is the most severe). Focusing on the destructive process of workplace bullying has led to a deeper understanding of what it feels like and how costly it is. This chapter instead focuses on levels of construction or how to survive and rebuild. In the following section, I discuss constructive strategies that Communication scholars have generated at the individual, interpersonal, organizational, and macrosocietal levels of analysis.

Individual Level

Gaining an awareness of the real lived experiences of those who experience it has been a major contribution of the field (Lutgen-Sandvik, 2007; Tracy, Lutgen-Sandvik, & Alberts, 2006; Tye-Williams & Krone, 2015). For example, in a metaphor analysis, participants likened the experience of bullying to a battle, water torture, nightmare, and noxious substance (Tracy et al., 2006). Tracy et al. found that workers framed bullies as narcissistic dictators, two-faced actors, and devil figures, while targets described themselves as vulnerable children, slaves, prisoners, animals, and heartbroken lovers. One participant in this study likened their experience to being a vulnerable child having an "abusive father and all the children—when they're dressed up on Sunday afternoon and guests come visiting to the house—everything is wonderful and perfect, and we have this deep dark secret about the abusive father that nobody will tell about" (p. 169). A deeper awareness of the harmfulness of bullying has led to a development of communication-based remedial strategies rooted in experience.

Target Resistance Strategies

A focus on how individuals experience (Tracy et al., 2006) and make sense (Lutgen-Sandvik & McDermott, 2011) of workplace mistreatment provides a foundation for understanding individual level responses. Workers believe that they are bullied because the perpetrator is evil, mentally ill, and power-hungry, and they cite the lack of intervention from upper management as part of the problem (Lutgen-Sandvik & McDermott, 2011). These perspectives explain, in part, why mistreatment often goes unreported. Additionally, targeted workers perceive themselves as having little power to effectively address it (Tracy et al., 2006). Bullying strips individual voice and agency to address confusing and unexpected workplace experiences. To address the silencing nature of workplace bullying, research extending from these findings explored the role of agency and an individual's ability to reclaim a sense of voice in the face of workplace mistreatment (Tracy et al., 2006; Tye-Williams & Krone, 2015).

Several strategies can be applied at the individual level, such as reporting abuse to organizational authorities or unions, filing formal complaints, and standing up to the bully. Unfortunately, individual efforts to correct it are often unsuccessful and can lead to more harm (Keashly, 2001; Lutgen-Sandvik et al., 2009). For example, when organizational authorities are made aware of abuse, they often do nothing (Lutgen-Sandvik & McDermott, 2011). This response results in further silencing. However, communication strategies can increase the likelihood that stories will be taken seriously. Research examining how targets communicate about their experience found that they tell chaos, quest, and report narratives about their experiences (Tye-Williams & Krone, 2015). According to Tye-Williams and Krone, organizational authorities (as well as friends and family members) more likely discounted chaos narratives, defined as those without a clear beginning, middle, and end. In light of this finding, scholars advise individuals to provide clear and convincing stories with little emotion (e.g., I excused myself to go outside and cry) (Tracy, Alberts, & Rivera, 2007; Tye-Williams & Ruble, 2017). Tye-Williams and Krone defined clear and convincing stories as ones that have a clear beginning, middle, and end and include specific details about the mistreatment. It is important to recognize that, even in instances where individuals tell clear and convincing stories, the bullying may persist. A study on productive and unproductive justice episodes found that "attaining justice may be a process or series of actions, rather than a one-shot attempt" (Cowan, 2009, p. 298). Based on her research, Cowan advised targets to utilize multiple responses in order to realize more productive episodes in their fight for justice.

Interpersonal Level

A great deal of popular press work on workplace bullying places the responsibility on the target to be able to navigate it (Horn, 2002). A focus only on what mistreated workers can do to resist individualizes the experience and limits the development of more potent solutions. Communication scholars have long recognized the impact of power on any one individual actor's ability to prompt or enact change in organizations. Therefore, research examines the role of multiple actors in attending to bullying. The Communication literature has focused on support as a mechanism with which to help individuals achieve self-preservation and resist mistreatment. Interpersonal level dynamics then become a crucial feature in an individual's ability to make sense of and address bullying. Key actors involved at the interpersonal level include family members, friends, and co-workers.

Family Members and Friends

Although we know little about the role of family members and friends in helping individuals cope, initial research has shown that they can be quite valuable in helping individuals navigate their difficult experiences (Lutgen-Sandvik, 2018). One caveat to this finding pertains to advice. Well-meaning friends and family members often want to provide advice and commonly advise others to report it to organizational authorities, stand up to the bully, and to quit. However, targets reported that these strategies are largely unhelpful. Research supports this perception. For example, according to Lutgen-Sandvik (2006), confronting the bully often aggravates the situation rather than improving it. Individuals reported that these common pieces of advice either would not have worked in their situation or, if they did follow the advice, it made their situation worse. Interestingly, when asked what advice they would give to others, they recommend that same advice they found problematic. A key takeaway for friends and family members, as well as co-workers, is to simply listen and help mistreated friends and family members to develop strategies that they feel would be more useful (Tye-Williams & Krone, 2017).

Co-Workers

Notably, co-workers can be complicit or even the main perpetrators in bullying situations (Namie & Lutgen-Sandvik, 2010). However, they can also play a crucial role in contesting it. For example, scholars commonly recommend that individuals find a trusted person to talk to about their experience (Tye-Williams & Krone, 2015, 2017). Co-worker support makes a difference in the ability for individuals enduring bullying to not only makes sense of their experience but also to communicate more effectively to organizational authorities about their mistreatment (Tye-Williams & Krone, 2015). The insider knowledge co-workers have about the organization and players involved help them provide potentially more useful strategies for their mistreated co-workers to utilize. Listening and letting individuals know they are not imagining what is happening to them is critical in helping people withstand bullying, although, the most effective resistance strategies comprise collective resistance whereby co-workers band together to talk to organizational authorities (Lutgen-Sandvik, 2006). Collective voices "give credence to affected workers' claims, bolster their courage to speak out, and encourage them to plan pooled resistance strategies" (Lutgen-Sandvik, 2006, p. 425). It can be difficult to generate this level of support from co-workers, as even though they may sympathize with a mistreated colleague, they are also at the same time fearful of the consequences speaking out against the abuse could bring. Co-workers fearful of becoming vocal advocates can still be tremendously helpful by providing behind the scenes support (e.g., sending flowers with an unsigned card), which has been shown to help mistreated workers make sense of their experience and communicate more effectively about it to others (Tye-Williams & Krone, 2015). An understanding of the roles family members, friends, and co-workers play in the generation of resistance strategies is useful in gaining an awareness of how individuals can create spaces where they can talk about and make sense of their painful experiences. Just as focus on the individual level of analysis was an incomplete view of how communication could be used to address bullying, stopping at the interpersonal level is also an incomplete view of the complexity of stopping it. I next turn to a discussion of the role of the organization in ameliorating bullying.

Organizational Level

The organizational level of analysis is focused on the formal and informal communication structures that perpetuate an environment where mistreatment is not only allowed but may even be rewarded. The most common outcome of bullying is that mistreated workers leave the organization (Lutgen-Sandvik et al., 2009), but simply leaving does not end the abuse. Although abused workers frequently leave the organization, perpetrators remain and are able to enact their abusive behavior on new employees, thus perpetuating a cycle of abuse in organizations (Lutgen-Sandvik, 2003). We should also consider another important organizational feature—the policies and procedures in place to handle situations where employees are mistreated. We know that cycles of abuse continue until the composition of workgroups is restructured or until the organization intervenes by implementing policies and working to transform corporate culture (Lutgen-Sandvik & McDermott, 2008). In the next section, I discuss communication-based strategies posited for human resource professionals and leaders.

Human Resource Professionals

HR professionals are "on the front lines" listening and responding to episodes of workplace bullying, positioning them as an important potential line of defense (Fox & Cowan, 2015). HR profession-als' attributions for why it happens impacts what action they take, if any. One study found that HR professionals attribute bullying to aggressive management styles, deficient communication, organiza-tional culture, a contemporary issue rooted in society, and personality clashes (Cowan, 2013). These attributions may negatively impact the likelihood that HR professionals would intervene. Similarly, HR professionals often report seeing bullying as a misinterpretation between parties and intervene only when they "get a feeling" that the situation was bad (Cowan, 2012). Waiting until the situation escalates makes it less likely for a workable solution to be reached. Communication-based training is one strategy to help HR professionals more effectively address mistreatment (Cowan, 2012). This training could involve storytelling scenarios where narratives that feature bullying are told to HR professionals who are given training on how to better respond when hearing target accounts with the hope of helping them better address it (Tye-Williams & Krone, 2015).

Gaining insight into how HR professionals understand and address mistreatment or fail to do so has been an important step toward opening up channels to ameliorate it. A related and important extension of research on HR professionals and workplace bullying pertains to policy. Unlike sexual harassment, no laws specifically address bullying (Yamada, 2011), making the development of clear and effective policies a crucial component of reform. One study of HR professionals versus worker perceptions of organizational policy determined that policy documents often communicated to workers that, "anti-bullying measures were not a priority, that bullying did not rise to the level of legal harassment, and that only some behaviors were explicitly prohibited" (Cowan, 2011, p. 321). HR professionals perceived that these policies communicated the expectation of professional behav-ior, that the organization cares about and addresses bullying, and that policies give workers an avenue to complain about it (Cowan, 2011). The disconnect between worker and HR professional percep-tions of policy elucidates the need to continue to investigate the development and implementation of effective anti-bullying policies. Ultimately, developing management supported policies that clearly convey the steps that should be taken to report and address maltreatment is crucial in better address-ing it (Cowan, 2011). I turn next to a discussion of managerial responses.

Managerial Responses

Research examining managers and leaders often situates them as part of the problem rather than considering how they can be part of the solution. Bullying can only thrive when it is supported implicitly and explicitly by management (Hoel & Cooper, 2001). Policies have to be supported and enforced by those in a position to enforce them. While the most typical managerial response, unfortunately, involves doing nothing (Lutgen-Sandvik, 2003), the reasons posited for such inaction give cause for hope. According to Lutgen-Sandvik (2011), managers fail to intervene for a variety of reasons; however, chief among them is that they lack the skill to do so and/or they are too appre-hensive about getting involved. One strategy to overcoming these obstacles comprises reframing managers as collaborating partners who simply lack the knowledge to intervene and, in turn, educat-ing them about bullying and appropriate interventions (Lutgen-Sandvik, 2011). Providing managers with communication-based conflict resolution training could improve their ability and willingness to more directly address it. Reframing the role of managers as part of the solution rather than the problem could be a fruitful way to develop even stronger strategies for addressing this complex individual, interpersonal, and organizational dilemma. In addition to exploring strategies for addressing bullying at each of these levels, we should also explore societal influences on our perceptions of targets and workplace mistreatment.

Macrosocietal Level

The macrosocietal level of analysis pertains to broader social and cultural issues. At this level, the analysis shifts from what is happening at the individual, interpersonal, and organizational levels to the social and cultural norms and attitudes that surround it. These norms, attitudes, and beliefs shape how we talk about societal issues. For example, when others ask me about my research and I share that I study bullying in the workplace, they tend to tilt their heads slightly to the side, smile awkwardly, and say, "I thought that only happened in elementary school." This simple and very common response illustrates the importance of examining the ways that we talk about abuse in the workplace. Responses like this one minimize the seriousness of workplace abuse and frames targets as children who cannot successfully function in organizational life. Broader discourses also normalize workplace mistreatment as simply a by-product of working in competitive environments (Lutgen-Sandvik & McDermott, 2008). Common phrases like "If you can't take the heat, get out of the kitchen" are proof positive of how entrenched we are into this way of thinking about organizational life. Lutgen-Sandvik and McDermott (2011) found that "the moral imperative that people should, 'fight the good fight' propels targets to battle injustice" (p. 18). However, they often use discourses of individualism, omnipotent leaders, and unbeatable evil to make sense of their situations, leading them to frequently conclude that they are powerless to alter their situation (Lutgen-Sandvik & McDermott, 2011).

Adding to this feeling of helplessness is the notion that we should blame the rigid and inflexible nature of organizations for producing environments where abusive behaviors are the norm. Importantly, abuse can only be normalized by people, and as such people have the power to transform abusive organizations. At the heart of this transformation lies communication. Organizations do not simply appear; they are created or constituted through communication (Cooren, Taylor, & Van Every, 2006). Communication can maintain long-standing organizational practices, but it can also alter them.

To extend this theorizing, bullying in the workplace is the product of previous and ongoing actions, and broader discourses of human value and work feed conversations that happen throughout the life of the organization (Lutgen-Sandvik & McDermott, 2008). If abusive workplace environments are created through communication, they can be changed by it as well. One possible way to do so is by re-storying bullying. Because such a reimagination would involve the generation of new research, I turn now to a discussion of future research.

Future Research Directions

For the past 20 years, Communication scholarship has increased our understanding of workplace bullying significantly. We now have a greater understanding of the enactment and experience of workplace bullying, the role of communication in supporting and hindering effective responses to workplace abuse, and the powerful influence of macrosocietal discourses in shaping how we communicate about and address it. Important breakthroughs are left to be made largely by privileging creativity over constraint. In the following section, I describe an imagination of possibilities.

Re-Storying Bullying

A powerful way to change bullying is to change the conversation or discourse surrounding it. Victim blaming is not a helpful strategy for altering toxic work environments. Normalizing these environments as "just the way things are in organizations" is highly problematic. Communication scholars have made important contributions to our understanding of target experiences through the collection and analysis of narratives (Tracy et al., 2006; Tye-Williams, 2015). We must imagine alternative ways to think about work through a process of re-storying the very way we talk about it. This process would require a great deal of creativity; however, the impact could be quite powerful. Innovative research methods could provide one way to aid in the production of alternative stories about work and workplace bullying.

Innovating Research

Innovative qualitative research methods that could advance our understanding of amelioration strategies include "bubble dialogue" techniques and participatory action theatre. Research on bullying in schools has used a bubble dialogue method to help students more creatively imagine how they could respond to various difficult scenarios (Bosacki, Marini, & Dane, 2006). Similar to the participant drawings generated by Tracy et al. (2006), "bubble dialogue" techniques involve asking participants to complete drawings about their experiences and answer questions such as: How do you think the bully feels? What is the bully thinking? How do you think the person being picked on feels? Why is he/she being picked on, and what could she/he do about it (Bosacki et al., 2006)? Asking multiple members of the organization to complete the same exercise asking about workplace bullying in general could help gain a multilevel perspective on the various actors involved along with organization specific strategies to address it. Additionally, asking participants to alter the plot and/or the ending could be useful in the generation of alternative responses.

Participatory theatre involves asking participants to act out a variety of responses to events. For example, in her study on healthcare workers, Quinlan (2009) asked participants to write bullying scenarios that they were later invited to act out as group. The study cites the power of participatory theatre to cultivate "imaginative capacities, enabling our potential to call forth something that has never been before and envision alternative norms and values" (p. 130). Although we have made great strides in developing amelioration strategies, the research is mixed on their ultimate effectiveness. Approaches that allow for the development of alternative strategies of addressing it could be key in the generation of more meaningful and helpful responses.

Attending to Nuances

Scholars who study bullying are often called upon to provide recommendations for how to solve it. Recommendations are difficult to provide because they depend on a variety of contextual factors. Responding with, "It depends," provides a less than satisfying but honest response. Communication research should continue to explore the nuances of workplace mistreatment as it applies to different age groups (Keashly, 2011; Lutgen-Sandvik, 2007) and racial and gender dynamics (Allen, 2009; see also Harris & Janovic, this volume; Razzante, Orbe, & Tracy, this volume). Research examining how it manifests in specific occupations has been limited. Future research should also explore specific occupations to develop a better understanding of possible nuances. Examples of specific occupations that have been explored in the field include faculty (Keashly, 2010), graduate students (Martin, Goodboy, & Johnson, 2015), and bus drivers (Goodboy, Martin, & Brown, 2016).

Cyberbullying

According to a recent report, a 31-year-old firefighter committed suicide due to being cyberbullied for years by her co-workers (Wright, 2016). Despite the harm inflicted, academic research on cyberbullying in the workplace is limited (Privitera & Campbell, 2009). Individuals may be cyberbullied by co-workers or leaders by sending aggressive emails or posting negative comments on social media, but it can also occur when people strategically neglect to send important emails or simply don't bother to respond. Cyberbullying does not simply occur between organizational members. With the rise of the service economy, a large segment of workers are frequently cyberbullied by angry and/or demanding customers (D'Cruz & Noronha, 2014). Communication scholars have the potential to make a profound impact by exploring how organizations and organizational members can respond to cyberbullying from co-workers and customers alike.

Exploring Relationship Dynamics

Family members and friends can offer important forms of support. Yet, we know little about how friends and family impact an individual's ability to cope with and develop solutions to address it. Conversely, an awareness of how workplace mistreatment impacts relationships outside of work is also largely unknown. It has been well-documented that that our personal and work spheres overlap and influence one another. A recognition of relational dynamics is important in generating a broader understanding of the harm bullying can cause along with the development of strategies to cope with and address it.

Blending Theory and Practice

The final call for future research pertains to the opportunity for communication scholars to use their expertise to influence positive change in organizations. For example, Tracy et al. (2007) created a white paper intended to help targets explain their mistreatment to key decision makers. Keashly (2010) provided answers to key questions about bullying directed at Ombudspersons. These efforts with their focus on translating research and theorizing for broader audiences is key to truly making a positive impact on organizations. Scholars should consider direct partnerships with workplace bullying practitioners. One such example that has had a strong influence on the field is the partnership between Pamela Lutgen-Sandvik and Gary and Ruth Namie at the Workplace Bullying Institute. This collaboration and others like it have and will continue to identify key questions and issues to keep moving the field forward. Such partnerships improve not only our understanding of workplace bullying but also what can be done about it.

Conclusion

This chapter explored the contributions that communication scholars have made to the awareness and understanding of bullying in the workplace. The last two decades have brought with them important advancements in the field. We now have a much deeper understanding of the nature of bullying. Communication scholars have also generated communication-based strategies to help targets, co-workers, family members and friends, human resources professionals, and leaders more effectively address it. Through the use of creative approaches, effective interventions to address bullying can be developed to positively transform toxic organizations.

8

THE THEORY OF BULLYING CONFLICT CULTURES

Developing a New Explanation for Workplace Bullying

Nathalie Desrayaud, Fran C. Dickson, and Lynne M. Webb[*]

As a community of scholars, Communication researchers are attempting to conceptualize bullying in communicative terms—an especially difficult task for bullying in higher education where we privilege academic freedom and the free exchange of ideas. The purpose of this chapter is to augment our current thinking by offering a new theory of workplace bullying, specifically the Theory of Bully Conflict Cultures (BCC) and to apply that theory to a particular type of workplace, higher education. In doing so, we offer the academy, and the accompanying research on bullying in higher education, as an exemplar of our new theory's ability to accurately describe and predict bullying. We anticipate that this new theoretical frame will expand the disciplinary thinking about bullying and how this insidious behavior might be effectively ameliorated to make academic workplaces more cooperative and less toxic.

In this chapter, we frame bullying as a type of conflict behavior, albeit a perverse, dysfunctional, and destructive form of conflict. We adopt Lewicki, Saunders, and Minton's (1997) classic definition of conflict as "the interaction of interdependent people who perceive incompatible goals and interference from each other in achieving those goals" (p. 15). Then, we review the negative effects of workplace bullying and offer evidence that those negative effects are especially apparent in the academy—the primary reason we selected higher educational organizations as the exemplar we employ throughout our chapter. Next, we review current conceptualizations of workplace bullying, offering our new theory as a means of connecting these divergent streams of scholarship. Finally, we present our new theory by proposing that organizational conflict cultures serve as facilitating agents of bullying. We argue that bullying can be examined more precisely by *not* focusing on the small behaviors that comprise bullying nor on the organizational culture as a whole. Instead, we propose focusing on one element within broad organizational culture, *conflict culture*, as a means for explaining, preventing, and addressing bullying. We posit that certain conflict cultures are far more likely to develop and encourage bullying practices than others. Thus, to change the conflict culture (the conflict norms in a given workplace) would be to actively encourage or discourage bullying.

Defining Workplace Bullying as Conflict

We begin by acknowledging the widespread view that bullying is overt, unwanted, negative attention that continues despite a clear request for cessation. We propose that such behavior can be classified as conflict behavior, albeit a dysfunctional, perverse, and destructive form of conflict. Certainly, we are not the first scholars to link bullying to conflict. Bullying typically develops in organizations where frequent interpersonal conflict exists (Baillien, Bollen, Euwema, & De Witte, 2014). Furthermore, one of the strongest predictors of bullying is whether the organization experiences and tolerates conflict escalation (Leon-Perez, Medina, Arenas, & Munduate, 2015). Finally, Einarsen (1999) introduced the label "dispute-related bullying" to describe situations when bullies escalate conflicts by employing coercive or aggressive conflict resolution strategies. Thus, multiple previous scholars have framed bullying as conflict.

In addition to the arguments offered by previous researchers noted above, we assert that workplace bullying is a conflict behavior in three inherent ways: (1) Because bullying is an unwanted behavior, the bully's and target's goals are inherently incompatible, thereby creating conflict. (2) The act of bullying in the workplace creates conflict between the bully, the target, and any supervisor who becomes involved. (3) Because responding to bullying from the perspective of the target, an observer, or the supervisor typically aggravates the situation, bullying can be viewed as a volatile, escalating conflict. If we view workplace bullying as conflict behavior, then the Theory of Conflict Cultures can be applied be the phenomenon. We briefly explain that theory below.

The Theory of Conflict Cultures provides a framework for differentiating organizations by the types of conflict behaviors they employ (Gelfand et al., 2008). This theory features two underlying dimensions of conflict that lie along opposing axes, forming four distinct conflict types (see Figure 8.1). The theory resembles other topological theories with two underlying dimensions that create four types such as family communication environments (Koerner, Schrodt, & Fitzpatrick, 2018). When conceptualizing bullying as a form of conflict, then the Theory of Conflict Cultures can be used to effectively predict which types of organizations are more or less likely to encourage bullying.

The theory proposes that conflict processes are inherently linked to the organizational context in which they occur through the organizational norms governing conflict. Based on these norms, an organizational member can predict other members' individual conflict behaviors (Gelfand et al., 2008). In sum, if bullying is a conflict behavior, then the Theory of Conflict Cultures can provide a framework for differentiating organizations more or less likely to encourage bullying. Bullying as a form of conflict is problematic for targets, supervisors, witnesses, and the organization itself, as we describe in detail below.

The Negative Effects of Workplace Bullying

Workplace bullying is a communication phenomenon worthy of study for two reasons: its iniquitousness and its negative effects. Over 27% of Americans report that they directly experienced bullying in the workplace, and over one-third reported that they are aware of workplace bullying (Namie, Christensen, & Phillips, 2014). From the managerial perspective, bullying negatively impacts productivity (Khan, Sabri, & Nasir, 2016), employees' absenteeism (Hollis, 2015; Raskauskas & Skrabec, 2011), and employment longevity (Sedivy-Benton, Strohschen, Cavazos, & Boden-McGill, 2014). From the target's perspective, bullying leads to low job satisfaction (Oladapo & Banks, 2013; Saricam, 2016), decreased work engagement (Park & Ono, 2017), low work productivity (Carroll & Lauzier, 2014; Khan et al., 2016), and health problems (Einarsen & Nielsen, 2015; Park & Ono, 2017).

The negative effects of bullying on targets can be profound; they include PTSD (Nielsen & Einarsen, 2012), depression and withdrawal from the workplace (Way, Jimmieson, & Bordia, 2016), physical health problems (Einarsen & Nielsen, 2015), and burnout, sleep problems, anxiety, and physical and psychological health problems (Nielsen & Einarsen, 2012). A recent study reported targets experiencing job anxiety, stress, and dissatisfaction (Goodboy, Martin, Knight, & Long, 2017). Workplace bullying can be life changing in that it can prompt job changes and withdrawal from careers. Narratives about workplace bullying reveal profound effects that parallel the negative outcomes of rape and physical assault. Such negative effects also occur in higher education, an incident-rich organization for examining bullying behavior.

Higher Education as an Exemplar

The academy offers a workplace environment that can provide fertile ground for bullying. Colleges and universities value academic freedom, which encourages sharing of diverse perspectives and sound arguments to defend those ideas; emergent differences of opinions can provide the basis for dispute-based bullying. Additionally, colleges and universities often provide opportunities for situations associated with higher incidences of bullying such as long-term employment with high job security (Gravois, 2006; Enwefa, Enwefa, Dansby-Giles, & Giles, 2010; Keashly & Wajngurt, 2016), jealousy among employees (Sedivy-Benton et al., 2014), and competitive, adversarial, highly political environments (Keashly & Wajngurt, 2016). An academic in the rough and tumble intellectual world of a highly competitive unit where colleagues often verbally clash might experience feelings of inadequacy; such feelings might lead to bullying. Misawa (2015) argued that academic bullies who experience a sense of inadequacy or lack of self-confidence can turn to bullying to experience empowerment.

Workplace bullying is quite common in educational organizations generally (Freedman & Vreven, 2016) and higher education specifically. Hollis (2012) reported that over 60% of higher education employees witnessed or were targets of bullying. This high incidence of bullying has not gone unnoticed. The past few years have witnessed a dramatic increase in discussion about bullying in the academy including articles in *The Chronicle of Higher Education* (e.g., Gluckman, 2017), books on the subject (e.g., Roderick, 2016; Twale, 2018), and reports of original research (e.g., Theiss & Webb, 2016).

Additionally, the higher-education workplace offers a desirable exemplar of workplace bullying because targets vary widely by rank. Bullying most often occurs when administrators target faculty; however, faculty-on-faculty bullying (Dentith, Wright, & Coryell, 2015; Keashly & Neuman, 2010; Peters, 2014; Wright & Hill, 2014) and mobbing (Celep & Konakli, 2013; Gorlewski, Gorlewski, & Porfilio, 2014; Saricam, 2016) also take place. Mobbing occurs when additional co-workers join in bullying behavior against a given target (Celep & Konakli, 2013; Gorlewski et al., 2014). Additionally, faculty-to-administrator bullying is not unknown (King & Piotrowski, 2015; Navayan & Chitale, 2016). Finally, research has examined undergraduate and graduate students' experiences of bullying as well as staff as perpetrators and targets (Fox & Stallworth, 2010). Keashly and Neuman (2010) reported that faculty (versus staff) members were more likely to experience mobbing, and faculty members reported that their experience of bullying/mobbing tended to last for more than five years. In sum, higher education offers an incident-rich exemplar of workplace bullying.

Thus far in this chapter, we defined bullying as a conflict behavior, identified the negative effects of bullying in the workplace, and described the academy as an incident-rich exemplar for examining a new theory of workplace bully. Next, we turn to a brief review of existing conceptualizations of workplace bullying with their associated lines of research. We offer our new theory, in part, as an opportunity to integrate these lines of research as well as provide a superior explanation of workplace bullying. In short, in the next section, we provide a review that provides justification for offering a new theory of workplace bullying.

Current Conceptualizations of Workplace Bullying

Workplace bullying began emerging as a distinct area of study in 1998 with its introduction at the World Health Organization (Namie & Namie, 2009). At that time, researchers characterized bullying as exposure to repeated aggression in the workplace (e.g., teasing, mocking, threats, harassment, taunting, hazing, social exclusion). Since then, understandings of workplace bullying evolved to include additional notions such as stigmatization (Einarsen, 1999). More recently, Theiss and Webb (2016) offered a data-based argument for a definition of workplace bullying that is broader in scope: Academic managers reported that employees can perceive aggression as bullying at the first instance (versus repeated aggression) if the aggressor is a known bully in the unit. Additionally, managers did not see bullying as limited to aggressive behaviors in interpersonal interaction but rather "in terms of the bully's behaviors *and the conditions surrounding the conflicts*" (p. 70, emphasis in the original). That is, workplace bullying can be viewed as a group or team phenomenon that can be described in terms of immediate as well as collateral damage. Finally, managers viewed bullying behaviors as both direct and indirect. Thus, from an organizational perspective, bullying can be envisioned as a larger phenomenon than two co-workers engaging in a given set of negative behaviors. In short, disciplinary thinking about bullying has expanded beyond initial research focused on identifying bullying behaviors in negative interpersonal communication encounters to include the broader perspective of organizational culture. (For additional information on interpreting bullying, review Spitzer as well as Turner & West, this volume).

To date, Communication scholarship has conceptualized bullying in two primary ways: (1) an undesirable set of repeated interpersonal communication behaviors (Way et al., 2016) or (2) an outgrowth of organizational cultures that either encourage or discourage bullying (Eddington & Buzzanell in this volume). We will explore each in turn.

Interpersonal Communication Behaviors

Much initial research on workplace bullying conceptualizes bullying as an interpersonal communication phenomenon in which certain kinds of interactants (e.g., the predatory bully) exhibit certain behaviors (e.g., filing unwarranted HR complaints) for certain reasons (e.g., feelings of inadequacy) to achieve certain goals (e.g., eliminating competition for promotion). For example, initial research examining bullying in academe framed such behaviors as incivility and harassment among peers (Piotrowski & King, 2016). Scholars often explain workplace bullying via the following scenario: One person feels threatened by a colleague. The threatened person's primary rationale for engaging in bullying is to inflict harm on the target (Weuve, Pitney, Martin, & Mazerolle, 2014; Mitsopoulou & Giovazolias, 2015); others may join in creating a mobbing effect to drive the target out of the unit (Goodboy, Martin, & Mills, this volume), further amplifying the negative consequences and suffering of the target (Celep & Konakli, 2013, Saricam, 2016).

Adopting this interpersonal communication view, scholars sought to identify specific bullying behaviors. For example, overt bullying behaviors include verbal aggression (Piotrowski, 2015), domineering (Piotrowski & King, 2016), and physical intimidation (de Wet, 2017). Other bullying behaviors are subtler, often leaving the target confused about whether the action was bullying. For example, a common bullying behavior is leaving the target out of important decision making processes (Sedivy-Benton et al., 2014). When the targets question this behavior, it is easy for the bullies to say that they thought the target received the meeting notice. Given that many employees are conflict-adverse, targets may want to believe that it was all a misunderstanding. Of course, *patterns* of such behavior are more difficult to ignore.

The line of research examining interpersonal communication behaviors used in bullying was augmented by communication researchers attempting to ascertain if the communication environment also influences bullying behavior (Erkutlu & Chafra, 2014; Goodboy, Martin, Knight, & Long, 2017; Piotrowski & King, 2016; Sedivy-Benton et al., 2014). Their research treats bullying, including the accompanying interpersonal behaviors, as an outgrowth of the organizational culture in which it occurs. We briefly review that research below.

Outgrowth of Organizational Cultures

An organization's culture shapes, constrains, and controls behaviors (O'Reilly, 2008), including those related to bullying. Organizational culture comprises the pattern of shared meanings and assumptions, constituted through communication, and into which new members are socialized (Keyton, 2005). Certain disciplines, industries, and organizations have cultures that normalize bullying behaviors, whereas others vilify bullies. In some cases, bullies may be attracted to organizations that privilege bullying. In other cases, individuals become bullies by complying with organizational norms. Regardless of how the organizational culture comes into being, members of some organizations more likely exhibit bullying behaviors than members of other organizations. In short, experts in workplace bullying strongly suggest that an organization's culture relates to the manifestation of hostile and aggressive behaviors in the workplace (Lester, 2009).

When examining bullying at the organizational level, two of the strongest predictors of bullying include poor working conditions (an organizational culture that supports bullying) and inadequate leadership practices (Erkutlu & Chafra, 2014; Hollis, 2016b; Piotrowski & King, 2016). We summarize the extensive research on these matters below by pointing out that bullying especially thrives in organizations

- that are competitive, adversarial, and highly political (Cleary, Walker, Andrew, & Jackson, 2013; Sedivy-Benton et al., 2014);
- that provide long-term employment with high job security culture (Eksi, Dilmac, Yaman, & Hamarta, 2015);
- that highly reward performance and productivity (Cooper-Thomas et al., 2013; Samnani & Singh, 2014);
- when resources are in short supply (Keashly & Wajngurt, 2016);
- when intimidating managers control the purse strings (Armstrong, 2011);
- when employees experience workload and role conflicts (Balducci, Cecchin, & Fraccaroli, 2012);
- that experience destructive leadership styles (Hauge, Skogstad, & Einarsen, 2007) and/or laissez-faire leaders (Dussault & Frenette, 2015); and
- whose leaders use unsupportive leadership practices, including unwillingness to listen, and who inadequately respond to hostile work conditions (Hauge et al., 2011).

Widespread acknowledgement exists among scholars that bullying occurs more frequently in organizational cultures that allow bullying to go unchallenged and fail to actively discourage bullying (see Goodboy et al., this volume). Given this acknowledgement, we propose that bullying can be explained *more precisely* by examining one aspect of the organizational culture, specifically *conflict culture*. Certain organizational practices may create cultures that provide fertile ground for bullying. Nonetheless, we assert that bullying need not flourish in that very organizational culture *if* the conflict culture normalizes cooperation instead.

Furthermore, a consideration of conflict cultures eloquently incorporates current lines of research. Conflict cultures are based on norms governing conflict. These norms regulate interpersonal behaviors in conflict, including interpersonal bullying behaviors. Additionally, leaders model norms and working conditions reinforce norms. Thus, conflict cultures provide a means to unite current streams of research on bullying under one theoretical umbrella.

Thus far, we have defined bullying as conflict, described its negative effects in the workplace, and reviewed current lines of research on communication and bullying. We noted that these two lines of research examine bullying in two discrete ways: by examining interpersonal behavior and organizational culture. Below, we offer a new theory of workplace bullying that provides the opportunity to integrate these existing lines of research while offering a fresh perspective on the etiology of bullying as well as its possible elimination in the workplace.

Constructing A New Theory: The Theory of Bullying Conflict Cultures (BCC)

We developed our new theory of BCC by integrating bullying into the existing Theory of Conflict Cultures (Gelfand et al., 2008). We begin our explanation of BCC theory with our theoretical assumptions. Next, we review the core elements of the existing Conflict Cultures Theory (its two dimensions and four types of conflict cultures) to describe how they apply to bullying. During that explanation, we provide examples from higher education for each type of BCC. We note the bullying behavior that each type of four BCC likely features. Finally, we present the new explanations for the etiology and disposition of bullying offered by the theory.

Assumptions

Definition: Bullying is a communicative behavior.

Mechanism: Individuals elect to enact specific communication behaviors based, in part, on the perceived appropriateness of the behavior within the social environment in which they are communicating in the given moment.

Action: Generally, individuals will engage in communicative behavior, including bullying, when they experience it as a fitting response, within the social context, to the situation in which they find themselves. A minority of individuals will engage in bullying whenever they desire to do so, regardless of the social setting, because (1) they are unaware of the social norms or (2) they are unable or unwilling to comply with social norms.

Operation: Generally, individuals will *not* engage in communicative behavior, including bullying, that they perceive as inappropriate for the current social setting. A minority of individuals will *not* engage in bullying in any context for a variety of reasons (e.g., they view such behavior as unprofessional or unethical).

Defining Conflict Cultures

We define *conflict culture* as an organization's norms, expectations, and shared understandings about how conflict should be initiated, managed, resolved, and interpreted. Conflict cultures are influenced by both their environments and constituent parts. For example, an academic unit's conflict culture is likely influenced by its environment, including the culture of the institution as a whole, the predominant culture of its geographic location, and the cultural influences of academe as a whole. Additionally, the unit's conflict culture will be affected by the administrators, faculty, staff, and students who are part of the specific unit.

Bullying in Conflict Cultures

As a viable means of combining the multiple perspectives on workplace bullying reviewed thus far (i.e., specific interpersonal communication behaviors such as bullying and organizational cultures encouraging/discouraging bullying, including working conditions and leadership styles), we propose viewing workplace bullying as a set of behaviors governed by the organization's conflict culture. The organization's conflict culture becomes the primary socializing agent for norms governing how to handle disagreement and conflict within the organization and thus the etiology of bullying. Employees decode bullying as a special type of conflict, albeit a dysfunctional, perverse, and destructive form of conflict. Then, based on the conflict culture and its accompanying norms, employees decode bullying in only two ways: (1) within the acceptable framework for how we engage in conflict in our organization (i.e., permitted within the organizational norms) or (2) outside the accepted norms for conflict resolution and thus not an acceptable behavior in our organization (i.e., an aberrant behavior that should be discouraged).

We propose that conflict cultures constrain conflict behaviors including bullying. When new members become socialized into an existing organization, they learn the norms and expectations for conflict processes through both observation and trial and error. If their behavior deviates from the norm, they receive negative feedback from colleagues, either directly or indirectly. A faculty member may say: "We don't do that here." Another colleague may display a negative facial expression or create more social distance to provide negative feedback. Conversely, when newcomers follow the norms, they may receive positive feedback (i.e., "I like how you handled that debate."). Existing members face the same kinds of sanctions for non-normative behaviors; most academics find negative feedback from colleagues sufficiently undesirable to avoid non-normative behaviors. These subtle but consistent feedback processes shape organizational members' behaviors. In turn, their behaviors reinforce the existing norms, and the norms reinforce the conflict culture. In addition to feedback and norms, organizational structures (that define working conditions) also may form and, in turn, reify conflict culture. For example, the frequency of meetings, availability of communication tools, and institutional traditions may reinforce certain conflict behaviors while constraining others. Below, we provide some evidence of our propositions from existing literature on higher education.

A recent study provides support for linking organizational norms governing conflict to the existence of workplace bullying. Einarsen, Skogstad, Rorvik, Lande, and Nielsen (2016) examined how effective conflict management in organizations related to reports of less bullying. Einarsen et al.'s (2016) "findings indicate that when employees perceive strong conflict management [norms that encourage collaborative problem solving], less bullying takes place, work engagement is strong, and any exposure to bullying is no longer associated with reduced work engagement" (p. 13). In other words, when an organization's conflict culture encourages employees to manage conflicts using collaborative strategies, less bullying takes place.

Proposition 1: Conflict cultures directly affect the amount of bullying that takes place in an organization.

Types of Conflict Cultures and Their Associated Bullying Behaviors

Gelfand et al. (2008) developed a typology of conflict cultures using Van de Vliert and Euwema's (1994) two conflict management dimensions: active-passive and agreeable-disagreeable.

- The active-passive dimension refers to how actively and readily parties engage in conflict. Discussing, confronting, and forcing conversation are active behaviors, whereas avoiding, ignoring, and tolerating comprise passive behaviors. Active conflict cultures encourage discourse about incompatible goals or ideas; passive conflict cultures discourage those same behaviors.
- Agreeableness includes communication that is accepting, concurs, and shows solidarity (van de Vliert & Euwema, 1994). In contrast, disagreeable conflict cultures encourage withholding help, ignoring, and refusing to acknowledge the validity of opposing views.

These dimensions describe the typical behaviors that epitomize the corresponding conflict cultures. For example, cultures high in activeness hold underlying norms specifying active behaviors as the "correct" or "expected" way to manage conflict.

One study queried the existence of these dimensions in higher education. Desrayaud (2013b) surveyed faculty at a large Midwestern university to assess conflict cultures in their units. Her results document the two-dimensional model of conflict culture (agreeableness and activeness), thus providing the first evidence of the theory's veracity in the academic workplace.

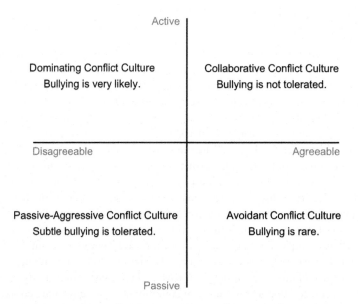

Figure 8.1 Typology of Workplace Conflict Cultures and Likelihood of Bullying Behaviors Figure
Based on Gelfand et al. (2008)

When the two dimensions of agreeableness and activeness are displayed on opposing axes (see Figure 8.1), they reveal Gelfand et al.'s (2008) four types of conflict cultures: collaborative, avoidant, dominating, and passive-aggressive. Desrayaud (2013b) reported evidence of each of the four types of conflict cultures in the university under examination. We describe each of the four conflict cultures in detail below.

Collaborative Conflict Cultures

Collaborative conflict cultures exhibit active and agreeable conflict norms. Organizations with this conflict culture expect members to collaborate or integrate when managing conflict. The norms encourage members to be engaged and actively voice their disagreements as well as to seek solutions that meet all parties' needs. Members highly value supportive communication and confirming messages.

Proposition 2: In collaborative conflict cultures, bullying behaviors are unlikely; bullies do not find support from organizational structures or colleagues.

Desrayaud's (2013b) study of tenured and tenure-track faculty uncovered the professorial view that an ideal conflict culture is an active, agreeable culture. The faculty members' reports of collaborative conflict cultures were associated with higher job satisfaction, higher organizational identification, and lower intent to leave. The absence of bullying in the faculty members' descriptions of these ideal, collaborative conflict cultures is consistent with Proposition 2 above.

Avoidant Conflict Cultures

Avoidant conflict cultures are passive; organizational members are expected to keep most conflict to themselves or to use highly structured and indirect methods to express their disagreements (e.g., suggestion box). Avoidant cultures are also agreeable; they strive to find solutions that work best for

The Theory of Bullying Conflict Cultures

all parties. However, members rarely discuss such solutions openly or negotiate them overtly. Organizations with an avoidant conflict cultures tend to value harmony and cohesiveness, making bullying behaviors less likely.

> *Proposition 3*: In avoidant conflict cultures, bullying behaviors are unlikely; bullies who use overt tactics do not find support from organizational structures or colleagues.

Dominating Conflict Cultures

Dominating conflict cultures are active and disagreeable. These organizations expect members to vocalize disagreements and advocate strongly for their individual positions. The most commonly used conflict management strategy is dominating or competing. In these environments, members envision every situation through the lens of competition, and the loudest, strongest, or most persistent competitor wins. In organizations with a dominating conflict culture, individuals likely use bullying as a strategy, and do so overtly and explicitly. Yelling at and insulting colleagues exemplify the type of bullying likely to take place. Dispute-related bullying (Einarsen, 1999) very likely takes place because they perceive being aggressive during disagreements as the correct way to manage conflict. Opportunist bullying (Namie & Namie, 2009) also may appear when savvy organizational members realize that they can use bullying to advance their careers. Given the wide acceptance of dominating and competing, members view mobbing as acceptable in a dominating conflict culture.

One qualitative study examining the relationship between a university athletic department's conflict culture and bullying found that workplace bullying occurred when administrators tolerated bullying (Weuve et al., 2014). Pressure to win from coaches and lack of administrative support comprised key factors that led to bullying (Weuve et al., 2014), creating what we would label a dominating conflict culture in which coaches overtly pressured trainers to get their way. This study was not conducted within an academic department but nonetheless demonstrates the link between tolerance for bullying and the presence of bullying within a unit, providing support for Proposition 4.

> *Proposition 4*: Dominating conflict cultures encourage overt bullying behaviors; bullies find support from organizational structures, supervisors, and/or colleagues, especially when their tactics are overt.
> *Proposition 5*: Overt mobbing may occur in dominating cultures.

Passive-Aggressive Conflict Cultures

Passive-aggressive cultures are passive and disagreeable. Competition occurs, but norms strictly regulate how to communicate that competition. Much like avoidant conflict cultures, individuals are expected to use highly structured and indirect methods when they express their disagreements. However, such organizations do not value harmony nor cohesiveness. Therefore, bullying results from this conflict culture, but that bullying is likely to be subtle and well hidden. For example, organizational members may file frivolous grievances to bully targets. Given passive-aggressive conflict cultures' strong rule-orientation, predatory bullying (Einarsen, 1999) more likely occurs than in other conflict cultures. Additionally, individuals may form coalitions to out-vote a target's suggestions, resulting in mobbing.

> *Proposition 6*: Passive-aggressive conflict cultures encourage tacit bullying behaviors; bullies who use covert tactics find support from organizational structures, supervisors, and/or colleagues.
> *Proposition 7*: In passive-aggressive conflict cultures, subtle mobbing may occur.

In sum, bullying can take place in any organization with any type of conflict culture (see assumptions regarding aberrant behavior and above discussion about socializing newcomers). However, organizations with certain conflict cultures are more likely to tolerate and encourage workplace bullying than organizations with other conflict cultures. Organizations with dominating and passive-aggressive conflict cultures, namely organizations with norms that allow disagreeable forms of conflict management, reinforce bullying behavior as the one right or correct way to manage conflict. As bullying behavior becomes more common, the disagreeable conflict culture is reified. Conversely, organizations with agreeable conflict cultures (i.e., collaborative and avoidant cultures) are unlikely to tolerate bullying.

New Explanations for the Etiology of Bullying

Stakeholders create, reify, and maintain conflict cultures at multiple levels. Therefore, multiple paths exist for creating and changing conflict cultures (Gelfand & colleagues, 2008). Below, we describe how conflict cultures, including BCC, are affected by top-down processes, through bottom-up processes, and by larger structural and environmental factors.

Formal Leadership

Individuals with access to power have great influence on BCC. Formal leaders play an important role in establishing conflict cultures because organizational members likely model leaders' conflict styles (Gelfand, Leslie, Keller, & de Dreu, 2012). Gelfand and associates (2010) concluded that collaborative leaders' behavior was negatively related to dominating cultures, where we propose bullying is likely to occur. Other research has attributed the causes of bullying to the supervisor's leadership style, concluding that laissez-faire leadership (Dussault & Frenette, 2015) and abusive leadership with no accountability (de Wet, 2017; et al., 2014), especially in a chaotic organization (de Wet, 2017), contribute to bullying in the workplace. For example, a unit administrator who uses bullying tactics helps to create a BCC in which bullying is acceptable and, one could argue, encouraged.

Informal Leadership

Other sources of power (i.e., tenure) afford the opportunity to influence BCC. One study offers a compelling example of that power. Theiss (2007) documented that, although administrators in higher education institutions attempted to manage bullying incidences, bullying persisted in their units when the perpetrator was a tenured faculty member. Academics often envision tenure as conferring recognition of high achievement and thus establishing positional power. In higher education, organizational members with tenure may influence BCC by example and by persuasion, similar to formal leaders.

> *Proposition 8*: Powerful people (including leaders, authority figures, and those with privilege) can directly influence conflict cultures through their bullying behaviors.

Organizational Membership

Influence on BCC also involves bottom-up processes. Although powerful individuals are influential, so too are lower-level organizational members, especially en masse. If a unit's BCC is entrenched, then a change in leadership may fail to change the unit's BCC, especially if a majority of the organizational members work to maintain the culture. For example, if the membership strongly supports

The Theory of Bullying Conflict Cultures

bullying, then simply changing to a collaborative leader may do little to change the BCC and its related bullying behaviors.

Overarching Organizational Context

Finally, environmental and structural factors influence BCC. Larger forces (i.e., societal level culture, institutional structures) may constrain BCC development. For instance, in their extensive review of research on bullying in higher education, Keashly and Neuman (2010) reported the following conclusions related to structural and environmental constrains in higher education: (1) Given the tenure system, faculty have little motivation to handle issues effectively with difficult colleagues. This lack of motivation can create a toxic work environment. (2) If institutions of higher education have mechanisms for addressing bullying, faculty are more likely to participate in informal processes that formal interventions. (3) The pattern of faculty autonomy in academe creates an environment where faculty are unfamiliar and unskilled in working collectively and collaboratively.

> *Proposition 9:* Multiple agents and paths exist for influencing and changing an organization's conflict culture, including tolerance of bullying.

New Explanations for the Disposition of Bullying

The BCC theory augments our options for defining, describing, addressing, and preventing bullying. Although the same behaviors comprise bullying and the definition of repeated, unwanted, negative attention can be applied, this theory offers the perspective that bullying behavior can be a situational response to organizational expectations of conflict behavior and that workplace bullying may occur *only when* individuals perceive themselves in conflict with a co-worker. Thus, bullying may be diminished by simply reducing conflict in the workplace as well as by changing the organization's BCC to be increasingly collaborative. This theory predicts that a change in BCC (the normative ways people engage in workplace conflict) will influence the amount of overt bullying in the organization. Additionally, the theory offers an explanation for the etiology of bullying behavior beyond the enactment of specific behaviors to a co-constructed reality we labeled BCC, as well as a movement beyond individual behaviors and interactions to a transactional and organizational perspective. In sum, the theory offers a direct and credible explanation for the etiology of bullying, manifestation of the behaviors that comprise and accompany it, and how to discourage workplace bullying.

As a caveat, we acknowledge that BCC does not explain all workplace bullying. For example, some bullies may engage in compulsive or chemically induced behavior; in these cases, such behaviors lie beyond the purview of organizational norms. Additionally, some bullying may be difficult to monitor, such as bullying in private conversations, and thus some bullying may occur without collegial monitoring. Such cases present difficult challenges for targets and unit administrators. Nonetheless, we believe the theory we here advocate, the Theory of BCC, explains the vast majority of workplace bullying and that cases such as those described above are aberrant events. Organizations may deal with bullying generally, and these aberrant situations specifically, through policies and procedures that reflect their particular BCC.

Given that BCC are norm-based, diminishing (if not eradicating) bullying involves changing conflict norms. Most members of most organizations will readily agree to a no-tolerance policy for workplace bullying. After the policy is in place, if formal and informal leaders will model collaborative conflict resolution and the larger organizational culture will support such efforts, then it becomes a matter of persuading rank and file organization members to practice collaborative behaviors and to "call out" colleagues who do not. Thus, the theory outlines a five-prong approach to changing a BCC (policy, formal leaders, informal leaders, institutional support, and finally garnering support from the wider membership). Although they await testing, these objectives seem achievable one by one and offer a road map for change.

Suggested Directions for Future Research

Our BCC theory-under-construction has heuristic implications. We propose that Communication scholars more carefully examine bullying at the micro level of the organization, specifically examining conflict cultures, to better contextualize workplace bullying. Empirical examinations can be conducted using recently developed assessments of conflict cultures (Desrayaud, 2013a). We believe this perspective offers a direct and credible explanation for the etiology of bullying, incorporating the behaviors that comprise and accompany bullying as well as organization-wide strategies to discourage bullying. Indeed, our proposed theory allows a simple and direct solution for addressing bullying in the workplace: change the conflict culture—a far easier task than changing the macro-level organizational culture as a whole.

Summary and Conclusions

A growing body of research links organizational conflict to workplace bullying; concurrently, a parallel set of studies has begun to document the existence of conflict cultures within organizations, including the academy. In this chapter, we argue for a new theoretical viewpoint that weds these ideas, the theory of Bullying Conflict Cultures. The theory offers a useful model, based on an existing conceptual framework, four assumptions, and nine propositions. We see this perspective as a particularly useful conceptualization of bullying because it allows communication scholars to continue their long tradition of teaching, training, and studying conflict behavior. Furthermore, we see this theory as providing helpful suggestions for diminishing and ultimately eliminating bullying in any given workplace by changing an organization's BCC. Finally, this approach provides thoughtful directions for future research.

Note

* The authors acknowledge their equal contribution to this essay.

9

UNDERSTANDING WORKPLACE BULLYING FROM TWO PERSPECTIVES

The Case of the Persian Gulf and the United States

Renee L. Cowan and Jaime E. Bochantin

Based on the idea that culture and cultural norms affect how bullying is understood in various countries, this chapter focuses on human resource (HR) professionals' perceptions of what bullying entails, why it occurs, and how culture might affect these perceptions from two perspectives; the United States (U.S.) and Persian Gulf countries (Saudi Arabia and Bahrain). Juxtaposing these perspectives will illuminate important similarities and differences that could be pertinent to multi-national and global organizations. Clearly, HR professionals are integral actors in bullying situations, as they are often the actors who work to legitimate claims of bullying, investigate these situations and offer insight on possible remedies (Bentley et al., 2012; Cowan, 2012; Jackson, Schuler, & Jiang, 2014).

We will discuss data collected though in-depth interviews with U.S. HR professionals and Persian Gulf HR professionals. Our interviews were part of a larger project consisting of perspectives from 15 countries (see Cowan, et al., 2015). We analyzed our interviews using a constant comparative analysis approach and produced supported themes from both datasets that address what bullying is and is not, why it occurs, and how culture might affect this understanding. In the following sections, we first discuss culture as a frame that affects how bullying is understood; we then discuss bullying and the role of the HR professional, describe the methodology, and detail our supported themes from both HR perspectives. Finally, we conclude with a comparison of the two perspectives and the implications of these findings for organizations and society.

Workplace Bullying and Culture

Workplace bullying refers to "actions and practices that a 'reasonable person' would find abusive, occur repeatedly or persistently, and result in adverse economic, psychological, or physical outcomes to the target and/or a hostile work environment" (Fox & Cowan, 2015). HR professionals in the West added the "reasonable person" standard in their own definitions of workplace bullying, referring to the legal standard that requires the behavior to be understood as abusive by a typical reasonable person in society (Willborn, Schwab, Burton & Lester, 2007). In the last 20 years, we have gathered much information about what constitutes workplace bullying, antecedents, outcomes, prevention strategies, and more (see Einarsen, Hoel, Zapf, & Cooper, 2011; Lutgen-Sandvik & Tracy, 2012). Organizational communication scholars joined the bullying conversation in the early 2000s, with research contributing to and expanding this body of work, especially the important work of Pamela Lutgen-Sandvik, Loraleigh Keashly, Sarah Tracy, and others (see Keashly, 1997; Lutgen-Sandvik et al., 2007; Tracy et al., 2006). Even though we are gaining a strong handle on bullying as a negative workplace phenomenon, most of this research is based on European and American samples. Although notable exceptions exist (see Celep & Konakli, 2013; D'Cruz & Noronha, 2010, 2011, 2012; Efe & Ayaz, 2010; Karatuna, 2014), we know of no studies focusing on Arab countries. However, we should not assume similarity, as these countries differ significantly in terms of cultural norms. For example, the U.S. embraces an individualistic approach (see Hofstede, 1984 for a review of cultural dimensions) to its culture in which members privilege autonomy, reserving deep connections only for very close family members and friends. Individualistic cultures emphasize "I" over the "we."

Conversely, the Persian Gulf tends to espouse a more collectivist culture, in which members value tightly integrated relationships, and work often gets carried out in groups. Within these groups, members demonstrate undoubted loyalty and support each other when a conflict arises with another. Importantly, Triandis and Gelfand (1998) argued that the relative salience of "in-groups" (e.g., groups that are important to members and for whom they will make sacrifices) differentiates individualistic and collectivistic cultures. Thus, in the U.S., many in-groups can influence behavior, whereas in the Persian Gulf, individuals tend to align with far less general in-groups, and, as a result, the influence of those groups becomes more salient (Gudykunst, 2005). With more and more opportunities to collaborate and interact in a global community, sensitivity to the differences between these two cultures is vital.

Workplace bullying is an issue pertinent to many organizations in the U.S. (Cowan, 2017); in the Middle East, an increase in workplace bullying has been reported in Lebanon (Alameddine, Kazzi, El-Jardali, Dimassi, & Maalouf, 2011), Iraq (AbuAlRub, Khalifa, & Habbib, 2007), and Egypt (Abbas, Fiala, Abdel Rahman, & Fahim, 2010), but no studies to our knowledge have examined the Persian Gulf countries. Additionally, most studies that have explored negative workplace behaviors in the Arab region focused on aggression and violence, with almost no research on workplace bullying specifically (Alswaid, 2014).

Workplace Bullying and the HR Professional

As previously discussed, we have extensive knowledge on the target's voice in workplace bullying situations. Understanding the target experience is important and has resulted in much needed information and concrete suggestions for action in bullying situations (Einarsen et al., 2011). We are still gathering the voices of additional important stakeholders, such as the HR professional. Cowan (2012) and Harrington, Rayner, and Warren (2012) have argued the HR professional is a particularly important voice to engage. The HR professional is often the organizational actor to whom targets report bullying, and they are often responsible for policy creation and enforcement as well as bullying investigations (Cowan, 2012; Cowan & Fox, 2015).

Although this HR role likely remains consistent across countries (Storey, 1993; Ulrich, Brockbank, Johnson, & Younger, 2010), cultural norms in terms of interpersonal communication vary (Gudykunst, 2005). Thus, HR professionals in the U.S. might understand employee mistreatment and negative workplace communication (as well as what constitutes bullying) differently from how HR professionals in the Persian Gulf orient to the same kind of behavior. For example, the Persian Gulf has a much higher power distance index compared to the U.S. (Hofstede, 1984). The power index comprises the extent to which the less powerful members of organizations accept and expect that power is distributed unequally and that an established hierarchy is in place and executed without question (Hofstede, 1984). Hofstede later updated his claims on power distance and cultural norms and stated that "culture sets the level of power distance at which the tendency of the powerful to maintain or increase power distances and the tendency of the less powerful to reduce them will find their equilibrium" (2001, pp. 83–84). Moreover, the acceptance of inequalities in power shapes views about how individuals with differing levels of power should interact (Javidan & House, 2001). In the Persian Gulf, individuals assume more of a hierarchical approach to business where they prioritize status and chain of command and expect deference (Yang, Mossholder, & Peng, 2007) as opposed to the U.S., where the index is much lower, and members question authority and attempt to distribute power (Javidan & House, 2001). As such, individuals could deem negative behavior toward a superior as unacceptable in the Persian Gulf, due to this norm of respecting the chain of command. This perspective would be particularly salient in workplace bullying situations where we know superiors are more often than not the perpetrators of bullying behaviors (Namie, 2017). It is important to shed light on possible similarities and differences in perceptions of what bullying entails, why it occurs, and how culture might affect these perceptions that could be pertinent to multi-national and global organizations.

Research Focus: How do those in HR in Bahrain/Saudi Arabia and the U.S. understand and define bullying? What are the cultural expectations that inform these perceptions?

Method

Sampling and Data Collection

In this study, we sought to examine perceptions of workplace bullying among HR professionals in both the U.S. and the Persian Gulf Coast region of the Middle East. All the HR professionals interviewed in both U.S. and Bahrain/Saudi Arabia were employed in HR professional roles at the time. We used convenience and purposive sampling to garner both samples. To participate in the study, participants had to be employees over the age of 18 working in an HR role either in U.S., Saudi Arabia or Bahrain.

We obtained the Bahrain and Saudi Arabia participants in two ways: (1) through accessibility via the HR graduate course that the second author was teaching in Bahrain and (2) through specifically targeting HR professionals working in Bahrain and Saudi Arabia. Our sampling technique yielded 11 total participants. Seven of the participants were women and four were men. All participants identified as being Arab-Muslim. We conducted in-depth interviews with all 11 participants in an office on campus, with interviews averaging 45 minutes in length.

For the U.S. sample, we accessed participants through the first author's personal and professional networks, using email invitations and posting invitations on social media sites and HR professional organization message boards. This technique yielded 15 U.S. participants, 12 women and three men. We conducted our interviews away from the participant's place of work and at locations that the participants considered to be comfortable. These interviews lasted between 40 and 120 minutes.

We conducted all the interviews in English, and we asked participants the same questions concerning what behaviors were considered workplace bullying, what constituted bullying, and how culture that could affect how bullying is understood and dealt with. We transcribed both datasets verbatim, resulting in 112 pages of analyzable text for the Bahrain/Saudi Arabia sample and 247 pages of single-spaced text for the U.S. sample. The appropriate Institutional Review Boards approved our research procedures. As noted previously, these interviews were a part of a larger project consisting of interviews with HR professionals across 15 countries (see Cowan et al., 2015).

Data Analysis

We utilized the constant comparative method for the systematic inductive analysis of data (Corbin & Strauss, 2008). The first author analyzed the U.S. data, and the second author analyzed the Persian

Gulf data. Both authors began data analysis with open coding where several readings of the transcribed interviews were done in order to obtain a preliminary understanding of the data. This open coding, as described by Strauss & Corbin (1998), served at a very general level as the first step in organizing the data into meaningful themes and clusters. The open codes uncovered in the Persian Gulf dataset regarding participants' perceptions of bullying included cultural expectations, religion, gender, ethnocentrism, supervisor discretion, social norms, workplace culture, respect for authority, and collegiality. The open codes uncovered in the U.S. dataset regarding perceptions of workplace bullying were media, capitalism, freedom, difference, lawsuits, individualism, competition, work expectations, and equality.

Once we completed the open-coding process, we began axial coding. During axial coding, we identified connections between the open codes and articulated larger categories (Charmaz, 2000). We came together to discuss the open codes generated and how they possibly fit together. We discussed how the open codes were similar, different, and what larger categories seemed to be present. We used words and other connections in the transcriptions to determine concepts within and between them. We combined initial codes and/or foregrounded to focus on participants' perceptions of workplace bullying and the role of culture (if any) in the acceptability of bullying behaviors. Though the axial coding process, we uncovered several major categories related to our focus questions. We found three prominent themes emerged in the Bahrain/Saudi Arabia sample: (1) participants considered all discourteous, aggressive, or inappropriate workplace behavior to constitute "bullying"; (2) an ethnocentric view seems to inform and constrain their perceptions of workplace bullying; and (3) cultural expectations reproduce perceptions of workplace bullying. In the U.S. sample, two themes emerged regarding perceptions of bullying behaviors: (1) with the exception of clearly aggressive behaviors (physical aggression, verbal abuse, and spreading rumors), participants perceived behaviors as ambiguous and contingent on organizational norms and the criteria of repetition, and (2) they oriented to cultural values such as freedom, diversity, and capitalism as drivers for the acceptability of bullying behaviors.

After constructing these themes and to ensure the trustworthiness of our findings, we conducted member checks. Member checks allow for the veracity of coding by ensuring that it resonates with the experience of the participants and also further informs themes (Creswell, 2007). Additionally, the trustworthiness of our findings is apparent through the use of thick, rich descriptions in the following section, which Creswell (2007) argued allows readers to evaluate the quality and transferability of the categories.

Findings and Interpretation

Perceptions of Bullying Behaviors in the Persian Gulf

We attempted to better understand the perceptions of those in HR in the Persian Gulf and the U.S., regarding potentially bullying behaviors (see Appendix A). From the Persian Gulf perspective, we found discourteous, aggressive, or inappropriate workplace behavior is considered bullying without fail—our participants categorized all of the behaviors presented as very clearly bullying. Interestingly, we found a continuum of these behaviors with regard to their severity. For instance, when asked what would be considered bullying, spreading rumors (particularly about women), yelling, and physical aggression comprised the worst forms of bullying, with 10 out of the 11 participants reporting these behaviors as being particularly egregious. Additionally, insulting and putting someone down, aggressive body language, and ignoring someone's opinions were very clearly labeled as bullying but perhaps to a lesser extent. Maryam, an HR Generalist for the Ministry of Interior (the law enforcement sector of the Bahrain government) with over 15 years of experience, explained, "Ignoring someone's opinion may not be a severe form of bullying, but it's still a type of inappropriate behavior in the workplace." Participants almost always perceived persistent criticism as a form of bullying, although some interviewees pointed out that constructive feedback from superiors is acceptable and expected. Replacing tasks, withholding information, and giving unmanageable workloads were other behaviors where the interviewees reflected upon specific circumstances that make them more or less acceptable, suggesting a range when it comes to orienting to such behavior. However, clearly, under the "right" circumstances, they could understand all of the behaviors as bullying.

For example, participants talked about jokes as the most ambiguous behavior. Some described all jokes as inappropriate in the workplace, while others specified that only certain jokes should be labeled as bullying, such as those that are meant to cause emotional harm or embarrassment.

How participants frame and perceive bullying largely comes from their worldview and geographical location. Participants espoused the ethnocentric notion that bullying is something that does not occur very often in Bahrain or Saudi Arabia because of the values that were instilled in them as children. As Mohammad, an HR Director for a large oil company in Saudi Arabia, explained,

> I don't think the Saudi culture even has a vocabulary for understanding or committing acts of bullying. I myself have never really experienced it here nor seen anyone engage in this sort of behavior. I don't want to say we are exempt from it but we kind of are based on our socialization as children.

Moreover, participants claim the experience of bullying is a Western phenomenon and, as a result, not something that occurs in Bahrain and Saudi Arabia, at least not involving native individuals. As Alex, an HR Director with ten years of experience working in the public sector, explained, "These are things that Muslims just don't do to one another. Doesn't happen here and if it does, then it's probably a Westerner." Najwa, an HR Generalist, echoed this sentiment,

> I have had friends from other countries that have had bullying happen but in most cases it was an expat or Western supervisor that did this. A non-Muslim. I would be very surprised if a Muslim treated a fellow Muslim this way. It would be rare.

Like Alex and Najwa, most participants in this study claimed they have never been a victim of workplace bullying, nor had they witnessed such an occurrence unless a Westerner was the perpetrator.

Perceptions of Bullying Behaviors in the U.S.

Notably, HR professionals interviewed in the U.S. envision bullying in similar and different ways than those HR professionals interviewed in the Persian Gulf. First, like those in the Persian Gulf, our participants in the U.S. understood practices such as physical aggression, spreading rumors, and verbal abuse as bullying. Actions such as "telling jokes or encouraging others to tell jokes about someone or engaging in practical jokes" and "insulting someone and putting them down" seemed ambiguous and contingent on criteria such as which person performed the act and if that person repeated it.

The U.S. participants discussed some behaviors as ambiguous in terms of bullying. Some behaviors (see Appendix A) could be understood as bullying based on different factors such as if they were repeated, who engaged in the behavior, how the other person perceived the behavior, and if that behavior was deemed acceptable in a particular organization. What behaviors might be acceptable in one organization (for example a blue-collar work environment such as construction) could be perceived differently in another context (white-collar office setting). Amanda commented,

> So you know, different organizations in the U.S., things can be more acceptable than others. I mentioned my father and my brother working in the construction industry and you

know there are things that they do that just may be acceptable that would not be in my organization.

Mina's comment underscores context as important when experiencing practical jokes:

> I guess it depends on the work environment. I've seen practical jokes where someone wraps someone's office up in foil in a very conservative environment and everyone got written up. In other situations, I've seen where they fill someone's office up with balloons and it was like oh this is fun, congratulations or congratulations on your promotion. So it really depends on the environment.

Mina referenced some organizational contexts that allow practical jokes and others that do not tolerate this kind of behavior. Linda also noted the ambiguity of the behavior of unreasonable deadlines:

> If one employee is consistently being given deadlines that they have no chance at hitting or assigned projects when they already have a ton of other things going on and other employees who are in the same level or craft and have the same manager are not receiving those types of assignments, I think then that could definitely be bullying because they're really hitting that one person. They're not treating everyone else the same way. Also again it goes to the culture of the company. Because I know a lot of companies today it's like everyone is slammed and everyone has that kind of workload.

Linda's comment points to the repetition of these unreasonable deadlines as important as well as the context in which the behavior is happening (i.e., the culture of the company) and if possible target is being singled out. Jen observed that persistent criticism also can be ambiguous and contingent on the situation:

> It's acceptable if it is warranted and if it's done in a respectable way. If you're having a private conversation with the employee and you're giving feedback that they need to hear. If they're having performance problems they're probably making errors and mistakes, they need that feedback. It wouldn't be acceptable if it's happening consistently in front of a group of people. If you're pointing out things that really aren't errors or mistakes but you're nit-picking. If it's persistent and constant, happens all the time, I think that would be, would definitely be falling more towards the category of bullying.

As Jen noted, the factors that could make persistent criticism bullying depends on how and when the criticism occurs as well as the frequency of the criticism. Organizational context mattered to the U.S. HR professionals, particularly for those behaviors most associated with managerial prerogative such as unreasonable deadlines, replacing tasks, and persistent criticism. These behaviors were not clearly bullying to U.S. HR professionals because the participants expressed the idea that oftentimes these behaviors comprise legitimate management behavior in organizations. We uncovered different expectations for our Persian Gulf participants.

Persian Gulf Cultural Expectations

Gender, respect of authority, social, and religious norms help to frame the perceptions of bullying among the Persian Gulf participants. First, our findings revealed a highly gendered context. Although our participants repeatedly suggested that perpetrator gender did not matter when it came to the perceived severity and acceptability of bullying behaviors, we still found stereotypical views of men and women when it came to perceptions and plausibility of these behaviors occurring. To reiterate, the Persian Gulf participants in this study very clearly did not believe that bullying occurred on a very regular basis in the Middle East. However, the participants were able to tease out *perceptions* of what they *believe* constitutes bullying (or what bullying would look like if it did occur). We also discovered that intra-cultural bullying (bullying among members of the same cultural groups) hardly ever occurred. The most illuminating discussions involved the idea that men respect women too much to engage in any of the behaviors presented to them. At least half of the participants reported that mistreatment of women in the workplace was unacceptable based on their cultural values. Our interviewees mentioned these behaviors as more severe when men target women. Nawal, an HR practitioner with 19 years of experience, said, "If a man mistreats a woman, especially women that you work with, you are ostracized and you will be fired." Others echoed this zero-tolerance policy.

Additionally, while participants expressed respect for authority in the workplace, they did not believe that hierarchy was an aggravating factor in bullying situations. Most often, the participants strongly emphasized that no one should be engaging in bullying behaviors, and it does not matter who is engaging in them. However, negative behavior toward a superior was understood as particularly disrespectful. These interviewees made it very clear that Muslims/Bahrainis/Saudis respect both their elders and their superiors and that upward bullying would be unthinkable.

Lastly, our interviews in the Persian Gulf voiced a strong adherence to social norms and religion, which guides the perception of bullying. Violating social norms seemed to be the most salient criteria for what makes a behavior bullying. The social norm that is referred to most often is the adherence to Islamic values and/or Muslim faith. Bullying or aggressive workplace behaviors would violate the social norms associated with these highly regarded values. As stated earlier, several participants mentioned that they learn these values as children. Thus, elders or Mohammed "would be ashamed" if these behaviors occurred. Overwhelmingly, the participants asserted that they do not mistreat *each other* because that would be deeply disrespectful and a disgrace to their religion.

U.S. Cultural Expectations

Cultural values, such as diversity, freedom and equality, and capitalism, were all understood as drivers for the acceptability of bullying behaviors in the U.S. sample. Participants mentioned diversity as something that made it hard to answer questions about the U.S. culture and how it might affect the acceptability of bullying behaviors. After being asked the question, Sandie stated, "I think that's going to be hard to answer because we don't just have one culture, honestly." Others suggested that it was hard to discuss what American culture actually was made up of because of the diversity in the society. Mark, an HR Director for a large aerospace corporation, had a hard time understanding the questions associated with American culture and what would make bullying behaviors more or less acceptable. He discussed America has a wide variety of people as well as norms in the workplace, and, just more generally in a civilized society, bullying is always unacceptable.

The U.S. participants extensively noted freedom as a cultural driver for acceptability of bullying behavior. Reasons why bullying behaviors may be more or less acceptable in the U.S. included freedom of speech, equality, freedom to treat others poorly and a more liberal attitude. Sandie, an HR professional at a large non-profit organization, discussed bullying behaviors being reported more or less acceptable because:

> People are not intimidated by authority as much . . . Freedom is valued. Individual freedom is valued and expression is valued and free speech is valued. So because of that, people will say so and so did this or so and so hurt me or whatever. More likely than in countries where there are strict societal norms. I've worked in countries and places where they are Muslims and women would have no voice regardless of what happened to them. I think because in

the U.S. we have that culture, it makes these things less prevalent because you can't do it for long without somebody speaking up.

In her comment, Sandie directly compared her country and those where some have less of a voice (e.g., women in Muslim countries). She argued that, because of freedom as a value and freedom of speech as a norm, bullying behaviors are likely to be less prevalent because someone will eventually speak up. Stacey, an HR professional with a PR firm, commented, "Americans are more outspoken . . . they are a little bit more vocal than other cultures." Further, Linda commented, "As a culture we are a more liberal country . . . I think it makes it easier or more acceptable to say things." Linda went on to say that there are probably things she doesn't think are appropriate to say or do at work, but people can act as they will within parameters in the U.S. She continued, "we are all so no filter," and the norms seems to more relaxed in the U.S.

In reference to equality, unlike the Persian Gulf sample, our participants did not perceive gender as an aggravating factor to bullying behaviors by the U.S. HR professionals, and, instead of focusing on a respect for authority in the workplace (e.g., that bullying behaviors would be more out of line if enacted towards a manager), several in the U.S. sample pointed to the more profound effect of a manager enacting the behaviors on a subordinate. The participants understood the behaviors as being amplified if conducted by a manager. For example, Mark (and others) commented that the behavior would be perceived as much worse if it was enacted by a manager. Mark claimed,

> Because we hold our managers to an even higher standard of workplace ethics and professionalism. So if a manager is intentionally spreading false rumors, for example, then they're driving a behavior, they're demonstrating a behavior that others may think is appropriate.

The U.S. HR professionals' comments clearly affirm that a manager enacting bullying behaviors was understood as much worse than if a regular employee enacted these behaviors.

Our interviewees also stressed capitalism, open markets, and economic factors as drivers for the acceptability of bullying behaviors in the U.S. Amy and others discussed the idea that, in the U.S., stakeholders value businesses and their success over the people in the organizations. Amy, an HR professional for over 15 years, commented:

> We're so focused on the success of the businesses. This is just over the years we focus so much on the success of business, paying taxes, and lobbying that you know really there hasn't been any funded interest in protecting the employees . . . just progressively as a nation we're so focused on output and outcome and finances. We're a very business oriented country.

Amy's comment suggests that valuing businesses and profits over the well-being of individuals could mean that protecting employees from bullying behaviors is not as much a priority as the success of the business, outcomes, and the business's finances. Pam, an HR professional for over 25 years, echoed this sentiment:

> Issues are profit driven. Individual compensation is tied to the progress of the employer.
> In those circumstances maybe bullying might be a little bit more acceptable because I think that everybody is in fact pursuing the same goal of growing the company, growing the business. So if a little bit of bullying occurs on the way it may be perceived as being for individual good and maybe okay for business.

HR professionals interviewed in the U.S. envision bullying in both similar and different ways than those HR professionals interviewed in the Persian Gulf. Both U.S. and the Persian Gulf participants consider behaviors such as physical aggression, spreading rumors and verbal abuse to be bullying. The most notable difference across the two samples is that, in the Persian Gulf, under the "right" circumstances, *all* of the behaviors could be understood as bullying and that the severity of the behaviors is contained on a continuum. Moreover, gender, respect of authority, and social/religious norms also contribute to the perceptions of bullying among participants in the Persian Gulf, which was not the case in the U.S. With regard to the U.S. sample, interviewees discussed several behaviors as being ambiguous in terms of bullying, contingent upon who was performing the behavior, how many times it has occurred and how the other person perceived the behavior. Furthermore, certain organizations seem more tolerant of bullying behaviors, such as blue-collar environments.

Discussion and Implications

Our analysis revealed stark similarities and differences across the U.S. and Persian Gulf samples when it comes to understanding workplace bullying. It is the notion of what gets privileged and when that helps piece together this phenomenon. Indeed, a critical/power-based view of bullying could be applied to our findings in that taken-for-granted assumptions, beliefs, and meanings frame (Mumby & Ashcraft, 2006) bullying and bullying perceptions.

We found bullying and all related inappropriate workplace behavior is unacceptable in the Bahraini and Saudi workplaces, due to their ethnocentric viewpoint and their strict adherence to religious, social, and cultural norms. Thus, stakeholders privilege relationships over the bottom line, while, in the U.S., our interviewees suggest that many bullying behaviors can be acceptable in businesses that are driven by profit and competition. In addition, tensions exist centered around how participants discursively perceive bullying in both samples. In the U.S., we found that HR professionals overwhelming feel context is important to understanding bullying behaviors and that the management perspective is privileged in that they are the ones that get to "make sense" of the bullying behavior (i.e., the behavior is okay because it is what managers do) (see Weick, 1995 on sensemaking theory). At the same time, the U.S. HR professionals discuss "freedom" as a cultural driver for and against bullying.

Our Persian Gulf participants asserted that a devout Arab-Muslim never engages in bullying behaviors toward *other* devout Arab-Muslims. However, it seems those norms may not apply when dealing with immigrants or people that do not share the devout norms and values, which is an interesting finding. For example, Maryam mentioned that she knew of some isolated incidents involving the abuse and mistreatment of Southeast Asian workers in Saudi Arabia and Bahrain. She claimed that those occurrences are rare and likely happen because either the perpetrator was not a devout Muslim (because s/he would know better) or because the behavior is acceptable since immigrants do not share the same cultural values, thus making them members of the out-group. Qureshi, Rasli, and Zaman (2014) explored this idea as well, asserting that immigrants might violate social norms and expectations in various ways. They may talk and look different, have foreign names, or might be unfamiliar with the culture in their new place of work/new country. They might involuntarily violate unwritten rules and regulations due to language barriers and become bullying targets more easily (Qureshi et al., 2014). Thus, based on cultural norms and adopting an ethnocentric perspective, it seems that excuses and exceptions could be made for engaging in bullying behaviors but only under the right circumstances, a finding similar to our U.S. sample in that organizations allow and almost accept bullying under these sorts of conditions (i.e., involving a non-Muslim or Western expatriate) as part of the business model.

A second implication is the idea that cultural values and expectations in both samples help to reproduce and perpetuate perceptions of bullying. The U.S. participants perceived freedom, diversity, and capitalism as drivers for the acceptability of bullying behaviors, while in the Persian Gulf, gender, respect of authority, and social/religious norms help to frame the perceptions of bullying among the participants. Thus, while these cultural values are in stark contrast to one another, they are both nonetheless important and salient in their respective settings, a finding especially important in certain business situations like cross-cultural negotiations, mergers, and the global expansion of multi-national enterprises (MNEs). Thus, sensitivity to cultural differences and understanding these differences is of the upmost importance. For example, multi-national companies doing business in both contexts or with branches in both would benefit from understanding which behaviors that members perceive as bullying and how these kinds of situations are interpreted in context. This lens should help with interpersonal relationships and policy development.

Taken together, these implications suggest that we may need to recognize how bullying is constituted at all levels within an organization, including the macro, meso, and micro levels when it comes to bullying across the globe. As Lutgen-Sandvik & Tracy (2012) argued, we need to create "interventions that get at the source of bullying rather than work on its surface symptoms" (p. 8), a contention true for bullying in the U.S., the Middle East, and all other parts of the globe. Seeking such culturally based resources continues to be a particularly salient struggle but one that communication scholars can and should continue to tackle.

Conclusions, Limitations, and Future Research

This chapter focused on HR professionals' perceptions of what bullying entails, why it occurs, and how culture might affect these perceptions from two perspectives; the United States and Persian Gulf countries (Saudi Arabia and Bahrain). Through in-depth interviews with participants from these countries, we gained the perspective of two different groups of HR professionals that should prove useful to global organizations. Obviously, no study is without limitations. First, because we relied exclusively on interview data, we cannot generalize beyond our participants. Future research might compliment this study with a survey of a much larger sample of HR professionals to capture additional insights. Second, we only included two different global perspectives (i.e., U.S. and Middle East). This study is part of a much larger study investigating HR perceptions of bullying in several countries (Cowan et al., 2015). To truly understand workplace bullying from a global perspective, similar efforts would be fruitful in shedding light on how culture matters to preventing and addressing workplace bullying.

Appendix A
LIST OF BEHAVIORS

- Spreading false rumors about someone or their work
- Insulting someone or putting them down
- Telling jokes or encouraging others to tell jokes about someone or engaging practical jokes
- Verbal abuse (e.g., yelling, cursing, angry outbursts)
- Making aggressive or intimidating eye contact or physical gestures (e.g., finger pointing, slamming objects, obscene gestures)
- Making unwanted physical contact such as hitting, pushing, poking, spitting
- Giving tasks with unreasonable deadlines assigning an unmanageable workload
- Persistent criticism of errors or mistakes
- Removing key areas of responsibility or replacing them with trivial or unpleasant tasks
- Ignoring someone's opinion
- Socially excluding or ignoring someone
- Intentionally withholding necessary information from someone

10

GREAT LEADERSHIP IN BUSINESS DOES NOT COMPENSATE IDLE MANAGEMENT IN WORKPLACE

Leadership, Organizational Culture, and Workplace Bullying in Startups in Japan

Masaki Matsunaga

Bullying in workplace instigates harm in the well-being of employees and their family and colleagues, as well as the performance of the organization/team (Dollard & Idris, 2017; Lutgen-Sandvik & Tracy, 2012). Research suggests that leadership is associated with the emergence of workplace bullying (Hoel, Glasø, Hetland, Cooper, & Einarsen, 2010); nonetheless, the underlying structure of such linkages is not clearly understood. Borrowing insights from complexity leadership theory (Lichtenstein, Uhl-Bien, Marion, Seers, Orton, & Schreiber, 2006), this study reveals how leadership manifests in different domains and relates to organizational culture and workplace bullying with the data collected from startup companies in Japan.

The major contributions of this article are threefold. First, it presents a theoretical model that links leadership, organizational culture, and workplace bullying. This model provides a scientific basis for practitioners about how leadership should be exercised for effective organizational management. Second, this article bridges two distinct bodies of literature—one on bullying and the other on leadership—and, in so doing, it informs scholars in those fields of the symbiotic nature regarding the two areas of study. Finally, this study demonstrates that the same leader may command different leadership styles across situations, and how the processes of such domain-specific manifestation of leadership are associated with workplace bullying. This insight problematizes the existing literature that treats "leadership" as though it were a monolithic, trait-like construct and, thereby deepens the discussion on the relationship between leadership and bullying in workplace. To contextualize these frameworks, relevant literature is reviewed below.

Workplace Bullying

Although workplace bullying has been interpreted in a myriad of ways (see Turner & West, this volume), for purposes of the current research, *workplace bullying* is defined as repeated and unwanted negative acts which organizational members experience within their work-related relationships. Similar to other forms of bullying, workplace bullying is characterized by power imbalance between the perpetrator/offender and the victim(s) (Ferris, Zinko, Brouer, Buckley, & Harvey, 2007). It can be verbal or nonverbal, targeted toward one's work-related issues (e.g., removed from information loop or having one's opinion ignored) or personal aspects (e.g., being humiliated or ridiculed). In many ways, workplace bullying is along the same continuum as harassment, although the latter has state and federal protections in various countries while bullying has not yet reached this legal threshold.

Not surprisingly, workplace bullying has detrimental impact, not only on victims but also their family members, colleagues, and work teams as well. Both victims and observers of bullying experience damage to their well-being (Lutgen-Sandvik & Tracy, 2012). As for team performance, bullying leads to reduced productivity and compromised psychological safety climate, increased attrition and absenteeism, and overall lower performance (Dollard & Idris, 2017).

Leadership and Bullying

With regard to the current research, research points to leadership as an important element of the workplace bullying process, because the way leaders attend to the issue of bullying determines whether and how bullying emerges in workplace (Hoel et al., 2010). *Leadership*, like other terms in communication literature, can be viewed in multiple ways. This research adopts the notion of leadership as a human-initiated process that involves others into a certain cause, makes them understand what should be done, and drives them to take actions to achieve the desired objectives collectively (Yukl, 1994). As Lutgen-Sandvik and Tracy (2012) note, leadership strongly affects social interactions among employees and managers, shaping organizational culture and workplace climate (see Zohar & Tenne-Gazit, 2008). Therefore, leadership provides an influential factor to determine whether and how bullying propagates in workplace.

At the same time, while research indicates that leadership is associated with workplace bullying, the underlying structure of this linkage remains to be explored. For example, Hoel et al. (2010) examined four leadership styles and found that each style is uniquely associated with workplace bullying. Autocratic leadership is positively associated with observed bullying (i.e., reports that one has seen someone else being bullied); non-contingent punishment, or an unpredictable style of leadership that rebukes subordinates independently of the target's demeanor, is found to have a strong association with personally experienced bullying; and *laissez-faire* leadership is related to both observed and experienced bullying. Yet, the mechanisms that undergird these associations are still unclear, and thus, more research is needed to disentangle the relationship between leadership and workplace bullying.

Structure of Leadership-Bullying Linkage

On this front, it seems worth noting that inspiration-driven, charismatic leadership may come with some "boomerang effect" when it comes to building healthy organizational culture. For example, Sarros, Cooper, and Santora (2008) found that transformational leaders may generate competitive organizational culture, which may, in turn, degrade mutually supportive climate in workplace.

At the same time, complexity leadership theory (Lichtenstein et al., 2006) suggests that leadership is not a fixed attribute, but rather a dynamic process that emerges at the intersection of given situations and people operating therein. Accordingly, the same leader may command different styles of leadership across different situations (Uhl-Bien & Marion, 2007; Yukl & Mahsud, 2010). In fact, anecdotal evidence suggests that more often than not, vision-driven, innovative leaders are not as effective in managing healthy organizational culture, and those who still succeeded in the history had a business partner who complemented that function; Soichiro Honda and Takeo Fujisawa for HONDA, Masaru Ibuka and Akio Morita for SONY, or the legendary two "Steves"—Steve Jobs and Steve Wozniak—for Apple, just to name a few (see Shenk, 2014).

Leadership and Workplace Bullying in Startup Companies

Nonetheless, little is known about whether and how leaders act in different domains—for instance, creating a new business versus nurturing workplace climate—and, moreover, how such domain-specific manifestation of leadership affects organization. To fill this gap, the current study scrutinizes the relationship between workplace bullying and leadership within startups in Japan. *Startup*, or a newly founded enterprise that creates new businesses and seeks rapid growth (Blank, 2012), is set as the primary research context because: (1) a startup founder is typically the only leader in the organization, especially in its early stage; (2) therefore, her/his leadership style has immediate impact on organizational members; and (3) a startup founder is generally seen as charismatic by employees (Hmieleski, & Ensley, 2007; Leitch & Volery, 2017; Vecchio, 2003).

This structure of startup companies provides an interesting research context of workplace bullying. On one hand, the founder's vision-driven, charismatic leadership, together with high-pressure environment that a startup company regularly faces, is likely to cultivate an unforgiving organizational culture. This may compromise a mutually supportive climate and employees' perceptions of psychological safety (Sarros et al., 2008). On the other hand, such leaders often command poor leadership when it comes to organizational culture management. Regarding the latter issue, it is speculated that because entrepreneurs are so passionate and enthusiastic to pursue their mission, they invest relatively less on nurturing their company's organizational culture (Leitch & Volery, 2017; Shenk, 2014). Based on these syntheses, the following hypothesis is advanced:

> H1: Leaders command different leadership styles upon different situations. More specifically: (1) they primarily take a transformational leadership style for business development, while (2) the same leaders primarily take a *laissez-faire* leadership style for organizational management and workplace climate nurturing.

How such domain-specific leadership relates to workplace bullying is still unclear and, therefore, the current research scrutinizes several alternative models. The first model postulates direct impact of leadership on both organizational culture and workplace bullying (Model A in Figure 10.1). Research suggests that two leadership styles typically employed by startup founders can be a source of unforgiving culture and workplace bullying. That is, the mission-driven, transformational leadership they command for business development generates a competitive workplace culture and reduces psychological safety climate. Still, their *laissez-faire* leadership for organizational affairs allows propagation of workplace bullying. Hence, the following hypotheses:

> H2: Transformational leadership is associated with increased perceptions of competitive organizational culture and reduced psychological safety climate.
> H3: *Laissez-faire* leadership is positively associated with workplace bullying.

A second model posits a full-mediation path—leadership frames an organization's culture, which, in turn, halts or breeds workplace bullying; in this model, the effects of leadership on workplace bullying is fully mediated by organizational culture (Figure 10.1, Model B). Finally, a third model hypothesizes a mixture of direct and indirect effects. Here, the impact of leadership is partially mediated by the association with organizational culture, while it also has a direct effect on workplace bullying (Figure 10.1, Model C). To examine these surmises, the following hypotheses are proposed:

> H4a: The association between leadership and workplace bullying is fully mediated by organizational culture (i.e., increased competitive organizational culture and reduced psychological safety climate).
> H4b: The association between leadership and workplace bullying is partially mediated by organizational culture.

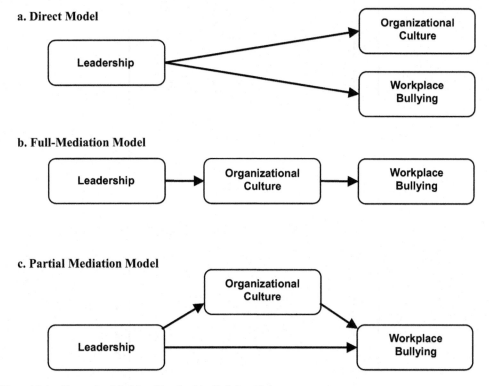

Figure 10.1 Alternative Models of Leadership-Bullying Linkage

Methods

To empirically test these hypotheses, the current study collected data from startup companies in Japan, which provide an ideal context because startup founders are typically the only leaders in the organization and, therefore, their leadership style has immediate impact on members (Hmieleski & Ensley, 2007; Leitch & Volery, 2017). Further, collecting data from both startup founders and employees enhances the current findings' generalizability and reduces the common method bias (Podsakoff, MacKenzie, Lee, & Podsakoff, 2003; but see also Conway & Lance, 2010). See Table 10.1 for descriptive statistics of the demographics and main variables of interest.

Respondents

Respondents were 695 employees recruited from 73 startup companies in Japan and their founders. On average, the companies had been operating for 6.97 years ($SD = 2.47$, $Min. = 2$, $Max. = 11$) and 9.52 employees per company participated in this study ($SD = 4.07$, $Min. = 4$, $Max. = 27$). For employees, average age was 33.20 ($SD = 5.24$, Min. = 25, Max. = 54) and 39% were female, while for founders, average age was 40.56 ($SD = 7.12$, $Min. = 27$, $Max. = 63$) and 26% were female.

Data Collection Procedure

Participation in this study was solicited through a convenience sampling method. Initially, I contacted the founders of the companies for which I had been providing consulting services and, through their

Table 10.1 Descriptive Statistics and Reliability Coefficients of Key Variables (n = 695)

Variable	M	SD	1.	2.	3.	4.	5.	6.	7.	8.	9.	10.	11.
1. Organizational Member's Sex[1]	0.39	0.49	—										
2. Organizational Member's Age	33.20	5.24	.01**	—									
3. Startup Founder's Sex[1]	0.26	0.45	.07**	−.05**	—								
4. Startup Founder's Age	40.56	6.70	.05**	−.05**	−.11**	—							
5. Transformational Leadership in Business Development	2.95	0.80	−.02**	.02**	.02**	.06**	.88**						
6. Laissez-Faire Leadership in Business Development	1.65	1.03	.07**	.03**	−.10**	.23**	−.46**	.78**					
7. Transformational Leadership in Organizational Management	1.39	1.03	−.05**	−.02**	−.06**	−.02**	.16**	−.08**	.89**				
8. Laissez-Faire Leadership in Organizational Management	2.61	1.06	.02**	.03**	.10**	.07**	−.20**	.27**	−.55**	.86**			
9. Competitive Culture	2.48	1.06	.02**	.08**	.10**	.03**	.25**	−.12**	−.15**	.13**	.90**		
10. Psychological Safety Climate	1.95	1.07	.00**	.00**	.00**	−.04**	.06**	.03**	.20**	−.37**	−.12**	.75**	
11. Workplace Bullying	1.31	1.06	.01**	.05**	.02**	.12**	−.10**	.13**	−.30**	.28**	.18**	−.22**	.78**

* $p < .05$. ** $p < .01$. Diagonal elements of the individual-level variables are reliability alpha coefficients.
[1] 0=Male; 1=Female

network, also a larger group of startup founders were contacted. Then I explained about the current research and asked if they would be interested. Upon obtaining the founders' agreement, an invitation was sent to the respective company's employees, who took an online survey. It was emphasized that taking the survey was voluntary and responses would be kept confidential. Upon the completion of the study, the founders received a summary of the overall analysis results (all they received was a summary report and they were not allowed to access raw data to maintain the confidentiality of the employee responses).

Instruments

Leadership Style

Startup founders' leadership styles were assessed using Avolio and Bass's (2004) MLQ-5x. Transformational leadership was assessed with 20 items tapping five elements—*idealized attribution, idealized behavior, inspirational motivation, intellectual stimulation,* and *individualized consideration*; example items included, "Our supervisor emphasizes the importance of having a collective sense of mission" and "Our supervisor talks optimistically about the future of our work group." *Laissez-faire* leadership was measured using four items from the MLQ-5x; an example item included "Our supervisor avoids making decisions."

For this study, respondents rated the leadership of their supervisor (i.e., startup founder) with respect to two distinct domains. They were presented with MLQ-5x items and asked to provided two sets of ratings on how frequently the founder would display the respective behavior, using a 5-point scale ("0 = Not at all" through "4 = Frequently, if not always"). One rating was for business development whereby respondents were presented with a prompt: "In terms of *business development* (e.g., generating new ideas, gathering resources, and/or exploring new business opportunities), our supervisor." A second rating was for organizational management and the prompt read: "In terms of *organizational management* (e.g., nurturing team spirit, promoting collaboration among employees, and/or organizing work flows), our supervisor." To minimize the order effect, half of the respondents provided ratings about business development first, while the other half gave ratings about organizational management first; t-tests revealed no significant differences ($ps = .20$ to $.56$).

To examine the factor structure of transformational leadership, two confirmatory factor analyses (CFAs) were conducted using the data tapping the business development domain. In one model, five latent factors were set up and the 20 items were specified to load onto each of those factors; in the other model, those five factors were further specified to load onto a second-order latent factor representing a single "transformational leadership" construct. CFAs indicated that the 5-factor model's fit was on the borderline (χ^2 [160] = 526.4, $p < .01$, χ^2/df = 3.29, CFI = .91, RMSEA = .09, SRMR = .06), whereas the hierarchical 1-factor model fit the data well (χ^2 [165] = 358.05, $p < .01$, χ^2/df = 2.17, CFI = .95, RMSEA = .06, SRMR = .04) (see Hu & Bentler, 1999, for a discussion of fit indices in latent factor modeling). These results provided empirical support to treat transformational leadership as a global construct, which is in line with previous studies.

Workplace Bullying

Workplace bullying was assessed using 12 items adopted from Einarsen, Hoel, and Notelaers's (2009) revised Negative Acts Questionnaire (NAQ-R), which assesses three interrelated domains of workplace bullying—*work-related bullying* (e.g., "Having opinions ignored"), *person-related bullying* (e.g., "Being humiliated or ridiculed"), and *physically intimidating bullying* (e.g., "Being shouted at or being the target of spontaneous anger").

Respondents evaluated their workplace experiences in terms of both experienced and observed bullying (Lutgen-Sandvik & Tracy, 2012), using a 5-point Likert-type scale ("0 = Never experienced/seen at all" through "4 = Experienced/Seen almost every day"). A 1-factor CFA model fit the data well: χ^2 (54) = 131.76, $p < .01$, χ^2/df = 2.44, CFI = .97, RMSEA = .05, SRMR = .04.

Competitive, Performance-Oriented Culture

A given startup's competitive, performance-oriented culture was assessed using the eight items from the Organizational Culture Profile (Sarros, Gray, Densten, & Cooper, 2005). Respondents evaluated their organization in terms of the phrases concerning competitiveness (e.g., "Achievement Orientation" and "Being Competitive") and performance orientation (e.g., "Having high expectations for performance" and "Being results oriented"). They rated the extent to which those phrases represent their organization, using a 5-point scale ("0 = Not at all" through "4 = Very much so"). A 1-factor CFA fit the data well: χ^2 (20) = 33.2, $p = .03$, χ^2/df = 1.66, CFI = .99, RMSEA = .03, SRMR = .01.

Psychological Safety Climate

A given startup's psychological safety climate was assessed using the 4-item scale developed by Dollard and Bakker (2010); example items included "All layers of the organization are involved in the prevention of stress" and "Our supervisor shows support for stress prevention through involvement and commitment." Respondents rated a 5-point Likert-type scale ("0 = Strongly disagree" through "4 = Strongly agree").

Results

This study examined four hypotheses on the relationships among leadership, organizational culture, and workplace bullying with the data collected from founders and employees of startup companies in Japan. Results of these analyses are reported in detail below.

H1: Domain-Specific Leadership

H1 posited that leaders command transformational leadership in business development, while they would take *laissez-faire* leadership for organizational management. To examine this hypothesis, two paired-sample *t*-tests were run. The first test revealed that, as predicted, leaders show more transformational leadership (M = 2.95) than *laissez-faire* leadership (M = 1.39) in business development: t (694) = 34.55, $p < .01$. On the other hand, the second *t*-test found that, when it comes to organizational management, they use *laissez-faire* leadership (M = 2.61) more than transformational leadership (M = 1.39): t (694) = 17.52, $p < .01$. Thus, H1 was supported.

H2–H4: Leadership, Organizational Culture, and Workplace Bullying

H2 through H4 of the current study postulated the structure of the associations among leadership, organizational culture, and workplace bullying.[1] To examine these hypotheses in a systematic manner, structural equation modeling (SEM) analyses were conducted.[2] To minimize the model complexity, items were aggregated into several parcels, which were used as the indicators of the respective construct (see Matsunaga, 2008, for a review of the parceling technique in SEM). This model, which specified leadership variables as exogenous variables, organizational culture as mediating variables, and workplace bullying as the endogenous variable (Figure 10.2), fit the data well: χ^2 (121) = 379.94, $p < .01$, χ^2/df = 3.14, CFI = .97, RMSEA = .04, SRMR = .04.[3] As a whole, this model accounted for approximately 15% of the variance of workplace bullying.

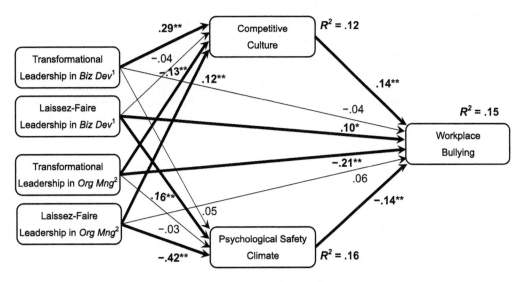

Figure 10.2 Structural Equation Model of Leadership, Organizational Culture, and Workplace Bullying

Note: All path coefficients are standardized. Correlations among exogenous variables (i.e., leadership variables), and between competitive culture and psychological safety climate, are not shown.

[1] Business Development. [2] Organizational Management.

* P < .05. ** p < .01.

H2 postulated the linkage between transformational leadership and organizational culture. In fact, transformational leadership in business development was positively associated with competitive culture (γ = .28, p < .01; cf. Sarros et al., 2008). On the other hand, interestingly, transformational leadership in organizational management had a *negative* association with competitive culture (γ = −.13, p < .01). Nonetheless, altogether, transformational leadership was positively associated with competitive organizational culture. Thus, H2 was supported.

H3 predicted that *laissez-faire* leadership would be positively associated with workplace bullying. This held true for both business development and organizational management domains at the bivariate level (rs = .13 and .28, respectively; see Table 10.1). Further, the direct effect of *laissez-faire* leadership in business development was statistically significant in SEM (γ = .10, p = .01); however, the direct effect of *laissez-faire* leadership in organizational management was not significant in SEM (γ = .06, p = .19). Thus, H3 was only partially supported.

Finally, H4a predicted that the link between leadership and workplace bullying would be fully mediated by organizational culture, whereas H4b postulated partial mediations. Both models supposed that at least some effects of leadership would be mediated by organizational culture; thus, the indirect effects via competitive culture and psychological safety climate were examined.

Analyses revealed that transformational leadership in business development indeed had a small but significant indirect effect to increase workplace bullying (γ = .03, p = .02). Similarly, *laissez-faire* leadership in business development had a negative indirect effect (γ = −.03, p < .01). The indirect effect of transformational leadership in organizational management was, however, not significant (γ = −.01, p = .17). Finally, the indirect effect of *laissez-faire* leadership in organizational management was positive and significant (γ = .08, p < .01).

Besides those significant mediation effects, leadership also had significant direct effects on workplace bullying (Figure 10.2). Specifically, as noted above, laissez-faire leadership in business development was positively associated with workplace bullying (γ = .10, p = .01); additionally, transformational leadership in organizational management had a direct negative effect (γ = −.21, p < .01).

This ran counter to H4a, which predicted that the effects of leadership on workplace bullying should be fully mediated (i.e., should diminish after the associations between organizational culture and bullying were taken into account), whereas H4b found partial empirical support.

Taken together, the total effect of transformational leadership in business development on workplace bullying was almost nil ($\gamma = -.01$, $p = .20$). Similarly, the total effect of *laissez-faire* leadership in business development was not significant ($\gamma = .07$, $p = 12$). In contrast, the total effects of both transformational leadership in organizational management ($\gamma = -.22$, $p < .01$) and *laissez-faire* leadership in organizational management were significant ($\gamma = .14$, $p < .01$).

Discussion

The current study examined a series of hypotheses about the relationships among leadership, organizational culture, and workplace bullying. The results revealed that leaders command different leadership styles in different situations. Further, such domain-specific leadership styles had distinct associations with organizational culture and workplace bullying. Underlying mechanisms of those linkages and their implications are discussed with reference to relevant literature in this section.

Domain-Specific Leadership Manifestation and Workplace Bullying

This study revealed that startup founders in Japan command different leadership styles across different domains. Specifically, they primarily take transformational leadership in business development, while the same leaders use *laissez-faire* leadership when it comes to organizational management. As Shenk (2014) points out, such domain-specific leadership manifestation is not uncommon; many great leaders who inspire team members and attend to details of business ideas can also be a poor orchestrator for building structured work flows or mutually supportive team culture. In fact, supplementary analyses of the current study's data suggested that, while 38.5% of the startup founders exhibit consistent leadership patterns (e.g., using transformational leadership in both business development and organizational management), the majority of 61.5% shows "codeswitching" patterns (e.g., using transformational leadership in business development while taking *laissez-faire* leadership in organizational management).

The results of the SEM analyses suggest that discussions of the leadership-bullying linkage should take this flexibility or fluidity of leadership processes into consideration. For example, transformational leadership in business development had little impact on workplace bullying (total-effect γ was $-.01$), while the same leader's same leadership style in a different domain—organizational management—was significantly associated with reduced workplace bullying (total-effect $\gamma = -.22$). Similarly, whereas the total effect of *laissez-faire* leadership in business development was not significant ($\gamma = .07$, $p = 12$), the same leadership shown in the organizational management domain had a significant association with workplace bullying ($\gamma = .14$, $p < .01$). These findings suggest that just being a great, inspirational leader in business does not necessarily mean she/he would make an effective leader in preventing workplace bullying or, more generally, building a healthy and supportive organizational culture (Lutgen-Sandvik & Tracy, 2012). More often than not, however, leadership is seen as a monolithic, trait-like construct, especially in the existing literature on workplace bullying (e.g., Hoel et al., 2010; Laschinger, Wong, & Grau, 2012). This study's findings problematize such unwavering views of leadership and call for more context-centered approaches to examine the impact of leadership on workplace bullying.

Underlying Mechanism of Leadership's Impact on Workplace Bullying

At the same time, the overall patterns found in the SEM analyses (Figure 10.2) point to certain structure undergirding the distinct relationship between leadership styles and workplace bullying. To illustrate, transformational leadership demonstrated negative associations and *laissez-faire* leadership had positive associations with workplace bullying; these patterns are consistent with previous findings (Hoel et al., 2010; Laschinger et al., Skogstad, Nielsen, & Einarsen, 2017).

Further, analyses of the indirect effects indicate that organizational culture provides a mediating mechanism which carries the impact of leadership on workplace bullying. Both transformational and *laissez-faire* leadership styles were significantly associated with the two organizational culture variables, which were, in turn, related to workplace bullying (Figure 10.2). As such, organizational culture was found to mediate some of the effects of leadership styles on workplace bullying. At the same time, even after taking into account those mediated effects, the associations of leadership with workplace bullying remained statistically significant, indicating the existence of certain mechanisms that were unexplored in the current research.

Research shows that not only weak leadership with little presence but strong, unformidable leadership can also pose problems vis-à-vis workplace bullying. Mathisen, Einarsen, and Mykletun (2011) suggest several unique paths connecting leadership with bullying; leaders may act in aggressive ways themselves, promote an organizational culture that is conducive to mistreatment of employees, or fail to intervene in workplace bullying (see also Woodrow & Guest, 2017).

Regarding the linkage between leadership and organizational culture, transformational leadership that emphasizes the importance of achieving inspirational goals may generate strenuous and unforgiving climate, which often engenders bullying and harassment (Sarros et al., 2008). Research also suggests that a charismatic leader is characteristically so dominant and convinced of her/his righteousness that employees feel their opinions would not have a chance to be heard and, therefore, shun raising their voice (Detert & Burris, 2007; House & Howell, 1992). As a result, inspiration- or charisma-driven leadership is likely to create, if inadvertently, a workplace environment that propagates and perpetuates bullying. This in fact seemed true in the current study; transformational leadership as a whole had a positive association with competitive, performance-oriented culture, which, in turn, was associated with increased workplace bullying (Figure 10.2). It should also be noted, however, that a large part of the effect of transformational leadership in organizational management was not mediated, indicating some unexplored mechanisms.

As for *laissez-faire* leadership, which is marked as a risk factor in the literature (Skogstad et al. 2007), the current study found that it is associated with compromised levels of psychological safety climate, increased competitive culture, and increased workplace bullying. One account for these associations would be that, because *laissez-faire* leaders are overly permissive or even avoiding, they fail to intervene when employees experience mistreatment in workplace; such failures result in reduced psychological safety, which, in turn, leaves employees particularly vulnerable to workplace bullying (Hoel et al., 2010).

Alternatively, the possibility of workplace climate driving leaders to minimize their commitment to organizational management and take *laissez-faire* leadership style may be worth a thought. Resolving widespread bullying in a workplace is a difficult undertaking, and entrepreneurs who are passionate to pursue their company mission might feel reluctant to commit themselves because they find other tasks more compelling and need their immediate attention. Theoretically, in the light of complexity leadership theory which posits leadership as a dynamic process manifesting at the intersection of given situations and people operating therein (Lichtenstein et al., 2006), it is plausible that an uncivil workplace culture reduces leaders' willingness to commit to organizational management. This reduced commitment, in turn, leads to the manifestation of *laissez-faire* leadership style. Future studies should explore this possibility to further elucidate the underlying structure of the relationship among leadership, organizational culture, and workplace bullying.

Practical Implications

The current study yields at least three implications for practitioners. First, one's leadership in organizational management should be evaluated in its own light, independently of her/his performance in business. The current findings provide empirical support for Lichtenstein et al.'s (2006) complexity leadership theory that posits leadership as a dynamic process. It stands to reason that promoting someone to a leadership position just because she/he is competent in business development may be a risky decision, for one's leadership in organizational management is a distinct competency. Great leaders in business do not necessarily make excellent managers.

Second, small teams—a newly founded startup is a typical example—might consider establishing the position of "Chief Relational Officer," who attends to the organizational management matters as her/his primary task. Relational troubles—workplace bullying is an extreme example of such troubles—damage a team's performance and members' well-being (Dollard & Idris, 2017; Lutgen-Sandvik & Tracy, 2012). It should be noted that having such a position is not "luxurious"; to the contrary, it is especially true for small teams and startups because, in those small organizations, the influence of the leader directly impacts employees. Given that workplace bullying severely harms the productivity of the team, small organizations with scarce resources should have structural means to prevent it from emerging and propagating.

Third, before making commitment, employees and shareholders should assess how a leader attends to organizational matters, separately from her/his leadership in business development. The current findings suggest that if a leader does not exercise effective leadership in organizational management, it would reduce psychological safety climate and even lead to widespread bullying in workplace (Figure 10.2). Because bullying is typically associated with attrition, absenteeism, and overall poor performance (Dollard & Idris, 2017), leaders' taking *laissez-faire* approach to organizational management should be considered too important a sign of risk to ignore.

Limitations and Future Directions

There are several limitations in the current research and they should be addressed in future studies. First, this study's data were collected from startups in Japan. Thus, future researchers should examine the extent to which the current findings apply to small teams within larger organizations and data collected from other cultures. Second, only transformational and *laissez-faire* leadership styles were examined in this study with regard to complexity leadership theory (Lichtenstein et al., 2006). There are, however, more nuanced typologies of leadership style or theories of leadership (e.g., Chemers, 1997; Friedrich, Griffith, & Mumford, 2016; Vroom & Sternberg, 2002); thus, the current findings should be reexamined in the light of those emerging theories. Third, the current study could not utilize multilevel approach to account for the nested structure of the data, due to the model convergence error (see endnote 2); future studies should try collecting more data and/or using different measures to address this issue. Fourth, the mechanism through which leadership and organizational culture is related to workplace bullying should be further explored in the future research. The current study has identified several important paths, but still some of the direct effects of leadership remained significant, even after accounting for the mediated effects via competitive culture and psychological safety climate. It indicates other mechanisms that are not examined in this study. In addition, how specifically organizational culture begets workplace bullying should be explored in the future studies as well.

Conclusion

Leaders play a critical role in the dynamics of workplace bullying, as they can prevent or permit the mistreatment of employees through their leadership. This study revealed that startup founders who command great, inspirational leadership to drive business may not necessarily be able or willing to maintain supportive workplace environment. The employees working under such leaders are more likely to experience a competitive culture, compromised psychological safety, and increased workplace bullying, than their counterparts whose leaders take transformational leadership in organizational management. These findings suggest that business development and organizational management are two distinct "arts," and leadership in one domain does not complement the other.

Notes

1 Although preliminary analyses found some correlations between members' or founder's sex and age with leadership and organizational culture (Table 10.1), no clear patterns were detected. Prioritizing model parsimony, those demographic variables were not included in SEM.
2 An alternative approach would be to run a multilevel SEM (Preacher, Zhang, & Zyphur, 2011). Nonetheless, the decision was made to employ a single-level SEM for this study because such multilevel models could not be made to converge with the current study's data. A second option could be to run a series of hierarchical linear modeling, or HLM, analyses (Raudenbush & Bryk, 2002). This option, however, would have overcomplicated analyses because HLM can take only one dependent variable and, thus, necessitated running separate models for competitive culture, psychological safety climate, and workplace bullying each.
3 More details of the results of this SEM analysis are available from the author upon request.

11

COPING WITH WORKPLACE INCIVILITY

A Qualitative Study of the Strategies Targets Utilize

Jennifer S. Linvill and Stacey L. Connaughton

News media are rife with examples of incivilities in the form of rudeness, microaggressions, bullying, and sexual harassment. Schools, politics, and workplaces are all sites for these destructive behaviors. Indeed, the Workplace Bullying Institute (WBI) 2017 National Survey indicated that 19% of U.S. employees (about 30 million targets[1]) "have suffered abusive conduct at work," while another 19% (about 30 million witnesses[2]) have witnessed abusive behavior (p. 1). As a consequence, U.S. organizations routinely lose billions of dollars annually due to events related to destructive workplace behaviors, including the costs associated with (target and witness) turnover, absenteeism, presenteeism, and costs associated with legal defense, dispute resolution, trials, settlements, and worker's compensation/disability insurance fraud investigations (Namie, 2017). Given that adults spend the majority of their time at work (Lutgen-Sandvik, 2013), workplace incivility is a critical, timely area for research.

Workplace Incivility

Workplace incivility has been defined as rude, disrespectful behavior that is often communicative in nature, and that demonstrates a lack of regard for others (Sypher, 2004). Even seemingly small acts of incivility are inappropriate and harmful to others. Although Sypher (2004) distinguishes destructive behaviors along two continua of intensity and intentionality, in this chapter, *workplace incivility* is an overarching concept that includes all forms of negative and destructive workplace behaviors, such as, but not limited to, ignoring, bullying, aggression, workplace violence (Sypher, 2004), and sexual harassment (Gill & Sypher, 2009).

Despite a growing body of literature on workplace incivility, little empirical research exists on how targets of workplace incivility cope with the incivility they experience. This study begins to fill this void. Studying targets' coping strategies is important, given that individuals often cannot leave their organization because they perceive they do not have an alternative, as the disruption and stress they experience often negatively affect their ability to remain productive and feel contented or connected (Sypher, 2004).

Coping

Coping constitutes the "cognitive and behavioral efforts to master, reduce, or tolerate the internal and/or external demands . . . created by [a] stressful transaction" (Folkman, 1984, p. 843) to avoid psychological damage (Pearlin & Schooler, 1978). Coping refers to how one handles what one perceives as a stressful situation (e.g., workplace incivility). Researchers have identified two coping strategies that individuals often use: problem-focused coping and emotion-focused coping (Hogh & Dofradottir, 2001). *Problem-focused coping* utilizes messages aimed at changing the situation the individual perceives as problematic (Babrow, 1992, p. 106), while *emotion-focused coping* messages focus on the emotions caused by the event (Hogh & Dofradottir, 2001). Researchers generally agree that these two strategies are often used in combination with one another (Hogh & Dofradottir, 2001). In the context of this study, targets of workplace incivility may emotionally cope with the incivility (emotion-focused) and/or confront the incivility (problem-focused) they experience.

A small body of research regarding how individuals cope with bullying from a problem-focused perspective informs this study. Djurkovic, McCormack, and Casimir (2005) examined how victims react to different types of workplace bullying (e.g., assertiveness, avoidance (doing nothing), seeking help). Additionally, Hogh and Dofradottir (2001) explored whether individuals who experienced bullying used the same problem-focused coping strategies as individuals who did not experience bullying but were experiencing other kinds of workplace stress. Hogh and Dofradottir identified key coping strategies as problem solving/take action, avoidance/selective ignoring, humor, resignation, seek support, it could be worse, and seek help for problem solving. They found that individuals do employ coping strategies when faced with bullying and that "it is not necessarily the quantity of the negative acts that cause the change in behaviour [sic] but more the fact of being exposed to such acts" (p. 485).

Indeed, workplace incivility constitutes an issue that some targets (perceive they) cannot escape, making it important to further examine how these individuals cope with incivility. Thus, the following research question was posed: How do targets cope with workplace incivility?

Method

This study examines workplace incivility using a social constructionist lens (Burr, 2003). This lens aligns with Sypher's (2004) call for communication scholars to study "the socio-cultural and political landscapes that foreground [destructive] behavior and the explicit, local knowledge and moral wisdom that can be gained from a social constructionist view of uncivil practices at work" (p. 261).

Participants

Initially, the first author utilized her personal and professional contacts to recruit participants (Lindlof & Taylor, 2017). Given the sensitive nature of workplace incivility, such a convenience sample helped to establish a high degree of trust between researchers and participants. We recruited additional participants using snowball sampling (Creswell, 2003).

Individuals qualified for participation in the study if they perceived they had experienced even seemingly small acts of workplace incivility. Participants could have either chosen to stay or chosen to leave the organization where they had experienced incivility.

Twenty-four individuals participated (female = 20; male = 4). Participants ranged in age from 26 to 58 years old (mean = 34.9 years). Participants had worked in jobs where they experienced various types of workplace incivility from 14 months to 9.5 years. Their average organizational tenure was approximately four years. Fifteen participants had earned a bachelor's degree or above; four had some college credits. Four participants had a high school diploma. Participants varied in profession (i.e., account clerk, architect, higher education professionals, paralegals). Although Sypher's (2004) definition of incivility includes behaviors high on the intensity/intentionality scale (i.e., physical violence), none of the participants interviewed for this study shared experiences with high intensity/intentionality behavior(s). Instead, participants perceived their experiences to be lower on the intensity/intentionality scale, yet nonetheless hurtful (i.e., rudeness, humiliation, low-intensity forms of bullying).

Procedures

We used in-depth, semi-structured interviews to gather rich descriptions of participants' experiences and perspectives for events that cannot otherwise be directly observed (Lindlof & Taylor, 2017). The first author asked participants to tell their stories of workplace incivility, how they cope(d) with or manage(d) uncivil behavior, and whether they utilize(d) any type of social support while/after the incivility took place. We audio recorded interviews and transcribed them verbatim. Interviews ranged from 60 minutes to 120 minutes, resulting in 343 pages of single-spaced transcripts. The first author wrote field notes both during and immediately after each interview. We concealed all identifying information and used pseudonyms.

Data Analysis

In keeping with a social constructionist approach, data analysis focused on examining the language participants used when describing their experiences as targets of workplace incivility. We analyzed data through a constant comparative approach, in which systematic gathering and inductive data analysis enables related concepts to emerge (Charmaz, 2000; Strauss & Corbin, 1998). Data analysis began during the interview and transcription processes when we independently wrote initial field notes and memos on the data (i.e., initial thoughts, reflections, and analytic questions; Creswell, 2003). We engaged in open, axial, and selective coding to refine categories, with the goal of revealing related themes and patterns among participants' descriptions (Lindlof & Taylor, 2017; Strauss & Corbin, 1998) that evidenced recurrence, repetition, and forcefulness (Owen, 1984). During analysis, we met after each phase to discuss the interpretations prior to proceeding with the next step (Creswell, 2003). We conducted member checks to help ensure validity (Lindlof & Taylor, 2017).

Coping With Workplace Incivility

Findings show that participants employ varied coping strategies to "master, reduce, or tolerate the internal and/or external demands that are created by the stressful transaction" (Folkman, 1984, p. 843; see Table 11.1). As the following sections show, in response to workplace incivility, individuals use both emotion-focused coping to confront the troublesome emotions (Hogh & Dofradottir, 2001) and problem-focused coping to try to change their situation (Babrow, 1992). Our participants considered coping strategies that focus on the cognitive feelings and efforts to manage their experiences to be emotion-focused, while they oriented toward coping strategies that focus on the behavioral efforts and responses of the individual in order to change conditions as problem-focused (Folkman, 1984).

Emotion-Focused Coping Strategies

Findings indicate that participants in this study utilized emotion-focused coping strategies more frequently than problem-focused coping strategies. According to participants, employing emotion-focused coping helped them deal with their experiences of workplace incivility even when engaging problem-focused coping strategies failed to actually change the situation.

Social Support

In these data, all participants (n = 24) utilized social support as a coping strategy. *Social support* occurs when one individual helps another individual cope with or mediate/moderate the stress felt in a particular situation (Davies, 1996; Sass & Mattson, 1999). Individuals sought social support when they felt that their own coping efforts need to be reinforced (MacGeorge, Feng, Butler, & Budarz, 2004).

Table 11.1 Coping Strategies, Descriptions, and Types

Coping Strategy	Description	Type
Change (re)Actions	Target changes reaction to uncivil behavior or changes actions in response to uncivil behavior.	Problem-focused
Complain	Target tells others about dissatisfaction, pain, resentment, etc. Also known as "venting."	Emotion-focused
Confront	Target presents a complaint regarding the uncivil behavior for acknowledgement by the instigator (either directly or through others).	Problem-focused
Continue Cycle of Incivility	Target is uncivil to others.	Emotion-focused
Engage in Activities Outside of Organization	Target becomes occupied with activities outside of the organization (i.e., watching television, reading).	Emotion-focused
Ignore	Target refrains from noticing the uncivil behavior (i.e., to "tune out" or to accept as normal to the organization).	Emotion-focused
Learn Skills or Techniques	Target learns ways in which the instigator can be managed or interacted with in order to minimize the uncivil behavior.	Problem-focused
Justify	Target makes sense of or justifies uncivil behavior.	Emotion-focused
Retaliate	Target intentionally returns like behavior (i.e., to requite).	Emotion-focused
React Emotionally	Target reacts with an emotional response (i.e., cry, use humor, internalize feelings).	Emotion-focused
Social Support	Target seeks support of others (i.e., colleagues, family, friends, management).	Emotion-focused
Withdraw	Target seeks to remove him/herself from the situation (i.e., avoid, disconnect).	Emotion-focused

For example, Lauren, a director at a university, reported receiving social support from colleagues who were also experiencing workplace incivility and could "commiserate about the effects of that behavior." Lauren's description echoes the experiences of many of these participants ($n = 15$) who indicated that they would combine their resources and efforts to confront similar emotion-based problem(s) (Lyons, Mickelson, Sullivan, & Coyne, 1998). Thus, emotional support (such as listening and empathy) assists individuals with coping (Monge & Contractor, 2001; Sass & Mattson, 1999).

In another example of social support, Lynette, a paralegal, explained how a counselor, available through her employer's Employee Assistance Program (EAP), was invaluable for her situation because she learned "tools" to cope with her experiences. As an example of social support through information (Monge & Contractor, 2001; Sass & Mattson, 1999), the counselor provided Lynette knowledge and resources to use as tools for coping with her situation.

Such examples highlight how dyadic coping occurs when another person recognizes an individual's stressful situation and then reacts in either a helpful or unhelpful manner (e.g., offering support, engaging in mutual problem solving, reacting with contempt; Maguire & Sahlstein, 2007). We found that participants generally used dyadic coping ($n = 20$) when they perceived these other people or groups could help them in some way (i.e., offering support; engaging in mutual problem solving). Specifically, targets reported seeking the support of counselors, co-workers, EAPs, family, friends, Human Resources, support groups, mentors, office managers, office mates, supervisors, and upper management.

Because organizations are formed through relationships where individuals communicate in order to create their organization's culture and interpret the context of their surroundings (Lutgen-Sandvik &

McDermott, 2008), communal and dyadic coping responses to uncivil behavior helped many participants (n = 11) navigate organizational relationships where uncivil behavior was present. When social support allows individuals to mediate the effects of stress they experience (Monge & Contractor, 1999) due to workplace incivility, they can remain with the organization.

Complain to Others

To cope with workplace civility, people often complain to other people (n = 17), including coaches, colleagues, counselors, EAP and/or HR, family, friends, managers, and mentors. For example, Kathryn, a paralegal at a large law firm, explained that sitting next to a co-worker whom she could talk to throughout the day made her feel "a little better" because she felt that person was able to share in her "pain" and "misery." Additionally, complaining allowed individuals to tell their "stories" to others. As Darla, a paralegal at another large firm, related: "Basically we kind of vent, get it out of our system, and move on." Often in telling their stories to others, individuals feel validated and are able to cope with workplace incivility.

Justify to Themselves

Many participants reported that they justify workplace incivility to cope (n = 14). Participants noted that, in some cases, a strange work environment or a unique situation could account for workplace incivility. For example, Lauren, the university director, felt that a blending of personal and professional lives might cause uncivil behavior to emerge. In her example, a husband and wife work together in her department, in an arrangement Lauren described as "very separate, but only by one step" because of a lack of boundaries between the two. She also mentioned other work colleagues who had a father-daughter relationship. For Lauren, these types of work arrangements "breed crossing those lines simply due to the fact that you've got people who have personal and professional relationships."

Ignore Uncivil Behavior

Other participants chose to ignore workplace incivility to cope with their situation (n = 8). Targets reported ignoring the instigator, the uncivil acts, or both. Some individuals chose to ignore the instigator or the uncivil acts to minimize the emotional pain they felt when experiencing uncivil behavior. For example, Caitlin, an administrative assistant at a university, explained that she's "not a confrontational person," and when confronted with uncivil behavior she ignores it so that it "rolls off of [her]." Similarly, Jessie, an administrative assistant who eventually confronted her instigator, first tried to ignore uncivil behavior by shaking it off and letting it go by putting it out of her mind. Yet, other participants ignore uncivil behavior by accepting the behavior as normal to the organization. As Darla, the paralegal, repeatedly noted: "It's just the way it is. And it's not going to change." For Darla, the uncivil behavior from the attorney with whom she works is common and will not be confronted by the organization. Consequently, Darla feels that she must ignore the behavior by accepting it as a normal part of her routine within the organization.

Engage in Activities Outside Work

In an effort to cope, some individuals engaged in activities or hobbies outside of the workplace (n = 8). For example, Lisa, an account clerk in an academic department, enjoys reading and completing sudoku puzzles, while Helena likes to "veg out" out by watching television. Some participants related that they enjoy going out with friends and colleagues for drinks after work or on weekends.

As Reece, the web vocations manager, explained, socializing with colleagues outside of the office allowed trust to be built. Reece told us how she was able to "[bond] over the personal things discussed over alcohol—things you don't talk about in the office." Similarly, Kathryn, the paralegal, shared that doing enjoyable things outside work allowed her to disengage from workplace incivility experienced during her work day. For these individuals, engaging in activities outside the workplace helped them cope with the uncivil work environment.

React Emotionally

Some individuals found themselves reacting emotionally to uncivil treatment ($n = 7$), in contrast to previously discussed coping strategies that were more active or participatory in nature. For example, some participants reported internalizing their feelings by not talking about them; others would cry when away from the organization and recalling their experiences. Lisa described being "thick skinned," and others, like Darla and Betsy, used humor to cope. As Darla explained, "It's a joke because everyone knows it goes on. And you kinda' laugh about it because there's not really much else you can do." Lauren, the university director, likens the uncivil behavior experienced to a game that must be survived (i.e., *Survivor*) where the winner is the last one remaining. Similarly, Lynette, the paralegal, likened the uncivil behavior to a battle that must be fought. The use of humor and the reframing of workplace incivility as a game or a battle constitute ways in which individuals attempt to emotionally cope with their situation and to describe the pain they feel. Such use of metaphors aligns with research that found targets of workplace bullying use metaphors to convey the magnitude of their resulting emotional pain (Tracy et al., 2006).

Retaliate

Some individuals ($n = 4$) were unable to use a coping technique that allowed them to feel validated. Instead, they turned to retaliation—purposefully getting back at an individual or an organization to feel vindicated. Participants report using retaliation, or responding to a behavior with the same or a similar behavior, as a coping method for the emotions felt when they experience workplace incivility. As Jonathan, an architect, explained, he no longer feels connected to his organization so he is continually "looking for clients basically to steal." Lisa, the account clerk, has become "thick skinned" and behaves in a "brash" manner to others. She feels that responding in any other way is a "waste of time" and often would not be worth the effort. Similarly, Reece, the web manager, provided an example of retaliating through back and forth email exchanges where she was rude back to an individual who she felt had been uncivil. As she explained, she and a colleague exchanged emails and her language became "catty." This type of exchange did not stop the uncivil behavior but seemed to perpetuate it. Yet, as participants explained, being able to retaliate allowed them to cope.

Continue the Cycle of Incivility

Some participants found that rather than, or in addition to, employing one or more of the coping techniques previously discussed, they began to enable incivility in various ways ($n = 3$). Perpetuating uncivil behavior was internal to the organization and external to others. As participants reflected, perpetuating incivility differs from retaliation because it is not intentional. Participants did not report using perpetuation to solve a problem, but instead to cope with the emotions being experienced as a result of the situation. For example, Helena, an administrative assistant at a large stock brokerage firm, found that she encouraged uncivil behavior from stock brokers by prioritizing tasks according to the "bigger headache." By placing the work of uncivil individuals first, she rewarded their uncivil behavior. Darla, the paralegal, also admitted that, at times, she could be uncivil back, which seemed to continue the pattern of incivility between her and the instigator. In her own words, "There are times when I can go overboard and I guess it does piss people off."

Withdraw

Yet for others, ignoring workplace incivility is not enough, and they must withdraw ($n = 13$) from the uncivil person, their job, and/or the organization. Withdrawal encompasses avoidance, disconnectedness, and in some cases leaving the organization. Withdrawal comprises an emotion-focused coping strategy because the individual seeks to limit experiencing negative emotions. For Helena, an administrative assistant, avoiding the uncivil behavior became one of the easiest ways to cope while at work. She found herself doing the actual work in the evenings after everyone had gone home. As a result, she worked many extra hours in a week and also physically disconnected herself from individuals outside the organization. Mitch, a software engineer, also avoided the uncivil person by leaving his desk, even though he said it hurt his productivity.

Other participants found themselves withdrawing from their jobs. For example, Helena, the administrative assistant, began to feel complacent and stopped caring about work. Similarly, Lauren, the university director, also withdrew from her job, spending as much time away from the office as she could by working in other locations. Glenda, a paralegal, pursued an internal transfer to a different part of the organization.

Other participants withdrew from the organization by thinking of their job as temporary and by planning a future outside of the organization. As Kathryn, a paralegal, described, "I realized that this is just a job. It was not a career for me." Joshua, a publisher in the automobile industry, held similar thoughts, "I was planning my future in line without that company for sure." Instead, he was planning how and when he would quit and what he would do for his next job. Jessica, a paralegal, actively looked for another job once her threshold for uncivil behavior had been reached, saying "I felt [that leaving the organization] was going to be an easy transition for me." In all of these cases, the targets became disconnected in some way from the uncivil person, the job, or the organization.

Problem-Focused Coping Strategies

Similar to the small body of scholarship regarding how individuals cope with bullying from a problem-focused perspective, this study found targets engaged three additional problem-focused coping strategies: confronting the instigator, changing their own (re)actions, and learning skills/tools. This research extends previous findings regarding the reactions of targets to different types of workplace bullying that included assertiveness, avoidance, and seeking help (Djurkovic et al., 2005). The following paragraphs further illustrate these findings regarding problem-focused coping.

Confront the Instigator

Other participants chose to confront the instigator by presenting a difference or something unpleasant for their acknowledgement. This confrontation varied in that it could be direct ($n = 8$), indirect through other individuals such as managers ($n = 12$), or both directly and indirectly ($n = 4$). Jessie, an administrative assistant, talked about directly confronting someone who was rude to her by throwing work on her desk instead of asking her for assistance and politely handing it to her. She recalled how she threw the work right back at the individual and told him not to throw work at her.

However, some individuals never directly confront the instigator of uncivil behavior. Instead, they confront the instigator indirectly through management at either the supervisory or human resources (HR) level. Elaine, a HR professional in a law firm, found herself in a situation where an attorney was upset and began calling her at her home to yell at her. When this incident occurred, Elaine notified her supervisor and asked for his assistance in resolving the problem. Similarly, Darla, the paralegal, turned to her office manager because the attorney that she worked for was being uncivil toward her on a daily basis. These individuals did not feel comfortable with direct confrontation, so they chose indirect confrontation through others to cope with their respective situations.

Change (re)Actions

While some individuals opted to withdraw from and/or leave the organization, others decided to simply change their own actions and/or reactions ($n = 10$) in an attempt to change their situation (problem-focused coping). Lauren, the university director, learned to utilize breathing techniques, take a walk, and divert her attention to other non-stressful areas of her work. Mitch, a software engineer, also changed his (re)action to uncivil behavior by using headphones at work.

Others took a more active approach to changing their (re)actions to the uncivil behavior. Cynthia, a director of financial affairs for a university department, began to develop relationships with her instigator(s) in an attempt to minimize the uncivil behavior she was experiencing. She explained that she put a lot of "time and effort" into developing these relationships in order to establish a rapport and build trust. She indicated that doing so made a "huge improvement" in her work experiences.

Similarly, Lisa, the account clerk, and Lynette, the paralegal, both reacted by learning not to take things personally. Lisa stated that she was practiced at "considering the source," and Lynette began to tell herself the uncivil behavior was "just how [my boss] is." These individuals monitored their reactions by not taking on blame through personalizing the situation. All of these participants took it upon themselves to place great effort into changing their own behaviors in order to avoid or minimize the effects of workplace incivility.

Learn Skills and Techniques

Some targets ($n = 7$) managed their situation through learning various skills to either combat or eliminate uncivil behavior. For example, Lacey, a fundraiser at a university, sought assistance from her organization's EAP when she found herself experiencing uncivil behavior from her direct supervisor. The EAP sent Lacey to a counselor who helped her develop a "tool kit" in order to cope with the situation. With this resource, Lacey read books and completed exercises that taught her how to deal with uncivil individuals. For example, she learned to keep all communication with the uncivil person fact-based. Lacey also mentally documented what she felt a manager should not do. She felt that this type of learning would be beneficial to her later in her career if she were to ever become a manager. As previously mentioned, Lauren, the university director, also acquired techniques for coping with uncivil individuals in the workplace. She began to see a counselor for support and strategies to divert her attention away from uncivil behaviors. During Lauren's counseling sessions for managing work stress, she attained breathing techniques and realized the value of taking a short walk or using another work project to divert her attention from the workplace incivility and the stress that she was experiencing. For these participants, actively confronting the uncivil behavior through skills they have learned to help combat or eliminate uncivil behavior enables them to cope with their situation.

Typology of Coping Strategies

Following Bell and Kozlowski (2007), this study developed a typology that created a "schema [to establish] similarities and differences" and then categorize the coping strategies into divergent types (Bell & Kozlowski, 2007, p. 21). Our findings show that individuals utilize various emotion- and problem-focused coping techniques in order to manage the uncivil behavior that they experience within the workplace (see Table 11.1). We also noted that participants' coping strategies varied along

		Regard for the Organization/Job	
Effort to maintain a positive relationship with the instigator	High	*High* Change (re)Actions Confront Complain Ignore Justify Learn React Emotionally Social Support	*Low*
	Low		Continue Cycle of Incivility Engage in Activities Outside of the Organization Retaliate Withdrawal

Figure 11.1 Participants' Coping Strategies Varied Along Two Dimensions: Regard for the Organization/Job and Effort to Maintain a Positive Relationship With the Instigator.

two dimensions—regard for their organization/job and effort made to maintain their relationship with the instigator. Participants could be described as having: (1) high regard for their organization/ job; (2) low regard for their organization/job; (3) making high effort to maintain a relationship with the instigator; and (4) making a low effort to maintain a relationship with the instigator. The next paragraphs describe the coping strategies that emerged in terms of these variations (see Figure 11.1).

Some participants had a high regard for the organization/job and made a high effort to maintain their relationships with the instigator. These individuals employed coping strategies including *change their (re)action* towards uncivil behavior, *utilize social support networks*, *react emotionally*, *confront* the individual directly, *learn* various skills, *justify* the uncivil behavior, *ignore* the uncivil behavior, and *complain* to others. We also noted another variation in that some participants had a low regard for their organization/job and also made a low effort to maintain their relationship with the instigator. These individuals employed coping strategies including *engaging in activities* outside of the workplace, *withdrawal* from the organization, *retaliating*, and *continuing the cycle of incivility*. Within these variations, those who have a high regard for their organization/job also made a high effort to maintain their relationship with the instigator. On the contrary, those who have a low regard for their organization/ job also made a low effort to maintain their relationship with the instigator.

These data revealed targets' coping strategies to be at two extremes of the four dimensions and also noted the intersection of these extremes. While some targets moved from one extreme (high regard for their organization/job and making a high effort to maintain their relationship with the instigator) to the next (low regard for their organization/job and making a low effort to maintain their relationship with the instigator), some for example moved from complaining to seeking new employment, the middle dimensions (high regard for their organization/job and making a low effort to maintain their relationship with the instigator; low regard for their organization/job and making a high effort to maintain their relationship with the instigator) and their intersection were not exposed by these data. This finding affirms the need for future research.

Discussion

Findings from this study present a complex and varied description of how individuals (targets) cope with or handle workplace incivility as it is perceived to be a stressful situation (Folkman, 1984).

The types of coping strategies that targets employ include utilizing social support, complaining, justifying, withdrawing, ignoring uncivil behavior, engaging in activities outside of work, reacting emotionally, retaliating, continuing the cycle of incivility, confronting the instigator, changing (re) actions, and learning skills and techniques. The current study constitutes a departure from the (limited) research regarding how individuals cope with destructive workplace behaviors (e.g., rudeness, bullying, humiliation, verbal abuse, workplace aggression) by positioning workplace incivility as an overarching construct that recognizes even seemingly small acts of uncivil behavior within the two dimensions of intensity and intentionality (Sypher, 2004).

Theoretical and Practical Contributions

This chapter contributes to and extends existing research by exploring workplace incivility through a communicative lens (see also Lutgen-Sandvik & Sypher, 2009; Lutgen-Sandvik, 2006; Sypher, 2004; Tracy et al., 2006). This study also extends scholarship (e.g., Djurkovic et al., 2005) by uncovering individuals' problem- and emotion-focused coping responses and showing that emotion-focused coping is employed more frequently than problem-focused coping strategies.

First, unlike previous empirical work, which has tended to focus on more intense forms of workplace incivility (i.e., bullying; aggression), this study empirically examines lower-intensity workplace incivility. In so doing, it reminds researchers and practitioners that even seemingly small acts of incivility may be consequential (Sypher, 2004) and introduces ways that targets may be coping with incivility in the workplace.

Second, the current study examines how individuals cope with emotionally painful or stressful situations that are experienced when a target is subjected to uncivil workplace behaviors. Tracy and colleagues (2006) examined participant interviews and drawings and conducted a metaphor analysis "to articulate and explore the emotional pain of workplace bullying and, in doing so, [help] to translate its devastation and encourage change" (p. 148). An inductive approach is important in that it helps make sense of bullying as an emotionally painful experience. By studying individuals' reactions to workplace incivility, this study offers empirical evidence that explores additional emotion-focused aspects of destructive workplace behavior(s).

Third, by examining how individuals manage workplace incivility, this study sheds light on how those individuals attempt to return the civil discourse to their organization, particularly in terms of the coping types (social support, justify, confront, withdraw, change (re)actions, ignore, engage in activities, learn). Targets' (re)actions to uncivil behavior reflected their perceptions about ways of minimizing or mitigating the uncivil discourse. These categories contrast with coping strategies such as complaining, reacting emotionally, retaliating, and continuing the cycle of incivility where often times the target would themselves engage in uncivil discourse as a coping strategy.

Fourth, this study shows that some targets ignore uncivil behavior by accepting the behavior as an organizational norm. This approach is problematic as doing so may create a socially constructed reality that allows workplace incivility to be normalized as acceptable behavior. Additionally, these data suggest that the targets of workplace incivility and those who provide them support are engaged in problem-focused and emotion-focused coping efforts to minimize either the uncivil behavior(s) they experience or the stress of being treated in an uncivil manner. Importantly, participants used emotion-focused coping more often, indicating that they are either unable or unwilling to employ problem-focused coping techniques.

Findings from this study are also of practical use to organizations. Because individuals are spending more time at work than they have in the past (Hewlett & Luce, 2006; Sypher, 2004), it is important to understand what allows workplace incivility to develop and persist. While many organizations have programs that specifically focus on sexual harassment or workplace violence, many lack policies that cover other forms of workplace incivility. Additionally, managers often turn a blind eye toward acts of incivility, especially within a hierarchical structure amid an individualistic culture (Namie, 2003). Management's unwillingness to acknowledge that workplace incivility is inappropriate, and perhaps even siding with the aggressor when the target seeks assistance, constitute fairly common management responses (Namie, 2003). Findings from this study may encourage organizations to consider policies governing acts of workplace incivility and to provide assistance to employees who are experiencing workplace incivility.

Limitations and Future Directions

We must acknowledge the limitations of this study. First, the participants interviewed in this study came from different work units and organizations, thus limiting the ability to understand any additional variations surrounding workplace incivility within organizations. For example, the nature of this particular sample limited the researchers' ability to determine whether the organization's culture or various power relationships within the organization played a role in contributing to incivility. For these reasons, future research should attempt to investigate incivility in *one* organization and do so longitudinally. Second, our participants were primarily women ($n = 20$). The disparity between the number of women and men in this study may limit our ability to understand any gender issues that may be present. For example, the nature of this study may limit our ability to discover whether gender roles or other gender-based factors play a role in contributing to workplace incivility and/or affect how individuals cope. Finally, this study relies on self-reported data and is therefore inherently subjective in nature as participants self-identified as targets of workplace incivility. Although we do not question the merits of these individuals' perceptions, we recognize that we obtained the perspectives of only one party. Tracy and colleagues (2006) noted that some critics of research that focuses only on the target's perspective(s) say these experiences sound too egregious to be true. Thus, future studies should be designed so that the relational aspects of incivility can be examined; that is, the ways in which incivility is constituted communicatively between the aggressor and target(s). Doing so will be important for future theorizing.

Notes

1 The terms target and victim have been used interchangeably (Namie, 2003) in research on workplace bullying, workplace incivility, workplace aggression, and workplace violence. For this chapter, the term target will be used to indicate those who are targets of or who have been victimized by those engaging in destructive workplace behaviors.
2 Experiences of third-party organizational members, often referred to as witnesses (Harvey et al., 2007; Lutgen-Sandvik, 2006; Pearson, Andersson, & Porath, 2000), are also important because witnesses to destructive workplace behaviors, or even those hearing about it secondhand, may also experience stress, decreased productivity, health issues, or engage in exiting the organization (Lutgen-Sandvik, 2006). However, witness accounts exceed the scope of this chapter, which is why the focus of this study is the target.

VOICES FOR VISIBILITY

It's More Than Personality Clash: The Escalation of Bullying

Anonymous

Immediately upon my doctorate graduation, I secured a tenure-track faculty job in a private liberal arts college. The demographic composite of the college was quite homogeneous, with over 90% of the faculty and 80% of the student body Caucasian. I was one of the two international professors on the campus. I was so excited about my first job in the U.S. and fully prepared to embark on a new journey in my career. I felt that fortune was smiling on me. Little did I know that this position was just the beginning of a nightmare.

On the first day of my work, I met my colleagues:

> *Kathy was very active in different social events, which made her well connected at the college. She just turned tenure that year, but without promotion because she didn't have any publications yet. Her husband, a senior faculty member, worked as Chair in another department.*
>
> *Andrew had worked as a temporary faculty member for three years. If he didn't transition to tenure-track after his fifth year, his contract could not be renewed any more. He seemed to align very closely with the Chair, first Emma and then Kathy.*
>
> *Emma, originally from Canada, was the Chair of the department in my first year. She seemed professional and easy-going.*

Everything seemed to go smoothly in my first year. My research and teaching performance had met the school standards with just a few comments on my accent, although the majority of the students didn't have a problem in understanding me. I totally understood as students were not used to the difference yet. To address that concern, I enrolled in a professional accent reduction program in the summer and received positive reactions from my students.

The Beginning of the Bullying: Is It Personality Clash?

In my second year, Emma left for some unknown reasons. Kathy became the new Chair. Being sociable, she liked to talk everything through. I often saw her chatting with others in the hallway. I also joined the chit-chat sometimes, but as a new faculty member, I had to focus on new course preparations and research in my office most of the time due to the busy work schedule. My efforts paid off; I got two publications after the first year. Despite our college's efforts to enhance the weight of faculty research, Kathy didn't seem to pay much attention to this aspect. Actually, she felt a little uncomfortable when talking about research since she didn't have any publications yet. She once said to me that I should focus more on teaching instead of research. I acknowledged her comments and worked harder to improve my teaching. Overall, I thought that we were on good terms, even though we had totally different personalities, cultural backgrounds, and work styles. I respected the difference.

However, after a semester, things started to change subtly. In department meetings, Kathy occasionally ignored me. Once, I proposed an internship opportunity for our majors that I found through my personal networks. She just responded coldly, "you should talk to career service." Yet, when Andrew or Maggie (a new hire) proposed similar opportunities, Kathy expressed appreciation and asked us to post flyers on the department board and inform our students in class. Kathy constantly interrupted me as I tried to contribute ideas. I lived close to campus, so I always volunteered to represent the department on Open Houses and family visitation days, whereas other faculty members opted not to attend such functions on weekend mornings. However, Kathy took those services for granted and never acknowledged my work on behalf of the department in any formal or informal talk. I was a little disappointed.

Things that evolved in the next semester made me even more confused. Although seemingly outgoing, she was the type of person who tended to avoid conflict. Whenever she was not satisfied with someone, she would talk behind his/her back instead of confronting directly. In an informal office chat, she mentioned Emma, the old Chair. I had never seen them have any problem when Emma was still here. After Emma left, I realized the seemingly good relationship was just on the surface. As always, Kathy talked about how much better our department had become without Emma. I only spent a year with Emma and barely knew her, so I didn't make any comments. While talking to Andrew and Maggie, she turned to me and asked, "Do you know Emma? . . . She was no good." Before I even responded, she said, "Oh, I forgot, she hired you." I was speechless at that moment.

I sensed something was wrong, but I didn't know what it was. I made efforts to socialize more with her and reduce the distance, but things didn't change for the better. She never talked to me as she spoke to the other two faculty members. I found her talking behind my back with the other two colleagues when I walked into the office suite, and they switched topics quickly after spotting me. Learning the Chair's attitude, the other two members also seemed to shun me. I felt a sense of isolation and exclusion, which added extra strain to my already busy work. I found myself constantly persuading myself that it might be just the cultural difference. The once ambitious and hard-working new graduate had turned into a stressful and confused member struggling to be recognized by the Chair.

A Critical Event: The Interim Review

An incident that happened just before my interim review pushed me further toward the abyss of despair. As a policy, all tenure-track faculty members have an interim review at the end of the second year. I was pretty confident about the approaching interim review as my publication record exceeded the school's expectations and my teaching performance and service had met the school's standards. However, a few weeks before the meeting with faculty personnel committee (FPC), Kathy had a talk with me in her office.

Kathy: *As you know, you're going through interim review this semester. Your publication record looks pretty good. Maybe you should try to apply for some research schools. I'd be glad to write a recommendation letter for you.*
         I was shocked and paused for a while . . .
Me: *Thank you. I like doing research as well as teaching, and I like my current job. Is there anything I should be concerned about for this interim review?*
Kathy: *No, nothing. I just want to let you get prepared just in case.*

Voices for Visibility

After this conversation, I talked to another senior faculty member outside my department. I wanted to know if I should worry about the interim review and if I should start looking for another job. She was equally shocked at what the Chair had said to me. In her ten years of experience at the college, it was only in very rare conditions that tenure-track faculty got terminated after the interim review, such as if the doctoral degree had not been completed yet. Given my strong record, I should have had nothing to worry about. I felt a little relieved after talking to the senior faculty member.

As expected, I successfully passed the interim review that semester. However, after the interim review, my work situation got even worse. The school policy stated that every faculty member should have one course release after the interim review in order to give them a break to reflect and improve. However, not only was I not granted the course release, but I was also assigned several completely new courses that semester. I had wondered if I should talk to Kathy, but I hadn't wanted to offend her in the critical interim review period when the class schedule for next semester was supposed to be made. Maybe she had thought I couldn't pass the interim? Maybe she just forgot? But, after knowing that I had passed my interim review, she still didn't grant the course release, which was a serious violation of our faculty handbook policy. I had to take the extra assignment as students had already registered for my classes. She acted as if nothing had happened and didn't even acknowledge my overload at any occasion—formal or informal. A few years later, when it was Andrew's turn for interim review, she had already made the plan in course reduction one semester before his review.

The constant exclusion, lack of recognition, and heavy workload finally took a toll on my health. I no longer felt excited, but depressed at work. No matter how hard I worked and what I accomplished, I simply could not get a single word of recognition from her. Instead, my weaknesses were always magnified. I almost felt like I was worthless and I didn't deserve this job. I started dreaming about a crystal ball inside which there was a little person—me: I shouted, but people outside could not hear me.

Only after I left this institution a few years later did I finally learn all that had transpired during my interim review. Before I left, I talked to the person who had chaired the faculty personnel committee (FPC) during my interim review. The FPC Chair told me that Kathy had made the worst comments about me in the meeting with the FPC as part of my interim review. Basically, she labeled me as a hiring mistake. However, after reviewing my records and talking to me, the FPC found out that Kathy's statements were far from the truth. Instead, the members of the FPC saw a promising young faculty member who had satisfactorily met every aspect of the college standards. The FPC realized that I was working in a hostile work environment. For the first time in the FPC's history, they even wrote a special letter to the Dean, recommending that she provide more "structural" support for me. However, the Dean didn't do anything to intervene. The Dean was not popular at the college. Faculty had complained about her practices in several college-wide faculty meetings. She connected closely with Kathy, and they often socialized outside the workplace.

The Tenure Drama

After the interim review, my work situation deteriorated further. Kathy was obviously surprised at my survival of the interim review, but pretended to be happy for me. I didn't know she had viciously attacked me in the meeting with the FPC. In a small liberal arts college, tenure review only takes one step. The Chair and the candidate submit the documents separately and meet the FPC separately. The candidate doesn't know the Chair's attitude beforehand. Thus, the process lacked transparency. I blindly believed that she supported me at the meeting, enabling me to pass the interim review. I appreciated her. Never did I realize that she evaluated me negatively in her letter and during the closed-door meeting with the FPC.

In the following years, she asked me to constantly open new courses every semester and join various committees on campus to represent the department even if I had more than enough service

129

for my position, providing no break for me to reflect on and consolidate the courses that I already taught and dragging down my professional development. I was out of breath. In addition, the numerous put-downs, ignoring, and exclusions shattered my self-esteem. I constantly felt that I was not good enough. Others in my department easily brushed aside my ideas and failed to recognize my contributions. I was an outcast in this group—I was different in appearance, accent, and the treatment I received.

Finally, it reached my tenure year. Kathy came to my office and offered to help me prepare for the meeting with the FPC. She asked me how I was going to answer some of the potential questions. I responded without any reservation and felt relieved that she was going to support me for my tenure. The reality proved me wrong again. Since she didn't beat me in my interim review, she just wanted to test my responses so that she could prepare her strategies in the meeting with the FPC, something that I learned only after receiving the letter from the FPC full of negative quotes from my Chair.

In addition, Kathy formed allies with another faculty member—Andrew, who had been converted to tenure-track and was going through his interim review the next semester. According to school policy, all tenure-track faculty in the department were allowed to submit an evaluation letter for my tenure review. Andrew submitted one, too. That semester, I often found Kathy and Andrew whispering in the office suite. When I stepped in, they would stop talking and go back to their own offices. Later, I found out that Andrew had written a negative letter about me, although he had never observed a single class of mine.

The big day came. As a rule, Kathy went inside to meet with the FPC for the first half hour. After she came out, I gave her a warm hug. I thought she supported me. Whenever I thought about that hug later, I felt so stupid and naïve. As soon as my meeting with FPC began, I sensed that the atmosphere was wrong; I faced very challenging questions, and my responses fell on absolute silence. I felt that they were closely examining whatever I said—more like an interrogation. The FPC Chair finally asked one question: "Do you feel like you have the support from the Chair?" I paused for a while and then said, "yes." I lied because I didn't want to give them the impression that I didn't get along well with the Chair. They might think that I "lacked collegiality." At that moment, I was not aware that my Chair already bad-mouthed me in the first half of the meeting, resulting in the challenges, doubts, and examinations from the committee. The Chair had already set up the tone before I even entered the room. I had been stabbed in the back, again!

The day after the meeting, Kathy pretended to show concern and asked me how the meeting had gone and if I had got any response. Soon after, I got the negative letter from the FPC, which used lots of negative direct quotes from my Chair. I was shocked. How could this happen? She had never mentioned those negative comments to me in annual reviews or in face-to-face conversations. I had thought she supported me! I wrote a letter responding to each of the negative evaluations from my Chair. I showed them evidence that the evaluations were far from the truth.

Strangely, the next day, I found that the annual reviews located in the department public drive had been replaced by some new ones which I'd never seen before. Kathy normally posted annual reviews on the department public drive for us to read at the end of each year, but she never asked me to sign any annual reviews before she submitted them to the Dean, which actually violated the faculty handbook policy. I read the annual reviews every year, and none of the comments in her FPC letter had ever been mentioned. However, the new ones she uploaded within one day after my FPC meetings were all negative, similar to her negative comments reflected in the FPC's letter. The computer system showed that the new annual reviews for the past five years were all created at the same time, the day after my FPC meeting. She falsified information to bring me down. I emailed the FPC Chair and learned that the FPC had requested additional evidence from her the preceding day. Finally, FPC decided to submit their recommendation, her letter, and my response letter together to the Dean, which had never happened in the history of FPC. Until now, everything came to light. She had stabbed me in the back throughout the process.

A few days later, the Dean met me and told me that I was going to receive a negative recommendation. Given the negative consequences of tenure denial, she suggested I submit the resignation letter myself. I refused. I had to appeal; the information on the letter was totally untrue. I needed to let people know what had happened throughout my years at the school.

A week later, I got another "offer" from the Dean—I could submit a "delayed resignation" within a week, meaning that I could submit the resignation at that point, but the resignation wouldn't become effective until the end of the following year. She emphasized the negative consequences of tenure denial again and told me that this outcome would give me some time to look for another job without the stigma of the tenure denial. I realize now why she pushed me to accept the offer. If I had appealed, she would have looked bad because she neglected to intervene and provide structural support according to the recommendations of the FPC at my interim review. The Dean didn't do anything when my Chair violated faculty handbook policies in my course release and annual review signature procedures.

I was frustrated with and angry at the "offers." If I accepted the offer, I would have to give up my right to appeal. I wouldn't be able to seek justice after years of unfair treatment and bullying. If I didn't accept, I was worried about whether any other institutions would care about the "stigma." I couldn't envision any way for me to explain the complicated story in the interviews. What if she retaliated by bad-mouthing me in my job search? I did not want to risk my entire career. After all, I had a family with two kids to support. I also heard that faculty who appealed at this institution stood almost no chance of winning. After a week's deliberation and sleepless nights, I submitted the resignation letter. After all the drama and torture, I was too exhausted to start another fight, especially one that might already be doomed from the beginning. I had been totally disappointed with the school and was tired of the politics. Maybe it was time to leave this institution and start a new life.

A few years passed since I left the institution. I moved on and obtained a new faculty job, but the trauma has not subsided yet. It was like a nightmare, one in which I was sucked into a downward swirl with no bottom. After the fall, I had to gradually pick up all the broken pieces—my self-esteem, my health, and my ability to trust people again. However, I know I will eventually recover and stand up firmly for myself one day, because no one deserves to be treated as I was in my very first faculty position.

★★Bullying in the Academy★★

12
U.S. K–12 BULLYING PREVENTION POLICY
A CHAT Analysis

Geoffrey Luurs

Bullying is prevalent in U.S. schools, with one in five students experiencing this negative communicative behavior at some point (National Center for Education Statistics, 2016). Because of bullying's prevalence, every U.S. state has passed laws for bullying prevention, legislation that can be enforced in primary and secondary education institutions (McCallion & Feder, 2013). Legislative requirements vary state-to-state, but many require school districts to adopt anti-bullying policies (StopBullying. gov, 2017b). K–12 bullying prevention programs have reduced bullying behaviors by 20–23% and bullying victimization by 17–20% (Farrington & Ttofi, 2009; McCallion & Feder, 2013). In spite of these promising results, continued analysis of anti-bullying policies and prevention techniques is required to sustain these efforts and advance policy into the future. This chapter examines a sample of district-wide anti-bullying policies through the lens of Cultural-Historical Activity Theory (CHAT, Engeström, 1987) to highlight strengths and gaps in K–12 bullying prevention policies. This study serves as a model for how districts in other parts of the United States can analyze and enhance their own policies. The analysis begins with an explication of the sample's characteristics.

Sample

I explored a representative sample of the five largest school districts in North Carolina. Currently, no federal laws specifically address bullying, but some targeted bullying violates several federal statutes (Ali, 2010). As noted elsewhere (West & Turner, this volume), bullying on the basis of race, color, national origin, sex, religion, or on the basis of disability falls under the purview of Title VI of the Civil Rights Act of 1964, Title IX of the Education Amendments of 1972, Section 504 of the Rehabilitation Act of 1973, and Title II of the Americans with Disabilities Act of 1990. Despite the lack of codified law regarding bullying, the U.S. Department of Health and Human Services (2014a) and the U.S. Department of Education (2010) have produced a guideline of key components for state-level anti-bullying policies.

A single U.S. state was analyzed because all districts' policies hold identical legal obligations under state law. While the policies detailed in this chapter share some similarities, they differ in terms of how the policies define and strive to prevent bullying. I selected North Carolina because it is one of seven states that has anti-bullying laws but no default policy that all school districts must follow (U.S. Department of Health and Human Services, 2014b). Interestingly, despite not having a uniform policy, North Carolina ranks near the bottom of all states in bullying prevalence (WalletHub, 2016). Further examination was merited. The districts and student enrollment included in this study were:

Wake County Public School System (159,462 students), Charlotte-Mecklenburg Schools (148,951), Guilford County Schools (71,710), Winston-Salem/Forsyth County Schools (54,552), and Cumberland County Schools (50,459). These five districts combined to serve 485,134 children, roughly one-third of all North Carolinian public school students, during the 2016–2017 school year (North Carolina State Board of Education, 2017). The Centers for Disease Control and Prevention (CDCP, 2016) found 20%, or roughly 97,000, of the students in these school districts have experienced bullying in their lifetime.

Bullying poses a health risk, and the anti-bullying policies used by these school districts can play an integral role in students' physical and mental well-being (Centers for Disease Control and Prevention, 2016). Furthermore, the CDC argues that developing positive problem solving skills, supportive families, and positive school climate all decrease bullying behaviors (Center for Disease Control and Prevention, 2016). As argued throughout this volume, Communication Studies is uniquely suited for informing bullying policies because bullying is a communicative practice. First, we must assess the existing policies for their strengths and weaknesses in how they communicate about bullying.

Policy Search

Data for this study reflect public policy information because policy dictates how schools within a district define and enforce anti-bullying measures. Additionally, these materials are accessible to students, parents, and school administrators alike and inform how stakeholders understand bullying and punishment for not adhering to the policy. After selecting the five largest school districts in the state, I searched publicly available data on each district's anti-bullying policy. For each district, I studied the first available district-administered "home page" with information about bullying as well as additional links to official policy manuals. I analyzed each home page and bullying policy for details about how the district defines, recognizes, and punishes bullying, using Cultural-Historical Activity Theory (CHAT) as a sensitizing framework. CHAT allows anti-bullying policies, and thus how bullying prevention is communicated by K–12 school districts, to be analyzed by the socio-cultural forces that contribute to the activity of "bullying prevention." Analyzing bullying prevention efforts as a system of actors, tools, and artifacts illuminates how bullying prevention outcomes are achieved through the policies themselves.

Defining Bullying Through Policy

I began by examining each district-administered home page for a definition of bullying. Three of five districts defined bullying on their respective home page. Charlotte-Mecklenburg Schools (2017a) described it as:

> Unwanted, aggressive behavior among school aged [sic] children that involves a real or perceived power imbalance. The bullying is repeated, or has the potential to be repeated, over time. Bullying includes actions such as making threats, spreading rumors, attacking someone physically or verbally, and excluding someone from a group on purpose.
>
> *(para. 2)*

Winston-Salem/Forsyth County Schools (2017) requires the behavior to be unwanted or aggressive, to intend harm, to propagate a real or perceived imbalance of power, and to be repeated. Wake County Public School System (2017) characterized bullying behaviors as "physical violence and attacks; extortion and theft; taunts, name calling and put-downs; peer group exclusion; threats and intimidation; [and] cyberbullying" (para. 1). Cumberland County Schools (2010a) provided advice for parents and community members but did not include a specific definition of bullying on their home page. Cumberland County School's policy manual defines bullying as:

> Any pattern of gestures or written, electronic or verbal communications or any physical act or any threatening communication that: (1) places a student or school employee in actual and reasonable fear of harm to his or her person or damage to his or her property; or (2) creates or is certain to create a hostile environment by substantially interfering with or impairing a student's educational performance, opportunities or benefits or by adversely altering the conditions of an employee's employment.
>
> *(sec. C, para. 2)*

Guilford County Schools (2017) provided links to their anti-bullying resources and a form to report bullying and discrimination but provided no definition on the home page. Guilford has separate bullying policies for staff (1994) and students (2009a). The staff policy (Guilford County Schools, 2009b) defines bullying as:

> Any pattern of gestures or written, electronic or verbal communications, physical act or any threatening communication . . . that places an employee in actual and reasonable fear of harm to his or her person or damage to his or her property; or creates or is certain to create a hostile environment by substantially interfering with an employee's ability to function successfully in the workplace. places a student or school employee in actual and reasonable fear of harm to his or her person or damage to his or her property or creates a hostile educational environment.
>
> *(Guilford County Schools, 2010, para. 5)*

Guilford's student policy further specifies "disrespect, intimidation, [and] threats" that interfere with a student's educational performance or a school employee's ability to do his or her work (Guilford County Schools, 2009a, para. 2).

Cultural-Historical Activity Theory for Bullying Policy Analysis

Engeström (1987) describes Cultural-Historical Activity Theory (CHAT) as a systems approach to analyzing organizational structures and behaviors. CHAT argues for prioritizing the analysis of activity systems and their motivations over individuals and their actions. CHAT suggests that the most effective units of analysis are the joint practices and behaviors that provide structure and reproduce a given system (or activity) by generating similar actions over time (Engeström & Sannino, 2010). Activity systems encompass six components, including tools, subjects, objects, rules, communities of practice, and divisions of labor. CHAT affirms that individual behaviors or actions must be situated contextually into the activity systems in which they occur in order to better understand what motivates behavior. Furthermore, activity theory elucidates the relationship among individuals, their (communicative) behaviors, and the (social) systems in which those individuals are ensconced by asking, "What is an actor doing and what motivated them to act in that way?" Using CHAT, I analyzed existing anti-bullying policies to identify institutional foci and gaps and to illuminate how institutions view, assess, and prevent bullying through policies.

Communities of Practice

A community of practice is a space (real or imagined) where groups of people share similar sets of problems, concerns, or passions about a topic. Communities help shape activity by establishing the conventions that mediate rules and labor of a given activity (Feller, 2014). In K–12 education systems, many communities of practice exist, through which behaviors are learned. Family systems, friendship groups, and school policy all shape the climate of the school environment and the behaviors practiced by individuals within a K–12 education system. Community practices inherently link with the outcomes of the activity (i.e., educating young people; preventing bullying) and the social strata that surround the activity (Ghobadi, 2013).

Bullying can happen in the physical spaces in which people congregate. The sample policies provided examples of any school building or on school premises, bus stops and on the school bus, any place where the subject is under the authority of school personnel, and any place where the behavior has direct and immediate effect on the school's ability to maintain order and discipline (Cumberland County Schools, 2010a; Wake County Public School Systems, 2015a). The policies also expanded their scope beyond on-campus behaviors. Students' off-campus behaviors that result in material disruption of school business and activities also fall under the purview of school policy (Charlotte-Mecklenburg Schools, 2008a). K–12 students also face cyberbullying in their online communities, especially on social media (Festl & Quandt, 2013; Kowalski & Limber, 2007). Time spent on the internet proportionally increases the likelihood that one will experience cyberbullying because the internet removes some physical and social barriers that prevent bullying, and some young people view the internet as a safe space for risky communicative behaviors (Arntfield, 2015; Erdur-Baker, 2010). Network positioning in a community is an important determinant of whether someone is bullied (Festl & Quandt, 2013). System-level data suggests those who only perpetrate or are victimized tend to reside on the outer fringes of the community's social strata, while those who are more centrally located in the system are more likely to be both perpetrator and victim.

The policies included in this chapter are compelling in their recognition of the types of spaces where bullying occurs. However, the policies fail to recognize bullying as a method by which some members of a community participate. The district's policies are not evident in their reflection on how bullying is viewed as a social behavior or how bullying may serve as an impetus to influencing young people in their navigation of their social spheres.

Rules

Any human activity always takes place in an environment that is constricted by the rules that constrain concepts and behaviors (Engeström, 1987). Two types of rules appeared in this sample of policies. First, definitional rules guide determinations of whether bullying has occurred. Definitional rules categorize behaviors by type and form and co-determine acceptable behavioral practices in a community. The Stop Bullying Now! Resource Kit (cf. Charlotte-Mecklenburg Schools, 2017b) describes bullying behaviors as "aggressive," "intentional," and an "imbalance of power or strength" between the bully and their target. The kit specifies that bullying behavior is often repetitive and can take on the forms of physical violence (hitting, punching, pushing), unwanted teasing or name calling (verbal aggression), intimidation using gesture or social exclusion (emotional bullying), and cyberbullying (Charlotte-Mecklenburg Schools, 2017b). The second type of rule includes those of a procedural nature that must be followed as per the guidelines of the bullying policy itself. Procedural rules include standards for reporting bullying, investigating the complaint, punishing improper behavior, and filing official reports with the State Board of Education (Cumberland County Schools, 2010b; Charlotte-Mecklenburg Schools, 2008a, 2008b; Guilford County Schools, 2009a; Wake County Public School System, 2015a; Winston-Salem/Forsyth County Schools, 2011).

Definitional and procedural rules work together to communicate to interlocutors what bullying behaviors look like and the formal processes to be followed should bullying occur. In all districts, complainants must file a report with a school administrator. Complainants should file the report with the principal or assistant principal if the bullying is perpetrated by a student (cf. Guilford County

Schools, 2009b), or the perpetrators' direct supervisor if the bullying is done by an employee (cf. Guilford County Schools, 1994). All districts require a formal investigation following a complaint where the investigator must interview all parties involved before determining a course of action. The results of that investigation, including punitive action, are then reported to the superintendent, who in turn files a yearly report to the North Carolina State Board of Education.

The sample policies clearly lay a foundation of rules that prohibits specific behaviors and provides a course of action should those rules be broken. In the education community, bullying might best be described as a rules violation. The procedural rules are reactionary in that they are only activated once a violation occurs. Developing prevention materials that are proactive in identifying where rules violations have frequently occurred in the past and are likely to occur in the future may assist in training staff to identify bullying before it happens.

Tools

Tools come in a variety of forms, both physical and abstract. Tools facilitate identification of a problem and provide a systemic response (Engeström, 1987). Tools mediate activity by helping individuals to internalize a problem and mediate a solution. They develop socially and are picked up, adapted, and used by members of a given community to participate in common cultural activities like using language, developing theory, creating technical artifacts, and establishing modes and norms of acting (Miettinen, 1999). Tools include physical objects, language choices and signs, and models used to communicate aggression or exclusion (Vandebosch & Van Cleemput, 2009). Tools help an individual accomplish a specific task or to solve specific problems by mediating behavior—tools are categorized by how they are used. Tools come in four forms: physical objects and acts, language tools, cyber tools, and prevention tools.

Physical Objects and Acts

The first category of tools are physical objects and acts used in physical bullying. Physical bullying includes gestures, pushing or shoving, hair pulling, striking, spitting, damaging personal property, physically impeding the target's movement, or any other unwelcomed physical contact or intimidation (Charlotte-Mecklenburg Schools, 2008a, 2008b; Winston-Salem/Forsyth County Schools, 2011). Wake County (2015b) specified "punching, pushing, shoving, kicking, inappropriate touching, tickling, headlocks, school pranks, teasing, fighting, or the use of available objects as weapons" as their inclusion criteria for physical bullying. Wake County's (2015a) policy manual also included "assault, impeding or blocking movement, [and] offensive touching." Two districts did not define physical tools, but forbade physical acts that produce a hostile work or learning environment (Cumberland County Schools, 2010a; Guilford County Schools, 2009a, 2010).

Language Tools

The second category of tools encompasses language tools and signs. Language tools include both verbal and nonverbal communication, such as name calling, false accusations, defamation, extorting money, directed foul language, profanity or epithets, putting down, taunting, tormenting, ganging up, laughing at others' expense, spreading rumors, extorting money, making negative comments about one's appearance, derogatory posters or cartoons, and planned social exclusion or ignoring (Charlotte-Mecklenburg Schools, 2008b; Cumberland County Schools, 2010a; Wake County Public School System, 2015b, Winston-Salem/Forsyth County Schools, 2011). Unlike physical tools, language travels beyond the immediate proximity of the bully. Rumors can spread virally. Because they attack a person's emotional well-being, the hurt may continue long after the bullying behavior has stopped (Pew Research Center, 2014).

Cyber Tools

The third type of tool involves cyber tools. Other chapters in this volume discuss the differences between bullying and cyberbullying; however, the policies included here conceptualize cyberbullying as any bullying done via digital media, including, but not limited to, email, instant messaging, short-messaging services (SMS)/text messages, social networking sites (SNS), photographs, video messages, and websites (Charlotte-Mecklenburg Schools, 2008b; Wake County Public School System, 2015b). Cyberbullying has unique features that must be considered, such as the possibility of asynchronous communication, the potential for anonymity, cyberbullies' around-the-clock access to their targets from any distance, and an amorphous but potentially large audience (Davis, Randall, Ambrose, & Orand, 2015). Cyberbullying is exceptionally dangerous because it employs both physical and language tools to affect a target's well-being.

Prevention Tools

Prevention tools comprise the category of tools. Prevention tools range from physical objects to report bullying, like a form or website, to the policies themselves, which mediate the course of action to take after a report is filed. Each district included in this sample has publicly available websites with resources that help readers to understand bullying and the districts' related policies (Charlotte-Mecklenburg Schools, 2017a; Cumberland County Schools, 2017; Winston-Salem/Forsyth County Schools, 2017; Guilford County Schools, 2017; Wake County Public School System, 2017). Four districts provided digital tools for reporting bullying, such as a phone number (WCPSS) or an online form (CMS; GCS; WS/FCS). All five districts encourage complainants to tell a teacher or school administrator, all of whom are mandatory reporters. The policies encourage students, parents, volunteers, and visitors to report as well (Charlotte-Mecklenburg Schools, 2008a, 2008b; Cumberland County Schools, 2010b; Guilford County Schools, 2009b, 2010; Wake County Public School System, 2015a; Winston-Salem/Forsyth County Schools, 2011). The internal investigation that results from the use of reporting tools also serves as a tool for preventing future bullying by determining proper recourse, needed training, and corrective actions to be taken by the school (Wake County Public School System, 2015a).

The dominant tools of an activity system are those that are deemed most useful (Engeström, 1987). The physical, language, and cyber tools used to bully have staying power, and although the policies in this sample attempt to dictate proper and improper tool usage, this volume clearly shows that bullying still occurs. Prevention tools and their related policies are the district's strongest means for action. The district's online and anonymous reporting tools invite victims and bystanders to report the bullying they experience.

Subjects and the Division of Labor

Bullying policies inherently must address the issue of subjects and labor. Subjects in an activity system are the individual actors whose behavior contributes to the overall activity. Learning behavioral norms is a part of complex interactions between subjects and the labor they produce. Engeström (1987) stated that the division of labor often allows individuals to participate in an activity system without them being fully aware of the system's objects or its motives. The issue of motivation, or intention, in anti-bullying policies ties together subjects with the actions they produce when identifying and responding to bullying behaviors. Aggression can manifest societally through the behaviors of an individual (i.e., the perpetrator) and be displayed through social processes, like interpersonal interactions. Extant bullying literature often defines bullying as an intentional behavior, which is motivated by the wants and needs of the perpetrator (Arntfield, 2015; Langos, 2012). The policies in the sample did not discuss intention and instead focused on describing labor through specific bullying behaviors and types of harassments. The policies never speculated as to why someone might bully in the first place and instead chose to classify subjects by the type of labor they produce in bullying interactions.

The policies in the sample constructed four broad categories of subjects: people who perpetrate negative behaviors (bullies), people who are targeted by those behaviors (victims), bystanders who witness the behaviors, and guardians, who provide guidance, support, and punishment should bullying occur. Those categories align with previous studies on bullying and cyberbullying (Arntfield, 2015; Salmivalli, Lagerspetz, Björkqvist, Österman, & Kaukiainen, 1996; Zych, Ortega-Ruiz, & Del Rey, 2015a). The labor of all four types of actors contributes to the formation of anti-bullying policies and, by proxy, related bullying prevention outcomes.

Bullying behaviors can be performed by anyone. The sample policies define bullies by how their behaviors violate community rules instead of by their role and function in the school system (i.e., teachers, students, administrators, visitors). The policies dictate that students follow a code of conduct, and employees, volunteers, and visitors follow board policies and school regulations (cf. Charlotte-Mecklenburg Schools, 2008a; Cumberland County Schools, 2010b). Bullying offenses may occur among fellow students, co-workers, supervisors and subordinates, employees and students, and non-employees/visitors (Cumberland County Schools, 2010a; Guilford County Schools, 2010). Upward bullying—bullying which targets someone in a higher position of power—can occur when students bully employees (Charlotte-Mecklenburg Schools, 2008a). Should a person file a complaint, the district identifies the person conducting the bullying behavior as an "alleged perpetrator" (cf. Cumberland County Schools, 2010b). Labeling a subject as an alleged perpetrator has a cascading effect as that person is then investigated and sometimes punished for their behavior.

Targets are those who have received "any pattern of gestures or written, electronic or verbal communications, or any physical act or any threatening communication" that causes the recipient to fear harm to one's self or one's property or which creates a hostile environment that impairs the educational workspace (Cumberland County Schools, 2010a). A target's labor comprises of bearing the brunt of the bullying behavior and (potentially) reporting the behavior to a school official. Every district policy asks those who are targeted by bullying to come forward as a complainant, although they can do so anonymously (Charlotte-Mecklenburg Schools, 2008a, 2008b; Cumberland County Schools, 2010a, 2010b; Guilford County Schools, 1994, 2009a, 2009b, 2010; Wake County Public School System, 2015a, 2015b; Winston-Salem/Forsyth County Schools, 2011).

Bystanders comprise individuals who witness or observe bullying behaviors but who do not participate in the behavior, nor are the target of said behaviors (Charlotte-Mecklenburg Schools, 2008a). Policy standards suggest bystanders should file an official report to school administrators on behalf of a target. Bystanders can voluntarily participate in an investigation or be drawn into the investigation as a witness by either the complainant, alleged perpetrator(s), or other possible targets who are not complainants (Cumberland County Schools, 2010b).

Policies in this sample mention guardians the most, especially in terms of bullying prevention. While the policies described actions of bullies, targets, and bystanders briefly, they recommend that guardians contribute to prevention policies in many significant ways not expected of other interlocutors. State law tasks local school boards with developing and implementing an anti-bullying policy, providing a framework for reporting and tracking investigations, and ensuring school officials enforce the policy without retaliation against complainants (North Carolina General Statues, 2009). After a bullying report is filed, an investigator is assigned and should begin interviewing involved parties immediately, concluding the investigation within 30 school days (cf. Cumberland County Schools, 2010b). The school's principal or assistant principal is the primary investigator for student complaints, while employee complaints should go to their direct supervisor (Charlotte-Mecklenburg Schools, 2008b Cumberland County Schools, 2010b; Guilford County Schools, 1994, 2009a).

Federal laws, such as Title VI, Title IX, Section 504, and the Americans with Disabilities Act dictate that a school superintendent must assign a coordinator to receive and investigate complaints related to each law (Cumberland County Schools, 2010b; Wake County Public School System, 2015a; Winston-Salem/Forsyth County Schools, 2011). Following the investigation, the policies require school officials to discipline students immediately in accordance with the school's behavioral management plan. Employees and visitors who violate the board's policy face disciplinary action as well, including dismissal for employees and removal from the property or contact with law enforcement for visitors (Cumberland County Schools, 2010a; Wake County Public School System, 2015a; Winston-Salem/Forsyth County Schools, 2011).

School superintendents must communicate official bullying policies with school administration through policy manuals and student handbooks in concordance with North Carolina state law (North Carolina General Statutes, 2009). State law and district-level policies require the school superintendent to provide copies of the bullying policy and reporting procedures to students and employees, establish and communicate a training program to eliminate bullying behaviors, determine the nature and severity of bullying offenses to decide whether individual level or school-wide recourse is required, provide remedial punishment for acts of retribution against complainants, record and report all investigations via the Discipline Data Collection Report required by the North Carolina State Board of Education, and evaluate the effectiveness of the anti-bullying program annually (Charlotte-Mecklenburg Schools, 2008a, 2008b; Cumberland County Schools, 2010b; Guilford County Schools, 2009b, 2010; North Carolina General Statues, 2009; Wake County Public School System, 2015a; Winston-Salem/Forsyth County Schools, 2011).

The five policies included in the sample for this chapter do little beyond show compliance to North Carolina state bullying law in a "paint-by-numbers" approach. School districts have the opportunity to demonstrate that bullying prevention is at the forefront of the administration's agenda through its policies; however, none of the districts took that opportunity. The policies were "canned" responses that cover the district legally but do little to attack the problem proactively. The prevalence of bullying in school systems suggests an entrenchedness of negative communicative behaviors in education communities (Heirman et al., 2015). Activity systems seek homeostasis in the behaviors people perform, the tools that mediate those behaviors, the artifacts the behaviors produce, and the outcomes that result from the activity (Engeström, Engeström, & Kärkkäinen, 1995). Subjects must take an active role to communicate pro-socially and admonish bullying behaviors. Bullying policies should clearly articulate the form and function of their anti-bullying training programs through official school policies. When policies begin to articulate the nuances of bullying participation and prevention beyond identifying individual behaviors, they can translate micro-level subject analysis to the macro-level of the education system at large. Analyzing how subjects and their labor protect or transgress against the system is paramount for workable policy initiatives.

Objects

Although the rules, tools, subjects, and divisions of labor are discussed explicitly, the artifacts of bullying loom as amorphous, assumed evidence without any of the policies providing specifics that could serve as exemplars of rules violations or banned behaviors—the policies fail to define their objects. Objects in an activity system are the processes and artifacts that are produced and left behind as subjects work within the system (Yamagata-Lynch, 2010). One of CHAT's strengths is its ability to analyze objects and place those objects within the framework of the activity. A CHAT approach to objects in bullying policy allows policymakers and policy enforcers to be able to identify how an object protects or transgresses against the homeostatic norms of the system—in this case the K–12 education system. The relevant objects to anti-bullying policy are the concrete messages and behaviors produced by bullying, and their related prevention processes and procedures—the district policies.

Perspective matters when analyzing objects. A holistic viewpoint of bullying is necessary because an object must be situated within the activity from which it is produced—an incomplete perspective would also produce an incomplete policy. Explicit language does not constitute bullying in and of itself, but repeated, targeted, and unwanted explicit language is bullying as defined by the policies included in this chapter's sample. Simply identifying objects, like negative messages, does not prevent their production. Instead, object analysis must root itself in understanding what motivated the object's production, the activity's operations, and the outcomes the object produced (Leontyev, 1977). Bullying artifacts include actions that are motivated to communicate actual or perceived differentiating characteristics or those which are motivated by actual or perceived association with those who have differentiating characteristics (e.g., taunting someone for being LGBTQ+; Cumberland County Schools, 2010a). Age-appropriate pedagogical techniques were mentioned, but never articulated in the policy (Cumberland County Schools, 2010a; Wake County Public School System, 2015a).

The anti-bullying policies and their associated paperwork are also artifacts of the activity. Guilford County Schools (2009a, 2010) noted the goal of their anti-bullying policy was to explicitly acknowledge "the dignity and worth of all employees," to "strive to create a safe, positive and caring environment to facilitate teaching and working," and to "maintain a teaching and working environment that is free from harassment, bullying and discrimination." Every district has publicly available websites with necessary resources that help readers to understand bullying and the district's policies more deeply (Charlotte-Mecklenburg County Schools, 2017a; Cumberland County Schools, 2017; Guilford County Schools, 2017; Winston-Salem/Forsyth County Schools, 2017; Wake County Public School System, 2017). Additionally, reports of bullying produce administrative paperwork artifacts as described in the sections above.

The district policies show some aptitude for addressing object analysis. The policies indicate an awareness of bullying artifacts by policymakers and school officials but show less awareness of the relationship between bullying objects and the activity system. Missing the latter relationship prevents them from speaking directly to the issue of intention. Although the policies do not address why the object was produced, they do address how bullying behaviors can hinder or prevent a workable education environment by constructing classes of behaviors that include those that can be construed as causing "fear or harm," or which create "a hostile environment" (cf. Cumberland County Schools, 2010a). Bullying policy decisions that seek long-term, sustainable prevention must find themselves strongly within one's motivation to bully. Policies and related training materials should take to task the objects and processes that contribute to bullying's occurrence by asking why an individual is motivated to bully and what end bullying behaviors serve for that individual.

Future Directions

Anti-bullying policies are a vital and necessary part of the K–12 education system. Millions of young people avoid and are able to manage bullying behaviors every year because of established K–12 bullying policies (Farrington & Ttofi, 2009; McCallion & Feder, 2013). As this chapter illustrates, despite what bullying policies do well, there is room for improvement. The policies included in this chapter were focused intensely on the labor of guardians while skimming over the labor of other subjects. It is understandable that a school board policy details the procedures that school administrators must follow after receiving a complaint, but, beyond passing notions of evaluating training materials, the policies do not clarify how they prevent bullying. Policies detail specific banned behaviors, but the training and procedures offer guidelines for reacting to a violation of the policy, rather than establishing processes and practices that foster prevention. Communication skills-based training has long been argued as an outlet for preventing aggression (Infante, Chandler, & Rudd, 1989). The corollaries between aggression and bullying research are sufficient to believe training young people to communicate more effectively will alleviate some aggressive behaviors. Future policies should specify how the district engages with students to assess the social motivations that call forth bullying behaviors and to provide students with the interpersonal communication skills needed to prevent, confront, and cope with bullying when they experience it.

Another route by which school administrators can effectively develop anti-bullying policies is by using CHAT to analyze their education environments. Mapping bullying behaviors into a CHAT framework allows policymakers to identify points of entry for bullying behaviors, which in turn can help them refine their policies to address those concerns. In that sense, bullying policies can proactively prevent bullying if policymakers are better equipped to predict and identify the points in the system where bullying emerges. Although the policies included in this chapter were clear in identifying subjects, their labor, and their communities of practice, rules related to bullying were less clear. The policies described individual, micro-level behaviors that violate rules, but did not explore those rules violations and their relationship to the processes and procedures involved in K–12 education. Furthermore, the policies in the sample do not point their readers toward related policies on acceptable behavior in an actionable way. A more robust policy would make clear to its readers both what they should do and what they should not. Additionally, the policies show concern at the administrative level about bullying's effect on the education process but do not clearly articulate how bullying disrupts that process outside of describing it as a disruption. Developing criteria for what constitutes a meaningful disruption to the education process would alleviate some ambiguity laden into bullying policies while still allowing them to be sufficiently amorphous to apply to new and evolving forms of bullying.

An object-oriented exploration of bullying in K–12 schools is the next necessary evolution of bullying research for communication scholars. Communication scholars have begun this process already. For example, some scholars currently explore the social processes of bullying, a venture capable of linking individuals and their actions to the activity systems of which they are a part (Barlett & Gentile, 2012; Festl, Scharkow, & Quandt, 2015; Festl & Quandt, 2013). Others relate subjects and their actions to the larger discourse of communities of practice and, more importantly, social norms within those communities of practice that may contribute to bullying perpetration (Heirman et al., 2015). Many scholars have studied the communicative features of bullying and the communication tools used in bullying (cf. Adler & Adler, 1995; Alvarez, 2012; Erdur-Baker, 2010; see also Charlotte-Mecklenburg Schools, 2017b). The logical next step is to combine findings, such as those listed above, using a CHAT framework to better situate existing knowledge of bullying, its perpetration, and its prevention within the activity system of a K–12 school district. Communication researchers are in an informed position to investigate these steps through multiple methods.

Bullying is a prevalent problem affecting the K–12 education system in the United States (National Center for Education Statistics, 2016). This chapter argues that proactive anti-bullying policy is possible, but it requires a new framework for studying bullying. The above pages show how school administrators can analyze their own policy to enhance their efforts and move from reactive punishment techniques for rules violations to proactive communication skills-based training in hopes that developing necessary pro-social coping skills will help prevent bullying behaviors (cf. Center for Disease Control and Prevention, 2016; Davis et al. 2015). Bullying pervades the education system at all levels (Festl et al., 2015; Pew Internet & American Life Project, 2011). Future policy must change the norms of the education system that allow and invite bullying behaviors; only then is durable change possible.

13

TO TELL OR NOT TO TELL

Bullied Students' Coping and Supportive Communication Processes

Carly M. Danielson and Lucas J. Youngvorst

As other chapters have underscored, bullying is a serious communicative act, impacting more than one out of every five students (20.8%; NCES, 2016). The issue becomes more extreme when considering the influence of computer-mediated modalities, as cyberbullying rates have nearly doubled (18% to 34%) over the past decade (Patchin & Hinduja, 2016). It can be challenging enough for students to break their silence and confide in someone about their victimization, and the problem is heightened when the confidant fails to appropriately and effectively respond (Matsunaga, 2010b). Considering the inherent communicative nature of bullying, studying this social problem from a communication perspective provides pragmatic insights for how prevention programs, researchers, and readers can effectively manage bullying. This chapter overviews coping processes and supportive communication as a coping mechanism to explicate *how* and *why* bullying influences the health and well-being of students. Readers should garner a better understanding of coping, as well as how to effectively *be there* and support bullied students.

Coping

When students face a stressor like bullying, they begin the coping process. *Coping* involves an individual's cognitive and behavioral efforts to manage stress. A widely utilized coping model is the Transactional Model of Stress and Coping (TMSC; Lazarus & Folkman, 1984, 1987). The TMSC suggests that stressors are appraised as a threat to an individual's well-being, which they manage with internal coping resources, such as mentally distancing from the stressor, along with external coping resources, including seeking support. Appraisals occur at two levels. *Primary appraisal* involves evaluating a situation to ascertain whether it is a threat by assessing the favorability and relevance of the event (e.g., is this message hurtful and about me?). *Secondary appraisal* includes examining one's power to change the situation and resources to manage stress (e.g., can I control this and manage the pain?). Individuals experience stress when they perceive an event as negative and the demand to manage the issue exceeds one's ability to accomplish it (Lazarus & Folkman, 1984, 1987). Stress triggers coping responses that can be problem- or emotion-focused. *Problem-focused* responses directly confront and deal with stressors (e.g., standing up to the tormentor), whereas *emotion-focused* responses manage stressful emotions (e.g., avoiding thoughts about bullying). Problem-focused responses often resolve the issue in the long run, but they can create anxiety that results from confronting the stressor. Emotion-focused, particularly passive, strategies can reduce stress and mitigate pain, but rarely resolve

Figure. 13.1   TMSC With Bullying

problems (Kochenderfer-Ladd, 2004; Lazarus & Folkman, 1984, 1987). Figure 13.1 illustrates coping with bullying based on the TMSC.

Lazarus and Folkman (1984, 1987) identify coping as dichotomous dimensions (problem *or* emotion), yet this dichotomy can be overly simplistic. Someone being bullied likely uses a range of problem- and emotion-focused responses simultaneously, such as avoidance, distraction, *and* seeking support (Elledge et al., 2010). A coping response can also be used to fulfill goals for both emotion- and problem-focused dimensions. For instance, bullied students described using distancing as a problem- (analyzed the stressor and decided to ignore it), emotion- (managed emotional pain by ignoring the stressor), and both problem-focused and emotion-focused response (avoided the problem to prevent escalation and manage pain; Tenenbaum, Varjas, Meyers, & Parris, 2011). The bullying literature is moving beyond a dichotomous approach to examine coping, although this research is limited (e.g., Danielson & Emmers-Sommer, 2016; Tenenbaum et al., 2011).

Scholars group coping strategies into five types (Lazarus & Folkman, 1984; Roth & Cohen, 1986). *Seeking social support* involves asking for assistance and help from others, such as family and friends. *Distancing* includes detaching from and avoiding stressors (e.g., avoiding the perpetrator). *Problem solving* involves thinking through options to manage stressors (e.g., planning on who to involve and ways to negotiate with the perpetrator). *Internalizing* involves keeping emotions inward and not involving others (e.g., rumination, reappraisal). *Externalizing* includes outwardly displacing energy and stress (e.g., retaliation, finding an expressive outlet).

Students often anticipate coping with bullying in adaptive ways, such as seeking help or reporting the incident (Paul, Smith, & Blumberg, 2012). Bullying includes repeated hurtful acts against a target with less power, so adaptive coping can be more challenging to carry out than expected (Donoghue, Almeida, Brandwein, Rocha, & Callahan, 2014). Bullied students tap various coping mechanisms, including problem solving, seeking support, ignoring the issue, and externalizing (Danielson & Emmers-Sommer, 2016; Davis et al., 2015), but they usually respond with passive and avoidant coping (Bitsch Hansen, Steenberg, Palic, & Elklit, 2012). Students report similar strategies when dealing with cyberbullying, yet they appear differently online (e.g., distancing: staying offline, blocking the cyberbully; Davis et al., 2015).

Coping Outcomes

How bullied students cope results in beneficial or detrimental effects. It is not sufficient to assume that certain strategies will be effective for all situations. For example, researchers have found mixed results about retaliation and seeking support (Danielson & Emmers-Sommer, 2016; Tenenbaum et al., 2011). Although advocates urge bullied students not to retaliate (PACER Center, 2018), some students view retaliation as helpful. Retaliation is *reactive aggression*: using aggression in response to aggression for protection or coping (Kochenderfer & Ladd, 1997). Students who respond aggressively to their own bullying plight likely face continued victimization, along with social and emotional difficulties (Kochenderfer & Ladd, 1997). Yet, retaliatory behaviors have reduced anxiety for frequently bullied students (Visconti & Troop-Gordon, 2010). Despite ongoing challenges, some students feel they have no other way to stop bullying than to aggress (Evans, Cotter, & Smokowski, 2017). Notably, retaliation often escalates bullying, which can make both parties appear as part of the issue.

Seeking help to cope with bullying is endorsed by advocates (PACER Center, 2018), albeit inconsistent findings for its effectiveness. Students who seek help report better emotional stability and likeliness to escape victimization than those who avoid, confront bullies, or seek revenge (Visconti & Troop-Gordon, 2010). Even if disclosure does not immediately resolve bullying, it can reduce stress (Matsunaga, 2010a). However, students can be hesitant to seek help due to fear of subsequent bullying. Bullies react poorly to being told on to persons of authority (Tenenbaum et al., 2011), so someone who seeks help might face payback. Students noted that teachers would send bullies to the principal's office as punishment, yet as soon as the bullies returned to class, the bullying continued (Evans et al., 2017). Students who receive unhelpful support can be more hesitate to report bullying, as being told to "ignore them" or "fight back" expresses minimal concern and care in ways that discourage future disclosures (Danielson & Emmers-Sommer, 2016). Current findings illuminate the importance of schools adopting a standard protocol to handle bullying so students feel cared for and acknowledged. Any standardized bullying management approach, however, is difficult when considering the various individual and contextual factors that influence the coping process. Coping is a dynamic process, and the best strategies to use depend on the individual(s) involved and specific situation.

Gender

Students' social role in accordance with their gender influences coping. Bullied boys tend to cope using aggressive externalizing and distancing responses (Craig, Pepler, & Blais, 2007; Tenenbaum et al., 2011). Passive strategies, such as ignoring the bully or walking away, often result in more repercussions for boys (A. J. Rose & Rudolph, 2006), likely due to cultural expectations for boys to "tough" it out (Oransky & Marecek, 2009). Girls who respond aggressively are at greater risk for maladjustment than boys, likely because other stakeholders expect them to reject violence and demonstrate understanding (Kochenfelder-Ladd & Skinner, 2002). Girls tend to cope with more relational and assertive strategies, including seeking support and problem solving (Craig et al.). For bullied girls, seeking support from a friend decreased internalizing and social problems (Shelley & Craig, 2010), whereas the same strategy increased social problems for boys (Kochenderfer-Ladd & Skinner, 2002). Bullied girls also use harmful internalizing behaviors (e.g., self-blame, self-harm; Danielson & Emmers-Sommer, 2016; Donoghue et al., 2014). High internalizing coping predicts social (Kochenfelder-Ladd & Skinner) and mental health issues (e.g., depression; Lohmann, 2012), justifying the need to educate students about productive coping. Parents, friends, and teachers should be aware of victimization signs (e.g., low self-esteem, isolation, cuts on body) so they can help students.

Age and Efficacy

Developmental influences also shape the coping process. Problem solving strategies tend to de-escalate bullying (Mahady Wilton & Craig, 2000), but involve a level of critical thinking that youth rarely enact. Rather, the use of cognitively demanding problem solving strategies increases throughout adolescence (Skinner & Zimmer-Gembeck, 2007). *Self-efficacy*, or one's confidence to implement desired behaviors in certain situations, is also associated with coping (Putter, 2007). High school students report experiencing a cognitive shift in which they learn to cope with and feel greater confidence in their ability to defend against bullying (Evans et al., 2017). Conversely, younger students with insufficient efficacy for resolving conflicts in nonaggressive ways tend to use aggressive externalizing (Fox & Boulton, 2005; O'Brennan, Bradshaw, & Sawyer, 2009). Younger students also endorse strategies suggested by and tend to seek help from adults (Olweus, 1993a), whereas older students handle problems independently or turn to friends for help (Skinner & Zimmer-Gembeck, 2007).

Bullying Type

The type and frequency of victimization also influences coping. Indirect bullying is covert and subtle, and it can be challenging to identify anonymous perpetrators. Girls more often experience indirect bullying (Catanzaro, 2011) and use internalizing behaviors (Hoglund, 2007), which is not the case for boys. Students favor passive responses for indirect bullying, whereas they prefer retaliation for direct bullying (Kanetsuna, Smith, & Morita, 2006). Males tend to be physically bullied and pressured to respond in aggressive ways to perhaps maintain status or avoid stigmas associated with being a victim (Hoglund; Oransky & Marecek, 2009). Frequently bullied students more often use passive and avoidance coping, which associates with poor emotional and social outcomes (Hunter & Boyle, 2004). Understanding how individual-difference factors influence coping processes offers practical insights for bullying programs to educate students, families, and schools about constructive bullying management strategies that reduce victimization and buffer negative outcomes.

Social Support

Although coping is largely researched in psychology, communication research often focuses on the processes of seeking support and supportive communication. Feeling supported by others is important for bullied students. Cohen and Wills (1985) theorized two models that describe the functions of social support. The *main effect model* posits individuals benefit from receiving social support in general; however, the *stress-buffering model* posits "support is related to well-being only for persons under stress" (Cohen, Underwood, & Gottlieb, 2000, p. 11). The main effect model suggests perceived support does not function as a coping strategy; rather, it is the nature of support itself, regardless of stressors, that benefits health. The *stress-buffering theory* suggests higher levels of support enable better coping with stressors, which enhances health. If someone appraises a stressful event (primary appraisal), their outcome can be positive if they know they have support (secondary appraisal). *Perceiving* that support will be available for bullying improves coping ability and well-being (Davidson & Demaray, 2007; Tanigawa, Furlong, Felix, & Sharkey, 2011). If one *receives* support for bullying, they likely experience this stress-buffering role (Matsunaga, 2010b, 2011).

Disclosure does not guarantee effective coping, but it is a first step to initiate the communication process. Exploring social support mechanisms is important due to discrepant findings about its outcomes, likely due to the type(s) of support provided. Supportive messages fulfill various functions (Cutrona, 1990; Cutrona & Russell, 1990). *Emotional support* conveys concern, comfort, and availability and helps affected individuals cope with difficult emotions stemming from bullying, such as sadness, fear, anger, and shame. Emotional support: (1) is an appropriate and helpful response to one's distress for various situations and cultures (Feng & Burleson, 2006), (2) produces physical and psychological benefits for support recipients (Burleson, Kunkel, Samter, & Working, 1996; Jones, 2004), (3) facilitates positive reappraisal and coping (Jones & Wirtz, 2006), and (4) fosters a climate for subsequent interactions (Burleson, 2003). *Esteem support* expresses respect and confirms competence to recipients. Esteem support is vital when experiencing failure events or rejection. When revealing a stressor that influences one's self-identity, esteem support is crucial (Holmstrom & Burleson, 2011). Bullying involves attacks against one's characteristics, which often evokes threats to one's self-esteem (Olweus, 1993a). Esteem and emotional support appear in the literature as the most used support types for various relationships (e.g., Harel, Shechtman, & Cutrona, 2012).

The third type of social support is *informational*, which offers advice or guidance for strategies the distressed person can use to fix the problem (MacGeorge, Feng, & Guntzviller, 2016), such as how to stop bullying. Advice must be carefully crafted to address the support recipient's needs and not be too blunt or insensitive (MacGeorge, Lichtman, & Pressey, 2002). Unwanted advice can be met with resistance, which can increase distress (Feng & MacGeorge, 2006). For that reason, Feng (2009, 2014) suggested that support providers should inquire about and analyze the support seeker's situation before offering advice. This process allows support providers to determine the relevance of advice and involve the support seeker in the analysis of the problematic situation. *Network support* involves the provision of social resources, such as referring people to experts or other confidants (Cutrona, 1990; Cutrona & Russell, 1990). Network support offers a sense of group membership with others who share similar interests and concerns. The kinds of network resources for bullied students include parents, school administrators, teachers, peers, and bullying prevention organizations. Researchers report mixed findings about the usefulness of network support for bullied students, likely due to their relationship with the support provider (e.g., friend versus teacher; Danielson & Jones, in press; Matsunaga, 2010b).

Supportive Communication

Communication researchers have contributed greater understandings of social support processes by exploring supportive message characteristics and health outcomes (Burleson & MacGeorge, 2002). Supportive communication is "verbal and nonverbal behavior produced with the intention of providing assistance to others perceived as needing that aid" (MacGeorge, Feng, & Burleson, 2011, p. 317). High-quality emotional supportive messages facilitate distressed individuals to verbalize their thoughts more often, resulting in more positive reappraisals of stressors and emotional improvement. Conversely, low-quality emotional supportive messages can create negative changes in the recipient's behavior and affect (Bodie & Burleson, 2008). The process of seeking and proving support during stressful events is complex, as both parties must simultaneously manage coping and relational needs (Albrecht & Goldsmith, 2003).

Support Providers

The support provider constitutes an important aspect of the supportive communication process. Students are often protected from health issues when they perceive high numbers of putative support providers, such as friend, peer, parental, teacher, and/or school administration (Davidson & Demaray, 2007; Tanigawa et al., 2011). *Perceived* support is particularly crucial, as support alleviates stress through a mediational process reflecting the support recipients' perceptions of the supportive interaction (Burleson & Goldsmith, 1998). Gaps between desired and received support can impede effective processing of bullying (Matsunaga, 2011). Bullied students rarely disclose *primarily* to parents and/or teachers, but rather talk with and rely on friends for help (Matsunaga, 2010a). The benefits of family support continue into college. Previously bullied college students who reported high family support were less likely to experience anxiety during college adjustment (Reid, Holt, Bowman, Espelage, & Green, 2016). Despite the importance of adults to manage the unequal power distribution in bullying dynamics, some research suggests that bullied students find adults as ineffective support sources (Danielson & Emmers-Sommer, 2016; Tenenbaum et al., 2011). Notably, whether support providers have or lack prior experience with bullying influences outcomes for support seekers. Cyberbullied support seekers reported more effective impressions of messages when delivered by a support provider who had experience being cyberbullied compared to a provider who did not (High & Young, 2018). Individuals are generally more receptive to supportive messages from similar others who share something in common, which facilitates coping (Feng & MacGeorge, 2010). Ultimately, bullied students value support from providers who have experience being targeted and coping with bullying.

To facilitate quality social support, research examines how certain support types offered by support providers elicits better outcomes over others. Expectations for support needs differ considerably for close-tie and weak-tie sources. *Close-tie* members (e.g., family, friends) are more emotionally attached to support seekers and resort to emotional support as primary supportive responses (Wellman & Wortley, 1990). Providing emotional support can be difficult for close-ties, though, who may fear that they further upset individuals who have experienced bullying or say the wrong things, particularly if it involves judgment and critique. Support seekers may experience fear of being patronized, stigmatized, incapable of handling one's own issues, and receiving unwanted support (Wright & Miller, 2010). They can also encounter difficulties in receiving helpful support from close-ties if they lack experience, knowledge, and information about specific stressors (Albrecht, Burleson, & Goldsmith, 1994; Brashers, Neidig, & Goldsmith, 2004). *Weak-tie* relationships (e.g., teachers, pediatricians) are less emotionally attached than close-ties. Weak-ties usually possess more tightly defined roles and behavioral expectations that make up those roles (Wright & Miller, 2010), as well as communication that explicitly addresses power and professionalism (Alderman & Green, 2011; Bigelow, Tesson, & Lewko, 1992). Weak-ties can afford advantages during problematic, threatening, and sensitive circumstances, as they can be more comfortable providing support even if it is unpleasant (Wright & Miller, 2010). Two social support contexts of interest to health communication include *face-to-face* (FtF) and *online contexts*.

FtF Supportive Communication

Supportive communication often occurs in a FtF context. Increased peer support is the most significant predictor of decreased bullying and negative emotions for students with and without disabilities (C.A. Rose, Espelage, Monda-Amaya, Shogren, & Aragon, 2013). A bystander who asks if the bullied student is okay, needs anything, and shows they care can help alleviate pain. In fact, bullied youth who received emotional support from a friend or peer were protected from internalizing problems (Yeung Thompson & Leadbeater, 2013). Clearly, schools should adopt bullying prevention programs that foster increased peer social support (e.g., PACER Center, 2018). Matsunaga (2010b, 2011) analyzed support outcomes for bullied students and found that emotional support best predicted positive reappraisal, communication satisfaction, and post-bullying adjustment. Matsunaga (2010b, 2011) also discovered positive effects for esteem support, no effects for informational support, and negative effects for network support. The studies largely included close-ties (e.g., parents, friends), which suggests that close-tie support providers should offer emotion or esteem support as an immediate and primary response during supportive conversations about bullying.

Although negative outcomes occurred for close-ties providing network support (Matsunaga, 2010b, 2011), bullied students perceived teachers who provided network support as most helpful (Danielson & Jones, in press). Teachers most often provided informational support to students (Malecki & Demaray, 2003). Individuals who have been bullied appreciate emotional and esteem support in close-tie contexts, but with weak-ties, informational and network support likely becomes more valuable. For instance, if a bullied student seeks out a school administrator, teacher, or bullying advocacy group (i.e., usually weak-ties) for help to stop bullying and they are provided with sympathy, comfort, and affirmation (i.e., emotional and esteem support), it can help the student cope with difficult emotions and improve distress, but this alone does not *do* anything to manage the issue. According to Danielson and Jones, students likely seek weak-ties with the expectation of getting something accomplished, such as problem solving, receiving advice, getting access to resources, and monitoring at school. Weak-tie support providers may have greater knowledge about and power to change bullying. An important unanswered question is: How does close-tie support influence weak-tie support and vice versa? For instance, how does "home" support influence the ways students seek support at school? Students may first expect emotion and esteem support from close-ties, then expect information and network support from weak-ties.

Supportive Communication Characteristics

Supportive interactions usually contain various messages implemented simultaneously and at different stages of the process (Jacobson, 1986). Yet, researchers often examine supportive communication using a competitive rather than complementary view, such as someone's preference for a specific support type being contrasted with another. Social support is not mutually exclusive (Feng, 2009). For instance, although informational and network support from weak-ties may be more useful for bullied students, emotional support provided *in conjunction with* informational (Feng, 2009) and network support (Danielson & Jones, in press) leads to better support evaluations. Danielson and Jones determined that bullied students rated the provision of emotional support *only* from teachers to bullied students as extremely unsupportive, whereas the provision of emotional *and* network support in conjunction with one another was evaluated as highly supportive. Informational or network support alone can come off as more cold and dismissive without emotional support. Respondents assessed supportive conversations about bullying that contain only a single-support type (e.g., emotion) as less helpful than conversations with two or three types (e.g., emotion and network). Clearly, students need various support types to cope. The placement of support types in conversations may be equally important.

Emotional Primacy

Different types of support might be more appropriate at different moments in a supportive response. Supportive communication and counseling research suggest that the initial response to someone's distress should be emotionally focused before working through problems, providing advice, or other support types. Research in the counseling field suggests that the provision of emotional support *first* creates a supportive climate before helping someone cope with problems (Heritage & Sefi, 1992; Vehviläinen, 2001), as it lets them know they are heard and cared for. Greenberg's Emotionally Focused Therapy, for instance, states that a therapist's first step is to create a supportive bond by acknowledging, expressing understanding, and validating the client's emotions (Greenberg & Paivio, 2003). Communication research poses similar recommendations. Burleson and Goldsmith's (1998) theory of conversationally induced reappraisal suggests the initial response to a distressed person should contain emotional support to facilitate cognitive reappraisals of the upsetting event. Providing emotional support *first* creates a climate where people can work through negative feelings and thoughts, which maximize the effects of working through issues (Burleson, 2003). Feng's (2009, 2014) Integrated Model of Advice contends that a conversation needs to begin with emotional support before problem solving with or suggesting advice to the distressed person.

Online Supportive Communication

Although traditional research examines the supportive communication process primarily in FtF settings, computer-mediated communication (CMC) venues both alleviate and exacerbate many challenges that bullied students face when seeking and receiving help. CMC modalities make it easier to experience bullying (Aboujaoude, Savage, Starcevic, & Salame, 2015), yet CMC venues also unite people in ways that foster supportive communication and coping (Wright, Johnson, Averbeck, & Bernard, 2011). Considering the prevalence of technology on our lives in general, and on the lives of bullied students in particular, we must examine how and why CMC venues influence bullying.

Technological Affordances

Importantly, we should not envision CMC venues monolithically but rather identify differences between channels that explain variations in communication therein (Fox & McEwan, 2017; Nass & Mason, 1990; Walther, Gay, & Hancock, 2005). Thus, CMC modalities must be differentiated on the basis of *affordances*. Gibson (1977) originally defined affordances as the action possibilities of an object or environment; specific actions and behaviors can only occur because of a certain feature. Hutchby

(2001) extended this definition to computer-mediated spaces and identified *technological affordances* as the inherent components of technology that directly influence the nature of computer-mediated interactions. Affordances, such as message editability (i.e., how much a message can be strategically crafted prior to sending) and temporal response delays, constitute action possibilities and structure normative communication practices of computer-mediated interactions (High & Solomon, 2011). For instance, a video/audio-based channel permits interactions that differ from text-based channels on the basis of transmitted social cues and temporal delays. Although multiple affordances exist, we highlight three that are particularly influential on how bullied targets seek and receive support.

ANONYMITY

Anonymity regards the degree to which an individual's identity is concealed (Lea & Spears, 1991). Highly anonymous channels allow users to choose whether or not to disclose their identity; conversely, venues low in anonymity require users to release personal information. FtF contexts are rarely anonymous because people are able to observe each other's identity throughout interactions. Although interactants may not know each other, such as brief contact with peers, their identity is salient. Non-anonymous FtF interactions bind people to social norms that drive their communication (Postmes, Spears, Sakhel, & De Groot, 2001). Several CMC channels, however, afford anonymity. Online chat rooms often allow users to interact with others without revealing their identity (e.g., displaying a picture, providing their name). This practice changes the nature of the interaction because users are no longer restricted by social norms inherent to FtF contexts and can engage in uninhibited communication.

Anonymity holds several implications for bullied support seekers. Anonymity promotes self-disclosure (Hollenbaugh & Everett, 2013; Suler, 2004). Because self-disclosure is a necessary precursor to social support (Chaudoir & Fisher, 2010), FtF support seekers reveal highly personal and potentially embarrassing information to others. Anonymous CMC allows users to avoid risks of disclosing information or requesting support due to decreased face threat (Caplan, 2003). Thus, users can more easily signal a need for support through self-disclosure online than FtF. Anonymity also helps establish supportive relationships. Wright (2000) noted that because people felt less judged and stigmatized within anonymous CMC venues, they were more comfortable revealing information that built intimacy and encouraged supportive communication.

Anonymity also influences the ways in which support providers engage in supportive communication. Providing effective support is a risky and face-threatening activity that requires individuals to interpret and evaluate other's complex needs during times of stress (Burleson, 2003; Goldsmith, 1994). How users respond to support seekers may vary depending on how well they can conceal their identity. Studies highlight the benefits of private channels when exchanging sensitive and sophisticated supportive messages (Vitak & Ellison, 2013; Youngvorst & High, 2018). Accordingly, support providers may feel unwilling or incapable of providing support in non-anonymous channels due to potential public securitization, but such concerns may be lessened in anonymous channels that are less risky. Some research does suggest that anonymity diffuses personal responsibility to support bullied targets and increases passive observing behavior (Brody & Vangelisti, 2016). Bystanders and support providers are especially likely to respond to and support bullied targets when they think the target knows that they are aware of the incident (Brody & Vangelisti, 2016). Ultimately, anonymity equips both bullied support seekers and support providers with unique ways in which to engage in supportive interactions.

SYNCHRONICITY

Synchronicity refers to how soon messages occur in succession, such that synchronous messages occur immediately after one another. Asynchronous messages, however, are temporally delayed

(High & Solomon, 2011). FtF interactions are always synchronous; not only must FtF support providers effectively process the message(s) they receive, they must then immediately attend and respond to the needs of the support seeker with little delay between messages. Conversely, CMC interactions usually occur asynchronously, granting users more time to formulate a response that meets the needs of the situation and enabling them to send and receive messages over time. While the cognitively demanding nature of providing effective support remains constant, the user has more time to strategically craft their messages and provide effective support. High (2011) reported that people provided more effective support when interacting through CMC venues as compared to FtF, illustrating how asynchronicity afforded by various CMC channels enables users to more effectively engage in complex interactions.

Synchronicity equally influences bullied support seekers. Online support groups frequently act in place of offline support networks (Rains & Keating, 2011), and High and Solomon (2011) identified their asynchronous nature as one of the main contributors to their widespread use and efficacy. Because online support groups usually communicate asynchronously, bullied users are able to come and go as support is needed. This flexibility allows users to view previous conversations that have happened through the group, gaining helpful information for their own problems and participating in conversations as time allows.

NUMBER OF USERS

The number of users who engage in an interaction is important to consider because some contexts may allow for more or less users than others. For FtF communication, interactions occur solely between those who can be in the physical presence of one another. Although not inherently limited to a certain number of people, geographical and temporal barriers limit an individual's ability to communicate with others in FtF contexts. CMC venues are not bound by these same limitations, given that people can communicate with a multitude of users at the touch of a button, expanding the possible communicative interactions that can occur, as users are not only able to communicate with more people, but also with unique populations that are otherwise difficult (or impossible) to contact.

The limited number of barriers within CMC significantly impacts bullied support seekers. To initiate a supportive interaction and seek support, people must have others with whom they can interact. Finding a support system can be difficult in FtF contexts because users may not have relationships that allow for information disclosure or support seeking. CMC networks, however, increase users' ability to connect with people who have similar problems and can provide effective support. Past research supports this claim, such that people experiencing low levels of FtF support increased their time spent on online message boards and listservs (Wright, 2000), resulting in various physical and psychological effects. As Rains and Young (2009) noted, participating in computer-mediated support groups "led to increased social support, decreased depression, increased quality of life, and increased self-efficacy to manage one's health condition" (p. 309).

The number of users in a CMC venue also influences when and if others will provide support. The ways in which support providers receive support seeking requests predicts whether they will respond or not. For example, support providers may feel less inclined to help bullied support seekers online if they send the request for help to multiple recipients (e.g., a public online post asking for help about bullying; Blair, Foster Thompson, & Wuensch, 2005; Brody & Vangelisti, 2016). Other research indicates that larger number of users may foster a sense of community among members that increases provider motivation to support others in need (Rains & Wright, 2016). Therefore, CMC venues alter supportive interactions because users attain greater access to diverse individuals and resources.

When considering anonymity, synchronicity, and number of users within the context of online supportive communication, clearly, these affordances significantly influence the ways bullied students seek and receive support. As High and Solomon (2011) concluded, it is likely "the interplay between features of support messages and characteristics of CMC venues that determines the experience of computer mediated social support" (p. 131). Ultimately, exploring these dimensions within various CMC contexts will enhance our understanding how such venues impact the social support process among bullied students.

Conclusion

Help-seeking is one of the most researched and crucial strategies to cope with bullying. The role of support providers in coping cannot be underestimated. Close-tie, school, community, and online support can positively influence the lives of bullied students. Providing social support is a free technique that can be taught and emulated in others. Some programs incorporate social support and supportive environments within their curriculum, such as the Olweus Bullying Prevention Program (2018) and PACER'S National Bullying Prevention Center (2018). These programs can be incorporated in school bullying reduction strategies, and we hope that additional programs can benefit from this knowledge. Research affirms advantages to creating support groups for bullied students that focus on increasing support from school staff and peers, as well as social skills lessons that focus on how to appropriately ask for help when faced with stressors. We are confident that this review of coping and social support informs scholars in communication about the complexity and importance of supportive communication.

14

BULLYING IN ACADEMIA AMONG COLLEGE PROFESSORS

Alan K. Goodboy, Matthew M. Martin, Carol Bishop Mills, and Cathlin V. Clark-Gordon

Perhaps there never was an ivory tower in academia. Any professor, administrator, graduate student, or staff member working in a college or university can attest that some professors can be difficult to work with and, at times, even cruel. On one hand, almost any organization will have a handful or more of unkind employees, and, just like any other organizational cohort, nothing special about academic departments deters higher education employees from potentially mistreating each other. On the other hand, some unique organizational features might make academic departments potentially susceptible to employee mistreatment. Professors can be self-involved and self-aggrandizing when it comes to their academic egos. Some professors perceive pressures to publish or to secure grants that might turn collaboration into academic competition. For the professors in positions of privilege, opportunities for tenure, which if granted, bestow career stability, even if they are not good department colleagues or university citizens. Given these academic considerations, perhaps unsurprisingly, bullying in academia is perpetrated most frequently by administrators and senior faculty (Keashly & Neuman, 2010; Wieland & Beitz, 2015).

However, as De Luca and Twale (2010) pointed out, "faculty members who have only their self-interests in mind and are not concerned with the successes or accomplishments of other faculty will bully anyone they feel is in their way, be the person tenured or not" (p. 2). Some of these features of academia, then, might make it a unique and important organizational context to study the bullying of employees (Taylor, 2013). Several researchers would agree. As Keashly and Neuman (2010) argued, "academic settings are worthy and in need of concerted attention by researchers in workplace aggression and bullying" (p. 49). Given these features of the academic life, such as publication demands, potentially high teaching loads, and the complexities of tenure, the research team explored varying workplace stressors that might increase perceptions of bullying, as well as organizational factors that might influence those perceptions. To do so, we employed the job demand-control-support (JDCS) model of workplace strain.

Although this volume of chapters contains various interpretations of workplace bullying, we embrace the view that workplace bullying refers to

> repeated actions and practices that are directed against one or more workers; that are unwanted by the victim; that may be carried out deliberately or unconsciously, but clearly cause humiliation, offense, and distress; and that may interfere with work performance and/ or cause an unpleasant working environment.
>
> *(Einarsen et al., 2011b, p. 9)*

Lutgen-Sandvik and Tracy (2012) described workplace bullying as "a toxic combination of unrelenting emotional abuse, social ostracism, interactional terrorizing, and other destructive communication that erode organizational health and damages employee well-being" (p. 5). Some common features that distinguish workplace bullying from other forms of aggression or discrimination (see Lutgen-Sandvik et al., 2009) include repetition (bullying reoccurs frequently at work and is not an isolated incident), duration (bullying occurs over period of time and not in the short term, often six months or longer), power disparity (targets of bullying are unable to easily defend themselves from a perpetrator/perpetrators), and harm (bullying damages employees' physical, mental, or occupational health).

Indeed, workplace bullying occurs too often in higher education (Hollis, 2012; Twale & De Luca, 2008). Although estimates of bullying prevalence vary, McKay, Arnold, Fratzl, and Thomas (2008) found that 52% of faculty, instructors, and librarians at a mid-sized Canadian university were bullied in the past five years, mostly through emails, or in office spaces, or in the classroom. Cassidy, Faucher, and Jackson (2014) noted that 9% of faculty experienced cyberbullying from a colleague in the past year; the majority of targets were female faculty. Keashly and Neuman (2013) reported the most comprehensive summary of the prevalence rates of bullying in higher education with ranges from 11.7% to 54.9% for faculty and higher education employees who experienced bullying, and ranges from 22% to 75% of these employees witnessing bullying. Keep in mind, however, that these data vary across the time in which bullying was reported (bullying in the prior six months up to the last five years) and across different countries (United Kingdom, Finland, United States, Canada, Turkey, New Zealand). Regardless of the variability in prevalence, we know that bullying happens in academia.

However, what does bullying in the academy look like? As asserted by Eddington and Buzzanell (this volume), bullying behaviors in academia appear to mirror many of those reported in other organizational contexts (Nielsen, Notelaers, & Einarsen, 2011). In a study among nursing faculty, the most frequently identified bullying tactics included withholding information, gossiping, silencing, isolating, lying, sabotaging, and creating unrealistic workloads, among others (Goldberg, Beitz, Wieland, & Levine, 2013). In a study with a community college sample, Lester (2009) revealed that workplace bullying among faculty included threats to professional status, including taunting and humiliation, coupled with isolation and marginalization. Likewise, Giorgi (2012) found that employees in universities most frequently bully targets by withholding information, expecting work outside the level of required competence, and gossiping. Although understanding the multitude of ways that faculty mistreat each other is important, we must also assess the academic work conditions that might encourage or discourage professors to mistreat each other.

Antecedents of Academic Bullying

Salin and Hoel (2011) argued that bullying occurs at work due stressful working environments that do not support employee autonomy. The job demand-control-support (JDCS) model of workplace strain has served as a valuable framework for operationalizing stress-induced work environments that cultivate workplace bullying (Goodboy, Martin, Knight, & Long, 2017). The JDCS model (Karasek, 1979; Karasek & Theorell, 1990) theorizes that employees' well-being is jeopardized in strained work environments featuring *high job demands* (i.e., having too many psychological demands related to the job and workload), *low control* (i.e., lacking the authority to make one's own decisions about how work is performed), and *low supervisor social support* (i.e., having a supervisor who is unhelpful or unavailable for social interaction). These work environments provide an isolation-strain (iso-strain) job where employees believe that they have an abundance of hard work to accomplish without the autonomy over how to complete it and without a boss who can be counted on to discuss problems.

An iso-strain work environment leads to reduced employee well-being in the form of physical and mental health, including depression and anxiety, fatigue, emotional exhaustion, and psychological distress, among other indicators of compromised well-being (Häusser, Mojzisch, Niesel, & Schulz-Hardt, 2010). Predictably, employees who work in an iso-strain environment also report more stress and dissatisfaction on the job, among other negative occupational outcomes (de Lange, Taris, Kompier, Houtman, & Bongers, 2003).

Although researchers use the JDCS model to make predictions about employee well-being and occupational outcomes (Van der Doef & Maes, 1999), it has recently been applied to explain antecedents of workplace bullying due to job strain in the work environment (Janssens, et al., 2016). Notelaers, Baillien, De Witte, Einarsen, and Vermunt (2013) found that employees with very high job demands were two times more likely to be a target of severe bullying and were four times more likely to be a target if they had very low job control. Tuckey, Dollard, Hosking, and Winefield (2009) revealed that police officers who were targets of bullying reported significantly higher job demands and lower control and support resources. Finally, Goodboy, Martin, Knight, and Long (2017) reported support for an iso-strain hypothesis, revealing that psychological job demands were a positive predictor, whereas job control and supervisor social support were negative predictors, of experiencing workplace bullying. Based on this empirical evidence, we expected the JDCS model to serve as a work environment explanation for bullying in academia. Therefore, we offered an iso-strain hypothesis predicting academic work antecedents of professor bullying:

H1: Professors who work in academic departments with (1) higher psychological job demands, (2) lower control, and (3) lower supervisor social support will experience more workplace bullying.

Consequences of Academic Bullying

This literature is replete with documented negative outcomes of workplace bullying or, as Lutgen-Sandvik et al. (2009) put it, "empirical and anecdotal evidence indicate that bullying affects all aspects of targets' lives" (p. 36), including mental health, suicidal ideation, daily functioning, chronic stress, and physical health, to name a few outcomes. The consequences of workplace bullying in academia are likely to be just as damaging as in other organizational contexts. Martin et al. (2015) discovered that professors who bully their graduate students make them disinterested in their education and increase their intentions to leave graduate school. Goodboy, Martin, and Johnson (2015) concluded that bullied graduate students report more burnout and less organizational citizenship behaviors. Giorgi (2012) found that bullying in academia is correlated with declines in health (psychological, physical, and general) as well as the organizational climate (job description, autonomy, development, communication, job involvement). McKay et al. (2008) noted that bullied academics experience stress, frustration, anger, demoralization, powerlessness, and anxiety, whereas DelliFraine, McClelland, Erwin, and Wang (2014) revealed that the most common outcomes for faculty included anger, stress, frustration, exhaustion, anxiety, irritability, demoralization, powerlessness, and a desire to retaliate.

From a university perspective, bullying is an expensive problem. In an attempt to monetize the effects of bullying in the academy, Hollis (2015) argued that even medium-sized universities can lose $4.6 million annually from workplace bullying when considering turnover, including approximately 150% of an annual salary for a replacement along with lost productivity. And, pragmatically, especially in smaller academic departments, unhappy and stressed faculty can have an enormous impact on the organizational culture for the other faculty and students. Even one faculty member leaving a department can be devastating to the course offerings, consistency for students, and the structure of the department (Heckert & Farabee, 2006).

Therefore, since our study focused on work environment antecedents of workplace bullying, we examined professors' occupational outcomes that result from bullying. In line with job strain research, we hypothesized the following consequences of workplace bullying in academia:

H2: Professors who experience more workplace bullying will report (1) less job satisfaction, (2) more occupational stress, and (3) greater intentions to leave academia.

Method

Participants

Participants included 119 college or university professors from 40 disciplines, including astrophysics, art history, ecology, education, neuroscience, philosophy, communication, and psychology. These professors held different ranks and job titles, including adjunct professor ($n = 9, 7.8\%$), instructor ($n = 8$, 6.9%), lecturer ($n = 12, 10.3\%$), assistant professor ($n = 42, 36.2\%$), associate professor ($n = 28, 24.1\%$), full professor ($n = 15, 12.9\%$), and administration roles, such as department chair ($n = 2, 1.7\%$). Of the 119 participants, our sample consisted of 37 male professors (31.1%) and 82 female professors (68.9%), with an average age of 40.47 years ($SD = 8.92$). The majority of participants achieved doctoral degrees ($n = 95, 80.5\%$); 21 earned a master's degree (17.8%), and 2 participants completed a bachelor's degree (1.7%). The highest degree offered by the professors' departments spanned a wide spectrum—from associate's ($n = 6, 5.1\%$), bachelor's ($n = 33, 28\%$), master's ($n = 24, 20.3\%$), to doctoral ($n = 55, 46.6\%$). On average, these professors worked in academia for 9.7 years ($SD = 8.22$) with an average salary of 72,643.77 U.S. dollars ($SD = \$33,434.50$). The race of the participants included White/Caucasian ($n = 109, 91.6\%$), Asian American ($n = 2, 1.7\%$), Black/African American ($n = 2$, 1.7%), Hispanic/Latino ($n = 2, 1.7\%$), and 4 participants who selected "other" as a race (3.4%).

Procedures and Measurement

After obtaining Institutional Review Board (IRB) approval, we administered an online survey via Qualtrics to professors who volunteered to respond through a variety of sampling methods. Our research team employed network sampling, asking colleagues to share the survey with other colleagues and friends in academia via social media posts. We also advertised via email to multiple interdisciplinary research-based listservs and posted on academic-related forums online. We sought to reach a wide variety of professors and disciplines, rather than sampling only the discipline of the research team. The online survey included the following measures:

Workplace Bullying

The Negative Acts Questionnaire-Revised (NAQR; Einarsen et al., 2009) uses 22 items to capture a wide range of bullying behaviors directed toward a target at work over the last six months (e.g., "being ignored or excluded"). Participants responded on a 5-point Likert-type scale ranging from 1 = Never to 5 = Daily. Plopa, Plopa, and Skuzińska (2017) reported a previous Cronbach's alpha of .94 for the measure. In this study, the NAQR produced a Cronbach's alpha of .94 ($M = 1.48, SD = .53$).

Job Demands-Control-Support

We measured the JDCS variables using the standard Job Content Questionnaire subscales (Karasek et al., 1998), asking our respondents to rate statements on a 5-point Likert response format ranging from 1 = Strongly disagree to 5 = Strongly agree. We examined job demands with eight items from the psychological demands subscale (e.g., "I am not asked to do excessive work"). Control was measured with three items from the decision authority subscale (e.g., "I have a lot to say about what happens on my job"). We obtained data regarding supervisor social support with five items from the supervisor support subscale (e.g., "My supervisor is successful in getting people to work together"). Previous Cronbach's alphas have ranged from .65 to .81 for the subscales (de Jonge, Reuvers, Houtman, Bongers, & Kompier, 2000). In this study, the subscales produced the following Cronbach's alphas: psychological job demands (α = .77; M = 3.44, SD = .73), control/decision authority (α = .60; M = 4.19, SD = .66), and supervisor social support (α = .89; M = 3.79, SD = .96).

Job Stress

We used four items from the Job Stress Measure (Netemeyer, Maxham, & Pullig, 2005) to operationalize stress-induced symptoms of employee health (e.g., "Problems associated with work have kept me awake at night."). This measure employed a 5-point Likert response format, ranging from 1 = Strongly disagree to 5 = Strongly agree. Mulki, Jaramillo, Malhotra, and Locander (2012) reported a previous Cronbach's alpha of .72 for the measure. In this study, the measure produced a Cronbach's alpha of .84 (M = 3.32, SD = .98).

Job Satisfaction

We incorporated four items from the Brief Index of Affective Job Satisfaction (Thompson & Phua, 2012) to operationalize general satisfaction on the job (e.g., "Most days I feel enthusiastic about my job"). This measure utilized a Likert response format, ranging from 1 = Strongly disagree to 5 = Strongly agree. Hirschi (2014) reported a previous Cronbach's alpha of .90 for the measure. In this study, the measure produced a Cronbach's alpha of .91 (M = 4.03, SD = .86).

Intent to Leave

We included five items from the Intent to Leave Academia Scale (Barnes, Agago, & Coombs, 1998) to probe professor's thoughts about leaving their discipline (e.g., "I am considering a permanent departure from academia"). This measure used a 4-point Likert-type response format, ranging from 1 = Not at all to 4 = Very much. Barnes et al. (1998) reported a Cronbach's alpha of .82. In this study, the measure produced a Cronbach's alpha of .91 (M = 1.64, SD = .80).

Results

Before testing our hypotheses, we calculated Pearson correlations between all variables that are displayed in Table 14.1.

Informed by the JDCS model, we tested the antecedents of academic bullying as an iso-strain hypothesis, predicting professors would report more workplace bullying in departments that feature higher job demands, lower control over how to complete these demands, and lower social support from the supervisor or chairperson. Results of an ordinary least squares regression analysis confirmed this hypothesis, as all three JDCS variables served as significant and unique predictors of workplace bullying, accounting for over 40% of the variance. As displayed in Table 14.2, controlling for each predictor, job demand was a positive predictor (B = .214), whereas control (B = −.144) and supervisor social support (B = −.236) were negative predictors of academic workplace bullying. To determine the importance of each predictor in the model, we performed a qualitative dominance analysis (Budescu, 1993) on all three predictors using all subsets regression from the regression and linear models (RLM) macro (Darlington & Hayes, 2017). Results of the dominance analysis revealed

Table 14.1 Pearson Correlations Between Variables

Variables	1	2	3	4	5	6	7
1. Workplace Bullying	—						
JDCS Variables							
2. Job Demands (Psychological)	.42*	—					
3. Decision Authority (Control)	−.36*	−0.17	—				
4. Supervisor Social Support	−.54*	−.22**	.31**	—			
Workplace Outcomes							
5. Job Satisfaction	−.46*	−.24**	.45*	.34*	—		
6. Job Stress	.46*	.48*	−.33*	−.23**	−.34*	—	
7. Intent to Leave (Academia)	.40*	.21**	−.21**	−.23**	−.47*	.36*	—

Note: $*p < .001$, $**p < .05$. Two-tailed.

Table 14.2 Iso-Strain Hypothesis

	B	95% CI	SE B	β	t
Job Demands	.214	[.108; .319]	.053	.299	4.022
Control	−.144	[−.265; −.024]	.061	−.182	−2.375
Supervisor Social Support	−.236	[−.321; −.151]	.043	−.425	−5.519

Note: $F(3, 111) = 26.97$, $p < .001$. Adjusted $R^2 = .406$; Shrunken R = .629.

that supervisor social support completely dominates job demand and control as the most important predictor.

Our hypothesis for the consequences of academic bullying predicted that professors would report less job satisfaction, more occupational stress, and a greater intent to leave academia due to academic bullying. Results of Pearson correlations confirm this hypothesis as workplace bullying was correlated negatively with job satisfaction ($r = −.462$) and correlated positively with occupational stress ($r = .460$) and intent to leave academia ($r = .400$).

Discussion

Keashly and Neuman (2010) noted that for all of the research on bullying done by faculty members of the academy, scant scholarship focuses on the bullying that actually occurs within the academy. To help fill this void, our chapter examined how job demands, job control, and social support from supervisors (JDCS model) can contribute to the perceptions of workplace bullying in academia, and how academic bullying can elicit job dissatisfaction, job stress, and the desire to seek employment outside of academia.

The findings of this chapter replicate and extend recent scholarship by Goodboy, Martin, Knight, and Long (2017), demonstrating that workplace bullying is associated with a host of negative outcomes that are predicted by high job demands, low control, and low supervisor support. However, our research is unique because it allows us to consider several ongoing concerns of working in the proverbial ivory tower. Although stereotypical representations of the professoriate suggest a leisurely life, with summers off and sporadic appearances in the office, results from our chapter suggest the prevalence of job demands such as doing excessive work, working quickly, and sensing inadequate time to accomplish tasks, are psychological stressors of academic life. Implications and explanations exist for job demands in academia. First, job demands and stress for faculty typically emerge from "publish or perish" pressures. Tenure-earning faculty at most institutions face a short window (e.g., five to seven years) in which they must produce adequate research to earn tenure or they will not be allowed to continue in their positions. Even after tenure, faculty typically need to continue publishing scholarship (or be successful in creative achievements instead of publishing) for promotion to full professor, as well as take on additional service responsibilities. In our sample, 60% of respondents were still tenure-earning or working toward the rank of full professor. The job demands and pressure for these faculty is likely to be substantial. However, even professors who are tenured might still be targeted for bullying as they are unlikely to leave academia given their accomplishments. Taylor (2013) explained that, "if an organization wishes to terminate a tenured faculty member, it may be easier to convince the person to leave through bullying tactics than to end employment through official processes" (p. 23).

However, the strain of high job demands is not reserved for research faculty only. Professors in non-research appointments often teach four or more courses per semester with several different course preparations, and sometimes at multiple institutions. Most teaching and research faculty have advising and mentoring responsibilities as well (Serrow, 2000). One national study of university faculty members discovered that an average full-time university faculty member works 53.4 hours per week while part-time faculty members average 40-hour work weeks (Cataldi, Fahimi, Bradburn, & Zimbler, 2005). Indeed, the demands of academia are abundant, yet our data show that, despite these demands, faculty who possess some control over how their work demands are met experience less bullying in their academic department.

In relation to low levels of supervisor supportiveness and bullying, our findings are, again, consistent with prior research (see Lutgen-Sandvik et al., 2009; Lutgen-Sandvik & McDermott, 2011). In addition to creating a positive climate, research indicates that supervisors themselves may be the bullies (Lutgen-Sandvik & McDermott, 2011; Ortega, Høgh, Pejtersen, & Olsen, 2009). Thus, not surprisingly, lower levels of supervisor support are associated with both job dissatisfaction and academic bullying. Twale and De Luca (2008) argued that academic supervisors are increasingly uncivil with faculty members because of their own increased pressure from upper-level administration for higher productivity and larger grant-generating activity, as well as increased credit-hour production and stronger teaching evaluations from their departments and colleges. Yet, as scholars have pointed out, even if the supervisors are not the bullies, if they do not provide appropriate support and instead ignore faculty complaints, shift blame, or stigmatize the target, they may be inadvertently contributing to the festering problems that characterize bullying (Keashly, 2001). This lack of support is vital to understanding how bullying can affect scholars. Previous research suggests report that poor workplace relationships impede workers' motivations to execute their tasks (Goodboy, Martin, & Bolkan, 2017), which may ironically undermine the initial reasons for some of the bullying activities.

Accordingly, supervisors must remain cognizant of their own supportive role with faculty. They need to be helpful and a resource for issues that arise, but they also should be aware of the needs of scholars to control their own work-related tasks by avoiding micromanagement and remaining flexible about how job tasks are completed, as long as they are competently fulfilled. Examining the isolation effect on faculty members, Fleming, Goldman, Correli, and Taylor (2016) found that new members can feel isolated and, thus, experience high levels stress and be more likely to exit. Not surprisingly, then, their research suggests that departments with supportive chairs who actively assist in scaffolding junior faculty networks helped set a positive tone for their departments, which, in turn, affected senior faculty members' willingness to engage in supportive network construction.

Our contention is that department chairs play the single most important role in deterring workplace bullying in academic departments. Other scholars would support our claim. As De Luca and Twale (2010) asserted,

> [B]ecause chairs have a major impact on the future of individual faculty members, they must be able to recognize when a faculty member is being bullied and intervene to stop

the bully while simultaneously respecting the privacy, professionalism, and integrity of the faculty member involved.

(p. 1)

Our chapter advances the understanding of the role of bullying in the academy and also provides several areas that deserve further investigation. This chapter did not provide indices of productivity or explore findings based on academic rank. Prior research suggests that organizational roles may affect not only the stress on scholars but also their ability to speak up and address the bullying (Keashly & Neuman, 2013). Furthermore, we did not investigate the role of race or gender, which are known to have an influence on victimization, as well as negative outcomes from bullying (see Meares, Oetzel, Derkacs, & Ginossar, 2004), especially in academia (Johnson-Bailey, 2015).

Moving forward, future research exploring the bully-victim paradox also could be particularly fruitful. As Mansson and Myers (2012) suggested, the faculty-student mentorship relationship is critical for academic success, yet some graduate students have abusive relationships with faculty in which they are bullied under the guise of academic training and mentorship (Martin et al., 2015). As these scholars noted, this faculty-student bullying manifests itself in several negative ways including decreased interest in the topics of study, desire to leave academia, and venting with their cohort. What needs further exploration is whether this hostile mentorship sets up young scholars as easier targets due to already decreased motivation and if it inadvertently trains targets to become bullies themselves through modeling learned bullying behaviors.

Our study did not identify the specific ways in which professors lack control over their academic duties or experience overwhelming demands (e.g., publication productivity and selectivity in journals, grant-writing and funding expectations, teaching loads and decisions, volunteer and mandatory service opportunities). Thus, future research can more closely explore the specific stressors at various academic ranks and perhaps determine more idiosyncratic bullying behaviors that are uniquely enacted in university settings. Professors who bully professors may use forms of mistreatment that are not captured by a general operationalization of negative acts (NAQR; Einarsen et al., 2009).

Moreover, noting the differences in self-reports of bullying when asked to identify behaviors versus labeling acts as bullying, Keashly and Neuman (2013) suggested that we spend a bit more time diagnosing our use of the term "bullying" itself (see West & Turner, this volume). They argued that the increased use of the term may be attributable to the stress of our workplace and need to accomplish difficult tasks (aspects captured in the JDCS model). Finally, in line with the findings of this chapter, the causes and consequences of academic bullying should be modeled as a conditional process. Specifically, scholars should determine if professors' control over job tasks and supervisor/chair social support buffer against high job demands and resulting job stress, which can encourage professors to bully each other in a strained working environment. The JDCS model makes predictions about these buffering effects of control and social support, which are tested as a multiplicative effect.

As we continue to explore the relationships among the role of support, perceptions of bullying and negative outcomes of bullying such as job dissatisfaction, stress, and desire to seek other career paths outside of academia, it is critical to further explore the role of supervisors in setting the tone for collegiality and support. Paradoxically, though, we must heed Keashly and Neuman's (2010) warning that faculty may envision collegiality as fundamental for success in an academic environment, yet it may pose a predicament because junior faculty speaking out against bullying, or standing up to aversive behaviors, might be perceived as disruptive. However, those with tenure also value academic freedom and the ability to speak one's mind without recourse. Thus, creating a supportive environment is not simply about telling people to "play nicely," but also creating ways of constructively handling conflicts to ensure that junior faculty voices are not silenced while tenured faculty perspectives are privileged. Left unaddressed, those power imbalances may unwittingly contribute to bullying.

Bullying in Academia

As we noted above, the role of the supervisor in creating a climate free of bullying cannot be ignored. Unlike non-academic positions, most employees cannot simply resign from a position and find employment immediately. The unique culture of academic job searches operates on academic calendar cycles, thus hiring often occurs in the spring for employment that starts five to seven months later in the fall. Even with tenure, faculty may have few options for mobility (Mitenko & O'Hara, 2008), given that searches need to be open to scholars looking for employees at their rank, with their research interests, and teaching expertise. That is, tenure can function as proverbial golden handcuffs in bad situations (Taylor, 2013).

We do, however, share some good news from our data. With increasing faculty perceptions of control and support, faculty reported less victimization, lower levels of reported stress, and less of a desire to leave the academy. Thus, as we talk about "social support," we can broaden our scope and work not just to help supervisors be supportive but also help them cultivate and encourage multiple lines of support for their faculty and encourage faculty to be autonomous in their work.

Overall, this chapter contributes data about the antecedents and consequences of bullying in the academy. Believing that life in the university community is an ivory tower has always been a myth; we have never been disconnected from the strains and pressures of organizational life and the subsequent mistreatment from colleagues that can arise in the academy. However, we can use our knowledge about the importance of using supportive communication and support networks to make high job demands more manageable, to encourage opportunities and improve communication that affords faculty more control in their job tasks, and ultimately reduce job dissatisfaction, stress, and the desire to leave academia. Despite the constant flow of job demands in academia, workplace bullying has less of a chance to beleaguer departments when professors are free to do their work autonomously, and their chairperson is a source of social support.

15
TENSIONS WITHIN BULLYING AND CAREER RESILIENCE IN HIGHER EDUCATION

Sean Eddington and Patrice M. Buzzanell

When Patrice invited me (Sean) to co-author this chapter with her, I accepted without hesitation. I had wanted to sort through, name, and figure out how to better handle situations that were not conducive to well-being, professionalism, and fulfillment. My own administrative work in higher education often brought me face to face with those who had experienced problematic workplaces and workplace relationships, based on bullying. To revisit and reflect on these moments, I employ an approach that legitimizes worker experiences and also enables them to engage in constructing a new normal that is both adaptive and transformative. *Resilience* is a discursive and material process through which individuals, communities, and organizations reintegrate during and after life's disruptions, losses, and disasters (Buzzanell, 2010). Within organizational life, a major form of disruption is bullying.

As evidenced with several chapters in this volume, a myriad of interpretations of workplace bullying exist in the literature. For our purposes, workplace bullying, or "repeated and persistent negative actions towards one or more individual(s), involves perceived power imbalances and create hostile work environments" (Salin, 2003, p. 1214). According to a compilation of 49 studies conducted by The Workplace Bullying Institute (Namie, 2014), 27% of U.S. workers have experienced abusive behaviors in the workplace, with current findings indicating that 19% are bullied, another 19% have witnessed bullying, and 61% are aware of such conduct. Two-thirds of bullies are male bosses, with women being targeted more than men. Further, according to Namie, almost half (40%) of targets suffer health problems, and 45% of those surveyed report worsening of workplace relationships since the Trump election.

Studies on causes of and strategies for remedying bullying in educational and workplace contexts document bullying among children and youths as well as adults and in face-to-face and online contexts (i.e., cyberbullying takes place over digital devices, such as social media, SMS, instant messaging, and email; U.S. Department of Health and Human Services, 2017). Interpersonal and organizational communication scholars have studied the content and nature of online and face-to-face bullying incidents to understand and design appropriate interventions (e.g., Brody & Vangelisti, 2017; Lutgen-Sandvik & Davenport Sypher, 2009). Organizational communication scholars emphasize how workplace cultural discourses engender and foster bullying as normative and constituted through interaction, organizational structures, and policy. However, bullying in U.S. higher education settings have not been explored sufficiently.[1]

This chapter begins with a discussion of interdisciplinary bullying literature within higher education. Then, given that individuals co-construct workplace cultures in which they work, we provide an overview of scholarship that investigates the effect of bullying on worker identities. Guided by a belief that our own stories provide insight into bullying as an embodied experience and means to understand, analyze, and know the world (Denzin & Lincoln, 2017; Ellingson, 2009), we engage in conversation with one another about our own lived experiences in higher education. Through our dialogue, we brainstorm how to navigate and manage bullying within the workplace. We conclude with a discussion about resilience practices within the context of career and offer strategies for enacting resilience within the workplace.

Workplace Bullying Within Higher Education

Workplace bullying as destructive organizational processes is not a new concept; scholarship has described, quantified, and characterized its patterns and traits. Since the 2000s, communicative "dimensions of bullying and the ways in which targets responded through narrative, metaphors, and identity-managing discourses" have taken center stage within bullying scholarship (Kassing & Waldron, 2014, p. 644).

Within communication studies, scholarship has examined workplace aggression (Corney, 2008), individual to organizational communicative processes that enact workplace bullying (Lutgen-Sandvik & Tracy, 2012), impact on and threats to worker identity (Gill & Davenport-Sypher, 2009; Lutgen-Sandvik, 2008), and the effects of emotional tyranny within the workplace (Waldron, 2009). The various strands of scholarship analyze the ways in which destructive behaviors within the workplace exist. Taking a constitutive view of communication, we note that communication is at the heart of these behaviors, providing a strong rationale for continued exploration of counterproductive communicative practices within higher education workplaces.

The Higher Educational Context

Higher education has only recently given bullying and incivility much attention (see Goodboy, Martin, & Bishop Mills, this volume). According to Keashly and Neuman (2010, p. 48), "although much research has been done on workplace aggression and bullying over the last two decades, academics have paid relatively little attention to bullying in their own institutions." *The Chronicle of Higher Education*'s 2016 survey indicated that workplace bullying is widespread, with 64% of the 830 participants responding that they had experienced workplace bullying and 77 % having observed the phenomena (Gluckman, 2017). Within the blogosphere, academics also illuminate workplace issues:

> "All of us had a story or two to tell about academic colleagues who had been rude, dismissive, passive aggressive or even outright hostile to us in the workplace," Inger Mewburn, director of research training at Australian National University, wrote in a recent post called "Academic Assholes and the Circle of Niceness" for her popular blog, *The Thesis Whisperer*. "As we talked we started to wonder: Do you get further in academe if you are a jerk?"
>
> *(Flaherty, 2013, para 2)*

This quotation challenges what makes productive academic members and connects to academic cultures that engender certain cultural ideals of workers. As Flaherty (2014a, 2014b) noted, faculty have called on their colleagues and institutions to address civility, but such pleas meet with mixed results. Some maintain that the call comprises as an affront to free speech within academe (Flaherty, 2014a). Other institutions, like the University of Wisconsin-Madison, passed faculty legislation formalizing anti-bullying policies with strong majority support within the Faculty Senate (Flaherty, 2014b).

Besides controversies and enactment of policies, studies have centered on the costs of bullying and incivility within academe. Hollis (2015) conducted a study of over 400 respondents from a varied departments and functional units to examine both the extent and economic costs of bullying. Findings indicated that 27% of the respondents experienced prolonged bullying, and nearly 28% described inaction from their organization to address bullying. Second, Hollis found that the economic cost of turnover required universities to invest 150% more into their workers. If a worker's salary was $50,000 and he/she left because of a hostile work environment, it cost the university $75,000 to replace, train, and socialize a new worker. The rising tide of employee disengagement emerging from hostile workplaces also factors into economic ramifications. Because of workplace bullying, universities lose nearly $7,000 per worker because of worker disengagement (Hollis, 2015). These costs of worker disengagement often result from consistent inaction from leaders in handling the bullying issues; frustration at leaders, themselves, being the source of bullying, and feelings of social isolation because senior and tenured faculty hold lifetime appointments.

Additionally, Simpson and Cohen (2004) examined workplace bullying in higher education through a gendered lens and found that both perceptions and experiences varied between men and women; however, women in higher education were targets of bullying through unfair criticism, extra workloads, and fear of failing promotions. Simpson and Cohen's study noted that women perceived unfair treatment more succinctly than men and more likely to report inappropriate treatment. However, they faced challenges if their bully was their direct supervisor. Men more often considered bullying and harassment within the workplace to be appropriate management tools, an orientation rooted in masculinist management discourses of power, control, competition, and hierarchy (Buzzanell, 1994).

Whereas Hollis (2015) and Simpson and Cohen do not center communication within their studies, they both illustrate bullying as a communicative act. Messages shared within the workplace about promotions, mentoring programs, reporting processes and structures, and leadership practices shape the lived realities in the workplace. Bullying pervades organizations because of failures to address the phenomena within the setting *and* because leaders often are the source. Because of these communicative constructions enacted within the workplace, issues emerge at micro through macro levels of academe. These intersections beg the question regarding how and why these workplace concerns seem intractably situated within higher educational institutions.

From a critical standpoint, the various discourses enacted around higher education provide potential insights into change. Patton (2004) argued that prevailing civility discourses shroud racist, sexist, classist, and other problematic issues. For instance, Patton (2004) described hegemony "in language (words of tolerating diversity), racial tracking (segregated education where often Euro and Asian American students are placed in college prep courses and Black and Latino students are placed on a vocational track), or the model minority stereotype" (p. 81). Patton asserted that the ways in which such university systems are phrased, activated, and sustained for the betterment of students, faculty, and larger communities mask critical interrogation of underlying interests and ways of treating others that subordinate minorities. Examining the use of "family" metaphors to describe university cultures, Patton contends that these metaphors mask or overshadow attrition and retention rates by non-White members. These forms of civility discourse continually decenter or sequester women and minorities' experiences while also maintaining systems of whiteness and power in the academy.

Whereas Patton's (2004) work does not centrally examine workplace bullying, her arguments provide an important connection to the organizational discourses that constitute academic realities and experiences. Organizational discourses regarding workplace cultures and power issues focus on how everyday interactions converge around shared meanings but also examine and illuminate workplace cultures as "sites of struggle where different groups compete to shape the social reality of organizations that serve their own interest" (Mumby & Clair, 1997, p. 182). In other words, critical approaches to organizational discourses interrogate the very nature of who has the power to control and assess workers' experiences.

As noted above, workplaces that describe bullying within a civility discourse often ignore the interconnections of race and gender (and other social identities) within their conversations. By invoking notions of civility as normative processes, other identities and experiences are ignored. White, masculine perspectives create power structures within the university (Acker, 1990; Patton, 2004). These perspectives drive the master narratives of excellence, quality, success, and persistence through which workplaces are enacted (van den Brink & Benschop, 2011), hiding counternarratives that belie workers' lived reality. Patton and others like Allen (1996) and B. J. Allen, Orbe, and Olivas (1999) have challenged universities' incongruity between their espoused values and their lived and enacted values. These paradoxes and disenchantments are echoed in B. J. Allen's (2000) description of her (and other women of color's) experiences as outsider-within as she navigated being a Black woman in the U.S. higher educational system. Using Black feminist standpoints, she detailed micro-practices within academe that resulted in tokenization, being seen as intellectually inferior, experiencing comments about departmental status as diversity hires, and persistent "messages implicitly or explicitly [that] question [their] right to be in [their] new role" (B. J. Allen, p. 187). In layering her own and others' experiences, she created the group-level basis for critique, interventions, and new theorizing about socialization that incorporates tensions, difference, and micro-meso-macro discourses for praxis. In short, higher education claims civility and inclusivity; however, these aspirational values, beliefs, and messages are often ignored or serve as public images that hide realities of bullying and prevent visibility of concerns. The reality is anything but civil and inclusive; often workplace bullying involves specific threats and challenges to professional identities.

The Effects of Bullying on Worker Identities

When workplace bullying occurs, professional identities are often the first site of threat (Lutgen-Sandvik, 2008). Members of the academy feel and experience threats in the workplace every day through subtle interactions like terse and cold conversations, excessive and harsh feedback, awkward glances or avoiding eye contact, and dodging individuals in hallways; these moments over time challenge professionals' sense of self. These microaggressions and more blatant hostilities can prompt workplace disengagement and threats to individuals' dignity.

Such messages and interactions often are couched within professional and strategic workplace activities that Keashly and Neuman (2010) described as "behaviors designed to undermine their professional standing, authority, and competence, or impede access to key resources for their work (such as money, space, time, or access to strong students)" (p. 53). These rhetorical strategies have been explored within Nelson and Lambert's (2001) ethnographic examination into the institutional and organizational structures that protect and defend bullies within academe. In academic discussions, bullies veil their bullying as professional feedback and use organizational systems to legitimize their behaviors. These individuals create negative workplace environments—enacting what Stohl and Schell (1991) described as a "farrago" model of group dysfunction. The farrago enacts "socially inappropriate and organizationally problematic" behaviors (p. 97). Despite organizational dysfunctions, academic bullies often are as high performers. According to Stohl and Schell, they hold leadership positions within organizations and/or are perceived as necessary for the functioning of the workplace.

More troubling are the identity threats to workers' dignity. Dignity comprises one of the key dimensions to career (Buzzanell & Lucas, 2013) and is integral to performance, well-being, and satisfaction. Workplace dignity entails the prevailing belief of one's value, one's respect for self and others (Hodson, 2001; Lucas, 2015). Workplaces should be sites where "people can build a sense of dignity by making important contributions, developing their personal competence, and being recognized as a valuable part of a larger whole" (Lucas, 2015, p. 644). Workplaces also encompass sites for destructive patterns that can destroy dignity.

Hodson and Roscigno (2004) conducted a meta-analysis of ethnographic studies on workplace dignity and job-level through organizational outcomes and uncovered that organizational structures, job descriptions, and workplace that encourage forms of organizational citizenship and engagement.

Relatedly, workplaces can bolster or stymy individual worker dignity (Sayer, 2007). Extending this argument, Lucas, Manikas, Mattingly, and Crider's (2017) study on workplace dignity determined that workplace cultures that focus on "autonomy (when coupled with safe and secure work) and learning and development predicted increases" of counterproductive work behaviors (p. 1520). Counterproductive behaviors have been broadly defined, but, more recently, scholars have examined them within the dual context of incivility (Sakurai & Jex, 2012) and bullying (Devonish, 2013). Lucas et al. (2017, p. 1509) described them as "abuse targeted towards others, production deviance, sabotage, theft, and withdrawal." These counterproductive behaviors emerge as an emotional response to cultural issues within the workplace. Cultural manifestations of bullying exist within these counterproductive work behaviors that threaten one's sense of identity.

Identity threats, in this vein, can be subtle and cause various forms of mental and emotional trauma (Lutgen-Sandvik, 2008). They challenge cultural assumptions about one's value within the workplace. Citing the Protestant Worker norm, Weiland, Bauer, and Deetz (2009) reasoned that the organizational social constructions of identity place productivity at the heart of the ideal worker through careerist orientations. Careerism bleeds into academic spaces through prevailing ideas on workers being only as good as their work quality. Within higher education, productivity and impact might mean anything from numbers of attendees at an educational program, to journal publications, grants awarded, numbers and placement of students advised, as well as awards for discovery, learning, mentorship, and engagement. When academic bullies covertly attack others' professional identity, they often attack these workers' ability to be productive departmental, university, and disciplinary members. These attacks stem from jealousy (Georgakopoulos, Wilkin, & Kent, 2011) or fear for a bully's own standing and perceived competence within their department (Simpson & Cohen, 2004). However, the fact remains that bullying within the higher education workplace creates unique identity threats that require different communicative processes to mitigate the workplace bullying challenges.

A Communicative Model of Career Resilience

One pathway to mitigating workplace challenges is through the cultivation of career resilience, which London (1983) defined as "a person's resistance to career disruption in a less than optimal environment" (p. 621). Career resilience has been further conceptualized in interdisciplinary career literature as a quality or trait (Jiang, 2017), protective skillset (Akkermans, Brenninkmeijer, Schaufeli, & Blonk, 2015; Vanhove, Herian, Perez, Harms, & Lester, 2016), and necessary component of career motivation (London, 1983). Mishra and McDonald (2017) contended that career resilience is an integral component of career longevity. However, these approaches overlook the central role that communication processes serve to organize and enact resilience. In this vein, career resilience focuses on processes that enable individuals (and academic units) to legitimize their experiences, thus adapting, resisting, and potentially changing sites of disruption (Buzzanell, 2010). In this perspective, career resilience illuminates the need to sustain and enlarge individuals' (and academic units') communication networks as protective strategies to retain intellectual capital and identity and as springboards for creating more satisfying new normals. Centering communication in career resilience processes spans micro to macro levels; therefore, career resilience does not solely rest in one or the other, but rather it is "fundamentally grounded in messages, d/Discourse, and narrative" (Buzzanell, 2010, p. 2). In sum, possible pathways toward the management and lessening of are is through incorporating and communicatively enacting resilience.

In Conversation: Interrogating Experiences

Resilience within career can include (but is not limited to) changing workplace cultures, leaving specific workplaces, or cultivating survival strategies. My own experience (Sean) is one that has lent

Tensions Within Bullying & Career Resilience

itself to all three of these types of strategies. For this section, we (Sean and Patrice) engage in discussions about bullying that has been witnessed, experienced, and/or related to us by situating these narratives and reflections in an integrative case (D'Enbeau, Buzzanell, & Duckworth, 2010). This kind of case analysis creates imaginary places and spaces for discussions fraught with real issues and situated in everyday materialities.

We imagine Sean driving Patrice to meet others for dinner at a new microbrewery. As he made a turn onto a busy street, he turned to Patrice with a troubled look on his face. "You know, Patrice, I've worked in different jobs and at a number of different sites in higher education. I believe in work toward student success and generation of new knowledge. I just never unexpected to see bullying to such an extent. It seems to be so prevalent in academe."

Patrice responded, "What do you mean?"

"As a young professional, I wanted to see the good and optimistically (or blindly) tried to see the positive—especially working within student services. We spout off student development theory, and we try to supervise our undergraduate workers developmentally—meeting them where they are at; challenging and supporting them. And yet, I was and remain stunned at how the same co-workers who believe in these things are often some of the most problematic, callous, politically self-serving individuals. They hold senior leadership positions within departments; organize our annual retreats; hold titles like Director of Student Leadership and Development. I find it preposterous that I should not be able to trust my co-workers with my professional goals and aspirations. Departmental leaders have used my naivete against me by taking things that I have said out of context—reporting my comments to supervisors with veiled concern. They claimed we were a 'family,' but then they'd be the first to stab you in the back."

"I can't help but smile, Sean, because you still are awfully trusting and hope to make such a difference in your work," Patrice replied. "Despite the many things I've seen and experienced, I still trust and believe that we can change the world. I've been in institutional cultures that uphold members' dignity and others that take no action when bullies lead. You can't lose hope, Sean. But I cut you off, and I apologize. When you started talking, I was re-collecting pieces of bullying and incivility puzzles that we've been discussing when writing our chapter."

"That's okay. I appreciate your insights. It's just that—" Sean paused. "Well, I'm preparing to search for a faculty position. How do I recognize the signs? My experiences have made me cautious about what I share, how I talk within the workplace, and with whom I interact. So much of the bad behavior within higher education gets ignored. As educators, we are presumably the 'good people.' Yet, it certainly seems more complicated than that. What do you think?"

Patrice looked out the car window at the falling snow before commenting. "You know, Sean, I have been blessed with wonderful opportunities, great colleagues and students, and work that challenges me every day. Not everyone can say how much they love their work and all that being a professor brings. But it has been hard and there have been tradeoffs. I remain perplexed at what I've seen and heard."

"Like what?"

"Do you really want to hear?"

"Yes. But I'll need to make a quick stop to get gas. Then let's continue." Sean filled up the gas tank, while Patrice remained in the car and checked her text messages. After Sean paid for the gas, he hopped back into the car. He started up the car and turned the heat on high, muttering to himself about the cold temperature. As he exited the gas station, he checked the side mirror and rear window before pulling into the road. He reset Google™ maps for directions to the microbrewery and said, "Okay, let's continue."

"Okay!" Patrice started by remarking, "I have cultivated a great network of scholars who would come and talk about their experiences with me. I knew that I could do so with them without any hesitation. They might name their experiences, but often have felt at a loss about what to do. These are very accomplished women and men. They talk about how both the structure and leadership within the academic unit can foster abusive behaviors."

"What do you mean, Patrice?"

"Well, consider two of our systems: heads and tenure. Within academic departments, heads report to deans. Deans don't want to disrupt departmental processes by highlighting dysfunctionalities—especially when heads have significant connections and links to powerful people like donors or university administrators. Tenure complicates things as an additional tension in hierarchical relationships where one professor's words can carry more weight than the voices of those lower in the 'academic food chain.' Unless there is some record, some form of documentation or witnesses, the burden of proof can fall on the person lower in the different hierarchies in academe. This happens despite policies against harassment, retaliation, and so on. Some faculty (and even deans) believe that they can wait until bullies 'die off' through retirement, voluntary exit, and/or death. However, by that time, others have learned the system and the deep cultural forces that maintain the status quo. People start to see bullying as normal—and when they realize that something is wrong and consider exiting, they wonder if the next place could be worse. You'd be horrified at how bad it can be sometimes. I've heard of heads demanding—even yelling at—professors and staff to come to work despite being ill, in danger from domestic abuse (with restraining orders), and in the middle of difficult family issues. These demands have endangered lives. These behaviors have resulted in the exit of highly productive and well-regarded faculty and staff. The time and energy spent on discussing these things and trying to figure out what to do is a drain. No one wants to document, no one wants to be the one to report. Even when reported, the grievances and mediations sometimes go nowhere. There are real costs to everyone and to institutions themselves, as you know from your research."

Patrice paused for a few seconds and stared out the car window. "An added complication is the damage that can be done in relatively small and close professional networks if students and junior faculty are not protected. Bullies who are big names say, 'who is going to believe their word against mine?' Bullies can destroy reputations and academic progress for reasons as seemingly minor as their not liking the students' advisors and their not feeling supported in self-serving initiatives. It gets especially bad when department chairs don't support—or they terminate—those most vulnerable within departments. Fortunately, human resources and faculty ombudspersons are getting better and more adept at being a source of support within these instances; however, the efficiency and effectiveness of these processes rely on careful and meticulous documentation of interactions, emails, and instances. It's not unheard of for faculty *and* students to get counseling because of the actions of bullies within these departments."

Sean shook his head in disbelief and exclaimed, "Really? What happens to the academic bullies? There has to be some recourse!"

"You would think so." Patrice closed her eyes for a few moments. "It's complicated and it depends. If bullies are critical to productivity and data analytic results (meaning that they publish or get funding a lot, are linked to key faculty or donors, are partnered with people higher in administration or with governing bodies), they keep their jobs. They may be removed from supervisory or leadership roles. But even when replaced or when they depart willingly, the culture may retain the vestiges of their presence. Their friends and allies may safeguard their positions. These supporters sometimes learn that they, too, can be subject to harassment and vindictiveness when the bully turns on them."

Sean's car pulled into the microbrewery parking lot and he remarked, "It looks like we got here before everyone else! I think we need beer and those bacon-wrapped, fried cheese curds we've heard all about!"

Patrice agreed, and they got seated at the microbrewery. They texted to find out where the others were and, after the IPAs and appetizers arrived, they resumed their conversation.

Between bites, Sean stated, "I'm still not sure how to go about this issue, Patrice."

Patrice remarked, "We can do this together. Take out your laptop so that we can take notes. It's helpful to have these conversations and to keep records because sometimes when we experience or witness bullying, we are a loss about what to do. We find it hard to believe people would treat others the way that they do."

Sean started a new document. "Ready!"

When Patrice began, it all came out in a rush. "Strategies vary and depend on my own or others' analysis of the situation and the kinds of support individuals think they would have if they wanted to initiate action. I typically try to figure out why bullies act as they do. Sometimes they don't realize how out of line their behaviors are, especially if they were treated in this way in the past. Sometimes they are open to suggestions that can help them reframe ways to achieve or reset their goals. Other times, they feel insecure and in positions of power—whatever someone says will be perceived as a threat to them personally and to their leadership. They are dangerous, especially if they have not been in power before. They want to surround themselves with people who will follow their direction and not be more competent than they are. The lesson here is to tread carefully, work from within, and keep options open. If these leaders stay in their positions despite complaints and challenges to their authority, then systems are protecting them."

"Between the extremes of unintentional bullying and deliberate malicious behavior, one can do varied things. Members of higher educational institutions can work with Human Resources, Offices of Institutional Equity, ombudspersons, support and professional networks—and derive strategies. I figured out that containment works effectively a while ago when reporting committee results to faculty. I timed the bully's contributions to meeting interactions (always 20 minutes) and then thanked the person and turned immediately to acknowledge others who wanted to speak. If I didn't allow for that time, I encountered immediate repercussions for me and for the committee that I was chairing from the bully or from one of this person's current supporters—I say current because they were always new departmental members who hadn't yet caught onto departmental politics and were flattered by the attention of a 'big name'."

Shaking his head, Sean stared at his beer. "Containment can only go so far. When I was an academic advisor, I had an ally in senior leadership who would advocate for young professionals and try to minimize the effects of bullying by a more senior academic advisor and the director of the program. However, when she left, I and the other young professionals had no one in the office to rely upon. It only got worse, and I quit shortly after her. If we want to try and be change agents, shouldn't we go beyond survival tactics?"

Patrice paused and smiled. "That's the crux of the matter, isn't it? It's like I said; even when the bullies leave the department, there may still be vestiges of their presence. It takes a critical mass to fight; it takes belief that you can make change; it takes knowledge of policies and strategies from research; and it takes willingness to go public. It's been my experience that sometimes individuals do not recognize their actions as incivility, microaggressions, or bullying. Sometimes they might not even recognize how and why they do the things that they do. I try to give them the benefit of the doubt. I often say something to them. It depends. I was and am fortunate to be part of an interdisciplinary group where we would talk out issues and possible interventions. I learned how I might deal with bullying."

Sean's eyes narrowed, and his eyebrows furled in thought. "Hmmm."

Between bites of a bacon-wrapped cheese curd, Patrice replied, "You don't look convinced. If we can help individuals understand the short- and long-term impact of their actions, we might be able to create a new normal within departments. If the bullying is from deep-seated insecurities and is embedded in malicious leadership, then tread carefully, learn how to activate systemic protections and change mechanisms, and consider forms of resistance, including leaving the position if you have tried everything. Now, leaving the position can be seen in a variety of ways; however, in this case, it would a sign of strength and resistance to leave a toxic workplace . . . a sign of moving on."

Sean took a final drink of his beer and smiled. "I like that."

Sean looked up and saw that their friends had arrived. After a great meal and much laughter, Sean and Patrice left the microbrewery.

"Sean, thanks for driving me. With Steve out of town and the kids having our cars, I wouldn't have joined everyone tonight without the ride."

"You're welcome, Patrice. It gave me time without tons of people around for me to ask you about these workplace issues that have been weighing on me." During the drive, Sean continued to reflect on the conversation. "We've been wrestling with some big questions that seem to be a major part of academe—particularly as it comes to dealing and coping with--maybe even leaving--toxic work cultures. I'm paraphrasing here, but you've basically been talking about safeguarding, even thriving, in work and career, which sounds an awful lot like your communication theory of resilience. Is there a place to apply that theory as a career strategy to lessen bullying episodes, and maybe even change these work cultures?"

Patrice replied, "Yes!! However, the thing is that one doesn't cultivate and enact resilience alone—and that's the basis for challenging bullying."

Sean considered these ideas. "Meaning?"

Patrice replied, "Well, it *sounds* simple, but the emotional labor, dissent strategies, identity struggles, and interactions are complicated."

Sean concluded, "I bet. Where would you like me to drop you off? Home? I'll continue to think about all this as I send out a couple more job applications tonight."

Final Reflections and Strategies

As both this review of literature and our conversation illuminates, the workplaces within higher education constitute a challenging site for conflict, bullying, and human resilience. People within workplaces enact resilience as a communicative process by talking and interacting in ways that encourage reintegration after disruptions or destructive situations (Buzzanell, Shenoy, Remke, & Lucas, 2009). Drawing from Buzzanell's (2010) five tensions or processes—crafting normalcy, backgrounding negative and foregrounding productive action, sustaining identity anchors, building and maintaining social networks, and engaging in alternative logics—workers are often engaged in an adaptive-transformative dialectic to cope with bullying and toxic cultures. The adaptive part enables stability, coping, and social support in the event or in anticipation of bullying. However, the transformative aspects are embedded in the resilience model because, if taken to extremes and fixed for long times in interactions and networks, processes could be counterproductive.

Individuals do not cultivate and enact resilience alone. Communication networks comprise a vital source of social support with academic departments. Academicians and staff should find both mentors and sponsors who can (1) provide advice, (2) advocate for others' interests, issues, or needs, and (3) help to minimize the impact of toxic cultures and systems. Organizational members can invest in conversations that help academic bullies understand the impact of their actions. These conversations can be in individual or group settings that help illuminate the ironies or unintended ways that individual actions, policies, or messages play in shaping bullying behaviors. By cultivating alternative behaviors and pathways of accountability, people can enact new workplace normalcies that both preserve individual dignity and create a more equitable, and inclusive workplace.

Note

1 In U.S. higher education, most research has focused on students and on the ways in which difference, such as gender, sexual orientation, and race/ethnicity, is associated with bullying online and offline (e.g., Watts, Wagner, Velasquez, & Behrens, 2017).

VOICES FOR VISIBILITY
Middle School Bullies Using Lies to Incite a Fight

Garry Bailey

In her eighth grade Career Development class, Annie and her classmates were doing project work at tables. Students across the classroom were talking. Emily and Hannah were at the table next to Annie's talking to the students at their table. They talked loudly enough to make sure Annie could hear her name, but not the content of their conversation. The teacher was at her desk on the opposite side of the classroom out of hearing range, unaware of the kind of conversation that occurred.

At the end of class, students funneled into the hallway on their way to the next period. The teacher stood in the doorway of her classroom, as was the practice of all teachers, to monitor the hallways. It must have been school policy to do that. The main hallway lacked classrooms so students who wanted to bully others waited until they got there before abusing their peers. Emily and Hannah approached Annie, one on each side, to tell her what they were talking to the other students about in the Career Development class. Many other students were also walking and talking in the hallway so everything must have seemed normal to any onlookers. The conversation was anything but normal for Annie.

Emily and Hannah intimidated Annie, gazing down at her and talking in very mean voices. They claimed that Annie was sending texts to other students, telling them that their classmate, Bonnie, was pregnant. These comments frightened Annie because a lot of people might believe these accusations and could easily be mad at Annie, even though it was a lie. Annie didn't know anything about Bonnie's real situation, but she knew that, if she didn't do anything, Emily and Hannah would successfully get Annie in a lot of trouble.

Annie quickly began thinking about all of the things that could happen. She knew this situation could easily negatively affect her reputation. She figured this claim would anger a lot of people, including classmates, teachers, the office, and even parents. She was pretty sure that her parents' anger, however, would be directed at the school, whereas everyone else would be angry with her. She decided that it would be best to tell her parents about it after school.

Emily and Hannah indicated that they were going to get Annie in trouble and that there was going to be a fight. Hannah seemed to be very emotionally invested, and Annie assumed that Hannah was the one who wanted to fight. As they continued walking down the main hallway with no presence of adult authority, Hannah began using more aggressive talk with foul language and a louder volume. It felt like a fight was about to happen. Annie couldn't wait to get into her classroom. Even the thought that someone wanted to fight her was terrifying to Annie. The whole experience was confusing to Annie because she had no background, context, or true events to help her with making sense of this encounter.

Fortunately, Annie was headed to History class, while Emily and Hannah were both going to English. The event in the hallway was so overwhelming to Annie that she broke down and cried in History class. Of course, several students knew what was happening from hearing what Emily and Hannah were doing. News quickly got back to Emily and Hannah about the effect that they had had on Annie.

The issue escalated quickly to almost out of control. Annie heard reports from her friends that Hannah was bragging about making Annie cry. Hannah's friends were laughing about it, and Annie's friends were mad about it. Annie kept thinking about the fact that she didn't even have a phone that could do texting. She also knew that it didn't really matter because the whole thing was way out of control. It was just so unfair because she didn't do anything to deserve being at the center of this problem.

By the end of the school day, Annie felt like everyone in the school knew about this growing conflict and that Hannah had the upper hand. Annie just wanted to leave school and never come back. She feared being cornered somewhere in the school and getting beat up. She worried about going to the bathroom and having Hannah follow her. Thankfully, she was going home so she didn't have to worry about it for the rest of the day.

Annie's next hurdle in dealing with this horrendous event was talking about it to her parents. She knew that some parents would not be understanding and might even add some punishment to the pain that she was already experiencing. The challenge in her family, she thought, was reliving the story without making it too emotional. An over-emotional telling of the story could make Dad's reaction unpredictable. A more rational telling of the story would hopefully lead to a thoughtful, strategic response from Mom and Dad.

Dinnertime in Annie's family comprised a time for everyone to talk about their respective day, with Mom and Dad asking how the day went for both Annie, the eldest child, and Ethan, the youngest child. Annie felt like her family situation was good because her parents were supportive and not controlling. As the time for dinner drew closer, she was pretty sure the conversation would go well, but she was also somewhat nervous and worried. Annie began thinking that she might have done something wrong and didn't know it. She might actually be in trouble, but she couldn't think of how she was in the wrong. It just felt like she was in trouble. Mom and Dad could help with that.

She then began thinking that, no matter how she told her parents, they might react toward the school in a way that could be really embarrassing for her and further ruin her reputation. Annie imagined that Dad might go to the school the next day with "guns blazing" and begin making demands. It was difficult for her to think about telling her parents, but, from her perspective, she really didn't have a choice.

Annie had a little time after school before dinner so she thought about what she would say. She had homework to do, but thinking about her story was more important right now. Not doing homework could mean a bad grade, but it had been a bad day. After rehearsing her story, dinnertime arrived, and she reported what happened during this awful day. Her parents asked questions in a remarkably calm manner. Annie felt very relieved, but she didn't eat much because her stomach was in such turmoil over what happened that day.

The big question, of course, was what to do about all of this mess. First, Dad wanted to know if she felt safe enough to be at school in such a volatile situation. If students were taking sides, with threats of fighting, the principal and the police officer needed to know about the potential for violence. Annie said that she felt confident that she could stay close enough to adults the next day so that no one would try anything. The class schedule alternated each day, and she had Keyboarding, with Annie on the opposite side of the classroom from Emily and Hannah. They had no reason to be anywhere near Annie.

The family decided, then, that Annie would go to school and see if the bullying was a one-day thing or if the threat persisted. She went to school, concerned about what students, and maybe even teachers, thought of her; however, she didn't worry that anyone would actually hurt her physically.

Voices for Visibility

The following day, it was obvious that students were taking sides, and threats were being made on behalf of Annie or against her. Annie just wanted all of this conflict to go away, but she began to realize that she would have to report the bullying to the office. Many of the threats were nonverbal in the form of obscene gestures, mean facial expressions and stares, and even avoidance from friends who didn't want to get involved.

Yet, the issue seemed easier to talk about, with the emotional shock wearing off. The time had come for thinking strategically, and talk about the day didn't wait until dinner. Her parents were at the school when the final bell rang, ready to pick up Annie and find out what the day had been like. Again, Mom and Dad listened carefully and then suggested that they needed to go to administration before the issue escalated any further.

Surprisingly, Dad didn't declare that this was the way it would be. Instead, he asked if Annie was okay with this plan. Mom and Dad were so gentle and did not push. They were thorough in questioning, though. They wanted to know what Annie might have done to make Emily and/or Hannah angry, but they were always supportive. Annie expressed her love for parents who supported her in this way. Annie always wanted to please her parents because they always wanted good things for her, including the expectation that Annie would do her best and treat people right.

The next morning was stressful. Waking up was hard because Annie woke up several times during the night, thinking about how the next day would go. It wasn't every day that a student made a complaint of bullying to the principal and police officer. In the morning, Annie expressed gratitude for developing a plan with Dad yet hoped that it wouldn't result in total embarrassment. Dad said he would go with Annie every step of the way and ask for a meeting with administration before she attended any class.

At school, everything seemed like an ordinary day. Students were filing into the school, and the principal stood at the front entrance, welcoming students. As Annie and her dad walked in, the principal initiated a greeting since fathers did not normally walk into school in such a manner, and, as the posted sign clearly indicated, any visitor must check in at the front office. Dad told the principal that Annie needed to report a bullying incident. The principal pointed to the front office and escorted Annie and her father to the office, asking staff to contact the police officer.

The police officer was also on patrol in the hallways, greeting students and ensuring that everyone realized the presence of law enforcement on the school premises. Annie and her father waited for a few minutes, but the police officer soon returned to the front office and walked with Annie and her father to the police office, which was adjacent to the front office. After a kind greeting to both Annie and her father, the officer turned to Annie to hear about what happened.

Annie told her story to the officer with most of the same facts, but she didn't go into as much depth as she did at home. The officer then asked Annie's dad if he wanted to add anything. Dad displayed the recent telephone bill, with a list of all texts that had been sent over the past two months. Dad also disclosed that Annie did not have a cell phone with texting capability, and he invited the police officer to investigate the family's cell phone usage. The officer noted that it wouldn't be necessary to do so.

The police officer mentioned that he knew the girls that Annie referenced, and he also knew Annie's character well enough to doubt that she would have willingly participated in any of this activity. He said that he would interview Emily and Hannah about what happened, but he figured that the story wouldn't be much different. He then pulled out a laminated sheet from his desk. It included some descriptions of what counted as bullying and what did not count as bullying. The descriptions suggested that fighting, pushing, name calling, rude talk, excluding, and teasing were negative behaviors but not necessarily bullying. The officer affirmed that he defined what Annie experienced as bullying because it satisfied three requirements: (1) the actions must include repeated threats; (2) a power difference exists between the one(s) bullying and the target(s); and (3) the situation comprised an obvious intention to harm the target(s).

The officer noted that he would call Emily and Hannah out of class for an interview to talk about what happened, explain to them what bullying was, and inform them what would happen if they engaged in any such behavior ever again while they were students at the school. He stressed that he would tell them that, if it happened again, he would go to their classroom, arrest them, put cuffs on their wrists in class, and then take them to juvenile detention. He assured Annie that he would be following up with her and make sure her school was safe for her.

The officer's comments shocked Annie, and she felt responsible for getting these girls in trouble. As she walked out of the police office and went to the front office to get a slip for going to class late, Dad encouraged her to remember that this situation was not her fault. He said that Emily and Hannah did something wrong and very dangerous. They needed to get a message from authority that their actions could not be repeated without serious repercussions.

Her father asked her if she was going to be okay and inquired if she wanted to stay at school or if she needed a day off. Annie said that she needed to face the day and that doing so would help her reputation. When it came time for Career Development class again, the police officer came to the classroom and interrupted class. He was holding his cuffs on one finger so the whole class could see, and he called Emily and Hannah to come with him for a conversation about bullying.

When Emily and Hannah returned, their faces were very red, and they had obviously been crying. Annie felt bad for them. She hadn't wanted that to happen. Again, she just wanted the whole thing to go away. Everyone in class knew what had happened, and Annie was quite certain that no one in class would ever choose to engage in bullying again. The police officer made getting caught for bullying a very scary experience.

Annie noticed that everything seemed normal afterward. The students that had taken Hannah's side didn't seem to have a problem with Annie anymore. Even Emily and Hannah had a civil attitude when interacting with Annie during collaborative assignments. It was surprising to Annie that it seemed like the whole thing actually did go away. However, word did quickly spread that the Police Officer busted someone for bullying, underscoring that bullying just wasn't fun anymore for anyone.

In the nine years after the incident took place, Annie survived the end of middle school, all of high school, and her undergraduate degree. She remains a happy person overall, with resilience to interpersonal attacks against her. With friends and people that she meets, she chooses to be open and welcoming. With people who reject her, exclude her, or say negative things about her, she chooses to let it go as someone else's problem. One valuable lesson that Annie learned from this incident is empathy for someone who is bullied. She knows what it is like, so she has a clear ability to empathize with someone who experiences bullying. She is the kind of person who would choose to walk alongside the bullied to be an understanding, supportive presence and a wise counsel for anyone seeking guidance about bullying.

★★ Bullying Within/Across the Lifespan ★★

16

EXPLORING BULLYING EXPERIENCES AMONG IMMIGRANT YOUTH IN CANADA

Rukhsana Ahmed

Introduction

Bullying comprises a complex and multidimensional social problem. According to Bullying Canada (2017, para 1), "Bullying happens when someone hurts or scares another person on purpose and the person being bullied has a hard time defending themselves." Bullying affects physical and mental health and creates family and social problems and academic difficulties (Abada, Hou, & Ram, 2008; Bullying Canada, 2017; Centers for Disease Control and Prevention, 2015; US Department of Health and Human Services, n.d.). In spite of a burgeoning body of research on different aspects of bullying, such as school bullying (Mills & Carwile, 2009; Ttofi & Farrington, 2011), workplace bullying (Lutgen-Sandvik & Tracy, 2012), cyberbullying (Goodboy & Martin, 2015), bystanders (Dillon & Bushman, 2015), and harassment (Spitzberg & Cupach, 2014), the intersection of culture and youth bullying remains under-investigated (Haines-Saah, Hilario, Jenkins, Ng, & Johnson, 2016; Maynard, Vaughn, Salas-Wright, & Vaughn, 2016). As such, this study aims to explore bullying experiences of immigrant youth, focusing on Canada.

According to the 2011 National Household Survey (NHS) (Statistics Canada, 2013), about 1,162,900 foreign-born persons arrived in Canada between 2006 and 2011, accounting for 3.5% of Canada's total population and contributing to the makeup of Canada's rapidly growing multicultural population in metropolitan areas. Although reports indicate that Canada has higher rates of bullying (Canadian Institute of Health Research, 2012; Public Safety Canada, 2016), we know little about the experiences of bullying among immigrants, especially immigrant youth. Notably, Canada has undertaken key anti-bullying initiatives such as Bill 14, Anti-Bullying Act, 2012 (Legislative Assembly of Ontario, 2011) and Anti-Cyberbullying Law, Bill C-13 (Puzic, 2015). The question thus arises as to how these initiatives can be successful if they are not tailored to the specific needs of the country's diverse population group needs. Interestingly, based on American study findings, Canadian scholars (Pottie, Dahal, Georgiades, Premji, & Hassan, 2015) concluded that first generation and non-native English speaking immigrant youth experience higher bullying rates than do youth who are third generation and native-born. Based on their review of existing literature, the authors identified associations between bullying and health-related problems generally and, more particularly, between ethnic bullying and mental health. More recently, though, researchers in Canada (Haines-Saah et al., 2016) examined the connection between the sources of emotional distress in youth's lives and peer-based bullying within their community in northern British Columbia, Canada. Through the use of an intersectional lens, their "findings suggests that youths' narratives about bullying reflect intersecting and socially embedded configurations of 'race,' neocolonialism, and place" (para 1). Therefore, using intersectionality as an analytical tool (Collins & Bilge, 2016), this chapter explores what immigrant youth in Ottawa-Gatineau, the sixth largest Canadian entry point for foreign-born residents (Statistics Canada, 2013), communicate about and how they deal with bullying. Findings from this study will contribute to an empirically grounded and theoretically informed understanding of bullying experiences at the intersection of culture and youth bullying. Advancing such understanding can help inform anti-bullying initiatives and interventions for ethnically, culturally, religiously, and linguistically diverse population groups in Canada and beyond.

The Context

According to the CIHR (2012) reported feature on *Tackling Bullying*, on a scale of 35 countries, Canada has the 9th highest rate of bullying in the 13-years-olds category. In Canada, one in three adolescents in schools have reported being subject to bullying, and 47% of Canadian parents disclosed that their child had been the victim of bullying. Moreover, students who identify as Lesbian, Gay, Bisexual, Trans-identified, Two-Spirited, Queer or Questioning (LGBTQ) are three times more likely than heterosexual youth to experience discrimination. With regard to cyberbullying, girls tend to be more prone to be bullied on the internet when compared to boys.

Between 1999 and 2008, immigrant youth (aged 15–24) arriving to settle in Canada increased from 28,125 to 37,425 (Shakya, Khanlou, & Gonsalves, 2010). One in every three newcomers was less than the age of 24 in 2011 (Statistics Canada, 2013). A large number of these youth who belong to visible minority groups (Shakya et al., 2010; Statistics Canada, 2008) face bullying, racism, and discrimination (Abada et al., 2008; Canadian Council on Social Development, 2000; Hilario, Vo, & Pottie, 2015; Salehi, 2010).

Intersectionality

In the backdrop of the research context discussed above, I embrace an intersectional approach in this study, which Collins and Bilge (2016) defined as "a way of understanding and analyzing the complexity in the world, in people, and in human experiences" (p. 2). Intersectionality allows for an examination of individual experiences based on multiple identities such as race, class, gender, ethnicity, and sexuality, working together "in diverse and mutually influencing ways" (p. 25) to produce and reinforce inequality and social exclusion. Historically, feminist scholars and practitioners spanning North America, Europe, and Asia have widely used intersectionality frameworks (Collins & Bilge, 2016). An intersectional approach has also been applied to various fields of studies such as political science (Erzeel & Mügge, 2016), education (Bhopal & Preston, 2012), healthcare (Caiola, Docherty, Relf, & Barroso, 2014), economics (Elu & Loubert, 2013), and, more recently, to bullying research (Stoll & Block, 2015), including in the Canadian context (Haines-Saah et al., 2016). However, an intersectional approach has not been applied much to communication research, in general, and to advancing understanding of bullying from a communication-based perspective, in particular. Employing an intersectional approach, this chapter contributes growing scholarship on bullying and youth grounded in communication-based work. Given that intersectionality provides a useful analytic tool that sheds light on the complexity of people's lives within an equally complex social context (Collins & Bilge, 2016, p. 25), this study seeks to explore how youth communicate about bullying experiences as a way to also identify the strategies they use to address bullying. Specifically, two research questions guide this study: What do immigrant youth in Canada communicate about bullying? How do immigrant youth in Canada deal with bullying?

Method

This study is part of my research on bullying experiences of immigrant youth and implications for mental healthcare. Drawing on focus group data, this chapter aims at producing empirical evidence on a complex, multifaceted social problem, such as bullying, by giving voice to vulnerable populations.

Participants

Participants for this study included four immigrant youth, two female and two male ranging in age from 16 to 25. Four of the three participants identified as Arab, and one identified as Chinese. Education ranged from being enrolled in high school to attending college and university.

Data Collection

Upon receiving approval from the Research Ethics Board, I conducted a focus group with the study participants in November 2017. I used a combination of stratified purposeful and snowball sampling strategies (Miles & Huberman, 1994) to obtain immigrant youth, who were between the ages of 16–25, both male and female, across generations (e.g., first generation, second generation, and so on), and able to communicate their experiences in English. Seven immigrant youth confirmed their participation, but four eventually showed up for the focus group discussion. At the beginning of the focus group session, participants completed a consent form that ensured their voluntary participation and guaranteed their anonymity by never using their actual names in any written form. After collecting demographic information, I utilized a semi-structured focus group guide to gather a diversity of perspectives and generate debate and discussion among participants on bullying (see related work by Cameron, 2010). I analyzed focus group data relating to participants' understanding of bullying (e.g., "In your opinion, what is bullying?" "Have you had any experience with bullying?") as well as the strategies that they employ to deal with bullying ("In your opinion, what are some of the possible ways to stop bullying?"). The focus group discussion lasted 142.43 minutes. I provided participants with snacks and refreshments as well as a CAD 10 Starbucks gift card as compensation for their time and contribution. I recorded the focus group session digitally with participants' written consent and transcribed verbatim, yielding 43 pages of single-spaced text.

Data Analysis

I analyzed the focus group data using Braun & Clarke's (2006) 6-phase guide to conducting thematic analysis. In the first phase, I familiarized myself with the data by performing repeated reading and taking notes about initial ideas. In the second phase, I produced initial codes based on interesting aspects in the data across the entire dataset. The third phase involved search for themes by sorting and collating the initial codes into possible themes. In the fourth phase, I reviewed the identified themes for possible refinement based on whether they appropriately reflected the data. This process was followed by defining and naming the final set of themes in the fifth phase. The sixth phase included the final analysis and production of a scholarly report of the analysis. I chose representative quotations from the transcripts to illustrate participants' viewpoints and emergent themes. In doing so, vocal filters were removed to improve clarity, but I kept the grammar as spoken. I preserved the confidentiality of participants by using pseudonyms to protect participants' identities in all reporting of the data.

Trustworthiness and Reliability

With a view to improving the trustworthiness and reliability of focus participants' responses, I used a range of quotations and engaged in interpretation of these quotations (Tracy, 2010). I also strived to ensure rigor and trustworthiness by performing member checks (Gall, Borg, & Gall, 1996). Specifically, I obtained feedback from the participants during the focus group discussion to make a transition to the next questions and offer the participants an opportunity to revise and extend their remarks. Moreover, the last focus group question stated: "Is there anything else that you would like to share with me?"

Findings

The focus group conversations generated a number of themes that revealed what immigrant youth in Canada communicate about bullying and how they deal with bullying. In this section, I discuss these themes under two headings: "communicating about bullying" and "dealing with bullying." Overall, participants believe bullying is prevalent in today's society, and they locate their experiences with bullying at the intersection of their racial and gender identities. Notwithstanding, the participants also discussed anti-bullying strategies that they espoused to help address issues of bullying.

Communicating About Bullying

In particular, three themes emerged from focus group participants' discussion about what they think bullying is and whether they had any experience with bullying: expressions of bullying as all-pervasive, being related to race, and gendered. Preceded by an illustration in Table 16.1, I discuss these themes below.

Bullying Is All-Pervasive

All participants discussed how bullying permeates every aspect of life—children beaten up at elementary school by other children, friends ganging up on a friend in high school, teachers being verbally abusive to little kids in school, parents fighting at home, racial remarks in the workplace. For example, Sabah, a high school student between 16 and 20 years of age, underscored how a bully does not have to be someone who is an enemy or a stranger. Sometimes, friends could be bullies

Table 16.1 Characterization of Communication About Bullying

Theme	Exemplary Quotes	
Bullying Is All-Pervasive	"I can bet you right now that in school this morning there was a kid punching another kid in kindergarten" (Sabah).	"So I'd say I definitely got bullied at work a few times. Especially if you . . . allow it to happen a bit. And if there's a lack of confidence, lack of speaking up" (Li).
Bullying Is Related to Race	"bullying . . . I feel like it's related or correlated to race as well" (Omar).	"So when it comes to jokes about race or looks or anything, and if you get offended then you're the loser" (Lina).
Bullying Is Gendered	"as soon as girl is prettier than them it's like, 'Oh, no. She's a slut. Yeah, whatever, she's pretty but she sleeps around'" (Lina).	"Rape culture as in 'boys will be boys'" (Sabah).

because of their personal dislikes, or even family members could bully by passing judgment. Sabah further shared:

> But it also comes from school and as a kid back home in my home country I got bullied all the time. I was a very loser kid I guess. It happened less here [Canada] but it still happened. Not so much for my appearance but for my religion. I am Muslim. I just think it's personal and just how you define it.

Hence, Sabah's exemplar also illustrates how her experience with bullying is subjective, embedded in her embodied religious identity and reproduced in social interactions.

Bullying Is Related to Race

All participants reported feeling bullied because of their racial identities. They felt that immigrant youth were more likely to be subject to racist bullying in terms of being the subject of race jokes in school, college, and in certain jobs. For example, Li, a college student between 21 and 25 years of age, shared:

> [B]eing in trade school it was a little uncomfortable at certain times. With a lot of people, especially the trades background being Caucasian and from outside of the city—at least maybe an hour this way or an hour that way or two hours this way and they come in every day so you know that their background, they wouldn't—they wouldn't see visible minorities that much. And I'm pretty sure I had a guy tell me he didn't like colored people or something like that.

Li further disclosed how, as an apprentice in a mechanic shop and the only visible minority, he would "get a little bit of race jokes coming up." These experiences mirror findings from prior research that found how immigrant youth were significantly more likely to experience bullying victimization than native-born youth (Maynard et al., 2016). Specifically, immigrant youth were more likely than their non-immigrant peers to report being victims of peer aggression "because of issues related to their race, religion, and family income" (Sulkowski, Bauman, Wright, Nixon, & Davis, 2014, p. 649).

Bullying Is Gendered

Existing research on gender differences in bullying presents mixed evidence. While some studies (Olweus, 1993a, 2013a) found higher likelihood for bullying victimization among boys than girls, other studies (Görzig & Olafsson, 2013; Kowalski & Limber, 2007; Kowalski, Limber, & Agatston, 2012; Mark & Ratliffe, 2011) indicated girls reporting being more exposed to bullying than boys. These mixed findings, mostly in the context of cyberbullying, bring attention to the underlying factors and mechanisms of bullying that still remain under-researched, especially in the Communication discipline.

In the present study, all participants noted how bullying experiences are gendered. While male participants tended to identify males (e.g., "teenage guys," "adults") as having more aggressive attitude as bullies and become physical, female participants portrayed female bullies ("girls") as judgmental, jealous, and engaging in more verbal abuse. Some participants also extended the gendered nature of bullying to non-binary gender identity and sexual orientation. For example, Omar, an undergraduate student between 21 and 25 years of age, opined:

> So when you're basically someone who's—yeah, it could be visible minority, you could have a different sexual orientation—that happens a lot—you could be someone who also [is] transgendered. You don't identify as male or female or you switch from being a male to female, female to male. So this is a factor of, or a cause of bullying. And it could be somebody who is vulnerable.

Omar's exemplar highlights how bullying can ensue from a double minority status and result in double discrimination experiences for people who identify with multiple racial and gender identities.

These gendered bullying experiences are also evident in communication-based scholarship focusing on bullying and gender. For example, when examining gender differences in the relationships between cyber and traditional bullying experiences, Erdur-Baker (2010) determined that male students were more likely to be victims of both traditional and cyberbullying than their female counterparts.

Dealing With Bullying

Three themes emerged from focus group participants' discussion about possible ways to stop bullying: engaging in self-"roasting" (e.g., mocking, teasing, poking fun, and ridiculing), playing the "cool" factor, and having a sense of confidence. Preceded by an illustration in Table 16.2, I detail these themes below.

"Roasting" Yourself

All participants discussed the idea of engaging in self-mocking, teasing, poking fun, and ridiculing as a strategy to stop being bullied, as a defense mechanism to stand up against the bully. Lina, a high school student between 16 and 20 years of age, explained this strategy:

> Because say something really traumatic happened, I will make a joke about it. And some people are, "Why would you make a joke about that?" But that's just how I would deal with things. Because in grade eight I was being bullied for being the emo kid, I use that in high school now. And also because now I am the minority. I make jokes about myself and that's just how I deal with my own insecurities [from being bullied].

Table 16.2 Strategies to Deal with Bullying

Theme	Exemplary Quotes	
"Roasting" Yourself	"I roast myself specifically just to make people feel like their roasts are useless" (Sabah).	"If someone [a bully] did start roasting, because I'm doing it to myself so much it could even get to the point it's like, 'Oh, [Li]'s so confident about himself.' Whoopsies!" (Li).
The "Cool" Factor	"We're all adults here, I may be the youngest out of you guys but I'm not cool with that. And I wanna let you know I'm not cool with that" (Li).	"I know that bullying happens but I feel like there are no boundaries unless you set them. You can't go up to a person and say the n-word—and if you're Arab and expect it to be cool with it just because you're Arab, you know?" (Sabah).
A Sense of Confidence	"there's a lot of factors when it comes to bullies. I feel it always, always . . . has to do with confidence" (Omar).	"if you're confident and happy with what actions you took yourself, then that's the best you can do" (Li).

Lina's exemplar also illustrates that, while she attributes her experience with bullying to her minority status, she exudes a proactive approach to addressing bullying.

These findings add to the growing literature on bullying and communication, especially how bullied individuals who belong to minority groups respond to bullying. The findings are also significant because what limited research is available found immigrant youth reporting "that their own responses to peer aggression were less likely to lead to positive outcomes" (Sulkowski et al., 2014, p. 649).

The "Cool" Factor

All participants shared how students in schools, mainly bullies, engage in verbal abuse by using hurtful words against other students, including friends just to act "cool." They associated this acting "cool" for the wrong reasons with bullies having feelings of insecurity, lots of friends, and/or being physically stronger than their victims. Participants recalled how they witnessed bullying against some peers in school but did not stand up against the bullies. All participants supported the strategy of playing the "cool" factor against the bullies. Saying to the bully—"it is not cool," "hey that wasn't cool."

Being "cool" comprised another strategy that participants identified to help stop bullying. They thought an effort to stand against bullying actually enabled them to do something when seeing someone getting bullied. Lina, a high school student between 16 and 20 years of age, elaborated this importance of taking action against bullying:

> [E]ven if you are scared of being an outsider or you wanna be in on the joke instead of being out of it, it's just one of those things that you're just better off just trying to stop what's [bullying] going on. And just start speaking out. Because I think if you're watching something happening—if you're watching bullying happening and you stop it, you seem like such a cool person. So I think that's the number one thing.

These findings support existing Communication scholarship that advocates for bystander intervention in order to putting a stop to bullying (Brody & Vangelisti, 2016), especially the employment of peer-to-peer communications (McWilliam, King, Drennan, & Cunningham, 2016). However, it is also important to note findings from prior research indicating how immigrant youth reported "that peer bystander interventions did not benefit them as much as these interventions benefited their non-immigrant peers" (Sulkowski et al., 2014, p. 649).

A Sense of Confidence

All participants referenced the importance of having a sense of confidence to deal with bullying. For them, the lack of confidence can result in being bullied, and, accordingly, they championed being confident to stand against bullies. Notably, participants also expressed awareness of the challenges that victims of bullying can face when working up the confidence and reporting the bully because of lack of social support and the fear of being bullied again. As such, they advocated the idea of developing a sense of confidence by embodying it. For example, Sabah shared how she acts confident as a defense mechanism to deal with bullying:

> I feel like I do this all the time where this is just my way of feeling confident. Where I'm not confident at all but I just make it seem like it. Just for people to feel like their thoughts about me or how judgmental they are specific things about me are useless. If I ever fight someone and they bring up how ugly I am, I'm like, again, "I have a mirror. I can see myself. I know what I look like. You don't need to tell me."

In addition to echoing the importance that current Communication research has placed on social support for positive outcomes for victims of bullying (Matsunaga, 2010b, 2011), these findings also add to the research by underscoring the significance of improving self-esteem as a proactive strategy as well as a coping mechanism to stand against and deal with bullying.

Discussion

Situating the focus group findings within an intersectional approach, this study unpacks the multiple aspects of identity that complicate bullying experiences of the participating immigrant youth in Canada. The small, yet diverse group of immigrant youth revealed how their individual and shared experiences of bullying can be linked to multiple grounds of discrimination intersecting with their manifold identities, including ethnicity, race, gender, religion, or sexual orientation. In doing so, the study findings provide important implications for research and practice.

The focus group findings indicate that participating immigrant youth perceive and experience bullying as a pervasive social problem, not so much an isolated fact and experience, despite for instance a UNICEF poll report that almost "97 percent of young people [in more than 18 countries] believe that bullying is a pervasive problem in their communities, and two-thirds say they have been bullied" (UN News Centre, n.d.). In short, youth around the globe are at risk for bullying, but some youth, as in the case of participants in this study, may be more at risk because of their intersectional experiences, including race and gender (Abada et al., 2008; Haines-Saah et al., 2016).

The immigrant youth in this study were acutely aware of their minority status, which cannot be separated from their experiences with bullying, evident in what they communicated about bullying and the strategies they articulated in order to address it. Thus, an important implication for bullying scholarship, including Communication scholars, is to extend bullying research across the lifespan to include different intercultural, cross-cultural, and international perspectives (for related work, see also Socha, this volume). While locating intersecting experiences of bullying among youth can be a complex undertaking, an intersectional approach can inform such investigation by considering the social contexts of the bully and the bullied (Haines-Saah et al., 2016).

The focus group findings revealed how the bullying experiences of these immigrant youth made them resilient, especially given the anti-bullying strategies that they advocated. For example, "roasting" has been termed "as the newest form of cyberbullying among children and youth in Canada" (PREVnet, 2017, para 1). The participating immigrant youth group participants seemed to have turned this new form of bullying into an anti-bullying strategy and a coping mechanism. Scant literature focuses on adolescent bullying and resilience (Sapouna & Wolke, 2013) and the intersections of discrimination, assault, and bullying among youth based on race/ethnicity, immigration status, sexual orientation, and weight (Garnett et al., 2014). Hence, current scholarship on bullying should extend examination of anti-bullying strategies to include an intersectional lens that can help address youth bullying experiences that are located within multiple identity markers and also to find out how they cultivate resilience for preventing bullying. By doing so, researchers and practitioners can realize how intersectionality can be employed as a tool for critical inquiry and praxis (Collins & Bilge, 2016) for anti-bullying initiatives. Such an alliance can lead to community and capacity building by also engaging study participants to develop recommendations regarding how to best deal with bullying that can contribute practically to the efficient delivery of different anti-bullying initiatives and interventions.

Considering the significant growth in the number of immigrant youth in Canada and beyond, as well as the greater chances of these youth being subject to bullying, it is important to advance empirical and theoretical understanding of bullying experiences among immigrant youth. As discussed above, little research has focused on exploring bullying experiences of immigrant youth in general and in particular these explorations are even scant from a communication-based perspective.

Given that bullying is a complex and multidimensional social problem, the experience of which is unique to immigrant youth, we need further research to address bullying victimization in immigrant youth and examine prevention strategies. To this end, the present study has documented the bullying experiences of immigrant youth in Canada as communicated by them. In doing so, I have made an attempt to build on existing scholarship on bullying, in general, and, in particular, to extend communication-based work to explorations of youth bullying experiences as they intersect with their immigration statuses.

Finally, because bullying is a multifaceted global concern, room remains for Communication scholars to make disciplinary contributions to unpack the underlying factors and mechanisms of bullying experiences among immigrant and ethno-culturally diverse youth, especially as they relate to relational factors, identity negotiation, and health-related implications. Through these explorations, Communication scholars can contribute to targeting and tailoring anti-bullying initiatives to the specific needs and circumstances of diverse population groups.

Study Limitations and Future Research Directions

Findings from this study shed light on how the bullying experiences of immigrant youth in Canada are located at the intersection of ethnicity, culture, gender, and religion, as well as the need for tailored anti-bullying initiatives and interventions for diverse population groups in Canada and beyond. Although this study offers important insights that will assist researchers and practitioners in the field, the findings should be considered in light of certain limitations and future research directions. The small sample size (i.e., one focus group with four participants) and limited geographical coverage of participants (i.e., Ottawa) may not fully represent the bullying experiences of the entire immigrant youth in Canada. Hence, future research should include a larger sample from diverse immigrant groups and cover other metropolitan areas to account for any population and place-based differences in the bullying experiences of immigrant youth. Since this study employed focus group methodology, I recommend that future research on this topic be conducted in combination with other complementary qualitative and quantitative data collection tools such as observations, focus groups, and surveys in order to gain deeper insights or follow up research to clarify findings from another method.

17

A LOOK AT BULLYING COMMUNICATION IN EARLY CHILDHOOD

Towards a Lifespan Developmental Model

Thomas J. Socha and Rachel Sadler

This chapter conceptualizes bullying communication as a type of dark-side communication process (see Spitzberg, this volume) that begins in early childhood and appears with varying degrees of sophistication and complexity in all stages of the human lifespan. Like the personality trait of aggressiveness (e.g., Bandura, 1973) and the social process of aggressive communication (Infante & Wigley, 1986), individuals differ in their orientations toward bullying communication and in their bullying communication abilities. This chapter begins by arguing the theoretical merits of conceptualizing bullying communication as a form of dark-side, lifespan, and developmental communication where aggressive messages are used strategically to breach the protective interpersonal bulwark of connected pairs, allowing for the formation of a parasitic relationship (Volk, 1995) between bully and victim. That is, bullies seek out specific conditions in which they can engage in bullying communication in service of their needs-satisfaction at the expense of a host or victim (e.g., Vlachou, Andreou, Botsoglou, & Didaskalou, 2011). Second, the chapter begins to describe bullying communication's lifespan-developmental arc by reviewing what is known about early bullying communication among very young children (infancy through age 5). Finally, the chapter concludes with recommendations for future research and interventions concerning bullying communication in early childhood, specifically the need for: (1) more observational research of early childhood bullying communication episodes grounded in a socio-ecological model (Bronfenbrenner, 1979, 1986), (2) continued inquiry into the role of communibiology in early childhood bullying communication, and (3) development and efficacy testing of primary and secondary bullying communication prevention interventions for early childhood programs.

Bullying Communication: Dark Side and Lifespan

All human communication, both positive and negative, is developmental. Following social learning theory (Bandura & Walters, 1963), children first learn primitive or simple forms of positive communication (Socha & Pitts, 2012) and dark-side communication such as aggression (e.g., Bandura, 1973; Spitzberg & Cupach, 2007) as they interact with family (Socha & Yingling, 2010) and children's groups (Socha, 1999), as well through media creation and use (e. g., see Strasburger, Wilson, & Jordan, 2014). They watch, interact, and mimic the communication of proximal adults and older children as well as view and imitate distal media personae. Over time, with continued engagement, cognitive-developmental maturation, and formal/informal communication education, children's primitive forms of communication develop or increase in sophistication and complexity over the lifespan (Nussbaum, 2014; Socha & Yingling, 2010). Included among these many and varied communicative forms is bullying communication. Let's take up the question of what bullying communication is, a question to which there is no easy response (see West & Turner, this volume).

Socha and Beck (2015) argued that dark-side communication features messages that create conditions that block or in some way inhibit the needs-satisfaction of others, while positive communication creates conditions that permit or in some way promote the needs-satisfaction of others. According to this conceptualization, bullying communication is, by definition, a form of dark-side communication. This conceptualization is consistent with a widely used definition of bullying: "a repeated pattern of intentional negative actions (physical and/or psychological) used by one or more persons with the intent to injure or disturb another, in which there is an imbalance of power" (Moran, 2011, p. 18). More generally, bullying entails "overbearing insolence; personal intimidation; petty tyranny" (*Oxford English Dictionary*, 2017). Before zooming in for a closer look at bullying communication and young children, let's use a panoramic lens and see what "bullying" patterns look like across a variety of contexts.

Tyler Volk (1995), in his book, *Metapatterns*, examined the similarities of patterns across physical, psychological, and socio-cultural systems. That is, Volk found that patterns in the physical also turn up in psychological, sociological, and cultural worlds. For example, humans, like all living beings, have "borders" (physical, psychological, and cultural) that separate inside from outside. Borders are penetrable. Human skin, for instance, contains pores allowing moisture and air (good things) into physiological systems along with parasites and diseases (bad things). Human physiological and psychological systems also contain sensory-cognitive openings that (like pores) allow constructive, affirming, and empowering messages (positive communication) to enter as well as destructive, disconfirming, and forbidding ones (dark-side communication). As humans communicate, they create symbolic borders (cultures) that welcome friends (in-groups) and keep out enemies (out-groups).

Let's follow Volk's (1995) logic and think about "bullying" as a kind of metapattern that occurs, albeit in different forms, across physical, biological, ethological, physiological-psychological, and cultural systems. Hurricanes seek warm water. Diseases seek healthy cells. Animal predators seek food. But what are bullies after? Researchers show that children (ages 8–12) who bullied were motivated in part by a desire to increase their popularity (a kind of power) as evidenced by choosing unpopular victims (Veenstra et al., 2005). "Bullies aren't looking to be loved . . . they are looking to be noticed" (Boyles, 2015, p. 1844). Of course, hurricanes, infectious diseases, and animal predators must do as nature dictates. They find a host, take what they need, and continue to do so until conditions change such that a host can no longer can support them or until the host is destroyed. Hurricanes, diseases, and animal predators (as well as human bullies) interact with the outside world, forming a metapattern that is characterized as parasitic (Volk, 1995). That is, when conditions are favorable, hurricanes, diseases, animal predators, and human bullies alike, unable to exist (or achieve needs-satisfaction) without a host, successfully penetrate a host's borders and form a parasitic bond. More specifically, human bullies seek out host-persons (victims) who appear weak, and when conditions are right, engage in bullying communication, inflict damage, and continue to do so until the conditions that gave rise to bullying are depleted and/or otherwise are no longer available (e.g., see Veenstra et al., 2005). Akin to the biology and chemistry of hurricanes, diseases, and animal predators, human bullies may possess genetic predispositions that can give rise to and influence bullying behaviors (for aggression, see Bandura, 1973; and see the communibiological approach in McCroskey & Beatty, 2000). However, unlike hurricanes, diseases, and animal predators, human bullies are also conscious and social beings who, in non-clinical populations, have the capacity to reflect on, halt, and/or change their patterns of behavior.

Thus, bullying communication can be conceptualized as a dark-side, developmental, and lifespan communication phenomenon that involves the strategic use of various forms of aggressive messages for specific purposes with specific targets in specific conditions forming parasitic bonds between bully and victim. However, what might these specific purposes, targets, and conditions be? And what does bullying communication look like in its earliest, most primitive forms?

Parameters of Bullying Communication and Childhood

According to Greene (2000), researchers who study human bullying agree on the following five necessary conditions for bullying to exist:

1. The bully intends to inflict harm or fear upon the victim.
2. Aggression toward the victim occurs repeatedly.
3. The victim does not provoke bullying behavior by using verbal or physical aggression.
4. Bullying occurs in familiar social groups.
5. The bully is more powerful (either real or perceived power) than the victim.

Following a lifespan developmental framing, let's start at the very beginning of communication development and examine these conditions in the context of early childhood.

Motivating Conditions

With respect to bullying communication, motivating conditions can include an intent to inflict harm (psychological, physical), intimidation, and/or to frighten someone in service of needs-satisfaction for attention and control (Veenstra et al., 2005). However, it is important that we draw additional distinctions when it comes to the motivations of children considered clinical (i.e., requiring psychiatric and psychological care) versus non-clinical as well as motivations to engage in acts of bullying that are criminal.

Music (2016) wrote about children as young as age 4, institutionalized at the Portman Clinic in the UK for severely disturbed children, who behave sadistically (bullying at its most extreme). These children displayed violent, cruel, and criminal behaviors and derived pleasure from doing so. Lacking the bio-psycho-physiological capacities to arrest these behaviors, and feeling no remorse, these clinical children committed violent and sadistic crimes, including murder.

> Before her 11th birthday she [Mary] had strangled a four-year-old boy in a derelict house. A few months later she strangled a three-year old in local wasteland. Chillingly, she returned to carve an "M" onto his stomach. She also reportedly took some scissors and cut his hair off, scratched his body and mutilated his penis. Of course, in part such behaviour is a reenactment of something already experienced. Mary's mother was a prostitute and "gave" a pre-school Mary to men to be sexually abused. Her mother's murderousness was seen in how Mary "accidentally" fell out of windows or in her mother giving her sleeping pills which she said were sweets.
>
> *(Music, 2016, p. 302)*

According to Music (2016), friends, teachers, and parents routinely labeled these clinical children "bullies." Undoubtedly, these children clearly fit Greene's (2000) bullying criteria. They intended to hurt others and did so repeatedly. They also did so only when they could wield power and influence over their victims. Music distinguished between the "hot" and "cold" aggression displayed by these clinical children, where hot aggression occurred spontaneously in the heat of the moment ("They feel upset, provoked and want to hurt back . . . because something feels unfair," p. 305). "This is very different to 'colder' more proactive kinds of aggression in which children and adults show more calculation. Proactive aggressors do not feel bad about their anger" (p. 305).

Bullying communication of clinical populations of children is not the intended focus of this chapter. However, we mention this population because adults sometimes mistakenly ascribe clinical qualities to very young children's aggressive behavior when, developmentally, they may lack boundary-management abilities, interpersonal skills, and/or an ability to self-control. Further, children (non-clinical) also vary developmentally in their levels of moral development insofar as they may not understand the harms they are inflicting (Socha & Eller, 2015). When studying the bullying communication of children, their social, cognitive, communicative, and moral developmental levels require consideration as well as psycho-physiological.

Regarding children's moral development, Davies (2011), for example, situated bullying in a discourse of moral order where "it is proposed that children learn a new form of ethical relationality in which they are open to difference and to their own ongoing creative evolution" (p. 278). Davies illustrated this approach by analyzing an episode of bullying in a UK prep school where two girls (assumed to be of high school age) bashed a Sudanese boy's head against a wall and knocked out a tooth. The girls wanted him to stop playing the game "Kiss and catch the girls" (p. 280). Davies argued that the girls' and boy's behaviors highlight a human moral order (and their shifting relative positions of power within it). When confronted, the girls cried and felt bad about what they did, but they also said that the boy should not have been playing a sexually offensive game and they wanted him to stop. In this framing, and following related literature (see Vlachou et al., 2011), the Sudanese boy is a bully-victim, and the girls are victim-bullies as they shifted positions of relative power across these situations. Davies speculated that the violent and criminal episode (that occurred among these non-clinical youth) was due in part to a kind of lag in their moral development and that it could have been prevented by means of teaching those involved about ways to manage conflicts pro-socially as well as to how to positively confront antisocial forms of power.

Targets and Situations

The fourth item on Greene's (2000) list identifies specific targets of bullies that include familiar others and those perceived by the bully to be vulnerable and weaker. Among young children (ages 3–5), boys tend to bully boys and girls tend to bully girls (Veenstra et al., 2005). Salmivalli et al. (1996) also found that episodes of bullying communication actually involve four additional communication roles beyond bullies and victims. These are: (1) ringleader bully (who starts the bullying), (2) assistant bully (who joins in the bullying, but does not start it), (3) reinforcer (who encourages the bully), (4) defender (who supports the victim), (5) outsider (who observes but keeps out of the bullying situation), and (6) victim. Similarly, Veenstra et al. (2005, 2007) also argued that childhood bullying should be contextualized as a kind of group communication behavior; they also stressed the importance of accounting for these varying perspectives when studying childhood bullying.

In order to increase the comprehensiveness of Salmivalli et al.'s (1996) list of six bullying communication roles, we add the following three roles: (7) proximal adults (parents and teachers), (8) older siblings, and (9) media personae. These three additional bullying communication roles function in distinct ways before, during, and after episodes of childhood bullying communication. For example, proximal adults and older sibling could play a bullying-inhibitive role by informing parents and teachers about a situation of bullying or victimization (an indirect defender) or, on the dark side, could function as an assistant bully. And, to the extent to which they might be invoked before, during, or after a bullying communication episode, media personae can also play either bullying-facilitative or bullying-inhibiting functions.

Finally, a potentially endless number of social conditions can give rise to bullying communication. That is, any and all interactions between a potential bully and a potential/actual victim can afford opportunities for a bully to explore and identify victims' weaknesses for exploitation. Further, the presence of bullying assistants and bullying reinforcers can be facilitative of bullying communication, whereas the presence of defenders, especially powerful ones, could inhibit bullying communication.

Next, we use this general conceptual framing to take a closer look at early childhood bullying and children's initial experiences with bullying communication.

Bullying Communication in Early Childhood

Difficulties in Defining, Labeling, and Operationalizing

How widespread is bullying in early childhood? Researchers face significant challenges when operationalizing, gathering, and reporting data about the occurrence of bullying communication among children in the primary grades (K–3) and younger. Turner, Finkelhor, Shattuck, Hamby and Mitchell (2014) reported a national study of childhood victimization patterns of children ages 6–17. They found that "[Experiences of] . . . verbal aggression was highest in the youngest group (6- to 9-year-olds)" (p. 9). However, they qualified this result:

> It is possible that we underestimated peer victimization and/or specific incident characteristics occurring among the younger 6- to 9-year-old group (for which information was obtained by caregiver reports), because parents may not be aware of or know the details of many incidents that occur away from home.
>
> *(p. 16)*

And, what about children, ages 2–5? According to Vlachou, Botsoglou, and Andreou (2013), "despite the growing interest in bully/victim problems in school, studies that have addressed this issue in the preschool years are extremely rare" (p. 1). What little data exist for this age range are often not aggregated by age but are reported in wide age-ranges of children. For example, one study compared two previous national surveys of U.S. childhood victimization (age range 2–17). Finkelhor, Turner, Ormrod, and Hamby (2010) found that in 2003, 46% of the caregivers of children ages 2–17 reported their charges experienced either bullying or emotional bullying, and in 2008 this percentage had declined to 40%. The method used to determine the occurrence of bullying or emotional bullying among these children was the Juvenile Victimization Questionnaire administered to parents and caregivers. In spite of serious measurement reliability concerns and the wide range of ages, the study attributed the decline in bullying to "many schools began to rapidly adopt anti-bullying and other violence-prevention policies and programs" (p. 241).

The reliability of parent/caregiver reports of the bullying experiences of children of widely varying ages is open to serious question (e.g., see Vlachou et al. 2013). Of course, episodes of early childhood bullying resulting in juvenile criminal charges could be counted reliably. However, most early childhood bullying episodes never rise to this level. Further, what adults count as episodes of "bullying" can include social slights (e.g., child did not get a birthday party invitation), minor displays of aggression (e.g., child has a tantrum, attempts bite, etc.), as well as intense displays of aggression (e.g., child punches, bites, etc.) (Vlachou et al., 2013).

Empirical research has documented some of the various difficulties that adults and children face when trying to identify and label "bullying communication," but what about young children's reports? According to Vlachou et al. (2011), "sociocognitive and linguistic constraints characterizing this period affect not only the way children perceive the term bullying but also the tools researchers are asked to apply in order to study bully/victim problems in preschool children" (p. 331). According to Monks and Smith (2006), due in part to children's developing communication abilities, most research on bullying during early childhood focuses on children age 8 (grade 3) and older. Specifically, Monks and Smith determined that at age 8 children can distinguish different types of bullying with reasonable reliability, as well as include the element of an imbalance of power and repetition in their attempts to define it (and are able distinguish bullying from "fighting").

In spite of concerns for reporting reliability, according to Vlachou et al. (2011) "aggressive behaviors that could be bullying, and peer victimization, have been identified in children as young as 4 years in several countries" (p. 332), including France (Alsaker, 1993), the United Kingdom (Monks & Smith, 2006), and the United States (Ladd & Ladd, 1998). However, when studying children under age 8, they also contend that it remains a difficult task for children, parents/caregivers, and researchers to accurately label a communication episode as pure "bullying."

Past research shows that children's (ages 2–4) understandings of the meanings of the term "bullying" can vary widely. This raises questions about exactly what very young children understand that they are doing during communication episodes that adults label as bullying (Vlachou et al., 2013). For example, Vlachou et al. (2013) discovered wide differences in identifying who is a "bully" as a function of three different methods: peer-nomination, teacher-observation, and self-reports of children (ages 4–6). They concluded:

> agreement between informants was either nonsignificant or moderate. This is extremely important when conducting relevant empirical research with preschool populations. It is probable that inconsistent results obtained in previous research may be due to the selection of one or another source of information. It is of primary importance to design methodological tools that are both valid and reliable if prevention programs against victimisation are to be consistent and effective.
>
> *(p. 1)*

These kinds of methodological studies that focus on problems of labeling the behavior of young children as "bullying" are important because they raise questions about children's and adults' abilities to accurately recognize the enactment of children's bullying. When and how does a child before age 8 (or a parent, teacher of children during this age range) "know" that she/he is "bullying" or is "being bullied"? Further, as children age, do their abilities to accurately distinguish bullying from other forms of interpersonal conflict behaviors improve? Has bullying become a catch-all term for a variety of aggressive forms of childhood communication? We know, for example, that individual differences exist in the extent of individuals' experiences of bullying, ranging from extensive to limited (e.g., see Zaklama & Wright, 2004). Extent of bullying experiences would seem to potentially affect the accuracy and reliability of labeling episodes of bullying.

Besides these aforementioned elements, communication research in early childhood, especially studies of bullying communication, must consider the hard-wiring of children's temperament and its communicative display. Regarding bullying communication, the personality traits of agreeableness (general concern for social harmony) and neuroticism (the tendency to experience negative emotions, such as anger, anxiety, or depression)—two of the big five personality traits (along with openness to experience, conscientiousness, and extraversion, see Poropat, 2009)—would seem to figure large in the processes of labeling, experiencing, and managing episodes of children's bullying communication as well as differentiating bullying from other forms of aggressive communication. Specifically, some children may possess personality tendencies that increase their likelihood of engaging in aggressive behaviors (e.g., children higher in neuroticism), while other children who repeatedly find themselves in circumstances at odds with others may also be low in trait agreeableness. Both of these personality traits would seem to set the stage for bullying communication potential. However, we do not wish to suggest or imply that biology is destiny when it comes to understanding or explaining children's bullying communication, or for that matter bullying communication across the lifespan. Rather, we argue that inherited communibiological personality traits, such as agreeableness and neuroticism, as well as children's experiences of aggressive behavior modeled by older communicators clearly stand out as two significant sources of children's early bully communication that require study. Further, it would seem important for parents and caregivers to be able to identify these kinds of primitive, hard-wired kinds of personality traits in their young children and then use this understanding to help guide them as they teach their children how to manage what might be inherited aggressive tendencies (from which aggressive displays and bullying tendencies may arise).

Facilitating and Inhibiting Conditions of Bullying Communication in Early Childhood

Attending preschool for children ages 3 and 4 is an important developmental step. It offers the first opportunity for young students to experience peer groups, participate in organized team activities, and engage in organizational school cultures. It is likely that preschool may be the first context beyond their homes where children's social interactions with peers can be observed and assessed by non-familial adults and professionals. According to Bonnet, Goossens, and Schuengel (2011, as well as Gómez-Ortiza, Romera, and Ortega-Ruiza (2015), identification of problems with the management of aggressive feelings and displays of aggression, as well as boundary management and self-control, at this young age is very important and might prevent their escalation in later years and minimize their negative impact on schooling.

> When preschoolers engage in relationally aggressive acts, they tend to do so in relatively simple, direct ways that typically involve a current situation or provocation [like] . . . telling a peer that she/he will not be a peer's friend unless the peer gives her/him a crayon.
>
> *(Vlachou et al., 2011, p. 335)*

Further, "due to the social skills instability in preschool children, the term 'unjustified aggression' might be more proper for describing 'bullying' in the early years" (p. 335). However it is labeled, children (ages 3–4) are certainly capable of various forms of direct and indirect bullying, including verbal and physical social exclusion and rumor spreading.

Like all heritable communication traits, the results of past research suggest that about 50% of the variance of children's physical aggression is determined by genes (e.g., see DiLalla, 2002; Rhee & Waldman 2002). Vlachou et al. (2011) further asserted:

> Physical aggression is already diminished at school entry . . . whereas social aggression may not be fully developed until age 8. . . Whether and when this shift occurs, however, seems to be determined by the extent to which the child is exposed to a social environment that specifically promotes the use of social aggression.
>
> *(p. 336)*

Since communication is developmental, and development can shift with new contexts, it is important to undertake future bullying communication studies, not only from a communibiological framing but also within a social-ecological, developmental model (Bronfenbrenner, 1979, 1986). According to our review, past research on bullying communication has focused almost exclusively on proximal causes (such as genetics, abuse, harsh parenting, etc.) but neglects potential distal forces such as exposure to TV violence and/or violent videogame play (e.g., see Strasburger et al., 2014). Such exposure, even indirect exposure, to violent games may play a significant role later on. Although children ages 3–5 might not be directly (or deliberately) exposed to aggressive or violent programming, such programming is commonplace in many U.S. households and could potentially pose many occasions for indirect exposure of violence to young children. In households with older siblings (especially with those who play first-person shooter games), the exposure of young children

Bullying Communication in Early Childhood

to violent gaming could be extensive. For example, an important longitudinal study by Huesmann, Moise-Titus, Podolski, and Eron (2003) interviewed and gathered data (archival records, interviews of spouses and friends) of 329 participants (ages 20–25) from an original 1977 study sample of when they were 6–10-year-olds. The results found that childhood exposure to TV violence predicted aggressive behavior for both males and females in adulthood. Additionally, identification with same-sex aggressive TV characters, as well as participants' ratings of perceived realism of TV violence, also predicted adult aggression in both males and females. The results suggest that, while aggressive children may choose to watch more violent TV programming, it is more plausible that early childhood exposure to TV violence may stimulate increases in aggression later in adulthood.

If bullies are seeking to be noticed, then peer acceptance and peer rejection would seem to be important to research as a precursor of bullying communication. Buhs and Ladd (2001) studied peer acceptance/rejection among children (ages 4–5) and determined it to be related to underachievement, negative school attitudes, and school adjustment. According to Buhs and Ladd, consistent rejection seems to be a precursor of antisocial coping and offers fertile ground for future bullying communication research.

What is the role of parents' communication in the development of early childhood bullying communication? Bonnet, Goossens, and Schuengel (2011) demonstrated that parents may directly shape their children's interactions with peers in at least four ways: (1) as designers prior to interactions, (2) as mediators for making interactions happen, (3) as supervisors during interactions, and (4) as consultants afterwards when children raise concerns (also see Colwell, Mize, Pettit, & Laird, 2002). Of course, each of these four roles typically assumes pro-social or positive communication (e.g., Socha & Yingling, 2010, chapter 5). However, given the power of the dark side and earlier accounts from abusive parents of clinical children, parents could exert direct influence as dark-side designers, mediators, supervisors, and consultants to facilitate victim-bullies. Sadly, past parent-child communication research focusing on dysfunctional parental communication (e.g., see Whipple & Wilson, 1996; Wilson & Whipple, 1995; Wilson, Rack, Shi, & Norris, 2008) shows it is far too easy to image a parent urging a son to "hit back harder" during a sandbox melee over a toy, or coaching a child in bullying communication strategies and tactics in responding to episodes of victimization and thus creating victim-bullies (e.g., "Here's how you can get even with that nasty kid and really hurt him/her more than she/he hurt you!"). This latter hypothetical scenario is sadly borne out by data from a meta-analytic study. Lereya, Samara, and Wolkec (2013) argued that "both victims and those who both bully and are victims (bully/victims) were more likely to be exposed to negative parenting behavior including abuse and neglect and mal-adaptive parenting" (p. 1091). And, Bonnet et al. (2011) concluded:

> strategies to stimulate the autonomy of children and autonomy neutral strategies might support the decrease of peer victimization early in the school year. However, in the second semester, protective effects of parental strategies were not sustained. No support was found for autonomy undermining strategies as amplifying the vulnerability for peer victimization.
>
> *(p. 394)*

Based on Bonnet et al.'s study, parents' instructions of how to navigate initial encounters with bullying communication can and do influence 4- and 5-year-olds, and parental effects might be strongest when children initially encounter bullying communication. This suggests that an inoculation kind of approach warrants future investigation where parents teach children about pro-social ways to manage bullying communication prior to encountering a bullying communication episode. Programs grounded in reflection-enhancing communication where parents adopt a constructivist model to teach children ways to increase their person-centeredness communication (Wilson, Cameron, & Whipple, 1997) would seem to hold promise on this front.

Towards Lifespan Developmental Study of Bullying Communication

Consistent with other chapters in this volume, this chapter argues that future research of bullying communication should be approached: (1) developmentally, (2) socio-ecologically, (3) as a form of dark-side communication, and (4) across the lifespan. The remainder of this chapter will offer research-based suggestions in building a future research agenda as well as the need for the development and testing of intervention programs.

First, research reviewed in this chapter makes it clear that bullying communication in some form, along with precursors of the development of later bullying communication, is occurring during early childhood (ages 2–5). However, until this chapter, bullying communication during early childhood has not been a topic of study in the field of communication. It is a sad fact that less than 3% of all published studies in the entire field of communication have focused on children, and most of these studies are about children's television and children age 8 and older (Miller-Day, Pezalla, & Chesnut, 2013). Even in the *Journal of Family Communication* (founded by the first author of this chapter), "fewer than 6% of the publications . . . focused on children as communicators" (p. 161).

Going forward, and building on this chapter, there are a number of topics related to bullying communication that require future inquiry from a developmental communication vantage point. First, based on this review, more conceptual and empirical testing of the processes of "bullying" labeling and attribution are needed. How do children, parents, and caregivers decide which children's behaviors constitute "bullying" and when (and how) should a child be labeled a "bully?" What are the sources of information that inform bully and bullying communication attributions? Research reviewed in this chapter concludes that age, cognitive-developmental factors (e.g., linguistic, perspective-taking, etc.), and experiential factors (e.g., extent of prior bullying experiences) will affect these processes. We also need to know more about how children who are labeled as "bullies" manage this label and how it affects their communication. Second, we need studies of the role of communibiology in early childhood bullying communication. We need to examine the relative contributions of children's temperament, its early management by parents and caregivers, and potential connections to the frequency of early experiences with bullying communication episodes. And, third, we need more observation studies of naturally occurring communication in preschools (e.g., see Meyer, 2003), because bullying communication, or conditions feeding bullying communication's development, is undoubtedly occurring. Anecdotally, Caroline Presno (2014), an early childhood education professor and therapist, published a blog about 4-year-old mean girls, where she wrote:

> pre-school aged mean girls use tactics like: excluding a child from playing with the group; telling other kids not to play with that child; withdrawing affection and friendship if their demands are not met; and completely ignoring someone they're mad at.
>
> *(no page)*

Second, consistent with the varied chapters, topics, and approaches that appear in this volume, this chapter makes it clear that bullying communication is optimally studied using a socio-ecological model (Bronfenbrenner, 1979, 1986). There are a number of both proximal and distal sources that can contribute to bullying communication and its early development that require study. Most of the research to date on bullying communication in early childhood has focused on micro-systems (families, preschools) and to a far lesser extent on what is happening in children's mesosystems (neighborhoods), exosystems (extended families), and macrosystems (government, media, class, and so on). For example, in the future, will exposure to today's increasingly aggressive mediated public discourse change children's learning about bullying communication during early childhood? We also identified research in this review that suggests exposure to violent media and videogame play will also continue to shape the development of aggressive forms of communication.

Bullying Communication in Early Childhood

Third, although to date research on the dark side of communication has focused exclusively on adults, most of the research topics studied on the dark side of communication could certainly extend to children and be studied developmentally, including bullying communication. For example, related to bullying communication, topics such as co-dependence (Le Poire, Hallett, & Giles, 1998), obsessional relational intrusion (Cupach & Spitzberg, 1998), and females' social aggression (Willer & Cupach, 2011) would make useful starting points for study during early childhood.

Third, as this chapter and volume make abundantly clear, bullying communication is a lifespan phenomenon (Nussbaum, 2014). Going forward, it is important to better describe and document the developmental arc of bullying communication during early, middle, and late childhood, but also continue through adolescence and into emerging, early, and later adulthood. Are communicators simply repeating patterns of bullying communication learned in early and middle childhood across the lifespan? A master's thesis by Claudia Ferreira Sepe (2015) suggests this might be the case. She found mean-girl patterns among elderly women (ages 65–85) residing in an assisted living facility:

> many older adults living in retirement homes are being bullied and many of them are not speaking up and isolating themselves for the purpose of avoiding their bullies. Moreover, . . . staff members of the retirement communities are lacking the knowledge of the bullying problem in their community.
>
> *(p. iii)*

According to Sepe, "older adults also use many bullying activities that children use" (p. 40). She described senior women engaging in: name calling, spreading false stories, telling lies about targeted victims, and more. Her study raises important lifespan, developmental communication questions like: Have these women been communicating as bullies throughout their entire lives? Did they learn this communicative form during early childhood, discovered that it worked for them, and, assuming no educational or familial interventions, or at least none that succeeded, simply continued to engage in bullying communication? Have their bullying communication skills improved over time? Did they possess personality precursors conducive to bullying communication during early childhood?

Finally, in response to the rise of bullying, intervention programs are being developed rapidly to address: elementary teachers bullying identification (Chen, Sung, & Cheng, 2017), family involvement in elementary and middle school bullying (Lester et al., 2017), and emergent whole school anti-bullying programs (Tunac De Pedro et al., 2017). Although to a far lesser extent, we are also seeing recent development of pre-K anti-bullying games (Lee, 2017). These intervention efforts are important, but also require efficacy testing, and should include children of preschool age (most do not).

The time is ripe for communication researchers who study families and children to join the efforts of those in this volume. Communication scholars, teachers, and practitioners are well positioned to make a difference in positive human communication development across the lifespan by helping to inform those seeking to raise the next generation to be competent, positive communicators, and to effectively manage bullying communication starting with its earliest and most primitive forms.

18

VERBAL AGGRESSIVENESS AS BULLYING IN THE EMERGING ADULT SIBLING RELATIONSHIP

Scott A. Myers, Carrie D. Kennedy-Lightsey, Christine K. Anzur, James P. Baker, and Sara Pitts

Across several types of family (e.g., husband–wife, parent–child) relationships, verbal aggressiveness comprises one message behavior that can have negative ramifications for both the relational partners and the relationship itself (for a review, see M. M. Martin, Weber, Anderson, & Burant, 2004 or Vogl-Bauer, 2010). Scholars have determined verbal aggressiveness, conceptualized as a person's use of verbally aggressive messages that attack another person's self-concept for the sole purpose of inflicting psychological harm (Infante & Wigley, 1986), to be a destructive communication behavior that leads to decreased relational satisfaction (Infante & Rancer, 1996), with its recipients experiencing negative emotions such as humiliation, inadequacy, depression, hopelessness, embarrassment, or anger (Infante, 1987, 1995). These verbally aggressive messages can take several forms, including attacking a person's competence, character, background, personality, personal failings, group memberships, and physical appearance as well as making threats against a person; ridiculing, teasing, or insulting a person; swearing at a person; or using specific nonverbal behaviors (e.g., eye contact, facial expressions, vocal tone) in an aggressive manner (Infante, 1995; Infante, Riddle, Horvath, & Tumlin, 1992; Kinney, 1994; Rancer, Lin, Durbin, & Faulkner, 2010).

Despite the negative emotions associated with verbal aggressiveness, however, the adult sibling relationship is perhaps the only intimate, interpersonal relationship in which the effects of verbal aggressiveness may not fully be realized due to the characteristics that define the sibling relationship. According to Mikkelson (2014), the adult sibling relationship is unique in that it is pervasive, involuntary, and permanent—meaning that, despite Rocca, Martin, and Dunleavy's (2010) claim that the sibling relationship becomes more voluntary as siblings grow older because they can now make a conscious decision as to whether, how, when, and why they want to communicate with each other, most siblings are bound to each other genetically, legally, or emotionally (Floyd, Mikkelson, & Judd, 2006), thus making it difficult to sever these ties. Moreover, siblings share a long family history with each other that begins at birth and culminates with death. Myers and Bryant (2008a) posited that, due to this family history, when it comes to realizing the effects of verbally aggressive messages in the sibling relationship, by the time siblings reach emerging adulthood (i.e., between the ages of 18 and 25 years; Arnett, 2000), targeted siblings may not only become immune to these messages, but they also develop ways to cope with these messages. As such, emerging adults who consistently direct verbally aggressive messages toward their siblings likely remain unaware of or apathetic toward how these messages affect their relationships (Myers & Bryant, 2008a), particularly if these verbally aggressive messages are one way in which they engage in bullying with their siblings.

Bullying in Emerging Adult Siblings

This chapter, then, explores how emerging adults reflect on their use of verbally aggressive messages with their siblings and whether they used verbally aggressive messages as a way to communicatively bully their siblings during childhood. We chose to focus on siblings in emerging adulthood for two reasons. First, as researchers have noted, emerging adulthood is the time period in which individuals begin to assert their independence from their families of origin in their attempts to become an adult (J. J. Arnett, 1997, 2000; Nelson & Barry, 2005). These attempts not only involve moving out of the family home (and away from both parents and siblings) but also focusing their energy on their friendships, romantic relationships, education, and vocation rather than their family of origin (J. J. Arnett, 2007, 2015; Sneed et al., 2006). At the same time, during emerging adulthood, individuals begin to recognize the significance of their sibling relationships (Halliwell, 2016; Scharf, Shulman, & Avigad-Spitz, 2005)—a recognition that is not always present during childhood and adolescence— and start to pay attention to how their communication behaviors signal their commitment to these relationships (Myers & Bryant, 2008b; Myers, Goodboy, & Members of COMM 201, 2013). Second, although aggression among siblings generally decreases as siblings grow older (Felson, 1983), families often times perceive bullying as normative for the sibling relationship during childhood and adolescence (Skinner & Kowalski, 2013; Wolke & Skew, 2012), in part because siblings themselves may not view verbal aggressiveness as a bullying behavior (Hoetger, Hazen, & Brank, 2015). As such, when individuals enter emerging adulthood and begin to view their sibling relationships more favorably, they are well-positioned to reflect upon the verbally aggressive messages that they used with their siblings during childhood, particularly if they employed the messages to bully their sibling.

Review of Literature

During childhood, the sibling relationship is plagued with conflict, rivalry, and relational aggressiveness (i.e., behaviors intended to harm an individual's social relationships such as spreading rumors or gossiping) that can persist well into the emerging adult sibling relationship (Stocker, Lanthier, & Furman, 1997; Updegraff, Thayer, Whiteman, Denning, & McHale, 2005), communicatively manifesting itself in the form of verbal aggressiveness (Myers & Goodboy, 2006). This manifestation becomes particularly ripe in family relationships, where relational participants feel less pressure to adhere to social politeness norms (Infante, Myers, & Buerkel, 1994). This lack of pressure, coupled with the aforementioned characteristics of the sibling relationship, may help explain the composition of the specific verbally aggressive messages adult siblings are known to use with each other.

To date, family communication researchers have developed three typologies of adult sibling verbally aggressive messages. Teven, Martin, and Neupauer (1998) developed the first typology, consisting of 14 messages that emerging adults reported receiving from their adult siblings that attacked their intelligence, made fun of their lack of romantic relationships, made fun of their friendships, called them derogatory names, made fun of their physical appearance, threatened to get them in trouble, complained about something they had done, attacked their self-esteem, threatened to destroy their possessions, embarrassed them, teased them, and swore at them. M. M. Martin, Anderson, and Rocca (2005) created a second typology by refining the Teven et al. typology, reducing it to 10 types of verbally aggressive messages adult siblings used with each other: attacked their intelligence, teased them about their relationships with others, called them uncomplimentary nicknames, made fun of their physical appearance, threatened to get them into trouble, complained to the rest of the family about them, made fun of the way they talked, told them that they lacked common sense, embarrassed them in front of others, and pointed out their faults to them. Not surprisingly, when emerging adults were the recipients of these two sets of messages, they indicated lower levels of relational satisfaction and communication satisfaction with their sibling relationships in addition to perceiving their siblings as less trustworthy and credible (M. M. Martin, Anderson, Burant, & Weber, 1997; M. M. Martin et al., 2005; Teven et al., 1998).

In the third typology, Myers and Bryant (2008a) identified seven types of verbally aggressive messages emerging adults use with their siblings. These messages were name calling; insulting a sibling's intelligence, abilities, or appearance; withdrawing from interaction (i.e., informing a sibling that his or her physical presence was not valued or wanted); engaging in either real or implied threats of physical harm; repudiating the relationship (i.e., questioning a sibling's place in the family); making an unfair comparison; and engaging in negative affect toward the sibling (i.e., expressing dislike or hatred for a sibling). Interestingly, although emerging adults perceived the repudiating the relationship message as the most hurtful, the making an unfair comparison message as the most intense, and the engaging in either real or implied threats of physical harm message as the most intentional, Myers and Bryant found that generally, emerging adult siblings did not perceive the seven messages as significantly differing in their degrees of hurtfulness, intensity, or intent.

Together, these findings indicate that emerging adults do, indeed, use a variety of verbally aggressive messages with their siblings. However, family communication researchers have yet to examine the extent to which adult siblings recall using these verbally aggressive messages with each other during their childhood. To correct this oversight and contribute further to this body of knowledge, we posed the first research question:

RQ1: To what extent do emerging adults recall using verbally aggressive messages with their siblings during childhood?

As researchers have found, however, the extent to which individuals employ verbally aggressive messages with a relational partner may depend on whether they are high or low in trait verbal aggressiveness. According to Infante et al. (1992), individuals who are high in trait verbal aggressiveness "send and receive more self-concept attacking messages than [individuals who are low in trait verbal aggressiveness]" (p. 117). More specifically, they found that high verbally aggressive individuals use messages that contain competence, background, and physical appearance attacks; teasing, ridicule, and swearing; and nonverbal emblems at a higher rate than low verbally aggressive individuals. Concomitantly, because verbally aggressive individuals are less compassionate or sensitive to other persons' needs (Cranmer & Martin, 2015), less predisposed to verbally praise other people (Wigley, Pohl, & Watt, 1989), and less responsive (M. M. Martin & Anderson, 1996), emerging adults who differ in their levels of trait verbal aggressiveness (i.e., high, low) will likely report using verbally aggressive messages at a differential rate with a sibling during childhood. To examine this idea, we posited the first hypothesis:

H1: Emerging adults who are high in trait verbal aggressiveness will report using verbally aggressive messages with a sibling during childhood more frequently than emerging adults who are low in trait verbal aggressiveness.

We further distinguished individuals who differ in their trait verbal aggressiveness by (1) their justification for engaging in a verbally aggressive with a relational partner and (2) the extent to which they perceive the message to be hurtful. Not only are verbally aggressive individuals more likely to perceive their use of verbally aggressive messages as justified (M. M. Martin, Anderson, & Horvath, 1996), but individuals who are high in trait verbal aggressiveness (as compared to those individuals who are low in trait verbal aggressiveness) identify specific justifications for using these messages, which include disdain for the targeted person, the desire to either appear tough or be mean to the targeted person, and a conversation that evolves into a verbal fight (Infante et al., 1992). Other reasons for using verbally aggressive messages include self-defense and reprimanding, manipulating, or teasing the targeted person (Infante, Bruning, & Martin, 1994). Individuals who are high in trait verbal aggressiveness also consider verbally aggressive messages to be less hurtful than individuals who are low in trait verbal aggressiveness (Infante et al., 1992). Based on this collective research, it stands to reason that emerging adults will rate their use of verbally aggressive messages similarly. To explore this notion, we advanced the second and third hypotheses:

H2: Emerging adults who are high in trait verbal aggressiveness will view their use of verbally aggressive messages with a sibling during childhood as more justified than emerging adults who are low in trait verbal aggressiveness.

H3: Emerging adults who are high in trait verbal aggressiveness will view their use of verbally aggressive messages with a sibling during childhood as less hurtful than emerging adults who are low in trait verbal aggressiveness.

As sibling bullying researchers have noted, several of the aforementioned verbally aggressive messages (e.g., teasing the sibling, making fun of the sibling, calling the sibling names) also are considered to constitute sibling bullying (Bowes et al., 2014; Skinner & Kowalski, 2013), which also results in siblings feeling angry, upset, embarrassed, or confused when they are the targets of these bullying messages (Skinner & Kowalski, 2013). Sibling bullying, which Menesini, Camodeca, and Nocentini (2010) considered to be "a specific type of aggression aimed at dominating another person and at causing physical or psychological harm" (p. 921), often includes verbal or relational aggression (Hoetger et al., 2015) that is not limited to a single occurrence but rather occurs frequently and repeatedly (Wolke & Skew, 2012). To extend the verbal aggressiveness literature and to contribute further to the sibling bullying literature, we posed the second research question and posited the fourth hypothesis:

RQ2: To what extent do emerging adults recall using verbally aggressive messages as a way to bully a sibling during childhood?

H4: Emerging adults who are high in trait verbal aggressiveness will report using verbally aggressive messages more frequently to bully a sibling during childhood than emerging adults who are low in trait verbal aggressiveness.

Method

Participants

Participants were 124 undergraduate students (46 males, 78 females) who were enrolled in one of several undergraduate communication courses at a large mid-Atlantic university. Their ages ranged from 18–32 years (M = 20.2, SD = 1.9). They reported on 62 male and 60 female siblings (the sex of two siblings was not provided) whose ages ranged from 18–42 years (M = 22.8, SD = 3.8) and who were largely biological siblings (n = 100; 18 siblings were half-siblings, 4 siblings were step-siblings, and 2 siblings were adopted). On average, participants estimated that they lived 352 miles (M = 352.33, SD = 778.21) from their sibling. The median number of children in their family was three (Mdn = 3.0; Mo = 3.0; range = 2–11 children), which included themselves and their sibling. No other demographic or relational data were collected.

Procedures

Following approval from the university's Institutional Review Board, we solicited participants from an advertisement placed on the department's research project board (located both outside the department office and on a website). The advertisement explained the purpose of the research study, identified the inclusion criteria for participation (i.e., 18 years of age or older, enrolled at the university, and have a living sibling who is 18 years of age or older), and provided the date, time, and location for participating in the research study. Upon arrival at the room in which the data were gathered, one of the research team members greeted the participants, reiterated the purpose and inclusion criteria of the study, and provided participants with a cover letter, a copy of the survey, and an envelope. We instructed participants to read (and keep) the cover letter and then complete the survey. Upon completion of the survey, we asked them to place the survey in the envelope, seal the envelope, and place the sealed envelope in a box located at the front of the room. We then thanked participants for their participation and exited the room. All participants received a minimal amount of extra credit determined by their respective course instructor.

Instrumentation

Participants completed a survey that inquired about the aforementioned demographic data, four versions of a measure of verbally aggressive messages created specifically for this study, and the Verbal Aggressiveness Scale (Infante & Wigley, 1986). Following the procedure used by Myers and Odenweller (2015), we instructed participants to (1) identify the sibling (by initials) whose birthday was closest (i.e., calendar month and day) to their own birthday and (2) complete all measures in reference to the identified sibling.

After completing several demographic data questions, we provided participants with a typology of 28 verbally aggressive messages (see Table 18.1). We created this typology based on the verbally aggressive messages used or obtained in prior research studies conducted on emerging adults' relationship with their siblings (Martin et al., 2005; Myers & Bryant, 2008a; Teven et al., 1998). We directed participants to follow these instructions:

> Keep the sibling you identified on the prior page in mind as you complete the following items. Listed below are examples of types of verbally aggressive messages siblings use with each other. During your childhood—which is defined as when you were between the ages of 5 and 18 years—indicate how often you engaged in each behavior with your sibling. There is neither a right nor a wrong answer.

We solicited responses using a 5-point Likert scale ranging from 1 = Almost never to 5 = Very often. Participants then completed the same typology assessing the extent to which they considered each message to be hurtful (the second version) and the extent to which they considered the use of each message to be justified (the third version); responses for both versions were solicited using a 5-point Likert scale ranging from 1 = To no extent to 5 = To a very great extent. Finally, participants responded to the fourth version of the typology, which assessed the frequency with which participants used each message to bully their sibling during childhood. The directions provided to the participants stated:

> Finally, we are interested in whether you used each of the following behaviors as a way to bully your sibling during childhood. Again, we define childhood as when you were between the ages of 5–18 years. Sibling bullying is considered to be a specific type of aggressive behavior that is repeated over time, intended both to cause harm and to dominate. There is neither a right nor a wrong answer.

We solicited responses using a 5-point Likert scale ranging from 1 = Almost never to 5 = Very often.

The participants then completed the Verbal Aggressiveness Scale, which is a 20-item self-report measure that assesses an individual's tendency to use verbally aggressive behaviors, using a 5-point Likert scale ranging from 1 = Almost never true to 5 = Almost always true. Previous reliability coefficients ranging from .82 to .87 have been reported for the scale (Beatty, Pascual-Ferra, & Levine,

Bullying in Emerging Adult Siblings

Table 18.1 Typology of Verbally Aggressive Messages

Called sibling a derogatory name
Attacked sibling's intelligence
Attacked sibling's abilities
Attacked sibling's physical appearance
Told sibling that I did not want to be physically present around him/her
Told sibling that I did not value his/her presence
Threatened sibling with bodily harm
Physically hurt sibling
Threatened to get sibling into trouble with a parent
Threatened to damage sibling's property
Damaged sibling's property
Rejected sibling's attempts to communicate with him/her
Was unwilling to communicate with sibling
Expressed hatred toward sibling
Expressed dislike for sibling
Downplayed sibling's feelings about an important topic to him/her
Made unfair comparisons of sibling's life to my life
Made inaccurate comparisons between events happening in our lives
Accused sibling of being a terrible sibling
Questioned whether sibling was a "good" family member
Hurled insults at sibling
Teased sibling about his/her relationships with other people
Called sibling uncomplimentary nicknames
Complained to family members about sibling
Made fun of the way sibling talks
Told sibling that he/she lacks common sense
Embarrassed sibling in front of family members
Pointed out sibling's faults to him/her

2015; Madlock & Kennedy-Lightsey, 2010). In this study, a Cronbach's alpha reliability coefficient of .77 (M = 48.79, SD = 10.90) was obtained for the measure.

Data Analysis

To arrive at the levels of trait verbal aggressiveness, we categorized participants' scores on the Verbal Aggressiveness Scale into three groups (i.e., high, moderate, low) using a 33% percentile break. Thirty-nine (n = 39) participants comprised the high trait verbal aggressiveness group, 39 participants comprised the moderate verbal aggressiveness group, and 40 participants comprised the low verbal aggressiveness group. (We excluded six participants from data analysis due to missing data.) Because this study focused on the differences between participants who were either high or low in trait verbal aggressiveness, we did not include the data gathered from the participants who were classified as moderate in trait verbal aggressiveness in the analyses. We then examined the four hypotheses using a series of independent sample t-tests. For each hypothesis, the 28 verbally aggressive messages served alternately as the dependent variables and the level of trait verbal aggressiveness (i.e., high, low) served as the independent variable. Due to the large number of t-tests conducted to test each hypothesis, an effect size (i.e., Cohen's d) for each t-test was calculated as a way to further substantiate any significant differences (Field, 2009). We answered both research questions by calculating the mean and standard deviation

Scott A. Myers et al.

scores for each of the 28 verbally aggressive messages and then ranking the messages in descending order of mean scores.

Results

Preliminary Analyses

Because sibling bullying is tied to sibling demographic variables such as sex, age, and birth order (Menesini et al., 2010; Wolke & Skew, 2012), we conducted several preliminary analyses between these three variables and emerging adults' use of the 28 verbally aggressive messages as a way to bully a sibling during childhood. The only significant findings were obtained for sibling sex. Male emerging adults reported using the "physically hurt sibling" (M_{Male} = 2.22, SD = 1.21; M_{Female} = 1.69, SD = 0.98; $t(122)$ = 2.63, p = .01, d = .48), "threatened to damage sibling's property" (M_{Male} = 2.46, SD = 1.28; M_{Female} = 1.69, SD = 0.98; $t(122)$ = 3.77, p < .001, d = .68), "damaged sibling's property" (M_{Male} = 2.30, SD = 1.36; M_{Female} = 1.63, SD = 1.05; $t(122)$ = 3.16, p = .002, d = .56), "teased sibling about his/her relationships with other people" (M_{Male} = 2.43, SD = 1.28; M_{Female} = 1.76, SD = 1.08; $t(122)$ = 3.15, p = .002, d = .57), "called sibling uncomplimentary nicknames" (M_{Male} = 2.78, SD = 1.23; M_{Female} = 2.23, SD = 1.34; $t(122)$ = 2.29, p = .024, d = .42), and "made fun of the way sibling talks" (M_{Male} = 1.98, SD = 1.15; M_{Female} = 1.56, SD = 0.98; $t(122)$ = 2.14, p = .034, d = .39) messages as a higher rate than female emerging adults as a way to bully their siblings during childhood.

Primary Analyses

The first question inquired about the extent to which emerging adults recalled using verbally aggressive messages with their siblings during childhood. Generally, emerging adults reported that they recalled either rarely or never at all using verbally aggressive messages with their siblings during childhood (see Table 18.2). Of the 28 messages, "threatening to get sibling into trouble with a parent" was the most frequently used message and "damaged sibling's property" was the least frequently used message.

The first hypothesis posited that emerging adults who are high in trait verbal aggressiveness would report using verbally aggressive messages with a sibling during childhood more frequently than emerging adults who are low in trait verbal aggressiveness. This hypothesis was partially supported. Of the 28 verbally aggressive messages, emerging adults who are high in trait verbal aggressiveness reported using nine messages more frequently than emerging adults who are low in trait verbal aggressiveness. These messages are "called sibling a derogatory name" (M_{HighVA} = 2.60, SD = 1.22; M_{LowVA} = 2.08, SD = 1.09; $t(77)$ = 2.02, p = .047, d = .50), "attacked sibling's abilities" (M_{HighVA} = 2.48, SD = 1.20; M_{LowVA} = 1.74, SD = 0.97; $t(77)$ = 2.98, p = .004, d = .68), "attacked sibling's physical appearance" (M_{HighVA} = 2.28, SD = 1.15; M_{LowVA} = 1.46, SD = 0.76; $t(77)$ = 3.70, p < .001, d = .84), "told sibling I did not value his/her presence" (M_{HighVA} = 2.10, SD = 1.28; M_{LowVA} = 1.41, SD = 0.88; $t(77)$ = 2.79, p = .007, d = .63), "damaged sibling's property" (M_{HighVA} = 1.83, SD = 0.96; M_{LowVA} = 1.41, SD = 0.79; $t(77)$ = 2.10, p = .039, d = .47), "hurled insults at sibling" (M_{HighVA} = 2.70, SD = 1.10; M_{LowVA} = 1.95, SD = 1.19; $t(77)$ = 2.65, p = .010, d = .60), "called sibling uncomplimentary nicknames" (M_{HighVA} = 2.43, SD = 1.36; M_{LowVA} = 1.87, SD = 1.08; $t(77)$ = 2.00, p = .049, d = .46), "made fun of the way sibling talks" (M_{HighVA} = 2.10, SD = 1.37; M_{LowVA} = 1.36, SD = 0.78; $t(77)$ = 2.94, p = .004, d = .66), and "pointed out sibling's faults to him/her" (M_{HighVA} = 2.38, SD = 1.33; M_{LowVA} = 1.69, SD = 0.86; $t(77)$ = 2.69, p = .009, d = .62).

The second hypothesis posited that emerging adults who are high in trait verbal aggressiveness would view their use of verbally aggressive messages with a sibling during childhood as more

Bullying in Emerging Adult Siblings

Table 18.2 Use of Verbally Aggressive Messages During Childhood

Rank	Behavior	M	SD
1	Threatened to get sibling into trouble with a parent	2.71	1.27
2	Complained to family members about sibling	2.52	1.38
3	Called sibling a derogatory name	2.43	1.19
4	Hurled insults at sibling	2.39	1.28
5	Attacked sibling's abilities	2.19	1.16
6	Attacked sibling's intelligence	2.14	1.14
7	Expressed dislike for sibling	2.12	1.22
8	Called sibling uncomplimentary nicknames	2.11	1.21
9	Embarrassed sibling in front of family members	2.10	1.12
	Told sibling that he/she lacks common sense	2.10	1.15
11	Told sibling that I did not want to be physically present around him/her	2.08	1.14
12	Accused sibling of being a terrible sibling	2.06	1.19
13	Pointed out sibling's faults to him/her	2.03	1.13
14	Teased sibling about his/her relationships with other people	2.02	1.10
	Was unwilling to communicate with sibling	2.02	1.19
16	Threatened sibling with bodily harm	1.99	1.21
17	Attacked sibling's physical appearance	1.96	1.16
18	Made unfair comparisons of sibling's life to my life	1.94	1.02
19	Physically hurt sibling	1.90	1.08
	Questioned whether sibling was a "good" family member	1.90	1.14
	Threatened to damage sibling's property	1.90	1.11
22	Rejected sibling's attempts to communicate with him/her	1.88	1.16
23	Made inaccurate comparisons between events happening in our lives	1.86	1.04
24	Made fun of the way sibling talks	1.81	1.18
25	Expressed hatred toward sibling	1.79	1.09
26	Downplayed sibling's feelings about an important topic to him/her	1.75	0.92
27	Told sibling that I did not value his/her presence	1.73	1.09
28	Damaged sibling's property	1.69	0.97

justified than emerging adults who are low in trait verbal aggressiveness. This hypothesis was partially supported. Of the 28 verbally aggressive messages, emerging adults who are high in trait verbal aggressiveness viewed their use of five messages with a sibling as more justified than emerging adults who are low in trait verbal aggressiveness. These messages are "told sibling that I did not want to be physically present around him/her" (M_{HighVA} = 2.68, SD = 1.31; M_{LowVA} = 1.95, SD = 1.40; $t(77)$ = 2.39, p = .019, d = .53), "told sibling that I did not value his/her presence" (M_{HighVA} = 2.50, SD = 1.20; M_{LowVA} = 1.72, SD = 1.28; $t(77)$ = 2.81, p = .006, d = .63), "expressed hatred toward sibling" (M_{HighVA} = 2.18, SD = 1.20; M_{LowVA} = 1.51, SD = 1.00; $t(77)$ = 2.67, p = .009, d = .61), "accused sibling of being a terrible sibling" (M_{HighVA} = 2.38, SD = 1.30; M_{LowVA} = 1.67, SD = 1.22; $t(77)$ = 2.50, p = .015, d = .56), and "pointed out sibling's faults to him/her" (M_{HighVA} = 2.58, SD = 1.24; M_{LowVA} = 1.95, SD = 1.32; $t(77)$ = 2.18, p = .032, d = .49).

The third hypothesis posited that emerging adults who are high in trait verbal aggressiveness would view their use of verbally aggressive messages with a sibling during childhood as less hurtful than emerging adults who are low in trait verbal aggressiveness. This hypothesis was partially supported. Of the 28 verbally aggressive messages, emerging adults who are high in trait verbal aggressiveness viewed their use of seven messages with a sibling as less hurtful than emerging adults who are low in trait verbal aggressiveness. These messages are "attacked sibling's physical appearance" (M_{HighVA} = 2.88, SD = 1.32; M_{LowVA} = 3.67, SD = 1.58; $t(77)$ = −2.42, p = .018, d = .54) "damaged sibling's property" (M_{HighVA} = 3.05, SD = 1.34; M_{LowVA} = 3.74, SD = 1.52; t(77) = −2.16, p = .034, d = .48), "expressed hatred toward sibling" (M_{HighVA} = 2.80, SD = 1.38; M_{LowVA} = 3.62, SD = 1.60; t(77) = −2.43, p = .018, d = .55), "expressed dislike for sibling" (M_{HighVA} = 2.65, SD = 1.31; M_{LowVA} = 3.38, SD = 1.48; t(77) = -2.34, p = .022, d = .52), "accused sibling of being a terrible sibling" (M_{HighVA} = 2.73, SD = 1.34; M_{LowVA} = 3.51, SD = 1.43; t(77) = −2.53, p = .014, d = .56), "questioned whether sibling was a 'good' sibling" (M_{HighVA} = 2.63, SD = 1.33; M_{LowVA} = 3.59, SD = 1.50; t(77) = −3.02, p = .003, d = .68), and "hurled insults at sibling" (M_{HighVA} = 2.73, SD = 1.28; M_{LowVA} = 3.44, SD = 1.42; t(77) = −2.33, p = .022, d = .52).

The second research question inquired about the extent to which emerging adults recalled using verbally aggressive messages as a way to bully a sibling during childhood. Generally, emerging adults reported that they recalled either rarely or never at all using verbally messages as a way to bully their siblings during childhood (see Table 18.3). Of the 28 messages, "threatening to get sibling into trouble with a parent" was the most frequently used message to bully a sibling and "made fun of the way sibling talks" was the least frequently used message to bully a sibling.

The fourth hypothesis posited that emerging adults who are high in trait verbal aggressiveness would report using verbally aggressive messages more frequently to bully a sibling during childhood than emerging adults who are low in trait verbal aggressiveness. This hypothesis was partially

Table 18.3 Use of Verbally Aggressive Messages to Bully Siblings during Childhood

Rank	Behavior	M	SD
1	Threatened to get sibling into trouble with a parent	2.58	1.36
2	Called sibling uncomplimentary nicknames	2.44	1.32
3	Complained to family members about sibling	2.36	1.41
4	Hurled insults at sibling	2.31	1.30
5	Expressed dislike for sibling	2.21	1.30
6	Called sibling a derogatory name	2.15	1.18
7	Was unwilling to communicate with sibling	2.08	1.19
8	Accused sibling of being a terrible sibling	2.06	1.22
	Rejected sibling's attempts to communicate with him/her	2.06	1.24
10	Told sibling that I did not want to be physically present around him/her	2.02	1.14
11	Teased sibling about his/her relationships with other people	2.01	1.20
12	Attacked sibling's abilities	1.99	1.11
13	Embarrassed sibling in front of family members	1.96	1.08
	Threatened to damage sibling's property	1.96	1.19
15	Downplayed sibling's feelings about an important topic to him/her	1.94	1.11
	Pointed out sibling's faults to him/her	1.94	1.24
	Threatened sibling with bodily harm	1.94	1.03
	Told sibling that he/she lacks common sense	1.94	1.14
19	Made inaccurate comparisons between events happening in our lives	1.91	1.10
	Made unfair comparisons of sibling's life to my life	1.91	1.07
21	Physically hurt sibling	1.89	1.10
22	Attacked sibling's intelligence	1.87	0.96
	Damaged sibling's property	1.87	1.23
	Expressed hatred toward sibling	1.87	1.19
25	Questioned whether sibling was a "good" family member	1.85	1.17
26	Attacked sibling's physical appearance	1.82	1.08
27	Told sibling that I did not value his/her presence	1.78	1.12
28	Made fun of the way sibling talks	1.72	1.06

supported. Of the 28 verbally aggressive messages, emerging adults who are high in trait verbal aggressiveness reported using 22 messages to bully a sibling than emerging adults who are low in trait verbal aggressiveness. These messages are "attacked sibling's intelligence" (M_{HighVA} = 2.25, SD = 1.28; M_{LowVA} = 1.82, SD = 1.00; t(77) = 2.93, p = .004, d = .37), "attacked sibling's abilities" (M_{HighVA} = 2.40, SD = 1.28; M_{LowVA} = 1.59, SD = 0.79; t(77) = 3.39, p < .001, d = .76), "attacked sibling's physical appearance" (M_{HighVA} = 2.30, SD = 1.16; M_{LowVA} = 1.31, SD = 0.61; t(77) = 4.74, p < .001, d = 1.07), "told sibling I did not want to be physically present around him/her" (M_{HighVA} = 2.25, SD = 1.17; M_{LowVA} = 1.64, SD = 1.04; t(77) = 2.44, p = .017, d = .55), "told sibling that I did not value his/her presence" (M_{HighVA} = 2.13, SD = 1.11; M_{LowVA} = 1.36, SD = 0.96; t(77) = 3.27, p = .002, d = .74), "physically hurt sibling" (M_{HighVA} = 2.20, SD = 1.09; M_{LowVA} = 1.59, SD = 1.02; t(77) = 2.57, p = .012, d = .58), and "threatened to damage sibling's property" (M_{HighVA} = 2.35, SD = 1.23; M_{LowVA} = 1.49, SD = 0.94; t(77) = 3.49, p < .001, d = .79).

Other messages are "damaged sibling's property" (M_{HighVA} = 2.35, SD = 1.27; M_{LowVA} = 1.28, SD = 0.92; t(77) = 4.27, p < .001, d = .96), "rejected sibling's attempts to communicate with him/her" (M_{HighVA} = 2.43, SD = 1.24; M_{LowVA} = 1.64, SD = 1.14; t(77) = 2.93, p = .004, d = .66), "expressed hatred toward sibling" (M_{HighVA} = 2.20, SD = 1.14; M_{LowVA} = 1.41, SD = 0.97; t(77) = 3.32, p < .001, d = .75), "expressed dislike for sibling" (M_{HighVA} = 2.53, SD = 1.30; M_{LowVA} = 1.77, SD = 1.09; t(77) = 2.80, p = .006, d = .63), "downplayed sibling's feelings about an important topic to him/her" (M_{HighVA} = 2.45, SD = 1.24; M_{LowVA} = 1.44, SD = 0.91; t(77) = 4.13, p < .001, d = .93), "made unfair comparisons of sibling's life to my life" (M_{HighVA} = 2.25, SD = 1.17; M_{LowVA} = 1.49, SD = 0.89; t(77) = 3.26, p = .002, d = .73), and "made inaccurate comparisons between events happening in our lives" (M_{HighVA} = 2.30, SD = 1.09; M_{LowVA} = 1.51, SD = 0.97; t(77) = 3.39, p = .005, d = .77).

Still other messages are "accused sibling of being a bad sibling" (M_{HighVA} = 2.40, SD = 1.13; M_{LowVA} = 1.67, SD = 1.13; t(77) = 2.89, p < .001, d = .65), "questioned whether sibling was a 'good' family member" (M_{HighVA} = 2.18, SD = 1.20; M_{LowVA} = 1.44, SD = 1.00; t(77) = 2.98, p = .004, d = .67), "hurled insults at sibling" (M_{HighVA} = 2.78, SD = 1.27; M_{LowVA} = 1.97, SD = 1.29; t(77) = 2.78, p = .007, d = .63), "teased sibling about his/her relationships with other people" (M_{HighVA} = 2.35, SD = 1.35; M_{LowVA} = 1.56, SD = 0.88; t(77) = 3.05, p = .003, d = .69), "called sibling uncomplimentary nicknames" (M_{HighVA} = 2.80, SD = 1.44; M_{LowVA} = 2.08, SD = 1.20; t(77) = 2.43, p = .018, d = .54), "made fun of the way sibling talks" (M_{HighVA} = 2.18, SD = 1.20; M_{LowVA} = 1.36, SD = 0.82; t(77) = 3.54, p < .001, d = .80), "told sibling that he/she lacks common sense" (M_{HighVA} = 2.25, SD = 1.19; M_{LowVA} = 1.59, SD = 0.99; t(77) = 2.67, p = .009, d = .60), and "embarrassed sibling in front of family members" (M_{HighVA} = 2.23, SD = 1.17; M_{LowVA} = 1.59, SD = 0.88; t(77) = 2.73, p = .008, d = .62).

Discussion

This chapter explored how emerging adults reflect on their use of verbally aggressive messages with their siblings and whether they used verbally aggressive messages as a way to communicatively bully their siblings during childhood. We obtained three general findings. First, emerging adults report that they rarely or never used verbally aggressive messages with their siblings during childhood. Second, few differences exist between those emerging adults high in verbal aggressiveness and those emerging adults low in verbal aggressiveness in regard to their use of specific verbally aggressive messages during childhood, the justification they had for using these messages, and the hurtfulness they associated with these messages. Third, although emerging adults report that they rarely or never used verbally aggressive messages as a way to bully their siblings during childhood, emerging adults who are high in verbal aggressiveness used 22 of these 28 verbally aggressive messages more frequently to bully their siblings than emerging adults who are low in verbal aggressiveness.

Of these findings, the third finding is the most intriguing because it begs the question as to why siblings intentionally use verbally aggressive messages use as a bullying tactic. That is, why do emerging adults who are high or low in trait verbal aggressiveness recall that they did not differ generally in their use of specific verbally aggressive messages with their siblings during childhood yet did recall using these many of these same types of messages to bully their siblings during childhood? This answer may lie with the intended effect of verbally aggressive messages, which is to make the recipient experience psychological pain (Infante, 1988). On a day-to-day basis, siblings may not feel the need to behave in a verbally aggressive manner toward each other because they can gain little from doing so. When they use the verbally aggressive message frequently and repetitively to bully a sibling, however, this message may have just as much of a painful impact as physical (e.g., hitting, kicking), verbal (e.g., verbal abuse, blackmail), or relational (e.g., ostracizing, ignoring) forms of bullying (Hoetger et al., 2015; Wolke & Skew, 2012). Moreover, because the verbally aggressive messages used by emerging adults with their siblings during childhood center on either devaluing the targeted sibling (e.g., attacks on intelligence and physical appearance, name calling) or denigrating the sibling relationship (e.g., expressed hated or dislike, accusing sibling of being terrible)—much like the findings obtained by Myers and Bryant (2008a)—the significance of the message may be further emphasized when used as a bullying tactic rather than as a remark made in a casual conversation.

Two important implications from this study should guide future research and praxis. First, this study affirms the need for family communication researchers and practitioners to examine the role that verbal aggressiveness plays in sibling bullying. Perhaps the foremost (and more salient) solution lies in identifying the reasons behind why family members—namely children—choose to communicate with each other in a verbally aggressive manner. Aside from psychopathology or disdain for another person (Infante, Trebing, Shepherd, & Seeds, 1984), Infante (1988) posited that a deficiency in argumentative skills best explains why some individuals engage in verbal aggressiveness. Individuals who adopt an "attack and defend" mentality when placed in a vulnerable communication situation tend to personalize the situation, which then provokes a verbally aggressive response. When individuals are not taught or trained how to respond constructively in such situations, they then are more likely to engage in verbal aggressiveness. Furthermore, Infante (1987) noted that "verbal aggression is learned by reinforcement and by modeling" (p. 183). For example, in terms of reinforcement, Bayer and Cegala (1992) found that parents who utilize an authoritarian parenting style tend to be high in trait verbal aggressiveness, whereas when it comes to modeling, for instance, children simply may imitate their parents' communication behaviors. For example, M. M. Martin and Anderson (1997) found that adult sons and daughters who are high in verbal aggressiveness have mothers who also are high in verbal aggressiveness.

Once these reasons have been identified, families then need to take steps to eradicate verbal aggressiveness in general—and verbally aggressive messages in particular—from the family communication repertoire. In some families, communicating in a verbally aggressive manner is a common behavior and may even be linked to their family communication patterns. Schrodt and Carr (2012), for example, discovered that a positive relationship exists between emerging adults' trait verbal aggressiveness and their family's use of conformity orientation and that a negative relationship exists between emerging adults' trait verbal aggressiveness and their family's conversation orientation. Booth-Butterfield and Sidelinger (1997) reported that emerging adults who are high in trait verbal aggressiveness consider their families to be less open in their communication.

Second, family communication researchers and practitioners need to develop, present, and assess intervention programs that teach family members not only how to recognize the presence of verbally aggressive behaviors and messages in their communication with one another but also how to replace these verbally aggressive behaviors and messages with constructive behaviors and messages. Infante (1995) suggested that such programs encapsulate three instructional goals: (1) enhance parents' and children's understanding of verbal aggressiveness (including how verbal aggressiveness can be regarded as another form of sibling bullying), (2) assist parents and children in developing strategies for controlling verbal aggressiveness, and (3) provide activities in which both parents and children can internalize their newly obtained knowledge and skills. Doing so will undoubtedly prove helpful for families (or individual family members) who either are unable or do not know how to refrain from engaging in verbally aggressive behaviors and messages with each other. Moreover, because parents often are present when sibling bullying occurs (Skinner & Kowalski, 2013), researchers should examine the degree to which parental awareness or involvement of their use of verbally aggressive messages affects whether their children (i.e., siblings) either engage in bullying behavior or use verbally aggressive messages as a specific way to bully each other.

Conclusion

Verbal aggressiveness constitutes a destructive communication behavior that almost always results in negative ramifications for its recipients (Infante, 1987). When siblings engage in verbally aggressive messages specifically for the purpose of bullying one another, these negative ramifications can increase substantially. Because "bullying starts at home" (Wolke & Skew, 2012, p. 8), family communication researchers and practitioners should consider educating families about how to prevent siblings from using verbal aggressiveness as a way to bully each other. Doing so not only can enhance the communication and relationships that family members develop with each other, but also may decrease the extent to which sibling bullying occurs. Because emerging adults often model the communicative behaviors they learn from their parents (Arroyo, Nevárez, Segrin, & Harwood, 2012; Floyd & Morman, 2000; Odenweller, Rittenour, Myers, & Brann, 2013), eradicating verbal aggressiveness from the family communication environment is one way to positively influence the learned behaviors that they take into their future relationships as spouses, parents, and extended family members.

19

BULLYING IN SENIORS' COMMUNITIES

What's Identity Got to Do With It?

Loraleigh Keashly

Much attention has been paid to elder abuse, which the Centers for Disease Control (2017) defined as "an intentional act, or failure to act, by a caregiver or another person in a relationship involving an expectation of trust that causes or creates a risk of harm to an older adult [*someone 60 years or older*]." Older adults are also vulnerable to abusive and aggressive treatment from peers/co-residents in seniors' communities (Bonifas, 2016). Scholars refer to such aggression as resident-to-resident elder mistreatment (RREM; Lachs et al., 2016). RREM encompasses aggressive behaviors that vary in terms of nature (verbal, social, physical) and frequency (Lachs et al., 2016). Bullying, as a persistent form of RREM, has become a recognized issue by staff in these communities, yet, until recently, it has drawn little systematic research attention (Bonifas, 2016). Older adults also recognize bullying as an issue in their communities (see West & Turner, this volume). In their study of seniors' subsidized apartment buildings, Goodridge, Heal-Salahub, PausJenssen, James, and Lidington (2017) report rates of 29% for being a target and 39% witnessing in the prior 12 months. Rex-Lear (2011) found a victimization rate of 24% among independent living seniors (own home or in retirement communities).

Existing research has come primarily from an elder care perspective and revealed a great deal about why the older adult may bully. Specifically, the transition to these varied living arrangements reflects a need for increased support in response to declines associated with aging. For people who have lived independent lives, these declines are challenging, reflecting decreasing autonomy and control, and a fundamental challenge to their identity as competent and experienced adults. The adjustment to being in closer community with others not of their choosing further challenges the individual's identity. Researchers have suggested that bullying could comprise an attempt on the part of an older adult to negotiate a new identity that is characterized by strength rather than loss (Barnhart & Peñaloza, 2012; Bonifas, 2016; Salari, 2006). In this chapter, I utilize a communication lens on identity negotiation to reveal ways to meet the older adult resident identity needs more constructively. I will situate this discussion of identity in the broader social discourse about aging and being "old." Specifically, I will explore how ageism and ageist communication frame "being old" as a devalued and stigmatized identity (decline, deficit, incompetence and dependence), which shapes communicative structures and practices of communities defined by age (seniors' communities) and influences people's experiences of themselves and others and how they embody and enact the identity of "old." Within this context, bullying is considered an agentic attempt to negotiate and (re) claim a more positive identity of competence and control (Nelson, 2005). The perspective of identity negotiation opens up possibilities for how to address problematic behaviors in these communities in ways that affirm the value, integrity, and agency of the actor/bully and the community.

The Graying of the United States

We are all getting older. Thus, each of us will grapple with incorporating into our self-view what it means to be older, old, and elderly. The overall life expectancy in the U.S. is 78.6 years (women 81.1 years and men 76.1 years; National Center for Health Statistics, 2017), but we aspire to live to 90 (Pew Research Center, 2013). Also, we hear about more and more "old people" all the time In the U.S., 10,000 people turn 65 every day (Cohn & Taylor, 2010). As of June 2017, 49 million Americans were 65 years and older, representing 15% of the U.S. population (United States Census Bureau, 2017). By 2050, the U.S. Census Bureau (Ortman, Velkoff, & Hogan, 2014) estimates the U.S. population will include 83.7 million "senior citizens," 22% of the population. This single largest and growing demographic increasingly shapes our economic (e.g., social security, Medicare) and social agendas. For example, at the 2015 White House conference on aging (www.hhs.gov/aging), participants discussed a number of initiatives focused on providing resources for "successful" or "positive aging" (Barnhart & Peñaloza, 2012), including the necessity of living and housing that respect and respond to the needs of an "older population" requiring at least some care or assistance. Living options range from:

- "aging in place"—the provision of services focused on keeping people in their homes;
- seniors' independent living communities, including age-restricted communities (+55), seniors' apartments, and cohousing (voluntary co-location with similar others);
- assisted living—varying degrees of supportive services
- nursing care facilities (aka "nursing homes")—highly skilled nursing care (Ginzler, 2009).

Continuing care retirement communities (CCRC) encompass a variety of care options ranging from independent living to skilled nursing care and are tied to the changing health status of residents. These housing options reflect variability in the degree of autonomy and freedom of choice residents have for decision making about, and control over, their activities and interactions. These communities also vary in extent of co-location and interaction with dissimilar "others." Residents may differ in terms of functional status (physical and cognitively) as well education, economic, and racial/ethnic backgrounds, i.e., neighbors but not by choice (Goodridge et al., 2017). Increasing levels of assistance position those providing support and care as ever more central in the management and control of the resident's life. Through their structure, composition, and communicative practices, these communities are rich with cues about aging and what it means to be "older" and "old." By making the "old" identity salient, these settings challenge residents' capacity to negotiate and maintain an identity as an experienced and competent adult. In the next section, what it means to be "old" as constituted in the social discourse of aging will be discussed.

The Meaning of "Old"

What does "old" mean? When does someone become "old"? The answers to these questions provide the descriptive anchors to which identity is tied (Degnen, 2007; Taylor, Morin, Parker, Cohn, & Wang 2009). To address these questions, it is important to consider how Americans think about "old" and then discuss the dominant discourse of aging.

In the most recent Pew Research Center survey (Taylor et al., 2009), the age of "becoming old" was related to the age of the respondent. Those under 30 years of age identified 60 years as when the average person becomes "old" while those 65 years and older identified 74 years. In essence, the age "old" is the one "at which I have not arrived yet" (Taylor et al., 2009, p. 21). To personalize "old," respondents were asked if they feel younger, older, or the same as their chronological age. In the 65 and older group, only 28% "felt old" while those 75 years and older, 31% "felt old." Interestingly, over half of respondents 18–29 years of age felt "older than their age," but, of those who were 30 and older, approximately 60% felt "younger." The gap between actual age and felt age also corresponded to the age of the respondent, with larger gaps associated with older age (e.g., 30–49-year-olds feel five years younger while those 65 and older report feeling ten years younger on average). These results underscore the subjectivity and dynamic nature of the identity and meaning of "old," drawing our attention to the socially constructive nature of identity.

We negotiate our identities through communication with others and within a social context (Burke, 1991; Westerhof, Whitbourne, & Freeman, 2011). Within a particular context, we distinguish identities as desirable or undesirable (stigmatized), and we define the expectations of an "effective" identity (Cohen & Sherman, 2014; Salari, 2006; Westerhof et al., 2011). Thus, we need to explore the macrosocietal discourse of what "being old" means and how that discourse shapes how we engage with and perceive people who are "old" (i.e., ageism and ageist communication; Berger, 2017; Nelson, 2017). These stereotypes influence an individual's own sense of self as "being old" and whether that identity is one to be embraced or to be shunned or from which to distance oneself. An undesirable identity of "being old" (e.g., decline, incompetence, incapacity) has implications for interactions with others the individual sees as reflecting that undesired identity, setting up the possibility for using aggression and bullying of the peer in an effort to distinguish oneself as not "that kind of old" (Nelson, 2005; Weiss & Freund, 2012). I will return to the dynamics of identity on behavior towards others in the section on identity threat. For now, it is important to explore what the image of old is.

On "Being Old" in the United States

Research on the meaning of "being old" reveals negative images dominated by the inevitability of decline and incompetence as a result of increasing loss of control over one's physical and cognitive capacities, features that are highly valued in a national culture of youth and vibrancy (Carney & Gray, 2015; Martens, Goldenberg, & Greenberg, 2005; Weiss & Staudinger, 2015; Westerhof et al., 2011). These stereotypes are pervasive and pernicious (Gullette, 2017; Nelson, 2004). They have been documented in the perceptions of younger others (Degnen, 2007; Nelson, 2005; Taylor et al., 2009) and also in the behavior of care staff in seniors' communities (e.g., Salari, 2006; Salari & Rich, 2001). Sadly, but not surprisingly, these images show up in older adults' beliefs about the nature of the aging process as inevitable and immutable (i.e., they will, indeed, become incompetent and dependent; Lagacé, Tanguay, Lavallée, Laplante, & Robichaud, 2012; Raina & Balodi, 2014; Weiss & Staudinger, 2015). Despite evidence that, by far, the majority of those over 65 and even over 80 live independently and remain physical and cognitively capable (Sneed & Whitbourne, 2005; Taylor et al., 2009), these beliefs regarding inevitability of physical and cognitive decline and associated incompetence and dependence persist. Indeed, stereotype research finds "older" being associated with "bad" (Nosek, Banaji, & Greenwald, 2002). Meaning of aging research (e.g., Weiss & Freund, 2012) shows that older adults resist these negative characterizations by seeking to distance themselves from images of the "old" person ("I am not old!"). These stereotypes are not without consequence, as they guide how people interact and communicate with older adults and also how older adults themselves behave (Nussbaum, Pitts, Huber, Raup, Krieger, & Ohs, 2005). Stereotype threat research (e.g., Barber, 2017) shows that negative attitudes about aging, when internalized, profoundly affect older adult themselves as they begin to behave in line with the aging stereotype. For example, adults who believe that aging involves cognitive decline will underperform on tests of memory. In essence, the older adult comes to embody the stereotype (embodied ageism; Levy, 2009).

This "master narrative of decline" (as cited in Lamb, 2014) and the associated image of aging as "second childhood" (Ryvicker, 2009; Salari, 2006) undergird the macro discourse of ageism (Carney & Gray, 2015; Lagacé et al., 2012; Martens et al., 2005; Raina & Balodi, 2014). R. N. Butler (1989) defined ageism as "those negative attitudes and practices that lead to discrimination against the aged" (p. 139). Ageism can be malignant/hostile (older people as a burden or drain on resources; worthless) or benign/benevolent (kind but incompetent, e.g., "sweet old dear"—patronizing; Barber, 2017; Butler, 1989). Barber argued that ageism is "one of the most socially condoned and acceptable forms of prejudice to hold" (p. 78.).

Ageist communication practices manifest ageism (Lagacé et al., 2012). Communication Accommodation Theory (Giles, Coupland, & Coupland, 1991) posits that we adjust our speech and gestures to reflect the stereotypes we have of the other. Ageist stereotypes show up in very specific types of speech with older people. Elderspeak (Ryan, Bourhis, & Knops, 1991) is characterized by over-accommodating speech including speaking louder and slower, higher pitch, simplified talk, secondary baby talk (as we do with pets and inanimate objects), and patronizing speech (Giles et al., 1991; Hummert, Shaner, Garstka, & Henry, 1998; Lagacé et al., 2012; Nussbaum et al., 2005; Raina & Balodi, 2014). These linguistic markers facilitate a process of infantilization of the older adult in their interaction with others. Infantilization is also manifested environmentally in the structure and programming of seniors' communities and institutions, e.g., engaging in activities designed for children (e.g., Ryvicker, 2009; Salari & Rich, 2001).

Residents of seniors' communities (even those with cognitive impairment) are keenly aware of, and frustrated by, "being treated as a child" (Ryvicker, 2009). The older adult's ability to actively resist infantilization is limited by the concern that their behavior will be taken as evidence of cognitive decline; a symptom of them "losing their minds" (Salari & Rich, 2001). Thus, many older adults accommodate, becoming more dependent and less situationally competent, i.e., self-fulfilling prophecy (Giles et al., 1991; Raina & Balodi, 2014). This communication further devalues the older adult's individuality (Raina & Balodi, 2014). Lagacé et al. (2012) documented the influence of these interactional and environmental communication features on older people's perceptions of the activity and care space as one of "denegation of their self, identity and dignity" (pg. 337).

Given the power and pervasiveness of ageist discourse, scholars and advocates have sought to redefine getting older as "successful" or "positive aging" (Sneed & Whitbourne, 2005). Lamb (2014) argued that this reframing is still problematic as it "overemphasizes independence, prolonging life and declining to decline at the expense of coming to meaningful terms with late-life changes, situations of (inter)dependence, possibilities of frailty, and the condition of human transience," in essence, viewing the "aging self as an ageless self" (p. 46). Such framing positions anyone who experiences (inevitable) bodily and cognitive changes and increasing need for help and support as a failure and "less than." This framing bifurcates older adults into the "well-derly" and the "ill-derly," creating intragroup tension, and highlights a need to defend one's identity as successful and legitimate (Barber, 2017; Lamb, 2014; Martens et al., 2005). Weiss and Freund's (2012) research on "subjective age" demonstrates that, when presented with an age-related image of functional decline and loss in the form of a same aged peer, older adults seek to differentiate and distance themselves from that peer as a self-protective response to maintain a positive view of self. This practice has implications for life in seniors' communities, particularly CCRCs where residents encounter daily exposure to peers with varying degrees of functionality or other signs of "negative" aging (Iecovich & Lev-Ran, 2006; Sandhu, Kemp, Ball, Burgess, & Perkins, 2013). Distancing can be enacted through avoidance or exclusion and differentiation through derogation of the peer. These strategies of identity management are also behaviors frequently identified and experienced as bullying by those on the receiving end (Monks & Coyne, 2011).

Taken together, many societies struggle with aging and mortality (Martens et al., 2005; Nelson, 2005). Being "old" is a societally stigmatized and undesirable identity (Barnhart & Peñaloza, 2012; Lamb, 2014; Nelson, 2005; Rapolienė, 2015). This identity becomes particularly salient when co-located with similar demographic others in seniors' communities; institutions defined by aging. Thus, these communities can be sites of identity threat and fuel the need to manage that threat. Bullying of peers is one way to assert an identity of strength rather than one of decline and weakness (Bonifas, 2016).

Seniors' Communities as Sites of Identity and Identity Threat

By their very existence, seniors' communities make salient aging and being old. On the upside, these communities enable people to live comfortable and enriching lives through various forms of assistance. They accomplish this lifestyle by co-locating similarly aged others, on the presumption of shared interests but also for efficient deployment of resources and services. This co-location, though, separates these older adults from younger others, concentrating interaction to similarly aged peers. This separation has several implications. First, it restricts the models available for social comparison to similarly aged peers. Social comparison is an important social cognitive process for assessing and evaluating identity. Pending the functional status and visibility of aging, infrequent contact with varied aged peers can create a situation of ego (identity) threat (Barber, 2017; Iecovich & Lev-Ran, 2006; Nelson, 2005). Second, separation runs the risk of marginalization, i.e., removing older adults from the dynamics of everyday life and their ability to influence those dynamics, reducing opportunities for manifesting competency critical to the older adult's identity. Third, separation increases the influence of the institutional context on the construction and manifestation of a "good" and "safe" life for the older adult generally, and the identity of "being old," specifically. The notion of "safe" environment presumes that older adults are "vulnerable" and in need of protection. Such presumption assumes the incapability of the older adult to do so, highlighting the identity of decline and incompetence. From a communication perspective, the structures, practices, management, and activities of these communities and restriction of contact to primarily similarly aged others construct and transmit the nature and value of the identity of "old." These messages, in turn, influence residents' behaviors, their views of themselves, and their interactions with their peers.

Ryvicker (2009) articulated the residents' challenge of a seniors' community context as one of "preservation of self," which involves navigating the connection between personal self and institutional identity. Specifically, residents must manifest "the ability to maintain an ongoing sense of individual identity and personhood in the context of physical and/or cognitive limitations as well as within the constraints of institutional life" (p. 13). In her comparative study of two nursing homes, Ryvicker (2009) identified contradictory staff practices that both supported and interfered with residents' preservation of self. Practices that supported residents' sense of self and agency included enabling residents' civic identities by arranging absentee voting and taking residents to the polls or providing opportunities for the residents to engage in activities they had enjoyed before entering the nursing home—a reminder of the personal self that exists beyond the institutional boundaries. Practices also ensued that infantilized (age inappropriate activities; treating as a child) and objectified the residents, resulting in the image of the resident as "bodies that needed maintenance rather than people who needed caring" (p. 16). These communicative practices, reflecting the two distinct institutional identities of autonomous adult and ill and dependent person, created notable challenges for residents' maintenance of a unique and strong personal identity.

Nursing homes comprise a viable housing option for older adults in need of skilled nursing care. In their study of two seniors' (adult care) day centers, Salari and Rich (2001) found that the centers varied in the opportunity for, and support of, autonomy and independence, i.e., the ability to exercise choice and control. Seniors had positive self-images and a sense of agency in the center environment that offered age appropriate activities (vs child-like activities) and where staff supported client choice whether to participate in these activities. Importantly, these centers supported the clients' ability to regulate their own privacy (openness and closedness to others). Salari, Brown, and Eaton's (2006) study of five seniors' centers documented how the style of staff management (authoritarian vs collaborative or client empowerment) and the physical layout of the center influenced conflicts between seniors. Specifically, "table society" culture where identity was based on table membership and exclusionary cliques (regulars vs newcomers) occurred in centers where there were limited settings for engagement and the dining room was *the* center of multiple activities. Exclusionary behavior is a

Bullying in Seniors' Communities

frequently identified form of peer bullying in seniors' communities (Bonifas, 2016; Goodridge et al., 2017; Rex-Lear, 2011; Sepe, 2015). In the centers with distinct settings for different activities and more collaborative participative management with staff, participants identified with the entire center (communal society culture). Their identity encompassed all center members as one group, a dynamic that is associated with less likelihood of bullying behavior.

These studies of institutional environments highlight how seniors' communities comprise vital sources of, and sites for, identity negotiation and threat. Infantilizing and objectifying practices and activities, co-location with others of different functional status, and restriction of resident autonomy and choice, can highlight an identity of "old" that can be threatening to a resident's sense of self (Ryvicker, 2009; Sandhu et al., 2013). These institutional practices are difficult for the residents to challenge, and thus, they need to seek alternative ways to assert a strong identity, which may be directed at their fellow residents in the form of bullying.

Managing Identity and Identity Threat

Self and identity comprise intrapersonal processes but also social constructions, constituted communicatively in interactions with others (Burke, 1991; Goffman, 1959; Westerhof et al., 2011). Identity Control Theory (Burke, 1991, 2007) and Identity Process Theory (Westerhof et al., 2011) highlight the processual and relational nature of identity. In essence, we continuously define and redefine our identity through a feedback loop, in which how we see ourselves (identity standards) is compared to how others perceive us (reflected appraisals). Reflected appraisals may be a result of specific communication from another of the older adult's undesirable identity (e.g., infantilization, objectification by staff, or criticism from peers; Ryvicker, 2009; Salari & Rich, 2001). The reflected appraisals may also be inferred from the presence of a similarly aged peer who embodies the undesired identity: Nelson's (2005) notion of the "feared future self" (p. 207). When this comparison reveals a discrepancy, the person experiences stress and is motivated to remediate it. A stigmatized identity (Goffman, 1963) is threatening to one's sense of self as it represents a negative discrepancy between ideal self (e.g., autonomous and experienced adult) and reflected self (e.g., dependent, frail old, in need of help; Burke, 1991; Ryvicker, 2009; Sneed & Whitbourne, 2005). While theories vary in the number of types of responses to identity threat (Burke, 1991; Holmes, Whitman, Campbell, & Johnson, 2016; Westerhof et al., 2011;), they distill down to two main ways individuals address this discrepancy: accommodation and resistance (Burke, 1991; Lagacé et al., 2012; Ryvicker, 2009). Accommodation occurs by changing one's identity to fit the current situation. In the face of infantilization, for example, the older adult succumbs to, and manifests, the "I am old," frail, and dependent identity (e.g., Salari, 2006).

Resistance can occur in at least two ways. First, the older adult enacts their ideal identity of "being younger" through behavior reflective of it. For example, the older adult behaves as an autonomous adult in command of their mind by making their own decisions or enhancing their memory, i.e., identity assimilation (Barnhart & Peñaloza, 2012; Westerhof et al., 2011). Such enactment makes visible to others and to themselves that the older adult is an *exception* to the old age stereotype (Cohen & Sherman, 2014; Rapolienė, 2015). Alternatively, an older adult could deny the reflected appraisal by challenging the situation or the person that initiated the discrepancy such as a disabled peer (Rapolienė, 2015). This challenge can be enacted directly or indirectly.

An assertive and constructive form of challenge occurs when the older adult attempts to convince the other through verbal argument of the validity of the ideal identity (Barnhart & Peñaloza, 2012). As noted earlier, this form of challenge can be risky, depending on the extent to which the seniors' community is structured to support autonomy, choice, and control. When the environment and the staff reflect ageist beliefs, such behavior can be framed as problematic or "symptomatic" of aging and loss of cognitive control (i.e., acting "old"; Ryvicker, 2009; Salari, 2006), further justifying the undesired treatment.

Creating psychological and physical distance from a peer who represents the stigmatized identity (Nelson, 2005; Rapolienė, 2015; Sandhu et al., 2013; Weiss & Freund, 2012) is another way to resist the stigmatized identity. A direct and potentially destructive form of challenge involves derogation of the other by criticizing their competency or making fun of them (Burke, 1991; Greenberg & Arndt, 2011; Holmes et al., 2016), highlighting how the older adult is "not like" the "old and frail" peer (Barber, 2017; Bonifas, 2016: Sandhu et al., 2013). In their study of everyday social identity threat situations, Holmes et al. (2016) found that derogation was perceived as effective in eliminating identity threat, suggesting it could become a favored strategy. The indirect rebuke manifests through avoidance of the other, e.g., excluding from the dining table or ignoring the person in the hallway. As noted earlier, bullied individuals and observers in a variety of contexts frequently identify and experience such derogation and exclusion/ignoring as aggression and bullying (Monks & Coyne, 2011).

In terms of seniors' communities, frequently identified behaviors include exclusion from the group, deliberately hurtful comments, calling people names, making fun of others, and spreading rumors (Goodridge et al., 2017; Rex-Lear, 2011; Sepe, 2015). These behaviors and the pattern of interaction are directed at disruption of, or harm to, an individual's connection to other residents, thus undermining the other's status and concomitantly enhancing one's own (Bonifas, 2016; Salari et al., 2006; Sandhu et al., 2013). Berdahl (2007) has tied such aggression to social status (identity) threat. Lachs et al. (2016) found that targets of aggression were more likely to be cognitively impaired relative to the actor, consistent with the notion of the peer as embodied identity threat and aggression as a way to resist such characterization (see Rapolienė, 2015).

These frequently identified behaviors work strategically as well because they tend to be indirect and thus hard to detect (Bonifas, 2016; Walker & Richardson, 1998). Walker and Richardson (1998) suggested that older adults, in general, are particularly "well-suited" to using indirect aggression because they have the social and verbal skills and the ability to strategically plan to inflict harm without being identified. The cognitive and emotional capability required for the sophistication of indirect aggression is consistent with findings that residents who bully tend to be "cognitively intact" relative to targets (Lachs et al., 2016). These covert behaviors also permit the resident to express aggression but within social parameters, thus reducing the likelihood of detection by staff or retaliation by the target (Cardinal, 2015), permitting these behaviors to continue unchecked. Bonifas (2016) asserted that bullying estimates may be low because staff and residents do not recognize or report much of this social/relational aggression.

In sum, seniors' communities provide ample opportunity for identity threat. Membership in these communities signals a change in identity and status, often framed as loss and "less than," which the older adult as a resident needs to manage. The composition, structure, and practices of the community shape the messages and cues about the appropriate or effective identity for residents (Ryvicker, 2009; Salari, 2006). These communities vary in the extent to which they reflect or challenge ageist discourse. To the extent that the resident's sense of self is discrepant with the institutional identity, the resident will experience identity threat, resultant distress, and be motivated to remediate the threat to preserve the self. Residents' responses range from accommodation to resistance (constructive and destructive). Bullying directed toward similarly aged peers who represent the undesired identity by derogation or exclusion may be an attempt to rectify and (re)establish a more agentic and autonomous self (Bonifas, 2016). Thus, efforts to address bullying need to address problematic institutional structures and practices and provide the means by which more constructive strategies are available for negotiating a strong identity.

Addressing Bullying as an Identity Threat Response

Taking the perspective of bullying and aggression as an identity threat response highlights the need to manage opportunities for, and responses to, threat as well as increase opportunities for more complex identities beyond the stigmatized one of "being old" (Martens et al., 2005). The root of identity threat for older adults in seniors' communities rests in the messages and cues with which these communities are communicatively constituted; these messages reflect the broader discourse of ageism. To root out the threat requires a challenge to, and change of, the societal discourse of ageism and the stereotypes about being old (Gullette, 2017; Martens et al., 2005; Nelson, 2004). While that task extends beyond the scope of this chapter, a more immediate focus will be on what can be done within the boundaries of the seniors' communities, specifically staff communicative practices and strategies for enhancement of identity.

Staff Communicative Practices

Infantilizing and objectifying speech and conduct by staff communicatively enact the old age stereotypes of dependence and incompetence, and challenges the older adult's self-integrity as good, productive, autonomous, and efficacious (Cohen & Sherman, 2014; Ryvicker, 2009). The insidious nature of these communicative practices needs to be surfaced and challenged (Nussbaum et al., 2005). This process necessitates education and training of staff focused on understanding (1) the process of "healthy" aging, including the "real facts" per the Pew Research Center survey (Taylor et al., 2009); (2) the (pernicious) nature and dynamics of ageism and ageist communication (Gullette, 2017; Nelson, 2017); (3) the staff member's own beliefs regarding aging and "being old" and how that influences their engagement with the residents; (4) the social nature and dynamics of identity (Burke, 1991; Cohen & Sherman, 2014; Westerhof et al., 2011); and (5) communicative practices that recognize and address the unique identity and needs of each resident such as affirming communication style (e.g., Hummert et al., 1998; Infante & Gorden, 1989; Williams, Kemper & Hummert, 2004) and activities that (re)affirm adult status such as opportunities to express and draw upon the resident's life experience, privacy regulation, and practices of collaborative and participatory decision making (Cardinal, 2016; Ryvicker, 2009; Salari, 2006; Salari & Rich, 2001).

Identity Enhancement

This set of strategies focuses on residents (and staff) taking a more expansive view of the self and their resources/strengths beyond the (threatening) focus on "being old" (Barber, 2017; Cohen & Sherman, 2014; Martens et al., 2005). Grounded in Self-Affirmation Theory (Sherman & Cohen, 2006), values (self) affirmation interventions involve having the older person articulate their core personal values. For example, residents could be asked to choose two or three values most important to them from a list (e.g., independence, being helpful, learning and gaining knowledge, honesty), and write or talk about situations in which these values were important and why. Staff and co-residents can help facilitate these affirmation strategies by asking the resident about their life history and experiences. Drawing on those experiences to address situations within the community such as advice giving or skill sharing (Salari, 2006; Ryvicker, 2009) can make these core values visible to self and others.

Activating other domains of accomplishment through engagement in pro-social activities within the community (e.g., maintaining the community garden or helping a fellow resident who is physically impaired get from one place to another; Sandhu et al., 2013) can function as an embodiment of the core values exercise. Barbera (2016) argued that participation in these activities enhances residents' sense of self and by extension the need to bully to feel better or stronger. Social wellness initiatives in seniors' communities (Cardinal, 2016) can contribute to self-affirmation and integrity as they engage residents and staff together in promoting a climate of supporting the whole individual. Finally, a six-week "social experiment" in the UK brought together 4-year-olds with older adults in a care home (The Conversation, 2017, August 7), dramatically improving residents' physical ability and mood. Intergenerational initiatives address separation and isolation of older adults and emphasize experiences that activate the broader sense of self as capable, needed, and adults with life experiences (Barber, 2017; Barnhart & Peñaloza, 2012; Weeks, 1996).

These guided self reflections, staff support, and engagement in, and processing of, a variety of activities provide opportunities for enactment of the multifaceted and rich nature of the older adult's self, many aspects of which the community values and needs (Barber, 2017; Bonifas, 2016; Cohen & Sherman, 2014). This broadened view of self (identity expansion and assimilation—Westerhof et al., 2011) can diminish the perceived threat of "being old" (Barber, 2017) and thus reduce defensive and destructive distancing responses such as bullying. Reduced defensive responding has implications for more constructive engagement with peers (Cohen & Sherman, 2014). Further, this enactment of a variety of identities challenges staff and others' ageist assumptions, which in turn may influence a richer and more positive societal narrative of "being old."

Conclusion

In this chapter, I utilized an identity perspective to frame peer-to-peer bullying as a response to the identity threat posed by ageist beliefs and stereotypes reflected in, and enacted through, the structures, composition, and communicative practices of seniors' communities. Faced with the image of "old" as a state of decline and a second childhood (Salari, 2006), the older adult must manage a negative discrepancy from their and society's desired image of competent, autonomous, and efficacious self in an environment marked by isolation and compliance. Active resistance can be constructive or destructive. Bullying a peer who represents the "feared future self" (Nelson, 2005) through derogation or exclusion may provide temporary relief from the distress of being "less than" (Burke, 1991). Taking a communicative perspective on senior bullying privileges the dynamic and co-creative nature of identity, identity threat, and response to threat in the form of bullying and focuses attention on altering communicative practices and structures. Actions aimed at addressing staff communicative practices and broadening resident identity beyond "being old" would help create a climate and community in which bullying is no longer required to express a strong competent identity. The broader resolution requires challenging our societal notions of aging, generally and ageist discourse specifically, so that "being old" is a valued and rich identity such as being "pioneers of longevity" (Carney & Gray, 2015, p. 125).

As researchers and practicing professionals, we are embedded in and shaped by this ageist society and discourse. We need to be aware of how our perceptions and even stereotypes are shaped by ageist discourse and influence how we think about and approach this topic of aging, "being old," and, by extension, bullying among seniors (Nussbaum et al., 2005). For example, extrapolation of our understanding of, and response to, bullying among children, teens, and emerging adults to adults in workplaces, communities, and now seniors' communities is common (Bonifas, 2016; Monks & Coyne, 2011; Salari, 2006; Utech & Garrett, 1992). What implicit and unchallenged assumptions undergird this comparison of childhood and elderhood (Salari, 2006)? Do we critically consider how adults are different than children and teens? Are we considering the ways in which life experience, emotional regulation, and greater cognitive control are developed with age and how that influences (or not) how we approach and conceptualize our questions and recommendations? We need to "take inventory of any personal biases toward the ageing process and ensure (*our*) research (*and recommendations*) does not serve to reify these stereotypes" (*italics* added; Nussbaum et al., 2005, p. 299).

★★Cyberbullying★★

20

DEFINING CYBERBULLYING

Analyzing Audience Reaction to Anti-Bullying Public Service Announcements

Kelly P. Dillon and Nancy Rhodes

The CDC has labeled cyberbullying as an important public health issue, affecting millions of Americans daily (David-Ferdon & Hertz, 2009). Researchers have found that the experience of being cyberbullied results in long-lasting physical and mental health effects for adolescents (Copeland, Wolke, Angold, & Costello, 2013) and young adults (Kowalski, Giumetti, Schroeder, & Reese, 2012; Goodboy, Martin, & Goldman, 2016). People who are online of any age appear to be at risk of encountering cyberbullying (Cho & Yoo, 2017). In a rapidly changing media environment, educating key stakeholders is an important step. Mass media campaigns aim to properly define bullying and cyberbullying in order to educate, generate awareness, and encourage intervention and prevention among the general public (e.g., Savage, Deiss, Roberto, Aboujaoude, & Deiss, 2017). Although expert definitions exist of what behaviors constitute cyberbullying, a connection to societal definitions has not been made. Indeed, research suggests that news reports of cyberbullying may be counterproductive in this regard (Young, Subramanian, Miles, Hinnant, & Andsager, 2017). If experts and the general public differ in how they define cyberbullying, these behaviors may not be reported or identified, resulting in continued harassment of targets[1] and the normalizing of harassment.

We conducted in-depth focus groups with 152 digital native informants who watched five existing public service announcements (PSAs) aiming to define cyberbullying for viewers. We collected layperson definitions of cyberbullying and compared them to academic definitions. Viewers identified key components presented in the PSAs leading to a better understanding of and improved vigilance in preventing and responding to cyberbullying in their real lives. This chapter explores our findings and identifies the themes that might be most effective in helping to establish a more comprehensive definition of cyberbullying in the general public.

Cyberbullying and Public Service Announcements

Bullying is a term that has been tossed around and, consequently, has resulted in multiple interpretations (see Turner & West, this volume). For our purposes, we adopt the definition of *bullying* as "aggressive behavior with certain special characteristics such as an asymmetric power relationship and some repetitiveness" (Olweus, 2013b, p. 756). When these behaviors appear online, they are cyberbullying (Tokunaga, 2010). The mediated environment is unique in that a single comment, meme, picture, or post can meet the criteria for cyberbullying because it can be seen repeatedly by different audiences and individuals. Not all online harassment meets the criteria for cyberbullying, but all types cyberbullying fit the definition of online harassment. However, because of the changing nature of technology, even communication and other social science experts are rarely in complete agreement in definitions. Thoroughly explicating behaviors as cyberbullying is important for practical, legal, and socially normative reasons. Without clear definitions, individuals would be ill-informed as to what behaviors to refrain from and in what incidents they should intervene.

Bullying and cyberbullying constitute socially constructed behaviors centered in communication between individuals; thus, a communication perspective is especially appropriate for examining how public health experts aim to educate the public on a destructive phenomenon. Symbolic Interactionism (Blumer, 1969) is a good first step to understanding choices of, and reactions to, content in PSAs. This theory assumes that "human beings act towards things on the basis of the meanings that the things have for them" (p. 2), and we construct this meaning through social interactions. Individuals construct meaning through the communication process of the individuals demonstrating specific behaviors in PSAs. The social nature of the focus group itself can assist in the construction of this meaning for the individual as well as the group. While this might be obvious for face-to-face bullying, cyberbullying interactions may not be as obvious, especially for bystanders. We may be able to construct more appropriate meanings for the viewer by framing textual cyberbullying as interpersonal interactions between a bully and his or her target, with bystanders present. The interpretive process used to construct and apply these meanings is the third assumption of Symbolic Interactionism. The PSA viewer "selects, checks, suspends, regroups, and transforms the meanings in light of the situation" (Blumer, 1969, p. 5) provided for him or her, and if successful, will choose to either engage in a positive health behavior or refrain from a negative health behavior.

In this work, we take a mental models approach (e.g., Morgan, Fischhoff, Bostrom, & Atman, 2002), which refers to a process of understanding how lay individuals understand an issue, as opposed to that of experts in the area. Mental models help us to discern the lay theories of the issue at hand so communication can be targeted to the ways that they understand it. In the present case, we conducted structured interviews with young adults in the context of watching anti-cyberbullying PSAs and elicited their lay definitions of cyberbullying. These mental models construct the symbolic meanings for the viewer through the social interactions portrayed.

Public health campaigns using PSAs have been implemented to prevent negative and promote positive behaviors (Bryn, 2011). Campaigns from Federal agencies like Department of Health and Human Services and the CDC have been designed to combat bullying and cyberbullying. Defining the behavior meant to be curbed or encouraged is an important feature of these campaigns (Glanz, Rimer, & Viswanath, 2008). However, PSAs may not be persuasive enough to make the concepts remain with the viewers (Paek, Hove, Ju Jeong, & Kim, 2011).

Many PSAs evoke emotions in order to be persuasive, which, in turn, can muddy the concepts and behaviors depicted (Dillard & Peck, 2000). Fear appeals, or persuading action based on fear of outcomes or behaviors, have been found to have mixed success in health campaigns, especially in remembering key instructions (Ruiter, Kessels, Peters, & Kok, 2014). Shame and guilt appeals, which invoke these moral emotions in the viewer for not following the suggested lifestyle or behavior, are also not uniformly successful (Boudewyns, Turner, & Paquin, 2013). No matter the type of appeal used, if the images, texts, or symbolism do not properly define behaviors to avoid, messages can be lost in translation.

The main purpose of this chapter is to determine if the lay definitions viewers construct and understand from anti-cyberbullying PSAs align with scholarly definitions. If viewers of these PSAs leave with a clear understanding of what does or does not constitute cyberbullying, they should be able to remain vigilant in noticing these behaviors in the real world. If the PSAs are unsuccessful in properly defining, clarifying, and illustrating cyberbullying to viewers, especially to stakeholders like college students, the message to "delete cyberbullying" will be missed.

Procedures

We recruited participants from undergraduate communication courses at a large, public university and awarded research credit for their time in the study. Prior to arriving to the focus group, we sent participants a link to complete an online pretest survey and their informed consent. Upon arrival to the focus group, participants were provided name tags for their first names (for ease of conversation) and free response forms to allow for two minutes of independent thought collection after each stimulus. A trained research assistant facilitated the focus group with IRB approved questions and scripts, while a second research assistant typed notes. We audio recorded and later transcribed all focus group sessions. At the conclusion of the focus group, we permitted participants another two minutes of free response "thought collection" to provide general feedback. A week following their focus group, we sent participants a second link to complete a posttest survey. We combined participants' pretest, free response writings, transcribed audio responses, and posttest results for analysis.

We collated audio recordings and free response forms for each focus group so all participant responses for each PSA across sessions were included in one document. We used a grounded theory approach (Glaser & Strauss, 1967) to develop a set of codes and concepts emerging from the data. The first author read these as a first-dive immersion into the data to identify any emerging themes "without losing the connections between concepts and their context" (Bradley, Curry, & Devers, 2007, p. 1761).

Stimuli

We chose five PSAs from various sources, with all between 30–60 seconds, in full color, English, and publicly available. The FBI's video "No Big Deal" (FBI, 2013) features a young girl at the end of class posting mean pictures about another girl on her laptop. A male friend tries to dissuade her, telling the cyberbully "this has to stop," reminding her the target's family would see the photos, while ghostly images of the target's family appears. Two Ad Council PSAs titled "Talent Show" (2008a) and "Kitchen" (2008b) depict a bully reading posts insulting a target face-to-face, rather than online, and in front of other shocked onlookers who do nothing. Both end with text reading, "If you won't say it in person, why would you do it online? Delete cyberbullying." An MTV (A Thin Line, 2011) PSA titled "Tattoo" depicts a young boy at a tattoo shop, with all sorts of insults already inked on his body. He receives another insult via text message and instructs the tattoo artist to use his back. A voiceover tells the audience "The hurt of digital harassment can last forever. There's a thin line between words and wounds." The only user generated PSA incorporated in this study was called "Erase It," (Submit the Documentary, 2013), which depicts a Facebook profile on a dry-erase board, with individuals approaching to write mean, terrible things while a voiceover explains why cyberbullying is wrong. The viewer hears "be more than a bystander" while a person is seen erasing all the posts.

Each of these PSAs took the act of cyberbullying off the computer or phone screen and illustrated the behavior in socially interactive terms. Each included the bully, their target, and a perceived public audience witnessing these events. They aimed to define cyberbullying as a public health concern. We sought to determine if they achieved this goal.

Surveys

We asked participants to report personal experience as a target of, or a bystander to, bullying or cyberbullying in pretest surveys. Other personality assessments and specifics about their bullying and cyberbullying experiences were also collected for a separate study. A week following their focus group, we asked participants how often they thought about the focus group, what they had thought about, what, if any, interpersonal conversations they had about the focus group, if they had noticed cyberbullying in the week since, and any actions they took or intended to take upon witnessing these incidents.

Participants

A total of 152 students completed the pretest surveys and participated in the focus groups. The majority of the sample identified as female (71%, $n = 107$), 29% ($n = 45$) as male, 77% as White ($n = 117$), 7% as Asian American ($n = 11$), 5% as African American ($n = 8$), and 11% ($n = 16$) as other, multiple races, or preferred not to answer. A total of 80 students (53%) completed the post-test surveys after their focus group participation, and 72 (47%) did not complete the surveys after multiple requests.

Results

Pretest survey data gave us an idea of the personal experience that participants had with bullying and cyberbullying prior to participating, and these data were pertinent to another study. We analyzed focus group free response forms and transcripts to determine the mental models and themes participants constructed. Posttest data helped us understand if the PSAs were persuasive in getting participants to think about or notice cyberbullying more.

Defining Cyberbullying

One main purpose of this study was to determine how participants defined cyberbullying after viewing anti-bullying PSAs. Without prompting of the academic or legal definitions of the behavior, we asked participants if they could define cyberbullying based on what they had seen. They made comparisons to offline or face-to-face bullying: "I would say it's bullying but behind a computer screen . . . It's verbal bullying on paper basically"; "Just like bullying, but using technology." One defined cyberbullying as "bullying through words, no physical harm," while another considered "teasing hurts just as much as getting beat up." Scholars often study bullying as a physical phenomenon (Perlus, Brooks-Russell, Wang, & Iannotti, 2014), and parents unfamiliar with the mediated world may draw parallels (DeHue, Bolman, & Völlink, 2008). An astute participant verbalized this very disconnect by stating, "I remember growing up when I was little it was, 'Sticks and stones may break my bones and words will never hurt me.' But I feel like our parents—that was their thing. Ours is actually the opposite."

Viewers mentioned explicit behaviors that constitute cyberbullying and the platforms typically used by bullies. For example, one participant defined it as "name calling, or writing over a photo, or putting up embarrassing photos, even something as simple as putting up an embarrassing photo that they wouldn't want." Cyberbullying, then was envisioned as "harassment that comes through social media, text messages, electronic sources, through technology." Although each PSA may have either shown or assumed a specific platform, participants were able to make connections beyond what was actually shown. One participant noted after watching "Erase It," which used a Facebook style profile, "It's not just on Facebook. It's Twitter, YouTube and everything. It's cyberbullying is [sic] everywhere." A danger in using only one platform or behavior, however, in a PSA may be viewers walking away with the idea that *only* these behaviors constitute cyberbullying, and thus, other behaviors would go unnoticed and not dealt with. A participant warned of this danger, "It shows one type outright. There are so many different kinds of cyberbullying. I don't think cyberbullying is just putting a picture. Obviously people know that, but just from this PSA that's what you get from it."

Responses explicitly incorporated the three characteristics of cyberbullying as defined by most academics and scholars: intentional harm, repetitive actions, and creating or maintaining a power imbalance. The clear intent of the sender, rather than accidentally being rude or mean, appeared in their discussions. Respondents defined cyberbullying as "any type of action intended to harm someone over the internet" or actions "meant to intentionally hurt and target a person." After watching the PSAs, participants constructed an understanding of cyberbullying as "purposely doing something knowing that is going to have a negative outcome on someone else."

The intentional degradation of another is a hallmark of cyberbullying, according to more than a few participants: "Whether it's via a keyboard or just straight to someone's face it's still gonna have the same effect on somebody, it's still gonna hurt someone's feelings and incite some anger." Cyberbullying, then, is "when you post something on technology that could or would hurt, degrade, or make someone feel uncomfortable, via words/pics"; or posting something "in a way that makes them feel uncomfortable or out of place for the world." The PSAs used in this study were explicit in the intent of the cyberbully in their actions.

The repetitive nature of cyberbullying is sometimes a sticking point to researchers and laypersons (Slonje & Smith, 2008). Some individuals may consider one cyberbullying post as one incident, while others acknowledge the viral potential of this same post. Some participants in our focus groups recognized this potential in the behaviors illustrated in the PSAs, saying "because once you look . . . it's one remark after another." Another participant observed, "When people think of bullying they think a reoccurring issue but it seems in this this sense, people are doing it but at different times." It should be noted that very few participants recognized this explicitly as a repetitive act.

Like other forms of harassment, cyberbullying has been defined as creating or maintaining some form of power imbalance (Bauman, Underwood, & Card, 2013). The complications of interpreting actions in the digital environment in the social world have rightfully questioned the necessity of power imbalance to define behaviors as cyberbullying (Englander, Donnerstein, Kowalski, Lin, & Parti, 2017). The target as "helpless" or the cyberbully "trying to put yourself ahead of that person [the target]" was a recurring theme. Participants often identified the cyberbully as "trying to reveal a flaw about somebody else" in order to make them "feel better or to tear that person down." Rather than the cyberbully having obvious power over his or her target, participants recognized the behavior as a means to establishing this power. One student defined cyberbullying as "people are degrading you or using derogatory terms against you to either make them feel empowered in order to make you feel less empowered, or both."

Focus Group Themes

Besides the literal definition of cyberbullying, we used focus groups as a means to understand how viewers constructed meaning from these PSAs. Through the social interactions with others in the focus group, five major themes emerged, suggesting viewers' mental models of cyberbullying after viewing the messages contained important elements of the expert definition of cyberbullying. These themes encompassed: (1) cumulative harm and offense, (2) effects of deindividuation, (3) textual persistence, (4) offline ramifications, and (5) lack of control. We are dedicated to honoring how a participant "selects, checks, suspends, regroups, and transforms the meanings in light of the situation" (Blumer, 1969, p. 5) and include their words as much as possible to convey their meanings.

Cumulative harm

Participants recognized the accumulative nature of cyberbullying, regardless of the number of offenders depicted. They perceived nearly all PSAs as showing how "words have a permanent effect good or bad," and each "shows the audience how hurtful it is when said out loud." Whether it was "people coming together to make the comments," or if "one person starts and their friends get peer pressured in and they gang up on one person," participants recognized the snowballing effect. The harm that cyberbullying can do to an individual's sense of worth was worrisome, especially if "people wear the words they are told, they begin to believe or wonder if it's true or not because if you are constantly being told something about yourself, then you really start to question if this is true."

The constant barrage of negative comments, and how each may invite others to pile on, was especially apparent in the PSA "Erase It." A participant who watched this PSA stated that "All the comments that were put and how many and like one word phrases just each person adding one like builds up." Another recognized that "just seeing it all together as one and realizing just like seeing it as a negative." Participants took notice of how bystanders must interrupt the event, with one stating that "if you don't step in it's going to continue."

Effects of Deindividuation

In each of the PSAs, participants recognized how mediated environment affords users to feel disinhibited, often leading to deindividuated behavior (Suler, 2004). The depiction of targets' reactions to cyberbullying made an impression: "when you're just typing something on a computer you don't know how the other person feels." Each PSA was successful in helping its audience to recognize that "even though you are behind a computer screen, the other person has feelings. You are not talking or texting to a computer." The deindividuated nature of computer-mediated communication "made sense that people kind of hide behind social media and it's easier to say things when you're not face to face with someone." How we perceive and process online communication exemplifies these effects where "people say things are a lot different over text than they are in person; you don't know if someone's being sarcastic or joking or if they're really being serious."

Seeing a target's reaction in real time to the cyberbullying was important to the participants with whom we spoke. One participant stated that "I liked how they showed the reaction of the children's faces and the specific close up of [target] herself, and you could just see the pain on her face," while another said, "they don't have to deal with it face to face or look anybody in the eye and tell them those kinds of things." Without seeing the target's reaction in real time, the online environment emboldens the cyberbully "to say whatever they want so I think that they're less afraid to say something online" and realize "there is a person on the other side getting the message." Some participants recognized the difficulty for cyberbystanders to interpret what was going on: "I don't think people take it quite as hard . . . because they can't really picture the words being said to the victim."

Textual Persistence

Importantly, these campaigns strive to educate the public on how permanent online communication can be (Roberto et al., 2014). The PSAs were effective as they "depict the permanence" for the target as well as the cyberbully who "can walk away from a screen—it won't go away from the internet but you can still walk away. You can't do that in real life." Viewers recognized the creative licensing taken in the PSAs, with one saying, "I mean it's obviously not literally realistic but I think the message is pretty realistic—that words affect people for a long time." One participant, upon viewing "Tattoos," acknowledged how "the imagery of all these hateful words all over this person permanently attached to them would stick with viewers." Another noted, "cyberbullying sticks with you forever; words are like scars and the tattoos made it like physical," and another marveled at how "words are permanent. Profound way to represent the idea of how words are everlasting like a tattoo."

Offline Consequences

Showing the offline consequences of online harassment and bullying is one main focus of these health campaigns and appeared successful: "It's important to connect the offline with the online especially with social media. People aren't just friends with school friends, there's family, friends of family . . . think about how hurt they would be in the long run." Those who are in the target's networks are affected by cyberbullying too. One insightful participant stated,

> [A] lot of people don't really think "oh if I post this picture" . . . how it's going to affect her, her family seeing it, her grandparents . . . You don't really think about who your audience really is.

The reach of a post came across in the PSAs: "It shows how many people you can affect, even though you only intend to affect one person, you affect a lot of people."

The possible long-term psychological effects of cyberbullying were depicted as physical violence in more than one PSA and clearly "demonstrated the power of words." For more than one participant, "it definitely hit home that words are just as hurtful as physical violence and bullying forms as in actions, body language," and how "people don't think of words as violence but they really are." The advertisements that showed how "one action could impact people's perspectives in different parts of their lives" stuck with many of our participants, who felt "worse for the victim because they discuss the consequences for her."

Lack of Control

Lack of control, on the target's part, was a common theme in all the videos and in many responses: "When I see all those things written up there, I realize I can't control what somebody else writes." Participants recognized targets are "not in control of what goes on around, what other people think, what they say, what they do." Some successfully saw themselves in the situations depicted in the PSAs: "I don't feel much power over what other people might choose to write on my wall or somebody else's wall." Participants understood the difference between a face-to-face conversation and the effects of the same words going online, "At least if you're one-on-one, you might be able to deal with it in a different way or talk about it. With cyberbullying, it's almost uncontrollable." The way things can spiral out of control online, with "the simplicity of 'it starts with one post'" symbolized the targets' "helplessness."

Focus group participants were clear in their construction of their mental models of the symbolism depicted in the chosen PSAs. They reported that each PSA defined cyberbullying typically: the intentional degradation of another person, online, while creating or maintaining some type of power imbalance. The PSA depicted less clearly that cyberbullying is truly repetitive. Very few participants recognized how posts can be seen repeatedly, but did communicate the cumulative nature of the harm it can effect. Given Symbolic Interactionism's first assumption that we "act towards things on the basis of the meanings that the things have for them" (Blumer, 1969, p. 2), participants should definitely act towards any cyberbullying that they notice in the near future after participating in our focus group.

Post-Focus Group Survey Results

A week after their participation, we sent each individual a posttest survey link, and we analyzed data from 80 students (53%). Nearly 78% ($n = 62$) of posttest respondents reported thinking about their participation in the week between the focus group and the posttest survey, leading to mindful musings of what they had seen and experienced. At least 45% ($n = 36$) reported having either face-to-face or online conversations about the focus group. One respondent wrote, "My roommate described something as being 'gay' and I decided to call her out on it, tell her that wasn't okay." Another participant perfectly summed the co-created meaning during the focus groups stating, "I thought about how the other participant perceived the forms of online bullying differently than I did . . . because of the people we surround ourselves with we each took the message differently."

Eleven participants (14%) reported noticing cyberbullying more after the focus group, with 50% of those attributing the focus group specifically as causing this hyperawareness. The call to be aware for these behaviors, inherent in each PSA, appears to have stuck with some participants. One wrote, "I have tried paying more attention while I'm scrolling through social media to see if I notice any cyber bullying. I have thought about what I would do if I did notice any cyber bullying." This comment suggests the PSA and focus group may have not only increased awareness and properly defined the problem but left the participant with the responsibility of responding to any incidents. Another wrote, "I thought about how much bullying is present on my own social media platforms," yet this response made no mention of intention to intervene. Only one of these 11 participants reported directly intervening in the cyberbullying incident.

Participants were reflective of their own behaviors in particular. One wrote, "Every time I said something I thought could be considered mean, I took a step back and avoided saying something to that caliber." Another commented that "I just thought about what the things I was saying and how they could effect [sic] people." One participant reported even taking note of their offline interactions after the focus group: "I have noticed thinking to myself before I say things to people in class that I usually don't talk to because something I say can be offensive."

A key goal of these PSAs was to make viewers more aware of the behaviors that could be considered cyberbullying, and the fact these behaviors are prevalent in the online spaces in which they spend time. A theme of higher self-awareness emerged from participants' posttest responses. For example, one participant wrote, "I thought that I should start looking a little harder for bullying in my everyday life. I would see friends sending risky potentially mean tweets and I would think back to the focus group," and another "I looked at my social media and wondered if some things could be considered cyberbullying." Some have taken it upon themselves to identify as a cyberbystander: "I have thought about what I would do if I did notice any cyber bullying [sic]," while another noted, "I want to be able to notify someone if I think there is cyberbullying going on." Though only one participant reported actually intervening, others reported noticing "a lot of how the things other people say are hurtful without them knowing how they are hurtful."

Discussion

If an individual has any online presence, or uses any twenty-first century communication technology such as text messaging, email, the internet, or social media, they have the opportunity to perpetrate, experience, or witness various versions of cyberbullying. PSAs comprise an important component of any public health campaign educating at-risk stakeholders of behaviors, environments, and reactions to avoid. Whether viewers recognize, and official PSAs include, key elements of cyberbullying are crucial to preventing and reacting to these behaviors.

Focus group participants were clear that the PSAs employed properly defined and illustrated cyberbullying. Participants' mental models of cyberbullying included that it is intentional and repetitive, and includes some form of power imbalance. Five key themes also emerged from these 152 undergraduate students. They recognized how the harmful nature of cyberbullying can accumulate for the target, how it festers in a deindividuated environment, the affordance of textual persistence online, the very real offline ramifications for all parties involved, and lack of control, especially on behalf of the target, over what happens online.

Using a Symbolic Interactionism frame and a mental models approach, we examined how the themes in the PSAs contributed to lay participants' understanding of cyberbullying. Because there was a close match between the definitions of cyberbullying that emerged in the focus groups and academic and legal definitions of cyberbullying, we feel these PSAs were effective in communicating the essential features of cyberbullying to their audience. Future campaigns to raise awareness of cyberbullying should model themselves after these. Testing messages using a combination of free response and focus group discussions is a good way to ensure the message is being conveyed in the manner intended by the designers and sponsors of the PSAs.

What may be most inspiring from our findings is the very act of viewing and then *discussing* the PSAs with other stakeholders appears to have some effects on participants' behaviors after the session. One participant remarked in their posttest survey, "I think it was an impactful experience for me to discuss the effects of bullying. I actually enjoyed discussing the topics because I think they are so very relevant today and should be brought to the discussion table." Another mentioned, "I liked that it was set up kind of like a discussion with others so people can hear the point of view of their peers." The social construction of what cyberbullying means to the individual, to society, and to others in the future was a valuable experience.

Most of those who completed the posttest surveys indicated they had given some thought to what they had talked about, and nearly half of respondents reported being more self-aware. Better awareness of their own actions, and others', on and offline, indicate the reach of the PSAs. While only one participant reported actually intervening in cyberbullying that they witnessed, we hope that the results of this research have helped others notice, interpret, and feel efficacious to respond to cyberbullying. Other public service announcements targeted towards additional audiences where bullying and cyberbullying may be prevalent—employers and employees in workplaces (Cowan, 2009), instructors and students in the academy (Vogl-Bauer, 2014), or younger audiences beginning to learn how to navigate their mediated social worlds—must continue the practice of properly defining behaviors for their viewers.

Note

1 A conscious effort is made to identify individuals directly affected by cyberbullying as "targets" rather than "victims" throughout this chapter. This is not to diminish the very real implications and reactions for individuals who are targeted by cyberbullies, but instead to describe the distinctive roles illustrated in the PSAs.

21

EXAMINING CYBERBULLYING BYSTANDER BEHAVIOR

Sarah E. Jones and Matthew W. Savage

Introduction

Cyberbullying occurs in a triadic social context among bully, victim, and bystander (Twemlow, Fonagy, & Sacco, 2004), and involves "the deliberate and repeated misuse of communication technology by an individual or group to threaten or harm others" (Roberto & Eden, 2010, p. 2). With increased communication via social networking sites (SNSs) comes increased exposure. Nearly 39% of SNS users have experienced cyberbullying, often resulting in psychosomatic and psychiatric issues associated with trauma (Sourander et al., 2010).

Communication literature, however, does not yet include focused investigation of cyberbullying bystanders. We argue that cyberbullying bystanders comprise those who witness the incident, either within or outside their personal social network(s), whose available responses range from inaction to intervention. Notably, we exempt "peers" from the definition because, while traditional bullying often occurs in primary and secondary school settings, cyberspace houses any individual with internet or cellular access, so bystanders vary in age amid a potentially broader audience. Although more bystanders might appear to translate into greater potential for victims to receive help, previous research has found that larger numbers of bystanders may decrease helpful and altruistic behaviors (Burton, Florell, & Wygant, 2013; Twemlow et al., 2004).

We contend that cyberbullying bystanders' awareness of their role and empathic attitude may ameliorate cyberbullying processes or reduce the consequences of victimization. In this way, cyberbullying interventions may be enhanced by systematic focus on how bystanders might stop or thwart cyberbullying interactions through specific behavioral responses. Therefore, this chapter explores the empirical associations among cyberbullying bystander behaviors, perpetration, and victimization, resulting in a typology of cyberbullying bystanders.

Literature Review

In contrast to traditional bullying, perpetration of cyberbullying can be all the more severe and threatening, due to anonymity and the ubiquitous nature of the internet (Patchin & Hinduja, 2006). Perpetration can involve impersonation, rumors, cyberstalking, embarrassment or humiliation, teasing, insults, and forms of "denigration" (Willard, 2007) through hacking and exhibition of unapproved photos, videos, or other multimedia (von Marées & Petermann, 2012). Cyberbullying affords novel tools to bullies with great potential for victimization (Belsey, 2005).

Bystanders of any age, however, are not often considered within cyberbullying studies (see Agatston, Kowalski, & Limber, 2007 or Mishna, Cook, Gadalla, Daciuk, & Solomon, 2012 for initial estimates of bystander frequencies). Nevertheless, bystander research in traditional bullying contexts, coupled with reflections on the digital, electronic nature of cyberspace, suggests that cyberbullying bystanders not only exist, but that bystanders are active parties inclusive of anyone who witnesses cyberbullying, either within or outside their personal social network(s), whose available responses range from inaction to intervention.

The Power of Cyberbullying Bystanders

Cyberbullies' power typically stems from technological skills and the exploitation of anonymity afforded by the asymmetrical nature of digital communication technologies (Patchin & Hinduja, 2006). Bystanders play an integral role in the establishment of power as a result of group norms. Traditional bullying literature, for example, has found that, when bystanders observe others continuing to reinforce the bully (Salmivalli & Voeten, 2004), a *normative* environment emerges, preventing attempts to thwart bullies' power (Dijkstra, Lindenberg, & Veenstra, 2008). Assimilation as adaptive behavior allows those who are not targeted meet socially accepted standards and avoid victimization (Garandeau & Cillessen, 2006).

The socialization of normative bystander behavior has two major implications. First, bystanders' physical proximity to the bully may be largely irrelevant (Juvonen & Ho, 2008). Bystanders have greater influence on each other; the bully simply assumes the role of the bystanding audience agent (Twemlow et al., 2004), rather than the sole focus and responsible party. Second, bystanders' adaption to the status quo fosters a power imbalance that benefits bullies and restricts pro-social interventions (O'Connell, Pepler, & Craig, 1999). Because power comprises a highly salient construct of cyberbullying, it follows that cyberbullying bystanders' place in the establishment, maintenance, and advancement of power deserves inquiry.

Clusters of bystanders create a social structure based on pro-bullying, pro-social, and non-involved roles (Salmivalli, Huttenen, & Lagerspetz, 1997), such that the consequences of cyberbullying are severe and affect all parties. Traditional bullying provides a starting point for exploring these consequences. Bullying reinforced by bystanding peers not only leads to more one-on-one encounters between bully and victim (Espelege, Holt, & Henkel, 2003) but also higher group cohesion (Garandeau & Cillessen, 2006). Inactive reinforcement is intensified in cyberbullying, as the exploitation of anonymity may make it easier to avoid the incident or make bystanders more reluctant to intervene. Though inaction may seem safe, nonintervention to repeated exposure impacts private and public behaviors and attitudes (Gini, Pozzoli, Borghi, & Franzoni, 2008), makes attempts at pro-social interventions obsolete (Salmivalli, 2010), and desensitizes bystanding peers (Cowie, 2000). However, when bystanders come to victims' defense, frequency decreases (Kärnä, Salmivalli, Poskiparta, & Voeten, 2008). Even one bystander who chooses to defend the victim can decrease deleterious effects, reducing the bully-victim power differential (Sainio, Veenstra, Huitsing, & Salmivalli, 2011).

Multiple Goals Theories

It is essential to expand cyberbullying research beyond the cyberbully-cybervictim dyad in order to reconceptualize cyberbullying as a distinctly interactive, social context—one that is typified by multiple levels of influence across micro and macro-social hierarchical structures (O'Connell et al., 1999; Twemlow et al., 2004). Multiple goals theories (Caughlin, 2010) may have a number of advantages for the study of cyberbullying bystanders. The framework suggests that interpersonal messages have a calculated effect on individuals' level of satisfaction within specific interactions, as well as relational well-being and message production. Goals do not simply shape messages; goals shape interpretation of messages. A multiple goals approach allows cyberbullying scholars to connect bystander behavior with social norms and victimization outcomes in distinct ways. First, cyberbullying bystanders can be strategic in managing their own and others' identity, and they can also initiate and maintain a specific relationship with other parties. Second, cyberbullying bystanders have the capability to exhibit differing behaviors because they likely have multiple, prioritized goals. Finally, cyberbullying bystanders may deal with internal goal conflicts by behaving in a way that adheres to norm(s) of the environment.

We argue that tracing the utility of bystander goals' shaping of messages and interpretations of messages will help us to learn how depth of cyberbullying aggression and victims' relational well-being are rooted in bystanders' behavior. To meet this objective, we posed the following research questions:

RQ1: What are the goal(s) of cyberbullying bystanders?

RQ2: How do cyberbullying bystanders' goals impact their behavior, such that perpetration and victimization are encouraged or restrained?

RQ3: In what ways do goals and behaviors combine to elicit a typology of cyberbullying bystanders?

Methods

The present study utilized focus group interviews (FGIs) among undergraduate students enrolled in intro-level communication courses at a large southeastern university. We conducted five focus groups with 5–10 participants each for 40 total participants (13 females; 27 males) who ranged from 18–26 years of age and were predominantly White/Caucasian (77.5%, $n = 31$). We could not ensure confidentiality, due to the group discussion format, so participants chose pseudonyms during the discussions. All reported access to a cell phone and computer with an internet connection, and each had witnessed cyberbullying via SNSs at least once.

We audio recorded the FGIs, and we reviewed transcripts through data immersion and coded for specific theoretical constructs: goals, behavioral responses, and impact on perpetration or victimization. We completed *first level*, *second level*, and *hierarchical coding* for each FGI question (Tracy, 2013). Together, we regularly visited the data, evaluated its conceptual clarity, and noted connections among codes and emerging themes through *memoing* and the *constant comparative method* (Creswell, 2013) to elicit a typology of cyberbullying bystanders. Finally, we organized data in a *loose analysis outline* to ensure that themes were salient in the actual data and connected well to the results, thereby guiding the actual writing process.

Results

Participants' conceptualization of their bystanding role, including bystander goals and resulting behavior(s), supports the proposed definition and ultimately results in a unique typology of cyberbullying bystanders. Participants described encountering aggressive behavior on a continuum, from teasing to the creation of fake profiles used to harass others through stolen or graphic images. Participants felt that online behavior "crossed the line" when it included intentional, repetitive threats targeting a specific individual, their relationships, or personal health and appearance. Even if they did not know all parties, participants recognized their part in the triadic interaction and argued that bystanders are often dismissive because they think the aggression is harmless. Yet, participants had unfavorable attitudes about cyberbullying writ large, referring to it as "immature," "annoying," and "demoralizing." Participants perceived cyberbullies' actions as purely for attention or "entertainment." Still, most felt the behavior was "hard to curtail effectively," a struggle that was reflected in participants' discussion of bystander goals and how those goals influenced their behavior.

Goals of Cyberbullying Bystanders

Analysis revealed five distinct bystander goals: honor proximity, respond according to severity, embrace the cultural environment, gauge from other's responses, and avoid personal consequences. All participants utilized multiple goals simultaneously when assessing their role as a cyberbullying bystander. In the following subsections, each goal is defined. Later, we contextualize these goals within corresponding behaviors using participants' own voices.

Honor Proximity

Bystander responses most often depended on degrees of separation or full knowledge of both "sides" of the story; they hinged on the depth of "connection" between parties in terms of *relational* or *informational proximity*, which participants spoke of in terms of loyalty, responsibility, and an obligation to protect. Several participants felt that success in reporting the incident to an authority figure depended on that proximity; if reported to someone who knows the cybervictim, they are more likely to "go that extra step to make sure it stops." Yet, like Víctor, participants described how knowing the cyberbully *and* cybervictim left them agonizingly "torn":

> I was really good friends with this guy and he stole this other guy's girlfriend. The other guy had a cleft lip when he was little and got it fixed. He made a tweet about the other guy mentioning his cleft lip, called him a bad name and everyone knew. It put me in an awkward position—I was torn as to what to say. Do I turn on my best friend or do I support this? Or do I look bad because I'm not like doing either?

Thus, a lack of proximity induced uncertainty. Participants spoke of not wanting to "get involved" when the cybervictim was a stranger. Bystanders not only distance themselves, but our participants also acknowledged feeling that it might be "out of line" to engage. For example, Shiloh explained, "I knew of them, but like I didn't feel comfortable being like, 'Oh, this person's my hero,' or whatever."

Finally, participants preferred to be informed bystanders, only becoming involved or "putt[ing] [themself] in that position" if they had in-depth knowledge of the dyadic interaction. In many ways, this aspect of honoring proximity contains an underlying defense mechanism. If bystanders were to get involved, tell friends, or report to an authority without knowing "all the details and stuff," the end result could be unpleasant. Participants shared that they preferred to do nothing than to "tell them the wrong story" and most likely "make it worse." In this way, bystanders may be restrained by the lack of proximity to information.

Respond According to Severity

Since participants consider cyberbullying on a continuum, the incident's degree of severity also influenced bystander goals. Some referred to the specific site used. For example, they perceived cyberbullying on YouTube as less personal because of the vast size of its user base and its purpose in broadcasting content rather than establishing social connections and community with others. Thus, less personal mediums equaled less severe cyberbullying, and therefore, bystanders "don't take it as seriously."

> If you're on YouTube, I have no connection to you. You have no connection to me. There's no way you can find anything about me on YouTube. You have no idea who my friends are. But if you're coming at me on Facebook ... that's more personal because now you're on a platform where I'm in a community of people.
>
> *(Josh)*

More often, severity referred to the aggression itself. Participants considered "making fun of" another as "amusing" rather than severe. When the situation progressed to "*really* serious" or "unusual" (i.e., incessant mocking of an individual or their friends, talking about someone's family, threats, or leaking controversial or graphic images), they defined the behavior as severe. At this point, participants felt that action needed to be taken as bystanders, whether telling an authority figure or stepping in themselves. Thus, bystanders may model their judgment and response in proportion to the severity of the incident so as to act most appropriately.

Embrace the Cultural Environment

The pressure to adhere to group norms functioned as a prominent determinant of bystanders' behavior, which they discussed in terms of age and immediate physical surroundings. They envisioned bystander responses as largely dependent on a maturity and moral development that "comes with age," especially when comparing high school to college: "You start to get into your mid-to-late 20s," Liz described, "and you have a more set-in-stone moral code that you more or less live your life by . . . who's watching isn't really gonna change that." As a result, our participants understood older bystanders as having "more incentive" to intervene. However, incentive may not translate into action. Participants also argued that, although they were mature enough to realize cyberbullying was "childish," their "moral code" could still be in flux: "when you're still at our age or younger," Liz continued, "you're still kind of discovering what's right and what's wrong from your point of view. So, you're more . . . careful."

Participants also pitted high school against college. Whereas high school students are "a little more interconnected" due to daily interactions in a "closer, smaller space," college students are exposed to thousands of others, leaving one with an abundance of alternative options: "If you get mad at one of your friends, there's 20,000 other people on campus that you can talk to." A college environment allows bystanders to apathetically blend in and absolve themselves of responsibility: "You have to be at least a little apathetic . . . you're in college," Austin declared. "You're too busy. You can't worry about everything. If you did, you wouldn't get anything done."

Gauge From Others' Responses

Participants used others' responses as a way to gauge what they should do and feel. For most, others' responses justified their own inaction, such that the more other bystanders engaged in support of the cybervictim, the less they felt obligated to act. They envisioned the public nature of cyberbullying as an out, or as Víctor described, "I'm not the only one held accountable. I'm not the only one that sees this. So, it's not all my responsibility to step up and defend the person. I would get judged for it." In other cases, bystander responses propelled them to become part of the solution; the larger the inclusive community, the safer bystanders felt:

> Her closer friends group posted on her wall saying, "Don't listen to them. They don't know what a relationship is like," and stuff like that. So, it made me want to post something . . . I felt like the more she got, the better she would feel. I mean if someone's really mean and more people agree that it's mean than agree that it's funny, then you're gonna be more—like it's less like dangerous for you to defend someone or come to someone's defense instead of like thinking it's funny.
>
> *(Andie)*

Collectively, these results suggest that gauging from others' responses propels deindividuation.

Avoid Personal Consequences

Participants understood that attempts at intervention or consolation may be met with additional aggression—this time, aimed at them. Despite the fact that bystanders "don't want [cyberbullying] to happen," the possibility that "say[ing] something" or "defend[ing] someone" might lead to their own victimization must be avoided at all costs. Andie explained how the potential for victimization manifested in this particular goal:

> I think when you put yourself out there and try to defend someone, you're putting yourself in the situation to get bullied too. So, I think by saying something and coming to someone's defense, you're putting yourself at risk of being bullied too.

Personal consequences may also take the form of bystanders' attempts at intervention being misconstrued. Participants do not just aim to avoid victimization but also to avoid being labeled as "defiant," as one who spoke out of line, or as an instigator. Some sought social support by finding someone "with more wisdom" like a parent or a peer to solicit advice or learn how to frame a response that could not be "construed as cyberbullying."

Impact of Goals on Bystander Behavior

Bystander goals manifested in four distinct bystander behaviors: ignoring, observing, instigating, and intervening. Collectively, these behaviors reveal bystanders' triadic power to encourage or restrain perpetration and victimization. In the following sections, composites of participants' own responses to cyberbullying incidents plus their observations of others are contextualized alongside corresponding goals.

Ignoring

Participants reported that they most often responded to cyberbullying by disengaging. Whether they opted to "just stay neutral" or distanced themselves by "moving on and away," bystanders intentionally "separate[d]" themselves from the incidents. Bystanders also chose not to observe the continued aggression past the initial exposure: "You just . . . keep scrolling," Max said. Participants reported that this behavior was propelled by *honoring proximity*, especially when the incident did not involve a close friend. Again, Max explained, "it doesn't pertain to you. It's not your business what's going on between them." Proximity to information also influenced bystander behavior. As Teresa argued, "I generally like to stay neutral if I have no knowledge of both sides." *Avoiding personal consequences* comprised another explanation; participants felt the most effective way to avoid consequences was simple—"don't get involved in it."

Overall, participants felt that *ignoring* was effective because it denied the cyberbully a main catalyst of their behavior: attention. By responding in some way or even observing the behavior from a distance, bystanders pacify the cyberbully, allowing them to "win." By ignoring the incident, bystanders obstruct the cyberbully's purpose insofar as, "if they don't have a reason, if they don't have people reading what they're saying, and they don't have people reacting, what's the point?" (Max).

Nonetheless, participants still acknowledged that ignoring may upset victims who "think everyone agrees." Allan summarized, "If they have nobody standing up for them and this person keeps going and going and nobody's saying anything, they're like, 'Oh, well nobody has my back so why should I be here?'" When asked what they would recommend as a course of action for other bystanders, not a single participant suggested *ignoring* or any variation thereof. This chasm between bystanders' actual behaviors and "model" behaviors suggests a sinister side of bystander goals, whereby bystanders' inner, altruistic attitudes are overtaken by goals that adheres to the group norm.

Observing

In contrast to ignoring the incident altogether, some participants "stood back" and watched the cyberbullying in action. As bystanders, participants not only mentioned it to friends—"Oh, did you see this?!"—but also explicitly invited others to watch with statements like Jayme's: "Go look at this page! Look what they did to this girl. That's messed up." Accepting the invitation was "almost like watching a fight." They characterized gossiping, laughing, and joking about the aggression as "naturally" apathetic ways to respond to the "amusing" incident. Aside from entertainment, some felt a true *need* to tell others. If the cyberbullying was particularly horrible, they did not treat it as appropriate nor comfortable to keep secret. Andie said, "I need to talk about it with someone," and, "If it's a big deal then you don't just want to keep it to yourself."

Some goals inspire observation, especially *gauge from others' responses*. The fact that others were "watching the fight go on" made participants "feel a little better about not partak[ing]" and "just witnessing it." In this way, observing quickly becomes the group norm with the bystander finding little incentive to deviate within the social structure. Bystanders may also feel that the cyberbullying is simply not severe enough to warrant engagement (*respond according to severity*). Jayme recalled, "Nobody cared. Everyone thought it was . . . amusing." Presumably, the bystander does not know the cybervictim well enough to feel comfortable intervening (*honor proximity*), or as Shiloh detailed, "I didn't really know any of the people getting attacked . . . I was kind of just an onlooker, so I didn't really get involved." College-aged bystanders' characterization of cyberbullying as "childish" also seemed to contribute to their "downplaying" of the incident (*embrace the cultural environment*).

Like *ignoring*, some participants felt observing denied cyberbullies their desire to be the "center of attention," suggesting that, even though they watched and commentated, they prevented the cyberbully from winning since they did not *publicly* respond. Like *ignoring*, no participants recommended observing exclusively, which suggests the behavior may be more of a coping mechanism than a solution.

Instigating

Participants described how some bystanders went beyond mere observation to instigate the aggression; in many cases, the instigation was intentional. All participants recalled times when bystanders "encouraged it to go on." Liz recalled bystanders reaching out to *both* the cyberbully and cybervictim, noting that "she was getting a lot of support too! There was a lot of opposition, but she was getting a lot of support for what she's saying too." Instigating also occurred by provoking the cybervictim, or as Allan modeled, "Aw, so you gonna let 'em talk to you like that?!" In these ways, the bystander "adds to the entertainment" by acting as a "co-conspirator" (Craig & Pepler, 1997). Participants aimed to *avoid personal consequences* by offering bystander support to the cyberbully as a strategy to avoid being "attacked" themselves. *Honoring proximity* also appeared when the bystander had a pre-existing connection with the cyberbully, allowing their relationship to prioritize aggression despite an internal goal conflict. Nonetheless, participants decided that *intentionally instigating* cyberbullying was ineffective, harmed all involved, and urged against it.

In other cases, the instigation was unintentional. Participants shared many examples of bystanders who intended to help but, in the end, did not. Austin noted that when his friends "jumped in" and began "going back and forth" with the cyberbully's friends, they did not allow her to "fight [her] battle." Bystanders inadvertently inflamed the aggression by striking back at the cyberbully and ignoring the fact that "it wasn't between me *and* all my friends *and* her." Similarly, when Seth told the cyberbully, "What the hell? Stop. You're pathetic!" the cyberbully only became defensive. Thus, while they may have good intentions, bystanders "gang[ing] up on" the cyberbully may provoke more bullying, which is likely to harm all involved.

Participants recognized that *honoring proximity* may not always ameliorate the situation. "I've seen that a lot," Liz shared. "They'll have 400 comments saying well, just attacking the cyberbully instead of trying to help." Participants also attempted to *gauge from others' responses* insofar as propelling one another to join in retaliation against the cyberbully rather than diffuse responsibility. While these bystanders may be trying to halt the incident, they remain distant from any solution. As every participant agreed, "fighting fire with fire" is a "dangerous path to tread." When striking back, the bystander—who may have been the cybervictim's hope—ends up intensifying the situation and risks hypocrisy. Therefore, participants implored others to avoid it: "Don't make yourself a bully in the process."

Intervening

With few exceptions, participants agreed that bystanders must "step up" and shared stories of how they would "try [their] damndest" to "get to the bottom of the issue." However, specific methods of intervening varied depending on the severity of the incident(s) or their proximity to the cybervictim. For example, bystanders may choose to intervene by reporting the incident(s) to authorities. Participants described reaching out to teachers, parents, or mentors in an effort to put a final stop to the cyberbully's attacks, especially when the incident was prolonged or severe. These reporting attempts were successful because cyberbullies were reprimanded, but at the great cost of timing. Max recalled, "It took awhile. It took several posts [from the cyberbully] to have someone of authority step in and say something about it." Otherwise, participants recommended bystanders "flag" the cyberbully's post to alert the site's administrators. While a quicker action, participants expressed skepticism that it would be "possible to govern or watch" all the aggression taking place.

Consequently, bystanders may circumvent authorities and instead respond directly to the cyberbully. Participants felt that this form of direct response was the surest way to make the cyberbully "realize the error of their own ways." By confronting the cyberbully in "a more respectful way" (e.g., "Maybe you shouldn't be subtweeting these things"), others are more protected from escalation. Víctor noted that when the bystander community responded directly, the cyberbully felt isolated and finally apologized: "He really saw then, 'Wow, I should not have said that.'" Participants remained optimistic that the cyberbully could "change for the better," but they felt that a "common, unaffiliated" bystander asking the cyberbully to stop would result in backlash, while someone closer may have more credibility, impact, and a "right to respond."

However, participants offered two cautions: (1) "come with a more respectful approach," and (2) "talk to [the cyberbully] privately." Participants explained that, by responding with kindness, the cyberbully will not feel attacked, thus making them more open to bystanders "explaining why they should stop" and realizing the hurt caused. Because public responses often result in too much "back and forth," bystanders felt that sending a direct, private message, such as a "DM" on Twitter, guarded against *their* responses turning into entertainment. "The easy way out is just to post something," Jayme shared, "versus actually confronting the bully." To that end, the easy response may not be the optimal response.

Finally, bystanders may also intervene by reaching out to the cybervictim to let them know "*somebody* [is] there for you." Participants described how some made an explicit call for support. For example, Víctor recalled a cybervictim posting a screenshot of the cyberbully's messages: "Obviously she was asking for attention," he elaborated, "but she needed it. So, I think her posting that was like her way of coping with it, instead of just letting it like sit there." To that end, extending a helping hand (e.g., "Don't listen to them," or, "You're beautiful . . .") makes the cybervictim "feel better about themselves" and more importantly, "less alone," which increases their self-confidence and security. Mia asked, "suppose that no one comes to their defense. Then how do they feel?" *Gauging from others' responses* largely influenced this form of bystander behavior. Though bystanders who are friends with the cybervictim may create "a more dynamic change," participants discovered that "from the victim's point of view," even one or two "random" bystanders can make a difference. With cybervictims' well-being as the primary concern, participants advocated most for this form of response. Seth summarized, "Nobody deserves to be pelted out with bullets . . . if you're having trouble dodging them you need somebody there to help you dodge them."

Typology of Cyberbullying Bystanders

From these exploratory results, a framework of the bystanding experience materializes. Table 21.1 offers a typology of cyberbullying bystanders, with contributing goals for each behavior.

Table 21.1 Typology of Cyberbullying Bystanders

Bystander Types	Contributing Goals	Resulting Behavior
the oblivious/ distant bystander	*Honor Proximity*: If it doesn't involve a friend or they don't know "both sides'" stories, it doesn't pertain to them and is therefore "not [their] business." *Avoid Personal Consequences*: The most effective way to avoid victimization or misconstrued attempts at intervention is "don't get involved." *Embrace the Cultural Environment*: College environments with near-infinite alternative interactions allows them to easily "move on," blend into a silent crowd, and "keep scrolling."	ignoring
the entertained bystander	*Gauge from Others' Responses*: A group norm is constructed when others accept an invitation to watch or gossip. A bystander evaluating their reaction in comparison may find no reason to deviate. *Respond According to Severity*: Incident is more amusing than severe enough to warrant engagement. *Honor Proximity*: Although interested in the interaction, they don't know the cybervictim well enough to feel comfortable intervening. *Embrace the Cultural Environment*: Because their age group typically thinks of cyberbullying as "childish," they often joke about and "downplay" the incident.	observing
the conspiring bystander	*Avoid Personal Consequences*: If they want to avoid victimization, it is "less dangerous" to back up the cyberbully or provoke the cybervictim. *Honor Proximity*: If close to the cyberbully, they feel an allegiance and support the aggression.	(intentional) instigating
the unintentional instigating bystander	*Honor Proximity*: If close to the cybervictim, they feel obligated to support but may do so by attacking the cyberbully. *Gauge from Others' Responses*: Supporters "ganging up on" the cyberbully and their supporters propels more bystanders to join in retaliation.	(unintentional) instigating
the active/ empowered bystander	*Respond According to Severity*: When severe or prolonged, authorities should be informed or cyberbullies should be approached to understand why the behavior is wrong. *Honor Proximity*: They are more likely to intervene if close to the cybervictim. *Gauge from Others' Responses*: A community of supportive bystanders encourages others to also reach out to the cybervictim.	Intervening (report; respond directly; reach out)

Discussion

The typology reveals bystanders to be integral members of the online community—an equal party in the triadic, interactive social context, whereby their reaction has a decided and direct impact on the longevity of the incident and severity of harm. The typology benefits practitioners' management of cyberbullying threats—by matching bystanders' goals to their behaviors, making their private attitudes and motivational struggles more salient, prediction of behaviors is more possible. Understanding bystanders' depth of influence reveals numerous opportunities to transform their brute power into "passionate statement and respectful communication," ultimately minimizing the harmful impact on cybervictims (Salmivalli, 2010; Twemlow et al., 2004). Here, we examine the implications of this study.

Practical Implications

This study contributes to emerging scholarship documenting cyberbullying in college. Participants were intimately familiar with the phenomenon, and bystanding experiences directly inform their attitudes and adherence to certain goals. The results also highlight the integral nature of integral bystanders to cyberbullying incidents as they unfold, suggesting that prevention and intervention efforts would be more effective if aimed at bystanders. Indeed, scholars investigating traditional bullying have argued that interventions should not "overemphasize therapeutic efforts with the victim or victimizer" (Twemlow et al., 2004, p. 218) but instead teach them to "attend to their discomfort" through assertion, support, and constructive resolution (Swearer, Espelage, Vaillancourt, & Hymel, 2010; O'Connell et al., 1999, p. 448). Participants exhibited pro-social, altruistic attitudes toward cybervictims and criticized cyberbullies. However, a chasm exists between bystanders' inner attitudes and ultimate responses when they reinforce cyberbullies through ignoring, observation, or encouragement, suggesting that goals evolve over a single incident (Keck & Samp, 2007). Normative bystander behavior, then, benefits the aggressor and restricts pro-social interventions.

If bystander intervention is key to terminating cyberbullying incidents (Pearce, Cross, Monks, Waters, & Falconer, 2011), we should look toward comprehensive approaches that make salient those goals that align with bystanders' pro-social attitudes. Snakenborg et al.'s (2011) analysis of prevention and intervention programs for cyberbullying highlights just one as bystander-related (*Cyber Bullying: A Prevention Curriculum*). Future interventions should help bystanders find ways to recognize their goals, evaluate those goals relative to the cybervictim's psychological well-being and physical safety, and perhaps offer examples of ways to confront the aggressor and/or support the cybervictim in a respectful and selfless manner, thereby empowering bystanders to abandon harmful *oblivious/distant, entertained, conspiring*, and *unintentional instigating* bystander roles.

Theoretical Implications

This investigation advances our understanding of cyberbullying bystanders as essential, goal-oriented communicators, which has implications for future theorizing. Goal-oriented communication allows for management and manipulation of relational identity (Clark & Delia, 1979), and bystander goals revealed strategic identity management. For every bystander ignoring the incident, others may engage differently, and individual bystanders may even alter their responses from incident to incident depending on internal goal conflicts. The direct impact bystander goals have on the establishment, maintenance, and advancement of power in cyberbullying incidents and victimization outcomes affirms Caughlin's (2010) assertion that goal inferences that shape meaning of communication behavior also shape impact.

In fact, this study extends multiple goals theories in two ways. It remedies a limitation of previous multiple goals research by avoiding a focus on isolated encounters, and instead looking at the "big picture," as we examined relationships holistically to identify bystanders' goals and link those goals to perpetration and victimization. Second, as seen in the typology, each goal is multifaceted—one goal does not equal one behavior, but rather, one goal may contribute to multiple behaviors, each in different ways. Understanding bystanders' actions as goal-oriented, communicative functions of proximity, severity, environment, audience, and potential consequences both affirms and extends communication theory in significant ways.

Strengths, Limitations, and Future Directions

This study provided a detailed analysis of cyberbullying bystanders' power and place in the triadic interaction and so exemplifies efforts to move toward translational work. For instance, the typology of cyberbullying bystanders can be helpful as a "classificatory system" (Tracy, 2013, p. 210). However, this study could have benefited from *member checking* to further ensure trustworthiness of data (Creswell, 2013, p. 252). Examining bystanders' class rank and age with their goals in future studies may also be an important step. Finally, future studies should engage in *triangulation* by combining multiple sources of data, such as real-time capture of cyberbullying interactions or any recorded bystander responses (Creswell, 2013).

Conclusion

By grounding the investigation in a multiple goals theoretical framework, participants' experiences established that bystanders are crucial to the initiation, maintenance, and prolonged presence of online aggression. Attending to bystander goals and their impact on behavioral responses clarifies this role by exposing bystanders' underlying cognitions and challenging the status quo of cybervictimization.

22

TEXTUAL HARASSMENT AS A FORM OF BULLYING, DRAMA, AND OBSESSIVE RELATIONAL INTRUSION

Erin M. Sumner, Nicholas Brody, and Artemio Ramirez Jr.

People behave in ways that emotionally and psychologically injure each other, and mediated interactions are no exception. In a PEW survey, 73% of online American adults had witnessed someone being harassed online, and 40% of respondents had been harassed themselves (Duggan, 2014). Though the concept of harassment is well-established in online contexts, mediated harassment also occurs via cell phones (Hoffman, 2010). Most existing research has selected a hostile behavior (i.e., cyberbullying) and described the channels thorough which it occurs; such as phone calls, text messaging (TM), instant messaging (IM), and websites (P. K. Smith et al., 2008). We take a different approach by exploring the various forms of interpersonal harassment that might occur within a single medium—text messaging.

The present study explores how TM is employed to enact various forms of interpersonal harassment. As reviewed in the following pages, cyberbullying involves a relatively specific set of behaviors, yet the term is sometimes erroneously applied to all antisocial mediated behaviors. This chapter will use TM as an example of the various forms of harassment—including but not limited to cyberbullying—that occur via mediated channels. We analyze participants' narratives to assert that harassment via TM can take the form of range of antisocial behaviors such as cyberbullying, drama, and obsessive relational intrusion.

Mobile Communication and the Nature of Online Harassment

Mobility is a defining feature of the modern technological landscape and has helped produce a "personal communication society" in which individuals are attached to wearable devices that enable nearly constant communication across geographic boundaries (Campbell & Park, 2008, p. 372). As Campbell and Park noted, individuals often treat smart phones, for example, as extensions of self that enable both micro-coordination (i.e., pursuit of instrumental goals) and hyper-coordination (i.e., enactment of expressive goals) within their social networks.

Despite the rapid development of cue-richer technology that facilitate near synchronous interactions involving both visual and aural cues (e.g., Facetime and Skype), communicators often employ cue-leaner media such as TM, IM, and email (Walther & Ramirez, 2009). TM provides several user affordances that lead 97% of cell phone owners to use it, making it the most popular cell phone feature (A. Smith, 2015). For example, TM is asynchronous (i.e., involves a time lag), which can be problematic when communicators differ in their expectations for response time (Kato & Kato, 2015), yet enables individuals to carefully edit messages before sending them. Moreover, TM allows users to communicate across geographic distance without internet access, enabling a state of nearly perpetual contact (Katz & Aakhus, 2002). Extant research has examined TM within relationships (e.g., Brody & Peña, 2015), but we know relatively little about TM as a channel for harassment. As such, we will review three forms of interpersonal harassment that are likely pertinent to TM and other cue-leaner channels.

Bullying and Cyberbullying

Researchers have struggled to conceptualize cyberbullying in relation to more traditional forms of bullying (Tokunaga, 2010). According to Olweus (1993b), traditional bullying encompasses repetition (i.e., harassment occurring more than once) and power imbalance (i.e., the bully is more socially and/or physically powerful than the victim). These features set bullying apart as a pattern of hostile behavior that is more intense and targeted than isolated acts of aggression, incivility, or harassment (Marwick & boyd, 2011). Tokunaga (2010) asserted that the characteristics of cyberbullying question the importance of repetition and power differentials as defining elements of bullying. For example, if someone creates a hurtful online message (e.g., a text, video, or web post) and then forwards it to other people, the perpetual sharing of that one message might feel like multiple distinct incidents of bullying. Likewise, power differentials related to physicality might dissipate online because a person's physical stature does not prevent him/her from typing a hurtful message. Based on these distinctions, Tokunaga defined cyberbullying as "any behavior performed through electronic or digital media by individuals or groups that repeatedly communicates hostile or aggressive messages intended to inflict harm or discomfort on others" (p. 278). Of note, this definition still identifies a persistent and targeted set of hostile behaviors. Although cyberbullying occurs in many different contexts, extant research reveals it is often related to romantic relational conflicts, jealousy, and breakups (Brody & Vangelisti, 2017; Hoff & Mitchell, 2009). Although TM might be used to enact bullying, other forms of harassment are also likely to occur via TM.

Drama

Adults and some scholars often label all antisocial online behaviors as cyberbullying; however, teens and young adults often evoke the term *drama* when discussing hostile online behaviors of a relatively less serious manner (Marwick & boyd, 2011). Drama is not a new phenomenon, but modern technologies allow these behaviors to play out in mediated environments, such as via TM. Marwick and boyd discussed five key components of drama: (1) it entails social and interpersonal dynamics; (2) it involves relational conflict; (3) it involves reciprocal hostility; (4) it is gendered; and (5) it is performed for and augmented by social networks. These components reveal that—unlike targeted bullying— drama involves the exchange of hostile messaging between two or more people who cannot be easily distinguished as targets or perpetrators. Moreover, drama is conceptualized as a more feminine and indirect style of communication, with girls seen as engaging in more drama behaviors such as "hostile texting" (K. P. Allen, 2012). Finally, Marwick and boyd contend that drama gains steam when it is performed for an audience. Audiences are often found on social media, but Allen noted that TM becomes performative when messages are forwarded. In sum, drama behaviors are hurtful, but could also be described as a somewhat inevitable aspect of teenage social life. Indeed, Allen observed that administrators typically claim that bullying is rare, yet drama is common at their schools.

Obsessive Relational Intrusion

Obsessive relational intrusion (ORI) constitutes the "repeated and unwanted pursuit and invasion of one's sense of physical or symbolic privacy by another person, either stranger or acquaintance, who desires and/or presumes an intimate relationship" (Cupach & Spitzberg, 1998, pp. 234–235). People connect relationships with higher-order life satisfaction goals, and will generally pursue relationships they believe are obtainable and desirable (Spitzberg, Cupach, Hannawa, & Crowley, 2014). Goal-motivated relation pursuit can be healthy within a reciprocal context, but morphs into ORI when one partner continues to pursue an unobtainable and unreciprocated relationship. Moreover, ORI perpetrators sometimes experience a shift in motives when their rejection triggers them to abandon intimacy attempts and instead seek revenge.

Spitzberg and Hoobler (2002) found evidence for three categories of ORI occurring in online contexts: hyperintimacy (i.e., making exaggerated claims of affection or disclosing in inappropriate ways), real-life transference (i.e., switching to offline behaviors), and threats (i.e., sending aggressive and threatening messages). Although mediated ORI behaviors are often lumped into the cyberbullying label, it is a distinct phenomenon because it is—at least initially—rooted in a desire for relational closeness rather than a desire to inflict harm. The relationally oriented nature of ORI may explain some of the underlying motivations for, and subsequent enactment of, TM harassment behaviors.

The Present Study

The present study explores the nature of harassment that occurs via text messaging. Extant research reveals that 43% of 11–18-year-olds have experienced text-based bullying (Raskauskas, 2010); however, all forms of mediated aggression or harassment were lumped under the label of cyberbullying. As previously reviewed, drama and ORI are unique from cyberbullying, and some forms of TM harassment might be better captured outside of the cyberbullying label. For example, reciprocal and relatively benign acts of TM harassment might be better understood using drama as a lens. Likewise, TM harassment born out of a desire for relational closeness (and/or retribution for unreciprocated affection) might be most accurately understood via the concept of ORI. These distinctions are, however, completely speculative because the harassment via TM remains understudied. To fill this void, this study explores narratives of harassment via TM using the following guiding questions.

RQ1: How do textual harassment targets describe the nature of their experience in regard to: (1) relational contexts, events, and consequences and (2) perceived harasser motives?

RQ2: To what extent does textual harassment follow the patterns of other interpersonal harassment behaviors such as cyberbullying, drama, and obsessive relational intrusion?

Methods

Participants and Procedures

We recruited our sample from undergraduate courses at a large university in the southwest region of the United States. The call for participation specified that this study sought to understand the perspectives of young adults who have been harassed via TM. Participants received a small amount of extra credit, with alternative credit options available.

We conducted seven focus groups with a total of 30 students (17 female and 13 male), who averaged 22 years of age. Upon arrival, participants signed consent forms allowing the focus groups to be audio recorded, transcribed, and used for research purposes. Focus groups employed a semi-structured protocol with consistent discussion prompts, yet flexibility for groups to organically direct the flow of conversation beyond the prompts (Tracy et al., 2006). At the onset, we asked each participant to tell their harassment story. Several participants had multiple experiences, resulting in 36 unique narratives. We then engaged participants in conversation to clarify and expand on their initial narratives.

The first focus group was cross-sex and included three men and three women who revealed that their experiences often involved cross-sex relational partners. We constructed the remaining focus groups as male-only (three groups) and female-only (three groups) to facilitate safe spaces for disclosure. The focus groups allowed for theoretical saturation, with the final groups confirming existing themes rather than raising new ones. The audio recordings were professionally transcribed to produce 121 pages of single-spaced data. The transcripts were analyzed using a constant comparison approach (Glaser & Strauss, 1967), which allowed for the iterative development and refinement of themes. We employed drama, bullying, and ORI as sensitizing concepts that provided a potential starting point for analysis (Charmaz, 2003).

Results

Regarding RQ1, TM harassment appeared to occur in many diverse forms. The content of harassing messages ranged from relatively innocent attempts at intimacy to vivid death threats. Likewise, the related events ranged from single-day spurts of emotionally charged texting to patterns of systematic bullying and stalking that spanned multiple years. When assessing the situation, some participants claimed to be innocent victims who ignored their harassers, while others admitted to reciprocating the hostility they received.

The consequences of TM harassment also varied greatly across narratives. One prevalent sub-theme was the belief that TM is somehow less real than FtF harassment. Within this sub-theme, participants attempted to dismiss the consequences of TM, and claimed that the harasser likely chose TM because they "lacked the guts" to pursue the aggression offline. In these situations, TM harassment was described as a mere annoyance that provoked momentary stress, yet no lasting repercussions. Conversely, a relatively less common sub-theme emerged among participants who believed that TM harassment might translate into offline violence. Within this sub-group of narratives, participants reported feeling scared for their physical safety, and took actions such as filing restraining orders and recruiting friends to "have their backs" in case an offline altercation occurred. Across both sub-groups, participants explained that harassment via TM led to sleep disruptions because they received late night messages, lay awake ruminating, or even had nightmares about their harasser. Some participants began to avoid their phone, with a few actually changing their phone numbers to escape the harasser.

In general, TM harassment appears to be an inherently relational phenomenon occurring between individuals with a pre-existing social connection. Almost all of the participants knew their harassers on a personal level and described them as (ex)romantic partners, dating prospects, friends, and acquaintances. The remaining participants were essentially one-degree of social separation from their harassers, and their harassment arose from conflict over their shared social tie (e.g., getting caught up in a love triangle). Hence, the act of sending private and personalized harassing TMs appears to be rooted in larger relational processes that are well-suited for analysis using existing interpersonal harassment concepts. Indeed, the use of drama, cyberbullying, and ORI as conceptual lenses (RQ2) provides further insight into why participants diverged so much when discussing the nature of their TM harassment.

Text Messaging as Drama

Drama-based harassment emerged between peers, (ex)romantic partners, and romantic rivals, and was characterized by three aspects: (1) although potentially distressing in the moment, the harassment did not produce lasting negative effects; (2) the series of hostile actions were short-lived; and (3) the behavioral pattern involved the reciprocation of hostile behaviors.

Relational Contexts, Events, and Consequences

First, although participants were somewhat affected by drama-based TM harassment, they downplayed its seriousness and noted an absence of long-term repercussions. As explained by one male participant, "it's not really even harassment, but it was super annoying and intrusive, like she was messing with me for no reason and starting issues to get a response." A female participant similarly noted, "it's not like I was horribly bullied, but it was really ridiculous." Some participants directly invoked the term "drama" in their accounts, recalling that "we were good friends for a couple years, then all this drama happened, like he said/she said."

The actual series of events varied, but drama-based harassment typically centered on interpersonal conflicts that spiraled out of control. One participant was harassed when her ex-boyfriend's best friend "started texting me that I was a liar and a bitch and all this stuff." She was not sure why he did this, but shared that "things were overblown because they were by text."

Relatedly, drama-based language was applied toward narratives of short-lived harassment. For example, one participant explained that she was spending time with a male friend when his girlfriend saw them and "started freaking out . . . sending all these texts like 'stay away from Jim' [name changed]." The situation was stressful, but stopped after a single day of back-and-forth texting. Likewise, another participant got into an altercation when his close friend accused him of stealing a parking permit and proceeded to barrage him threats via TM:

> It was a little nerve-wrecking for the hour or two between when we had the textual argument and when he apologized. At the same time, I was thinking "This kid's been my friend for a while. The fact that he's freaking out . . . this is absurd. I'm sure it'll blow over."

Despite the stressful and overtly threatening nature of this interaction, the participant evoked a drama-based framework by claiming that his friend was just blowing off steam and that their friendship was not affected by this short-lived altercation.

Other instances of drama-based harassment reportedly transpired over slightly longer periods, such as a week or two, yet participants still downplayed them as relatively short-lived cycles of conflict regarding a precipitating event, rather than patterns of sustained and targeted abuse. One participant explained, "I had a relationship that kind of spiraled out of control at the end . . . my girlfriend was being 'it's all your fault, you're a piece of shit' and all this stuff." He admitted that they were both going back-and-forth with hostile communication in person, via TM, and over social media for a couple of weeks attempting to blame each other for the break-up. He believed they were both protecting their egos and image, yet ultimately reached a sense of closure and moved on without any real repercussions.

Finally, although all 30 participants maintained that they were innocent at the onset of the harassment, those who invoked drama-based language admitted that they got defensive and "probably fueled the fire" by reciprocating the hostility. For example, one participant explained that he found out his girlfriend had another out-of-state boyfriend when this rival began to send him threatening texts. He admitted that "I sent threats back to him just because he was threatening me. I said come and find me, it's not that hard . . . Obviously, your girlfriend knows where I live." A female participant succinctly captured the reciprocal nature of drama-based harassment by explaining "I feel like one person has to instigate it . . . but the text is just so potent where it really pisses you off and you reply back to it, and that's how things spiral."

Perceived Harasser Motives

The drama aspect of TM harassment was evident in the attributions that participants assigned to their harassers. In drama-based TM, participants tended to downplay the maliciousness of their harassers, by describing them as "immature," "silly," "attention-seeking," "just being stupid," "wanting to cause drama," or "wanting to get a rise out of me." Likewise, participants often described drama-based TM using gendered descriptors, such as a female harasser being "catty," and a male harasser performing "the whole aggressive testosterone thing." Tapping into the performative nature of drama, one participant noted that her harassers were putting on a show to look cool because, "they have their clique to satisfy, like their image to uphold." Another noted that his harassment was actually quite silly, yet seemed to be a source of amusement for his harasser and her friends by saying, "I mean come on! Just grow up a bit here ... What kind of game are you trying to play?" TM appeared to be a common vessel for drama-based harassment because "with texting it's easy to start stuff, but it's not real. If he doesn't have the balls or whatever to give me a call or even come meet me FtF then that's his problem." As summarized by one participant, "Some people get their jollies off textual harassment ... maybe they wouldn't do it that much in person. Like big thumbs and a small mouth." As such, drama-based harassment was downplayed as motivated by social entertainment: a way for immature people to create a spectacle from the safety of their phone.

Text Messaging as Bullying

Bullying also emerged as a useful framework for understanding TM harassment and emerged in narratives involving targeted and persistent patterns of abuse that tended to transcend the boundaries of any one channel.

Relational Contexts, Events, and Consequences

Participants described bullying by TM as one component of a larger pattern that included social media and FtF behaviors aimed at destroying the target and his/her reputation. Unlike drama, bullying-based TM harassment persisted, felt extremely targeted, and provoked significant fear and severe consequences.

One participant described moving to a new town and befriending a girl in her class. She recalled that the girl's friends then "singled me out and were like we basically hate you!" TM played a key role in this situation; the bullies ignored the participant at school, while simultaneously sending her harassing TM and circulating mean rumors to other classmates via TM. At first, the participant tried to smooth over what she thought was a misunderstanding, but she quickly resorted to passively ignoring the texts and rumors because she felt powerless from "not having a strong support system, having just moved to town." The participant affirmed that this situation left lasting repercussions on her ability to form friendships with other women.

A different participant discussed a similar situation in which her group of four best friends suddenly became divided, and two of the girls proceeded to engage in mediated and FtF bullying that lasted more than a year.

> They started texting me, like, "we're going to tell our softball coach this about you" ...just all these malicious lies, like I cheat on tests and whatever. I sleep around. I was just like, "Are you kidding me?" They would send them over and over. And they'd get different friends phones and they'd send them, like our mutual friends.

This experience was incredibly isolating; "being harassed by your peer group is the hardest thing. Like you don't want to go to your parents in a way because you don't think they'll understand. So, it's like, if you don't have any friends anymore, who do you to go to?"

A male participant who identified as "openly gay" explained that he went to a Sadie Hawkins dance with a female friend and began to receive harassing texts from her boyfriend. Although the bully never confronted the participant in person, he threatened to do so: "He got really mad and was texting like 'I'm gonna fuck you up, faggot'." The participant explained, "I didn't want to be caught seeing or talking to her . . . I was legit scared." Overall, these accounts highlight ways that TM harassment can reflect a pattern of bullying when it becomes persistent, targeted, and produces severe consequences for the target.

Perceived Harasser Motives

Whereas drama-based TM harassment was often downplayed, participants were very unforgiving when interpreting why their bullies harassed them via TM. They described their harassers as "bullies" and "bad kids" who were "legit crazy" and "probably on drugs." The participant who was bullied after moving to a new town believed that being new made her an easy target, and explained that her bullies were "mean girls, but too scared to say it to my face." The participant who was bullied by her former best friends believed that TM was selected very malicious reasons:

> It's manipulative control . . . they can control when you receive the message. They can formulate what they want to say, whereas FtF maybe they can't really think quickly on what they want to say. And they want this message to be powerful . . . and they want to hurt you right then and there, but it's not always possible FtF.

Thus, TM provides a venue for bullies to enact patterns of targeted and sustained abuse.

Text Messaging as Obsessive Relational Intrusion

Finally, a subset of TM harassment narratives seemed to fit the profile of ORI in which their harasser was—at least initially—using TM as a way to seek relational closeness.

Relational Contexts, Events, and Consequences

TM harassment followed a pattern of ORI in three contexts: acquaintances, ex-romantic partners, and romantic rivals. First, several participants described situations of unrequited affection in which an acquaintance, or someone with whom they had gone on only one or two dates, sent persistent affection-seeking messages. One participant met a guy at a party who began to text her:

> I tried to nicely tell him "oh sorry I'm not interested," but he just wouldn't stop and it kept going and going. I didn't change my number, but I was actually considering it, because I started ignoring him but he kept texting me and it was getting creepy.

Another participant described a similar situation in which a group of her male classmates developed a sudden interest in her. "I would get repeated, repeated text messages like 'you need to come out. We're going to have somebody come pick you up' or 'come party with us.' I'd be like hey, I have plans today, sorry." The participant explained "I tried to politely make excuses until one of them texted 'I just want you to know I love you' or something like that, and it really freaked me out." Initially, these participants politely brushed off the unwanted affection, but their harassers did not pick up on the polite rejection. As the situation went on, one participant summarized that she "started to be more direct. I started to get a bit short with him." Some cases involving ORI from acquaintances eventually fizzled out when the other person got the hint and moved on. In other instances, the acquaintances became quite angry and shifted their motives toward retaliating with hostile text messages.

In the second set of narratives, participants received TM from an ex-romantic partner as part of a larger ORI pattern. These stories constituted some of the most extreme examples of TM harassment, perhaps due to greater investment and shared relational history. One participant summarized that her verbally abusive ex-boyfriend began to text her after their break-up:

> At first like "I'm so sorry, come back" and then when I wouldn't respond to that, it would be like "you're such a whore. I hate you. You're so worthless." It was just really bad things. "I never loved you." Just trying to get a reaction. This literally happened every day for probably two and a half months ... But I started dating somebody and I don't know how he found out, but he found out his name and where he works. He sent me text messages telling me all this information, like he was going to go to his work and beat him up and all this other stuff ... and still to this day ... probably once every other month, I'll get a nasty text message.

Another participant's ongoing experiences with her ex-partner similarly typified the erratic nature of TM as a channel for ORI:

> He would send "I'm going to kill you, you fucking bitch." Stuff like that "you're never going to be anything but a stripper. You should just drop out of school." Like stuff that doesn't even relate to my life at all ... just like hey call a girl a stripper. But then he would send me HUGE bouquets of flowers every single week and text or call saying he's sorry. Even after I blocked his number he would find a way.

A male participant experienced ORI when his ex-girlfriend harassed him via TM for months after breaking up. He noted that she had a way to "get the personal out and just kinda like drill it, and make it like I know I can hurt you. I can do this. I know things that I can hurt you with."

The final set of examples involved love-triangle situations. In these instances, individuals intruded on an ex-romantic partner's life by harassing his/her current romantic partner. Situations involving third-parties often became quite heated. For example, one participant had been dating his girlfriend for a while when he started receiving messages from an unknown number saying "Hey, faggot ... that's my ex-girlfriend." This ex-boyfriend continued to text the participant for over six months, calling him names and challenging him to a fight. The exchange led to an altercation in a parking lot where "he shoved me, and I punched him in the face," which effectively ended the pattern of TM harassment.

Perceived Harasser Motives

In ORI-based harassment involving acquaintances, participants' lack of relational history with their harasser factored into their perceptions of the situation. Initially, participants were simply frustrated that their harassers were "not getting the hint." These participants felt their pursuer's repeated messaging crossed a line, yet acknowledged that their own lack of directness left room for misinterpretation. When the harassment persisted despite increased directness, participants often noted that their lack of knowledge about an acquaintance provoked fear and uncertainty. One participant, for example, began to receive naked photos from a guy that she had rejected after one date. She reasoned that "maybe in the beginning he hoped it would entice me. I have no idea. After that I feel it was just to get a rise out of me, but I really don't know." Another participant explained feeling "a lot of fear and uncertainty ... You don't have ultimate control over that other person. You are helpless. You just have to hope that they come to a healthy state of mind and back off." This participant, and others, admitted that they did not know enough about their harasser to know whether to be afraid.

Participants offered very harsh attributions of why their ex-romantic partners engaged in ORI-based harassment via TM. One participant was intensely harassed by her ex-boyfriend for many months and reasoned; "I think he wanted me to feel bad. At first, I think he wanted to get me back, but then I think he just wanted to get back at me after that. It did get very dangerous." Another participant explained her ex's goal was "to get me back, then make me pay. I was blocking all contact on social media and calls. But he knows I'll have to open my phone to delete a text message and will see it on the screen." Another participant explained that TM harassment allowed his ex-girlfriend to prevent him from moving on; "I don't want you to be happy. Right now, I know you're probably being happier than I am, but I want you to be as unhappy as I am." In these cases, ORI's tendency to involve a shift in motivations was apparent.

Finally, in ORI involving third-party harassers, participants believed their harassers were displacing anger and sadness onto their ex's new partner. One participant explained;

> I think that he was finally realizing that breaking up means I don't get to be with that person. Because he kept trying to be with her after they broke up and he was like "oh I can't have my cake and eat it too?" And I was the person that was taking his cake.

In these cases, participants believed that sending harassing TM to a third-party served as a form of ORI that allowed the jealous harassers to insert themselves back into their ex's lives.

Discussion

The present study explored the nature of harassment occurring via TM. In regard to RQ1, TM harassment constitutes a diverse phenomenon with many different characteristics. In some cases, participants dismissed harassing texts as a mere annoyance, while in other cases, participants experienced persistent abuse through TM. Notably, harassment via TM encompasses an inherently relational behavior that is motivated by and enacted within the context of offline social networks and relationships. As such, RQ2 analyzed TM harassment narratives using established concepts such as drama, (cyber)bullying, and ORI.

Teenagers and young adults invoke the term drama to explain reciprocal interpersonal conflicts that get overblown, and that are not targeted or serious enough to be considered as cyberbullying (Marwick & boyd, 2011). Similar trends emerged in the present study. Drama-based narratives occurred between peers or romantic partners of relatively equal social standing, involved reciprocal acts of aggression, and were attributed to understated harasser motives such as pettiness and immaturity. Participants explained that the affordances of TM make it incredibly easy to pursue drama from anywhere and at any time.

Our results also hint at ways in which drama-based TM harassment might differ from previous conceptualizations of drama. First, participants described drama as semi-public behavior that is performed for audiences (Marwick & boyd, 2011), and TM typically involves private messaging. Our participants explained that their private messages sometimes became fodder for discussion within their social networks, supporting Allen's (2012) claim that TM can take on a performative nature. That said, our participants also asserted that TM provided a way for their harasser to pursue a type of one-on-one drama; they could essentially hide behind their phones and say hurtful things that they were unwilling to say in front of other people.

Second, previous research presents drama as a gendered concept that is commonly enacted by women (Marwick & boyd, 2011), yet our data paints a more complicated picture. Although participants asserted that sending mean or harassing texts commonly occurs among young women, they also acknowledged that texting allows young men to act tough by sending insults and threats that they would not pursue offline. Several participants believed that their situation amounted to a form of chest-puffing regarding which of them was more manly. In this way, TM harassment enabled both feminine and masculine forms of drama.

In addition to drama, several TM harassment narratives included elements that fit existing scholarly definitions of cyberbullying (e.g., Tokunaga, 2010). Participants evoked bullying language to describe experiences in which they felt that they were personally targeted for an extended time period in ways that they were afraid to reciprocate or even defend against. Persistence was a key factor; participants became afraid and depressed when the bully "just kept at it." Likewise, although the bullies in this study did not tend to hold formal power over their targets—which Olweus (1993b) describes as a characteristic of traditional bullying—the participants felt at a social disadvantage that provoked a sense of isolation and helplessness. Some of the bullies were described as physically intimidating; others had reputations as "bad kids" or "mean girls" who were widely feared or simply had more social clout than their targets.

Overall, most bullying TM incidents reported in this study emerged from incidents relating to close relationships gone awry. This trend parallels recent work indicating romantic relationships, friendships, and sexual activities frequently trigger cyberbullying on Facebook (Brody & Vangelisti, 2017), and that romantic relationship issues are the most common source of cyberbullying among high school students (Hoff & Mitchell, 2009). The present findings, therefore, reinforce the relational nature of bullying in mediated contexts while offering a unique additional dimension—bullying can result from perceived third-party relational rivalry. Indeed, multiple participants claimed to be targeted because they spent time with someone that the bully had already claimed as a best friend or romantic interest.

Finally, some TM harassment narratives most closely resembled a pattern of obsessive relational intrusion in the form of unreciprocated attempts to initiate a relationship, unreciprocated attempts to continue a relationship that had ended, and attempts to destroy an ex-partner's current romantic relationships. Our categories of ORI-based TM harassment also extend Spitzberg and Hoobler's (2002) three categories of mediated ORI; attempts at hyperintimacy (e.g., repeatedly stating their love), threats (e.g., threatening the participant or his/her current romantic partner, and real-life transference (e.g., meeting for a physical fight). Similar to past research about ORI (e.g., Cupach & Spitzberg, 1998) our participants revealed that their harassment began as an earnest (albeit unreciprocated) attempt at intimacy, yet spiraled into ORI-based harassment when the perpetrator refused to give up, and in some cases became angry enough to stop seeking intimacy and being seeking revenge.

Limitations, Implications, and Future Directions

Our small convenience sample and focus-group methodology fit our exploratory purposes, but limit our ability to make generalizations beyond this study. As such, follow up studies should build on our framework using quantitative research designs.

Extant research and the present results suggest that cyberbullying, drama, and ORI provide useful lenses for exploring (more broadly) harassment that occurs via TM and other mediated contexts. Although it is tempting to lump all negative mediated behaviors under the label of cyberbullying, past research—coupled with our data—reveal that there are likely important yet somewhat subjective and blurry distinctions between bullying, drama, and ORI. For example, it is hard to determine whether drama is actually distinct from bullying, or whether it represents a self-protective attempt to save face by downplaying the severity of harassment (Marwick & boyd, 2011). Indeed, some participants' experiences began as drama and spiraled into bullying when the behaviors persisted and began to truly harm the participant's well-being. Likewise, romantic relationships are a prominent context for cyberbullying (Brody & Vangelisti, 2017; Hoff & Mitchell, 2009) that might overlap with ORI in some situations. Many cases of post-breakup TM harassment began as a pattern of ORI aimed at winning an ex-partner back but took on a persistent and sadistic nature that could ultimately qualify as targeted bullying. As such, it might be useful to conceive of drama, bullying, and ORI as overlapping dimensions or components of interpersonal harassment that might be enacted using TM and other media. Most importantly, although adults (including scholars and school administrators) often refer to all forms of online harassment as cyberbullying (Marwick & boyd, 2011), the present study reinforces that young adults see nuanced differences between various forms of TM harassment.

In sum, the present study helped clarify some of the characteristics that distinguish cyberbullying, drama, and ORI as dimensions of both online and offline harassment that occur via TM. Characteristics such as persistence, power dynamics, the severity of consequences, and perceived harasser motives seemed to play a role in the ways that people experience TM harassment. Future research can build on the above limitations by specifying and quantitatively examining the unique features of harassment that occur via TM (i.e., textual harassment). For instance, when defining textual harassment and considering its effects on those who are targeted, the structural features of TM (i.e., messages are narrowcast, often targeted to an individual, and private) might interact with characteristics of the incident itself (i.e., drama, ORI, and bullying).

EPILOGUE
Looking Forward

Christina S. Beck and Richard West

Although this anthology concludes here, regrettably, incidents of bullying persist in unimaginable ways. This behavior continues to impact the daily lives of people across the globe—from playgrounds to offices, from homes to the internet. Particularly in the United States, the harsh and divisive socio-political climate, exacerbated by the outcome of the 2016 U.S. presidential election, undercuts cultural preferences for civility and kindness, inciting angry discourse on television and social media, as well as in the streets. We're continually inundated with images of trauma and tragedy from horrific violence, often occurring in schools or offices. Although not all such episodes can be linked to bullying, too many involve an individual who is/was a bully or was bullied at some point.

The *Routledge Handbook of Communication and Bullying* provides a wide-ranging examination of varied contexts in which bullying occurs. A myriad of stakeholders suffer from and/or participate in bullying episodes--from schools to workplaces, from youth to senior citizens, from bullies to bystanders to those who have been bullied. We conceptualized this book with the primary goal of showcasing the direction and influence of Communication research in the area of bullying. We accomplished this objective by including chapters that spanned multiple contexts with diverse and varied lenses. We cannot overemphasize the value of this approach. Incorporating both quantitative and qualitative approaches to topics related to the bullying act ensures a robust data set. Moreover, in doing so, we simultaneously honored the words of the target/victim, both through varied "Voices" and through the words of the scholars and their research populations. As we close, we highlight four key themes that emerged across the chapters.

First, this volume spotlights the implicitly communicative nature of bullying and underscores the importance of Communication scholarship for improved understanding of this complex, multifaceted societal problem. Throughout this collection of theoretical, empirical, and practical contributions, authors aimed to unpack the enactment of and responses to bullying as inherently communicative and relationally consequential.

Second, researchers who study bullying produce this work to be used. Chapters in this volume include theoretical discussions as well as application-based reflections. Four pieces share a "Voice from the Margins," ensuring that the issues resonate with our readers in concrete ways. Moreover, as the first comprehensive collection of Communication research focusing on bullying, we recognized our responsibility in delivering a thorough treatment of the subject for various stakeholders. We hope that, among the takeaways, individuals who work day-to-day trying to understand and modify the climate of bullying will find something of value in this anthology. Our contributors embraced

Epilogue: Looking Forward

myriad ways to investigate bullying as they offered both theoretical and pragmatic implications of their conclusions.

If practitioners apply even one conclusion from the exemplary scholarship contained in this volume, we will feel that we have accomplished the goal of making a difference through our research (Carragee & Frey, 2016; Kahl, 2010). Indeed, Communication researchers who examine bullying generate research that matters by striving to right social injustice (see related work by Frey & Carragee, 2016). As we reflect on the contributions to this volume, we recognize the underlying imperative that resonates across chapters: Educate. Equip. Empower. We hope that this work educates relevant constituencies, equipping them with meaningful information and perspectives and, ultimately, enabling them to empower themselves through experience, witness, and action.

To do so, we stress that, third, all participants implicitly frame the bullying incident through their responses or lack thereof. Obviously, bullies communicate a particular orientation toward the objects of their bullying. However, both shouting and silence (and the range in between) constitute communicative actions. Administrators who dismiss complaints . . . classmates who walk by without intervening . . . bullied individuals who accept attacks without responding in their own defense . . . All wordlessly communicate volumes, and those (in)actions reflexively define what has happened and frame what awaits.

A fourth theme related to the volume's chapters reveals the global nature of bullying. This anthology affirms the need for scholars across the international community to tackle the subject of bullying with commitment and passion. This anthology provides an international perspective—both via authorship and through content. Yet, we recognize that much more can and should be done. Communication scholars in the U.S., for example, should find scholarly soulmates around the world who share interests in the investigation of bullies, bullying, and relevant communication processes. Few efforts have more potential to shift the conversation to more productive levels than global scholarly partners dedicated to investigating a crisis that has no geographical boundaries.

In closing, the *Routledge Handbook of Communication and Bullying* highlights some of the important work on bullying that has been produced by Communication scholars--thus far. Much remains to be done in terms of getting this compendium, for instance, into the hands of those who could broaden its impact and application through education and policy. In that spirit, we urge researchers from all academic backgrounds to continue their study of bullying. Concurrently, we encourage practitioners and policymakers to employ Communication research as they work to develop interventions and resources, resulting in safer, inclusive, and more accepting environments.

REFERENCES

Abada, T., Hou, F., & Ram, B. (2008). The effects of harassment and victimization on self-rated health and mental health among Canadian adolescents. *Social Science & Medicine, 67*, 557–567. doi:10.1016/j.socscimed.2008.0 4.006Aboujaoude, E., Savage, M. W., Starcevic, V., & Salame, W. O. (2015). Cyberbullying: Review of an old problem gone viral. *Journal of Adolescent Health, 57*, 10–18. doi:10.1016/j.jadohealth.2015.04.011

Abbas, M. A., Fiala, L. A., Abdel Rahman, A. G., & Fahim, A. E. (2010). Epidemiology of workplace violence against nursing staff in Ismailia Governorate, Egypt. *Journal of the Egyptian Public Health Association, 85*(1–2), 29–43.

AbuAlRub, R. F., Khalifa, M. F., & Habbib, M. B. (2007). Workplace violence among Iraqi hospital nurses. *Journal of Nursing Scholarship, 39*(3), 281–288. doi:10.1111/j.1547- 5069.2007.00181.x

Acker, J. (1990). Hierarchies, jobs, bodies: A theory of gendered organizations. *Gender & Society, 4*(2), 139–158. doi:10.1177/089124390004002002

Adams, F. D., & Lawrence, G. J. (2011). Bullying victims: The effects last into college. *American Secondary Education, 40*, 4–13. Retrieved from www.jstor.org/stable/23100410

Adams, T. E. (2011). *Narrating the closet: An autoethnography on same-sex attraction.* New York, NY: Routledge.

Ad Council. (2008a, December 3). *Talent show—Cyberbullying prevention commercial* [Video file]. Retrieved from www.youtube.com/watch?v=bdQBurXQOeQ

Ad Council. (2008b, December 3). *Kitchen—Cyberbullying prevention commercial* [Video file]. Retrieved from www.youtube.com/watch?v=NbtajOvAU10

Adler, P. A., & Adler, P. (1995). Dynamics of inclusion and exclusion in preadolescent cliques. *Social Psychology Quarterly, 58*(3), 145–162.

Agatston, P. W., Kowalski, R., & Limber, S. (2007). Students' perspectives on cyber bullying. *Journal of Adolescent Health, 41*, S59–S60. doi:10.1016/j.jadohealth.2007.09.003

Akkermans, J., Brenninkmeijer, V., Schaufeli, W., & Blonk, R. (2015). It's all about CareerSKILLS: Effectiveness of a career development intervention for young employees. *Human Resource Management, 54*, 533–551. doi:10.1002/hrm.21633

Alameddine, M., Kazzi, A., El-Jardali, F., Dimassi, H., & Maalouf, S. (2011). Occupational violence at Lebanese emergency departments: Prevalence, characteristics and associated factors. *Journal of Occupational Health, 53*(6), 455–464. doi:10.1539/joh.11–0102-OA

Albrecht, T. L., Burleson, B. R., & Goldsmith, D. J. (1994). Supportive communication. In M. L. Knapp & G. R. Miller (Eds.), *Handbook of interpersonal communication* (2nd ed., pp. 419–449). Thousand Oaks, CA: Sage.

Albrecht, T. & Goldsmith, D. J. (2003). Social support, social networks, and health. In T. Thompson, A. Dorsey, K. Miller, & R. Parrott (Eds.), *Handbook of health communication* (pp. 263–284). Mahwah, NJ: Lawrence Erlbaum Associates.

Alderman, G. L., & Green, S. K. (2011). Social power and effective classroom management. *Intervention in School and Clinic, 47*, 39–44. doi:10.1177/1053451211406543

Ali, R. (2010). *Federal law on bullying.* Office of Civil Rights, U.S. Department of Education. Retrieved from www.wcpss.net/cms/lib/NC01911451/Centricity/Domain/46/BullyingPrevention-FederalLaw.pdf

References

Allen, B. J. (1996). Feminist standpoint theory: A black woman's (re)view of organizational socialization. *Communication Studies, 47*, 257–271. doi:10.1080/10510979609368482

Allen, B. J. (2009). Racial harassment in the workplace. Lutgen-Sandvik, P., Namie, P., & Namie, R. (2009). In P. Lutgen-Sandvik and B. D. Sypher (Eds.), *Destructive organizational communication: Processes, consequences, and constructive ways of organizing* (pp. 164–183). New York: Routledge.

Allen, B. J. (2000). "Learning the ropes": A Black feminist standpoint analysis. In P. M. Buzzanell (Ed.), *Rethinking organizational and managerial communication from feminist perspectives* (pp. 177–208). Thousand Oaks, CA: Sage.

Allen, B. J. (2011). *Difference matters: Communicating social identity* (2nd ed.). Long Grove, IL: Waveland Press.

Allen, B. J. (2017, July). Engaging difference matters: Critical perspectives and practices. Keynote remarks presented at the annual meeting of the Aspen Conference on Engaged Scholarship, Aspen, CO.

Allen, B. J., Orbe, M., & Olivas, M. (1999). The complexity of our tears: Dis/enchantment and (in)difference in the academy. *Communication Theory, 9*, 402–429. doi:10.1111/j.1468- 2885.1999.tb00206.x

Allen, K. P. (2012). Off the radar and ubiquitous: Text messaging and its relationship to "drama" and cyberbullying in an affluent, academically rigorous US high school. *Journal of Youth Studies, 15*, 99–117. doi:10.1080/13676261.2011.630994

Alsaker, F. D. (1993). Isolement et maltraitance par les pairs dans les jardins d'enfants: Comment mesurer ces phénomènes et quelles sont leurs conséquences? [Isolation and bullying in kindergarten: How can these phenomena be measured and what are their consequences?]. *Enfance, 47*(3), 241–260. doi:10.3406/enfan.1993.2060

Alswaid, E. (2014). Workplace bullying among nurses in Saudi Arabia: An exploratory qualitative study. Published Master's Thesis. Retrieved from http://mro.massey.ac.nz/bitstream/handle/10179/5701/02_whole.pdf?sequence=2&isAllw ed=y

Alvarez, A. R. G. (2012). "IH8U": Confronting cyberbullying and exploring the use of cybertools in teen dating relationships. *Journal of Clinical Psychology, 68*(11), 1205–1215. doi:10.1002/jclp.21920

Alzheimer's Association. (2017). *Alzheimer's association releases dementia care practice recommendations for end of life care.* Retrieved from www.alz.org/national/documents/release_082807_dcrecommends.pdf

Americans with Disabilities Act of 2004, Title II, 28 C.F.R. Part 35 (2004).

Andreou, E. (2006). Social preference, perceived popularity and social intelligence: Relations to overt and relational aggression. *School Psychology International, 27*(3), 339–351. doi:10.1177/0143034306067286

Appiah, K. A. (2006). *Cosmopolitanism: Ethics in a world of strangers.* New York, NY: Norton.

Armstrong, P. (2011). Budgetary bullying. *Critical Perspectives on Accounting, 22*, 632–643. doi:10.1016/j.cpa.2011.01.011

Arnett, J. J. (1997). Young people's conceptions of the transition to adulthood. *Youth & Society, 29*, 3–23. doi:10.1177/0044118x97029001001

Arnett, R. C. (1987). The status of communication ethics scholarship in speech communication journals from 1915 to 1985. *Central States Speech Journal, 38*, 44–61.

Arnett, J. J. (2000). Emerging adulthood: A theory of development from the late teens through the twenties. *American Psychologist, 55*, 469–480. doi:10.1037//0003–066X.55.5.469

Arnett, J. J. (2007). Emerging adulthood: What is it, and what is it good for? *Child Development Perspectives, 1*, 68–73. doi:10.1111/j.1750–8606.2007.00016.x

Arnett, J. J. (2015). *Emerging adulthood: The winding road from the late teens through the twenties* (2nd ed.). New York, NY: Oxford University Press.

Arnett, R. C. (1981). Toward a phenomenological dialogue. *Western Journal of Speech Communication, 45*, 201–212. doi:10.1080/10570318109374043

Arnett, R. C. (2011). Situating a dialogic ethics: A dialogic confession. In G. Cheney, S. May, & D. Mushi (Eds.), *The handbook of communication ethics* (pp. 45–63). New York, NY: Routledge.

Arnett, R. C., Fritz, J. M. H., & Bell, L. M. (2009). *Communication ethics literacy: Dialogue and difference.* Thousand Oaks, CA: Sage.

Arntfield, M. (2015). Toward a cybervictimology: Cyberbullying, routine activities theory, and the anti-sociality of social media. *Canadian Journal of Communication, 40*, 371–388. doi:10.22230/cjc.2015v40n3a2863

Arroyo, A., Nevárez, N., Segrin, C., & Harwood, J. (2012). The association between parent and adult child shyness, social skills, and perceived family communication. *Journal of Family Communication, 12*, 249–264. doi:10.1080/15267431.2012.686941

Austin, E. (1993). Exploring the effects of active parental mediation of television content, *Journal of Broadcasting and Electronic Media, 37*, 147–158. doi:10.1080/08838159309364212

Austin, E., Bolls, P., Fujioka, Y. & Engelbertson, J. (1999). How and why parents take on the tube. *Journal of Broadcasting and Electronic Media, 43*, 175–192. doi:10.1080/08838159909364483

References

Avery, J. B., Wernsing, T. S., & Luthans, F. (2008). Can positive employees help positive organizational change? Impact of psychological capital and emotions on relevant attitudes and behaviors. *The Journal of Applied Behavioral Science, 44*, 48–70. doi:10.1177/0021886307311470

Avolio, B. J., & Bass, B. M. (2004). *Multifactor leadership questionnaire: Manual and sampler set* (3rd ed.). Redwood City, CA: Mind Garden.

Azeredo, C. M., Rinaldi, A. E. M., de Moraes, C. L., Levy, R. B., & Menezes, P. R. (2015). School bullying: A systematic review of contextual-level risk factors in observational studies. *Aggression and Violent Behavior, 22*, 65–76. doi:10.1016/j.avb.2015.04.006

Babrow, A. S. (1992). Communication and problematic integration: Understanding diverging probability and value, ambiguity, ambivalence, and impossibility. *Communication Theory, 2*, 95–130. doi:10.1111/j.1468–2885.1992. tb00031.x

Baillien, E., Bollen, K., Euwema, M., & De Witte, H. (2014). Conflict and conflict management styles as precursors of workplace bullying: A two-way longitudinal study. *European Journal of Work and Organizational Psychology, 23*, 511–524. doi:10:1080/1359432X.2012.752899

Baillien, E., Escartin, J., Gross, C., & Zapf, D. (2017). Towards a conceptual and empirical differentiation between workplace bullying and interpersonal conflicts. *European Journal of Work and Organizational Psychology, 26*, 870–881. doi:10/1080/1359432X.2017.1385601

Balducci, C., Cecchin, M., & Fraccaroli, F. (2012). The impact of role stressors on workplace bullying in both targets and perpetrators, controlling for personal vulnerability factors: A longitudinal analysis. *Work & Stress, 26*, 195–212. doi:10.1080/02678373.2012.714543

Bandura, A. (1973). *Aggression: A social learning analysis*. Englewood Cliffs, NJ: Prentice Hall.

Bandura, A., & Walters, R. (1963). *Social learning and personality development*. New York, NY: Holt, Rinehart, & Winston.

Barber, S. J. (2017). An examination of age-based stereotype threat about cognitive decline. *Perspectives on Psychological Science, 12*(1), 62–90. doi:10.1177/1745691616656345

Barbera, E. F. (2016). Bullying assessment strategies and interventions. In R. P. Bonifas (Ed.), *Bullying among older adults: How to recognize and address an unseen epidemic.* (Chapter 7). Baltimore, MD: Health Professionals Press, Inc.

Barlett, C. P., & Gentile, D. A. (2012). Attacking others online: The formation of cyberbullying in late adolescence. *Psychology of Popular Media Culture, 1*(2), 123–135. doi:10.1037/a0028113

Barlett, C. P., Gentile, D. A., & Chew, C. (2016). Predicting cyberbullying from anonymity. *Psychology of Popular Media Culture, 5*(2), 171–180. doi:10.1037/ppm0000055

Barnes, L. L. B., Agago, M. O., & Coombs, W. T. (1998). Effects of job-related stress on faculty intention to leave academia. *Research in Higher Education, 39*, 457–469. doi:10.1023/A:1018741404199

Barnhart, M., & Peñaloza, L. (2012). Who are you calling old? Negotiating old age identity in the elderly consumption ensemble. *Journal of Consumer Research, 39*(6), 1133–1153. doi:10.1086/668536

Bauman, S. (2013). Why it matters. In S. Bauman, D. Cross, & J. Walker (Eds.), *Principles of cyberbullying research: Definitions, measures, and methodology* (pp. 23–25). New York, NY: Routledge.

Bauman, S., Toomey, R. B., & Walker, J. L. (2013). Associations among bullying, cyberbullying, and suicide in high school students. *Journal of Adolescence, 36*(2), 341–350. doi:10.1016/j.adolescence.2012.12.001

Bauman, S., Underwood, M. K., & Card, N. A. (2013). Definitions: Another perspective and a proposal for beginning with cyberaggression. In S. Bauman, D. Cross, & J. Walker (Eds.), *Principles of cyberbullying research: Definitions, measures, and methodology* (pp. 41–46). New York, NY: Routledge.

Bayer, C. L., & Cegala, D. J. (1992). Trait verbal aggressiveness and argumentativeness: Relations with parenting style. *Western Journal of Communication, 56*, 301–310. doi:10.1080/10570319209374418

Bazelon, T. (2014, January 15). The online avengers. *The New York Times.*

Beatty, M. J., Pascual-Ferra, P., & Levine, T. R. (2015). Two studies examining the error theory underlying the measurement model of the Verbal Aggressiveness Scale. *Human Communication Research, 11*, 55–81. doi:10.1111/hcre.12039

Bell, B. S., & Kozlowski, S. W. J. (2007). A typology of virtual teams: Implications for effective leadership. *Group & Organization Management, 27*, 14–48. doi:10.1177/1059601102027001003

Belsey, B. (2005). Cyberbullying: An emerging threat to the "always on" generation. Retrieved from www.cyber bullying.ca/pdf/Cyberbullying_Article_by_ Bill_Belsey.pdf

Benson, J. (n.d.). *Relational aggression and subjective well-being in independent senior living communities.* Retrieved from www.matherlifewaysinstituteonaging.com/wpcontent/uploads/2012/03/Relational-Aggression.pdf

Bentley, T. A., Catley, B., Cooper-Thomas, H., Gardner, D., O'Driscoll, M. P., Dale, A., & Trenberth, L. (2012). Perceptions of workplace bullying in the New Zealand travel industry: Prevalence and management strategies. *Tourism Management, 33*(2), 351–360. doi:10.1016/j.tourman.2011.04.004

Berdahl, J. L. (2007). Harassment based on sex: Protecting social status in the context of gender hierarchy. *Academy of Management Review, 32*(2), 641–658. doi:10.5465/amr.2007.24351879

References

Berger, R. (2017). Aging in America: Ageism and general attitudes toward growing old and the elderly. *Open Journal of Social Sciences, 05*(08), 183–198. doi:10.4236/jss.2017.58015

Bergeron, R., & Gray, B. (2003). Ethical dilemmas of reporting suspected elder abuse. *Social Work, 48(1)*, 96–104. doi:10.1093/sw/48.1.96

Berkowitz, L. (1962). *Aggression: A social psychological analysis.* New York, NY: McGraw-Hill.

Bernardo, R. (2016, August 16). *2016's states with the biggest bullying problems.* Retrieved from https://wallethub.com/edu/best-worst-states-at-controlling-bullying/9920/#main-findingsBerry, K. (2013). Spinning autoethnographic reflexivity, cultural critique, and negotiating selves. In T. E. Adams, S. Holman Jones, & C. Ellis (Eds.), *The handbook of autoethnography* (pp. 209–227). Walnut Creek, CA: Left Coast Press.

Berry, K. (2016). *Bullied: Tales of torment, identity, and youth.* New York, NY: Routledge.

Berry, K., & Adams, T. E. (2016). Family bullies. *Journal of Family Communication, 16*(1), 51–63. doi:10.1080152 67431.2015.1111217

Bhopal, K., & Preston, J. (Eds.). (2012). *Intersectionality and "race" in education.* New York, NY: Routledge.

Bigelow, B. J., Tesson, G., & Lewko, J. H. (1992). The social rules that children use: Close friends, other friends, and "other kids" compared to parents, teachers, and siblings. *International Journal of Behavioral Development, 15*, 315–335. doi:10.1177/016502549201500303

Bishop, V., & Hoel, H. (2008). The customer is always right? Exploring the concept of customer bullying in the British Employment Service. *Journal of Consumer Culture, 8*(3), 341–367. doi:10.1177/1469540508095303

Bitsch Hansen, T., Steenberg, L. M., Palic, S., & Elklit, A. (2012). A review of psychological factors related to bullying victimization in schools. *Aggression and Violent Behavior, 17*, 383–387. doi:10.1016/j.avb.2012. 03.008

Bittman, M., Rutherford, L., Brown, J., & Unsworth, L. (2012). *Digital natives? New and old media and children's language acquisition.* Retrieved August 19, 2014, from www.aifs.gov.au/institute/pubs/fm2012/fm91/fm91b. html

Blair, C. A., Foster Thompson, L., & Wuensch, K. L. (2005). Electronic helping behavior: The virtual presence of others makes a difference. *Basic and Applied Social Psychology, 27*, 171–178. doi:10.1207/s15324834basp2702_8

Blank, S. (2012). *The startup owner's manual: The step-by-step guide for building a great company.* New York, NY: BookBaby.

Blumer, H. (1969). *Symbolic interactionism: Perspective and method.* Englewood Cliffs, NJ: Prentice Hall.

Bodie, G. D., & Burleson, B. R. (2008). Explaining variations in the effects of supportive messages: A dual-process framework. In C. S. Beck (Ed.), *Communication yearbook 32* (pp. 355–398). New York, NY: Routledge.

Bonifas, R. P. (2016). *Bullying among older adults: How to recognize and address an unseen epidemic.* Baltimore, MD: Health Professionals Press, Inc.

Bonnet, M., Goossens, F. A., & Schuengel, C. (2011). Parental strategies and trajectories of peer victimization in 4 to 5 year-olds. *Journal of School Psychology, 49*, 385–398. doi:10.1016/j.jsp.2011.04.002

Booth-Butterfield, M., & Sidelinger, R. J. (1997). The relationship between parental traits and open family communication: Affective orientation and verbal aggression. *Communication Research Reports, 14*, 408–417. doi:10.1080/08824099709388684

Bosacki, S. L., Marini, Z. A., & Dane, A. V. (2006). Voices from the classroom: Pictorial and narrative representations of children's bullying experiences. *Journal of Moral Education, 35*, 231–254. doi:10.1080/03057240600 681769

Boudewyns, V., Turner, M. M., & Paquin, R. S. (2013). Shame-free guilt appeals: Testing the emotional and cognitive effects of shame and guilt appeals. *Psychology & Marketing, 30*(9), 811–825. doi:10.1002/mar.20647

Bowes, L., Wolke, D., Joinson, C., Lereya, S. T., & Lewis, G. (2014). Sibling bullying and risk of depression, anxiety, and self-harm: A prospective cohort study. *Pediatrics, 134*, e1032–e1039. doi:10.1542/peds.2014–0832

Bowes-Sperry, L., & O'Leary-Kelly, A. M. (2005). To act or not to act: The dilemma faced by sexual harassment observers. *Academy of Management Review, 30(2)*, 288–306. doi:10.5465/AMR.2005.16387886

boyd, D. (2014). *it's complicated- the social lives of networked teens.* New Haven, CT: Yale University Press.

Boyles, S. (2015). What motivates kids who are bullies. *WebMD.* Retrieved from www.webmd.com/parenting/news/20100325/what-motivates-kids-who-are-bullies#1

Boylorn, R. M., & Orbe, M. (Eds.). (2014). *Critical autoethnography: Intersecting cultural identities in everyday life.* Walnut Creek, CA: Left Coast Press.

Bradley, E., Curry, L., & Devers, K. (2007). Qualitative data analysis for health services research. *Health Services Research, 42*(4), 1758–1772. doi:10.1111/j.1475–6773.2006.00684.x

Brandl, B., & Raymond, J. (2012). Policy implications of recognizing that caregiver stress is not the primary cause of elder abuse. *Generations, 36*(3), 32–39. Retrieved from www.ingentaconnect.com/content/asag/gen/2012/00000036/00000003/art00009

References

Brandtzæg, P. B. (2010). Towards a unified Media-User Typology (MUT): A meta-analysis and review of the research literature on media-user typologies. *Computers in Human Behavior, 26*(5), 940–956. doi:10.1016/j.chb.2010.02.008

Brashers, D. E., Neidig, J. L., & Goldsmith, D. J. (2004). Social support and the management of uncertainty for people living with HIV or AIDS. *Health Communication, 16*, 305–331. doi:10.1207/S15327027HC1603_3

Braun, V., & Clarke, V. (2006). Using thematic analysis in psychology. *Qualitative Research in Psychology, 3*(2), 77–101. doi:10.1191/1478088706qp063oa

Brock, C. H., Oikonomidoy, E. M., Wulfing, K., Pennington, J. L., & Obenchain, K. M. (2014). "Mean girls" go to college: Exploring female—female relational bullying in an undergraduate literacy methods course. *Peace and Conflict: Journal of Peace Psychology, 20*(4), 516. Retrieved from http://psycnet.apa.org/buy/2014-33462-001

Brody, N., & Peña, J. (2015). Equity, relational maintenance, and linguistic features of text messaging. *Computers in Human Behavior, 49*, 499–506. doi:10.1016/j.chb.2015.03.037

Brody, N., & Vangelisti, A. L. (2016). Bystander intervention in cyberbullying. *Communication Monographs, 83*, 94–119. doi:10.1080/03637751.2015.1044256

Brody, N., & Vangelisti, A. L. (2017). Cyberbullying: Topics, strategies, and sex differences. *Computers in Human Behavior, 75*, 739–748. doi:10.1016/j.chb.2017.06.020

Bronfenbrenner, U. (1979). *The ecology of human development: Experiments by nature and design.* Cambridge, MA: Harvard University Press.

Bronfenbrenner, U. (1986). Recent advances in research on the ecology of human development. In R. K. Silbereisen, K. Eyferth, & G. Rudinger (Eds.), *Development as action in context: Problem behavior and normal youth development* (pp. 287–309). New York, NY: Springer-Verlag.

Brubacher, J. S., & Rudy, W. (1997). *Higher education in transition: A history of American colleges and universities* (4th ed.). New Brunswick, NJ: Transaction.

Bryn, S. (2011). Stop bullying now! A federal campaign for bullying prevention and intervention. *Journal of School Violence, 10*(2), 213–219. doi:10.1080/15388220.2011.557313

Budescu, D. V. (1993). Dominance analysis: A new approach to the problem of relative importance of predictors in multiple regression. *Psychological Bulletin, 114*, 542–551. doi:10.1037/0033–2909.114.3.542

Buhs, E. S., & Ladd, G. W. (2001). Peer rejection as an antecedent of young children's school adjustment: An examination of mediating processes. *Developmental Psychology, 37*, 550–560. doi:10.1037//0012–1649.37.4.550

Bullying Canada. (2017). *What is bullying.* Retrieved from www.bullyingcanada.ca/what-is-bullying

Burke, P. J. (1991). Identity processes and social stress. *American Sociological Review, 56*(6), 836–849. doi:10.2307/2096259

Burke, P. J. (2007). Identity control theory. In *The Blackwell Encyclopedia of Sociology* (pp. 2202–2207). doi:10.1002/9781405165518.wbeosi002

Burleson, B. R. (2003). Emotional support skills. In J. O. Greene & B. R. Burleson (Eds.), *Handbook of communication and social interaction skills* (pp. 551–594). Mahwah, NJ: Erlbaum.

Burleson, B. R., & Goldsmith, D. J. (1998). How the comforting process works: Alleviating emotional distress through conversationally inducted reappraisals. In P. A. Anderson & L. K. Guerrero (Eds.), *Handbook of communication and emotion: Research, theory, applications, and contexts.* (pp. 245–280). San Diego, CA: Academic Press.

Burleson, B. R., Kunkel, A. W., Samter, W., & Working, K. J. (1996). Men's and women's evaluations of communication skills in personal relationships: When sex differences make a difference—and when they don't. *Journal of Social and Personal Relationships, 13*, 201–224. doi:10.1177/0265407596132003

Burleson, B. R., & MacGeorge, E. L. (2002). Supportive communication. In M. L. Knapp & J. A. Daly (Eds.), *Handbook of interpersonal communication* (3rd ed., pp. 374–424). Thousand Oaks, CA: Sage.

Burr, V. (2003). *Social constructionism* (2nd ed.). London: Routledge.

Burton, K. A., Florell, D., & Wygant, D. B. (2013). The role of peer attachment and normative beliefs about aggression on traditional bullying and cyberbullying. *Psychology in the Schools, 50*, 103–115. doi:10.1002/pits.21663

Butler, J. (1994). Contingent foundations for a careful reading. In S. Benhabib, J. Butler, D. Cornell, & N. Fraser (Eds.), *Feminist contentions: A philosophical exchange* (pp. 35–57, 127–143). New York, NY: Routledge.

Butler, R. N. (1989). Dispelling ageism: The cross-cutting intervention. *The ANNALS of the American Academy of Political and Social Science, 503*(1), 138–147. doi:10.1177/0002716289503001011

Buzzanell, P. M. (1994). Gaining a voice: Feminist organizational communication theorizing. *Management Communication Quarterly, 7*, 339–383. doi:10.1177/0893318994007004001

Buzzanell, P. M. (2010). Resilience: Talking, resisting, and imagining new normalcies into being. *Journal of Communication, 60*, 1–14. doi:10.1111/j.1460–2466.2010.01469.x

Buzzanell P. M., & Lucas K. (2013). Constrained and constructed choices in career: An examination of communication pathways to dignity. *Annals of the International Communication Association, 37*, 3–31, doi:10.1080/23808985.2013.11679144

References

Buzzanell, P. M., Shenoy, S., Remke, R., & Lucas, K. (2009). Creating resilience to foster human dignity and hope. In P. Lutgen-Sandvik & B. Davenport Sypher (Eds.), *Destructive organizational communication: Processes, consequences, and constructive ways of organizing.* (pp. 291–315). New York, NY: Routledge.

Bybee, C., Robinson, D. & Turow, J. (1982). Determinants of parental guidance of children's television viewing for a special subgroup: Mass media scholars. *Journal of Broadcasting, 26*, 697–710. doi:10.1080/08838158209364038

Caiola, C., Docherty, S., Relf, M., & Barroso, J. (2014). Using an intersectional approach to study the impact of social determinants of health for African-American mothers living with HIV. *ANS: Advances in Nursing Science, 37*(4), 287–298. doi:10.1097/ANS.0000000000000046

Cameron, J. (2010). Focusing on the focus group. In I. Hay (Ed.), *Qualitative methods in human geography* (3rd ed., pp. 152–172). Oxford, UK: Oxford University Press.

Campbell, S. W., & Park, Y. J. (2008). Social implications of mobile telephony: The rise of personal communication society. *Sociology Compass, 2*, 371–387. doi:10.1111/j.1751–9020.2007.00080.x

Canadian Council on Social Development. (2000). *Immigrant youth in Canada.* Ottawa. Retrieved from www.ccsd.ca/subsites/cd/docs/iy/index.htm

Canadian Institute of Health Research. (2012). *Canadian bullying statistics.* Retrieved from www.cihr-irsc.gc.ca/e/45838.html

Caplan, S. E. (2003). Preference for online social interaction a theory of problematic Internet use and psychosocial well-being. *Communication Research, 30*, 625–648. doi:10.1177/0093650203257842

Card, N. A. (2013). Psychometric considerations for cyberbullying research. In S. Bauman, D. Cross, & J. Walker (Eds.), *Principles of cyberbullying research: Definitions, measures, and methodology* (pp. 188–201). New York, NY: Routledge.

Cardinal, K. P. (2015). *From social bullying in schools to bullying in senior housing: A new narrative & holistic approach to maintaining residents' dignity* (Unpublished Master's thesis). University of Massachusetts, Boston, MA.

Cardinal, K. P. (2016). Social wellness initiatives to reduce bullying among older adults. In R. P. Bonifas (Ed.), *Bullying among older adults: How to recognize and address an unseen epidemic* (Chapter 9). Baltimore, MD: Health Professionals Press, Inc.

Carney, G. M., & Gray, M. (2015). Unmasking the 'elderly mystique': Why it is time to make the personal political in ageing research. *Journal of Aging Studies, 35*, 123–134. doi:10.1016/j.jaging.2015.08.007

Carragee, K. M., & Frey, L. R. (2016). Communication activism research: Engaged communication scholarship for social justice. *International Journal of Communication, 10*, 3975–3999.

Carroll, T. L., & Lauzier, M. (2014). Workplace bullying and job satisfaction: The buffering effect of social support. *Universal Journal of Psychology, 2*(2), 22–39. doi:10.13189/ujp.2014.02020

Cassidy, W., Faucher, C., & Jackson, M. (2014). The dark side of the ivory tower: Cyberbullying of university faculty and teaching personnel. *Alberta Journal of Educational Research, 60*, 279–299. Retrieved from http://ajer.journalhosting.ucalgary.ca/index.php/ ajer/article/view/1250

Cataldi, E. F., Fahimi, M., Bradburn, E. M., & Zimbler, L. (2005). 2004 National study of postsecondary faculty (NSOPF: 04) report on faculty and instructional staff in Fall 2003. ED TAB. NCES 2005–172. US Department of Education.

Catanzaro, M. F. (2011). Indirect aggression, bullying and female teen victimization: A literature review. *Pastoral Care in Education, 29*, 83–101. doi:10.1080/02643944.2011.573495

Caughlin, J. P. (2010). A multiple goals theory of personal relationships: Conceptual integration and program overview. *Journal of Social and Personal Relationships, 27*, 824–848. doi:10.1177/0265407510373262

Cavezza, C., & McEwan, T. E. (2014). Cyberstalking versus off-line stalking in a forensic sample. *Psychology, Crime & Law, 20*, 955–970. doi:10.1080/1068316X.2014.893334

Celep, C., & Konakli, T. (2013). Mobbing experiences of instructors: Causes, results, and solution suggestions. *Educational Sciences: Theory and Practice, 13*(1), 193–199. Retrieved from www.estp.com.tr/

Centers for Disease Control. (n.d.). *Bullying statistics.* Retrieved from www.cdc.gov/features/prevent-bullying/index.html, para. 4.

Centers for Disease Control and Prevention. (2015). *Fact sheet: Understanding bullying.* Retrieved from www.cdc.gov/violenceprevention/pdf/bullying_factsheet.pdf

Centers for Disease Control and Prevention. (2016). *Prevent bullying.* Retrieved from www.cdc.gov/features/prevent-bullying/index.html

Centers for Disease Control and Prevention. (2017). *Elder abuse: Definitions.* Retrieved December 6, 2017, from www.cdc.gov/violenceprevention/elderabuse/definitions.html

Chapin, J., & Coleman, G. (2017). The cycle of cyberbullying: Some experience required. *Social Science Journal, 54*(3), 314–318. doi:10.1016/j.soscij.2017.03.004

**Charlotte-Mecklenburg County Schools. (2008a). *Policy Code: JICK bullying.* Retrieved from https://board policyonline.com/?b=charmeck&s=145183

References

**Charlotte-Mecklenburg County Schools. (2008b). *Regulation code JICK-R bullying prevention.* Retrieved from https://boardpolicyonline.com/?b=charmeck&s=145183

*Charlotte-Mecklenburg Schools. (2017a). *Bullying prevention.* Retrieved from www.cms.k12.nc.us/parents/Pages/BullyingPrevention.aspx

**Charlotte-Mecklenburg Schools. (2017b). *What we know about bullying.* Retrieved from www.cms.k12.nc.us/mediaroom/backtoschool/Documents/Bullying-Prevention%20Tips%20for%20Parents/Tips-What%20We%20Know%20About%20Bullyingpdf.pdf

Charmaz, K. (2000). Grounded theory: Objectivist and constructivist methods. In N. K. Denzin & Y. S. Lincoln (Eds.), *Handbook of qualitative research* (pp. 509–535). Thousand Oaks, CA: Sage.

Charmaz, K. (2003). Grounded theory: Objectivist and constructivist methods. In N. K. Denzin & Y. S. Lincoln (Eds.), *Strategies for qualitative inquiry* (2nd ed., pp. 249–291). Thousand Oaks, CA: Sage.

Charmaz, K. (2006). *Constructing grounded theory: A practical guide through qualitative research.* London, UK: Sage.

Chaudoir, S. R., & Fisher, J. D. (2010). The disclosure processes model: Understanding disclosure decision-making and post-disclosure outcomes among people living with a concealable stigmatized identity. *Psychological Bulletin, 136,* 236–256. doi:10.1037/a0018193

Chávez, L. R. (2008). *The Latino threat narrative: Constructing immigrants, citizens, and the nation.* Stanford, CA: Stanford University Press.

Chemers, M. (1997). *An integrative theory of leadership.* New York, NY: Lawrence Erlbaum.

Chen, L., Sung, Y., & Cheng, W. (2017). How to enhance teachers' bullying identification: A Comparison among providing a training program, a written definition, and a definition with a checklist of bullying characteristics. *Asia-Pacific Education Researcher, 26*(6), 351–359. doi:10.1007/s40299-017-0354-1

Cheney, G., Munshi, D., May, S., & Ortiz, E. (2011). Encountering communication ethics in the contemporary world: Principles, people, and contexts. In G. Cheney, S. May, & D. Mushi (Eds.), *The handbook of communication ethics* (pp. 1–11). New York, NY: Routledge.

Chesebro, J. (1969). A construct for assessing ethics in communication. *Central States Speech Journal, 20,* 104–114.

Cho, Y., & Yoo, J. (2017). Cyberbullying, internet and SNS usage types, and perceived social support: A comparison of different age groups. *Information, Communication & Society, 20*(10), 1464–1481. doi:10.1080/1369118X.2016.1228998

Christensen, L. T., Morsing, M., & Thyssen, O. (2011). The polyphony of corporate social responsibility: Deconstructing accountability and transparency in the context of identity and hypocrisy. In G. Cheney, S. May, & D. Mushi (Eds.), *The handbook of communication ethics* (pp. 457–474). New York, NY: Routledge.

Christians, C. G., & Traber, M. (Eds.). (1997). *Communication ethics and universal values.* Thousand Oaks, CA: Sage.

Ciavarella, M. A. (1968). The counselor as a participant in minimizing curricular Frustration. *Counselor Education and Supervision, 7*(2), 132–136. doi:10.1002/j.1556-6978.1968.tb02078.x

Cisneros, J. D. (2008). Contaminated communities: The metaphor of "immigrant as a pollutant" in media representations of immigration. *Rhetoric & Public Affairs, 11,* 569–602. doi:10.1353/rap.0.0068

Civil Rights Act of 1964, Public Law 88–352, 78 Stat. 241, (1964).

Clark, L. S. (2011). Parental mediation theory for the digital age. *Communication Theory, 21,* 323–343. doi:10.1111/j.1468-2885.2011.01391.x

Clark, R. A., & Delia, J. G. (1979). *Topoi* and rhetorical competence. *Quarterly Journal of Speech, 65,* 187–206. doi:10.1080/00335637909383470

Cleary, M., Walter, G., Andrew, S., & Jackson, D. (2013). Negative workplace behaviours at the University of Hard Knocks. *Contemporary Nurse: A Journal for the Australian Nursing Profession, 44,* 253–256. doi:10.5172/conu.2013.44.2.253

Cohen, G. L., & Sherman, D. K. (2014). The psychology of change: Self-affirmation and social psychological intervention. *Annual Review of Psychology, 65,* 333–371. doi:10.1146/annurev-psych-010213-115137

Cohen, S., Underwood, L. G., & Gottlieb, B. H. (2000). *Social support measurement and intervention: A guide for health and social scientists.* Oxford, UK: Oxford University Press.

Cohen, S., & Wills, T. A. (1985). Stress, social support, and the buffering hypothesis. *Psychological Bulletin, 98,* 310–357. doi:10.1037/0033-2909.98.2.310

Cohn, D., & Taylor, P. (2010). *Baby boomers approach 65—glumly.* Retrieved November 24, 2017, from www.pewsocialtrends.org/2010/12/20/baby-boomers-approach-65-glumly/

Collins, P. H., & Bilge, S. (2016). *Intersectionality.* Cambridge, UK: Polity Press.

Colwell, M. J., Mize, J., Pettit, G. S., & Laird, R. D. (2002). Contextual determinants of mothers' interventions in young children's peer interactions. *Developmental Psychology, 38,* 492–502. doi:10.1037/0012-1649.38.4.492

Cone, J. D. (1978). The behavioral assessment grid (BAG): A conceptual framework and a taxonomy. *Behavior Therapy, 9*(5), 882–888. doi:10.1016/S0005-7894(78)80020-3

References

Connell, N., El Sayed, S., Gonzalez, J., & Schell-Busey, N. (2015). The intersection of perceptions and experiences of bullying by race and ethnicity among middle school students in the United States. *Deviant Behavior, 36*(10), 807–822. doi:10.1080/01639625.2014.977159

The Conversation. (2017, August 7). What happened when we introduced four-year-olds to an old people's home. Retrieved December 6, 2017, from http://theconversation.com/what-happened-when-we-introduced-four-year-olds-to-an-old-peoples-home-82164

Conway, J. M. & Lance, C. E. (2010). What reviewers should expect from authors regarding common method bias in organizational research. *Journal of Business & Psychology, 25*, 325–334. doi:10.1007/s10869-010-9181-6

Cooperrider, D., & Godwin, L. (2012). Positive development: Innovation-inspired change in an economy and ecology of strengths. In K. Cameron & G. Spreitzer (Eds.), *The Oxford handbook of positive organizational scholarship* (pp. 737–750). Oxford, UK: Oxford University Press.

Cooper-Thomas, H., Gardner, D., O'Driscoll, M. P., Catley, B., Bentley, T., & Trenberth, L. (2013). Neutralizing workplace bullying: The buffering effects of contextual factors. *Journal of Managerial Psychology, 28*, 384–407. doi:10.1108/JMP-12-2012-0399

Cooren F., Taylor, J. R., & Van Every, E. J. (2006). Introduction. In F. Cooren, Jr. R. Taylor, & E. J. Van Emery (Eds.). *Communication as organizing*. (pp. 1–18). Mahwah, NJ: Lawrence Erlbaum.

Copeland, W. E., Wolke, D., Angold, A., & Costello, E. J. (2013). Adult psychiatric outcomes of bullying and being bullied by peers in childhood and adolescence psychiatric outcomes of bullying and being bullied. *JAMA Psychiatry*, 1–8. doi:10.1001/jamapsychiatry.2013.504

Corbin, J., & Strauss, A. (2008). *Basics of qualitative research: Techniques and procedures for developing grounded theory*. Thousand Oaks, CA: Sage Publications.

Corney, B. (2008). Aggression in the workplace: A study of horizontal violence utilising Heideggerian hermeneutic phenomenology. *Journal of Health Organisation and Management, 22*, 164–177. doi:10.1108/14777260810876321

Cose, E. J. (1993). *The rage of a privileged class: Why are middle-class Blacks angry? Why should America care?* New York, NY: HarperCollins.

Coulter, R. W., Herrick, A. L., Friedman, M. R., & Stall, R. D. (2016). Sexual-orientation differences in positive youth development: The mediational role of bullying victimization. *American Journal of Public Health, 106*(4), 691–697. doi:10.2105/AJPH.2015.303005

Cowan, R. L. (2009). "Rocking the Boat" and "Continuing to Fight": Un/Productive justice episodes and the problem of workplace bullying. *Human Communication, 12*(3), 283–302. doi:10.1.1.485.8997

Cowan, R. L. (2011). "Yes, we have an anti-bullying policy, but . . .": HR professionals' understandings and experiences with workplace bullying policy. *Communication Studies, 62*, 307–327. doi:10.1080/10510974.2011.553763

Cowan, R. L. (2012). It's complicated: Defining workplace bullying from the Human Resource professional's perspective. *Management Communication Quarterly, 26*, 377–403. doi:10.1177/0893318912439474

Cowan, R. L. (2013). "★★it rolls downhill" and other attributions for why adult bullying happens in organizations from the human resource professional's perspective. *Qualitative Research Reports in Communication, 1*, 97–104. doi:10.1080/17459435.2013.835347

Cowan, R. L. (Expected 2017). When workplace bullying and mobbing occur: The impact on organizations. In D. C. Yamada & M. Duffy (Eds.), *Workplace bullying and mobbing in the United States (two volume set)*. Westport, CT: Praeger.

Cowan, R. L., & Fox, S. (2015). Being pushed and pulled: A model of US HR Professionals' roles in bullying situations. *Personnel Review, 44*(1), 119–139. https://doi.org/10.1108/PR-11-2013-0210

Cowan, R. L., Salin, D., Bochantin, J. E., Apospori, E., D'Cruz, P., Işık, I., et al. (2015, August). *Human resource professionals perceptions of workplace bullying from around the globe: Culture matters*. Symposium accepted for presentation at the 2015 Academy of Management Convention, Vancouver, Canada.

Cowie, H. (2000). Bystanding or standing by: Gender issues in coping with bullying in English schools. *Aggressive Behavior, 26*, 85–97. doi:10.1002/(SICI)1098-2337(2000)26:1<85::AID-AB7>3.0.CO;2-5

Coyne, I., Chong, P. S. L., Seigne, E., & Randall, P. (2003). Self and peer nominations of bullying: An analysis of incident rates, individual differences, and perceptions of the working environment. *European Journal of Work and Organizational Psychology, 12*, 209–228. doi:10.1080/13594320344000101

Craig, W. M., & Pepler, D. J. (1997). Observations of bullying and victimization in the school yard. *Canadian Journal of School Psychology, 13*, 41–60. doi:10.1177/082957359801300205

Craig, W., Pepler, D., & Blais, J. (2007). Responding to bullying: What works? *School Psychology International, 28*, 465–477. doi:10.1177/0143034307084136

Cranmer, G. A., & Martin, M. M. (2015). An examination of aggression and adaption traits with moral foundation. *Communication Research Reports, 32*, 360–366. doi:10.1080/08824096.2015.1089848

References

Craven, R. G., Marsh, H. W., & Parada, R. H. (2013). Potent ways forward: New multidimensional theoretical structural models of cyberbullying, cyber tragetization, and bystander behaviors and their potential relations to traditional bullying constructs. In S. Bauman, D. Cross, & J. Walker (Eds.), *Principles of cyberbullying research: Definitions, measures, and methodology* (pp. 68–85). New York, NY: Routledge.

Crawford, N. (1997). Bullying at work: A psychoanalytic perspective. *Journal of Community and Applied Social Psychology, 7*, 219–225. doi:10.1002/(SICI)1099–1298(199706)7:3<219::AID-CASP420>3.0.CO;2-Q

Crawshaw, L. (2009). Workplace bullying? Mobbing? Harassment? Distraction by a thousand definitions. *Consulting Psychology Journal: Practice and Research, 61*(3), 263–267. doi:10.1037/a0016590

Creswell, J. W. (2003). *Research design: Qualitative, quantitative, and mixed methods approaches* (2nd ed.). Thousand Oaks, CA: Sage.

Creswell, J. W. (2007). *Qualitative inquiry and research design Choosing amoung five approaches*. Thousand Oaks, CA: Sage Publications.

Creswell, J. W. (2013). *Qualitative inquiry and research design: Choosing among five approaches* (3rd ed.). Thousand Oaks, CA: Sage.

**Cumberland County Schools. (2010a). *Policy code: 1710/4021/7230 prohibition against discrimination, harassment and bullying*. Retrieved from https://boardpolicyonline.com/bl/?b=cumberland&s=127715#&&hs=127713

**Cumberland County Schools. (2010b). *Policy code: 1720/4015/7225 discrimination, harassment and bullying complaint procedure*. Retrieved from https://boardpolicyonline.com/bl/?b=cumberland&s=127715#&&hs=127713

*Cumberland County Schools. (2017). *Cumberland County Schools anti-bullying task force*. Retrieved from http://counselors.ccs.k12.nc.us/cumberland-county-schools-anti-bullying-task-force/

Cupach, W. R., & Spitzberg, B. H. (1998). Obsessive relational intrusion and stalking. In B. H. Spitzberg & W. R. Cupach (Eds.), *The dark side of close relationships* (pp. 233–264). Mahwah, NJ: Lawrence Erlbaum.

Cutrona, C. E. (1990). Stress and social support-in search of optimal matching. *Journal of Social and Clinical Psychology, 9*(1), 3–14. doi:10.1521/jscp.1990.9.1.3

Cutrona, C. E., & Russell, D. W. (1990). Types of social support and specific stress: Toward a theory of optimal matching. In B. R. Sarason, I. G. Sarason, & G. R. Pierce (Eds.), *Social support: An interactional view* (pp. 319–366). New York, NY: Wiley.

Danielson, C. M., & Emmers-Sommer, T. M. (2016). "She stopped me from killing myself": Bullied bloggers' coping behaviors and support sources. *Health Communication*. doi:10.1080/10410236.2016.1196419

Danielson, C. M., & Jones, S. M. (in press). "Help, I'm getting bullied": Examining sequences of teacher support messages provided to bullied students. *Western Journal of Communication*.

Darlington, R. B., & Hayes, A. F. (2017). *Regression analysis and linear models: Concepts, applications, and implementation*. New York, NY: Guilford Press.

Datta, P., Cornell, D., & Huang, F. (2016). Aggressive attitudes and prevalence of bullying bystander behavior in middle school. *Psychology in the Schools, 53*(8), 804–816. doi:10.1002/pits.21944

David-Ferdon, C., & Hertz, M. F. (2009). *Electronic media and youth violence: A CDC issue brief for researchers*. Atlanta, GA: Centers for Disease Control.

Davidson, L. M., & Demaray, M. K. (2007). Social support as a moderator between victimization and internalizing-externalizing distress from bullying. *School Psychology Review, 36*, 383–405. Retrieved from https://search.proquest.com/openview/59ac0e33c4f11bb798be50e5d868d8bb/1?pq-origsite=gscholar&cbl=48217

Davies, B. (2011). Bullies as guardians of the moral order or an ethic of truths? *Children & Society, 25*(4), 278–286. doi:10.1111/j.1099–0860.2011.00380.x

Davies, G. (1996). The employment support network—An intervention to assist displaced workers. *Journal of Employment Counseling, 33*, 146–154. doi:10.1002/j.2161.1920.1996.tb00447.x

Davis, K., Randall, D. P., Ambrose, A., & Orand, M. (2015). "I was bullied too": Stories of bullying and coping in an online community. *Information, Communication & Society, 18*(4), 357–375. doi:10.1080/1369118X.2014.952657

D'Cruz, P., & Noronha, E. (2010). The exit coping response to workplace bullying: The contribution of inclusivist and exclusivist HRM strategies. *Employee Relations, 32*(2), 102–120. doi:10.1108/01425451011010078

D'Cruz, P., & Noronha, E. (2011). The limits to workplace friendship: Managerialist HRM and bystander behaviour in the context of workplace bullying. *Employee Relations, 33*(3), 269–288. doi:10.1108/01425451111121777

D'Cruz, P., & Noronha, E. (2012). Clarifying my world: Identity work in the context of workplace bullying. *The Qualitative Report, 17*(8), 1. Retrieved from http://nsuworks.nova.edu/tqr/vol17/iss8/2/

D'Cruz, P., & Noronha, E. (2014). The interface between technology and customer cyberbullying: Evidence from India. *Information and Organization, 24*, 176–193. doi:10.1016/j.infoandorg.2014.06.001

Deccan Herald. (2015, April 19). *Cyberbullying rampant in India, legal vacuum persists*. Retrieved from www.deccanherald.com/content/472554/cyber-bullying-rampant-india- legal.html

References

Deetz, S. A. (1992). *Democracy in an age of corporate colonization: Developments in communication and the politics of everyday life.* Albany, NY: State University of New York Press.

Degnen, C. (2007). Minding the gap: The construction of old age and oldness amongst peers. *Journal of Aging Studies, 21*(1), 69–80. doi:10.1016/j.jaging.2006.02.001

DeHue, F., Bolman, C., & Völlink, T. (2008). Cyberbullying: Youngsters' experiences and parental perception. *CyberPsychology & Behavior, 11*(2), 217–223. doi:10.1089/cpb.2007.0008

de Lange, A. H., Taris, T. W., Kompier, M. A. J., Houtman, I. L. D., & Bongers, P. M. (2003). "The very best of the Millennium": Longitudinal research and the demand-control-(support) model. *Journal of Occupational Health Psychology, 8*, 282–305. doi:10.1037/1076–8998.8.4.282

de Lara, E. W. (2016). *Bullying scars: The impact on adult life and relationships.* New York, NY: Oxford University Press.

de Lara, E. W., & Garabino, J. (2003). *An educator's guide to school-based interventions.* Boston, MA: Houghton Mifflin.

DelliFraine, J. L., McClelland, L. E., Erwin, C. O., & Wang, Z. (2014). Bullying in academia: Results of a survey of health administration faculty. *The Journal of Health Administration Education, 31*, 147–163. Retrieved from www.ingentaconnect.com/content/aupha/jhae/2014/00000031/00000002/art00005

De Luca, B. M., & Twale, D. J. (2010). Mediating in the academic bully culture: The Chair's responsibility to faculty and graduate students. *The Department Chair, 20*, 1–3. doi:10.1002/dch.20037

Dempsey, A. G., Sulkowski, M. L., Nichols, R., & Storch, E. A. (2009). Differences between peer victimization in cyber and physical settings and associated psychosocial adjustment in early adolescence. *Psychology in the Schools, 46*, 962–972. doi:10.1002/pits.20437

D'Enbeau, S., Buzzanell, P. M., & Duckworth, J. (2010). Problematizing classed identities in father-hood: Development of integrative case studies for analysis and praxis. *Qualitative Inquiry, 16*, 709–720. doi:10.1177/1077800410374183

de Jonge, J., Reuvers, M. M. E. N., Houtman, I. L. D., Bongers, P. M., & Kompier, M. A. J. (2000). Linear and non-linear relations between psychosocial job characteristics, subjective outcomes, and sickness absence: Baseline results from SMASM. *Journal of Occupational Health Psychology, 5*, 256–268. doi:10.1037/1076–8998.5.2.256

den Hamer, A., Konijn, E. A., & Keijer, M. G. (2014). Cyberbullying behavior and adolescents' use of media with antisocial content: A cyclic process model. *Cyberpsychology, Behavior, and Social Networking, 17*(2), 74–81. doi:10.1089/cyber.2012.0307

Dentith, A. M., Wright, R. R., & Coryell, J. (2015). Those mean girls and their friends: Bullying and mob rule in the academy. *Adult Learning, 26*(1), 28–34. doi:10.1177/1045159514558409

Denzin, N. K., & Lincoln, Y. S. (2017). Introduction: The discipline and practice of qualitative research. In N. K Denzin & Y. S. Lincoln (Eds.), *The SAGE handbook of qualitative research* (5th ed., pp. 1–35) Thousand Oaks, CA: SAGE.

DeSmet, A., Veldeman, C., Poels, K., Bastiaensens, S., Van Cleemput, K., Vandebosch, H., & De Bourdeaudhuij, I. (2014). Determinants of self-reported bystander behavior in cyberbullying incidents amongst adolescents. *Cyberpsychology, Behavior, and Social Networking, 17*(4), 207–215. doi:10.1089/cyber.2013.0027

Desrayaud, N. (2013a, November). *Measuring perceived and ideal conflict cultures in academe.* Paper presented at the 99th annual convention for the National Communication Association, Washington, DC. Retrieved from www.natcom.org

Desrayaud, N. (2013b). *This is how we fight: Developing a measure of perceived conflict cultures.* Doctoral dissertation. Retrieved from www.proquest.com/products-services/dissertations/Dissertations-Abstract-International.html

Detert, J. R., & Burris, E. R. (2007). Leadership behavior and employee voice: Is the door really open? *Academy of Management Journal, 50*, 869–884. doi:10.5465/AMJ.2007.26279183

DeTurk, S. (2011). Allies in action: The communicative experiences of people who challenge social injustice on behalf of others. *Communication Quarterly, 59*(5), 569–590. doi:10.1080/01463373.2011.614209

Devonish, D. (2013). Workplace bullying, employee performance and behaviors. *Employee Relations, 35*, 630–647. doi:10.1108/ER-01–2013–0004

de Wet, C. (2017). Educators' perceptions on bullying prevention strategies. *South African Journal of Educa-tion, 27*(2), 191–208. Retrieved from www.sajournalofeducation.co.za

Dijkstra, J. K., Lindenberg, S., & Veenstra, R. (2008). Beyond the class norm: Bullying behavior of popular ado-lescents and its relation to peer acceptance and rejection. *Journal of Abnormal Child Psychology, 36*, 1289–1299. doi:10.1007/s10802-008-9251-7

DiLalla, L. F. (2002). Behavior genetics of aggression in children: Review and future directions. *Developmental Review, 22*, 593–622. doi:10.1016/s0273–2297(02)00504-x

Dillard, J. P. (1990). A goal-driven model of interpersonal influence. In J. P. Dillard (Ed.), *Seeking compliance: The production of interpersonal influence messages* (pp. 41–56). Scottsdale, AZ: Gorsuch Scarisbrick.

References

Dillard, J. P., & Peck, E. (2000). Affect and persuasion: Emotional responses to public service announcements. *Communication Research, 27*(4), 461–495. doi:10.1177/009365000027004003

Dillard, J. P., Segrin, C., & Harden, J. M. (1989). Primary and secondary goals in the production of interpersonal influence messages. *Communication Monographs, 56*, 19–38. doi:10.1080/03637758909390247

Dillon, K. P., & Bushman, B. J. (2015). Unresponsive or un-noticed?: Cyberbystander intervention in an experimental cyberbullying context. *Computers in Human Behavior, 45*, 144–150. doi:10.1016/j.chb.2014.12.009

Djurkovic, N., McCormack, D., & Casimir, G. (2005). The behavioral reactions of victims to different types of workplace bullying. *International Journal of Organization Theory and Behavior, 8*, 439–460. doi:10.1108/IJOTB-08–04–2005-B001

Doane, A. N., Kelley, M. L., Chiang, E. S., & Padilla, M. A. (2013). Development of the Cyberbullying Experiences Survey. *Emerging Adulthood, 1*(3), 207–218. doi:10.1177/2167696813479584

Doane, A. N., Pearson, M. R., & Kelley, M. L. (2014). Predictors of cyberbullying perpetration among college students: An application of the Theory of Reasoned Action. *Computers in Human Behavior, 36* 154–162. doi:10.1016/j.chb.2014.03.051

Dobry, Y., Braquehais, M., & Sher, L. (2013). Bullying, psychiatric pathology and suicidal behavior. *International Journal of Adolescent Medical Health, 25*(3), 295–299. doi:10.1515/ijamh-2013–0065

Dollard, M. F., & Bakker, A. B. (2010). Psychosocial safety climate as a precursor to conducive work environments, psychological health problems, and employee engagement. *Journal of Occupational & Organizational Psychology, 83*, 579–599. doi:10.1348/096317909X470690

Dollard, M. F., & Idris, M. A. (2017). Climate congruence: How espoused psychosocial safety climate and enacted managerial support affect emotional exhaustion and work engagement. *Safety Science, 96*, 132–142. doi:10.1016/j.ssci.2017.03.023

Donoghue, C., Almeida, A., Brandwein, D., Rocha, G., & Callahan, I. (2014). Coping with verbal and social bullying in middle school. *The International Journal of Emotional Education, 6*, 40–53. Retrieved from https://search.proquest.com/openview/28135e038185a9af79a2c25c73899925/1?pq-origsite=gscholar&cbl=2031381

Dooley, J. J., Pyżalski, J., & Cross, D. (2009). Cyberbullying versus face-to-face bullying: A theoretical and conceptual review. *Journal of Psychology, 217*, 182–188. doi:10.1027/0044–3409.217.4.182 Duck, S., Foley, M. K., & Kirkpatrick, D. C. (2006). Uncovering the complex role behind the "difficult" coworker. In J. M. H. Fritz & B. L. Omdahl (Eds.), *Problematic relationships in the workplace* (pp. 3–19). New York, NY: Peter Lang.

Duffy, M., & Yamada, D. C. (Eds.) (2018). *Workplace bullying and mobbing in the United States.* Santa Barbara, CA: ABC-CLIO.

Duggan, M. (2014). *Online harassment.* Retrieved from www.pewinternet.org/2014/10/22/online-harassment/

Dussault, M., & Frenette, E. (2015). Supervisors' transformational leadership and bullying in the workplace. *Psychological Reports, 117*, 724–733. doi:10.2466/01.PRO.117c30z2

Dutton, J. (2003). *Energizing your workplace.* Ann Arbor, MI: University of Michigan Press.

Education Amendments of 1972, Title IX, 20 U.S.C. §§ 1681–1688; 34 C.F.R. § 106.1 et seq., 34 C.F.R. Parts 106.51–106.61 (1972).

Edwards, L., Kontostathis, A. E., & Fisher, C. (2016). Cyberbullying, race/ethnicity and mental health outcomes: A review of the literature. *Media & Communication, 4*(3), 71. doi:10.17645/mac.v4i3.525

Edwards, O. W., & Batlemento, P. (2016). Caregiver configurations and bullying among high school students. *Journal of Child and Family Studies, 25*(9), 2885–2893. doi:10.1007/s10826-016-0442-5

Efe, S. Y., & Ayaz, S. (2010). Mobbing against nurses in the workplace in Turkey. *International Nursing Review, 57*(3), 328–334. doi:10.1111/j.1466–7657.2010.00815.x

Einarsen, S. (1999). The nature and causes of bullying at work. *International Journal of Manpower, 20*, 16–27. doi:10.1108/01437729910268588

Einarsen, S. (2000). Harassment and bullying at work: A review of the Scandinavian approach. *Aggression and Violent Behavior, 5*, 379–401. doi:10.1016/S1359–1789(98)00043–3

Einarsen, S., Hoel, H., & Notelaers, G. (2009). Measuring exposure to bullying and harassment at work: Validity, factor structure and psychometric properties of the Negative Acts Questionnaire-Revised. *Work & Stress, 23*, 24–44. doi:10.1080/02678370902815673

Einarsen, S., Hoel, H., Zapf, D., & Cooper, C. L. (2003). The concept of bullying at work: The European tradition. In S. Einarsen, H. Hoel, D. Zapf, & C. L. Cooper (Eds.), *Bullying and emotional abuse in the workplace* (pp. 3–30). London: Taylor and Francis.

Einarsen, S., Hoel, H., Zapf, D., & Cooper, C. L. (Eds). (2011a). *Bullying and harassment in the workplace: Developments in theory, research and practice* (2nd ed.). Baton Rouge, FL.: Taylor & Francis Group.

Einarsen, S., Hoel, H., Zapf, D., & Cooper, C. L. (2011b). The concept of bullying and harassment at work: The European tradition. In S. Einarsen, H. Hoel, D. Zapf, & C. L. Cooper (Eds.), *Bullying and harassment in the workplace: Developments in theory, research, and practice* (2nd ed., pp. 3–39). Boca Raton, FL: CRC Press.

References

Einarsen, S., & Nielsen, M. K. (2015). Workplace bullying as an antecedent of mental health problems. *International Archives of Occupational and Environment Health, 88*(2), 131- 142. doi:10.1007/s00420-014-0944-7

Einarsen, S., Skogstad, A., Rorvik, E., Lande, A. B., & Nielsen, M. B. (2016). Climate for conflict management, exposure to workplace bullying and work engagement: A moderating mediation. *International Journal of Human Resource Management, 1, 1–22*. doi:10.1080/09585192.2016.1164216

Eisenberg, M. E., Gower, A. L., McMorris, B. J., & Bucchianeri, M. M. (2015). Vulnerable bullies: Perpetration of peer harassment among youths across sexual orientation, weight, and disability status. *American Journal of Public Health, 105*, 1784–1791. doi:10.2105/ajph.2015.302704

Ekşi, F., Dilmaç, B., Yaman, E., & Hamarta, E. (2015). The predictive relationships between the values of university employees, mobbing, and organizational commitment. *Turkish Journal of Business Ethics, 8*, 311–322. doi:10.12711/tjbe.2015.8.0007

Elledge, L., Cavell, T. A., Ogle, N. T., Malcolm, K. T., Newgent, R. A., & Faith, M. A. (2010). History of peer victimization and children's response to school bullying. *School Psychology Quarterly, 25*, 129–141. doi:10.1037/a0020313

Ellingson, L. L. (2009). *Engaging crystallization in qualitative research: An introduction*. Los Angeles, CA: SAGE.

Elu, J. U., & Loubert, L. (2013). Earnings inequality and the intersectionality of gender and ethnicity in Sub-Saharan Africa: The case of Tanzanian manufacturing. *American Economic Review, 103*(3), 289–92. doi:10.1257/aer.103.3.289

Engeström, Y. (1987). Learning by expanding: An activity theoretical approach to research. Helsinki, Finland: Orienta-Konsultit Oy.

Engeström, Y., Engeström, R., & Kärkkäinen, M. (1995). Polycontextuality and boundary crossing in expert cognition: Learning and problem solving in complex work activities. *Learning and Instruction, 5*, 319–336. doi:10.1016/0959–4752(95)00021–6

Engeström, Y., & Sannino, A. (2010). Studies of expansive learning: Foundations, findings and future challenges. *Education Research Review, 5*, 1–24.

Englander, E., Donnerstein, E., Kowalski, R., Lin, C. A., & Parti, K. (2017). Defining cyberbullying. *Pediatrics, 140* (S2): S148–S151. doi:10.1542/peds.2016–1758U

Enwefa, S. C., Enwefa, R. L., Dansby-Giles, G., & Giles, F. (2010). Terror in the academy: Breaking the cycle of silence on bullying, mobbing, and emotional abuse in the workplace. *NAAAS & Affiliates Conference Monographs*, 978–991. Retrieved from www.naaas.org/publications/monograph-series/

Erdur-Baker, O. (2010). Cyberbullying and its correlation to traditional bullying, gender and frequent and risky usage of internet-mediated communication tools. *New Media & Society, 12*(1), 109–125. doi:10.1177/1461444809341260

Erkutlu, H., & Chafra, J. (2014). Ethical leadership and workplace bullying in higher education. *Hacettepe University Journal of Education, 29*(3), 55–67. Retrieved from www.voced.edu.au/

Erzeel, S., & Mügge, L. (2016). Introduction: Intersectionality in European political science research. *Politics, 36*(4), 341–345. doi:10.1177/0263395716665331

Escartín, J., Ceja, L., Navarro, J., & Zapf, D. (2013). Modeling workplace bullying behaviors using catastrophe theory. *Nonlinear Dynamics, Psychology, and Life Sciences, 17*(4), 493–515. Retrieved from http://hdl.handle.net/2445/102671

Espelege, D. L., Holt, M. K., & Henkel, R. R. (2003). Examination of peer-group contextual effects on aggression during early adolescence. *Child Development, 74*, 205–220. doi:10.1111/1467–8624.00531

Espelage, D. L., Hong, J. S., Kim, D. H., & Nan, L. (2017). Empathy, attitude towards bullying, theory-of-mind, and non-physical forms of bully perpetration and victimization among U.S. Middle school students. *Child & Youth Care Forum*. doi:10.1007/s10566–017–9416-z

Espelage, D. L., Rao, M. A., & Craven, R. G. (2013). Theories of cyberbullying. In S. Bauman, D. Cross, & J. Walker (Eds.), *Principles of cyberbullying research: Definitions, measures, and methodology* (pp. 49–67). New York, NY: Routledge.

Eterovic-Soric, B., Ashman, H., Mubarak, S., & Choo, K. R. (2017). Stalking the stalkers—detecting and deterring stalking behaviours using technology: A review. *Computers & Security, 70*, 278–289. doi:10.1016/j.cose.2017.06.008

Evans, C. B. R., Cotter, K. L., & Smokowski, P. R. (2017). Giving victims of bullying a voice: A qualitative study of post bullying reactions and coping strategies. *Child and Adolescent Social Work Journal, 34*, 543–555. doi:10.1007/s10560-017-0492-6

Evans, C. R., & Smokowski, P. R. (2016). Theoretical explanations for bullying in school: How ecological processes propagate perpetration and victimization. *Child & Adolescent Social Work Journal, 33*(4), 365–375. doi:10.1007/s10560-015-0432-2

References

Evans, S. K., Pearce, K. E., Vitak, J., & Treem, J. W. (2017). Explicating affordances: A conceptual framework for understanding affordances in communication research. *Journal of Computer-Mediated Communication, 22*(1), 35–52. doi:10.1111/jcc4.12180

Faris, R., & Felmlee, D. (2014). Casualties of social combat: School networks of peer victimization and their consequences. *American Sociological Review, 79*, 228–257. doi:10.1177/0003122414524573

Farrington, D. P., & Ttofi, M. M. (2009). School-based programs to reduce bullying and victimization. *The Campbell Collaboration Crime and Justice Groups, 6*, 1–143. doi:10.1037/e528362010–001

Fast, J., Fanelli, F., & Salen, L. (2003). How becoming mediators affects aggressive students. *Children & Schools, 25*, 161–171. doi:10.1093/cs/25.3.161

Feaster, J. (2010). Expanding the impression management model of communication channels: An information control scale. *Journal of Computer-Mediated Communication, 16*(1), 115–138. doi:10.1111/j.1083–6101.2010.01535.x

Feaster, J. C. (2013). Great expectations: The association between media-afforded information control and desirable social outcomes. *Communication Quarterly, 61*(2), 172–194. doi:10.1080/01463373.2012.751434

Federal Bureau of Investigation. (2013, July 9). *Cyber bullying: A public service announcement* [Video file]. Retrieved from www.youtube.com/watch?v=WAEvLJqIG_0

Feeley, K. M. (2013). *Workplace bullying lawyers' guide: How to get more compensation for your client.* Los Angeles, CA: Strategic Book Publishing. Felix, E. D., & You, S. (2011). Peer victimization within the ethnic context of high school. *Journal of Community Psychology, 39*(7), 860–875. doi:10.1002/jcop.20465

Feller, S. (2014). The good, the bad, and the ugly: The co-construction of identities in dialog. *Language and Dialogue, 4*(3), 341–356. doi:10.1075/ld.4.3.01fel

Felson, R. B. (1983). Aggression and violence between siblings. *Social Psychology Quarterly, 46*, 271–285. doi:10.2307/3033715 Feng, B. (2009). Testing an integrated model of advice giving in supportive interactions. *Human Communication Research, 35*(1), 115–129. doi:10.1111/j.1468–2958.2008.01340.x

Feng, B. (2014). When should advice be given? Assessing the role of sequential placement of advice in supportive interactions in two cultures. *Communication Research, 41*(7), 913- 934. doi:10.1177/0093650212456203

Feng, B., & Burleson, B. R. (2006). Exploring the support seeking process across cultures: Toward an integrated analysis of similarities and differences. *International and Intercultural Communication Annual, 28*, 243–266.

Feng, B., & MacGeorge, E. L. (2006). Predicting receptiveness to advice: Characteristics of the problem, the advice-giver, and the recipient. *Southern Communication Journal, 71*(1), 67–85. doi:10.1080/10417940500503548

Feng, B., & MacGeorge, E. L. (2010). The influence of message and source evaluations on advice outcomes. *Communication Research, 37*, 553–575. https://doi.org/10.1177/0093650210368258

Ferris, G. R., Zinko, R., Brouer, R. L., Buckley, M. R., & Harvey, M. G. (2007). Strategic bullying as a supplementary, balanced perspective on destructive leadership. *Leadership Quarterly, 18*, 195–206. doi:10.1016/j.leaqua.2007.03.004

Festl, R., & Quandt, T. (2013). Social relations and cyberbullying: The influence of individual and structural attributes on victimization and perpetration via the internet. *Human Communication Research, 39*, 101–126. doi:10.1111/j.1468–2958.2012.01442.x

Festl, R., Scharkow, M., & Quandt, T. (2015). The individual or the group: A multilevel analysis of cyberbullying in school classes. *Human Communication Research, 41*, 535–556. doi:10.1111/hcre.12056

Field, A. (2009). *Discovering statistics using SPSS* (3rd ed.). Los Angeles, CA: Sage.

Finkelhor, D., Turner, H. A., Ormrod, R. K., & Hamby, S. L. (2010). Trends in childhood violence and abuse exposure: Evidence from two national surveys. *Archives of Pediatrics & Adolescent Medicine, 164*(3), 238–242. doi:10.1001/archpediatrics.2009.283

First Post. (2016, June 17). *Stop Cyberbullying: Indian teens face biggest risk among Asian countries.* Retrieved from www.firstpost.com/business/stop-cyberbullying-indian-teens-face-biggest-risk-among-asian-countries-2840552.html

Fisher, S., Middleton, K., Ricks, E., Malone, C., Briggs, C., & Barnes, J. (2015). Not just Black and White: Peer victimization and the intersectionality of school diversity and race. *Journal of Youth & Adolescence, 44*(6), 1241–1250. doi:10.1007/s10964-014-0243-3

Flaherty, C. (2013, February 2103). *Academic jerks.* Retrieved from www.insidehighered.com/news/2013/02/26/blog-post-asks-whether-nice- academics-finish-last

Flaherty, C. (2014a, September, 9). *The problem with civility.* Retrieved from www.insidehighered.com/news/2014/09/09/berkeley-chancellor-angers- faculty-members-remarks-civility-and-free-speech

Flaherty, C. (2014b, December 2). *Bully-free zone.* Retrieved from www.insidehighered.com/news/2014/12/02/u-wisconsin-madison-faculty- approves-anti-bullying-policy

Fleming, S. S., Goldman, A. W., Correli, S. J., & Taylor, C. J. (2016). Settling in: The role of individual and departmental tactics in the development of new faculty networks. *The Journal of Higher Education, 87*, 544–572. doi:10.1080/00221546.2016.11777413

References

Fleschler Peskin, M. F., Tortolero, S. R., & Markham, C. M. (2006). Bullying and victimization among black and Hispanic adolescents. *Adolescence, 41*(163), 467–484. Retrieved from https://search.proquest.com/openview/ec526a86dbf5422a7d2ff67c2bee5bf0/1?pq-origsite=gscholar&cbl=41539

Floyd, K., Mikkelson, A. C., & Judd, J. (2006). Defining the family through relationships. In L. H. Turner & R. West (Eds.), *The family communication sourcebook* (pp. 21–39). Thousand Oaks, CA: Sage.

Floyd, K., & Morman, M. T. (2000). Affection received from fathers as a predictor of men's affection with their own sons: Tests of the modeling and compensation hypotheses. *Communication Monographs, 67*, 347–361. doi:10.0180/03637750009376516

Folkman, S. (1984). Personal control and stress and coping processes: A theoretical analysis. *Journal of Personality and Social Psychology, 46*, 839–852. doi:10.1037/0022–3514.46.4.839

Forssell, R. (2016). Exploring cyberbullying and face-to-face bullying in working life—Prevalence, targets and expressions. *Computers in Human Behavior, 58*454–460. doi:10.1016/j.chb.2016.01.003

Foss, S. K., & Foss, K. A. (2011). *Inviting transformation: Presentational skills for a changing world.* Long Grove, IL: Waveland Press.

Foucault, M. (1977). *The history of sexuality: An introduction, volume I* (Robert Hurley, trans.). New York, NY: Vintage.

Foucault, M. (1990). *Discipline and punish: The birth of the prison* (Alan Sheridan, trans.). New York, NY: Vintage.

Fox, C. L., & Boulton, M. J. (2005). The social skills problems of victims of bullying: Self, peer and teacher perceptions. *British Journal of Educational Psychology, 75*, 313–328. doi:10.1348/000709905X25517

Fox, J., & McEwan, B. (2017). Distinguishing technologies for social interaction: The perceived social affordances of communication channels scale. *Communication Monographs, 84*(3), 298–318. doi:10.1080/03637751.2017.1332418

Fox, S., & Cowan, R. L. (2015). Revision of the workplace bullying checklist: The importance of human resource management's role in defining and addressing workplace bullying. *Human Resource Management Journal, 1*, 116–130. doi:10.1111/1748–8583.12049

Fox, S., & Spector, P. E., & Miles, D. (2001). Counterproductive work behavior (CWB) in response to job stressors and organizational justice: Some mediator and moderator tests for autonomy and emotions. *Journal of Vocational Behavior, 59*, 291–309. doi:10.1006/jvbe.2001.1803

Fox, S., & Stallworth, L. E. (2005). Racial/ethnic bullying: Exploring links between bullying and racism in the US workplace. *Journal of Vocational Behavior, 66*, 438–456. doi:10.1016/j.jvb.2004.01.002

Fox, S., & Stallworth, L. E. (2010). The battered apple: An application of stressor-emotion-control/support theory to teachers' experience of violence and bullying. *Human Relations, 63*, 927–954. doi:10.1177/0018726709349518

Freedman, S., & Vreven, D. (2016). Workplace incivility and bullying in the library: Perception or reality? *College & Research Libraries, 77*, 727–748. doi:10.5860/crl.77.6.727

Freeman, J. (1993). Metaphor and inquiry in Mark Tansey's 'Chain of Solutions.' In *Mark Tansey*. San Francisco, CA: L.A. County Museum of Art/Chronicle Books.

Frey, L. R., & Carragee, K. M. (2016). Seizing the social justice opportunity: Communication activism research at a politically critical juncture. *International Journal of Communication, 10*, 4027–4033.

Friedrich, T. L., Griffith, J. A., & Mumford, M. D. (2016). Collective leadership behaviors: Evaluating the leader, team network, and problem situation characteristics that influence their use. *Leadership Quarterly, 27*, 312–333. doi:10.1016/j.leaqua.2016.02.004

Fritz, J. M. H. (2013a). Ethics matters: Why ethical communication makes a difference in today's workplace. In J. Wrench (Ed.), *Workplace communication for the 21st century: Tools and strategies that impact the bottom line* (pp. 39–60). Santa Barbara, CA: Praeger.

Fritz, J. M. H. (2013b). *Professional civility: Communicative virtue at work.* New York, NY: Peter Lang.

Fritz, J. M. H. (2014). Professional civility: Creating a culture of leadership. In C. B. Illés, A. Dunay, & A. Słocińska (Eds.), *New trends in management in the 21st century* (pp. 237–244). Częstochowa, Poland: Czestochowa University of Technology.

Fritz, J. M. H. (2016). Interpersonal communication ethics. In C. Berger & M. Roloff (Eds.), *International encyclopedia of interpersonal communication* (pp. 889–902). Chichester, England: Wiley-Blackwell.

Fritz, J. M. H. (2018). Communication ethics. In N. Snow (Ed.), *Oxford handbook of virtue* (pp. 700–721). New York, NY: Oxford University Press.

Fritz, J. M. H., O'Neil, N. B., Popp, A. M., Williams, C. D., & Arnett, R. C. (2013). The influence of supervisory behavioral integrity on intent to comply with organizational ethical standards and organizational commitment. *Journal of Business Ethics, 114*, 251–263. doi:10.1007/s10551–012–1345-z

Gage, N. A., Prykanowski, D. A., & Larson, A. (2014). School climate and bullying victimization: A latent class growth model analysis. *School of Psychology Quarterly, 29*(3), 256–271. doi: 10.1037/spq0000064.

Gall, M. D., Borg, R. D., & Gall, J. P. (1996). *Educational research: An introduction.* New York, NY: Longman.

References

Garandeau, C. & Cillessen, A. (2006). From indirect aggression to invisible aggression: A conceptual view on bullying and peer group manipulation. *Aggression and Violent Behavior, 11*, 641–654. doi:10.1016/j.avb.2005.08.005

Garfinkel, H. (1967). *Studies in Ethnomethodology*. Englewood Cliffs, NJ: Prentice-Hall.

Garlough, D. (2016). Beyond bullying. *Access, 30*, 17–20.

Garnett, B., Masyn, K., Austin, S., Miller, M., Williams, D., & Viswanath, K. (2014). The intersectionality of discrimination attributes and bullying among youth: An applied latent class analysis. *Journal of Youth and Adolescence, 43*(8), 1225–1239. doi:10.1007/s10964-013-0073-8

Garnett, B. R., Masyn, K. E., Austin, S. B., Williams, D. R., & Viswanath, K. (2015). Coping styles of adolescents experiencing multiple forms of discrimination and bullying: Evidence from a sample of ethnically diverse urban youth. *Journal of School Health, 85*(2), 109–117. doi:10.1111/josh/12225

Gelfand, M. J., Leslie, L. M., & Keller, K. M. (2008). On the etiology of conflict cultures. *Research in Organizational Behavior, 28*, 137–166. doi:10.1016/j.nob.2008.06.001

Gelfand, M. J., Leslie, L. M., Keller, K., & de Dreu, C. K. (2010). Cultures and conflict: How leaders and members shape conflict organizations. *Academy of Management Proceedings, 1*, 1–6. doi:10.5465/AMBPP.2010.5449399ACAD

Gelfand, M. J., Leslie, L. M., Keller, K., & de Dreu, C. (2012). Conflict cultures in organizations: How leaders shape conflict cultures and their organizational-level consequences. *Journal of Applied Psychology, 97*, 1131–1147. doi:10.1037/a002993

Georgakopoulos, A., Wilkin, L., & Kent, B. (2011). Workplace bullying: A complex problem in contemporary organizations. *International Journal of Business and Social Science, 2*, 1–20. Retrieved from www.ijbssnet.com/journals/Vol._2_No._3_[Special_Issue_-_January_2011]/1.pdf

Gergen, K. J. (2009). *Relational being: Beyond self and community*. New York, NY: Oxford.

Ghobadi, S. (2013). Application of activity theory in understanding online communities of practice: A case of feminism. *The Journal of Community Informatics, 9*(1). Retrieved from http://ci-journal.net/index.php/ciej/article/view/828/1017

Gibson, J. (1977). The theory of affordances. In R. Shaw & J. Bransford (Eds.) *Perceiving, acting, and knowing: Toward an ecological* (pp. 67–82). Hillsdale, NJ: Erlbaum.

Giles, H., Coupland, N., & Coupland, J. (1991). Accommodation theory: Communication, context, and consequence. In *Contexts of accommodation: Developments in applied sociolinguistics* (pp. 1–60). Cambridge, UK: Cambridge University Press.

Giles, H., & Sassoon, C. (1983). The effects of speaker's accent, social class background, and message style on British listeners' social judgments. *Language & Communication, 3*, 305–313. doi:10.1016/0271–5309(83)90006-X

Gill, M., & Davenport Sypher, B. (2009). Workplace incivility and organizational trust. In P. Lutgen-Sandvik & B. Davenport Sypher, (Eds.), *Destructive organizational communication: Processes, consequences, and constructive ways of organizing* (pp. 53–74). New York, NY: Routledge.

Gini, G., & Pozzoli, T. (2009). Association between bullying and psychosomatic problems: A meta analysis. *Pediatrics, 123*(3), 1059–1065. Retrieved from http://pediatrics.aappublications.org/content/123/3/1059.full-text.pdf

Gini, G., Pozzoli, T., Borghi, F., & Franzoni, L. (2008). The role of bystanders in students' perception of bullying and sense of safety. *Journal of School Psychology, 46*, 617–638. doi:10.1016/j.jsp.2008.02.001

Ginzler, E. (2009). *Which type of housing meets your needs*. Retrieved from www.aarp.org/home-garden/housing/info-08-2009/ginzler_housing_choices.html November 13, 2017

Giorgi, G. (2012). Workplace bullying in academia creates a negative work environment: An Italian study. *Employee Responsibilities and Rights Journal, 24*, 261–275. doi:10.1007/s10672-012-9193-7

Glanz, K., Rimer, B. K., & Viswanath, K. (2008). *Health behavior and health education: Theory, research, and practice*. Chicago: John Wiley & Sons.

Glaser, B., & Strauss, A. (1967). *Discovery of grounded theory*. Chicago, IL: Aldine.

Gluckman, N. (2017, April 11). *You're not the only one getting put down by your colleagues, survey finds*. Retrieved from www.chronicle.com/article/You-re-Not-the-Only-One/239756

Goffman, E. (1959). *The presentation of self in everyday life*. New York, NY: Anchor Books.

Goffman, E. (1963). *Stigma: Notes on the management of spoiled identity*. New York, NY: Simon and Schuster.

Goldberg, E., Beitz, J., Wieland, D., & Levine, C. (2013). Social bullying in nursing academia. *Nurse Education, 38*, 191–197. doi:10.1097/NNE.0b013e3182a0e5a0

Goldsmith, D. (1994). The role of facework in supportive communication. In B. R. Burleson, T. L. Albrecht, & I. G. Sarason (Eds.), *Communication of social support: Messages, interactions, relationships, and community*. (pp. 29–46). Thousand Oaks, CA: Sage.

Goldweber, A., Waasdorp, T. E., & Bradshaw, C. P. (2013). Examining associations between race, urbanicity, and patterns of bullying involvement. *Journal of Youth and Adolescence, 42*(2), 206–219. doi:10.1007/

References

s10964-012-9843-7Gómez-Ortiza, O., Romera, E., & Ortega-Ruiza, R. (2015). Parenting styles and bullying: The mediating role of parental psychological aggression and physical punishment. *Child Abuse and Neglect, 51,* 132–143. doi:10.1016/j.chiabu.2015.10.025

Goodboy, A. K., & Martin, M. M. (2015). The personality profile of a cyberbully: Examining the Dark Triad. *Computers in Human Behavior, 49,* 1–4. https://doi.org/10.1016/j.chb.2015.02.052

Goodboy, A. K., Martin, M. M., & Bolkan, S. (2017). Workplace bullying and worker engagement: A self-determination model. *Journal of Interpersonal Violence.* Advance online publication. doi:10.1177/0886260517717492

Goodboy, A. K., Martin, M., & Brown, E. (2016). Bullying on the school bus: Deleterious effects on public school bus drivers. *Journal of Applied Communication Research, 44,* 434–452. doi: 10.1080/00909882.2016.1225161

Goodboy, A. K., Martin, M. M., & Goldman, Z. W. (2016). Students' experiences of bullying in high school and their adjustment and motivation during the first semester of college. *Western Journal of Communication, 80,* 60–78. doi:10.1080/10570314.2015.1078494

Goodboy, A. K., Martin, M. M., & Johnson, Z. (2015). The relationships between workplace bullying by graduate faculty with graduate students' burnout and organizational citizenship behaviors. *Communication Research Reports, 32,* 272–280. doi:10.1080/08824096.2015.1052904

Goodboy, A. K., Martin, M. M., Knight, J. M., & Long, Z. (2017). Creating the boiler room environment: The job demand-control-support model as an explanation of workplace bullying. *Communication Research, 44,* 244–262. doi:10.1177/0093650215614365

Goodboy, A. K., Martin, M. M., & Rittenour, C. E. (2016). Bullying as an expression of intolerant schemas. *Journal of Child & Adolescent Trauma, 9*(4), 277–282. doi:10.1007/s40653-016-0089-9

Goodridge, D., Heal-Salahub, J., Pausjenssen, E., James, G., & Lidington, J. (2017). Peer bullying in seniors' subsidized apartment communities in Saskatoon, Canada: Participatory research. *Health & Social Care in the Community, 25*(4), 1439–1447. doi:10.1111/hsc.12444

Gorlewski, J., Gorlewski, D., & Porfilio B. (2014). Beyond bullies and victims: Using case story analysis and Freirean insight to address academic mobbing. *Workplace, 24,* 9–18. www.workplace-gsc.com.

Görzig, A., & Olafsson, K. (2013). What makes a bully a cyberbully? Unraveling the characteristics of cyberbullies across twenty-five European countries. *Journal of Children and Media, 7*(1), 9–27. doi:10.1080/17482798.2012.739756

Gradinger, P., Stohmeier, D., & Spiel, C. (2009). Traditional bullying and cyberbullying: Identification of risk groups for adjustment problems. *Journal of Psychology [Zeitschrift für Psychologie], 217,* 205–213. doi:10.1027/0044–3409.217.4.205

Gravois, J. (2006, April 14). Mob rule: In departmental disputes, professors can act just like animals. *Chronicle of Higher Education,* p. A32. Retrieved from www.chronicle.com/

Greenberg, J., & Arndt, J. (2011). Terror management theory. *Handbook of Theories of Social Psychology: Volume 1,* 398–415. doi:10.4135/9781446249215.n20

Greenberg, L. S., & Paivio, S. C. (2003). *Working with emotions in psychotherapy* (Vol. 13): Guilford Press.

Greene, M. B. (2000). Bullying and harassment in schools. In R. S. Moser, & C. E. Franz (Eds.), *Shocking violence: Youth perpetrators and victims—A multidisciplinary perspective* (pp. 72–101). Springfield, IL: Charles C. Thomas.

Greenleaf, R. K. (1977). *Servant leadership: A journey into the nature of legitimate power and greatness.* New York, NY: Paulist Press.

Grigg, D. W. (2010). Cyber-aggression: Definition and concept of cyberbullying. *Australian Journal of Guidance & Counselling, 20*(2), 143–156. doi:10.1375/ajgc.20.2.143

Grigg, D. W. (2012). Definitional constructs of cyber-bullying and cyber-aggression from a triangulatory overview: A preliminary study into elements of cyber-bullying. *Journal of Aggression, Conflict & Peace Research, 4*(4), 202–215. doi:10.1108/17596591211270699

Gudykunst, W. (2005). *Theorizing about intercultural communication.* Thousand Oaks, CA: Sage.

**Guilford County Schools. (1994). Staff harassment, bullying, and discrimination free environment. GAMA-P. Retrieved from http://www1.gcsnc.com/policies/pdf/GAMA-P.pdf

**Guilford County Schools. (2009a). Student harassment, bullying, and discrimination free environment. JCDAD. Retrieved from http://www1.gcsnc.com/policies/pdf/JCDAD-%20Student%20Harassment%20Bullying%20%20Discrimination%20Free%20Environment-%20approved%2006%2026%2008%20%20.pdf

**Guilford County Schools. (2009b). Student harassment, bullying, and discrimination free environment. JCDAD-P. Retrieved from http://www1.gcsnc.com/policies/pdf/JCDAD-P.pdf

**Guilford County Schools. (2010). Staff harassment, bullying, and discrimination free environment. GAMA. Retrieved from http://www1.gcsnc.com/policies/pdf/GAMA.pdf

*Guilford County Schools. (2017). Bullying prevention. Retrieved from www.gcsnc.com/Page/39670

Gullette, M. M. (2017). *Ending ageism: Or how not to shoot old people.* New Brunswick, NJ: Rutgers University Press.

References

Guntarto. (2001). Internet and the new media: Challenge for Indonesian children. *Media Asia, 28*, 195–203. doi :10.1080/01296612.2001.11726651

Haines-Saah, R. J., Hilario, C. T., Jenkins, E. K., Ng, C. K.Y., & Johnson, J. L. (2016). Understanding adolescent narratives about "bullying" through an intersectional lens: Implications for youth mental health interventions. *Youth & Society*, Article first published online: February 1, 2016. doi:10.1177/0044118X15621465

Hall, J.A. (2016). When is social media use social interaction? Defining mediated social interaction. *New Media & Society*. doi:10.1177/1461444816660782

Halliwell, D. (2016). "I know you, but I don't know who you are:" Siblings' discursive struggles surrounding experiences of transition. *Western Journal of Communication, 80*, 327–347. doi:10.1080/10570314.2015.109 1493

Harel, Y., Shechtman, Z., & Cutrona, C. (2012). Exploration of support behavior in counseling groups with counseling trainees. *The Journal for Specialists in Group Work, 37*, 202–217. doi:10.1080/01933922.2011.64 6087

Harrington, S., Rayner, C., & Warren, S. (2012). Too hot to handle? Trust and human resource practitioners' implementation of anti-bullying policy. *Human Resource Management Journal, 22*, 392–408.

Harvey, M. G., Buckley, M. R., Heames, J.T., Zinko, R., Brouer, R. L., & Ferris, G.R. (2007). A bully as an archetypal destructive leader. *Journal of Leadership & Organizational Studies, 14*, 117–129. doi:10.1177/1071791907308217

Harvey, S., & Keashly, L. (2003). Predicting the risk for aggression in the workplace: Risk factors, self-esteem, and time at work. *Social Behavior and Personality, 31*, 807–814. doi:10.2224/sbp.2003.31.8.807

Hauge, L. J., Einarsen, S., Knardahl, S., Lau, B., Notelaers, G., & Stogstad, A. (2011). Leadership and role stressors as departmental level predictors of workplace bullying. *International Journal of Stress Management, 18*, 305–323. doi:10.1037/a0025396

Hauge, L. J., Skogstad, A., & Einarsen, S. (2007). Relationship between stressful work environments and bullying: Results of a large representative study. *Work & Stress, 21*, 220–242. doi:10.1080/02678370701705810

Haun, D., & Tomasello, M. (2011). Conformity to peer pressure in preschool children. *Child Development, 82*(6), 1759–1767. doi:10.1111/j.1467–8624.2011.01666.x

Häusser, J. A., Mojzisch, A., Niesel, M., & Schulz-Hardt, S. (2010). Ten years on: A review of recent research on the job demand-control (-support) model and psychological well-being. *Work & Stress, 24*, 1–35. doi:10.1080/02678371003683747

Haynie, D., L., Nansel, T., Eitel, P., Crump, A. D., Saylor, K., Yu, K., & Simons-Morton, B. (2001). Bullies, victims, and bully/victims: Distinct groups of at-risk youth. *Journal of Early Adolescence, 21*, 29–49. doi:10.1177/0272431601021001002

Heckert, T. M., & Farabee, A. M. (2006). Turnover intentions of the faculty at a teaching focused university. *Psychological Reports, 99*, 39–45. doi:10.2466/pr0.99.1.39–4

Heirman, W., Angelopoulos, S., Wegge, D., Vandebosch, H., Eggermont, S., & Walrave, M. (2015). Cyberbullying-entrenched or cyberbullying-free classrooms? A class network and class composition approach. *Journal of Computer-Mediated Communication, 20*, 260–277. doi:10.1111/jcc4.12111

Heritage, J., & Sefi, S. (1992). Dilemmas of advice. In P. Drew & J. Heritage (Eds.), *Talk at work: Interaction in institutional settings* (pp. 359–417). Cambridge, UK: Cambridge University Press.

Hewlett, S. A., & Luce, C. B. (2006). Extreme jobs: The dangerous allure of the 70-hour workweek. *Harvard Business Review, 84*(12), 49–58. Retrieved from http://imaginal-labs.com/wp-content/uploads/2013/10/Allure-of-70-Hour-Workweek.pdf

Hicks, J., Jennings, L., Jennings, S., Berry, S., & Green, D. A. (2018). Middle school bullying: Student reported perceptions and prevalence. *Journal of Child and Adolescent Counseling*, 1–14. doi:10.1080/23727810.2017.1 422645

Hickson, M., & Roebuck, J. B. (2009). *Deviance and crime in colleges and universities: What goes on in the halls of ivy*. Springfield, IL: Charles C. Thomas.

High, A. C. (2011). The production and reception of verbal person-centered social support in face-to-face and computer-mediated dyadic conversations (Unpublished doctoral dissertation). The Pennsylvania State University, State College, PA.

High, A. C., & Solomon, D. (2011). Locating computer-mediated social support within online communication environments. In K. B. Wright & L. M. Webb (Eds.), *Computer- mediated communication in personal relationships* (pp. 119–136). New York, NY: Peter Lang Publishing.

High, A. C., & Young, R. (2018). Supportive communication from bystanders of cyberbullying: Indirect effects and interactions between source and message characteristics. *Journal of Applied Communication Research, 46*, 28–51. doi:10.1080/00909882.2017.1412085

Hilario, C. T., Vo, D., & Pottie, K. (2015). Immigrant adolescent health: Background and context. *Caring for Kids New to Canada*. Retrieved from www.kidsnewtocanada.ca/culture/adolescent-health-background

References

Hinduja, S., & Patchin, J. W. (2010). Bullying, cyberbullying, and suicide. *Archives of Suicide Research*, *14*(3), 206–221. doi:10.1080/13811118.2010.494133

Hinduja, S., & Patchin, J. W. (2017). Cultivating youth resilience to prevent bullying cyberbullying victimization. *Child Abuse & Neglect*, *73*, 51–62. doi:10.1016/j.chiabu.2017.09.010

Hirschi, A. (2014). Hope as a resource for self-directed career management: Investigating mediating effects on proactive career behaviors and life and job satisfaction. *Journal of Happiness Studies*, *15*, 1495–1512. doi:10.1007/s10902–013–9488–x

Hmieleski, K. M., & Ensley, M. D. (2007). A contextual examination of new venture performance: Entrepreneur leadership behavior, top management team heterogeneity, and environmental dynamism. *Journal of Organizational Behavior*, *28*, 865–889. doi:10.1002/job.479

Hodson, R. (2001). *Dignity at work*. Cambridge, UK: Cambridge University Press.

Hodson, R., & Roscigno, V. (2004). Organizational success and worker dignity: Complementary or C\contradictory? *American Journal of Sociology*, *110*, 672–708. doi:10.1086/422626

Hoel, H., & Cooper, C. L. (2001). Origins of bullying: The theoretical frameworks for explaining bullying. In N. Therani (Ed.), *Building a culture of respect: Managing bullying at work* (pp. 3–20). London: Taylor and Francis.

Hoel, H., Glasø, L., Hetland, J., Cooper, C. L., & Einarsen, S. (2010). Leadership styles as predictors of self-reported and observed workplace bullying. *British Journal of Management*, *21*, 453–468. doi:10.1111/j.1467–8551.2009.00664.x

Hoel, H., Sheehan, M. J., Cooper, C. L., & Einarsen, S. (2011). Organisational effects of workplace bullying. In S. Einarsen, H. Hoel, D. Zapf, & C. L. Cooper (Eds.), *Bullying and harassment in the workplace: Developments in theory, research, and practice* (2nd ed., pp. 129–147). Boca Raton, FL: CRC Press/Taylor & Francis Group.

Hoetger, L. A., Hazen, K. P., & Brank, E. M. (2015). All in the family: A retrospective study comparing sibling bullying and peer bullying. *Journal of Family Violence*, *30*, 103–111. doi:10.1007/s10896–014–9651–0

Hoff, D. L., & Mitchell, S. N. (2009). Cyberbullying: Causes, effects, and remedies. *Journal of Educational Administration*, *47*, 652–665. doi:10.1108/09578230910981107

Hoffman, J. (2010, December 4). Parents struggle with cyberbullying. *The New York Times*. Retrieved from www.nytimes.com/2010/12/05/us/05bully.html

Hofstede, G. (1984). *Culture's consequences: International differences in work-related values* (2nd ed.). Beverly Hills, CA: Sage. ISBN 0–8039–1444-X.

Hofstede, G. (2001). *Culture's consequences: Comparing values, behaviors, institutions, and organizations across nations*. Thousand Oaks, CA: Sage. Hogh, A., & Dofradottir, A. (2001). Coping with bullying in the workplace. *European Journal of Work and Organizational Psychology*, *10*, 485–495. doi:10.1080/13594320143000825

Hogh, A., Mikkelsen, E. G., & Hansen, A. M. (2011). Individual consequences of workplace bullying/mobbing. In S. Einarsen, H. Hoel, D. Zapf, & C. L. Cooper (Eds.), *Bullying and harassment in the workplace: Developments in theory, research, and practice* (2nd ed., pp. 107–128). Boca Raton, FL: CRC Press/Taylor & Francis Group.

Hoglund, W. L. G. (2007). Functioning in early adolescence: Genderlinked responses to peer victimization. *Journal of Educational Psychology*, *99*, 683–699. doi:10.1037/0022–0663.99.4.683

Hollenbaugh, E. E., & Everett, M. K. (2013). The effects of anonymity on self-disclosure in blogs: An application of the online disinhibition effect. *Journal of Computer-Mediated Communication*, *18*(3), 283–302. doi:10.1111/jcc4.12008

Hollis, L. P. (2012). *Bully in the ivory tower: How aggression and incivility erode American higher education*. Wilmington, DE: Patricia Berkly.

Hollis, L. P. (2015). Bully university? The cost of workplace bullying and employee disengagement in American higher education. *Sage Open*, *5*, 1–11. doi:10.1177/2158244015589997

Hollis, L. P. (2016a). Bruising the bottom line: Cost of workplace bullying and the compromised access for underrepresented community college employees. In L. P. Hollis (Ed.), *The coercive community college: Bullying and its costly impact on the mission to serve underrepresented populations* (pp. 1–26). Bingley, UK: Emerald Group Publishing.

Hollis, L. P. (2016b). Canary in the mine: Ombuds as first alerts for workplace bullying on campus. *Journal of the International Ombudsman Association*, *9*(1), 23–31. www.ombudsassociation.org/.

Holloway, S., & Valentine, G. (2003). *Cyberkids: Children in the information age*. London, UK: Routledge Falmer.

Holmes IV, O., Whitman, M. V., Campbell, K. S., & Johnson, D. E. (2016). Exploring the social identity threat response framework. *Equality, Diversity and Inclusion: An International Journal*, *35*(3), 205–220. doi:10.1108/edi-08–2015–0068

Holmstrom, A. J., & Burleson, B. R. (2011). An initial test of a cognitive-emotional theory of esteem support messages. *Communication Research*, *38*(3), 326–355. doi:10.1177/0093650210376191

Holt, M. K., Vivolo-Kantor, A. M., Polanin, J. R., Holland, K. M., DeGue, S., Matjasko, J. L., & Reid, G. (2015). Bullying and suicidal ideation and behaviors: A meta-analysis. *Pediatrics*, *135*(2), e496–e509. doi:10.1542/peds.2014–1864

References

Horn, S. (2002). *Take the bully by the horns.* New York, NY: St. Martin's.

Horton, P. (2016). Portraying monsters: Framing school bullying through a macro lens. *Discourse: Studies in the Cultural Politics of Education, 37,* 202–214, dx.doi.org/10.1080/01596306.2014.951833

House, R. J., & Howell, J. M. (1992). Personality and charismatic leadership. *Leadership Quarterly, 3,* 81–108. doi:10.1016/1048–9843(92)90028-E

Hu, L. T., & Bentler, P. M. (1999). Cutoff criteria for fit indexes in covariance structure analysis: Conventional criteria versus new alternatives. *Structural Equation Modeling, 6,* 1–55. doi:10.1080/10705519909540118

Huesmann, L. R., Moise-Titus, J., Podolski, C., & Eron, L. D. (2003). Longitudinal relations between children's exposure to TV violence and their aggressive and violent behavior in young adulthood: 1977–1992. *Developmental Psychology, 39,* 201–221. doi:10.1037//0012–1649.39.2.201

Hummert, M. L., Shaner, J. L., Garstka, T. A., & Henry, C. (1998). Communication with older adults: The influence of age stereotypes, context and communicator age. *Human Communication Research, 25*(1), 124–151. doi:10.1111/j.1468–2958.1998.tb00439.x

Hunter, N. (2011). *Cyber bullying.* London: Raintree.

Hunter, S. C., & Boyle, J. M. (2004). Appraisal and coping strategy use in victims of school bullying. *British Journal of Educational Psychology, 74,* 83–107. doi:10.1348/000709904322848833

Hutchby, I. (2001). *Conversation and technology.* Cambridge, UK: Polity Press/Blackwell.

Hyde, M. J. (2005). *The life-giving gift of acknowledgement.* West Lafayette, IN: Purdue University Press.

Hymel, S., McClure, R., Miller, M., Shumka, E., & Trach, J. (2015). Addressing school bullying: Insights from theories of group processes. *Journal of Applied Developmental Psychology, 37,* 16–24. doi:10.1016/j.appdev.2014.11.008

Hymel, S., & Swearer, S. S. (2015). Four decades of research on school bullying. *American Psychologist, 70,* 293–299. doi:10.1037/a0038928

Iecovich, E., & Lev-Ran, O. (2006). Attitudes of functionally independent residents toward residents who were disabled in old age homes: The role of separation versus integration. *Journal of Applied Gerontology, 25*(3), 252–268. doi:10.1177/0733464806288565

Infante, D. A. (1987). Aggressiveness. In J. C. McCroskey & J. Daly (Eds.), *Personality and interpersonal communication* (pp. 157–192). Newbury Park, CA: Sage.

Infante, D. A. (1988). *Arguing constructively.* Long Grove, IL: Waveland Press.

Infante, D. A. (1995). Teaching students to understand and control verbal aggression. *Communication Education, 44,* 51–63. doi:10.1080/03634529509378997

Infante, D. A., Bruning, S. D., & Martin, M. M. (1994, November). *Circumstances for favorable and unfavorable experiences with verbal aggression.* Paper presented at the meeting of the Speech Communication Association, New Orleans, LA.

Infante, D. A., Chandler, T. A., & Rudd, J. E. (1989). Test of an argument skill deficiency model of interspousal violence. *Communication Monographs, 56,* 163–177. doi:10.1080/03637758909390257

Infante, D. A., & Gorden, W. I. (1989). Argumentativeness and affirming communicator style as predictors of satisfaction/dissatisfaction with subordinates. *Communication Quarterly, 37*(2), 81–90. doi:10.1080/01463378909385529

Infante, D. A., Myers, S. A., & Buerkel, R. A. (1994). Argument and verbal aggression in constructive and destructive family and organizational disagreements. *Western Journal of Communication, 58,* 73–84. doi:10.1080/10570319409374488

Infante, D. A., & Rancer, A. S. (1996). Argumentativeness and verbal aggressiveness: A review of recent theory and research. In B. R. Burleson (Ed.), *Communication yearbook 19* (pp. 319–351). New York, NY: Routledge.

Infante, D. A., Riddle, B. L., Horvath, C. L., & Tumlin, S. A. (1992). Verbal aggressiveness: Messages and reasons. *Communication Quarterly, 40,* 116–126. doi:10.1080/01463379209369827

Infante, D. A., Trebing, J. D., Shepherd, P., & Seeds, D. E. (1984). The relationship of argumentativeness to verbal aggression. *Southern Speech Communication Journal, 50,* 67–77. doi:10.1080/10417948409372622

Infante, D. A., & Wigley, C. J., III. (1986). Verbal aggressiveness: An interpersonal model and measure. *Communication Monographs, 53,* 61–69. doi:10.1080/03637758609376126

Intel Security India. (2015). *Teens, tweens and technology study 2015.* Retrieved October 10, 2017, from http://apac.intelsecurity.com/digitalsafety/2015/10/27/research-india-ttt/

Internet in India. (2017). IAMAI media release, dated February 20, 2018. Retrieved June 1, 2018, from http://www.iamai.in/media/details/4990

Jackson, S. E., Schuler, R. S., & Jiang, K. (2014). An aspirational framework for strategic human resource management. *Academy of Management Annals, 8*(1), 1–56. doi:10.1080/19416520.2014.872335

Jacobson, D. E. (1986). Types and timing of social support. *Journal of Health and Social Behavior, 27,* 250–264. doi:10.2307/2136745

References

Jacobson, K. C., & Crockett, L. J. (2000). Parental monitoring and adolescent adjustment: An ecological perspective. *Journal of Research on Adolescence, 10*, 65–97. doi:10.1207/sjra1001_4

Janssens, H., Braeckman, L., De Clercq, B., Casini, A., De Bacquer, D., & Kittel, F. (2016). The indirect association of job strain with long-term sickness absence through bullying: A mediation analysis using structural equation modeling. *BMC Public Health, 16*, 851–863. doi:10.1186/s12889–016–3522-y

Jara, N., Casas, J. A., & Ortega-Ruiz, R. (2017). Proactive and reactive aggressive behavior in bullying: The role of values. *International Journal of Educational Psychology, 6(1)*, 1. doi:10.17583/ijep.2017.2515

Javidan, M., & House, R. J. (2001). Cultural acumen for the global manager: Lessons from Project GLOBE. *Organizational Dynamics, 29*, 289–305.

Jiang, Z. (2017). Proactive personality and career adaptability: The role of thriving at work. *Journal of Vocational Behavior, 98*, 85–97. doi:10.1016/j.jvb.2016.10.003

Johannesen, R. L. (2001). Communication ethics: Centrality, trends, and controversies. In W. B. Gudykunst (Ed.), *Communication yearbook 25* (pp. 201–235). Mahwah, NJ: Erlbaum.

Johnson-Bailey, J. (2015). Academic incivility and bullying as a gendered and racialized phenomena. *Adult Learning, 26*, 42–47. doi:10.1177/1045159514558414

Jones, S. M. (2004). Putting the person into person-centered and immediate emotional support: Emotional change and perceived helper competence as outcomes of comforting in helping situations. *Communication Research, 31*, 338–360. doi:10.1177/0093650204263436

Jones, S. M., & Wirtz, J. G. (2006). How does the comforting process work? An empirical test of an appraisal-based model of comforting. *Human Communication Research, 32*, 217–243. doi:10.1111/j.1468–2958.2006.00274.x

Juvonen, J., Graham, S., & Schuster, M. A. (2003). Bullying among young adolescents: The strong, the weak, and the troubled. *Pediatrics, 112*(6), 1231–1237. Retrieved from http://pediatrics.aappublications.org/content/112/6/1231.short

Juvonen, J., & Ho, A. (2008). Social motives underlying antisocial behavior across middle school grades. *Journal of Youth and Adolescence, 37*, 747–756. doi:10.1007/s10964-008-9272-0

Kahl, D. H. (2010). Making a difference: (Re) connecting communication scholarship with pedagogy. *Journal of Applied Communication Research, 38*, 298–302.

Kahle, L., & Peguero, A. A. (2017). Bodies and bullying: The interaction of gender, race, ethnicity, weight, and inequality with school victimization. *Victims and Offenders, 12*, 323–345. doi:10.1080/15564886.2015.1117551

Kalman, I. (2011). *Why anti-bullying programs aren't working*. Retrieved from https://bullies2buddies.com/why-anti-bully-programs-arent-working/

Kanetsuna, T., Smith, P. K., & Morita, Y. (2006). Coping with bullying at school: Children's recommended strategies and attitudes to school-based interventions in England and Japan. *Aggressive Behavior, 32*, 570–580. doi:10.1002/ab.20156

Kaplan, D. M. (2014). Career anchors and paths: The case of gay, lesbian, & bisexual workers. *Human Resource Management Review, 24*(2), 119–130. doi:10.1016/j.hrmr.2013.10.002

Karasek, R. A. (1979). Job demands, job decision latitude, and mental strain: Implications for job design. *Administrative Science Quarterly, 24*, 285–308. doi:10.2307/2392498

Karasek, R., Brisson, C., Kawakami, N., Houtman, I., Bongers, P., & Amick, B. (1998). The job content questionnaire (JCQ): An instrument for internationally comparative assessments of psychosocial job characteristics. *Journal of Occupational Health Psychology, 3*, 322–355. doi:10.1037/1076–8998.3.4.322

Karasek, R., & Theorell, T. (1990). *Healthy work: Stress, productivity, and the reconstruction of working life*. New York, NY: Basic Books.

Karatuna, I. (2014). Targets' coping with workplace bullying: A qualitative study. *Qualitative Research in Organizations and Management: An International Journal, 10*(1), 21–37. doi:10.1108/QROM-09–2013–1176

Kärnä, A., Salmivalli, C., Poskiparta, E., & Voeten, M. (2008, May). Do bystanders influence the frequency of bullying in a classroom? Paper presented at the XIth Biennial EARA Conference, Turin, Italy.

Kassing, J., & Waldron, V. (2014). Incivility, destructive workplace behavior, and bullying. In L. L. Putnam & D. K. Mumby (Eds.), *The SAGE handbook of organizational communication* (pp. 643–664). Thousand Oaks, CA: Sage.

Kato, Y., & Kato, S. (2015). Reply speed to mobile text messages among Japanese college students: When a quick reply is preferred and a late reply is acceptable. *Computers in Human Behavior, 44*, 209–219. doi:10.1016/j.chb.2014.11.047

Katz, J. E., & Aakhus, M. (2002). *Perpetual contact: Mobile communication, private talk, Public performance*. Cambridge: Cambridge University Press.

Keashly, L. (1997). Emotional abuse in the workplace: Conceptual and empirical issues. *Journal of Emotional Abuse, 1*, 85–117. doi:10.1300/J135v01n01_05

References

Keashly, L. (2001). Interpersonal and systemic aspects of emotional abuse at work: The target's perspective. *Violence and Victims, 16*, 233–268.

Keashly, L. (2010). Some things you need to know but may have been afraid to ask: A researcher speaks to Ombudsmen about workplace bullying. *Journal of the International Ombudsman Association, 3*, 10–23. Retrieved from https://greenvillemed.sc.edu/ombuds/doc/Keashly_2011.pdf

Keashly, L., & Jagatic, K. (2003). By any other name: American perspectives on workplace bullying. In S. Einarsen, H. Hoel, & C. L. Cooper (Eds.), *Bullying and emotional abuse in the workplace: International perspectives in research and practice* (pp. 31–61). London: Taylor and Francis.

Keashly, L., & Jagatic, K. (2011). North American perspectives on hostile behaviors and bullying at work. In S. Einarsen, H. Hoel, D. Zapf, & C. L. Cooper (Eds.), *Bullying and harassment in the workplace: Developments in theory, research, and practice* (2nd ed., pp. 41–71). Boca Raton, FL: CRC Press/Taylor & Francis Group.

Keashly, L., & Neuman, J. H. (2010). Faculty experiences with bullying in higher education: Causes, consequences, and management. *Administrative Theory & Praxis, 32*, 48–70. doi:10.2753/ATP1084–1806320103

Keashly, L., & Neuman, J. H. (2013). Bullying in higher education: What current research, theorizing, and practice tells us. In J. Lester (Ed.), *Workplace bullying in higher education* (pp. 1–22). New York, NY: Routledge.

Keashly, L., & Wajngurt, C. (2016). Faculty bullying in higher education. *Psychology and Education: An Interdisciplinary Journal, 53*(1), 79–90. doi:10.2753/ATP1084- 1806320103

Keck, K.L., & Samp, J.A. (2007). The dynamic nature of goals and message production as revealed in a sequential analysis of conflict interactions. *Human Communication Research, 33*, 27–47. doi:10.1111/j.1468–2958.2007.00287.x

Keinan, G., Shrira, A., & Shmotkin, D. (2012). The association between cumulative adversity and mental health: Considering dose and primary focus of adversity. *Quality Of Life Research: An International Journal of Quality of Life Aspects of Treatment, Care & Rehabilitation, 21*(7), 1149–1158. doi:10.1007/s11136-011-0035-0

Kennedy, T. & Wellman, B. (2007). The networked household. *Information, Communication & Society, 10*, 645–670. doi:10.1080/13691180701658012

Kessel Schneider, S., O'Donnell, L., Stueve, A., & Coulter, R. S. (2012). Cyberbullying, school bullying, and psychological distress: A regional census of high school students. *American Journal of Public Health, 102*(1), 171–177. doi:10.2105/AJPH.2011.300308

Keyton, J. (2005). *Communication and organizational culture: A key to understanding work experiences.* Thousand Oaks, CA: Sage.

Khan, S., Sabri, P. U., & Nasir, N. (2016). Cost of workplace bullying for employees: An anti- bullying policy through introduction of workplace spirituality in higher education sector of Lahore, Pakistan. *Science International, 28*(1), 541–549. Retrieved from http://sci-int.com

Khomami, N. (2016). *NSPCC records 88% rise in children seeking help for online abuse.* Retrieved from www.theguardian.com/society/2016/nov/14/nspcc-records-88-rise-in-children-seeking-help-for-online-abuse

Kilpatrick, H., & Joiner, W. (2012). *The drama years: Real girls talk about surviving middle School—bullies, brands, body image, and more.* New York, NY: Simon and Schuster.

Kim, Y.Y. (2005). Adapting to a new culture: An integrative communication theory. In W. B. Gudykunst (Ed.), *Theorizing about intercultural communication* (pp. 375–400). Thousand Oaks, CA: Sage.

King, C., & Piotrowski, C. (2015). Bullying of educators by educators: Incivility in higher education. *Contemporary Issues in Education Research, 8*(4), 257–262. Retrieved from www.cluteinstitute.com/ojs/index.php/CIER/index

King, D. (1988). Multiple jeopardy, multiple consciousness: The context of black feminist ideology. *Signs: Journal of Women in Culture and Society,* 14(1), Autumn, 42–72.

Kinney, T. A. (1994). An inductively derived typology of verbal aggression and its association to distress. *Human Communication Research, 21*, 183–222. doi:10.1111/j.1468–2958.1994.tb00345.x

Kinney, T. A. (2012). Workplace bullying as interpersonal violence? A reconceptualization in progress. In B. L. Omdahl & J. M. H. Fritz (Eds.), *Problematic relationships in the workplace, volume 2* (pp. 68–84). New York, NY: Peter Lang.

Kirton, H. (n.d.). *More than a third of LGBT people bullied at work.* Retrieved from www.peoplemanagement.co.uk/experts/research/more-than-third-lgbt-experience- workplace-bullying

Kirwil, L. (2009). The role of individualistic-collectivistic values in childrearing culture for European parents' mediation of Internet. *Journal of Children and Media, 3*, 394–409. doi:10.1080/17482790903233440

Kisamore, J. L., Jawahar, I., Liguori, E. W., Mharapara, T. L., & Stone, T. H. (2010). Conflict and abusive workplace behaviors: The moderating effects of social competencies. *Career Development International, 15*(6), 583–600. doi:10.1108/13620431011084420

Kochenderfer-Ladd, B. (2004). Peer victimization: The role of emotions in adaptive and maladaptive coping. *Social Development, 13*, 329–349. doi:10.1111/j.1467–9507.2004.00271.x

References

Kochenderfer, B. J., & Ladd, G. W. (1997). Victimized children's responses to peers' aggression: Behaviors associated with reduced versus continued victimization. *Development and Psychopathology, 9*, 59–73. doi:10.1017/S0954579497001065

Kochenfelder-Ladd, B., & Skinner, K. (2002). Children's coping strategies: Moderators of the effects of peer victimization? *Developmental Psychology, 38, 267–278*. doi:10.1037/0012–1649.38.2.267

Koerner, A. F., Schrodt, P., & Fitzpatrick, M. A. (2018). Family communication patterns theory: A grand theory of family communication. In D. O. Braithwaite, E. A. Suter, & K. Floyd (Eds.), *Engaging theories in family communication: Multiple perspectives* (2nd ed., pp. 142–153). Thousand Oaks, CA: Sage.

Komolsevin, R. (2002). Education, encouragement, self-regulation: Children and the Internet in Thailand. In K. Shetty (Ed.), *Kids online: Promoting responsible use and a safe environment on the Net in Asia* (pp. 154–186). Singapore: AMIC/NTU.

Koolstra, C. & Lucassen, N. (2004). Viewing behaviour of children and TV guidance by parents: A comparison of parent and child reports. *Communications, 29*, 179–198. doi:10.1515/comm.2004.012

Kowalski, R., Giumetti, G. W., Schroeder, A. N., & Reese, H. (2012). Cyber bullying amongst college students: Evidence from multiple domains of college life. In L. A. Wankel & C. Wankel (Eds.), *Misbehavior online in higher education*. Bingley, UK: Emerald Publishing.

Kowalski, R. M., & Limber, S. P. (2007). Electronic bullying among middle school students. *Journal of Adolescent Health, 41*(6), 22–30. doi:10.1016/j.jadohealth.2007.08.017

Kowalski, R. M., Limber, S. P., & Agatston, P. W. (Eds.). (2012). *Cyberbullying: Bullying in the digital age* (2nd ed.). Heboken, NJ: Wiley-Blackwell.

Kraft, E. M., & Wang, J. (2010). An exploratory study of the cyberbullying and cyberstalking experiences and factors related to victimization of students at a public liberal arts college. *International Journal of Technoethics, 1*(4), 74–91. doi:10.4018/jte.2010100106

Kuiper, E., Volman, M., & Terwel, J. (2008). *Students' use of Web literacy skills and strategies: Searching, reading and evaluating Web information*. Retrieved August 10, 2014, from www.informationr.net/ir/13-3/paper351.html

Kumar, R. (2016). ICT uses by 14–20-year-olds in India: Imperatives of parental intervention, *Interactions: Studies in Communication & Culture,* 7(2), 197–216 doi:10.1386/iscc.7.2.197_1

Kuykendall, S. (2012). *Bullying*. Santa Barbara, CA: Greenwood/ABC-CLIO.

Lachs, M. S., Teresi, J. A., Ramirez, M., Van Haitsma, K., Silver, S., Eimicke, J. P., & Luna, M. R. (2016). The prevalence of resident-to-resident elder mistreatment in nursing homes. *Annals of Internal Medicine, 165*(4), 229–236. doi:10.7326/m15–1209

Ladd, G. W., & Ladd, B. K. (1998). Parenting behaviors and parent—child relationship: Correlates of peer victimization in kindergarten? *Developmental Psychology, 34*, 1450–1458. doi:10.1037/0012–1649.34.6.1450

LaFollette, H., & Graham, G. (1986). Honesty and intimacy. *Journal of Social and Personal Relationships, 3*, 3–18. doi:10.1177/0265407586031001

Lagacé, M., Tanguay, A., Lavallée, M. L., Laplante, J., & Robichaud, S. (2012). The silent impact of ageist communication in long term care facilities: Elders' perspectives on quality of life and coping strategies. *Journal of Aging Studies, 26*, 335–342. doi:10.1016/j.jaging.2012.03.002

Lam, S., Law, W., Chan, C., Wong, B. H., & Zhang, X. (2015). A latent class growth analysis of school bullying and its social context: The self-determination theory perspective. *School Psychology Quarterly, 30*(1), 75–90. doi:10.1037/spq0000067

Lamb, S. (2014). Permanent personhood or meaningful decline? Toward a critical anthropology of successful aging. *Journal of Aging Studies, 29*, 41–52. doi:10.1016/j.jaging.2013.12.006

Langos, C. (2012). Cyberbullying: The challenge to define. *Cyberpsychology, Behavior, and Social Networking, 15*(6), 285–289.

Larochette, A., Murphy, A., & Craig, W. (2010). Racial bullying and victimization in Canadian school-aged children individual and school level effects. *School Psychology International, 31*(4), 389–408. doi:10.1177/0143034310377150

Laschinger, H. K. S., Wong, C. A., & Grau, A. L. (2012). The influence of authentic leadership on newly graduated nurses' experiences of workplace bullying, burnout and retention outcomes: A cross-sectional study. *International Journal of Nursing Studies, 49*, 1266–1276. doi:10.1016/j.ijnurstu.2012.05.012

Lazarus, R. S. & Folkman, S. (1984). *Stress, appraisal and coping*. New York, NY: Springer-Verlag.

Lazarus, R. S. & Folkman, S. (1987). Transactional theory and research on emotions and coping. *European Journal of Personality, 1*, 141–169. doi:10.1002/per.2410010304

Lea, M., & Spears, R. (1991). Computer-mediated communication, deindividuation, and group decision-making. *International Journal of Man-Machine Studies, 34*, 283— 301. doi:10.1016/ 0020–7373(91)90045–9

Leary, M. R., Kowalski, R. M., Smith, L., & Phillips, S. (2003). Teasing, rejection, and violence: Case studies of the school shootings. *Aggressive Behavior, 29*(3), 202–214. doi:10.1002/ab.10061

References

Lee, D. (2000). An analysis of workplace bullying in the UK. *Personnel Review, 29,* 593–613. doi:10.1108/00483480010296410

Lee, D. (2017). The cooperative games bullying prevention program: Cooperative games for a warm school climate Pre-K to Grade 2. *Multicultural Education, 24*(3/4), 51–52.

Lee, S., & Chae, Y. (2007). Children's Internet use in a family context: Influence on family relationships and parental mediation. *Cyber Psychology & Behavior, 10,* 640–644. doi:10.1089/cpb.2007.9975

Legislative Assembly of Ontario. (2011). Retrieved from www.ontla.on.ca/web/bills/bills_detail.do?locale=en&BillID=2550

Leitch, C. M., & Volery, T. (2017). Entrepreneurial leadership: Insights and directions. *International Small Business Journal, 35,* 147–156. doi:10.1177/0266242616681397

Leon-Perez, J. M., Medina, F. J., Arenas, A., & Munduate, L. (2015). The relationship between interpersonal conflict and workplace bullying. *Journal of Managerial Psychology, 30,* 250–260. doi:10.1108/JMP-01–2013–0034

Leontyev, A. N. (1977). Activity and consciousness. In *Philosophy in the USSR: Problems of dialectical Marxism* (R. Daglish, trans.) (pp. 180–202). Progress Publishers: Moscow.

Le Poire, B., Hallett, J. S., & Giles, H. (1998). Co-dependence: The paradoxical nature of the functional-afflicted relationship. In B. H. Spitzberg & W. R. Cupach (Eds.), *The dark side of close relationships* (pp. 153–176). Mahwah, NJ: Erlbaum.

Lereya, S., Samara, M., & Wolkec, D. (2013). Parenting behavior and the risk of becoming a victim and a bully/victim: A meta-analysis study. *Child Abuse and Neglect, 37,* 1091–1108. doi:10.1016/j.chiabu.2013.03.001

Lereya, S. T., Winsper, C., Heron, J., Lewis, G., Gunnell, D., Fisher, H. L., & Wolke, D. (2013). Being bullied during childhood and the prospective pathways to self-harm in late adolescence. *Journal of the American Academy of Child & Adolescent Psychiatry, 52*(6), 608–618. doi:10.1016/j.jaac.2013.03.012

Lerner, R. M. (2012). Developmental science: Past, present, and future. *International Journal of Developmental Science, 6,* 117–126. doi:10.3233/DEV-2012–12102

Lerner, R. M., & Callina, K. S. (2014). The study of character development: Towards tests of a relational developmental systems model. *Human Development, 57*(6), 322–346. doi:10.1159/000368784

Lester, J. (2009). Not your child's playground: Workplace bullying among community college faculty. *Community College Journal of Research and Practice, 33,* 444–462. doi:10.1080/10668920902728394

Lester, L., Pearce, N., Waters, S., Barnes, A., Beatty, S., & Cross, D. (2017). Family involvement in a whole-school bullying intervention: Mothers' and fathers' communication and influence with children. *Journal of Child & Family Studies, 26*(10), 2716–2727. doi:10.1007/s10826-017-0793-6

Levi, J. (n.d.). *Bullying and the laws pertaining to it.* Retrieved from http://digitalcommons.law.wne.edu/facschol/327/

Levy, B. (2009). Stereotype embodiment: A psychosocial approach to aging. *Current Directions in Psychological Science, 18*(6), 332–336. doi:10.1111/j.1467–8721.2009.01662.x

Lewicki, R., Saunders, D. M., & Minton, J. M. (1997). *Essentials of negotiation.* Chicago, IL: Irwin.

Lewis, D., & Gunn, R. (2007). Workplace bullying in the public sector: Understanding the racial dimension. *Public Administration, 85*(3), 641–665. doi:10.1111/j.1467–9299.2007.00665.x

Leymann, H. (1990). Mobbing and psychological terror at workplaces. *Violence and Victims, 5,* 199–126. Retrieved from www.mobbingportal.com/LeymannV%26V1990(3).pdf

Leymann, H. (1996). The content and development of mobbing at work. *European Journal of Work and Organizational Psychology, 5,* 165–184. doi:10.1080/13594329608414853

Lichtenstein, B. B., Uhl-Bien, M., Marion, R., Seers, A., Orton, J. D., & Schreiber, C. (2006). Complexity leadership theory: An interactive perspective on leading in complex adaptive systems. *Complexity & Organization, 8,* 2–12. Retrieved from http://digitalcommons.unl.edu/managementfacpub/8

Lindlof, T. R., & Taylor, B. C. (2017). *Qualitative communication research methods* ($_{4th}$ ed.). Thousand Oaks, CA: Sage.

Lippi-Green, R. (2003). *English with an accent: Language, ideology, and discrimination in the United States.* New York, NY: Routledge.

Livingstone, S. (2002). *Young people and new media.* New Delhi, India: Sage.

Livingstone, S. & Bovill, M. (2001). *Children and their changing media environment: A European comparative study.* Mahwah, NJ: Lawrence Erlbaum. Lohmann, R. C. (2012). Helping adolescents deal with anger and other emotions effectively. *Psychology Today.* Retrieved from www.psychologytoday.com/blog/teen-angst/ 201202/silent-cry-help-understanding-self-harm

London, M. (1983). Toward a theory of career motivation. *Academy of Management Review, 8,* 620–630. doi:10.5465/AMR.1983.4284664

Lucas, K. (2015). Workplace dignity: Communicating inherent, earned, and remediated dignity. *Journal of Management Studies, 52,* 621–646. doi:10.1111/joms.12133

References

Lucas, K., Manikas, A., Mattingly, E., & Crider, C. (2017). Engaging and misbehaving: How dignity affects employee work behaviors. *Organization Studies, 38*, 1505–1527. doi:10.1177/0170840616677634

Ludwig, S., & de Ruyter, K. (2016). Decoding social media speak: Developing a speech act theory research agenda. *Journal of Consumer Marketing, 33*(2), 124–134. doi:10.1108/JCM-04-2015-1405

Luker, J. M., & Churchak, B. C. (2017). International perceptions of cyberbullying within higher education. *Adult Learning, 28*, 144–156. doi:10.1177/1045159517719337

Lund, E. M., & Ross, S. W. (2017). Bullying perpetration, victimization, and demographic differences in college students: A review of the literature. *Trauma, Violence, & Abuse, 18*(3), 348–360. doi:10.1177/152483801 5620818

Lutgen-Sandvik, P. (2003). The communicative cycle of employee emotional abuse: Generation and regeneration of workplace mistreatment. *Management Communication Quarterly, 16*, 471–501. doi:10.1177/08933189032 51627

Lutgen-Sandvik, P. (2006). Take this job and. . . : Quitting and other forms of resistance to workplace bullying. *Communication Monographs, 73*(4), 406–433. doi:10.1080/03637750601024156

Lutgen-Sandvik, P. (2007). ". . . But words will never hurt me," abuse and bullying at work: A comparison between two worker samples. *Ohio Communication Journal, 45*, 81–105.

Lutgen-Sandvik, P. (2008). Intensive remedial identity work: Responses to workplace bullying trauma and stigmatization. *Organization, 15*, 97–119. doi:10.1177/1350508407084487

Lutgen-Sandvik, P. (2013). *Adult bullying—a nasty piece of work: Translating a decade of research on non-sexual harassment, psychological terror, mobbing, and emotional abuse on the job.* St. Louis, MO: ORCM Academic Press.

Lutgen-Sandvik, P. (2018). Vicarious and secondary victimization in adult bullying and mobbing: Co-workers, targets-partners, children, and friends. In M. Duffy & D. Yamada (Eds.), Santa Barbara, CA: Praeger.

Lutgen-Sandvik, P., & Davenport Sypher, B. (2009). Introduction. In P. Lutgen-Sandvik & B. Davenport Sypher (Eds.), *Destructive organizational communication: Processes, consequences, and constructive ways of organizing* (pp. 1–7). New York, NY: Routledge.

Lutgen-Sandvik, P., Hood, J. N., & Jacobson, R. P. (2016). The impact of positive organizational phenomena and workplace bullying on individual outcomes. *Journal of Managerial Issues, 28*(1/2), 30–49. Retrieved from www.researchgate.net/profile/Pamela_Lutgen-Sandvik/publication/ 292145009_The_ Impact_of_Positive_Organizational_Phenomena_and_Workplace_Bullying_on_Individual_Outcomes/ links/575c826308ae414b8e4c1cb4.pdf

Lutgen-Sandvik, P., & McDermott, V. (2008). The constitution of employee-abusive organizations: A communication flows theory. *Communication Theory, 18*, 304–333. doi:10.1111/j.1468–2885.2008.00324.x

Lutgen-Sandvik, P., & McDermott, V. (2011). Making sense of supervisory bullying: Perceived powerlessness, empowered possibilities. *Southern Communication Journal, 76*, 342–368. doi:10.1080/10417941003725307

Lutgen-Sandvik, P., Namie, G., & Namie, R. (2009). Workplace bullying: Causes, consequences, and corrections. In P. Lutgen-Sandvik & B. Davenport Sypher (Eds.), *Destructive organizational communication: Processes, consequences, & constructive ways of organizing* (pp. 27–52). New York, NY: Routledge.

Lutgen-Sandvik, P., Riforgiate, S., & Fletcher, C. (2011). Work as a source of positive emotional experiences and the discourses informing positive assessment. *Western Journal of Communication, 75*, 2–27. doi:10.1080/1057 0314.2010.536963

Lutgen-Sandvik, P., & Tracy, S. (2012). Answering five key questions about workplace bullying: How communication scholarship provides thought leadership for transforming abuse at work. *Management Communication Quarterly, 26*(1), 3–47. 10.1177/0893318911414400

Lutgen-Sandvik, P., Tracy, S. J., & Alberts, J. K. (2007). Burned by bullying in the American workplace: Prevalence, perception, degree, and impact. *Journal of Management Studies, 44*, 837–862. doi:10.1111/j.1467–6486.2007.00715.x

Lwin, M. O., Stanaland, A. J. S., & Miyazak, A. D. (2008). Protecting children's privacy online: How parental mediation strategies affect website safeguard effectiveness. *Journal of Retailing, 84*, 205–217. doi:10.1016/j. jretai.2008.04.004

Lyons, R. F., Mickelson, K. D., Sullivan, M. J. L., & Coyne, J. C. (1998). Coping as a communal process. *Journal of Social and Personal Relationships, 15*, 579–605. doi:10.1177/0265407598155001

MacGeorge, E. L., Feng, B., & Burleson, B. R. (2011). Supportive communication. In M. L. Knapp & J. A. Daly (Eds.), *Handbook of interpersonal communication* (4th ed., pp. 317–354). Thousand Oaks, CA: Sage.

MacGeorge, E. L., Feng, B., Butler, G. L., & Budarz, S. K. (2004). Understanding advice in supportive interactions: Beyond the facework and message evaluation paradigm. *Human Communication Research, 30*, 42–70. doi:10.1111/j.1468–2958.2004.tb00724.x

MacGeorge, E. L., Feng, B., & Guntzviller, L. M. (2016). Advice: Expanding the communication paradigm. In E. L. Cohen (Ed.), *Communication yearbook 40* (pp. 213–244). New York, NY: Routledge.

References

MacGeorge, E. L., Lichtman, R. M., & Pressey, L. C. (2002). The evaluation of advice in supportive interactions: Facework and contextual factors. *Human Communication Research, 28*, 451–463. doi:10.1111/j.1468–2958.2002. tb00815.x

MacIntosh, J., Wuest, J., Gray, M. M., & Aldous, S. (2010). Effects of workplace bullying on how women work. *Western Journal of Nursing Research, 32*, 910–931. doi:10.1177/0193945910362226

Madlock, P. E., & Kennedy-Lightsey, C. (2010). The effects of supervisors' verbal aggressiveness and mentoring on their subordinates. *Journal of Business Communication, 47*, 42–62. doi:10.1177/0021943609353511

Maguire, K., & Sahlstein, E. (2007). Pro-social, a-social, and anti-social coping in long distance romantic relationships. In T. A. Kinney & M. Pörhölä (Eds.), *Current advances in anti- & pro-social communication: An examination of theories, methods, and applications* (pp. 127–138). New York, NY: Peter Lang.

Mahady Wilton, M. M., & Craig, W. M. (2000). Emotional regulation and display in classroom victims of bullying: Characteristic expressions of affect, coping styles and relevant contextual factors. *Social Development, 9*, 226–244. doi:10.1111/1467–9507.00121

Malecki, C. K., & Demaray, M. K. (2003). What type of support do they need? Investigating student adjustment as related to emotional, informational, appraisal, and instrumental support. *School Psychology Quarterly, 18*, 231. doi:10.1521/scpq.18.3.231.22576

Mancini, A. D., Littleton, H. L., & Grills, A. E. (2016). Can people benefit from acute stress? Social support, psychological improvement, and resilience after the Virginia Tech campus shootings. *Clinical Psychological Science, 4(3)*, 401–417. doi:10.1177/2167702615601001

Mansson, D. H., & Myers, S. A. (2012). Using mentoring enactment theory to explore the doctoral student-advisor mentoring relationship. *Communication Education, 61*, 309–334. doi:10.1080/03634523.2012. 708424

Marcum, C. D., Higgins, G. E., & Nicholson, J. (2017). I'm watching you: Cyberstalking behaviors of university students in romantic relationships. *American Journal of Criminal Justice, 42(2)*, 373–388. doi:10.1007/s12103-016-9358-2

Marcum, C. D., Higgins, G. E., & Ricketts, M. L. (2014). Juveniles and cyber stalking in the United States: An analysis of theoretical predictors of patterns of online perpetration. *International Journal of Cyber Criminology, 8(1)*, 47–56. Retrieved from https://search.proquest.com/openview/194a2e3dca60708ae8691107c6467ce3/1?pq-origsite=gscholar&cbl=55114

Marini, Z. A., & Volk, A. A. (2017). Towards a transdisciplinary blueprint to studying bullying. *Journal of Youth Studies, 20(1)*, 94–109. doi:10.1080/13676261.2016.1184239

Mark, L., & Ratliffe, K. T. (2011). Cyber worlds: New playgrounds for bullying. *Computers in the Schools, 28(2)*, 92–116. doi:10.1080/07380569.2011.575753Martens, A., Goldenberg, J. L., & Greenberg, J. (2005). A terror management perspective on ageism. *Journal of Social Issues, 61(2)*, 223–239. doi:10.1111/j.1540–4560.2005. 00403.x

Martin, F., Wang, C., Petty, T., Wang, W., & Wilkins, P. (2018). Middle school students' social media use. *Journal of Educational Technology & Society, 21(1)*, 213–224. Retrieved from www.jstor.org/stable/26273881

Martin, J. N., & Nakayama, T. (1999). Thinking dialectically about culture and communication. *Communication Theory, 9*, 1–19. doi:10.1111/j.1468–2885.1999.tb00160.x

Martin, M. M., & Anderson, C. M. (1996). Argumentativeness and verbal aggressiveness. *Journal of Social Behavior and Personality, 11*, 547–554. Retrieved from https://search.proquest.com/openview/5e39c15b76a5be352c6dec3906b0fed4/1?pq-origsite=gscholar&cbl=1819046

Martin, M. M., & Anderson, C. M. (1997). Aggressive communication traits: How similar are young adults and their parents in argumentativeness, assertiveness, and verbal aggressiveness? *Western Journal of Communication, 61*, 299–314. doi:10.1080/10570319709374579

Martin, M. M., Anderson, C. M., Burant, P. A., & Weber, K. (1997). Verbal aggression in sibling relationships. *Communication Quarterly, 45*, 304–317. doi:10.1080/01463379709370067

Martin, M. M., Anderson, C. M., & Horvath, C. L. (1996). Feelings about verbal aggression: Justifications for sending and hurt from receiving verbally aggressive messages. *Communication Research Reports, 13*, 19–26. doi:10.1080/08824099609362066

Martin, M. M., Anderson, C. M., & Rocca, K. A. (2005). Perceptions of the adult sibling relationship. *North American Journal of Psychology, 7*, 107–116.

Martin, M. M., Goodboy, A. K., & Johnson, Z. (2015). When professors bully graduate students: Effects on student interest, instructional dissent, and intentions to leave graduate education. *Communication Education, 64*, 438–454. doi:10.1080/03634523.2015.1041995

Martin, M. M., Weber, K., Anderson, C. M., & Burant, P. A. (2004). Destructive communication in stepfamilies. In J. P. Morgan (Ed.), *Focus on aggression research* (pp. 41–52). Hauppauge, NY: Nova Science.

Martocci, L. (2015). *Bullying: The social destruction of self*. Philadelphia, PA: Temple University Press.

References

Marwick, A. E., & boyd, d. (2011). *The drama! Teen conflict, gossip, and bullying in networked publics* (SSRN Scholarly Paper No. ID 1926349). Rochester, NY: Social Science Research Network. Retrieved from http://papers.ssrn.com/abstract=1926349

Mathisen, G. E., Einarsen, S., & Mykletun, R. (2011). The relationship between supervisor personality, supervisors' perceived stress and workplace bullying. *Journal of Business Ethics, 99,* 637–651. doi:10.1007/s10551-010-0674-zMatsunaga, M. (2008). Item parceling in structural equation modeling: A primer. *Communication Methods & Measures, 2,* 260–293. doi:10.1080/19312450802458935

Matsunaga, M. (2008). Item parceling in structural equation modeling: A primer. *Communication Methods & Measures, 2,* 260–293. doi:10.1080/19312450802458935

Matsunaga, M. (2009). Parents don't (always) know their children have been bullied: Child- parent discrepancy on bullying and family-level profile of communication standards. *Human Communication Research, 35*(2), 221–247. doi:10.1111/j.1468- 2958.2009.01345.x

Matsunaga, M. (2010a). Individual dispositions and interpersonal concerns underlying bullied victims' self-disclosure in Japan and the US. *Journal of Social and Personal Relationships, 27,* 24–48. doi:10.01177/0265407510380084

Matsunaga, M. (2010b). Testing a mediational model of bullied victims' evaluation of received support and post-bullying adaptation: A Japan-U.S. cross-cultural comparison. *Communication Monographs, 77,* 312–340. doi:10.1080/0363775100378235

Matsunaga, M. (2011). Underlying circuits of social support for bullied victims: An appraisal- based perspective on supportive communication and postbullying adjustment. *Human Communication Research, 37,* 174–206. doi:10.1111/j.1468–2958.2010.01398.x

Matthiesen, S. B., & Einarsen, S. (2001). MMPI-2 configurations among victims of bullying at work. *European Journal of Work and Organizational Psychology, 10,* 467–484. doi:10.1080/13594320143000753

Maunder, R. E., & Crafter, S. (2018). School bullying from a sociocultural perspective. *Aggression and Violent Behavior, 38,* 13–20. doi:10.1016/j.avb.2017.10.010

Maynard, B. R., Vaughn, M. G., Salas-Wright, C. P., & Vaughn, S. R. (2016). Bullying victimization among school-aged immigrant youth in the United States. *The Journal of Adolescent Health: Official Publication of the Society for Adolescent Medicine, 58*(3), 337–344. doi:10.1016/j.jadohealth.2015.11.013

McCallion, G., & Feder, J. (2013). Student bullying: Overview of research, federal initiatives, and legal issues. *Congressional Research Service.* Retrieved from https://fas.org/sgp/crs/misc/R43254.pdf

McCroskey, J. C., & Beatty, M. J. (2000). The communibiological perspective: Implications for communication in instruction. *Communication Education, 49,* 1–6. doi:10.1080/03634520009379187

McKay, R., Arnold, D. H., Fratzl, J., & Thomas, R. (2008). Workplace bullying in academia: A Canadian study. *Employee Responsibilities and Rights Journal, 20,* 77–100. doi:10.1007/s10672-008-9073-3

McWilliam, K., King, R., Drennan, J., & Cunningham, S. (2016). Investigating the potential of peer-to-peer communications in Australian bullying campaigns targeting youth. *Communication Research and Practice, 2*(2), pp. 213–228. doi:10.1080/22041451.2016.1185929

Meares, M. M., Oetzel, J. G., Torres, A., Derkacs, D., & Ginossar, T. (2004). Employee mistreatment and muted voices in the culturally diverse workplace. *Journal of Applied Communication Research, 32,* 4–27. doi:10.1080/0090988042000178121

Mendez, J. J., Bauman, S., Sulkowski, M. L., Davis, S., & Nixon, C. (2016). Racially-focused peer victimization: Prevalence, psychosocial impacts, and the influence of coping strategies. *Psychology of Violence, 6,* 103–111. Retrieved from http://psycnet.apa.org/buy/2014-44483-001

Mendoza, K. (2009). Surveying parental mediation: Connections, challenges, and questions for media literacy. *Journal of Media literacy Education, 1,* 28–41. Retrieved from http://digitalcommons.uri.edu/jmle/vol1/iss1/3

Menesini, E., Camodeca, M., & Nocentini, A. (2010). Bullying among siblings: The role of personality and relational variables. *British Journal of Developmental Psychology, 28,* 921–939. doi:10.1348/026151009x479402

Merrin, G. J., Espelage, D. L., & Hong, J. S. (2018). Applying the social-ecological framework to understand the associations of bullying perpetration among high school students: A multilevel analysis. *Psychology of Violence, 8*(1), 43. doi:10.1037/vio0000084

Messias, E., Kindrick, K., & Castro, J. (2014). School bullying, cyberbullying, or both: Correlates of teen suicidality in the 2011 CDC Youth Risk Behavior Survey. *Comprehensive Psychiatry, 55*(5), 1063–1068. doi:10.1016/j.comppsych.2014.02.005

Meyer, J. (2003). *Kids talking: Learning relationships and culture with children.* Lanham, MD: Rowan & Littlefield.

Microsoft Corporation Survey. (2012). *Online bullying among youth 8–17 years old—India.* Retrieved from Microsoft Download Centre.

References

Miettinen, R. (1999). The riddle of things: Activity theory and actor-network theory as approaches to studying innovations. *Mind, Culture, and Activity, 6*(3), 170–195. doi:10.1080/10749039909524725

Mikkelson, A. C. (2014). Adult sibling relationships. In K. Floyd & M. T. Morman (Eds.), *Widening the family circle: New research on family communication* (2nd ed., pp. 19–34). Los Angeles, CA: Sage.

Miles, M. B., & Huberman, A. M. (1994). *Qualitative data analysis* (2nd ed.). Thousand Oaks, CA: Sage.

Miller-Day, M., Pezalla, A., & Chesnut, R. (2013). Children are in families tool: The presence of children in communication research. *Journal of Family Communication, 13*(2), 150–165. doi:10.1080/15267431.2013.768251

Mills, C. B., & Carwile, A. M. (2009). The good, the bad, and the borderline: Separating teasing from bullying. *Communication Education, 58*(2), 276–301. http://dx.doi.org/10.1080/03634520902783666

Misawa, M. (2015). Cuts and bruises caused by arrows, sticks, and stones in academia: Theorizing three types of racist and homophobic bullying in adult and higher education. *Adult Learning, 26*, 6–13. doi:10.1177/1045159514558413

Mishna, F. (2012). *Bullying: A guide to research, intervention, and prevention.* New York, NY: Oxford University Press.

Mishna, F., Cook, C., Gadalla, T., Daciuk, J., & Solomon, S. (2012). Cyber bullying behaviors among middle and high school students. *American Journal of Orthopsychiatry, 80*, 362–374. doi:10.1111/j.1939–0025.2010.01040.x

Mishra, P., & McDonald, K. (2017). Career resilience: An integrated review of the empirical literature. *Human Resource Development Review.* doi:10.1177/1534484317719622

Mitenko, G., & O'Hara, M. (2008). Assessing the mobility value of tenure to the faculty member. *Economics and Business Journal: Inquiries and Perspectives, 1*, 1–16. Retrieved from www.nebeconandbus.org/journal/v1n1p1.pdfMitsopoulou, E., & Giovazolias, T. (2015). Personality traits, empathy and bullying behavior: A meta-analytic approach. *Aggression and Violent Behavior, 21*, 61–72. doi:10.1016/j.avb.2015.01.007

Monge, P. R., & Contractor, N. S. (1999). Emergence of communication networks. In F. M. Jablin & L. L. Putnam (Eds.), *Handbook of organizational communication* (2nd ed.), pp. 441–501. Thousand Oaks, CA: Sage.

Monge, P. R., & Contractor, N. S. (2001). Emergence of communication networks. In F. M. Jablin & L. L. Putnam (Eds.), *The new handbook of organizational communication* (pp. 440–502). Thousand Oaks, CA: Sage.

Monks, C. P. (2011). Peer-victimisation in preschool. In C. P. Monks & Coyne, I. (Eds.), *Bullying in different contexts* (pp. 12–35). Cambridge: Cambridge University Press.

Monks, C. P., & Coyne, I. (Eds.) (2011). *Bullying in different contexts.* Cambridge: Cambridge University Press.

Monks, C. P., & Smith, P. K. (2006). Definitions of bullying: Age differences in understanding of the term, and the role of experience. *British Journal of Developmental Psychology, 24*, 801–821. doi:10.1348/026151005x82352

Monks, C. P., Smith, P. K., Naylor, P., Barter, C., Ireland, J. L., & Coyne, I. (2009). Bullying in different contexts: Commonalities, differences and the role of theory. *Aggression and Violent Behavior, 14*(2), 146–156. doi:10.1016/j.avb.2009.01.004

Moon, A. (2000). Perceptions of elder abuse among various cultural groups: Similarities and differences. *Generations, 24*(2), 75–81. Retrieved from https://search.proquest.com/docview/212184435/fulltextPDF/34B81F06E050419DPQ/1? accountid=12954

Moran, C. (2011). *The moderating effects of social support on the relationship between bullying and self-esteem in the elderly.* MA Thesis, Trent University, Canada. Retrieved from The Library and Archives of Canada, http://collectionscanada.gc.ca/ourl/res.php?url_ver=Z39.88–2004&url_tim=2017–10–08T16%3A36%3A44Z&url_ctx_fmt=info%3Aofi%2Ffmt%3Akev%3Amtx%3Actx&rft_dat=40777915&rfr_id=info%3Asid%2Fcollectionscanada.gc.ca%3Aamicus&lang=eng

Morgan, M. G., Fischhoff, B., Bostrom, A., & Atman, C. J. (2002). *Risk communication: A mental models approach.* New York, NY: Cambridge University Press.

Mueller, A. S., James, W., Abrutyn, S., & Levin, M. L. (2015). Research and practice. Suicide ideation and bullying among US adolescents: Examining the intersections of sexual orientation, gender, and race/ethnicity. *American Journal of Public Health, 105*(5), 980–985. doi:10.2105/AJPH.2014.302391

Mulki, J. P., Jaramillo, F., Malhotra, S., & Locander, W. B. (2012). Reluctant employees and felt stress: The moderating impact of manager decisiveness. *Journal of Business Research, 65*, 77–83. doi:10.1016/j.jbusres.2011.01.019

Mumby, D. K., & Ashcraft, K. L. (2006). Organizational communication studies and gendered organization: A response to Martin and Collinson. *Gender, Work & Organization, 13*(1), 68–90.

Mumby, D., & Clair, R. (1997). Organizational discourse. In T. A. van Dijk (Ed.), *Discourse studies II: Discourse as social interaction* (pp. 181–205). London: Sage.

Mumby, D. K., & Putnam, L. I. (1992). The politics of emotion: A feminist reading of bounded rationality. *Academy of Management Review, 17*(3), 465–486. doi:10.2307/258719

Music, G. (2016). Angels and devils: Sadism and violence in children. *Journal of Child Psychotherapy, 42*(3), 302–317. doi:10.1080/0075417x.2016.1238142

References

Myers, S. A., & Bryant, L. E. (2008a). Emerging adult siblings' use of verbally aggressive messages as hurtful messages. *Communication Quarterly, 56*, 268–283. doi:10.1080/01463370802240981

Myers, S. A., & Bryant, L. E. (2008b). The use of behavioral indicators of sibling commitment among emerging adults. *Journal of Family Communication, 8*, 101–125. doi:10.1080/15267430701857364

Myers, S. A., & Goodboy, A. K. (2006). Perceived sibling use of verbally aggressive messages across the lifespan. *Communication Research Reports, 23*, 1–11. doi:10.1080/17464090500535798

Myers, S. A., Goodboy, A. K., & Members of COMM 201. (2013). Using equity theory to explore adult siblings' use of relational maintenance behaviors and relational characteristics. *Communication Research Reports, 30*, 275–281. doi:10.1080/08824096.2013.836627

Myers, S. A., & Odenweller, K. G. (2015). The use of relational maintenance behaviors and relational characteristics among sibling types. *Communication Studies, 66*, 238–255. doi:10.1080/10510974.2014.930918

Nadal, K. L. (2011). The racial and ethnic microaggressions Scale (REMS): Construction, reliability, and validity. *Journal of Counseling Psychology, 58*(4), 470–480. doi:10.1037/a0025193

Nadal, K. L., Griffin, K. E., Wong, Y., Hamit, S., & Rasmus, M. (2014). The impact of racial microaggressions on mental health: Counseling implications for clients of color. *Journal of Counseling & Development, 92*(1), 57–66. doi:10.1002/j.1556–6676.2014.00130.x

Namie, G. (2003, November/December). Workplace bullying: Escalated incivility. *Ivey Business Journal Online*, 1–6. Retrieved from www.workplacebullying.org/multi/pdf/N-N-2003A.pdf

Namie, G. (2014, February). *2014 WBI U.S. Workplace Bullying Survey*. Retrieved from www.workplacebullying.org/wbiresearch/wbi-2014-us-survey/

Namie, G. (2017, June). *2017 WBI U.S. Workplace Bullying Survey*. Retrieved from www.workplacebullying.org/wbiresearch/wbi-2017-survey/

Namie, G., Christensen, D., & Phillips, D. (2014). *2014 WBI U.S. Workplace Bullying Survey*. Retrieved from www.workplacebullying.org/wbiresearch/wbi-2014-us-survey

Namie, G., & Lutgen-Sandvik, P. E. (2010). Active and passive accomplices: The communal character of workplace bullying. International Journal of Communication, 4, 343-373. doi: 1932-8036/20100343

Namie, G., & Namie, R. (2009). *The bully at work: What you can do to stop the hurt and reclaim your dignity on the job*. Naperville, IL: Sourcebooks.

Namie, G., Namie, R., & Lutgen-Sandvik, P. (2010). Challenging workplace bullying in the United States: An activist and public communication approach. In S. Einarsen, H. Hoel, D. Zapf, & C. L. Cooper (Eds.), *Bullying and harassment in the workplace: Developments in theory, research, and practice* (pp. 447–467). Boca Raton, FL: CRC Press.

Nansel, T. R., Craig, W., Overpeck, M. D., Saluja, G., & Ruan, W. J. (2004). Cross-national consistency in the relationship between bullying behaviors and psychosocial adjustment. *Archives of Pediatrics & Adolescent Medicine, 158*(8), 730–736.

Näsi, M., Keipi, T., Räsänen, P., & Oksanen, A. (2015). Cybercrime victimization among young people: A multination study. *Journal of Scandinavian Studies in Criminology & Crime Prevention, 16*(2), 203–210. doi:10.1080/14043858.2015.1046640

Nass, C., & Mason, L. (1990). On the study of technology and task: A variable-based approach. In J. Fulk & C. Steinfield (Eds.), *Organizations and communication technology* (pp. 46– 67). Newbury Park, CA: Sage.

Nassem, E., & Harris, A. (2015). Why do children bully? *School Leadership Today, 6*, 68–73.

National Center for Education Statistics. (2016). *Student reports of bullying: Results from the 2015 school crime supplement to the National Crime Victimization Survey*. U.S. Department of Education. Retrieved from https://nces.ed.gov/pubs2017/2017015.pdf

National Center for Health Statistics. (2013). *Health, United States, 2012: With special feature on emergency care*. Hyattsville, MD. Retrieved November 24, 2017, from www.cdc.gov/nchs/data/hus/hus12.pdf#018

National Center for Health Statistics. (2017). *Mortality in the United States, 2016*. Hyattsville, MD. Retrieved from www.cdc.gov/nchs/products/databriefs/db293.htm

National Center for Mental Health Promotion and Youth Violence Prevention. (2011). *Bullying prevention state laws*. Retrieved from www.promoteprevent.org/sites/www.promoteprevent.org/files/resources/Bullying%20Prevention%20State%20Laws_2.pdf

National Public Radio (2013, September 12). *How one unkind moment gave way to 'Wonder.'* Retrieved from https://www.npr.org/2013/09/12/221005752/how-one-unkind-moment-gave-way-to-wonder

Navayan, P. K., & Chitale, C. M. (2016). Mobbing of teaching faculties in higher education with Special reference to scheduled caste faculties: A phenomenological study. *Khoj Journal of Indian Management Research & Practices, 2016 Special Issue*, 87–96. Retrieved from www.mitsom.org

NCES. (2016). *Indicators of school crime and safety: 2015*. U.S. Department of Education. Retrieved from https://nces.ed.gov/fastfacts/display.asp?id=719

References

Nelson, E., & Lambert, R. (2001). Sticks, stones and semantics: The ivory tower bully's vocabulary of motives. *Qualitative Sociology, 24*, 83–106. doi:10.1023/A:1026695430820

Nelson, L. J., & Barry, C. M. (2005). Distinguishing features of emerging adulthood: The role of self-classification as an adult. *Journal of Adolescent Research, 20*, 242–262. doi:10.1177/0743558404273074

Nelson, T. D. (Ed.). (2004). *Ageism: Stereotyping and prejudice against older persons.* Boston, MA: MIT Press.

Nelson, T. D. (2005). Ageism: Prejudice against our feared future self. *Journal of Social Issues, 61*(2), 207–221. doi:10.1111/j.1540–4560.2005.00402.x

Nelson, T. D. (2017). *Ageism, stereotyping and prejudice against older persons.* Boston, MA: MIT Press.

Netemeyer, R. G., Maxham, J. G. III, & Pullig, C. (2005). Conflicts in the work-family interface: Links to job stress, customer service employee performance, and customer purchase intent. *Journal of Marketing, 69*, 130–143. doi:10.1509/jmkg.69.2.130.60758

Nguyen, T. M. P. & Nguyen, T. Q. C. (2002). Stealing access: A case study in Hanoi. In K. Shetty (Ed.), *Kids on-line: Promoting responsible use and a safe environment on the Net in Asia*, (pp. 216–233). Singapore: AMIC/NTU.

Nielsen, M. B., & Einarsen, S. (2012). Outcomes of exposure to workplace bullying: A meta- analytic review. *Work & Stress: An International Journal of Work, Health & Organisations, 26*, 309–332. doi:10.1080/02678373.2012.734709

Nielsen, M. B., Notelaers, G., & Einarsen, S. (2011). Measuring exposure to workplace bullying. In S. Einarsen, H. Hoel, D. Zapf, & C. L. Cooper (Eds.), *Bullying and harassment in the workplace: Developments in theory, research, and practice* (2nd ed., pp. 149–174). Boca Raton, FL: CRC Press.

Nikken, P. (2011). *Parental mediation of young children Internet use, EU kids online.* II Final Conference, September 2011. Retrieved from http://www2.lse.ac.uk/media@lse/research/EUKidsOnline/Conference%202011/Nikken.pdf

Nikken, P., & Jansz, J. (2006). Parental mediation of children's videogame playing: A comparison of the reports by parents and children. *Learning, Media and Technology, 31*, 181–202. doi:10.1080/17439880600756803

Nobles, M. R., Reyns, B. W., Fox, K. A., & Fisher, B. S. (2014). Protection against pursuit: A conceptual and empirical comparison of cyberstalking and stalking victimization among a national sample. *JQ: Justice Quarterly, 31*(6), 986–1014. doi:10.1080/07418825.2012.723030

No Bullying.com. (2014, February 25). *Six unforgettable cyberbullying cases.* Retrieved from https://www.prweb.com/releases/2014/02/prweb11609229.htm

NoBullying.com. (2017, March 26). *Bullying in India reaches epic proportions.* Retrieved from nobullying.com/bullying-in-india-2

North Carolina General Statues, Chapter 115, Article 29c (2009).

North Carolina State Board of Education. (2017). *Reports and statistics.* Retrieved from www.ncpublicschools.org/data/reports/

Norton Cyber Security Insights Report. (2016). Published by Symantec. Retrieved from us.norton.com/cyber-security-insights

Nosek, B. A., Banaji, M., & Greenwald, A. G. (2002). Harvesting implicit group attitudes and beliefs from a demonstration web site. *Group Dynamics: Theory, Research, and Practice, 6*, 101–115. doi:10.1037/1089–2699.6.1.101

Notelaers, G., Baillien, De Witte, Einarsen, S., & Vermunt, J. K. (2013). Testing the strain hypothesis of the demand control model to explain severe bullying at work. *Economic and Industrial Democracy, 34*, 69–87. doi:10.1177/0143831X12438742

Nussbaum, J. F. (Ed.). (2014). *The handbook of lifespan communication.* New York, NY: Peter Lang.

Nussbaum, J. F., Pitts, M. J., Huber, F. N., Krieger, J. L. R., & Ohs, J. E. (2005). Ageism and ageist language across the life span: Intimate relationships and non-intimate interactions. *Journal of Social Issues, 61*(2), 287–305. doi:10.1111/j.1540–4560.2005.00406.x

Nyborg, K., Anderies, J. M., Dannenberg, A., Lindahl, T., Schill, C., Schlüter, M., & Polasky, S. (2016). Social norms as solutions. *Science, 354*(6308), 42–43. doi:10.1126/science.aaf8317

Oakley, J., & Cocking, D. (2001). *Virtue ethics and professional roles.* New York, NY: Cambridge University Press.

Obermaier, M., Fawzi, N., & Koch, T. (2016). Bystanding or standing by? How the number of bystanders affects the intention to intervene in cyberbullying. *New Media & Society, 18*(8), 1491–1507. doi:10.1177/1461444814563519

O'Brennan, L. M., Bradshaw, C. P., & Sawyer, A. L. (2009). Examining developmental differences in the social-emotional problems among frequent bullies, victims, and bully/victims. *Psychology in the Schools, 46*, 100–115. doi:10.1002/pits.20357

O'Connell, P., Pepler, D., & Craig, W. (1999). Peer involvement in bullying: Insights and challenges for intervention. *Journal of Adolescence, 22*, 437–452. doi:10.1006/jado.1999.0238

References

Odenweller, K. G., Rittenour, C. E., Myers, S. A., & Brann, M. (2013). Father-son family communication patterns and gender ideologies: A modeling and compensation analysis. *Journal of Family Communication, 13,* 340–356. doi:10.1080/15267431.2013.823432

O'Farrell, C., & Nordstrom, C. R. (2013). Workplace bullying: Examining self-monitoring and organizational culture. *Journal of Psychological Issues in Organizational Culture, 3*(4), 6–17.

Ofe, E. E., Plumb, A. M., Plexico, L. W., & Haak, N. J. (2016). School-based speech-language pathologists' knowledge and perceptions of autism spectrum disorder and bullying. *Language, Speech, and Hearing Services in Schools, 47*(1), 59–76. doi:10.1044/2015_LSHSS-15–0058

Ofe, E. E., Plumb, A. M., Plexico, L. W., Haaka, N. J., Nippold, M., & Kelly, E. (2016). School- based speech-language pathologists' knowledge and perceptions of Autism spectrum disorder and bullying. *Language, Speech & Hearing Services in Schools, 47*(1), 59–76.

Ogle, C. M., Rubin, D. C., & Siegler, I. C. (2013). The impact of the developmental timing of trauma exposure on PTSD symptoms and psychosocial functioning among older adults. *Developmental Psychology, 49*(11), 2191. doi:10.1037/a0031985

Oladapo, V., & Banks, L. T. (2013). Management bullies: The effects on employees. *Journal of Business Studies Quarterly, 4*(4), 107–120. Retrieved from http://jbsq.org/

Olweus, D. (1993a). *Bullying at school.* Oxford, UK: Blackwell.

Olweus, D. (1993b). Victimization by peers: Antecedents and long-term outcomes. In K. H. Rubin & J. B. Asendorpf (Eds.), *Social withdrawal, inhibition, and shyness in childhood* (pp. 315–341). Hillsdale, NJ: Erlbaum.

Olweus, D. (1997). Bully/victim problems in school: Facts and intervention. *European Journal of Psychology of Education, 12,* 495–510. doi:10.1007/BF03172807

Olweus, D. (2013a). *Bullying at school.* Hoboken, NJ: Wiley & Sons.

Olweus, D. (2013b). School bullying: Development and some important challenges. *Annual Review of Clinical Psychology, 9,* 751–780. doi:10.1146/annurev-clinpsy-050212–185516

Olweus Bullying Prevention Program. (2018). Retrieved from https://olweus.sites.clemson.edu/index.html

Oransky, M., & Marecek, J. (2009). "I'm not going to be a girl": Masculinity and emotions in boys' friendships and peer groups. *Journal of Adolescent Research, 24,* 218–241. doi:10.1177/0743558408329951

Orbe, M. P. (1998). *Constructing co-cultural theory: An explication of culture, power, and communication.* Thousand Oaks, CA: Sage. doi:10.4135/9781483345321

Orbe, M. P. & Batten, C. (2017). Diverse dominant group responses to contemporary co-cultural concerns: U.S. intergroup dynamics in the Trump era. *Journal of Contemporary Rhetoric, 7*(1), 19–33. ISSN: 2161539X.

Orbe, M. & Harris, T. M. (2015). *Interracial communication: Theory to practice* (3rd ed.). Thousand Oaks, CA: Sage.

O'Reilly, C. A. (2008). Corporations, culture and commitment: Motivation and social control in organizations. *California Management Review, 31,* 9–25. doi:10.2307/41166436

Ortega, A., Høgh, A., Pejtersen, J. H., & Olsen, O. (2009). Prevalence of workplace bullying and risk groups: A representative population study. *International Archives of Occupational and Environmental Health, 82,* 417–426. doi:10.1007/s00420-009-0409-6

Ortman, J. M., Velkoff, V. A., & Hogan, H. (2014, May). *An aging nation: The older population in the United States.* Retrieved November 24, 2017, from www.census.gov/prod/2014pubs/p25-1140.pdf

O'Sullivan, P. B., & Carr, C. T. (2017). Masspersonal communication: A model bridging the mass-interpersonal divide. Online first: doi:10.1177/1461444816686104

Owen, F. (1984). Interpretive themes in relational communication. *Quarterly Journal of Speech, 70,* 274–287. doi:10.1080/00335638409383697

Oxford English Dictionary online. (2017). Retrieved from www.oed.com

PACER Center. (2018). *Pacer's national bullying prevention center.* Retrieved from www.pacer.org/bullying/

Paek, H. J., Hove, T., Ju Jeong, H., & Kim, M. (2011). Peer or expert? The persuasive impact of YouTube public service announcement producers. *International Journal of Advertising, 30*(1), 161–188. doi:10.2501/IJA-30-1-161-188

Palmer, S. B., & Abbott, N. (2018), Bystander responses to bias-based bullying in schools: A developmental intergroup approach. *Child Developmental Perspectives, 12,* 39–44. doi:10.1111/cdep.12253

Pan, S., & Spittal, P. (2013). Health effects of perceived racial and religious bullying among urban adolescents in China: A cross-sectional national study. *Global Public Health, 8*(6), 685–697. doi:10.1080/17441692.2013.799218

Park, J. H., & Ono, M. (2017). Effects of workplace bullying on work engagement and health: The mediating role of job insecurity. *International Journal of Human Resource Management, 28,* 3202–3225. doi:10.1080/09585192.2016.1155164

Patchin, J. W., & Hinduja, S. (2006). Bullies move beyond the schoolyard: A preliminary look at cyberbullying. *Youth Violence and Juvenile Injustice, 4,* 148–169. doi:10.1177/1541204006286288

References

Patchin, J. W., & Hinduja, S. (2016). Summary of our cyberbullying research (2004–2016). *Cyberbullying Research Center*. Retrieved from http://cyberbullying.org/summary-of-our-cyberbullying-research

Patton, T. O. (2004). In the guise of civility: The complicitous maintenance of inferential forms of sexism and racism in higher education. *Women's Studies in Communication, 27*, 60–87. doi:10.1080/07491409.2004.101 62466

Paul, S., Smith, P. K., & Blumberg, H. H. (2012). Comparing student perceptions of coping strategies and school interventions in managing bullying and cyberbullying incidents. *Pastoral Care in Education, 30*, 127–146. doi :10.1080/02643944.2012.679957

Pearce, N., Cross, D., Monks, H., Waters, S., & Falconer, S. (2011). Current evidence of best practice in whole-school bullying intervention and its potential to inform cyberbullying interventions. *Australian Journal of Guidance and Counselling, 21*, 1–21. doi:10.1375/ajgc.21.1.1

Pearlin, L. I., & Schooler, C. (1978). The structure of coping. *Journal of Health and Social Behavior, 19*, 2–21. doi:10.2307/2136319

Pearson, C. M., Andersson, L. M., & Porath, C. L. (2000). Assessing and attacking workplace incivility. *Organizational Dynamics, 20*, 123–137. Retrieved from www.researchgate.net/profile/Christine_Porath/publi cation/228079608_Assessing_an_attacking_workplace_incivility/links/5663616108ae192bbf8ef07a/ Assessing-an-attacking-workplace-incivility.pdf

Pearson, C., & Porath, C. (2009). *The cost of bad behavior: How incivility is damaging your business and what to do about it.* New York, NY: Portfolio.

Peguero, A. A. (2012). Schools, bullying, and inequality: Intersecting factors and complexities with the stratification of youth victimization at school. *Sociology Compass, 6*, 402–412. doi:10.1111/j.1751–9020.2012.00459.x

Peguero, A. A., & Williams, L. M. (2013). Racial and ethnic stereotypes and bullying victimization. *Youth & Society, 45*(4), 545–564. doi:10.1177/0044118X11424757

Pepler, D., & Cummings, J. (2016). Bullying in early childhood. In O. Saracho (Ed.), *Contemporary perspectives on research on bullying and victimization in early childhood education* (pp. 35–59). Charlotte, NC: Information Age.

Pereira, F., Spitzberg, B. H., & Matos, M. (2016). Cyber-harassment victimization in Portugal: Prevalence, fear and help-seeking among adolescents. *Computers in Human Behavior, 62*, 136–146. doi:10.1016/j.chb.2016.03.039

Perlus, J., Brooks-Russell, A., Wang, J., & Iannotti, R. (2014). Trends in bullying, physical fighting, and weapon carrying among 6th-through 10th-grade students from 1998–2010: Findings from a national study. *American Journal of Public Health, 104*(6), 1100–1106. doi:10.2105/AJPH.2013.301761

Peters, A. B. (2014). Faculty to faculty incivility: Experiences of novice nurse faculty in academia. *Journal of Professional Nursing, 30*, 213–227. doi:10.1016/j.profnurs.2013.09.007

Pew Internet & American Life Project. (2011). *Teens, kindness and cruelty on social network sites.* Retrieved from www.pewinternet.org/Reports/2011/Teens-and-social-media.aspx

Pew Research Center. (2013). *Living to 120 and beyond: Americans' views on aging, medical advances and radical life extension.* Retrieved November 24, 2017, from www.pewforum.org/2013/08/06/living-to-120-and-beyond-americans-views-on-aging-medical-advances-and-radical-life-extension/

Pew Research Center. (2014). *Online harassment.* Retrieved from www.pewinternet.org/2014/10/22/ online-harassment/

Picchi, A. (2017). *A workplace epidemic of bullying LGBT employees.* Retrieved from www.cbsnews.com/news/ bullying-lgbt-employees-workplace-epidemic/

Pigliucci, M. (2013). The demarcation problem: A (belated) response to Laudan. In M. Pigliucci & M. Boudry (Eds.), *Philosophy of pseudoscience: Reconsidering the demarcation problem* (pp. 9–28). Chicago, IL: University of Chicago Press.

Piotrowski, C. (2015). Adult bullying syndrome: A bibliometric analysis on concordance with personality disorder traits. *Journal of Instructional Psychology, 42*(1), 1–3. Retrieved from www.learntechlib.org

Piotrowski, C., & King, C. (2016). The enigma of adult bullying in higher education: A research-based conceptual framework. *Education, 136*(3), 299–306. Retrieved from www.projectinnovation.com/education.html

Planalp, S., & Fitness, J. (2011). Interpersonal communication ethics. In G. Cheney, S. May, & D. Munshi (Eds.), *The handbook of communication ethics* (pp. 135–147). New York, NY: Routledge.

Plopa, M., Plopa, W., & Skuzińska, A. (2017). Bullying at work, personality and subjective well-being. *Journal of Occupational Health Psychology, 22*, 19–27. doi:10.1037/a0040320

Podnieks, E. (2008). Elder abuse: The Canadian experience. *Journal of Elder Abuse & Neglect, 20*(2), 126–150. doi:10.1080/08946560801974612

Podsakoff, P. M., MacKenzie, S. B., Lee, J-Y., & Podsakoff, N. P. (2003). Common method biases in behavioral research: A critical review of the literature and recommended remedies. *Journal of Applied Psychology, 88*, 879–903. doi:10.1037/0021-9010.88.5.879

Popper, K. (1974). The problem of demarcation. In D. Miller (Ed.), *Popper selections* (pp. 118–130). Princeton, NJ: Princeton University.

References

Popper, K. (1980). Science: Conjectures and refutations. In E. D. Klemke, R. Hollinger, & A. D. Kline (Eds.), *Introductory readings in the philosophy of science* (pp. 19–34). Buffalo, NY: Prometheus.

Porath, C. L., & Erez, A. (2009). Overlooked but not untouched: How rudeness reduces onlookers' performance on routine and creative tasks. *Organizational Behavior and Human Decision Processes, 109*, 29–44. doi:10.1016/j.obhdp.2009.01.003

Pörhölä, M., Karhunen, S., & Rainivaara, S. (2006). Bullying at school and in the workplace: A challenge for communication research. In C. S. Beck (Ed.), *Communication yearbook 30* (pp. 249–301). New York, NY: Routledge. doi:10.1080/23808985.2006.11679059

Poropat, A. E. (2009). A meta-analysis of the five-factor model of personality and academic performance. *Psychological Bulletin, 135*, 322–338. doi:10.1037/a0014996

Postigo, S., González, R., Montoya, I., & Ordoñez, A. (2013). Theoretical proposals in bullying research: A review. *Anales De Psicología, 29*(2), 413–425. doi:10.6018/analesps.29.2.148251

Postmes, T., Spears, R., Sakhel, K., & De Groot, D. (2001). Social influence in computer- mediated communication: The effects of anonymity on group behavior. *Personality and Social Psychology Bulletin, 27*, 1243–1254. doi:10.1177/01461672012710001

Pottie, K., Dahal, G., Georgiades, K., Premji, K., & Hassan, G. (2015). Do first generation immigrant adolescents face higher rates of bullying, violence and suicidal behaviours than do third generation and native born? *Journal of Immigrant Minority Health, 17*(5), 1557–1566. doi:10.1007/s10903-014-0108-6

Preacher, K. J., Zhang, Z., & Zyphur, M. J. (2011). Alternative methods for assessing mediation in multilevel data: The advantages of multilevel SEM. *Structural Equation Modeling, 18*, 161–182. doi:10.1080/10705511.2011.557329

Presno, C. (2014). *Four-year-old mean girls, really? Manipulation starting in preschool.* Retrieved from www.psychologytoday.com/blog/parenting-your-preschooler/ 201401/four-year-old-mean-girls-really

PREVnet. (2017, September 5). *"Roasting" is the new cyberbullying.* Retrieved from www.prevnet.ca/news/in-the-news/roasting-is-the-new-cyberbullying

Priest, N., King, T., Bécares, L., & Kavanagh, A. M. (2016). Bullying victimization and racial discrimination among Australian children. *American Journal of Public Health, 106*(10), 1882–1884. doi:10.2105/ajph.2016.303328

Privitera, C., & Campbell, M. A. (2009). Cyberbullying: The new face of workplace bullying? *CyberPsychology & Behavior, 12*, 395–400. doi:10.1089/cpb.2009.0025

Public Safety Canada. (2016). *Bullying prevention: Nature and extent of bullying in Canada.* Retrieved from www.publicsafety.gc.ca/cnt/rsrcs/pblctns/bllng-prvntn/index-en.aspx

Puckett, M. B., Aikins, J. W., & Cillessen, A. N. (2008). Moderators of the association between relational aggression and perceived popularity. *Aggressive Behavior, 34*(6), 563–576. doi:10.1002/ab.20280

Putter, S. (2007). Peer victimization: The role of self-efficacy in children's coping strategies. *Journal of Undergraduate Research, 5*, 82–86. Retrieved from http://hdl.handle.net/1802/5163

Puzic, S. (2015, March 9). Anti-cyberbullying law, Bill C-13, now in effect. *CTV News.* Retrieved from www.ctvnews.ca/politics/anti-cyberbullying-law-bill-c-13-now-in-effect-1.2270460

Pyżalski, J. (2012). From cyberbullying to electronic aggression: Typology of the phenomenon. *Emotional and Behavioural Difficulties, 17*, 305–317. doi:10.1080/13632752.2012.704319

Quinlan, E. (2009). New action research techniques: Using participatory theatre with health care workers. *Action Research, 8*, 117–133. doi:10.1177/1476750309335204

Quinn, P. (2015). Adult bullying—are we taking it seriously? *Therapy Today, 26*, 18–21.

Qureshi, M., Rasli, A., & Zaman, K. (2014). A new trilogy to understand the relationship among organizational climate, workplace bullying and employee health, *Arab Economics and Business Journal, 9*, 133–146. doi:10.1016/j.aebj.2014.05.009

Raina, D., & Balodi, G. (2014). Ageism and stereotyping of the older adult. *Scholars Journal of Applied Medical Sciences, 2*(2), 733–739. doi:10.21276/sjams

Rains, S., & Wright, K. B. (2016). Social support and computer-mediated communication: A state-of-the-art review and agenda for future research. In E. L. Cohen (Ed.), *Communication yearbook 40* (pp. 175–211). New York, NY: Routledge. doi:10.1080/23808985.2015.11735260

Rains, S. A., & Keating, D. M. (2011). The social dimension of blogging about health: Health blogging, social support, and well-being. *Communication Monographs, 78*, 511–534. doi:10.1080/03637751.2011.618142

Rains, S. A., & Young, V. (2009). A meta-analysis of research on formal computer-mediated support groups: Examining group characteristics and health outcomes. *Human Communication Research, 35*, 309–336. doi:10.1111/j.1468-2958.2009.01353.x

Rananand, P. R. (2002). Defining responsibility: A report from Thailand. In K. Shetty (Ed.), *Kids on-line: Promoting responsible use and a safe environment on the net in Asia* (pp. 236–254). Singapore: AMIC/NTU.

References

Rancer, A. S., Lin, Y., Durbin, J. M., & Faulkner, E. C. (2010). Nonverbal "verbal" aggression: Its forms and its relation to trait verbal aggression. In T. A. Avtgis & A. S. Rancer (Eds.), *Arguments, aggression, and conflict* (pp. 267–284). New York, NY: Routledge.

Randall, P. (1997). *Adult bullying: Perpetrators and victims.* London: Routledge.

Randall, P. (2001). *Bullying in adulthood: Assessing the bullies and their victims.* East Sussex, UK: Brunner-Routledge.

Rapolienė, G. (2015). Aging identity: Do theories match experiences? *Corvinus Journal of Sociology and Social Policy, 6*(1), 3–24. doi:10.14267/cjssp.2015.01.01

Raskauskas, J. (2010). Text-bullying: Associations with traditional bullying and depression among New Zealand adolescents. *Journal of School Violence, 9*(1), 74–97. doi:10.1080/15388220903185605

Raskauskas, J., & Huynh, A. (2015). The process of coping with cyberbullying: A systematic review. *Aggression and Violent Behavior, 23,* 118–125. doi:10.1016/j.avb.2015.05.019

Raskauskas, J., & Skrabec, C. (2011). Bullying and occupational stress in academia: Experiences of victims of workplace bullying in New Zealand universities. *Journal of Intergroup Relations, 35*(1), 18–36. Retrieved from www.iaohra.org/

Raudenbush, S. W., & Bryk, A. S. (2002). *Hierarchical linear models: Applications and data analysis methods.* Thousand Oaks, CA: Sage.

Razzali, N. (2002). Security over safety: A report from Malaysia. In K. Shetty (Ed.), *Kids on-line: Promoting responsible use and a safe environment on the Net in Asia* (pp. 84- 108). Singapore: AMIC/NTU.

Razzante, R. J. (2017, November). *Identifying dominant group communication strategies: A phenomenological study.* Paper presented at the annual meeting of the National Communication Association, Dallas, TX.

Razzante, R. J., & Orbe, M. P. (2017, November). *Two sides of the same coin: Conceptualizing dominant group theory in the context of co-cultural theory.* Paper presented at the annual meeting of the National Communication Association, Dallas, TX.

Razzante, R. J., & Orbe, M. P. (2018). Two sides of the same coin: Conceptualizing dominant group theory in the context of co-cultural theory. *Communication Theory, 28*(1), 1–22. doi: 10.1093/ct/qtx008/4972627

Reed, K. P., Nugent, W., & Cooper, R. L. (2015). Testing a path model of relationships between gender, age, and bullying victimization and violent behavior, substance abuse, depression, suicidal ideation, and suicide attempts in adolescents. *Children and Youth Services Review, 55,* 128–137. doi:10.1016/j.childyouth.2015.05.016

Rehabilitation Act of 1973, Section 504, Public Law No. 93–112, 87 Stat. 394 (Sept 26, 1973).

Reid, G. M., Holt, M. K., Bowman, C. E., Espelage, D. L., & Green, J. G. (2016). Perceived social support and mental health among first-year college students with histories of bullying victimization. *Journal of Child and Family Studies, 25,* 3331–3341. doi:10.1007/s10826-016-0477-7

Reigle, R. (2016). *Bullying of adjunct faculty at community colleges and steps toward resolution.* Retrieved from https://eric.ed.gov/?id=ED563989

Rex-Lear, M. (2011). *Not just a playground issue: Bullying among older adults and the effects on their physical health.* Unpublished doctoral dissertation, University of Texas, Arlington, TX. Retrieved from https://dspace.uta.edu/bitstream/handle/ 10106/6207/REXLEAR_uta_2502D_11293.pdf?sequence=

Rhee, S., & Waldman, I. D. (2002). Genetic and environmental influences on antisocial behavior: A meta-analysis of twin and adoption studies. *Psychological Bulletin, 29,* 490—529. doi:10.1037/0033–2909.128.3.490

Rideout, V. J., Foehr, U. G., & Roberts, D. F. (2010). *Generation M^2 media in the lives of 8-to 18-year-olds.* Menlo Park, CA: Kaiser Family Foundation. Retrieved from https://files.eric.ed.gov/fulltext/ED527859.pdf

Rivera, D. P., Forquer, E. E., & Rangel, R. (2010). Microaggressions and the life experience of Latina/o Americans. In D. W. Sue (Ed.), *Microaggressions and marginality: Manifestation, dynamics, and impact* (pp. 59–83). New York, NY: Wiley & Sons.

Rivers, I. (2013). What to measure? In S. Bauman, D. Cross, & J. Walker (Eds.), *Principles of cyberbullying research: Definitions, measures, and methodology* (pp. 222–237). New York, NY: Routledge.

Rivers, I., & Duncan, N. (2013). *Bullying: Experiences and discourses of sexuality and gender.* London: Routledge.

Roberto, A. J. & Eden, J. (2010). Cyberbullying: Aggressive communication in the digital age. In T. A. Avtgis & A. S. Rancer (Eds.), *Arguments, aggression, and conflict: New direction in theory and research* (pp. 198–216). New York, NY: Routledge.

Roberto, A. J., Eden, J., Savage, M. W., Ramos-Salazar, L,. & Deiss, D. M. (2014). Outcome evaluation results of school-based cybersafety promotion and cyberbullying prevention intervention for middle school students. *Health Communication, 29*(10), 1029–1042. doi:10.1080/10410236.2013.831684.

Rocca, K. A., Martin, M. M., & Dunleavy, K. N. (2010). Siblings' motives for talking to each other. *Journal of Psychology, 144,* 205–219. doi:10.1080/00223980903356099

Roderick, L. (Ed.). (2016). *Toxic Fridays: Resources for addressing faculty bullying in higher education.* Anchorage, AK: University of Alaska.

References

Rodríguez-Hidalgo, A. J., Ortega-Ruiz, R., & Monks, C. P. (2015). Peer-victimisation in multicultural contexts: A structural model of the effects on self-esteem and emotions. *Psicologia Educativa, 21*(1), 3–9. doi:10.1016/j.pse.2015.02.002

Rose, A. J., & Rudolph, K. D. (2006). A review of sex differences in peer relationship process: Potential trade-offs for the emotional and behavioral development of girls and boys. *Psychological Bulletin, 132*, 98–131. doi:10.1037/0033–2909.132.1.98

Rose, C. A., Espelage, D. L., Monda-Amaya, L. E., Shogren, K. A., & Aragon, S. R. (2013). Bullying and middle school students with and without specific learning disabilities. *Journal of Learning Disabilities, 3*, 239–254. doi:10.1177/0022219413496279

Roth, S., & Cohen, L. J. (1986). Approach, avoidance, and coping with stress. *American Psychologist, 41*, 813–819. doi:10.1037/0003–066X.41.7.813

Ruiter, R. A., Kessels, L. T., Peters, G. J. Y., & Kok, G. (2014). Sixty years of fear appeal research: Current state of the evidence. *International Journal of Psychology, 49*, 63–70. doi:10.1002/ijop.12042

Ryan, E. B., Bourhis, R. Y., & Knops, U. (1991). Evaluative perceptions of patronizing speech addressed to elders. *Psychology and Aging, 6*, 442–450. doi:10.1037//0882–7974.6.3.442

Ryvicker, M. (2009). Preservation of self in the nursing home: Contradictory practices within two models of care. *Journal of Aging Studies, 23*(1), 12–23. doi:10.1016/j.jaging.2007.09.004

Sainio, M., Veenstra, R., Huitsing, G., & Salmivalli, C. (2011). Victims and their defenders: A dyadic approach. *International Journal of Behavioral Development, 35*, 144–151. doi:10.1177/0165025410378068

Sakurai, K., & Jex, S. (2012). Coworker incivility and incivility targets' work effort and counterproductive work behaviors: The moderating role of supervisor social support. *Journal of Occupational Health Psychology, 17*, 150–161. doi:10.1037/a0027350

Salari, S. M. (2006). Infantilization as elder mistreatment: Evidence from five adult day centers. *Journal of Elder Abuse & Neglect, 17*(4), 53–9. dio:10.1300/j084v17n04_04

Salari, S., Brown, B. B., & Eaton, J. (2006). Conflicts, friendship cliques and territorial displays in senior center environments. *Journal of Aging Studies, 20*(3), 237–252. dio:10.1016/j.jaging.2005.09.004

Salari, S. M., & Rich, M. (2001). Social and environmental infantilization of aged persons: Observations in two adult day care centers. *The International Journal of Aging and Human Development, 52*(2), 115–134. doi:10.2190/1219-b2gw-y5g1-jfeg.

Salehi, R. (2010). Intersection of health, immigration, and youth: A systematic literature review. *Journal of Immigrant and Minority Health, 12*(5), 788–97. doi:10.1007/s10903-009-9247-6

Salin, D. (2003). Ways of explaining workplace bullying: A review of enabling, motivating and precipitating structures and processes in the work environment. *Human Relations, 56*, 1213–1232. doi:10.1177%2F00187267035610003

Salin, D., & Hoel, H. (2011). Organisational causes of workplace bullying. In S. Einarsen, H. Hoel, D. Zapf, & C. L. Cooper (Eds.), *Bullying and harassment in the workplace: Developments in theory, research, and practice* (pp. 227–243). Boca Raton, FL: CRC Press.

Salmivalli, C., Lagerspetz, K., Björkqvist, K., Österman, K., & Kaukiainen, A. (1996). Bullying as a group process: Participant roles and their relations to social status within the group. *Aggressive Behavior, 22*, 1–15. doi:10.1002/(SICI)1098–2337(1996)22:1<1::AID-AB1>3.0.CO;2-T.

Salmivalli, C. (2010). Bullying and the peer group: A review. *Aggression and Violent Behavior, 15*, 112–120. doi:10.1016/j.avb.2009.08.007

Salmivalli, C., Huttenen, A., & Lagerspetz, K. (1997). Peer networks and bullying in schools. *Scandinavian Journal of Psychology, 38*, 305–312. doi:10.1111/1467–9450.00040

Salmivalli, C., & Voeten, M. (2004). Connections between attitudes, group norms and behavior associated with bullying in schools. *International Journal of Behavioral Development, 28*, 246–258. doi:10.1080/01650250344000488

Samnani, A. K., & Singh, P. (2012). 20 years of workplace bullying research: A review of the antecedents and consequences of bullying in the workplace. *Aggression and Violent Behavior, 17*(6), 581–589. doi:10.1016/j.avb.2012.08.004

Samnani, A-K., & Singh, P. (2014). Performance-enhancing compensation practices and employee productivity: The role of workplace bullying. *Human Resource Management Review, 24*, 5–16. doi:10.1016/j.hrmr.2013.08.013

Sampasa-Kanyinga, H., Roumeliotis, P., & Xu, H. (2014). Associations between cyberbullying and school bullying victimization and suicidal ideation, plans and attempts among Canadian schoolchildren. *Plos One, 9*(7). doi:10.1371/journal.pone.0102145

Sandhu, N. K., Kemp, C. L., Ball, M. M., Burgess, E. O., & Perkins, M. M. (2013). Coming together and pulling apart: Exploring the influence of functional status on co-resident relationships in assisted living. *Journal of Aging Studies, 27*(4), 317–329. doi:10.1016/j.jaging.2013.07.001

References

Sandvig, C. (2006). The Structural Problems of the Internet for Cultural Policy. In D. Silver & A. Massanari (Eds.), *Critical cyberculture studies* (pp. 107–118). New York, NY: NYU Press.

Sapouna, M., & Wolke, D. (2013). Resilience to bullying victimization: The role of individual, family and peer characteristics. *Child Abuse Neglect, 37*(11), 997–1006. doi:10.1016/j.chiabu.2013.05.009

Sarıçam, H. (2016). The mediator role of social safeness and pleasure in relation between mobbing and meaning of work in academicians. *Education & Science, 41*(184), 349–361. doi:10.15390/EB.2016.6201

Sarros, J. C., Cooper, B. K., & Santora, J. C. (2008). Building a climate for innovation through transformational leadership and organizational culture. *Journal of Leadership & Organizational Studies, 15*, 145–158. doi:10.1177/1548051808324100

Sarros, J. C., Gray, J., Densten, I. L., & Cooper, B. (2005). The organizational culture profile revisited and revised: An Australian perspective. *Australian Journal of Management, 30*, 159–182. doi:10.1177/031289620503 000109

Sass, J. S., & Mattson, M. (1999). When social support is uncomfortable: The communicative accomplishment of support as a cultural term in a youth intervention program. *Management Communication Quarterly, 12*, 511–543. doi:10.1177/0893318999124002

Savage, M. W., Deiss, D. M., Roberto, A. J., Aboujaoude, E., & Deiss, D. J. (2017). Theory-based formative research on an anti-cyberbullying victimization intervention message. *Journal of Health Communication, 22*(2), 124–134. doi:10.1080/10810730.2016.1252818

Sayer, A. (2007). Dignity at work: Broadening the agenda. *Organization, 14*, 565–581. doi:10.1177/1350508407078053

Scharf, M., Shulman, S., & Avigad-Spitz, L. (2005). Sibling relationships in emerging adulthood and in adolescence. *Journal of Adolescent Research, 20*, 64–90. doi:10.1177/0743558404271133

Schef, S. (n.d.). *How workplace bullying is impacting LGBT employees.* Retrieved from www.psychologytoday.com/blog/shame-nation/201710/how-workplace-bullying-is-impacting-lgbt-employees

Schenk, A. M., & Fremouw, W. J. (2012). Prevalence, psychological impact, and coping of cyberbully victims among college students. *Journal of School Violence, 11*(1), 21–37. doi:10.1080/15388220.2011.630310

Scherr, T. G. (2012, March 5). Bullying others: Factoring in race, ethnicity and immigration. *Education.com.* Retrieved from www.education.com/reference/article/bullying-factoring-race-ethnicity-immigration/

Schmidt, E., & Cohen, J. (2013). *The new digital age: Reshaping the future of people, nations and business.* New York: Knopf.

Schrag, C. O. (1997). *The self after postmodernity.* New Haven, CT: Yale University Press.

Schrock, A. R. (2015). Communicative affordances of mobile media: Portability, availability, locatability, and multimediality. *International Journal of Communication, 91*, 229–1246. Retrieved from http://ijoc.org/index.php/ijoc/article/viewFile/3288/1363

Schrodt, P., & Carr, K. (2012). Trait verbal aggressiveness as a function of family communication patterns. *Communication Research Reports, 29*, 54–63. doi:10.1080/08824096.2011.639914

Schumann, L., Craig, W., & Rosu, A. (2013). Minority in the majority: Community ethnicity as a context for racial bullying and victimization. *Journal of Community Psychology, 41*(8), 959–972. doi:10.1002/jcop.21585

Scully, M., & Rowe, M. (2009). Bystander training within organizations. *Journal of the International Ombudsman Association, 2*(1), 1–9. Retrieved from www.bu.edu/fafc/files/2012/05/bystander.pdf

Sedivy-Benton, A., Strohschen, G., Cavazos, N., & Boden-McGill, C. (2014). Good ol'boys, mean girls, and tyrants: A phenomenological study of the lived experiences and survival strategies of bullied women adult educators. *Adult Learning, 26*, 35–41. doi:10.1177/1045159514558411

Seeger, M. W. (1997). *Ethics and organizational communication.* Cresskill, NJ: Hampton.

Seery, M. D., Leo, R. J., Lupien, S. P., Kondrak, C. L., & Almonte, J. L. (2013). An upside to adversity?: Moderate cumulative lifetime adversity is associated with resilient responses in the face of controlled stressors. *Psychological Science, 24*(7), 1181–1189. doi:10.1177/0956797612469210

Sekerka, L. E., Comer, D. R., & Goodwin, L. N. (2014). Positive organizational ethics: Cultivating and sustaining moral performance. *Journal of Business Ethics, 119*, 435–444. doi:10.1007/s10551-013-1911-z.

Sen, S. (2016). *Paradigm shift in cyber crime.* Retrieved from www.scribd.com/doc/294873811/Paradigm-Shift-in-Cyber-Crime-by-Srikanta-Sen

Şentürk, Ş., & Bayat, S. (2016). Internet usage habits and cyberbullying related opinions of secondary school students. *Universal Journal of Educational Research, 4*, 1103–1110. doi:10.13189/ujer.2016.040520

Sepe, C. (2015). *Bullying among older adults in retirement homes: An unknown epidemic* (Unpublished undergraduate thesis). California State University, San Bernardino, CA.

Serrow, R. C. (2000). Research and teaching at a research university. *Higher Education, 40*, 449–463. Retrieved from www.jstor.org/stable/3448010

Shakya, Y., Khanlou, N., & Gonsalves, T. (2010). Determinants of mental health for newcomer youth: Policy and service implications. *Canadian Issue/Themes Canadiens,* Summer 2010, 98–102. Retrieved from http://

References

accessalliance.ca/wp-content/uploads/2015/03/Determinants_of_Mental_Health_for_Newcomer_Youth-Cdn_Issues.pdf

Shelley, D., & Craig, W. M. (2010). Attributions and coping styles in reducing victimization. *Canadian Journal of School Psychology, 25*, 84–100. doi:10.11771082957350957067

Shenk, J. W. (2014). *Power of two: Finding the essence of innovation in creative pairs.* New York, NY: Eamon Dolan/Houghton Mifflin Harcourt.

Sheridan, L. P., & Grant, T. (2007). Is cyberstalking different? *Psychology, Crime & Law, 13*, 627–640. doi:10.1080/10683160701340528

Sherman, D. K., & Cohen, G. L. (2006). The psychology of self-defense: Self-affirmation theory. *Advances in Experimental Social Psychology, 38*, 183–242. doi:10.1016/s0065–2601(06)38004–5

Shin, J. Y., D'Antonio, E., Son, H., Kim, S., & Park, Y. (2011). Bullying and discrimination experiences among Korean-American adolescents. *Journal of Adolescence, 34*, 873–883. doi:10.1016/j.adolescence.2011.01.004

Simpson, R., & Cohen, C. (2004). Dangerous work: The gendered nature of bullying in the context of higher education. *Gender, Work and Organization, 11*, 163–186. doi:10.1111/j.1468–0432.2004.00227.x.

Skinner, E. A., & Zimmer-Gembeck, M. J. (2007). The development of coping. Annual *Review of Psychology, 58*, 119–144. doi:10.1146/annurev.psych.58.110405.085705

Skinner, J. A., & Kowalski, R. M. (2013). Profiles of sibling bullying. *Journal of Interpersonal Violence, 28*, 1726–1736. doi:10.1177/0886260512468327

Skogstad, A., Einarsen, S., Torsheim, T., Aasland, M. S. & Hetland, H. (2007). The destructiveness of laissez-faire leadership. *Journal of Occupational Health Psychology, 12*, 80–92. doi:10.1037/1076–8998.12.1.80

Skogstad, A., Nielsen, M. B., & Einarsen, S. (2017). Destructive forms of leadership and their relationships with employee well-being. In E. K. Kelloway, K. Nielsen & J. K. Dimoff (Eds.), *Leading to occupational health and safety: How leadership behaviours impact organizational safety and well-being* (pp. 163–196). West Sussex, UK: Wiley.

Slonje, R., & Smith, P. K. (2008). Cyberbullying: Another main type of bullying? *Scandinavian Journal of Psychology, 49*(2), 147–154. doi:10.1111/j.1467–9450.2007.00611.x.

Smith, A. (2015, April 1). *U.S. Smartphone Use in 2015.* Retrieved from www.pewinternet.org/2015/04/01/us-smartphone-use-in-2015/

Smith, P., Ananiadou, K., & Cowie, H. (2003). Interventions to reduce school bullying. *Canadian Journal of Psychiatry, 48*, 591–599. doi:10.1177/070674370304800905

Smith, P. K. (1997). Bullying in life-span perspective: What can studies of school bullying and workplace bullying learn from each other? *Journal of Community and Applied Social Psychology, 7*, 249–255. doi:10.1002/(SICI)1099–1298(199706)7:3<249::AID-CASP425>3.0.CO;2

Smith, P. K. (2011). Bullying in schools: Thirty years of research. In C. P. Monks & I. Coyne (Eds.), *Bullying in different contexts* (pp. 36–60). Cambridge: Cambridge University Press.

Smith, P. K. (2014). *Understanding school bullying: Its nature & prevention strategies.* Los Angeles, CA: Sage.

Smith, P. K., Del Barrio, C., & Tokunaga, R. S. (2013). Definitions of bullying and cyberbullying: How useful are the terms? In S. Bauman, D. Cross, & J. Walker (Eds.), *Principles of cyberbullying research: Definitions, measures, and methodology* (pp. 26–40). New York: Routledge.

Smith, P. K., Mahdavi, J., Carvalho, M., Fisher, S., Russell, S., & Tippett, N. (2008). Cyberbullying: Its nature and impact in secondary school pupils. *Journal of Child Psychology and Psychiatry, 49*(4), 376–385. doi:10.1111/j.1469–7610.2007.01846.x.

Smith, P. K., Singer, M., Hoel, H., & Cooper, C. L. (2003). Victimization in the school and the workplace: Are there any links? *British Journal of Psychology, 94*, 175–188. doi:10.1348/000712603321661868

Smoker, M., & March, E. (2017). Predicting perpetration of intimate partner cyberstalking: Gender and the Dark Tetrad. *Computers in Human Behavior, 72390*–396. doi:10.1016/j.chb.2017.03.012

Smorti, A., Menesini, E., & Smith, P. K. (2003). Parents' definitions of children's bullying in a five-country comparison. *Journal of Cross-Cultural Psychology, 34*(4), 417–432. doi:10.1177/0022022103034004003

Snakenborg, J., Acker, R. V. & Gable, R. A. (2011). Cyberbullying: Prevention and intervention to protect our children and youth. *Preventing School Failure: Alternative Education for Children and Youth, 55*, 88–95. doi:10.1080/1045988X.2011.539454

Sneed, J. R., Johnson, J. G., Cohen, P., Gilligan, C., Chen, H., Crawford, T. N., & Kasen, S. (2006). Gender differences in the age-changing relationship between instrumentality and family contact in emerging adulthood. *Developmental Psychology, 42*, 787–797. doi:10.1037/0012–1649.42.5.787

Sneed, J. R., & Whitbourne, S. K. (2005). Models of the aging self. *Journal of Social Issues, 61*(2), 375–388. doi:10.1111/j.1540–4560.2005.00411.x.

Socha, T. J. (1999). Communication in family units: Studying the first 'group'. In L. R. Frey (Ed.), *Handbook of group communication theory & research* (pp. 475–492). Thousand Oaks, CA: Sage.

References

Socha, T. J., & Beck, G. A. (2015). Positive communication and human needs: A review and proposed organizing conceptual framework. *Review of Communication, 15,* 173–199. doi:10.1080/15358593.2015.1080290

Socha, T. J., & Eller, A. (2015). Parent/caregiver-child communication and moral development: Toward a conceptual foundation of an ecological model of lifespan communication and good relationships. In V. Waldron & D. Kelley (Eds.), *Moral talk across the lifespan: Creating good relationships* (pp. 15–34). New York, NY: Peter Lang.

Socha, T. J., & Pitts, M. J. (Eds.). (2012). *The positive side of interpersonal communication.* New York, NY: Peter Lang.

Socha, T. J., & Yingling, J. A. (2010). *Families communicating with children.* Cambridge, UK: Polity.

Solis, B. (2007). *The social media manifesto.* Retrieved February 10, 2013, from www.briansolis.com/2007/06/future-of-communications-manifesto-for/

Sommer, F., Leuschner, V., & Scheithauer, H. (2014). Bullying, romantic rejection, and conflicts with teachers: The crucial role of social dynamics in the development of school shootings—A systematic review. *International Journal of Developmental Science, 8*(1–2), 3–24. doi:10.3233/DEV-140129

Sontag, L. M., Clemans, K. H., Graber, J. A., & Lyndon, S. T. (2011). Traditional and cyber aggressors and victims: A comparison of psychosocial characteristics. *Journal of Youth & Adolescence, 40,* 392–404. doi:10.1007/s10964-010-9575-9

Sourander, A., Klomek, A. B., Ikonen, M., Lindroos, J., Lutamo, T., Koskelainen, M., Ristkari, T., & Heneius, H. (2010). Psychosocial risk factors associated with cyberbullying among adolescents: A population-based study. *Archives of General Psychiatry, 67,* 720–728. doi:10.1001/archgenpsychiatry.2010.79

Southern Poverty Law Center (2016, November 28). *The trump effect: The impact of the 2016 Presidential election on our nation's schools.* Retrieved from www.splcenter.org/20161128/trump-effect-impact-2016-presidential-election-our-nations-schools

Spitzberg, B. H. (2014). Toward a model of meme diffusion (M^3D). *Communication Theory, 24,* 311–339. doi:10.1111/comt.12042

Spitzberg, B. H. (2015). Assessing the state of assessment: Communication competence. In A. F. Hannawa & B. H. Spitzberg (Eds.), *Communication competence* (pp. 559–584). Boston, MA: De Gruyter Mouton.

Spitzberg, B. H. (2017). Acknowledgement of unwanted pursuit, threats, assault and stalking in a college population. *Psychology of Violence, 7*(2), 265–275. http://dx.doi.org.libproxy.sdsu.edu/10.1037/a0040205

Spitzberg, B. H., & Cupach, W. R. (Eds.) (1998). *The dark side of close relationships.* Mahwah, NJ: Erlbaum.

Spitzberg, B. H., & Cupach, W. R. (Eds.) (2007). *The dark side of interpersonal communication* (2nd ed.) Mahwah, NJ: Erlbaum.

Spitzberg, B. H., & Cupach, W. R. (2014). *The dark side of relationship pursuit: From attraction to obsession and stalking* (2nd ed.). New York, NY: Routledge.

Spitzberg, B. H., Cupach, W. R., Hannawa, A. F., & Crowley, J. P. (2014). A preliminary test of a relational goal pursuit theory of obsessive relational intrusion and stalking. *Studies in Communication Sciences, 14*(1), 29–36. doi:10.1016/j.scoms.2014.03.007

Spitzberg, B. H., & Hoobler, G. (2002). Cyberstalking and the technologies of interpersonal terrorism. *New Media & Society, 4*(1), 71–92. doi:10.1177/14614440222226271

Spradlin, A. (1998). The price of "passing:" A lesbian perspective on authenticity in organizations. *Management Communication Quarterly, 11*(4), 598–605. doi:10.1177/0893318998114006

Spriggs, A. L., Iannotti, R. J., Nansel, T. R., & Haynie, D. L. (2007). Adolescent bullying involvement and perceived family, peer and school relations: Commonalities and differences across race/ethnicity. *Journal of Adolescent Health, 41,* 283–293. doi:10.1016/j.jadohealth.2007.04.009

Sridhar, S. (2001). Protecting children in cyberspace. *Media Asia, 28,* 135–144. doi:10.1080/01296612.2001.11726643

Standen, P., Paull, M., & Omari, M. (2014). Workplace bullying: Propositions from Heider's balance theory. *Journal of Management & Organization, 20*(6), 733–748. doi:10.1017/jmo.2014.57

Statistics Canada. (2008). Census snapshot—Immigration in Canada: A portrait of the foreign-born population, 2006 census. Technical Report. 11–008-X. Ottawa, ON: Statistics Canada.

Statistics Canada. (2013). Immigration and ethnocultural diversity in Canada: National Household Survey, 2011. Analytical document. Statistics Canada Catalogue No. 99–010-XWE2011001. Ottawa, Ontario: Statistics Canada. Retrieved from http://www12.statcan.gc.ca/nhs-enm/2011/as-sa/99-010-x/99-010-x2011001-eng.pdf

Stewart, J. (2011). A contribution to ethical theory and praxis. In G. Cheney, S. May, & D. Mushi (Eds.), *The handbook of communication ethics* (pp. 15–30). New York, NY: Routledge.

Stocker, C. M., Lanthier, R. P., & Furman, W. (1997). Sibling relationships in early adulthood. *Journal of Family Psychology, 11,* 210–221. doi:10.1037/0893-3200.11.2.210

Stohl, C., & Schell, S. (1991). A communication-based model of a small-group dysfunction. *Management Communication Quarterly, 5,* 90–110. Retrieved from www.egosnet.org/os

References

Stoll, L. C., & Block, R. Jr. (2015). Intersectionality and cyberbullying: A study of cybervictimization in a Midwestern high school. *Computers in Human Behavior, 52,* 387–397. doi:10.1016/j.chb.2015.06.010

Stopbullying.gov. (n.d.). *Key components in state anti-bullying laws: Policies and laws.* Retrieved from www.stopbullying.gov/laws/keycomponents/index.html

StopBullying.gov. (2017a). *U.S. Department of Health & Human Services.* Retrieved from www.stopbullying.gov

StopBullying.gov. (2017b). *U.S. Department of Health & Human Services.* Retrieved from www.stopbullying.gov/laws/index.html

Stone, A. L., & Carlisle, S. K. (2017). Racial bullying and adolescent substance use: An examination of school-attending young adolescents in the United States. *Journal of Ethnicity in Substance Abuse, 16*(1), 23–42. doi:10.1080/15332640.2015.1095666

Storey, J. (1993). The take-up of human resource management by mainstream companies: Key lessons from research. *International Journal of Human Resource Management, 4,* 529–553. doi:10.1080/09585199300000035

Strasburger, V. C., Wilson, B. J., & Jordan, A. B. (2014). *Children, adolescents, and the media* (3rd ed.). Thousand Oaks, CA: Sage.

Strauss, A., & Corbin, J. (1998). *Basics of qualitative research: Techniques and procedures for developing ground theory.* Thousand Oaks, CA: Sage.

Streiner, D. L. (2003). Being inconsistent about consistency: When coefficient alpha does and doesn't matter. *Journal of Personality Assessment, 80*(3), 217–222. doi:10.1207/S15327752JPA8003_01

Submit the Documentary. (2013, July 19). *It's not physical it's personal: Cyberbullying PSA* [Video file]. Retrieved from www.youtube.com/watch?v=gyAtYa6qMWM

Sue, D. W., Capodilupo, C. M., Torino, G. C., Bucceri, J. M., Holder, A. M., Nadal, K. L., & Esquilin, M. E. (2007). Racial microaggressions in everyday life: Implications for counseling. *American Psychologist, 62,* 271–286. doi:10.1037/0003–066X.62.4.271

Suler, J. (2004). The online disinhibition effect. *Cyberpsychology & Behavior, 7,* 321–326. doi:10.1089/1094931041291295

Sulkowski, M. L., Bauman, S., Wright, S., Nixon, C., & Davis, S. (2014). Peer victimization in youth from immigrant and non-immigrant US families. *School Psychology International, 35*(6), 649–669. doi:10.1177/0143034314554968

Sutcliffe, A. G., Gonzalez, V., Binder, J., & Nevarez, G. (2011). Social mediating technologies: Social affordances and functionalities. *International Journal of Human-Computer Interaction, 27*(11), 1037–1065. doi:10.1080/10447318.2011.555318

Swearer, S. M., Espelage, D. L., Vaillancourt, T. & Hymel, S. (2010). What can be done about school bullying? Linking research to educational practice. *Educational Researcher, 39,* 38–47. doi:10.3102/0013189X09357622

Swearer, S. M., Siebecker, A. B., Johnsen-Frerichs, L. A., & Wang, C. (2010). Assessment of bullying/victimization: The problem of comparability across studies and across methodologies. In S. M. Swearer, S. R. Jimerson, D. L. Espelage, S. R. Jimerson, S. M. Swearer, & D. L. Espelage (Eds.), *Handbook of bullying in schools: An international perspective* (pp. 305–327). New York, NY: Routledge.

Sypher, B. D. (2004). Reclaiming civil discourse in the workplace. *Southern Communication Journal, 69,* 257–269.

Takizawa, R., Maughan, B., & Arseneault, L. (2014). Adult health outcomes of childhood bullying victimization: Evidence from a five-decade longitudinal British birth cohort. *American Journal of Psychiatry, 171,* 777–784. doi:10.1176/appi.ajp.2014.13101401

Tanigawa, D., Furlong, M. J., Felix, E. D., & Sharkey, J. D. (2011). The protective role of perceived social support against the manifestation of depressive symptoms in peer victims. *Journal of School Violence, 10,* 393–412. doi:10.1080/15388220.2011.602614

Tattum, D. P., & Herbert, G. (Eds.). (1997). *Bullying: Home, school and community.* London: David Fulton Publishers.

Taylor, B. C., & Hawes, L. C. (2011). What are we, then? Postmodernism, globalization, and the meta-ethics of contemporary communication. In G. Cheney, S. May, & D. Mushi (Eds.), *The handbook of communication ethics* (pp. 99–118). New York: Routledge.

Taylor, C. (1989). *Sources of the self: The making of the modern identity.* Cambridge, MA: Harvard University Press.

Taylor, P., Morin, R., Parker, K., Cohn, D., & Wang, W. (2009, June 29). *Growing old in America: Expectations vs. reality. Pew Research Center: A social and demographic trends report.* Retrieved from www.pewsocialtrends.org/2009/06/29/growing-old-in-america-expectations-vs-reality/

Taylor, S. (2013). Workplace bullying: Does tenure change anything? The example of a Midwestern research university. In J. Lester (Ed.), *Workplace bullying in higher education* (pp. 23–40). New York, NY: Routledge.

Tedeschi, J. T., & Felson, R. B. (1994). *Violence, aggression, and coercive actions.* Washington, DC: American Psychological Association.

Tehrani, N. (2001). A total quality approach to building a culture of respect. In N. Tehrani (Ed.), *Building a culture of respect: Managing bullying at work* (pp. 135–154). London: Taylor & Francis.

References

Tenenbaum, L. S., Varjas, K., Meyers, J., & Parris, L. (2011). Coping strategies and perceived effectiveness in fourth through eighth grade victims of bullying. *School Psychology International, 32,* 263–287. doi:10.1177/0143034311402309

Teo, A. (2012). Social isolation associated with depression: A case report of hikikomori. *International Journal of Social Psychiatry, 56*(2), 339–341. doi:10.1177/0020764012437128

Teven, J. J., Martin, M. M., & Neupauer, N. C. (1998). Sibling relationships: Verbally aggressive messages and their effect on relationship satisfaction. *Communication Reports, 11,* 179–186. doi:10.1080/08934219809367699

Theiss, S. L. (2007). *Intervention strategies used by academic administrators in cases of bullying among employees.* M. A. thesis. Retrieved from www.proquest.com/products-services/pqdtglobal.html

Theiss, S., & Webb, L. M. (2016). Workplace bullying: U.S. academic manager's intervention strategies. In E. S. Gilchrist-Petty & S. D. Long (Eds.) *Contexts of the dark side of communication* (pp. 50–74). New York, NY: Peter Lang.

A Thin Line. (2011, March 9). *Tattoo—The hurt of digital harassment can last forever* [Video file]. Retrieved from www.athinline.org/videos/1-tattoo

Thompson, E. R., & Phua, F. T.T. (2012). A brief index of affective job satisfaction. *Group & Organization Management, 37,* 275–307. doi:10.1177/1059601111434201

Thornberg, R. (2015). School bullying as a collective action: Stigma processes and identity struggling. *Children & Society, 29*(4), 310–320. doi:10.1111/chso.12058

The Times of India. (2015, March 10). CBSE directs schools to form anti-bullying committee. Retrieved October 19, 2017, from https://timesofindia.indiatimes.com/city/allahabad/CBSE-directs-schools-to-form-anti-bullying-committee/articleshow/46521102.cms

Tokunaga, R. S. (2010). Following you home from school: A critical review and synthesis of research on cyberbullying victimization. *Computers in Human Behavior, 26*(3), 277–287. doi:10.1016/j.chb.2009.11.014

Tokunaga, R. R., & Aune, K. S. (2017). Cyber-defense: A taxonomy of tactics for managing cyberstalking. *Journal of Interpersonal Violence, 32*(10), 1451–1475. doi:10.1177/0886260515589564

Tracy, S. J. (2010). Qualitative quality: Eight "big-tent" criteria for excellent qualitative research. *Qualitative Inquiry, 16,* 837–851. Retrieved from http://qix.sagepub.com/

Tracy, S. J. (2013). *Qualitative research methods: Collecting evidence, crafting analysis, communicating impact.* Hoboken, NJ: Wiley-Blackwell.

Tracy, S. J., Alberts, J. K., & Rivera, K. D. (2009). *How to bust the office bully: Eight tactics for explaining workplace abuse to decision-makers.* Retrieved from https://staffombuds.berkeley.edu/sites/default/files/how_to_bust_the_office_bully.pdf

Tracy, S. J., & Donovan, M. C. J. (2018). Moving from practical application to expert craft practice in organizational communication: A review of the past and OPPT-ing into the future. In P. J. Salem & E Timmerman (Eds.), *Transformative practices and research in organizational communication* (pp. 202–220). Hershey, PA: IGI Global.

Tracy, S. J., Franks, T., Brooks, M. M., & Hoffman, T. K. (2015). An OPPT-in approach to relational and emotional organizational communication pedagogy. *Management Communication Quarterly, 29,* 322–328. doi:10.1177/0893318915571350

Tracy, S. J., Lutgen-Sandvik, P., & Alberts, J. K. (2006). Nightmares, demons and slaves: Exploring the painful metaphors of workplace bullying. *Management Communication Quarterly, 20,* 148–185. doi:10.1177/0893318906291980

Triandis, H. C., & Gelfand, M. J. (1998). Converging measurement of horizontal and vertical individualism and collectivism. *Journal of Personality and Social Psychology, 74,* 118–128.

Ttofi, M. M., & Farrington, D. P. (2011). Effectiveness of school-based programs to reduce bullying: A systematic and meta-analytic review. *Journal of Experimental Criminology, 7*(1), 27–56. doi:10.1007/s11292-010-9109-1

Tuckey, M. R., Dollard, M. F., Hosking, P. J., & Winefield, A. H. (2009). Workplace bullying: The role of psychosocial work environment factors. *International Journal of Stress Management, 16,* 215–232. doi:10.1037/a0016841

Tunac De Pedro, K., Pineda, D., Capp, G., Moore, H., Benbenishty, R., & Astor, R. A. (2017). Implementation of a school district wide grassroots anti-bullying initiative: A school staff and parent-focused evaluation of because nice matters. *Children & Schools, 39*(3), 137–145. doi:10.1093/cs/cdx008

Turner, H. A., Finkelhor, D., Shattuck, A., Hamby, S., & Mitchell, K. (2014, October 20). Beyond bullying: Aggravating elements of peer victimization episodes. *School Psychology Quarterly.* http://dx.doi.org/10.1037/spq0000058

Twale, D. J. (2018). *Understanding and preventing faculty-on-faculty bullying: A psycho-social-organizational approach.* New York: Routledge.

Twale, D. J., & De Luca, B. M. (2008). *Faculty incivility: The rise of the academic bully culture and what to do about it.* San Francisco, CA: Jossey-Bass.

References

Twemlow, S. W., Fonagy, P., & Sacco, F. C. (2004). The role of the bystander in the social architecture of bullying and violence in schools and communities. *Annals New York Academy of Sciences, 1036,* 215–232. doi:10.1196/annals.1330.014

Tye-Williams, S. (2005, April). *Workplace bullying: A narrative analysis of "The Vortex of Evil."* Paper presented at the annual meeting of the Central States Communication Association, Indianapolis, IN.

Tye-Williams, S., & Krone, K. J. (2015). Chaos, quests, and reports: Narrative agency and co- workers in stories of workplace bullying. *Management Communication Quarterly, 29,* 3–27. doi:10.1177/0893318914552029

Tye-Williams, S., & Krone, K. J. (2017). Identifying and re-imagining the paradox of workplace bullying advice. *Journal of Applied Communication Research, 45,* 218–235. doi:10.1080/00909882.2017.1288291

Tye-Williams, S., & Ruble, R. (2017). Perceptions of workplace bullying narratives: Exploring attributions. *Ohio Journal of Communication, 55,* 1–15. Retrieved from www.researchgate.net/profile/S_Tye-Williams/publication/322255761_Perceptions_of_Workplace_Bullying_Narratives_Exploring_Attributions/links/5a4e88470f7e9bbfacfc319c/Perceptions-of-Workplace-Bullying-Narratives-Exploring-Attributions.pdf

Uhl-Bien, M., & Marion, R. (Eds.). (2007). *Complexity leadership: Part 1: Conceptual foundations.* Charlotte, NC: IAP.

Ulrich, D., Brockbank, W., Johnson, D., & Younger, J. (2010). Human resource competencies. *RBL White Paper.* Retrieved from https://rbl.net/index.php/search/library/#show=dave-ulrich-ideas-on-hr-competencies

UN News Centre (n.d.). *Two-thirds of young people in more than 18 countries say they have been bullied—UNICEF poll.* Retrieved from www.un.org/apps/news/story.asp?NewsID=54674#.WjB_C5WWxPI

United States Census Bureau. (2017, June 22). *The nation's older population is still growing, Census Bureau Reports.* Retrieved November 24, 2017, from https://census.gov/newsroom/press-releases/2017/cb17-100.html

Updegraff, K. A., Thayer, S. M., Whiteman, S. D., Denning, D. J., & McHale, S. M. (2005). Relational aggression in adolescents' sibling relationships: Links to sibling and parent-adolescent relationship quality. *Family Relations, 54,* 373–385. doi:10.1111/j.1741–3729.2005.00324.x

U.S. Department of Education. (2010). *Key policy letters from the education secretary and deputy secretary.* Retrieved from https://www2.ed.gov/policy/gen/guid/secletter/101215.html

U.S. Department of Health and Human Services. (2014a). *Key components in state anti-bullying policies.* Retrieved from www.stopbullying.gov/laws/key-components/index.html

U.S. Department of Health and Human Services. (2014b). *Laws & policies.* Retrieved from www.stopbullying.gov/laws/index.html

U.S. Department of Health and Human Services. (2017, September 18). *Cyberbullying.* Retrieved from www.stopbullying.gov/cyberbullying/what-is-it/index.html

US Department of Health and Human Services. National Institutes of Health. (n.d.). *How does bullying affect health and well-being?* National Institute of Child Health and Human Development. Retrieved from www.nichd.nih.gov/health/topics/bullying/conditioninfo/Pages/health.aspxUtech, M. R., & Garrett, R. R. (1992). Elder and child abuse: Conceptual and perceptual parallels. *Journal of Interpersonal Violence, 7*(3), 418–428. doi:10.1177/088626092007003010

Vaillancourt, T., Hymel, S., & McDougall, P. (2003). Bullying is power: Implications for school- based intervention strategies. *Journal of Applied School Psychology, 19*(2), 157–176. doi:10.1300/J008v19n02_10

Valkenburg, P., Krcmar, M., Peeters, A. & Marseille, N. (1999). Developing a scale to assess three styles of television mediation: "instructive mediation," "restrictive mediation," and "social co viewing." *Journal of Broadcasting and Electronic Media, 43,* 52–66. doi:10.1080/08838159909364474

Vandebosch, H., & Van Cleemput, K. (2009). Cyberbullying among youngsters: Profiles of bullies and victims. *New Media & Society, 11*(8): 1349–1371. doi:10.1177/1461444809341263van de Vliert, E., & Euwema, M. C. (1994). Agreeableness and activeness as components of conflict behaviors. *Journal of Personality and Social Psychology, 66,* 674–687. doi:10.1037/0022–3514.66.4.674

van den Brink, M., & Benschop, Y. (2011). Gender practices in the construction of academic excellence: Sheep with five legs. *Organization, 19,* 507–524. doi:10.1177/1350508411414293

Van der Doef, M., & Maes, S. (1999). The job demand-control (-support) model and psychological well-being: A review of 20 years of empirical research. *Work & Stress, 13,* 87–114. doi:10.1080/026783799296084

Van der Voort, T., Nikken, P. & Van Lil, J. (1992). Determinants of parental guidance of children's television viewing: A Dutch replication study. *Journal of Broadcasting and Electronic Media, 36,* 61–74. doi:10.1080/08838159209364154

Van der Voort, T., Van Lil, J. & Peeters, A. (1998). Determinants of parental television guidance as reported by parents versus children. *Medienpsychologie, 10,* 165–183. Retrieved from http://psycnet.apa.org/record/1998-11462-001Vanhove, A., Herian, M., Perez, A., Harms, P., & Lester, P. (2016). Can resilience be developed at work? A meta-analytic review of resilience-building programme effectiveness. *Journal of Occupational and Organizational Psychology, 89,* 278–307. doi:10.1111/joop.12123

References

Vecchio, R. P. (2003). Entrepreneurship and leadership: Common trends and common threads. *Human Resource Management Review, 13*, 303–327. doi:10.1016/S1053–4822(03)00019–6

Veenstra, R., Lindenberg, S., Oldehinkel, A. J., De Winter, A. F., Verhulst, F. C., & Ormel, J. (2005). Bullying and victimization in elementary schools: A comparison of bullies, victims, bully/victims, and uninvolved preadolescents. *Developmental Psychology, 41*(4), 672–682. doi:10.1037/0012–1649.41.4.672

Veenstra, R., Lindenberg, S., Zijlstra, B. J. H., De Winter, A. F., Verhulst, F. C., & Ormel, J. (2007). The dyadic nature of bullying and victimization: Testing a dual-perspective theory. *Child Development, 78*, 1843–1854. doi:10.1111/j.1467–8624.2007.01102.x

Vega, G., & Comer, D. R. (2005). Sticks and stones may break your bones, but words can break your spirit: Bullying in the workplace. *Journal of Business Ethics, 58*(1), 101–109. doi:10.1007/s10551-005-1422-7

Vehviläinen, S. (2001). Evaluative advice in educational counseling: The use of disagreement in the "stepwise entry" to advice. *Research on Language and Social Interaction, 34,* 371— 398. doi:10.1207/S15327973RLSI34–3_4

Visconti, K. J., & Troop-Gordon, W. (2010). Prospective relations between children's responses to peer victimization and their socioemotional adjustment. *Journal of Applied Developmental Psychology, 31*, 261–272. doi:10.1016/j.appdev.2010.05.003

Vitak, J., & Ellison, N. B. (2013). 'There's a network out there you might as well tap': Exploring the benefits of and barriers to exchanging information and support-based resources on Facebook. *New Media & Society, 15*, 243–259. doi:10.1177/1461444812451566

Vlachou, M., Andreou, E., Botsoglou, K., & Didaskalou, E. (2011). Bully/victim problems among preschool children: A review of current research evidence. *Educational Psychology Review, 23*, 329–358. doi:10.1007/s10648–011–9153–z

Vlachou, M., Botsoglou, K., & Andreou, E. (2013). Assessing bully/victim problems in preschool children: A multimethod approach. *Journal of Criminology,* Article ID 301658, 1–8. doi:10.1155/2013/301658

Vogl-Bauer, S. (2010). Aggressive expression within the family: Effects on processes and outcomes. In T. A. Avtgis & A. S. Rancer (Eds.), *Arguments, aggression, and conflict* (pp. 318–339). New York: Routledge.

Vogl-Bauer, S. (2014). When disgruntled students go to extremes: The cyberbullying of instructors. *Communication Education, 63*(4), 429–448. doi:10.1080/03634523.2014.942331

Volk, A. A., Dane, A. V., & Marini, Z. A. (2014). What is bullying? A theoretical redefinition. *Developmental Review, 34*(4), 327–343. doi:10.1016/j.dr.2014.09.001

Volk, T. (1995). *Metapatterns: Across space, time, and mind.* New York, NY: Columbia University Press.

von Marées, N., & Petermann, F. (2012). Cyberbullying: An increasing challenge for schools. *School Psychology International, 33*, 467–476. doi:10.1177/0143034312445241

Vroom, V., & Sternberg, R. J. (2002). Theoretical letters: The person versus the situation in leadership. *Leadership, 13*, 301–323. doi:10.1016/S1048–9843(02)00101–7

Waasdorp, T. E., Pas, E. T., Zablotsky, B., & Bradshaw, C. P. (2017). Ten-year trends in bullying and related attitudes among 4th-to 12th-graders. *Pediatrics, 139*(6), e20162615. Retrieved from http://pediatrics.aappublications.org/content/early/2017/04/27/peds.2016-2615

Wajngurt, C. & Keashly, L. (in press). Faculty bullying in higher education. In C. Kowalski, J. P. Cangemi, & A. Rokach (Eds), *Bullying: A critical problem in education, work environments and society.* Bloomington, IN: Xlibris Publishing.

**Wake County Public School System. (2015a). *Policy manual.* Wake County, NC: Author. Retrieved from https://boardpolicyonline.com/bl/?b=wake_new#&&hs=194147

**Wake County Public School System. (2015b). *Types of bullying.* Wake County, NC: Author. Retrieved from www.wcpss.net/cms/lib/NC01911451/Centricity/Domain/46/typesofbullying.pdf

*Wake County Public School System. (2017). *Bullying prevention.* Retrieved from www.wcpss.net/domain/46

Waldron, V. (2009). Emotional tyranny at work: Suppressing the moral emotions. In P. Lutgen- Sandvik & B. Davenport Sypher (Eds.), *Destructive organizational communication: Processes, consequences, and constructive ways of organizing* (pp. 9–26). New York, NY: Routledge.

Walker, S., & Richardson, D. R. (1998). Aggression strategies among older adults: Delivered but not seen. *Aggression and Violent Behavior, 3*(3), 287–294. doi:10.1016/s1359–1789(96)00029–8

Walraven, A., Brand- Gruwel, S., & Boshuzen, H. P. A. (2009). How students evaluate sources and information when searching the World Wide Web for information. *Computer and Education, 52*, 234–46. doi:10.1016/j.compedu.2008.08.003

Walther, J. B., Gay, G., & Hancock, J. T. (2005). How do communication and technology researchers study the internet? *Journal of Communication, 55*, 632–657. doi:10.1111/j.1460–2466.2005.tb02688.x

Walther, J. B., & Ramirez, A., Jr. (2009). New technologies and new directions in online relating. In S. W. Smith & S. R. Wilson (Eds.), *New directions in interpersonal communication research* (pp. 264–284). Thousand Oaks, CA: Sage.

References

Wang, C., & Chang, Y. (2010). Cyber relationship motives: Scale development and validation. *Social Behavior and Personality, 38*(3), 289–300. doi:10.2224/sbp.2010.38.3.289

Wang, F., Leary, K. A., Taylor, L. C., & Derosier, M. E. (2016). Peer and teacher preference, student–teacher relationships, student ethnicity, and peer victimization in elementary school. *Psychology in the Schools, 53*(5), 488–501. doi:10.1002/pits.21922

Wang, J., Nansel, T. R., & Iannotti, R. J. (2011). Cyber bullying and traditional bullying: Differential association with depression. *Journal of Adolescent Health, 48*, 415–417. doi:10.1016/j.jadohealth.2010.07.012

Warren, R. & Bluma, A. (2002). Parental mediation of children's Internet use: The influence of established media. *Communication Research Reports, 19*, 8–17. doi:10.1080/08824090209384827

Watts, L., Wagner, J., Velasquez, B., & Behrens, P. (2017). Cyberbullying in higher education: A literature review. *Computers in Human Behavior, 69*, 268–274. doi:10.1016/j.chb.2016.12.038

Way, K. A., Jimmieson, N. L., & Bordia, P. (2016). Shared perceptions of supervisor conflict management style. *International Journal of Conflict Management, 27*, 25–49. doi:10.1108.IJCMA-07–2014–0046

Weeks, J. (1996). *Developing opportunities for senior citizens and 3-and 4-year-old children in a Northeast US Jewish community center to interact* (Unpublished master's practicum report). Nova Southeastern University, Ft. Lauderdale, FL.

Weick, K. (1995). *Sensemaking in organizations.* Thousand Oaks, CA: Sage.

Weiland, S. M. B., Bauer, J., & Deetz, S. (2009). Excessive careerism and destructive life stresses: The role of entrepreneurialism in colonizing identities. In P. Lutgen-Sandvik & B. Davenport Sypher (Eds.), *Destructive organizational communication: Processes, consequences, and constructive ways of organizing* (pp. 99–120). New York: Routledge.

Weiss, D., & Freund, A. M. (2012). Still young at heart: Negative age-related information motivates distancing from same-aged people. *Psychology and Aging, 27*(1), 173. doi:10.1037/a0024819

Weiss, D., & Staudinger, U. M. (2015, November). Threat or challenge? Essentialist beliefs, age stereotypes, and cognitive performance in old age. *Gerontologist, 55* (suppl_2), 611–612. doi:10.1093/geront/gnv321.04

Wellman, B., & Wortley, S. (1990). Different strokes from different folks: Community ties and social support. *American Journal of Sociology*, 558–588. doi:10.1086/229572

West, R., & Turner, L. H. (2017). *IPC: Interpersonal Communication.* Boston, MA: Cengage.

West, R., & Turner, L. H. (2019). *Communication: An introduction.* Cambridge: Cambridge University Press.

Westerhof, G. J., Whitbourne, S. K., & Freeman, G. P. (2011). The aging self in a cultural context: The relation of conceptions of aging to identity processes and self-esteem in the United States and the Netherlands. *Journals of Gerontology Series B: Psychological Sciences and Social Sciences, 67*(1), 52–60. doi:10.1093/geronb/gbr075

Weuve, C., Pitney, W. A., Martin, M., & Mazerolle, S. M. (2014). Perceptions of workplace bullying among athletic trainers in the collegiate setting. *Journal of Athletic Training, 49*, 706–718. doi:10.4085/1062–6050–49.3.13

Whipple, E. E. & Wilson, S. R. (1996). Evaluation of a parent education program for families at risk of physical child abuse. *Families in Society, 77*(4), 227–239. doi:10.1606/1044–3894.904

Wieland, D., & Beitz, J. M. (2015). Resilience to social bullying in academia: A phenomenological study. *Nurse Education, 40*, 289–293. doi:10.1097/NNE.000000000000169

Wigley, C. J., III, Pohl, G. H., & Watt, M. G. S. (1989). Conversational sensitivity as a correlate of trait verbal aggressiveness and the predisposition to verbally praise others. *Communication Reports, 2*, 92–95. doi:10.1080/08934218909367488

Willard, N. E. (2007). *Cyberbullying and cyberthreats: Re-sponding to the challenge of online social aggression, threats, and distress.* Champaign, IL: Research Press.

Willbornm S. L., Schwab, S. J., Burton, J. F., & Lester, G. L. L. (2007). *Employment Law: Cases and Materials.* Newark, NJ: LexisNexis.

Willer, E. K., & Cupach, W. R. (2011). The meaning of girls' social aggression: Nasty or mastery? In W. R. Cupach & B. H. Spitzberg (Eds.), *The dark side of close relationships II* (pp. 297–326). New York, NY: Routledge.

Williams, K., Kemper, S., & Hummert, M. L. (2004). Enhancing communication with older adults: Overcoming elderspeak. *Journal of Gerontological Nursing, 30*(10), 17–25. doi:10.3928/0098-9134-20041001-08

Wilson, S. R., Cameron, K. A., & Whipple, E. E. (1997). Regulative communication strategies within mother–child interactions: Implications for the study of reflection-enhancing parental communication. *Research on Language and Social Interaction, 30*(1), 73–92. doi:10.1207/s15327973rlsi3001_3

Wilson, S. R., Rack, J., Shi, X., & Norris, A. (2008). Comparing physically abusive, neglectful, and non-maltreating parents during interactions with their children: A meta-analysis of observational studies. *Child Abuse & Neglect, 32*, 897–911. doi:10.1016/j.chiabu.2008.01.003

Wilson, S. R., & Whipple, E. E. (1995). Communication, discipline, and physical child abuse. In T. J. Socha & G. Stamp (Eds.), *Parents, children, and communication: Frontiers of theory and research* (pp. 299–317). Hillsdale, NJ: Erlbaum.

References

**Winston-Salem/Forsyth County Schools. (2011). *Policy code: 5131.1 prohibition against discrimination, harassment and bullying.* Retrieved from https://boardpolicyonline.com/?b=forsyth

*Winston-Salem/Forsyth County Schools. (2017). *What is bullying?* Retrieved from www.forsyth.k12.ga.us/page/689

Wolke, D., & Skew, A. J. (2012). Bullying among siblings. *International Journal of Adolescent Medicine and Health, 24,* 1–9. doi:10.1515/IJAMH.2012.004

Wolke, D., Woods, S., Bloomfield, L., & Karstadt, L. (2001). Bullying involvement in primary school and common health problems. *Archives of Disease in Childhood, 85*(3), 197–201. doi:10.1136/adc.85.3.197

Woodrow, C., & Guest, D. E. (2017). Leadership and approaches to the management of workplace bullying. *European Journal of Work & Organizational Psychology, 26,* 221–233. doi:10.1080/1359432X.2016.1243529

Workplace Bullying Institute. (2010). Results of the 2010 and 2007 WBI U.S. Workplace Bullying Survey. Retrieved February 10, 2017, from www.workplacebullying.org/wbiresearch/2010-wbi-national-survey/

Wright, A. D. (2016, May 13). What can HR do about cyberbullying in the workplace? *Society for Human Resource Management.* Retrieved from www.shrm.org/resourcesandtools/hr-topics/technology/pages/what-hr-can-do-about-cyberbullying-in-the-workplace.aspx

Wright, K. B. (2000). Perceptions of online support providers: An examination of perceived homophily, source credibility, communication and social support within online support groups. *Communication Quarterly, 48,* 44–59. doi:10.1080/01463370009385579

Wright, K. B., Johnson, A. J., Averbeck, J., & Bernard, D. (2011). Computer-mediated social support groups: Promises and pitfalls for individuals coping with health concerns. In T. L. Thompson, R. Parrott, & J. F. Nussbaum (Eds.), *Handbook of health communication* (pp. 349–362). Thousand Oaks, CA: Sage.

Wright, K. B., & Miller, C. H. (2010). A measure of weak-tie/strong-tie support network preference. *Communication Monographs, 77,* 500–517. doi:10.1080/03637751.2010.502538

Wright, M., & Hill, L. H. (2014). Academic incivility among health science faculty. *Adult Learning, 26*(1), 28–34. Retrieved from http://journals.sagepub.com/home/alxa

Wright, M. F., & Li, Y. (2013). The association between cyber victimization and subsequent cyber aggression: The moderating effect of peer rejection. *Journal of Youth and Adolescence, 42*(5), 662–674. doi:10.1007/s10964-012-9903-3

Wu, I., Lyons, B., & Leong, F. (2015). How racial/ethnic bullying affects rejection sensitivity: The role of social dominance orientation. *Cultural Diversity & Ethnic Minority Psychology, 21*(1), 156–161. Retrieved from http://psycnet.apa.org/buy/2014-43051-001

Yamada, D. C. (2010). Workplace bullying and American employment law: A ten- year progress report and assessment. *Comparative Labor Law & Policy Journal, 32,* 251.

Yamada, D. (2011). Workplace bullying and the law: Emerging global responses. In S. Einarsen, H. Hoel, D. Zapf, & C. Cooper (Eds.), *Bullying and harassment in the workplace: Developments in Theory, Research and Practice* (2nd ed.). Boca Raton, FL: Taylor & Francis.

Yamagata-Lynch, L. C. (2010). *Activity systems analysis methods: Understanding complex learning environments.* New York, NY: Springer Science & Business Media.

Yang, J., Mossholder, K. W., & Peng, T. K. (2007). Procedural justice climate and group power distance: An examination of cross-level interaction effects. *Journal of Applied Psychology, 92,* 681–692. doi:10.1037/0021–9010.92.3.681

Yeung Thompson, R. S., & Leadbeater, B. J. (2013). Peer victimization and internalizing symptoms from adolescence into young adulthood: Building strength through emotional support. *Journal of Research on Adolescence, 23,* 290–303. doi:10.1111/j.1532–7795.2012.00827.x

Yoon, J., Sulkowski, M. L., & Bauman, S. A. (2016). Teachers' responses to bullying incidents: Effects of teacher characteristics and contexts. *Journal of School Violence, 15*(1), 91–113. doi:10.1080/15388220.2014.963592

Young, R., Subramanian, R., Miles, S., Hinnant, A., & Andsager, J. L. (2017). Social representation of cyberbullying and adolescent suicide: A mixed-method analysis of news stories. *Health Communication, 32*(9), 1082–1092. doi:10.1080/10410236.2016.1214214

Youngvorst, L. J., & High, A. C. (2018). "Anyone free to chat?" Using technological features to elicit quality support online. *Communication Monographs.* Advance online publication. doi:10.1080/03637751.2018.1426871

Yukl, G. (1994). *Leadership in organizations.* Englewood Cliffs, NJ: Prentice Hall.

Yukl, G., & Mahsud, R. (2010). Why flexible and adaptive leadership is essential. Consulting *Psychology Journal, 62,* 81–93. http://dx.doi.org/10.1037/a0019835

Zaklama, C., & Wright, R. (2004). The bullying spectrum in grade schools: Parents, teachers, child bullies and their victims. *ProQuest Dissertations and Theses.*

References

Zeine, R., Boglarsky, C. Daly, E., Blessinger, P., Kurban, M., & Gilkes, A. (2014). Considerate leadership as a measure of effectiveness in medical and higher education: Analysis of supervisory/managerial leadership. *Organizational Culture: An International Journal, 15*(1), 1–13. Retrieved from www.commongroundpubli shing.com/

Zohar, D., & Tenne-Gazit, O. (2008). Transformational leadership and group interaction as climate antecedents: A social network analysis. *Journal of Applied Psychology, 93*, 744–757. doi:10.1037/0021–9010.93.4.744

Zych, I., Ortega-Ruiz, R., & Del Rey, R. (2015a). Scientific research on bullying and cyberbullying: Where have we been and where are we going. *Aggression and Violent Behavior, 24*, 188–198. doi:10.1016/j.avb.2015.05.015

Zych, I., Ortega-Ruiz, R., & Del Rey, R. (2015b). Systematic review of theoretical studies on bullying and cyberbullying: Facts, knowledge, prevention, and intervention. *Aggression and Violent Behavior, 2, 31*–21. doi:10.1016/j.avb.2015.10.001

*Indicates primary district-administered home page for anti-bullying policy.

**Indicates secondary policy information linked on primary district-administered home page.

CONTRIBUTORS

Rukhsana Ahmed (Ph.D., Ohio University) is Associate Professor, Department of Communication, University of Ottawa, Canada, with primary research interests at the intersection of health, communication, and culture. She is co-author and co-editor of *Health Literacy in Canada: A Primer for Students* (2014); *New Media Considerations and Communication Across Religions and Cultures* (2014); *Health Communication and Mass Media: An Integrated Approach to Policy and Practice* (2013), and *Medical Communication in Clinical Contexts* (2012; Distinguished Edited Book Award by the Applied Communication Division of NCA). She is the principal investigator in a collaborative project, Staying in Touch, Connecting, Integrating: Social Media Use of Newly Arrived Syrian Refugee Youth in Canada (2016–2018), funded by IRCC and SSHRC. Between 2010 and 2015, she was an Expert Advisory Committee member of the Health Profile on Immigrant and Refugee Children and Youth in Canada in *The Health of Canada's Children and Youth: A CICH Profile*.

Wilfredo Alvarez (Ph.D., University of Colorado Boulder) is Associate Professor in the Department of Communication at Southern Connecticut State University. Dr. Alvarez teaches courses in communication and difference, intercultural, interpersonal, organizational, conflict, and leadership communication. Dr. Alvarez's research examines cross-cultural symbolic meaning negotiation, particularly how relationships between communication processes, power dynamics, and social identity categories (i.e., race, social class, immigration, gender, sexuality, and ability status) in organizational, relational, and intercultural contexts mediate embodied and institutional lived experiences. Dr. Alvarez's research has appeared in *Management Communication Quarterly*; *Liminalities: A Journal of Performance Studies*; and *Inter/Cultural Communication: Representation and Construction of Culture in Everyday Interaction* (A. Kurylo, Editor).

Christine K. Anzur (M.A., West Virginia University) is a Ph.D. student in the Department of Communication Studies at West Virginia University. She has taught interpersonal communication, intercultural communication, and gender and communication. Her research interests are family and interpersonal communication, and she is most interested in the communication between parents and their emerging adult children, particularly in nontraditional families.

Garry Bailey (Ph.D., University of Oklahoma) is at Abilene Christian University teaching conflict resolution courses in identity and culture (within the contexts of race, gender, poverty, and religion), ethics, systems design, negotiation, and mediation strategies. Garry conducts workshops and trainings in mediation, peace circles, and restorative justice practices to help people work through conflict. He does research about working through bullying experiences and applying the ethics of fairness and caring in cultural contexts. It has always been his desire to help people work through conflicts, build good relationships, and find peace.

James P. Baker (M.A., California State University, Sacramento) is a Ph.D. student in the Department of Communication Studies at West Virginia University, where he teaches introductory communication courses. His primary research interests focus on instructional communication, with specific emphasis on the student-centered paradigm and the overlap of interpersonal communication. His secondary area of interest centers on the overlap between interpersonal communication and mass media, specifically the social uses of media.

Keith Berry (Ph.D., Southern Illinois University) is Associate Professor in the Department of Communication at the University of South Florida. His research and teaching focus on relational communication, particularly the ways in which conversation partners co-create, interpret, and use meaning within social interactions and relationships. He primarily examines ways people negotiate identities through relating, especially as this process pertains to vulnerable populations. His research has been published in journals such as *Journal of Family Communication, Journal of Applied Communication Research, Qualitative Inquiry*, and *International Journal of Qualitative Methods*, and in edited book collections such as the *Handbook of Autoethnography* and *Popular Culture as Everyday Life*. His book, *Bullied: Tales of Torment, Identity and Youth*, was named Best Book by NCA's Ethnography Division. Dr. Berry served as Co-Chair of NCA's Anti-Bullying Task Force and past Chair of NCA's Ethnography Division.

Jaime E. Bochantin (Ph.D., Texas A&M University) is Assistant Professor at the University of North Carolina, Charlotte. She teaches classes in organizational communication, leadership, research methods, and the dark side of organizational communication. Her research examines the social issues, member behavior, and cultural landscape of organizations to provide managers and HR practitioners with implementation strategies that will better the organization. Most recently, she has begun work on an occupational health study that examines police officers over the career length. Additionally, Dr. Bochantin co-runs the HERO lab (High reliability, Emotion, and Risk in Organizations). Her research has appeared in a number of venues, including *Academy of Management Journal, Communication Monographs, Management Communication Quarterly*, and *Negotiations and Conflict Management Research*, among others.

Nicholas Brody (Ph.D., University of Texas at Austin) is Assistant Professor of Communication Studies at the University of Puget Sound. His research interests include cyberbullying and the interplay of mediated communication and personal relationships. His recent research has examined bystander behavior in cyberbullying episodes, relational maintenance via text messaging, social networking site use in relationships, language use in break-up accounts, and communication in on-again/off-again relationships. This research appears in *Communication Monographs*, the *Journal of Social and Personal Relationships, Social Media + Society*, the *Journal of Language and Social Psychology, Personal Relationships*, and *Computers in Human Behavior*.

Patrice M. Buzzanell (Ph.D., Purdue University) is Professor and Chair of the Department of Communication at the University of South Florida and Endowed Visiting Professor for the School of Media and Design at Shanghai Jiaotong University. Fellow and Past President of the International

Communication Association (ICA), she served as President of the Council of Communication Associations and the Organization for the Study of Communication, Language and Gender. She is a Distinguished Scholar of the National Communication Association. Her research focuses on career, work-life policy, resilience, gender, and engineering design. She is co/editor of four books and more than 210 articles and chapters, plus proceedings in engineering education and other disciplines. She received ICA's Mentorship Award and the Provost Outstanding Mentor Award at Purdue, where she was University Distinguished Professor and Endowed Chair and Director of the Susan Bulkeley Butler Center for Leadership Excellence.

Cathlin V. Clark-Gordon (M.A., Clemson University, 2016) is a Ph.D. student in the Department of Communication Studies at West Virginia University, where she teaches introductory and social media courses. Her emphases are computer-mediated communication and instructional communication, and she is presently interested in the affordances of anonymity and pseudo-anonymity, studying their implications in social media and online learning environments.

Stacey L. Connaughton (Ph.D., The University of Texas at Austin) is Associate Professor in the Brian Lamb School of Communication at Purdue University. Her research examines leadership and identification in geographically distributed contexts, particularly as these issues relate to virtual organizing, political parties, and peacebuilding. Her research has been funded by the National Science Foundation, the Carnegie Foundation, and the Russell Sage Foundation. Her published academic work has appeared in journals such as *Journal of Applied Communication Research, Journal of Communication,* and *Management Communication Quarterly,* among others, and her book, *Inviting Latino Voters: Party Messages and Latino Party Identification,* was published by Routledge. Dr. Connaughton currently serves as Principal Investigator and Director of the Purdue Peace Project, an externally funded engaged research initiative with projects in Ghana, Liberia, Nigeria, El Salvador, and the United States.

Renee L. Cowan (Ph.D., Texas A&M University) is Affiliate Assistant Professor in the Knight School of Communication at Queens University of Charlotte. She is Co-Chair of the National Communication Association's Anti-Bullying Task Force. Her recent research focuses on workplace bullying and the human resource professional as well as how workplace bullying is understood and prevented across the globe. Her research appears in such peer-reviewed journals as *Human Resource Management Journal; Personnel Review; Management Communication Quarterly; Journal of Computer-Mediated Communication; Communication Education; International Journal of Business Communication; Communication Research Reports;* and others.

Carly M. Danielson (M.A., University of Nevada, Las Vegas) is a doctoral candidate at the University of Minnesota, Twin Cities. Her research focuses on bullying prevention and bystander interventions. She has presented at various national and international conferences about bullying and has published bullying research in *Health Communication* and the *Journal of Health Communication.* She is the recipient of the 2015 Outstanding Thesis Award in Health Communication by the International Communication Association. She also works at PACER Center in the National Bullying Prevention Center division.

Nathalie Desrayaud (Ph.D., Purdue University) is Assistant Professor of Communication at Florida International University. She previously served on the faculty of Missouri State University. Her research centers on perceptions and interpretations of conflict in both personal and professional relationships. Her work has appeared in prestigious journals including *Management Communication*

Quarterly, the *International Journal of Conflict Management*, and *Basic and Applied Social Psychology*. She has presented regularly at the National Communication Association and the International Communication Association.

Fran C. Dickson (Ph.D., Bowling Green State University, 1982) is Professor of Communication Studies in the Department of Communication at Eastern Kentucky University. Her teaching interests are interpersonal and personal relationships, later-life marriages, health communication, communication and aging, research methods, and communication and conflict. She has published book chapters and referred articles in the area of family communication, communication and aging, and health communication. Dr. Dickson's most recent projects include exploration of parenting challenges among families that are homeless, conflict among later-life married and remarried couples, and HIV/AIDS among later-life dating adults. Her work appears in *Handbook of Marriage and the Family* (2nd ed.), *Engaging Theories in Family Communication: Multiple Perspectives*, and *The Family Communication Sourcebook*. In addition, she has published articles in the *Southern Communication Journal*, *Qualitative Research Reports in Communication*, *Journal of Applied Communication Research*, *Journal of Social and Personal Relationships*, and *Journal of Family Communication*. She is also past Chair of the Family Communication Division of the National Communication Association.

Kelly P. Dillon (Ph.D., The Ohio State University, 2016) is an Assistant Professor of Communication at Wittenberg University. Her research interests are broadly focused on media, media effects, and computer-mediated communication. Her work has mainly focused on cyber-bystander behavior in cyberbullying, and the differences in direct and indirect intervention tactics. Dr. Dillon's work has appeared in *Computers in Human Behavior, Pediatrics, Psychology of Popular Media Culture*, and at international and national conferences. She has helped secure grant funding from the National Institutes of Health, Office of Special Education Programs, and the National Science Foundation.

Sean Eddington (M.S., Northwest Missouri State University) is a doctoral candidate in the Brian Lamb School of Communication studying organizational communication, and successfully defended his dissertation, *Networks of Outrage and Identity: Organizational Identity and Identification in r/TheRedPill*, in May 2018. He earned his B.A. in History from Purdue University, and his M.S. from Northwest Missouri State University. Eddington's research interests exist at the intersections of organizational communication, online organizing, resilience, and gender. He has researched diversity and inclusion and professional formation in engineering contexts, which has been published in *2015, 2017, and 2018 Proceedings of the American Society for Engineering Education* along with his research team. Eddington's work on online organizing is forthcoming in *Social Media and Society*. Finally, Eddington has also served as a series editor, contributed to trade publications, and facilitated workshops all related to higher education administrators' work experiences.

Janie Harden Fritz (Ph.D., University of Wisconsin-Madison) is Professor of Communication & Rhetorical Studies at Duquesne University. She is a past President of both the Eastern Communication Association and the Religious Communication Association. Her research focuses on communicative practices that constitute, sever, and restore the ties that bind individuals to institutions, with a specific focus on communication and virtue ethics, professional civility, troublesome workplace relationships, communication ethics and leadership, and religious communication. She is the author of *Professional Civility: Communicative Virtue at Work*, co-author of *Communication Ethics Literacy: Diversity and Difference*, co-editor of volumes 1 and 2 of *Problematic Relationships in the Workplace*, and co-editor of *Communication Ethics and Crisis: Negotiating Differences in Public and Private Spheres*.

Contributors

Alan K. Goodboy (Ph.D., West Virginia University, 2007) is Professor and Ph.D. Coordinator in the Department of Communication Studies at West Virginia University. His recent research examines the causes and consequences of bullying in educational and organizational settings. Dr. Goodboy is an Eastern Communication Association Research Fellow with publications in *Communication Research*, *Journal of Applied Communication Research*, and *Communication Education*.

Tina M. Harris is Professor in the Department of Communication Studies at the University of Georgia. Her expertise is in the area of interracial communication, where she explores the ways in which individuals communicate about race. Her research addresses how racial identities play a critical role in how people choose to communicate with others from a different race and the strategies that are used to navigate those difficult conversations. She is the co-author of the textbook *Interracial Communication: Theory Into Practice* (2015, Sage Publications). Other research interests include diversity and media representations and race and ethnic disparities and religious frameworks in health communication. Her current research explores the impact of racial microaggressions on the mental, physical, and emotional health of students of color at predominantly White institutions. Her commitment to communication scholarship and pedagogy is evidenced in her recognition as the 2017 Engaged Scholar Award (Office of the Vice President for Public Service and Outreach), a Distinguished Josiah T. Meigs Teaching Professors (highest teaching honor), 2009 recipient of the Scholarship of Teaching and Learning award (University System of Georgia Board of Regents' (BOR)) for her research on pedagogy and race, and the 2012 recipient of the International Diversity Award Recipient from the UGA Offices of International Education and Institutional Diversity. Her primary interest as a communication scholar is in the area of interracial communication. Harris has published many articles and book chapters on race and communication, served as reviewer for many top tier communication journals, and fulfilled many service roles within the discipline, the National Communication Association, the Southern States Communication Association, and other communication organizations. Her commitment to translating research from theory into practice is evidenced in her continued service to the department, university, discipline, and community through work that facilitates critical engagement with race

Anastacia Janovec is an accelerated Ph.D. student in Interpersonal and Health Communication. Prior to enrolling at the University of Georgia, Anastacia earned her B.S. in Communication Studies at the University of Wisconsin-La Crosse with minors in Psychology and Business Administration. Her research interests include family communication, children and adolescents' bullying experiences, bullying victims' disclosure process, and aggression. She is also involved in research with racial microaggressions on predominantly White campuses and family communications' impact on mental health.

Sarah E. Jones (M.A., University of Kentucky) is a doctoral candidate in the Hugh Downs School of Human Communication at Arizona State University. Her research spans interpersonal and organizational divisions, including management of interpersonal crises and technology use, and critical difference studies of gender, sexuality, and feminisms in the workplace. Currently, she is engaged in projects that address negotiations of identity amongst groups, including cyberbullying bystanders, transgender employees, and mothers in the milk banking industry. Ultimately, she aims to use both community-engaged and critical approaches to explore how hegemonic discourses surrounding marginalized corporealities and organizational norms formulate identities and police behavior. Her work has also been published in *Queer Communication Pedagogy: Intersectionality and Activism* (Routledge) and *Mental Health in the Digital Age: Grave Dangers, Great Promise* (Oxford University Press). Sarah is a certified facilitator with the Institute for Civil Dialogue® and previously served as Co-President of ASU's Graduate Women's Association. She is the recipient of ASU's 2016 Jeanne Lind Herberger Fellowship in Communication, 2017 Award for Sustained Innovation in Creative Inquiry, and several Teaching Excellence Awards. Sarah's work in milk banking has also earned her a Top Paper Award from NCA's Rhetoric & Communication Theory Division.

Loraleigh Keashly (Ph.D., University of Saskatchewan) is Professor in the Department of Communication at Wayne State University. She also serves as Associate Dean, Curricular and Student Affairs, College of Fine, Performing, and Communication Arts. Her research and consulting focus on quality of work relationships and conflict and conflict resolution at the interpersonal, group, and intergroup levels. Her current research focus is on the nature, effects, and amelioration of uncivil, hostile, and bullying behaviors in the workplace, with a particular interest in the role of organizational structure and culture in the facilitation or prevention and management of these behaviors. Her work has appeared in *Violence and Victims*; *Work & Stress*; *Administrative Theory & Practice*; *Journal of Management & Organization*; and *Employee Rights and Employment Policy Journal*, among many others.

Carrie D. Kennedy-Lightsey (Ph.D., West Virginia University) is Assistant Professor in the Department of Languages, Cultures, and Communication at Stephen F. Austin State University, where she teaches courses in the dark side of interpersonal communication, communication theory, and research methods. Her research interests center on romantic and parent-child relationships, with a specific focus on how individuals respond to jealousy, hurt, and privacy invasion. Her research is published in the *Journal of Family Communication, Communication Quarterly, Southern Communication Journal*, and *Communication Reports*.

Rajesh Kumar (Ph.D., Babasaheb Bhimrao Ambedkar Bihar University-Muzaffarpur) is Associate Professor at the School of Media and Communication Studies, Doon University, Dehradun, India. His teaching and research interests are relevant to important areas, including communication for development and social change, media and society, political economy of communication, and development of communication programs and campaigns. Dr. Kumar sees media and communication as an essentially multidisciplinary field and largely technology-driven. His research has appeared in *New Media and Society, Interactions: Studies in Communication and umarCulture*, and *Media Asia* (Routledge). He is also published in *The Routledge Companion to Social Media and Politics*. Before joining academia, he worked as a public service television broadcaster in India, where he oversaw research-based television productions for developmental communication.

Jennifer S. Linvill (Ph.D., Purdue University) is the IRB Administrator at Purdue University. Her research interests include destructive workplace behaviors, identity/identification, resilience, leadership, and virtual teams, particularly in the context of organizations. She has presented her work at national and international conferences. Linvill was awarded Purdue University's 2016 Above and Beyond Award by the Office of the Executive Vice President for Research and Partnerships and Purdue University's 2009 College of Liberal Arts Distinguished Master's Thesis Award.

Geoffrey Luurs (Ph.D., North Carolina State University, 2018) is an Assistant Professor in the Department of Organizational Communication at Murray State University. His research examines interpersonal and family communication with a focus on taboo topics. Dr. Luurs is interested in how people in close relationships communicate about difficult topics and the effect that communication has on one's physical and emotional health. Furthermore, his research

Contributors

focuses on applied communication and how effective communication can be used for building communities. His work has been published in *Hypperhiz* and the *Journal of Computer-Mediated Communication*.

Matthew M. Martin (Ph.D., Kent State University, 1992) is Professor in the Department of Communication Studies at West Virginia University. He has been chair of the department since 2001. His research focuses on aggressive communication, communication traits, and instructional communication. Recently he has worked with Dr. Alan Goodboy on numerous bullying studies, leading to publications in *Communication Education, Journal of Applied Communication Research, Communication Research, Journal of Child & Adolescent Trauma*, and the *Western Journal of Communication*. At their 100th anniversary celebration, Dr. Martin was recognized as a Centennial Scholar of Interpersonal Communication by the Eastern Communication Association.

Masaki Matsunaga (Ph.D., Pennsylvania State University, 2009) is Research Associate Professor at Robert T. Huang Entrepreneurship Center of Kyushu University, Fukuoka, Japan. His research interests span the manifestation of leadership in the communicative environment, interpersonal dynamics of information management, and communication issues in workplace. Dr. Matsunaga's research has been published in such outlets as *Communication Monographs; Human Communication Research; Human Resource Management; Japanese Journal of Communication Studies; Journal of Cross-Cultural Psychology;* and *Journal of Social and Personal Relationships*, among others. He also has contributed chapters to *International Encyclopedia of Communication Research Methods* and *International Encyclopedia of Interpersonal Communication*. He has been the recipient of more than a dozen top-paper awards at various regional, national, and international conferences.

Carol Bishop Mills (Ph.D., Purdue University, 2001) is Associate Professor and Graduate Coordinator in the Department of Communication Studies at the University of Alabama. Her research focuses on relational and health communication, with a focus on bullying and teasing across the lifespan. Her work has been published in outlets such as *Journal of Social and Personal Relationships, Communication Education*, and the *Southern Communication Journal*. In 2014, she was honored with the UA College of Communication and Information Sciences Board of Visitors Teaching Award. For four years, Dr. Mills served on the Board of Directors for the National Down Syndrome Congress and also served as their communication expert, helping the larger medical and education communities improve interactions with people with Down syndrome and their families. She is currently on the National Communication Association Anti-Bullying Task Force.

Scott A. Myers (Ph.D., Kent State University) is Professor and Peggy Rardin McConnell Chair in the Department of Communication Studies at West Virginia University, where he teaches courses in instructional communication, positive communication, and communication pedagogy. His research interests center on the adult sibling relationship, with a specific focus on how emerging adult siblings maintain their relationships. His research is published in the *Journal of Family Communication, Communication Quarterly*, and *Communication Research Reports*, among many others.

Mark P. Orbe (Ph.D., Ohio University) is Professor in the School of Communication at Western Michigan University. Orbe's teaching and research interests center on the inextricable relationship between culture and communication as played out in a number of contexts (intrapersonal, interpersonal, intergroup, mass media). Accordingly, he teaches a wide variety of undergraduate courses and is actively involved in numerous research projects. He is responsible for the conceptualization and theoretical refinement of Co-Cultural Theory.

Contributors

Sara Pitts (M.A.E., Western Kentucky University) is a Ph.D. student and graduate teaching assistant in the Department of Communication Studies at West Virginia University, where she teaches courses in small group communication and presentational speaking. Her research interests include advisee/advisor relationships and college student success related to family support.

Artemio Ramirez, Jr. (Ph.D., University of Arizona) is Professor in the Zimmerman School of Advertising and Mass Communications at the University of South Florida. His research focuses on the social and relational aspects of computer-mediated communication. His research has appeared in numerous outlets, including in the *Journal of Computer-Mediated Communication*; *Journal of Communication*; *Communication Monographs*; *Communication Research*; *New Media & Society*; and *Cyberpsychology, Behavior, and Social Networking*. Dr. Ramirez serves on several journal editorial boards and is a frequent invited reviewer. He is a recipient of the Franklin Knower Article Award from the Interpersonal Division of the National Communication Association.

Robert J. Razzante (M.Ed., Ohio University) is a Ph.D. student in the Hugh Downs School of Human Communication at Arizona State University. His research interests center on studying the ways in which we communicate power, privilege, and oppression in varying contexts. More specifically, he is interested in studying the variety of ways critical-intercultural communication occurs in interpersonal encounters within organizations, sports, and the family. Rob has contributed to a book chapter publication on communicating through prejudice toward authentic relationships.

Nancy Rhodes (Ph.D., Texas A&M University) is Assistant Professor of Advertising and Public Relations at Michigan State University. Her research interests are broadly focused on persuasion and social influence—particularly how they affect health and safety behaviors. Her work has recently focused on how normative influences contribute to substance use and on how norms might contribute to resistance toward health-related messages. Her work has appeared in journals such as *Communication Research*, *Communication Monographs*, and *Media Psychology*, as well as in specialty health and safety journals. She has received funding from the CDC for work on cigarette smoking among young teenagers living in poverty in the Southern United States, as well as for research on the attitudes and norms that contribute to youth risky driving behavior.

Rachel Sadler (B.A., Old Dominion University) is an M.A. candidate in the Lifespan & Digital Communications Program at Old Dominion University. She has been an educator for seven years with the Virginia Beach City Public Schools in Virginia as well as Hillsborough County Public Schools in Florida. Her research interests include adolescent female cyberbullying via social media and examining adolescent African American female friendship patterns in relationship to reality television consumption.

Matthew W. Savage (Ph.D., Arizona State University) is Assistant Professor of Health Communication at San Diego State University. His research interests focus on the intersection of health, interpersonal, and mass communication. Rooted in team science and community approaches, Dr. Savage aims to create and support health communication campaigns to deter risky behaviors among young adults. Currently, he is working on various projects that address adolescent bullying/cyberbullying, oral health promotion, and reciprocal violence. His research has been translated to clinical practice, supported by the Appalachian Regional Commission and internal grants at college and university levels. In terms of teaching, Dr. Savage's philosophy emphasizes participatory engagement and the importance of establishing the relevance of course material to real-world experiences. He has been recognized with prestigious teaching awards from the University of Kentucky, the University of

Contributors

Hawaii, and Arizona State University, as well as numerous research fellowships and competitive course development grants.

Thomas J. Socha (Ph.D., University of Iowa) is Professor of Communication, University Professor for Distinguished Teaching, and Director of the Graduate Program in Lifespan and Digital Communication at Old Dominion University. He was founding Editor of the *Journal of Family Communication* and is current Editor of the *Lifespan Communication: Children, Families and Aging* book series published by Peter Lang Publishing International. He is past President of the Southern States Communication Association.

Brian H. Spitzberg (Ph.D., University of Southern California) is Senate Distinguished Professor in the School of Communication at San Diego State University. His primary areas of research include communication competence, the dark side of communication, stalking, and social media communication diffusion. He has authored or co-authored over 125 scholarly articles, chapters and books, and he has co-edited four scholarly books. His two editions of the co-authored book *The Dark Side of Relationship Pursuit* won both the biennial International Association for Relationship Research Book Award (1996), and the Gerald Miller Book Award from the NCA Interpersonal Communication division (2016). His 2014 article on meme diffusion won the NCA Human Communication and Technology division article award. He has been awarded the WSCA Scholar Award, the Outstanding Biennial Best JLSP Reviewer Award, the NCA Larry Kibler Memorial Award, and the NCA Mark Knapp Interpersonal Communication award.

Erin M. Sumner (Ph.D., Arizona State University) is Associate Professor of Human Communication at Trinity University. Her primary research interests examine the interpersonal and relational dynamics of computer-mediated communication. Her research has appeared in journals such as *Communication Monographs*; *Journal of Computer-Mediated Communication*; *New Media & Society*; *Journal of Social and Personal Relationships*; *Journal of Interpersonal Violence*; *Communication Methods and Measures*; and *Communication Reports*. She has spoken at the SXSW Interactive conference and worked as a doctoral research intern with the Socio-Digital Systems group at Microsoft Research in Cambridge, UK.

Sarah J. Tracy (Ph.D., University of Colorado) is Professor in The Hugh Downs School of Human Communication at Arizona State University. Dr. Tracy's scholarly work examines emotion, communication, and identity in the workplace, with particular focus on workplace bullying, emotional labor, compassion, leadership, and work-life wellness. Her award-winning research has resulted in over 65 monographs and two books, including *Leading Organizations through Transition and Qualitative Research Methods*. She regularly provides academic and professional workshops related to her research, and favorite courses to teach include "Being a Leader," "Qualitative Methods," and "Communication and the Art of Happiness."

Lynn H. Turner (Ph.D., Northwestern University) is Professor of Communication Studies in the Diederich College of Communication at Marquette University. Her research examines interpersonal, gendered, and family communication. She is the co-author/co-editor of over a dozen books as well as over 50 journal articles and book chapters. Lynn has served in a number of different administrative positions in the discipline: President, National Communication Association (NCA); President, Central States Communication Association (CSCA); President, Organization for the Study of Communication, Language, and Gender (OSCLG). Together with Rich West, she has served as co-editor of the Journal of Family Communication several times. She is the recipient of various research and service awards from OSCLG, CSCA, Marquette University, and NCA including NCA's Bernard J. Brommel Award in Family Communication.

Contributors

Stacy Tye-Williams (Ph.D., University of Nebraska) is Assistant Professor of Communication Studies in the Department of English at Iowa State University. Her research focuses on how people narratively construct meaning in and about organizations. She examines dark and bright side processes in organizational life ranging from workplace bullying to the power of collective storytelling to bring about positive change. Her ultimate focus is how people use communication to organize and create positive outcomes in their organizations and the communities in which they are embedded along with the ways we fail to do so. Along with several book chapters, she has published articles in *Journal of Applied Communication Research, Management Communication Quarterly, Women and Language, Western Journal of Communication,* and *Communication Studies.*

Lynne M. Webb (Ph.D., University of Oregon) is Professor of Communication, Florida International University. She held previous tenured appointments in Florida, Memphis, and Arkansas. Her research examines interpersonal communication in a variety of forms, venues, and relationships. Dr. Webb has co-edited three scholarly readers and authored over 85 publications, including research reports, methodological pieces, and pedagogical essays. Her work has appeared in national and international journals including the Journal of Applied Communication, Health Communication, Computers in Human Behavior, and the International Journal of Social Research and Methodology as well as in Communicating Interpersonal Conflict in Close Relationships, Transforming Conflict through Communication, and Contexts of the Dark Side of Communication. Dr. Webb is past President of the Southern States Communication Association as well as the 2015 recipient of its Osborn Teacher-Scholar Award.

Lucas J. Youngvorst (M.A., Minnesota State University, Mankato) is a doctoral candidate at the University of Minnesota, Twin Cities. His research focuses on the intersection of supportive communication and computer-mediated communication, examining the influence of various factors (e.g., technology, cognitive processes, pro-social orientations) on supportive interactions. His research has been presented at various national and international conferences and has appeared in *Communication Monographs* and *Communication Quarterly.*

INDEX

Page numbers in *italic* indicate a figure and page numbers in **bold** indicate a table on the corresponding page.

abilities 49, 193; boundary-management 191; communication 55, 188, 192; cultural 13; human 27; intellectual 11; linguistic 65; personal 13; physical 11; sibling's 200, 204, 207; societal 13

Adams, A. 73

adult sibling bullying *see* sibling relationship bullying

aggressive dismantling 52, **52**, 194

aggressive impediment 51, **52**

Allen, B. J. 56n1, 167

Allen, K. P. 242

all-pervasiveness 182–183

Americans with Disabilities Act 135, 142

Anti-Bullying Act 179

anti-bullying public service announcements *see* public service announcements, anti-bullying

Anti-Cyberbullying Law 179

Arnold, D. H. 156

assertive dismantling **52**, 55

assertive impediment 50, 51, **51**, 55

assertive reinforcement 50, **51**

Baillien, E. 157

Bakker, A. B. 110

Barbera, E. F. 217

Bauer, J. 168

Bayer, C. L. 208

BCC *see* Bullying Conflict Cultures

Beck, G. A. 189

Berdahl, J. L. 216

Bilge, S. 180

Bill C-13 179

Bill 14 179

Bluma, A. 60

Bonnet, M. 194, 195

boundary-management abilities 191

Bowes-Sperry, L. 48

boyd, d. 61–62, 242

Braun, V. 181

Bryant, L. E. 198, 200, 208

bubble dialogue technique 79

Buhs, E. S. 195

bullying, collective: consequences 68–69; disciplinary 65–68; immigrant-host encounters 65–68

bullying, definition 3–4

bullying and race 38, 39–44; effect on students of color 44–45; intersectionality 42–44; interventions for critical social issue 45; marginalized status triggers victim status 41–42; race as an influencing factor 40–41

bullying communication, early childhood *see* early childhood bullying

Bullying Conflict Cultures (BCC) 86–92; assumptions 86; avoidant conflict cultures 89–90; collaborative conflict cultures 88; definition of conflict cultures 86; disposition of bullying 91–92; dominating conflict cultures 89; new explanations for the etiology 90–91; passive-aggressive conflict

Index

cultures 89–90; types of conflict cultures and their associated bullying behaviors 87–90, *88*

bullying in academia: antecedents 156–157; consequences 157–158; discussion 160–163; intent to leave 159, 160; Intent to Leave Academia Scale 159; isolation-strain (iso-strain) 156–157, 159, **160**; job demand-control-support (JDCS) 155, 156, 157, 158, 159, 160, 162; job satisfaction 158, 159, 160; job stress 159, 160, 162; method 158–159; method: participants 158; method: procedures and measurement 158–159; results 159–160; Pearson correlations 159, 160, **160**

bullying in seniors' communities 10–11, 210–218; bullying as an identity threat response 216–218; graying of the United States 211; identity enhancement 217–218; managing identity and identity threat 215–216; meaning of "old" 211–213; on "being old" in the United States 212–213; sites of identity and identity threat 214–215; staff communicative practices 217

bullying in the higher education workplace *see* workplace bullying in higher education

bullying prevention policy, U.S. K–12: communities of practice 137–138; Cultural-Historical Activity Theory (CHAT) 135, 136, 137, 142, 144; defining bullying through policy 136–137; future 143–144; objects 142–143; policy search 136; rules 138–139; sample 135–136; subjects and division of labor 140–142; tools 139–142; tools: cyber 140; tools: language 139, 140; tools: physical objects and acts 139; tools: prevention 140

bullying type 17–18, 148

Buzzanell, P. M. 156, 172

bystander behavior in cyberbullying *see* cyberbullying bystander behavior

Camodeca, M. 201

Campbell, S. W. 241

Canada *see* immigrant youth in Canada

Carlisle, S. K. 43

Carr, C. T. 20

Carr, K. 208

Casimir, G. 117

Caughlin, J. P. 239

Cegala, D. J. 208

Centers for Disease Control (CDC) 136, 210

Central Board of Secondary Education 59

Chae, Y. 60

Charlotte-Mecklenburg School 136

CHAT *see* Cultural-Historical Activity Theory

Chiang, E. S. 18

Chronicle of Higher Education, The 83, 165

CIHR: *Tackling Bullying* 180

Civil Rights Act 135

Clark, L. S. 61

Clarke, R. A. 181

close-tie support 149–150, 154

CMC *see* computer-mediated communication

co-cultural ally 51, **52**, 55

Co-Cultural Theory 46, 48, 49

codes, procedures, and standards approaches 27

Cohen, C. 166

Cohen, J. 62

Cohen, S. 148

Colbert, S. 3

collective bullying: consequences 68–69; disciplinary 65–68; immigrant-host encounters 65–68

college 8–9, 33, 37, 53, 83, 127, 129, 149

college professor bullying *see* bullying in academia

Collins, P. H. 180

Columbine High School 5

coming to terms with bullying: college 8–9; contextual approach 5; high school 7–8; holistic approach 11–12; middle school 7; preschool 6; schools 5–6; senior living communities 10–11; workplaces 9–10

communication abilities 55, 188, 192

communication ethics: codes, procedures, and standards approaches 27; deontological ethics 25–26; ethical responses 28–29; frameworks 25; implications 23–25; utilitarian ethics 26–27; virtue ethics 24, 25, 27–28, 29

complain to others 120, 124

computer-mediated communication (CMC) 63, 151, 152, 153, 154, 226

Cone, J. D. 18

confronting oppressive rhetoric 51, **52**, 55

Connell, N. 42–43

constant comparative method 95, 232

"cool" factor 184, 185

Cooper, B. K. 105

coping for bullied students 145–148; age and efficacy 147; bullying type 17–18, 148; coping and gender 147; coping outcomes 146–148; social support 148–154 (*see also* social support); Transactional Model of Stress and Coping (TMSC) with bullying 145, 146, *146*

coping fatigue 67

310

Index

Corbin, J. 96
Cose, E. J.: *The Rage of a Privileged Class* 67
Cowan, R. L. 28, 75, 94
Craven, R. G. 5
Creswell, J. W. 96
Crider, C. 168
Crockett, L. J. 59
cultural abilities 13
Cultural-Historical Activity Theory (CHAT) 135, 136, 137, 142, 144
Cumberland County Schools 136—137
Cummings, J. 6
cumulative harm 225–226
cyberbullying 242; communication research 80; cumulative harm 225–226; deindividuation 226, 234; discussion 228–229; focus group themes 225–227; lack of control 227, 228; offline consequences 226–227; participants 224; post-focus group survey results 227–228; procedures 223; public service announcements 221–224; results 224–228; stimuli 223; surveys 223–224; textual persistence 226, 228
cyberbullying, India 58; parental mediation 59–62; tackling cyberbullying 58–62
cyberbullying bystander behavior: avoidance of personal consequences 235; cultural environment 234; discussion 239–240; gauge from others' responses 234; goals 233–235; honor proximity 233, 236; ignoring 235–236; impact of goals 235–238; instigating 236–237; intervening 237–238; literature review 230–232; methods 232; multiple goals theories 231–232; observing 236; power 231; practical implication 239; respond according to severity 233–234; results 232–238; strengths, limitations, and future directions 240; theoretical implications 239–240; typology 238, **238**
cyberstalking 20, 230
cyber tools 140

Danielson, C. M. 150, 151
Davies, B. 191
De Luca, B. M. 155, 161–162
deontological ethics 25–26
Desrayaud, N. 87, 88
De Witte, H. 157
DGT *see* Dominant Group Theory
Diagnostic and Statistical Manual (DSM) 18
Digital India 63

Dillard, J. P. 25
dispute-related bullying 82, 89
Djurkovic, N. 117
Doane, A. N. 18
Dofradottir, A. 117
Dollard, M. F. 110, 157
Dominant Group Theory (DGT) 46, 48–52, 53, 54, 55–56, 56n2, 64, 65, 67; Co-Cultural Theory 49; communication orientations and strategies 50–52; factors influencing communication 49–50; premises 48–49; sample dominant group strategies by communication orientation **51–52**
drama years 7
Dunleavy, K. N. 198
Dutton, J. 48, 52

early childhood bullying: dark side and lifespan 188–190; difficulties in defining, labeling, and operationalizing 192–194; facilitating and inhibiting conditions 194–195; lifespan developmental study 196–197; motivating conditions 190–191; parameters 190–192; targets and situations 191–192
Eddington, S. M. 156
Education Amendments 135
Einarsen, S. 82, 87, 109, 113, 157
emotional support 119, 148, 149–150, 151
emotion-focused coping strategies 117, 118–122, **119**, 125, 146–147; complain to others 120–121, 124; continue the cycle of incivility 121–122; engage in activities outside work 120–121, 125, 214; ignore uncivil behavior 120, 125; justify to themselves 120; react emotionally 121, 124; retaliation 121, 141, 146–147, 148, 157, 216, 237; social support 47, 118–119, 120, 124, 125, 146, 148–150, 151, 152, 153, 154, 163, 172, 185, 186, 235; supervisor social support 156, 157, 159, 160, 162; withdraw 122
Employment Non-Discrimination Act 10
engage in activities outside work 120–121, 125, 214
"Erase It" 223, 224, 226
Erdur-Baker, O. 184
Eron, L. D. 195
esteem support 148, 150
etiology 90–91; formal leadership 90; informal leadership 90; organizational membership 90–91; overarching organizational context
EU Kids Online 59

Index

Facebook 58, 223, 224, 233, 250
FBI 223
Ferreira, C. 197
field of experience 49, 55
First Post 57
Fisher, S. 42
Fitness, J. 23
Fleschler Peskin, M. F. 43
Fletcher, C. 29
Folkman, S. 146
Foucault, M. 65
Fratzl, J. 156

Garnett, B. 42, 44
Gelfand, M. J. 87, 88, 90, 94
Gibson, J. 151
Gini, G. 8
GLBT 8, 9, 10
Goldsmith, D. J. 151
Goodboy, A. K. 157, 160
Google 47, 169; Science Fair 59
Goossens, F. A. 194, 195
Greene, M. B. 190, 191
Guilford County Schools 136, 137
Guntarto 61

Halder, D. 58
Hamby, S. 192
Harrington, S. 94
Harris, T. M. 38, 39
High, A. C. 153, 154
higher education, workplace bullying in *see* workplace bullying in higher education
high school 3, 4, 7–8, 10, 12, 31, 40, 64, 65, 117, 147, 176, 181, 182, 184, 185, 191, 234
Hodson, R. 167
Hoel, H. 105, 109, 156
Hofstede, G. 94
Hogh, A. 117
Hollis, L. P. 5, 83, 157, 165–166
honoring proximity 233, 235, 236, 237
Hoobler, G. 243, 250
Horton, P. 23–24
Hosking, P. J. 157
Huesmann, L. R. 195
human abilities 27
human resource professionals 47, 77
human resource professionals in the Persian Gulf and United States, workplace bullying *see* workplace

bullying and HR professionals in the Persian Gulf and United States
"hypodermic" analogy 13

Identity Control Theory 215
Identity Process Theory 215
ignore uncivil behavior 120, 125
ignoring someone's opinion 96–97
immigrant youth in Canada 182–184; communicating about bullying 182–184, **182**; confidence 185–186; context 180; data analysis 181; "cool" factor 184, 185; data collection 181; dealing with bullying **184**, 184–186; discussion 186–187; findings 182–186; and gender 183–184; intersectionality 180; and race 183; "roasting" yourself 184–185, 186; sense of confidence 184, 185–186; study limitations and future research 182, 187
individual level 74–75, 76, 142; target resistance strategies 75
Infante, D. A. 200–201, 208
Institutional Review Board 95, 158, 201
insulting someone or putting them down 97
intellectual abilities 11
intentional harm 3, 224
intent to leave 48, 88, 159, 160
Intent to Leave Academia Scale 159
interactional outcome 49, 50, 55, 56n2
Internet and Mobile Association of India 57
interpersonal level 75–76; co-workers 76; family members and friends 75–76
intersectionality 180, 186; race in bullying 42–44
intimate partner violence 13, 17
isolation-strain (iso-strain) 156–157, 159, **160**
It Act 62

Jacobson, K. C. 59
JDCS *see* job demand-control-support
Job Content Questionnaire 158
job demand-control-support (JDCS) 155, 156, 157, 158, 159, 160, 162
job satisfaction 82, 88, 158, 159, 160
job stress 159, 160, 162
Johnson, Z. 157
Jones, S. M. 150, 151
Journal of Family Communication 196

Kahle, L. 25, 43–44
Kantianism 25

Index

Keashly, L. 80, 83, 91, 94, 155, 156, 160, 162, 165, 167
Kelley, M. L. 18
Kinney, T. A. 25
Kirwil, L. 50
Knight, J. M. 157, 160
Komolsevin, R. 61
Krone, K. J. 50, 75
Kumar, R. 61

lack of control 227, 228
Ladd, G. W. 195
laissez-faire leadership 90, 105, 106, **108**, 109, 110, 111, 112–113, 114
Lambert, R. 167
Lande, A. B. 87
language tools 139, 140
Lazarus, R. S. 146
leadership in business startups in Japan: competitive, performance-oriented culture 110; descriptive statistics and reliability coefficients of key variables **108**; domain-specific leadership 110, 112; instruments 109–110; leadership 110–112; leadership style 109; limitations and future directions 114; methods 107; practical implications 113–114; psychological safety climate 110; respondents 107–108; results 110–112; structural equation modeling (SEM) 110, 111, *111*, 112, 115nn1–3; structure of leadership-bullying linkage 105, *107*; underlying mechanism of leadership's impact 112–113
Lee, S. 60
Lereya, S. 195
levels of construction 74–78; individual 74–75, 76, 142; interpersonal 75–76; organizational 76–78
Lewicki, R. 81
Leymann, H. 73, 74
linguistic abilities 65
Long, Z. 157, 160
Lucas, K. 168
Lutgen-Sandvik, P. 29, 77, 78, 102, 105, 156, 157
Lwin, M. O. 60

macrosocietal level 78
main effect model 148
managerial responses 77–78
Manikas, A. 168
Mansson, D. H. 162
Marsh, H. W. 5

Martin, M. M. 157, 160, 198, 199, 208
Marwick, A. E. 242
Matsunaga, M. 150
Mattingly, E. 168
McCormack, D. 117
McDermott, V. 78
McDonald, K. 168
McKay, R. 156, 157
Mendez, J. J. 40, 42
Menesini, E. 201
microaffirmations 46, 51, **52**, 55, 56n2
Microsoft Corporation 58
middle school bullies 7; use of lies 173–176
Mikkelson, A. C. 198
Minton, J. M. 81
Mishra, P. 168
Miyazak, A. D. 60
mobile communication and online harassment 241–243
models to understand bullying: behavioral assessment grid *19*; concept-generator for cyber-aggression **15**; "dark side" 14–17, *16*; measure what you theorize 17–19; verification should yield theoretically to falsification 19–21
Moise-Titus, J. 195
Monks, C. P. 44, 192–193
Mueller, A. S. 44, 45
Music, G. 190
Myers, S. A. 162, 198, 200, 202, 208

National Communication Association 24
National Household Survey 179
negative acts 104, 117, 162
Negative Acts Questionnaire 109, 158
Nelson, E. 167
network support 149, 150, 151
Neuman, J. H. 83, 91, 155, 156, 160, 162, 165, 167
Neupauer, N. C. 199
Nguyen, T. M. P. 61
Nguyen, T. Q. C. 61
Nielsen, M. B. 87
Nikken, P. 60
Nocentini, A. 201
nonassertive dismantling 51, **52**, 55
nonassertive impediment 50, **51**
nonassertive reinforcement 50, **51**, 54
"No Big Deal" 223
Notelaers, G. 109, 157
nuances 38, 56, 56n2, 65, 79, 114, 142

Index

obsessive relational intrusion 17, 18, 242–243, 247, 250

offline consequences 226–227

Ogle, C. M. 11

O'Leary-Kelly, A. M. 48

Olweus, D. 242, 250

Olweus Bullying Prevention Program 154

opportunist bullying 89

Orbe, M. P. 38, 39, 50, 167

organizational level 76–78, 85; human resource professionals 77; macrosocietal 78; managerial responses 77–78

Ormrod, R. K. 192

O'Sullivan, P. B. 20

PACER: National Bullying Prevention Center 154

Padilla, M. A. 18

Pan, T. S. 45

Parada, R. H. 5

parental mediation 57, 59–62, 63

Patton, T. O. 166, 167

Peguero, A. A. 25, 41, 43–44

Pepler, D. 6

perceived costs and rewards 49, 55

perceived harasser motives 245–246, 247, 248–249, 251

perceived support 148, 149

persistent criticism 97, 98

personal abilities 13

personality clash 77; beginning of bullying 127–128; critical event 128–129; tenure drama 129–131

Pew Research Center 211, 217

physical abilities 11

physical bullying 11, 139

physical objects and acts tools 139

Planalp, S. 23

Podolski, C. 195

Popper, K. 19–20

Porath, C. L. 26

Post-Traumatic Stress Disorder (PTSD) 11, 18, 66, 82

Pozzoli, T. 8

Prabhu, T. 58–59

preschool 6, 192, 193, 194, 196, 197

Presno, C. 196

prevention tools 140

problem-focused coping strategies 122–123; change (re)actions 123; confront the instigator 122–123; learn skills and techniques 123

PTSD see Post-Traumatic Stress Disorder

public service announcements, anti-bullying: cumulative harm 225–226; deindividuation

226, 234; discussion 228–229; focus group themes 225–227; lack of control 227, 228; offline consequences 226–227; participants 224; post-focus group survey results 227–228; procedures 223; public service announcements 221–224; results 224–228; stimuli 223; surveys 223–224; textual persistence 226, 228

race and bullying 38, 39–44, 183; effect on students of color 44–45; intersectionality 42–44; interventions for critical social issue 45; marginalized status triggers victim status 41–42; race as an influencing factor 40–41

race, ethnicity, and culture on personal violations: race and bullying 38, 39–44 (see also race and bullying); race as social construct 38–39

Rains, S. A. 153

Randall, P. 5

Rayner, C. 94

Razzali, N. 61

Razzante, R. J. 50

react emotionally 121, 124

Rehabilitation Act 135

Research Ethics Board 181

resilience: bullying 17, 28–29, 30–34; bullying of immigrant youth 186; career/workplace 164, 165, 168, 172, 176

re-storying bullying 78, 79

restrictive mediation 60

retaliation 121, 141, 146–147, 148, 157, 216, 237

ReThink 58–59

Riforgiate, S. 29

"roasting" yourself 184–185, 186

Rocca, K. A. 198

Rock, R. 3

Rodríguez-Hidalgo, A. J. 44

Rorvik, E. 87

Roscigno, V. 167

Rubin, D. C. 11

Ryvicker, M. 214

Salin, D. 156

Salmivalli, C. 191

Samara, M. 195

Samnani, A. K. 68

Sandvig, C. 62

Santora, J. C. 105

Sarros, J. C. 105

Saunders, D. M. 81

Index

Schell, S. 167
Scherr, T. G. 45
Schrag, C. O. 33
Schmidt, E. 62–63
Schrodt, P. 208
Schuengel, C. 194, 195
Schumann, L. 39, 40
Self-Affirmation Theory 217
self-efficacy 28, 147, 153
seniors' communities, bullying in *see* bullying in
    seniors' communities
sense of confidence 184, 185–186
sexual identity 43, 44
sibling relationship bullying: data analysis 201–204;
    discussion 207–209; study participants 201;
    preliminary analyses 204; primary analyses 204–207;
    procedures 201–202; review of literature 199–201;
    results 204–207; typology of verbally aggressive
    messages **203**; use of verbally aggressive messages
    during childhood **205**; use of verbally aggressive
    messages to bully siblings during childhood **206**
Siegler, J. C. 11
Simpson, R. 166
Singh, P. 68
situational context 49, 50, 55, 56n2
Skogstad, A. 87
Smith, P. K. 7, 13, 74, 192
SNSs *see* social networking sites
Socha, T. J. 189
social networking sites (SNSs) 230, 232
social support 47, 118–119, 120, 124, 125, 146,
    148–154, 163, 172, 185, 186, 235; anonymity
    152; communication 149–150; communication
    characteristics 150–151; emotional primacy 151;
    FtF supportive communication 150; number of
    users 153–154; online supportive communication
    151–154; supervisor 156, 157, 159, 160, 162;
    support providers 149–150; synchronicity
    152–153; technological affordances 151–152
societal abilities 13
Solomon, D. 153, 154
Southern Poverty Law Center 37, 45
Spittal, P. 45
Spitzberg, B. H. 243, 250
spreading false rumors 100
Spriggs, A. L. 43
stalking 14, 16, 17, 18, 20, 244; cyberstalking 20, 230
Stanaland, A. J. S. 60
Stewart, J. 24

Stohl, C. 167
Stone, A. L. 43
Stop Bullying Now! 138
Strauss, A. 96
stress-buffering model/theory 148
structural equation modeling (SEM) 110, 111, *111*,
    112, 115nn1–3
supervisor social support 156, 157, 159, 160, 162
Sypher, B. D. 116, 117

Tansey, M. 14
Tansey wheel 14
Tehrani, N. 48
Teven, J. J. 199
textual harassment: bullying and cyberbullying
    242; discussion 249–250; drama 242; limitations,
    implications, and future directions 250–251;
    methods 243–244; mobile communication and
    online harassment 241–243; obsessive relational
    intrusion 17, 18, 242–243, 247, 250; participants
    and procedures 243–244; perceived harasser
    motives 245–246, 247, 248–249, 251; present study
    243; relational contexts, events, and consequences
    245, 247–248; results 244–246; text messaging
    as bullying 246–247; text messaging as drama
    244–246; text messaging as obsessive relational
    intrusion 247–249; textual persistence 226, 228
Theiss, S. 83, 90
Theory of Conflict Cultures 82, 86
Thomas, R. 156
Times of India, The 59
Title II 135
Title VI 135, 142
Title IX 135, 142
TMSC *see* Transactional Model of Stress and Coping
Tracy, S. J. 56, 74, 79, 80, 93, 105, 125, 126, 156
Transactional Model of Stress and Coping (TMSC)
    with bullying 145, 146, *146*
Triandis, H. C. 94
Tuckey, M. R. 157
Turner, H. A. 192
Twale, D. J. 155, 161
Twitter 224, 237
Tye-Williams, S. 50, 75

UNICEF 186
unreasonable deadlines 98
unwanted actions 3
U.S. Department of Education 135

Index

U.S. Department of Health and Human Services 135
U.S. K–12 bullying prevention policy *see* bullying prevention policy, U.S. K–12
utilitarian ethics 26–27

verbal abuse 96, 97, 101, 125, 183, 185, 208
verbal aggressiveness in adult sibling relationship *see* sibling relationship bullying
Verbal Aggressiveness Scale 202, 203
Vermunt, J. K. 157
virtue ethics 24, 25, 27–28, 29
Vlachou, M. 192, 193, 194
Volk, T.: *Metapatterns* 189

Wake County Public School System 136
Warren, R. 60
Warren, S. 94
weak-tie support 149, 150, 151
Webb, L. M. 83
Weiland, S. M. B. 168
White supremacy 67
Williams, L. M. 41, 43
Wills, T. A. 148
Winefield, A. H. 157
Winston-Salem/Forsyth County School 136
Wolkec, D. 195
workplace bullying: communication 9–10; resilience 164, 165, 168, 172, 176
workplace bullying, communication research on: cyberbullying 80; future 78–80; innovation 79; levels of construction 74–78; nuances 38, 56, 56n2, 65, 79, 114, 142; relationship dynamics 80; re-storying bullying 78, 79; theory and practice 80; workplace bullying research 73–74
workplace bullying and culture 93–94; Persian Gulf cultural expectations 98–99
workplace bullying and HR professionals in the Persian Gulf and United States: culture 93–94; data analysis 95–96; discussion and implications 101–102; findings and interpretation 96–101; method 95—96; perceptions of bullying behaviors in the Persian Gulf 96–97; perceptions of bullying behaviors in the United States 97–98; Persian Gulf cultural expectations 98–99; sampling and data collection 95; U.S. cultural expectations 99–101
workplace bullying as conflict: Bullying Conflict Cultures 86–92 (*see also* Bullying Conflict Cultures); conceptualization 83–85; future research 92; higher education as an exemplar

83; interpersonal communication behaviors 84; negative effects 82; outgrowth of organizational cultures 84–85
workplace bullying escalation in personality clash 77; beginning of bullying 127–128; critical event 128–129; tenure drama 129–131
workplace bullying in higher education 81, 91, 156, 165–172; communicative model of career resilience 168; context 165–167; effects of bullying on worker identities 167–168; interrogating experiences 168–172; *see also* bullying in academia; human resource professionals in the Persian Gulf and United States
workplace bullying in startups in Japan: competitive, performance-oriented culture 110; descriptive statistics and reliability coefficients of key variables **108**; domain-specific leadership 110, 112; instruments 109–110; leadership 110–112; leadership style 109; limitations and future directions 114; methods 107; practical implications 113–114; psychological safety climate 110; respondents 107–108; results 110–112; structural equation modeling (SEM) 110, 111, *111*, 112, 115nn1–3; structure of leadership-bullying linkage 105, *107*; underlying mechanism of leadership's impact 112–113
Workplace Bullying Institute 80, 116
workplace bullying transformation: constructed vignette: Paws for Love 53–55; Dominant Group Theory 46, 48–52, 53, 54, 55–56, 56n2, 64, 65, 67 (*see also* Dominant Group Theory); moving from critiquing the problem to inspiring transformation 46–48; OPPT-in approach to power and privilege 55–56
workplace incivility: coping with 116–117, 118–23; data analysis 118; emotion-focused coping strategies 117, 118–122, **119**, 125, 146–147; limitations and future directions 126; method 117–118; participants 117–118, *124*; problem-focused coping strategies 122–123; procedures 118; theoretical and practical contributions 125–126; typology of coping strategies 123–124, *124*
World Health Organization 83
Wu, J. 39, 44
www.NoBullying.com 58

Young, V. 153
YouTube 7, 224, 233